Classical Arabic
Philosophy

An Anthology of Sources

Classical Arabic

Philosophy

An Anthology of Sources

Translated with Introduction,
Notes, and Glossary by

JON MCGINNIS AND DAVID C. REISMAN

Hackett Publishing Company, Inc.
Indianapolis/Cambridge

12 11 10 09 08 07   1 2 3 4 5 6

For further information, please address:

Hackett Publishing Company, Inc.
P.O. Box 44937
Indianapolis, IN 46244-0937

www.hackettpublishing.com

Cover design by Abigail Coyle
Text design by Carrie Wagner
Printed at Edwards Brothers, Inc.

Library of Congress Cataloging-in-Publication Data

Classical Arabic philosophy : an anthology of sources / translated with introduction, notes, and glossary by Jon McGinnis and David C. Reisman.
       p.   cm.
Includes bibliographical references and index.
ISBN-13: 978-0-87220-871-1 (pbk. : alk. paper)
ISBN-13: 978-0-87220-872-8 (cloth : alk. paper)
 I. Philosophy, Islamic.   I. McGinnis, Jon.   II. Reisman, David C.
B741.C52 2007
181'.92–dc22   2007018579

The paper in this publication meets the minimum requirements of
American National Standard for Information Sciences—
Permanence of Paper for Printed Library Materials,
ANSI Z39.48-1984

To our sons

Lorcan, Morgan, and Gage

Contents

Preface

Any translator, but particularly a translator of philosophical texts, faces the Scylla and Charybdis of translating a text in either an excessively literal or excessively literary way. If the text is translated too literally, there is the danger that the translation and its philosophical content will be inaccessible to those reading it in the target language. If the text is translated in a style that is too literary, there is the danger that the translation will reflect more the translator's own, perhaps idiosyncratic, understanding of the text rather than the original author's intent. As a general rule, where the arguments and thought of a given thinker are ambiguous or crabbed in the original Arabic, we have tried to retain that ambiguity rather than overinterpret the text in our translation, whereas when the intent of the text is relatively clear, we have felt free to render it in more accessible and idiomatic English.

The same also holds for certain individual words. For instance, the Arabic verb *ʿaqala, yaʿqilu, ʿaql* (and the Latin counterpart *intellego, intellegere, intellexi, intellectum*), at least in philosophical parlance, refers to the identifying activity of the intellect. Since the precise meaning of this verb is of considerable importance to philosophical psychology and this activity might be understood differently by different thinkers, we have followed the translation found in much of the secondary literature and chosen the cumbersome, but literal, verb "to intellect." In this same vein, we have sometimes also preferred the literal translation of a term rather than some technical expression, even though the technical term may have become standard in the secondary literature or other translations. For example the Arabic *fāḍa, yafīḍu, fayaḍān* is commonly translated in the technical vocabulary of the Neoplatonists as "to emanate" or "emanation," whereas we have translated it in the more literal sense of "to flow" or "to pour forth." Conversely, in other cases we have preferred to translate a word or phrase in a technical sense even though the literal translation may be more common in the secondary literature or in other translations. For example *rūḥānī*, which literally means "spiritual," is frequently contrasted with *māddī* ("material" or "corporeal") in such a way that the two terms are clearly meant to be exclusive of one another. Thus, to bring out the contrary nature of these two terms, we have in certain cases translated *rūḥānī* as "immaterial" or "incorporeal."

The term *maʿná* brings with it a whole set of issues and problems, as any one who has read medieval philosophy written in Arabic can testify. Literally it means "sense," "meaning," "account," or "intention"; however, its semantic range in philosophical writings came to cover a whole gamut of notions that are not strictly conceptual. Included within its semantic range are such meanings as "(an existentially thin) thing," and so even "nonexistence" might be thought of as a *maʿná*, as in the sentence "nonexistence is a difficult *thing* to understand." *Maʿná* also can have a much more (existentially) robust sense and may be translated as "explanatory account" or even "form"; in this respect *maʿná* does not merely signify some concept in the mind, but the very object in the world that the concept reflects. The difficulty is that virtually every author included in this anthology goes back and forth between using *maʿná* in a nontechnical sense and in a technical sense, and it is not always obvious when one sense is being used as opposed to another. The problem is compounded by the fact that *maʿná* is such a common expression in Arabic philosophical prose that it virtually precludes our noting every single occurrence. Consequently, we have only indicated those cases where *maʿná* is in the underlying Arabic, and we have not translated it by one of its literal translations, namely, "sense," "meaning," or "account."

As for the structure of this collection of texts, we have tried to provide a broad sampling from each of the philosophers represented here and to cover most of the major areas of philosophical study. These areas include logic or *propaedeutica*, natural philosophy or physics, philosophical psychology, that is, theories of the soul, metaphysics, and cosmology, as well as value theory, that is, ethics and politics (although admittedly our anthology has disproportionally fewer texts in this last area, primarily because a very good source of such works is already available in Lerner and Mahdi's *Medieval Political Philosophy*).[1] It has not always been possible to fulfill this ambition completely. Still, we believe that what we have included will provide readers with a sense of the vast extent of topics treated by philosophers writing in the medieval Islamic world. In certain instances several philosophical fields are covered in a single treatise, in which case we have simply translated the treatise as a whole and made no attempt to break it up into the relevant fields. Such is the case for al-Fārābī's *The Principles of Beings* (also known as the *Governance of Cities*), which provides a systematic presentation of most of the relevant fields of philosophy. Similarly, Ibn Bājja's *Conjunction of the Intellect with Man* discusses issues in psychology, metaphysics, and the ethical issue of the ultimate goal of human perfection.

When there are preexisting and readily available translations of a work and author, we only provide new translations of important passages of that work rather than retranslate the entire text *de novo* and instead refer the reader to the earlier translation. For example, there are two English translations of Ibn Ṭufayl's *Ḥayy ibn Yaqẓān*, and thus we have contented ourselves with merely providing new translations of certain central passages. Similarly, if an author wrote multiple treatises on the same subject, and one of those treatises is in translation and readily available whereas the other is not, we have preferred to translate the lesser-known work. Thus, for example, the extant portion of al-Kindī's *On First Philosophy* is available in English translation; however, many of the topics treated in *On First Philosophy* were obviously dear to al-Kindī's heart, and he frequently returned to them in shorter treatises, where he would either repeat the

---

[1] R. Lerner and M. Mahdi, eds., *Medieval Political Philosophy* (Ithaca, NY: Cornell University Press, 1972).

arguments of *On First Philosophy* or develop them further. Here we have chosen to include some of these smaller, less readily available, or even until now untranslated, treatises rather than retranslate *On First Philosophy*. Our general aim was to paint as broad a picture of the philosophical and scientific work being undertaken in the medieval Islamic world as is reasonably possible in a single anthology without significantly repeating the work of those who preceded us.

We should also note that in the bibliography, we have included primarily philosophical texts by the philosophers that are available in translation, the editions used for our translations, and a limited selection of secondary references. We have not, however, tried to compile a list of the "most important" secondary literature, which seemed prudent given the frequently significant differences of opinion among scholars in the field of Arabic and Islamic philosophy. Instead, in the footnotes to the individual translations, we have referenced those secondary sources that might be of help in understanding that particular text. Those who are interested in a more general bibliography of relevant secondary literature, for either a particular figure or subject, can consult the following sources: (1) Hans Daiber, *Bibliography of Islamic Philosophy*; (2) Thérèse-Anne Druart's online bibliography for literature available after 1999; and for those interested specifically in Ibn Sīnā, (3) Jules L. Janssens, *An Annotated Bibliography on Ibn Sīnā (1970–1989)* and *An Annotated Bibliography on Ibn Sīnā: First Supplement (1990–1994)*.[2]

There are two final remarks about the structure of this anthology. First, we have reserved the numbered footnotes primarily for quick clarifications, cross-references, and historical references, especially when the historical sources are available in English translation. The lettered textual notes provide the bibliographical information for the Arabic editions that we have used and any textual emendations that we may have made to them. They have been gathered at the end of this anthology and are intended primarily for those who know Arabic and are interested in various textual and philological points. In those notes we have observed the scholarly conventions of textual criticism. The manuscript references, unless otherwise stated, are indicated by the sigla used for them in the edition noted. Second, instead of having a standard index we have preferred to provide a relatively exhaustive glossary of technical terms, both from English to Arabic and Arabic to English. Consequently we have not tried to index every use of a given term; however, in the case of certain key philosophical concepts, we have provided the page numbers when the term is the subject of an extended discussion.

A brief explanation seems warranted for our use of the phrase "Arabic philosophy" in the title of this reader. Much ink has been spilled in the field of medieval Middle-Eastern studies over whether *falsafa* should be translated, or better interpreted, as "Islamic philosophy" or "Arabic philosophy" or even the apropos, but awkward,

---

2 Hans Daiber, ed., *Bibliography of Islamic Philosophy*, 2 vols.; Jules L. Janssens, *An Annotated Bibliography on Ibn Sīnā (1970–1989)*; and Jules L. Janssens, *An Annotated Bibliography on Ibn Sīnā: First Supplement (1990–1994)*.

"Islamicate philosophy." Those who prefer "Islamic philosophy" often argue that with very few exceptions the practitioners of *falsafa* were not ethnically Arabs but came from virtually all the different ethnic groups and countries that were under the control of Islam in the medieval period. Thus, calling this enterprise "Islamic philosophy" seems most fitting. In response, those who prefer "Arabic philosophy" note that a considerable amount of *falsafa* was not produced by Muslims but by Arabic-speaking Jews and Christians as well, and so the adjectives "Muslim" or "Islamic" to modify "philosophy" is not appropriate.

A deeper issue, even if not always explicitly stated as such, seems to involve the very nature of this enterprise: Does *falsafa* have an inherently religious, and particularly Islamic, element to it, or is it just philosophy, plain and simple, albeit done in Islamic lands? Those who think that there is an inherent religious element might point to the apparent religious natures of many of the central issues treated in *falsafa*, such as proofs for the existence of God and such divine attributes as simplicity (*tawḥīd*), the eternity or temporal origination of the world, the immortality of the soul and the possibility of bodily resurrection, as well as an explanation of prophecy and revelation. In response it is observed that every one of these issues was part and parcel of the Greek philosophical and scientific tradition bequeathed to the Near East and was treated in its Greek setting by pagan and monotheistic thinkers alike, regardless of religious affiliation. Thus, to call these topics "religious," let alone inherently "Islamic," is to succumb to anachronism; namely, one treats these issues, which we today consider to be topics of religion or philosophy of religion, as having been likewise categorized in the past.

Whatever the deeper issue may be for preferring one label to another, we do not intend to adjudicate it here but merely to explain it. Our use of "Arabic philosophy" is for no other reason than that during the time period covered by this anthology—that is, the beginning of the ninth century to the end of the twelfth century—the Arabic language was the primary vehicle through which philosophy was being practiced in the Near East, and it is the sole language in which all the works translated here were originally written. In this respect, the use of "Arabic philosophy" to describe this intellectual phenomenon is no different than the use of such labels as "Greek philosophy" or "Latin philosophy" to describe those intellectual phenomena. For this reason, then, Suhrawardī, the last figure included in this collection, marks a fitting closure to the classical period of Arabic philosophy, since he is the first to write a substantial number of philosophical treatises in Persian.[3] Moreover, it is with Suhrawardī, the founder of the Illuminationist

---

[3] See Hossein Ziai, "Shihāb al-Dīn Suhrawardī: Founder of the Illuminationist School," S. H. Nasr and O. Leaman, ch. 28, especially p. 436. In fact, Ibn Sīnā also wrote some philosophical allegories in Persian as well as a Persian philosophical encyclopedia, the *Dānishnāma-yi ʿalāʾī*; still, the preponderance of his vast outpouring of philosophical works—and it is voluminous—is in Arabic.

school, that we see the first sustained criticism of neo-Aristotelianism coupled with an alternative philosophical system intended to replace it.

Finally, it remains for us to acknowledge our considerable debt to a number of our friends and colleagues for their invaluable help with this anthology. We gratefully thank Peter Adamson and Peter Pormann for providing us with advance copies of their translations of al-Kindī's *The Proximate Efficient Cause for Generation and Corruption* and *On Dispelling Sorrow*. Peter Adamson and Richard Taylor also went through the whole manuscript and made numerous helpful suggestions. We benefited from both of their comments. Alexander Jones assisted us with many of the finer points of Ptolemaic astronomy that appear in al-Kindī's *The Proximate Efficient Cause*. We also appreciate Joel L. Kraemer's willingness to share his manuscripts of as-Sijistānī's *On the Proper Perfection of the Human Species*. Qasim Zaman clarified much of the legal terminology assumed by al-Ghazālī in his *Concerning That on Which True Demonstration Is Based*. The selections from Ibn Rushd's *Long Commentary on De anima* were suggested by Richard C. Taylor, and Shane Duarte graciously and meticulously went over our entire translation of those sections, improving the end result tremendously. Many thanks are extended to Nora Hendren and Josh Eaves for their practical help in putting together a work of this sort. Rick Todhunter and Carrie Wagner of Hackett Publishing should also be mentioned for their constant encouragement and support. We would both like to acknowledge the Institute for Advanced Study in Princeton, where we each successively enjoyed a year's membership. Also, Jon McGinnis would like to acknowledge and thank the National Endowment for the Humanities, which supported much of his work on this anthology. Finally, we are both grateful to Dimitri Gutas and Everett Rowson for kindling our passion for Arabic philosophy.

Introduction

I. *FALSAFA* AND THE ARABIC TRANSLATION MOVEMENT

Falsafa, which is derived from the Greek *philosophia*, was the standard term used by intellectuals in the medieval Near East to describe the enterprise we today call "philosophy," although they sometimes used the Arabic translation of *philosophia*, *ḥikma* or "wisdom," to refer to this activity as well. The use of the Greek loan word *falsafa* as the primary description of this intellectual movement suggests this activity's initial origins and primary impetus, namely, the Greek philosophical and scientific traditions to which thinkers in the Islamic world were heirs. We might, then, tentatively define *falsafa* as a continuation and refinement, undertaken at least initially in the Arabic language, of the Greek philosophical and scientific tradition. This tradition, in turn, extended back at least as far as the thought of Socrates, Plato, and Aristotle, if not to the pre-Socratics themselves, and then proceeded through the Neoplatonizing Aristotelianism of later Greek commentators, particularly as that system of thought was articulated at the Academy in Alexandria.[1] This is not to say that there were not other influences also shaping *falsafa* that were indigenous to its Islamic milieu. Indeed, within two centuries of the founding of Islam in 622 C.E. there were interesting theological debates going on within Islam itself as well as between Muslims and Greek, or more precisely, Syrian Christians. It thus would be foolish, and historically inaccurate, to think that the *falāsifa* (i.e., the practitioners of *falsafa*) were not aware of these theological debates, for the philosophers did react to such discussions. Still, it is with the translation of Greek philosophical and scientific works that *falsafa* arises within the medieval Arabic-speaking world as an independent intellectual enterprise.

The translation of Greek philosophical and scientific works into Arabic, the so-called "Graeco-Arabic translation movement," must be reckoned as one of the great human intellectual achievements of all times.[2] It certainly would be difficult to overstate its importance for the history of Western philosophy. With this movement virtually the entire ancient Greek philosophical and scientific corpora were translated into Arabic.

---

[1] For a discussion of the Neoplatonized Aristotelianism and course curriculum to which medieval Arabic speakers were heir, see Cristina D'Ancona, "Greek into Arabic: Neoplatonism in Translation" in *Cambridge Companion to Arabic Philosophy*, Peter Adamson and Richard Taylor, eds., 10–31.

[2] For studies of the Arabic translation movement see F. E. Peters, *Aristotle and the Arabs*, and Dimitri Gutas, *Greek Thought, Arabic Culture: The Graeco-Arabic Translation Movement in Baghdad and Early ʿAbbāsid Society (2ⁿᵈ–4ᵗʰ / 8ᵗʰ–10ᵗʰ Centuries)*.

With the possible exception of the translation of Arabic and Greek philosophical and scientific works into Latin, there seems to be no other translation movement that approaches the Graeco-Arabic translation movement in scale and magnitude.

The early seeds of the Arabic translation movement were sown in the middle of the fourth century C.E. when the Roman emperor, Jovianus, ceded a large tract of land (which included modern-day Syria) to the Sassanian, or Persian, Empire. Later, when Christian authorities in the Roman Empire began to persecute various heterodox Christian sects, such as the Monophysites and Nestorians, these groups were able to escape to these ceded lands, bringing with them books of Greek learning, which were in turn translated into Syriac. These translations, together with Syrian Christian translators, gave rise to the Arabic translation movement and so ultimately made *falsafa* itself possible. The movement may roughly be said to have begun with the accession of the ʿAbbāsid dynasty in 762 C.E. Among the first works translated were pieces on Aristotelian logic, followed shortly thereafter by works in the natural sciences, medicine, and metaphysics. The initial impetus for the movement appears to have been to provide Muslims with the intellectual tools to engage Christian theologians in religious debate; however, a general desire for knowledge seems to have been what perpetuated it thereafter.

The movement itself might be divided loosely into three stages. The first and earliest stage was characterized by a very literal style, and included such figures as Ibn al-Muqaffaʿ, Usṭāth, and members of the Kindī circle.[3] The second stage might be thought to begin with the caliphate of al-Maʾmūn (r. 813–833). Here we reach the high point of the movement, which was carried out primarily under the directorship of the Syrian Christian Ḥunayn ibn Isḥāq (809–877) with the help of his son Isḥāq ibn Ḥunayn (d. 910 or 911), his nephew Ḥubaish, and his disciple ʿĪsā ibn Yaḥyá, although one must also mention the Ḥarrānian, Thābit ibn Qurra, as a leading translator at this stage of the movement. For the most part it would be the polished translations of the Ḥunayn circle and their revisions of earlier translations that would provide the sources and foundation for *falsafa*. The third and final stage of the Arabic translation movement most frequently consisted of revisions and school editions of older versions by the Baghdad Peripatetics, such as Abū Bishr Mattá (d. 940) and Yaḥyá ibn ʿAdī (d. 974).

In a relatively short period of time, this handful of translators rendered practically the entire corpus of classical Greek scientific learning into Arabic. A brief list of some of the more important authors translated will give a sense of the magnitude of this undertaking. Virtually all the works of Aristotle were translated into Arabic. Plato's *Republic* and the *Laws* along with paraphrastic summaries of the philosophical content

---

[3] See Peter Adamson, *The Arabic Plotinus: A Philosophical Study of the* "Theology of Aristotle" for a discussion of the role of the Kindī circle in the early translation movement.

of many of his dialogues found their way into the Islamic world. The translators made available many of the works of later Greek Peripatetics, such as the paraphrases of Themistius as well as commentaries and treatises by Alexander of Aphrodisias. The writings of later Greek Neoplatonists also were translated, which would include many of their commentaries on the works of Aristotle as well as some of their commentaries on Plato. (Interestingly, the commentaries of the great Neoplatonic expositor, Simplicius, do not seem to have made it into Arabic translation.) A redaction of Proclus' *Elements of Theology*, which was known to medieval Arabic speakers under the title *The Pure Good* (*Fī l-Khayr al-maḥḍ*) (the *Liber de Causis* of the Latins), was erroneously attributed to Aristotle, as was a redaction of books IV–VI of Plotinus' *Enneads* under the title *The Theology of Aristotle*. Almost the entire Greek mathematical corpus was translated into Arabic, which would include the works of such luminaries as Euclid and Archimedes. Much of the voluminous medical corpus of Galen as well as the astronomical and scientific works of Ptolemy were translated as well. The Stoics and Skeptics seem to be the only Greek thinkers not translated into Arabic; if they were translated, virtually nothing of these translations is still extant, although Arabic-speaking philosophers certainly knew elements of their thought. A complete list of Greek works translated into early medieval Arabic can be found in an-Nadīm's *Fihrist*.[4]

II. THE INTELLECTUAL WORLD OF THE ANCIENT AND MEDIEVAL MEDITERRANEAN

Since all the figures included in this anthology assumed at least some and often quite a bit of familiarity with the thought of Aristotle and later developments in Greek philosophy and science, some attempt should be made to provide an historical and intellectual context for the *falsafa* movement. It would be impossible in a few pages, or even a book, to summarize the philosophical and scientific content of the Greek learning that the Islamic world inherited. Still, at least some general sketch of it is needed if one is to appreciate the advances made by philosophers writing in Arabic. Greek thinkers and the Near Eastern thinkers who followed them, used an Aristotelian framework to build their systems of logic and natural philosophy; they then supplemented Aristotle's thought with that of Galen in medicine, Ptolemy in Astronomy, and Neoplatonism in metaphysics and cosmology. The classical and medieval school curriculum began with logic and a good dose of mathematics, which were followed by natural philosophy, that is, the study of nature and the physical universe, which included the sciences of physics, psychology, biology, and astronomy. The high point of study was metaphysics or theology. The course curriculum ended with ethics and statescraft.

---

[4] An English translation is available: Bayard Dodge, *The Fihrist: A 10th Century AD Survey of Islamic Culture*. Great Books of the Islamic World.

Logic itself was considered a tool for practicing science and philosophy, which directed the intellect towards truth and preserved it from formal fallacies of reasoning. The objects of logical reasoning were the predicables, which in their most general divisions are genera, species, differences, properties, and accidents. Using these predicables the ancient and medieval logician and scientist would construct definitions as well as the philosophical and scientific propositions used in the given sciences. Thus, by giving something's genus and difference, the definition of a species resulted. For example, the species "human" might be defined as an animal (a genus) that is capable of rational thought (a difference). Properties and accidents could also be predicated of subjects to provide further scientific statements, such as "All humans are capable of laughter (a property)" or "Some humans are black (an accident)."

In addition to the general predicables—genus, species, difference, properties, and accidents—ancient philosophers also spoke of the predicables that corresponded with one of the ten ways of existing identified in Aristotle's *Categories*, that is, existing as a substance (*ousia*),[5] quantity, quality, relation, at a place, during a time, in a position, having a possession, and existing as an action or passion. For example, one might say of Socrates that he is a substance, but one might also say that Socrates is pale or short. The category of substance was considered the most basic or primary category, for the existence of all the other categories, the so-called "accidents," is dependent upon the existence of substances. That is because everything other than the primary substances can either be said of or is in a substance, as in "Socrates (a substance) is snub-nosed (an accident)," but substances are not said of and do not exist in anything else—one does not say, "*x* is a Socrates"—at least not in the primary signification of substance.[6]

Aristotle's *Categories*, however, not only was intended to provide a logical framework for composing premises, but also was intended to provide an ontology depicting the way the world itself is. This ontology is frequently referred to as Aristotle's "Substance Ontology." For Aristotle, and those following him, to exist as a substance is the primary way of existing, whereas any of the other categories merely indicate a qualified existence of a substance, for example, existing as snub-nosed. Intuitively, the reasons for making substances primary are obvious: while one can happily admit that Socrates, or any other substance for that matter, need not exist as snub-nosed (or any other accidental feature), one is less inclined to think that snub-nosed-ness exists independently of any substance.

---

[5] The notion of *ousia* or substance is that of a self-subsistent being that does not inhere in a subject but is ultimately the subject of the other modes of existence, that is, the so-called accidents.

[6] Aristotle accepts that genus and species, such as animal and human, respectively, are substances in a secondary sense, whereas particulars, such as Socrates, are substances in the primary sense. Thus, animal and human can be said of Socrates; however, substances in the primary sense are neither said of nor exist in a substance.

Given these categories of predication and existence, one can couple them together to form propositions or premises. Aristotle treats the various ways one might form well-constructed logical statements in *On Interpretation*. Next, given these well-formed premises, one can manipulate pairs of premises to form valid inferences; in the *Prior Analytics*, Aristotle indicated the various logically valid inference patterns. According to Aristotle's *Posterior Analytics*, scientific knowledge (Grk. *epistēmē*, Arb. *ʿilm*) involves the possession of premises that are true, primitive, and immediate (that is, they are not themselves inferred from some more basic premises), as well as a body of valid inferences based on such premises in which one has a demonstration (Grk. *apodeixis*, Arb. *burhān*). In addition, these first principles of a science must be better known than, prior to, and explanatory of the conclusion of the inference.

If the premises, and the inferences based upon them, are to fulfill these criteria, then they should concern causal interrelations among things. In his *Physics*, Aristotle identifies four types of causes that are investigated in the sciences. These are the material cause, the formal cause, the efficient cause, and the final cause. Loosely, the material cause is whatever underlies and is necessary if a given structure is to exist, such as the gold of a ring, while the formal cause is the structure imposed upon that underlying thing, such as the circular, hollow shape of the ring. The efficient cause is that which imposes the form upon the matter, in our example, the jeweler, and the final cause is the purpose or reason for imposing the form on the matter, for instance, adornment. Later commentators would further classify the material and formal causes as "internal causes" and the efficient and final causes as "external causes."

The primary subject matter of physics, according to Aristotle, is motion or change. Change, Aristotle argued, involves three factors: an underlying thing, privation, and form. The underlying thing is that which undergoes the change and is often identified with matter. In the physical systems of the ancient and medieval Mediterranean world, the basic physical stuff underlying change was some mixture of the four primary elements: earth, water, air, and fire, and perhaps underlying these was some even more basic stuff, which is wholly undifferentiated and as such frequently referred to as prime matter. Privation is also a necessary element of change, since if the underlying thing already possessed a given feature, there would be no sense in which the object changes, at least not with respect to that feature. Finally, the form is that aspect or quality that the underlying thing takes on at the end of the change. Thus, change involves a certain privation associated with an underlying thing that in its turn is replaced by a form at the end of the change. For example, consider a skillet's becoming hot. The skillet is the underlying thing; the initial coolness or lack of heat is the privation; and the heat that the skillet acquires when heated is the form.

Aristotle also took it as an obvious fact that if something is undergoing motion or change, then there must be some cause of this motion or change. One of the pressing issues in Aristotle's *Physics* concerns the nature of the ultimate cause of change, which Aristotle argued must be an Unmoved Mover. He reasoned thus: Since the cosmos obviously is undergoing motion it must be either (1) self-moved or (2) moved by another, where that other might be either (2a) itself moved by another or (2b) unmoved. The cosmos cannot be (1) wholly self-moved, continued Aristotle, because whenever something is moved, there is what is moved and what does the moving.[7] "Being moved," however, is an effect, whereas "what does the moving" is a cause. Thus, if the cosmos were wholly self-moved it simultaneously would be the effect and the cause of that very effect, which is absurd. If the cosmos is moved by another, call that other x, then one can pose the initial question of x: is x (1) self-moved, (2a) moved by another, or (2b) unmoved? For the reasons just stated, x cannot be wholly self-moved, but if it is moved by another, call that third thing y, then one is on the way to an infinite regress, since one can ask the initial question of y. In the case of an infinite regress, however, there would need to be an infinite number of actually existing causes to explain the motion of the cosmos, a position that most Aristotelians took to be absurd. Consequently, concluded Aristotle, the motion of the cosmos must be due to (2b) an Unmoved Mover.

As a historical note, whereas Aristotle had framed the question in terms of the *motion* of the cosmos and placed the discussion within the science of physics, later philosophers, particularly the Neoplatonists, generalized the question to the very being or existence of the cosmos itself. Thus, these later thinkers moved the discussion to the science of metaphysics, whose primary subject matter some thought was being *qua* being, that is, existence in whatever way it might be found, and others thought to be immaterial beings, such as "God."

Another pressing issue, which, like the previous topic, was discussed in both physics and metaphysics, is whether the motion of the cosmos, and indeed the cosmos itself, is eternal or was moved or came to exist at some first moment in time. Two of the most common arguments for the eternality of the cosmos were drawn from Aristotle: the first is taken from the relation between change and the cause of change, and the second is taken from time's relation to change. Let us consider the relation between change and the cause of change in the case of a first moment of change. If there were a first moment of change with respect to the cosmos, then the cause of this change, that is, the Unmoved Mover, would have changed from not causing the motion of the cosmos to causing it; however, in that case there is a change in the Unmoved Mover, which entails not only that the *Unmoved* Mover changes and so is moved, which is absurd, but also that there is a change before the first change, which is likewise absurd. The absurdities arise because it was assumed that the change in the cosmos was the first change, but this change requires the prior change in the cause of the change. If one shifts grounds and now claims that the change in the cause of motion is the first change, then Aristotle could simply ask about the cause of this change, and one is on the road to infinite regress.

---

[7] This analysis holds even in the case where, for example, I move myself to pick up an apple, for there is my body that is moved, and my desire for an apple that moves me to pick up the apple.

Similarly, one who maintains the temporal origin of the universe seems committed to a claim that is something like the following: "There *was* nothing *after* which there *is* something." The claim relies on both tense and a temporal particle, both of which presuppose the existence of time. According to Aristotle and those following him, however, time requires the existence of some changing thing of which time is its measure. In that case, however, if there were a time when there was nothing, there would also need to be some changing thing that time is measuring. Consequently, there would be something when purportedly there was nothing, which is absurd.

The majority of Greek- and Arabic-speaking philosophers who followed Aristotle maintained that the cosmos is eternal; nonetheless, there were those in both traditions, such as John Philoponus (ca. 490–570 C.E.) in the Greek tradition and al-Kindī in the Arabic tradition, who argued for the temporal origin of the world. Although they used several variations of argument against the thesis that the world is eternal, at their root all these arguments held that the eternality of the world would entail some absurdity involving the infinite. Thus, Philoponus argued that since the human soul is immortal, if there had been an infinite number of days, which an eternal cosmos seems to imply, and if only one person died per day but the soul continued to exist, then there currently would exist an actually infinite number of immortal souls; however, it is absurd that an actual infinite exists. Thus, concluded Philoponus, the cosmos must temporally be finite and so is not eternal.

Al-Kindī claimed that the eternality of the world lands one in a different sort of absurdity involving the infinite. He began by asserting that the infinite cannot be traversed, a premise that Aristotle and virtually all of those following him likewise maintained. Now if the cosmos were eternal, then an infinite number of days must have passed. Thus in order for the cosmos to have reached the present day, which it obviously has, then it would have traversed an infinite number of days. Again, reasserted al-Kindī, traversing an infinite is impossible. Thus, only a finite number of days could have been traversed, and as such the cosmos must have a temporal origin.

Despite differences of opinion concerning the duration of the cosmos, there was fairly widespread agreement about the topography of the cosmos. The Earth was fixed at the center of the universe and did not move. The element earth, which was thought to be the heaviest element, tended toward the center of the universe; then surrounding earth was the element water, followed by air, which surrounded both earth and water. Finally, the lightest element, fire, extended just to the sphere of the Moon. Beyond the sublunar realm were the seven known "planets": the Moon, Mercury, Venus, the Sun, Mars, Jupiter, and Saturn, which loosely might be thought to occupy concentric spheres around the Earth. The final sphere was that of the fixed stars. Approximately once every twenty-four hours the sphere of the fixed stars would complete a westward rotation around the Earth, sweeping with it all the planets below it and thus producing day and night. In addition to this diurnal westward motion, each of the planets also had a much slower eastward motion, which would account for changes in their placement as viewed against the fixed stars. In order to bring astronomical theory in line with empirical observation, Ptolemy (ca. 150 C.E.) had further worked out a system of deferents and epicycles, where a "deferent" is a larger sphere upon whose circumference there is a smaller sphere or epicycle. By manipulating the size, speed, and directions of the deferent and epicycle, ancient and medieval astronomers were able to provide close approximations of the heavens' apparent movements as seen from the Earth.

The motion of the heavens in turn produced motions in the elements of the sublunar realm. In general, the elements were in a sense constituted by four fundamental qualities: hot-cold, and wet-dry. Earth was a cold-dry mixture, water a cold-wet mixture, air a hot-wet mixture, and fire a hot-dry mixture. Thus, as the planets moved and brought about a motion in the elements, there came to be more complex mixtures of these four fundamental qualities, which in turn underlay the more complex substances. Among the more important mixtures, at least for ancient and medieval medicine following Hippocrates (460–377 B.C.E.) and Galen (131–201 C.E.), there were the four so-called humors: black bile, yellow bile, phlegm, and blood, which in human and higher animals mirrored the four elements. Black bile was a cold-dry mixture, yellow bile a hot-dry mixture, phlegm a cold-wet mixture, and blood a hot-wet mixture. The health as well as the temperament and disposition of a person were very much associated with which one of these humors predominated or whether there was a proper balance of these various humors.

Also within the domain of natural philosophy was a series of psychological questions concerning the soul: whether the soul exists, and if so, what are its nature and functions, and whether part of the soul can survive the death of the body. The locus classicus for these issues was again Aristotle, particularly his *De anima*. Aristotle defined the soul as "the first actuality of an organic body having life in it potentially."[8] Simply put, the soul is whatever it is that explains why living things are alive. Since living things are different from nonliving things, and there must be something that explains this difference, it was a short step for Aristotle and his followers to prove the existence of the soul. It should be noted, however, that since plants and other animals are also alive, having a soul is not unique to humans; rather, it is something common to all living things regardless of how primitive that life might be.

As for the nature of the soul, Aristotle identified it with the substantial form that belongs to a living thing; for if the soul were identified with the matter, then all material things, such as rocks, water, and the like, would also be living, and it is fairly clear that these latter sorts of things are not alive. Living things are in turn identified by the various functions proper to them as living things, such as self-nourishment, growth, and reproduction at the most basic level, as well as movement, perception, and even

---

[8] See Aristotle, *De anima* II 1, 412a27–28.

intelligence in the higher forms of animals. Since the soul is what explains being alive, it must explain these various operations and functions as well. Certainly for later Greek- and Arabic-speaking philosophers, the uniquely human function of thinking was the most pressing issue needing explanation.

Human cognition was explained on the model of perception. Perception involved something that was in potency to perceiving. For example, when a well-functioning visual system is put in the proper causal relation, such as being in the presence of an illuminated object, then that object causes that which potentially perceives actually to perceive. Similarly, in human cognition there must be what potentially thinks, the so-called "potential intellect," or what Alexander of Aphrodisias (fl. late second and early third century C.E.) and much of the later tradition called the "material intellect," as well as what causes that potential intellect actually to think, the so-called "Active Intellect" or "Agent Intellect." When these two intellects are in the correct causal relation, the human thinks.

What marks thinking apart from mere perception in Aristotelian psychology is that the manner in which the perceptible form is received in perception is quite different from the manner in which the intelligible form is received in thinking. In perception the perceiver receives a particular perceptible form from some external material thing, that is, the form inasmuch as it exists in a particular place at a particular time along with all the particular features of the perceived thing. This is not to say that the elemental matter of the perceived object is received into the perceiver, but only that the particularity of the perceived object as a material thing is received. In contrast, in the case of thinking, the human comes to have a wholly *immaterial* intelligible form, and so one that is not particularized. In other words, the intelligible form is something universal and not particular to a certain set of conditions. As such the universal intelligible form of, for example, a human is of what-it-is-to-be human rather than of this or that human. Since in thinking the human intellect receives something immaterial, namely, the intelligible form, then some aspect of the intellect likewise must be immaterial; for it was a general maxim that a thing is received only according to the manner of the receiver. Inasmuch as some aspect of the soul is immaterial, it would be unaffected by the death of the material body.

At least two debates ensued in both the classical and the medieval Islamic period concerning this immortal aspect of the soul. First, Aristotle's *De anima* III 5 strongly suggests that he thought that the Active Intellect is immortal. The question that arose among Aristotle's later commentators was whether the Active Intellect was common to or shared by all humans and as such was an independent substance distinct from any particular human intellect. If the Active Intellect was a separate substance, and so in some way existed apart from particular humans, then the death of any given individual human body would entail the death of the soul that is particular to that individual. This was the position of Alexander of Aphrodisias. Philoponus, in contrast, maintained that a unique Active Intellect belongs to each individual human, and so each individual human has an immortal part that survives the death of the body. Of course, between these two extreme positions there was room for many variations.

A second and related issue was whether the Active Intellect is the only immortal part, as Aristotle seemed to suggest, or might both the potential intellect and the Active Intellect be immortal. If both the potential and active intellects were immortal, then one might follow Alexander's position that the Active Intellect is a separate substance—which among the figures represented in this anthology was clearly the received view—and yet still maintain the subjective immortality of a part of the soul, namely, the potential intellect. Indeed, by the end of the classical period of Arabic philosophy, one of the most pressing issues in psychology focused on the nature of the potential or material intellect understood as something receptive.

As in natural philosophy, the foundation for metaphysical enquiry in the ancient and medieval world was Aristotle's thought, as embodied in his *Metaphysics*. In *Metaphysics*, the Unmoved Mover of *Physics* is transformed into "Thought Thinking Itself,"[9] a being that wholly transcends the physical world and would be identified as "God" by later thinkers. Despite the fact that Aristotle's God has no direct contact with our world, nor even thinks about our world, it causes the motion of the cosmos inasmuch as it is an object of desire that the cosmos desires to imitate. Obviously a moving or changing cosmos cannot imitate an Unmoved Mover in being unmoved, but it can do the next best thing, which is to rotate eternally in a stable way around the Earth; and as we have seen, this rotation is the proximate cause of the various changes and different mixtures that make up our world.

The metaphysical thought of Aristotle was further supplemented in significant ways by the thought of various later Neoplatonic thinkers, most notably Plotinus (204–270 C.E.) and Proclus (411–485 C.E.), but also Aristotle's later Neoplatonic commentators as well, such as Philopinus. We have already mentioned one such addition; namely that, for Aristotle, the Unmoved Mover was simply a cause of the motion or change in the world, not of the forms and matter that constitute the world and so of the world's very existence, whereas for later Neoplatonists the "One" was the source of being itself.

One can approach the subject of the One from the Neoplatonic principle of prior simplicity. This principle claims that in every composite thing there must be a principle of unity that makes the diverse components or constituents of the composite to be a unified thing and so to be; for a thing only is or has being insofar as it is one or has unity. Wholly nonunified components are no more an existing thing than scattered chalk dust is a piece of chalk. Given this principle, Neoplatonists argued that there must be an ultimate principle of unity—the One—that explains the unity and so being

---

[9] See Aristotle, Metaphysics Λ (XII, 6–9).

in all things. Since the One is in a sense the cause of being, it must itself be beyond being, while everything else that is, ultimately depends upon the One for its being. Since the One is wholly one and unified, nothing can be said or predicated of it, since such predication would suggest a composition in it. In short, the One is beyond understanding and words, and all the philosopher can hope to do is talk *around* the One.

The "causal mechanism" used by Neoplatonists to explain how the One is a source of all being is an emanationist schema. According to this schema, there emanates or flows from whatever is perfect a certain secondary activity. For example, light emanates from the Sun and heat emanates from fire; light and heat are not identical with the Sun and fire, but given the Sun or fire, light and heat necessarily follow. Similarly, being flows from the One. Thus, from the One, Intellect flows, and by Intellect's contemplating the One it is made determinate and so has being. Intellect itself also has a certain perfection, and thus it too has its own secondary activity that flows from it, namely, the Soul, and when Soul contemplates Intellect it is made determinate and so has being. Soul in its turn pours forth the World Soul, which is followed by the souls or intellects associated with all the planets of ancient and medieval astronomy. With each successive emanation the subsequent being is less perfect than the being from which it emanated, and with each successive stage of imperfection the subsequent being becomes less actual and more potential until the process of emanation terminates at the potentiality that is the matter of the sublunar realm. Here one reaches the physical world, where the physical system of Aristotle once again applies.

In general, medieval Arabic-speaking philosophers were less attracted by the ethical and political theories of the Greeks than they were by their logical, physical, and cosmological theories and rather preferred their own indigenous ethical and political systems of thought. In fact, at best only one or perhaps two books of Aristotle's *Politics* were translated into Arabic,[10] and although it seems that the whole of Aristotle's *Nicomachean Ethics* was translated, it did not receive the same close attention and popularity as his other writings.[11] Interestingly, it was Plato's *Republic* to which Arabic-speaking philosophers turned in those cases where they appropriated classical thought in their theories of statecraft. More specifically, it was the description of Plato's "philosopher-king" that inspired them, which, with relative ease, could be appropriated to the Islamic notion of an ideal caliph. Thus it is Plato's philosopher-king that is the climax of

---

[10] For a full discussion of the fortunes of Aristotle's *Politics* in the Arab world, see Shlomo Pines, "Aristotle's *Politics* in Arabic Philosophy," 150–60; reprinted in *The Collected Works of Shlomo Pines*, 146–56.

[11] Having said that, it should be noted that al-Fārābī did write a commentary on the *Nicomachean Ethics*, which is no longer extant, and the final part of Ibn Sīnā's "Pointers and Reminders" (*Al-Ishārāt wa-t-tanbīhāt*)] is clearly inspired by the meta-ethics of the *Nicomachean Ethics*.

al-Fārābī's magisterial *The Principles of the Opinions of the People of the Excellent City*, and it is the *Republic* that fills the spot of political theory in Ibn Rushd's monumental commentary project. Again, however, as a general rule the philosophical interests of most *falāsifa*, at least with respect to what they appropriated from classical Greek learning, were logic, natural philosophy, and metaphysics rather than subjects in value theory.

III.   THE PHYSICAL THEORY AND COSMOLOGY OF ISLAMIC SPECULATIVE THEOLOGY (*KALĀM*)

Alongside the classical Greek tradition there were also indigenous Islamic traditions, most notably the tradition surrounding the Qur'ān as well as *kalām* or Islamic speculative theology, both of which made claims that Arabic-speaking philosophers felt obliged to address. The Qur'ān was of particular importance for Muslims working in the *falsafa* tradition, who would occasionally cite verses from it as proof texts for their own philosophical positions. Still, the Qur'ān is not, nor was it intended to be, a philosophical textbook that systematically lays out arguments and rigorously defines philosophical concepts; rather, the Qur'ān is a religious text intended for all, whether philosophers or nonphilosophers. Be that as it may, the Qur'ān nonetheless does assert a number of what might be thought of as philosophical theses. Examples would include the affirmation that God exists as well as his having certain attributes, such as being perfect, unchanging, omnipotent, and omniscient; the claim that God is a creator and at least the strong suggestion that God created the world out of nonbeing at some first moment in time; and likewise the position that the human soul is immortal and the strong suggestion that there will be a bodily resurrection. Given the number of "philosophical" claims made in the Qur'ān and its ubiquitous influence on Islamic culture, it would have been virtually impossible for those philosophers working within the *falsafa* tradition, who were ostensibly Muslim, at least not to address some of the more apparent discrepancies between certain of their philosophical positions and claims of the Qur'ān. Consequently, certain philosophers at times felt obliged to reconcile their philosophical theses with the Qur'ān. Although this might be done in a number of ways, it was most frequently done by arguing that Qur'ānic claims that seemed contrary to demonstrative philosophical and scientific theses were in fact metaphorical restatements of those same philosophical and scientific positions, albeit presented in a way accessible to the masses who lacked proper intellectual training.

Although most of the Muslim *falāsifa* took a conciliatory approach towards the claims of the Qur'ān, they were considerably less willing to do so towards the claims of Islamic speculative theologians and frequently were outright hostile towards them. Unfortunately, assessing the exact extent of the intellectual exchange between *falsafa* and *kalām* is difficult, primarily because of the paucity of extant early *kalām* sources. In light of the work that still needs to be done on early *kalām*, the following survey should be viewed as an extremely rough sketch of the physical system and cosmology of *kalām*, intended merely to help provide a context for understanding some of the philosophers' arguments and criticisms.[12]

In general, the world of the Islamic speculative theologian could be divided up into God and then atoms (literally, indivisible bodies) and accidents. In addition, some theologians suggested that void space must also be included in this ontology as the space in which God creates. One of the standard *kalām* arguments for the existence of God begins with a proof that we have already encountered in al-Kindī. It observes that an infinite is impossible; however, if the world were eternal, then necessarily there would have been an infinite amount of time or an infinite number of days, which, by the initial assumption, is impossible. Thus, the world must have been created. If there is a creation, however, then there must be a Creator; for creation and Creator are correlative terms. Thus, a Creator, or God, must exist.

That there can be only one God is argued in the following way. Assume for the sake of argument that there were two gods, then it would be at least possible that these two gods could desire contrary things, such as an individual's dying or living right now. Under this scenario one is left with three options: (1) both of their desires are accomplished; (2) neither of their desires is accomplished; or (3) the desire of only one of them is accomplished. As for (1), since the desires are assumed to involve contrary outcomes, they both cannot be accomplished simultaneously; how could one be simultaneously both alive and dead? If (2) neither of their desires are accomplished, then both are wanting in power, whereas God is omnipotent, and so neither is in fact God. Finally, in the case of (3) where only one of their desires is accomplished, the one whose desire is accomplished is God, since the other is wanting in power and so is not God. This argument was in turn generalized to show that God must be wholly one or unified, a doctrine known as *tawḥīd*.

As for the physical world, most, though not all, of the Islamic speculative theologians took it to be a composition of atoms and accidents. Atoms are the minimal units of a wholly simple quantity. As such, atoms have no internal features into which they even could be divided. Although atoms function as the components of the various magnitudes composed of them, such as lines, planes, and solids, they technically cannot be said to have length, width, and depth, for length, width, and depth define bodies whereas atoms are the components out of which bodies are constituted. Since atoms are simple and have no internal features, whatever determinations they do have are accidents. Accidents are in turn defined as any and every attribute or determination that belongs to atoms and appear in the world, such as colors, tastes, being alive or

---

12 The following are additional resources for those interested in learning more about *kalām*: Harry A. Wolfson, *The Philosophy of Kalam*; Richard M. Frank, *Beings and Their Attributes: The Teaching of the Basrian School of the Muʿtazila in the Classical Period*; and Alnoor Dhanani, *The Physical Theory of Kalām: Atoms, Space, and Void in Basrian Muʿtazilī Cosmology*.

being ignorant, and the like. Atoms never exist separate from accidents; for inasmuch as atoms have no determinate features or attributes of their own, and to be wholly indeterminate is simply not to exist, there would be no meaningful sense in which it might be said that atoms exist without accidents. Moreover, every atom has every accident or its contrary. So, for example, an atom must have either the accident of being colored or the accident of being not-colored and similarly for taste/no-taste, living/not-living, knowing/ignorant as well as all the rest of the possible accidents and their contraries.

Considered in themselves, both atoms and accidents are incapable of sustaining their own existence; that is to say, if left alone they would cease to exist in a moment, where a "moment" is frequently understood as some atomic temporal unit or minimal amount of time. Since atoms and accidents do not endure, God must constantly re-create the atoms along with their accidents at every moment.

This constant re-creation of the atoms and their accidents, also called "occasionalism," entails that atoms and accidents are incapable of causal interaction. This conclusion follows since no atom, accident, or purported causal influence survives the constant annihilation that every atom and accident suffers such that it could cause the events of some later moment. Instead, it is God, and only God, who causes those events. In this vein, as well as one that the eighteenth-century Scottish philosopher Hume would develop several hundred years later, Islamic theologians were keen to note that when, for example, one observes fire's being brought into contact with cotton and then observes the cotton's burning, one does not in fact observe the fire's causing the cotton to burn. All one experiences is a constant conjunction of these two events, not a causal relation. In short, for the Islamic speculative theologian there is no empirical basis for assuming causal relations, and based upon their physical system, there are theoretical reasons for denying natural causal relations.

Given this occasionalist worldview, most Islamic theologians analyzed motion not as a smooth progression over a continuous space but as a series of discrete events during which an atom or set of atoms is re-created in different locations at different moments along an anticipated trajectory. Slower motions were explained by an atom or set of atoms being re-created for a number of moments at a given spot (or "resting") before being re-created in a different spot, and faster motions by the atoms' having fewer intervals of rest.

The notable exception to this atomic picture of motion was the Islamic theologian an-Naẓẓām (d. ca. 840) and his theory of the "leap" (ṭafra), which in salient ways is a hybrid of kalām atomic theories of motion and Aristotelian continuous theories of magnitude. On his theory an object moves from one spatial position to another by means of a series of discrete leaps without being in the intervening places, and so an-Naẓẓām's theory is akin to an atomic account of motion; however, the space over which the object leaps is continuous space, and so the theory is akin to a continuous theory of magnitude. The advantage of this otherwise odd theory is that it allowed an-Naẓẓām to avoid the unsavory consequences of certain Zeno-like paradoxes[13] that plagued more traditional Islamic atomic theories.

Even given the paucity of sources on early *kalām*, the above does not come close to describing the content of *kalām*'s physical theory and many of the issues debated by early Muslim theologians. Still, it is hoped that the preceding sketch does provide an adequate historical context to understand and evaluate some of the arguments presented by the philosophers treated in this anthology.

---

[13] The most common Zeno-like paradox in the medieval Islamic world was the ant-sandal paradox. It observed that if magnitudes were continuous, then should an ant attempt to cross a sandal, it would first need to reach the halfway point on the sandal, but before it could reach the halfway point, it would need to reach its halfway point and so on infinitely. Since an infinite cannot be traversed, the ant could never cross the sandal, but of course a body such as a sandal can be crossed, and thus bodies cannot be continuous, but must be composed of a finite number of atomic parts. As an-Naẓẓām noted that if the ant makes discontinuous "leaps" between points, it need not traverse an infinite number of such halfway points, and so the paradox does not arise.

AL-KINDĪ

Abū Yūsuf Yaʿqūb Ibn Isḥāq aṣ-Ṣabbāḥ al-Kindī, also known as "the philosopher of the Arabs," was born around 801 and died in Baghdad around 866. He was associated with the ʿAbbāsid courts of the Caliphs al-Maʾmūn (r. 813–833), al-Muʿtasim (r. 833–842), and al-Wāthiq (r. 842–847), but lost influence at the end of his life during the Caliphate of al-Mutawakkil (r. 847–861), who opposed the philosophical and theological positions of his predecessors—positions, it might be added, with which al-Kindī had sympathized. Al-Kindī flourished during the period of the Arabic translation movement of Greek philosophical and scientific texts, in which he played a limited translating role—most likely simply advising on philosophical and scientific content rather than undertaking any translating himself. He also was engaged to some extent in the controversy between the "rationalist" Muʿtazilite theologians and the "traditionalist" Sunni theologians, in which al-Kindī appeared to have affinities with Muʿtazilism.

A significant contribution of al-Kindī is his assimilation and appropriation of Greek science and philosophy. He wrote nearly two hundred and fifty treatises on philosophy and science, of which less than forty are extant. Examples of this assimilation and appropriation are his adaptation of a general Aristotelian scientific outlook on the cosmos, with such concepts as the act/potency, form/matter, and substance/accident distinctions, and the four causes. One also finds strains of Neoplatonism in his discussion of the "One" and the "many" in *On First Philosophy*, his most important philosophical work, and his subsequent positing of the "One True Being." Still, al-Kindī did not blindly follow the Greeks. He notably rejected the eternity of the world, a doctrine held by most Greek philosophers and most other Islamic *falāsifa* (e.g., al-Fārābī, Ibn Sīnā, and Ibn Rushd). Among al-Kindī's scientific achievements are works on mathematics, optics, medicine, and music. Again, although Greek scientists such as Hippocrates, Euclid, and Ptolemy influenced him, his work shows originality, especially in optics and medicine.

I. THE EXPLANATION OF THE PROXIMATE EFFICIENT CAUSE FOR GENERATION AND CORRUPTION[a]

1. [214] May God grant you long life in the happiest of states and the purest of deeds, O son of noble lords and pious leaders, the beacon of faith, the precious gem, the best of both worlds! May God suffice you in all needs and inspire you to perform all virtuous deeds!

2. Within those things that are clear to the senses (may God disclose the hidden things) lies the clearest evidence of an order by a First Ruler. I mean a Ruler of every

1

ruler, an Agent of every agent, a Creator of every creator, a First of every first, and a Cause of every cause. [This evidence is obvious] for anyone whose sensory apparatus is joined with the lights of his intellect, whose intentions are to find the truth and to associate himself with it specifically, whose aim is to trace causes back to the truth, to discover and evaluate it, and in any case where there is a dispute between himself and his soul, the intellect attests to the truth in his opinion. Whoever is like this will have the dark veils of ignorance ripped away from his soul's eyes, and his soul [thereafter] will abstain from drinking the dregs of vanity and will scorn the shallow-minded strife of pride. He will feel repelled at entering into the evils of sophisms and cease to rely on what is not examined critically. He will be ashamed of wanting to acquire what is not serious or to neglect what is serious. Thus, [the soul] will not oppose itself nor cling fanatically to those things that oppose it.

3. If you are like this (may God be your aid, O you of laudable form and precious substance!), then it will be clear to you that God—exalted is His praise as the True Being Who never was not and never will not be!—has always existed and ever will exist; that He is the single living being that in no way has a share in multiplicity; and that He is the First Cause that has no cause, the Agent that has no agent, the Perfector that has no perfector, the One Who gives the universe being from non-being, and the One Who makes some things reasons and causes for others. [This will be clear to you], just as will that which was explained to you in our remarks in *On First Philosophy*.

4. The greatest sign of a most perfect order and a wisest wisdom, together with their corollaries, namely, One Who rules and is wise (since all of these are correlatives), is to be found in the universe's order and regulation, in the action, subjugation, and subordination of some of its parts in relation to others, and in the perfection of its design, which follows the best possible manner with respect to the generation and corruption of all that is subject to generation and corruption, the permanence of all that is permanent, and the impermanence of all that is impermanent.

5. Were it not for [the benefit that] will transpire from granting your request (may God grant you all good things!) for an exposition concerning God's unity (exalted is His praise, awesome is His power, perfect is the ordering He brings about, boundless is His wisdom, superabundant [216] is His generosity) on behalf of many of the heirs to truth who have not reached the point of ascending the lofty summits of first philosophy and diving into the profoundest depths of its tumultuous swelling seas whose outer limits not even skilled mariners seek without the most thorough preparation and the most accomplished help, then the effort to complete our treatment of the deeply profound topics,[1] which you wanted to be completed for those who speak Arabic, would have been a most decisively strong and most pressing obstacle [to granting your request]. The merchants of any trade, however, are persuaded to take less of their profits when it is for the sake of the common good. We

---

[1] This is a reference to al-Kindī's already completed work, *On First Philosophy*.

beseech the One Who bestows all power to make easy the paths that we take to our goal of illuminating the truth, to strengthen us through the power of His wisdom, and to be a guide to His good order.

6.   It has already been explained through demonstrative propositions that every motion is either (1) locomotion, (2) augmentation or diminution, (3) alteration, or (4) generation or corruption. Locomotion is <the exchange of place of the body's parts and its center, or every part of a body only [but not its center in the case of rotation]>.[b] Augmentation is the motion that takes the terminations of the body to [an extremity] farther from the extremity at which it initially terminated by increasing [the body's] quantity. Diminution is the contrary of augmentation in essence and definition. I mean that it is that which makes the terminations of the body fall short of the extremity at which it initially terminated by decreasing the quantity. [217] Alteration is the motion that takes place through the change of some of a thing's states, while the thing itself is the same thing, as [when] the very same man is white, and then becomes pale owing to the white light of dawn[c] or an illness or the like. Generation and corruption is the motion that transforms something from its kind to another kind, like the nourishment whose kind was drink, or some other nourishment, and is then transformed into blood. So this motion ushers forth a generation of the blood and a corruption of the drink, I mean a motion corrupting the drink and generating the blood.

7.   We say that every motion is either essential or accidental. I mean by "essential" that which is part of the essence of the thing, whereas by "accidental" I mean that which is not part of the essence of the thing. I mean by "being part of the essence of the thing" whatever does not depart from the thing in which it is except through the corruption of its substance, like the life of the living thing, which does not depart from the living thing except through the corruption of its substance and its transformation into a nonliving thing. I mean by "what is not part of the essence of the thing" whatever departs from the thing without its substance being corrupted, like life in body; for life might depart from the living *body*, but the corporeality [of the body] continues in its state and is not corrupted.

8.   Let us now investigate the cause of generation and corruption. We have already made clear elsewhere in our accounts concerning natural philosophy that natural causes are either material, formal, efficient, or final. I mean by "material" the matter of a thing from which the thing is, like the gold that is the matter of the coin (lit. *dīnār*) from which the coin comes into being. By the "form," I mean the form of the coin, which, by virtue of its becoming one with the gold, there is the coin. [218] I mean by the "efficient [cause]" the craftsman of the coin, who makes the form of the coin become one with the gold. By "final [cause]" I mean that for the sake of which the craftsman makes the form of the coin one with the gold, that is, to gain something of benefit by the coin and to obtain what is sought by it. Since the natural causes do not exceed these four causes, these four that we have mentioned are causes of the generation and corruption of everything subject to generation and corruption.

9.   Every thing subject to generation, then, is in some matter or other, and so one cause of the generation and corruption of everything subject to generation and corruption is a material [cause], which is [the thing's] matter from which it was generated or corrupted. [The reason is] because if it were to have no matter, then it would be neither generated nor corrupted, because generation and corruption require a subject in which the generation and corruption successively occur. As for the formal cause, the generable thing comes to be by virtue of the fact that its form is made one with its matter, and it is by virtue of the fact that [the form] is separated from its matter that it corrupts.

10.   As for the efficient cause, this is the very object of our investigation, and it is only by identifying it that we shall find the final cause. [This is] because the final cause is either above the efficient cause (I mean as what compels one to act) or it is itself the efficient cause (I mean that nothing forced [the efficient cause] to act, but that it acted only because of itself, not on account of something else). Now, if the efficient cause is not something that exists, but is [itself] the final [cause], then the final cause does not exist. Whatever is above the <non>existent[d] also does not exist, because whatever does not exist is indeterminate, and with anything that is indeterminate, whatever is above it and is indeterminate [219] also does not exist. So if the efficient cause does not exist, then the final cause does not exist.

11.   The efficient cause is either proximate or remote. The remote efficient cause is like someone who shoots an arrow at an animal and kills it. The one who shoots the arrow is the remote cause of killing the animal, whereas the arrow is the proximate cause of its being killed; for the one who shoots with the intention of killing the animal produces the piercing action of the arrow, but the arrow produces the killing of the living thing by wounding it and by [causing] the living thing to receive an effect from the arrow when it strikes. As for the remote efficient cause of everything that is subject to generation and corruption as well as every perceptible and intelligible thing, we have already explained in our book, *On First Philosophy*,[2] that the First Cause—I mean God (exalted is His praise!)—is the One Who creates and completes[3] the universe, the Cause of causes and the One Who creates every agent. So let us now investigate the proximate efficient cause of everything that is subject to generation and corruption so that it will become clear to us how the universal order is through prior divine wisdom.

12.   The following have been explained in the propositions related to natural philosophy:

12.1.   Generation and corruption apply only to things that possess contrary qualities.

---

2 The reference is to *On First Philosophy*, ch.3.

3 The term here is *mutammim*, which comes from the same root used for "final cause." Thus, the suggestion is that God is both the remote efficient and final cause of the universe.

12.2. Hot, cold, wet, and dry are the primary contrary qualities.

12.3. The outermost body of the universe—I mean what is between the perigee of the Moon up to the last extremity of the body of the celestial sphere—is neither hot, cold, wet, nor dry, and [220] is not subject to generation and corruption for the period of time that God (exalted is His praise!) has appointed to it. Generation and corruption affect only whatever is below the sphere of the Moon.

12.4. Below the sphere of the Moon are the four dominant elements, namely, fire, air, water, earth, and whatever is composed of them. These four elements are neither generated nor corrupt *in toto,* but parts of each one of them do generate and corrupt into one another. *In toto,* however, their individuals remain for the period of time that God (exalted is His praise!) appointed to them. As for those things composed from [the elements] (I mean plants, animals, minerals, and the like) they are subject to generation and corruption completely in their individuals, but what remains of them, as in the case of the elements, is their forms, such as humanness, horseness, woodness, and mineralness.

12.5. Time, place, and locomotion are associated with each of these elements and what is composed from them; for <within>ᵉ the celestial sphere the totality of these four elements and what is composed from them have a place, while time is the number of the motion of the celestial sphere.

12.6. Fire and air are moved naturally away from the middle [of the universe, that is, the center of the earth] to their proper places. The proper place of fire is between <the lunar sphere's lowest point>ᶠ down to air's highest point, and the proper place of air is between fire's lowest point down to the outside surface of earth and water. Next, the proper place of earth and water is between air's lowest point down to the center of the universe, and their natural locomotion is towards the center of the universe. Earth as a whole is situatedᵍ at the center of the universe, and its parts move toward the center of the universe.

12.7. The surface of fire [221] and of air (I mean what is within its highest and lowest points) are both spherical. Also, the surface of earth and air together, while being composites, are spherical to the senses.

13. Now, the proximate cause of the generation and corruption that occurs in the parts of the four elements must be either from them [alone] or from something else, and either one of the two is the cause of that, or several of them and something else together. If it is only from [the elements], then either (1) one of them is the cause, or (2) several of them (that is, more than one) are the cause, or (3) each one of them is a cause of [the generation and corruption] in the others.

14. If, (1 and 2), one or several of them (that is, more than one) is the cause of that [namely, generation and corruption], then the one that is the cause (whether one or more) [must be] incorruptible entirely. Now it would not be one of [the elements] without its parts sometimes being corrupted and becoming many [from 12.4]. So it would be subject to generation and corruption in its parts, while not being subject to

generation and corruption in its parts, which is an impossible contradiction. Therefore, neither one nor many of [the four elements alone] can be the cause of generation
and corruption.

15.   If (3) each one of them is the cause of the generation and corruption
of the rest, then each one of them is the cause of all of them and the effect of all of
them. Now all of them come into contact with one another at spherical surfaces [from
12.6 and 12.7]. So the generation of air from fire and fire from air is either (3a) at
their common boundaries or (3b) it is not. [222] If (3b) it is not at their [common]
boundaries, then fire is affected so as to be air in a part of it where the air does
not touch. What necessarily follows, then, is that there would be an alteration of
every part of the fire whose distance from the surface of air is the [same] distance
as that part, and so the affected fire would be a sphere whose distance and height
from the surface of the sphere of air would be identical throughout. Otherwise some
of the air would have the power to transform the fire and some of it would not. In
that case, the air that is at the extremity of air's sphere, [which by supposition is not
affecting the fire], would either not be of the same nature [as the air that is affecting
the fire] or the cause for the difference of its [powers] is something else. But air is of
the same nature. So if the agent [causing the difference in the air's powers] is not
something else, [air] would invariably transform [any] identical sphere of fire whose
distance from its surface is the same, and so turn it into air. Fire would act on the air
in the same way. So there would be many spheres, some surrounding others, with air
between all of them. It necessarily results from this that each one of the neighboring
spheres would transform any sphere at one and the same distance and height from it
until each one of the spheres of fire and air would actually become entirely air and
entirely fire. But in that case, each one them would be simultaneously and actually
what it is and not what it is, but this is the most repugnant absurdity. The same
follows for the remaining elements. Therefore, there is another agent acting on it, but
we assumed that there was no other agent acting on it, which is an impossible contradiction. So, even if [the elements] are causes of generation and corruption, [223]
their generation and corruption cannot but be at their common boundaries [that is,
not (3b)].⁴

16.   If, (3a), [generation and corruption] occur at their common boundaries,
then either it is along the whole of the boundary or along some part of it and not
others. Now if it is along some part of it and not others, then—assuming that they
do not have a cause other than themselves—they must differ by nature, but we have
already stated that [the elements] do not differ by nature. Therefore, it remains that
the fire that is adjacent to their common boundary would be a sphere of air of uniform
height, and the air [that is adjacent to their common boundary] would be a sphere of
fire of uniform height. Then, as we have stated, there would be many spheres, some
of which surround other contiguous ones—fire surrounding air, for instance—and

---

4   Literally, "it is impossible that their generation and corruption is at their common boundary."

necessarily each one of them would be exerting that [very same] influence on what is adjacent to it until each one of them simultaneously and actually becomes entirely fire, but each one of them would simultaneously and actually be what it is and not what it is, but this is the most repugnant absurdity. The same follows for the rest of the elements. Therefore, the agent acting on it is something else, but it was assumed that there was no other efficient cause of its generation and corruption, which is an impossible contradiction. So it is not the case that each one of them is the proximate cause of the generation and corruption of the others. The only remaining option, then, is that the cause of [generation and corruption] in them is from something else or from them and something else together.

17.   In that case the other cause of [generation and corruption] must necessarily be either together with them or separate [from them]. Now it had been stated in the natural sciences by means of commonly accepted propositions that motion produces heat in the elements and anything composed from the elements. In that case, the elements are acted upon by either motion or contact. What is in contact with the last of them [that is, the outermost celestial sphere, which is in contact with the sphere of fire] neither [acts] by heating nor by cooling nor by moistening nor by drying [from 12.3], and so [the elements] receive only the influence of motion from its contact. Now what is in contact [with the sphere of fire] is made up of individuals varying in motion and position, because some of them are larger, others smaller, some of them are slower, [224] others faster, and some are farther away, some closer, but all of them have limits with respect to fastness and slowness, and additionally with respect to highness and lowness and how far or close [they are].

18.   Now we find that the things that heat others by motion do so more intensely the greater, closer, faster, or lower they are in relation to the position [of the heated object]. Therefore, the cause of the heat that comes to be in the elements as a result of the first element's being moved above them is in virtue of motion, time, place, and quantity. So the influences on the elements vary by virtue of the placement of their parts in relation to the bodies of the first element, and the amount of the time of the rotation over them, whether fast or slow, as well as how many or how few are the things moved above them. When the bodies in motion above a part [of the elements] are greater in number, faster, closer, lower, and bigger, then the heat of that part intensifies, whereas when some part is deprived of that, then it returns to its natural state. So when [those moved bodies] are distant from a part of earth [and water] and anything composed from them, then earth and water remain in their natural state, which is to be cold. (As for the air that surrounds us, it is not pure air; rather, it is mixed with water and earth, and so it descends because in this state the watery and earthy [natures] predominate.)

19.   In the propositions related to the natural sciences, it has already been stated that the primary active qualities [see 12.2 above] are hot and cold, whereas wetness and dryness are passive. So whenever celestial bodies are far from the earth's zenith, cold predominates, and whenever they are near, heat predominates. Then the wetness and dryness associated with hotness and coldness come to be, and from these four

qualities, the rest of the qualities come to be, and in proportion to the deficiency and excess of each one of these, a given thing comes to be.

20.   It was found that the actions of the soul follow upon the elemental mixtures of the [composite] bodies, and the elemental mixtures differ [225] by virtue of the variations of the higher individuals, [that is, the heavenly bodies], with respect to place, motion, time, and quantity, as we said previously. Thus, we can see that the inhabitants of the lands under the equator are turned black, like something cooked by fire, owing to the intense heat [caused] by the return of the Sun there twice during the year as well as to the fact that [the Sun] is directly above the equator, revolving in the greatest sphere.[5] [This also turns] their hair curly and frizzy, as when hair is close to fire and then quickly is [dropped] into it. It makes their lower parts (I mean their limbs) thin, their noses wide, their eyes large and bulging, their lips protuberant. It makes them tall because the moisture of their lower parts is attracted to their higher parts. They are more irritable and infuriated as a result of the excess of heat and dryness in them. Also their judgments change erratically because they are overcome by anger and passion.

21.   We also see that those who live near the arctic region are the opposite of that, owing to the intense cold of the land. For example, their eyes, lips, and noses are small; their color is white; their hair straight; their lower parts are thick as a result of the predominance of cold and wet in them. The heat is concentrated in their internal organs, and so they are sedate, hard-hearted, self-restrained, and frigid with respect to passion. Thus, they are most abstinent and of a middling sort.

22.   [226] Now the inhabitants of moderate climes, because of their moderate humoral mixtures, have a strong capacity for discursive reasoning. Scientific research and speculation is common among them. Moreover, their temperaments are moderate.

23.   We likewise observe that the body of every animal comes to have a temperament commensurate with its elemental mixture. Thus, temperaments follow upon the proximity and distance from us of the [celestial] individuals and how high or low or fast or slow they are, as well as whether they are in conjunction or opposition. Moreover, [our temperament] is proportionate to the elemental mixtures of our bodies at the time that the semen is produced as well as when it settles in the wombs. If that is the case, what would prevent something even finer than that existing through the motion of these celestial bodies at the will of the Creator (exalted is His praise!), since the most obviously discernible thing is their immediate proximate effect and they are its proximate cause? Why would it not be[h] that the rest of the things are only the consequences that follow upon this wondrous generation—I

---

[5] That is, (1) the Sun is directly above at the two equinoxes, and (2) throughout the whole year (summer and winter) the days are all nearly twelve hours.

mean the generation of nature and soul![i] Our thought will have gone far, then, if we establish this.

24.　The most significant evidence that these celestial bodies are the cause of our generation is what we observe of the motion of the Sun and planets, since these motions are very obvious to visual perception [even] setting aside mathematical computation; for these planets are singled out among all the heavenly bodies. [Further evidence] is their relative ordering; the change of their distances from the natural things subject to [227] generation and alteration; the numbers of their motion (some of which are westward and others eastward); as well as their proximity and remoteness to the center. [The motions of these celestial bodies] provide better evidence than the other celestial individuals [namely, the fixed stars] that they are the cause of the generation of things subject to generation, corruption, and alteration, and [the cause of] the continuation of their forms for the time that their Creator (exalted is His praise!) has allotted to them.

25.　This is particularly obvious in the case of the Sun, because it is the largest of the [celestial] bodies, as has been explained according to mathematical theorems. When compared to its magnitude, [the Sun] is the most proximate [celestial] body to us, because the [radius of] the Moon at its greatest distance from the Earth is equivalent[j] to the radius[k] of the Sun at its greatest distance, but the proportional measure of the body of [the Moon] to the body of [the Sun] is less than part[l] of a part. [Therefore], the body of [the Sun] in relation to its magnitude is considerably more proximate than the Moon in relation to its magnitude.

26.　Also, it moves over us faster than the Moon, because if the two are together at some point on the horizon, then the sphere with the Sun will revolve around us, returning [the Sun] to the point on the horizon in 360[m] degrees,[6] 59 minutes, and 8 seconds (or a little more or less to account for variation), whereas the sphere returns the Moon by its motion to its location (I mean the point on the horizon) in 373 degrees (or a little more or less to account for variation). Even if Saturn returns to the point on the horizon [228] only by an addition of 2 minutes to the 360, [the Sun] is still more proximate and larger than [Saturn] while the speed of motion is comparable.

27.　Moreover, of all the lofty bodies [the Sun] has the most obvious effect on what is subject to generation and corruption; for (1) calculating its position in relation to the Earth with reference to height and lowness, remoteness, and proximity from us, [and] (2) with reference to the inclined sphere;[7] and (3) its being tied to the motion of the greater sphere (I mean the one going from east to west); and (4) the difference

---

[6] The Arabic *juz'* here very likely refers to the Greek astronomical term *kronos*, given al-Kindī's use of it in the present argument, in which case it corresponds with $1/360^{th}$ of a sidereal day.

[7] That is, the apparent motion of the Sun is not parallel to the Earth's equator or any lines of latitude; rather, it has an inclination, and as such it crosses all of the Earth's parallels during the sidereal year.

of its centers[n] from the center of the Earth—all will provide the most obvious evidence for that.

28.   That is [so because] we find the places far from the northern tropic [that is, the tropic of Cancer] towards the North Pole are so excessively cold that there are almost no plants or animals there, and the human population is sparser the closer one is to these places. We also see that the places that are under the [celestial] equator are so excessively hot that human population is extremely sparse, and there are very few plants and animals as well. As one passes [the equator] towards the south pole until one comes to the position [whose latitude] corresponds with Sagittarius 5 degrees, 30 minutes [that is, 21 degrees, 35 minutes south of the terrestrial equator], where the Sun at perigee is at its highest and so is at its closest proximity to the Earth, its heat is so strong that the area is absolutely uninhabitable because of the Sun's extreme proximity to the center of the Earth. The farther one goes from these places, the more balanced and well-ordered the elemental mixtures become until one arrives at the places equidistant from the places of extreme cold and [extreme hot].

29.   Moreover, because of the shortening of the winter day, when the Sun is far from the zenith, we find that the moisture and cold increases, owing to the fact that the Sun is far from us and that it appears [only] briefly above us and that its ability to attract moisture away from us [229] and to warm the area and atmosphere around us weakens. During the opposite [season], however, we see the contrary of that.

30.   Now if the Sun's distance from the Earth were not so well-positioned but were higher, then it would heat (in one position) the atmosphere here to such a lesser degree that it would not exert the obvious influence on us that it does. In that case, everything on the Earth would be frozen, just as it is in the regions that are close to the poles, and so there would be no plants or animals or any other generated thing. If it were much closer, then everything on the Earth would be scorched, and again there would be no plants or animals or anything else, just as one finds in places where the Sun is much closer.

31.   Also, if [the Sun's] distance from the Earth were as well-positioned as it now is, but it were not <inclined>[o] (I mean its particular sphere in which it travels from west to east), and its motion were along the sphere of the equator or one of the other spheres parallel to the sphere of the equator, there would be neither winter, summer, autumn, nor spring, but a single season for every place on Earth, either always summer or always winter or one of the other seasons, but never varying. Now if this were the case, then generation and corruption would not continue, and things would be one without any generation and corruption occurring among them. Moreover, [as a result of this] the forms of generation would wholly cease, just as we see at different seasons; for when the dryness of the summer lasts too long, plants and animals perish and there are plagues, and similarly, if it is too brief, there is little heat. The same holds for every season; if it varies from the elemental mixture that it has, then plagues and corruption occur.

32.   If [the Sun's] motion were in an inclined sphere and at [the present] distance, but it were not to set due to [230] the westward diurnal revolution of the

greatest sphere and [instead] it were suspended facing any region on the Earth for half a year (since its revolution is a complete year), then animals would have no rest and also [the Sun] would consume all the moisture in the region so oppressed by it for half of the year. [This is so] because animals rest only when there is day and night. The same holds for the nourishment of plants; for some wither during the day but grow strong and take nourishment during the night, while for others it is just the opposite.

33. If [the Sun] were not eccentric from the Earth, there would not be four seasons but rather two, since [the Sun's] remoteness and proximity during each of its two intervals of declination in the north would be the same from the center of the Earth, and the same would hold [during its declination] in the south.[p] So [the Sun's] action during the northern declination would be one season, and [its action] during the southern declination would be one season.[8] The year would be two seasons only, resembling two of the four elements, and so these two elements would remain and the other two would be transformed into them, since they would have nothing to aid them against the transformation into the other two, unless it is by means of [the other two],[q] but these are strongly opposed to them. Now if there is hot, there is cold necessarily, and if there is dry, there is wet necessarily, and from the composition of the four qualities there are four elements necessarily. If there are two seasons, the elements will not be four; but then in that case it is required that what is necessary is necessarily not, which is an impossible contradiction.

34. How perfect is what the Creator (exalted is His praise!) has designed. For example, the Sun is nearly over our head while it is drawing near to us. It then rises high in the sky and moves away from the face of the earth until [231] it reaches <one inclination>,[r] and then it move towards us until it arrives at the other inclination. It then retreats [from us] until the equinox and descends in a different [direction, passing through] the distance in degrees whose inclination in one direction is the same inclination [as in the other direction].[9] [All of this] is in order that there will be two seasons during each inclination, in which case there will be four seasons corresponding to the qualities of the four elements. Moreover, between any two seasons during a single inclination there will be a quality common to both seasons in order that the natures are not wholly incompatible as a result of all of their qualities' being contrary to one another. If [the natures of the elements were wholly incompatible], then there would be no animals or anything else subject to generation; for the causes that prevent

---

[8] Al-Kindī's idea apparently is that since the Sun's ecliptic is both slightly inclined and slightly off center from the Earth, one can explain the four seasons by the four different relative locations of the Sun to the Earth. Thus, different seasons are correlated with the Sun's being (1) north and near the Earth, (2) north and far from the Earth, (3) south and near the Earth, and (4) south and far from the Earth. If, however, the Sun were only inclined but not eccentric, there would only be the Sun's northern and southern declinations, and so only two seasons.

[9] What al-Kindī is describing in this passage is the Sun's apparent motion between the times of the vernal equinox and the summer solstice, and then the autumnal equinox and the winter solstice.

generation in the places from which the Sun is far or to which it is near, and the places over which the Sun's rising and setting takes great time, or the places in which the seasons are not properly balanced, would be [the same causes] that prevent [generation] if the Sun had been farther or nearer [to the Earth], or its appearance or absence had been longer, or it had not produced a proper balance of seasons in any place.

35.   It has become clear that the normal state of things subject to generation and corruption, and the permanence of their forms to the end of the time that the Creator of generation (exalted is His praise!) intended for generation, and the conservation of their organization are [all] solely due to the following facts: (1) the Sun is well-positioned with respect to its distance from the Earth; (2) it travels in the inclined sphere; (3) it is tied to the motion of the greatest sphere, which imparts to it a westward motion; and (4) its sphere is eccentric in relation to the Earth (I mean with regard to its alternately being near to or far from the center of the Earth). [All of this] is so that there is a limit to the time in which events subject to generation occur.

36.   The Moon may also be a good example of this, because if its distance were not as well-positioned from the Earth as it is now, but rather it were closer, then it would prevent the generation of clouds and rain. [This is so] because it would disperse, dissipate, and rarify the vapors without bringing them together and condensing them. This is just like what we observe during the phases of the new [232] and full Moons; for rainfall is greatest during new Moons and at the first of the month when [the Sun and Moon] are close to conjunction, whereas during full Moons the rainfall is usually less because the Moon's light is stronger and it heats the atmosphere more intensely when compared with the time of conjunction. [In the latter case], the vapors are dissipated and rarefied by the Moon's heating the atmosphere, and so there is usually no rainfall during the full Moon, whereas there usually is rainfall during conjunction, because the conjunction brings [the vapors] together and condenses them, and the atmosphere cools in the absence of the Moon's light.

37.   If [the Moon] had the distance it has, but it were in one of the spheres parallel to the equator or the equator [itself], then we would not see the beneficial effects of its being in the inclined sphere, namely that when the Moon is full in the winter it is in the Sun's summer course, whereas when it is full during <summer>[10] nights it is in the Sun's winter course. In that case, when it is full during the [summer] night, its heating effect is decreased, and consequently the air is moderate. As a result of that, the land and its bounty grow at the time when it needs warmth, and the atmosphere is cooled at just the time that it needs it.

38.   If the Moon had all these [characteristics] but it were not eccentric and did not have an epicycle, then it would not be proximate and remote from the Earth during its four different phases; for it is because [it is eccentric and has an epicycle] that the full Moon is high during conjunction and is low during the quadratures; it descends and waxes during one of the four [phases], whereas it ascends and wanes

---

[10] The text has "winter night," but the context seems to demand that it be "summer night."

during another. Moreover, in addition to what we mentioned, it speeds up during one and slows down during another. Now with each of these circumstances, we observe a generation and corruption in some particular thing. With [the Moon's] descent, that is, with its increasing proximity to the Earth, we observe an increase in moisture on the Earth, and with its increasing remoteness from the Earth we observe a decrease in moisture. [233] Thus, it is obvious that because the Moon has the characteristics that it has, it greatly assists the Sun in generation and change in this world.

39. The other planets also clearly have a use in [the generation and preservation of things in the sublunar realm], because each of them has the following: inclined motion like the Sun's motion with respect to the inclined sphere; motion with respect to the eccentric sphere like the Sun and Moon; motion with respect to the epicycle like the Moon's motion; as well as the motion that the Moon has that deviates from the ecliptic[11] (I mean from the revolution that the sphere traces around the pole). [All of this] produces many configurations for them, like what happens to the Moon, for example, sinking below or rising above the Earth's central [region] and being in alignment with one region after another; or moving faster or slower; or deviating from the ecliptic; or being aligned with [the Sun] during its conjunction and opposition. [The planets] also produce influences that the Moon produces through its proximity and remoteness, its fastness and slowness, and its rising and sinking. Also, as a result of the change of [the planets'] apogees, there is a change of the relative periods of time for each one of them, like a planet's apogee in relation to certain motions when it is at the apex of its epicycle. When at that point it is at the highest point on [its] eccentric sphere and its lowest point is directly opposite that point, then as a result of the motion of the apogee the periods of time of [the motions] begin to be irregular along every part of the sphere during a given time.[12]

40. Everything we noted has a significant use in the generation and corruption of those things subject to generation. The empirical evidence for that is what we find concerning the difference in the seasons; for the spring in one year differs from the spring in another year, and likewise midsummer, autumn, and winter, even if the Moon's positions during them match up. If the action [that affects the things subject to generation and corruption] were due solely to the Sun and Moon without

---

11 Literally, "the bearing (samt) of the Sun's sphere." Al-Kindī is describing the motion of the moon and planets along the zodiac relative to the ecliptic. During the revolutions of all of these bodies they rise above and sink below the ecliptic in a periodic fashion.

12 Since before Ptolemy, astronomers had recognized that the Sun, Moon, and planets did not move at a uniform speed during their regular course, but rather sometimes apparently sped up and at other times apparently slowed down. Ptolemy, and ancient and medieval astronomers following him, explained this irregular motion by appealing to an epicycle/deferent system, and al-Kindī is giving here the general model for explaining such irregularities. For a more detailed discussion of this irregular motion and the Ptolemaic solution to it, see Thomas Kuhn, "Ptolemaic Astronomy," in *The Copernican Revolution: Planetary Astronomy in the Development of Western Thought*, 64–72.

the planets, then [any] day during which the Moon coincides with the Sun in the same part [of the heavens] would be exactly like any other day like it (I mean [any] day during which the two coincided in that part [of the heavens]), while we often find a clear difference in that. Also, we find that when a planet is close to [the Sun and the Moon] in part [of the heavens], then [the day] is hot, if the opposition is in the northern inclination, whereas if it is in the southern [234] inclination, it is much colder on that day, where the severity of the heat and cold during the periods of heat and cold will be proportionate to the closeness of the Sun and Moon.

41.   We also observe that things that exert a heating influence on us by their coming into contact with our bodies exert different influences on us commensurate with both the difference in the strength or weakness of the heat in relation to us *and* the difference of our bodies in relation to [their] dryness and wetness or the equilibrium [between them]. Thus, if we are equally balanced in terms of wetness and dryness, and the thing that comes into contact with us has a heat comparable to ours, it produces digestion. If its heat is greater than ours, it produces decomposition. If it is still greater, it produces attraction. If it is even greater than that, it produces desiccation. If it is even still greater than that, it produces burning. If our bodies are inclined towards wetness but are balanced between heat and cold, then the first degree of heat having an influence on us produces putrefaction, the second digestion, the third decomposition, the fourth attraction, the fifth desiccation, and the sixth burning. If our bodies are inclined toward dryness but are equally balanced between hot and cold, the first degree produces stagnation, the second more thickening and less decomposition, the third more desiccation and less attraction, the fourth more burning and less dissolution, the fifth more dissolution and less rarefaction, and the sixth intense rarefaction.

42.   In the same way, we should understand that the influence that the higher [celestial] individuals exert on us by heating our bodies and the air surrounding us corresponds with the influence of each one of them in proportion to its speed, proximity, [235] lowness, magnitude, and their contraries, as well as how many or few of them there are, whether they are in conjunction or opposition, and the variation of their states. Moreover, we often sensibly experience that [influence], as when we find that the North Wind blows heavily when Saturn descends into Cancer, and that the South Wind blows heavily when Mars descends into Capricorn. Also it is unseasonably damp in relation to prior damp periods when Venus is in conjunction with the Sun and so too when Venus descends into Aquarius and Pisces. Also, the varying and heavy wind together with the dampness are all unseasonable when Mercury descends into Aquarius. Thus, the usefulness of the other planets in the generation and corruption of things subject to generation and corruption is well known.

43.   Again the use that the fixed stars play in [generation and corruption] is well known from the fact that they too produce consequences similar to those that follow from the planets' being large or small, or in conjunction with the Sun, Moon, and other planets, since <every>s single equatorial circle produces an effect on the longitude

and latitude that it is directly above (like what we observe as a result of the conjunction of Sirius and the Sun in longitude, namely, most of the grass dries out and most
of the fruits ripen, and, moreover, the state of most of the cultivated and wild parts
of the locations change, as well as [the commensurate changes] in <temperaments>[t]
and habits of their inhabitants.) [The reason is that] everything that is in one of the
circles paralleling the equatorial circle passes over one circle of the Earth that parallels
the Earth's great circle through which the equator passes, [236] and so during its
rotation over that circle it produces a quantity of heat, cold, wet, and dry in the lands
under it during the whole time owing to the susceptibility of the various kinds of
temperaments, habits. and desires of the soul in proportion to their more general elemental mixture resulting from [the rotation] and the more specific elemental mixture
of each of the generable and corruptible things under [the rotation]. So, as a result of
that, new ambitions and desires occur that are different from the earlier ones, and so
the former outward appearance and customs also change. Consequently, dynasties and
their like change because the periodic change of all things subject to generation is in
accordance with the change brought about by the inclined sphere. Hence, the distance
of every [star] from the equator varies at the times during which there appears longitudinal[u] motion in [the star], whereas their distance from the circle of the Zodiac is
always the same in order that their actions in conjunction with the Sun are always
the same.

44.   This [influence of the heavenly bodies on terrestrial regions] is evident by
comparing the [terrestrial] locale along the parallel circles; for every type of them has
a unique condition that is common to them, unless the substance of the region[v]
happens to be altered by a sea, mountain, steppe, salt marsh, valley, or plateau, whether
lying to the east, west, north, or south of them.

45.   So it has become clear that the proximate efficient cause of the generation
and corruption of what is subject to generation and corruption is that the heavenly
bodies are over the locale that they are over, which is the earth, water, and air, where
the latter are arranged in layers and are equitably distributed. I mean [by "proximate
efficient cause"] the cause that, at the will of its Creator, produces this ordering that
is itself the cause of generation and corruption. [It has also become clear] that this is
the result of an order of a wise, omniscient, powerful, good, intelligent Being who
brings to perfection what He has made. Moreover, [it has become clear] that this order
is most perfect, since He imposes the most fitting command [237], as has become
clear, and we have now proven concerning whatever follows as a result of the eternal
perpetuation of the One Who possesses complete power, the True One, the One Who
creates, holds, and perfects the universe. [This is] because there is not a trace of craftsmanship in a door, bed, or chair in what is visible of them that is [comparable] with
the preordained harmony of the most perfect command. For those possessing the pure
eyes of the intellect, the most obvious case of that is this universe, with its arrangement
and its preordination according to the most beneficial and perfect command in its
generation, and that some of it became a cause for the generation of others, and that
some of it is a cause for the rectification of others as well as the appearance of the

perfection of power (I mean the emergence into act of whatever is not necessarily impossible).

46. All that we have mentioned is obvious for whomever's level of knowledge [includes] astronomy and natural science.[13] As for the one who lacks that, he will be unable to understand what we have said, because of his lack of knowledge of astronomy and natural science. Thus, beseech the One Who possesses complete power to be successful in completing the necessary steps that will indicate His unity, wisdom, power, and existence.

47. The first part of al-Kindī's book on elucidating the cause [of the generation and corruption in the world] is complete, many praises to God, the Lord of both worlds.

II. ON THE INTELLECT[a]

1. [353] May God cause you to understand all of the benefits [He bestows] and grant you happiness in the world of the living and the world of the dead. I understood your request for a brief explanatory discourse on the description of the doctrine concerning the intellect according to the opinion of the praiseworthy ancient Greeks. The most praiseworthy of them is Aristotle and his teacher Plato the wise. Since what is available of Plato's doctrine on that is the doctrine of his student Aristotle, we will discuss that according to the explanatory method.

2. Aristotle's opinion is that there are four types of intellect. The first of them is the intellect that is always actual. The second intellect is the one that is potential and belongs to the soul. The third intellect is the one in the soul when it is brought from potentiality to actuality. The fourth [354] intellect is the one that he calls the second[b] when he likens the intellect to sensation,[14] because of the close [association] of sensation to the living being and its encompassment of it more generally; for he says that there are two forms. One of them is the material form that falls under the senses. The other is not possessed of matter and is perceptible to the intellect, being the specificity of things as well as what is above that.[15] So the form that is in matter is the one that is actually an object of the senses, because if it were not actually perceptible by the senses, it would not fall under the senses.

3. When the soul has the use of [the form], it is in the soul, but the soul has use of it only because it is in the soul in potentiality. Then, when the soul makes a connection to it, it actually comes to be in the soul; however, it does not come to be in the soul like something that is in a container nor like a pattern in the body; for the soul [355] is neither corporeal nor divisible. So [the form] is in the soul, but the soul is one thing not another thing, nor an otherness like the otherness[c] of predicates.

---

[13] Here and below, literally, "of the universe's design and things natural."

[14] See *De anima* III, 4.

[15] That is, the genera of things.

Similarly, the faculty of sense is not something other than the soul, nor is it in the soul the way that an organ is in a body; instead, it is the soul, and it is what senses. Equally, the form perceptible to the senses is not in the soul as some other thing[d] or an otherness. Thus, what is sensed in the soul is what senses.[16] As for the matter, what is sensed of it is other than the soul that senses. Therefore, with respect to the matter, what is sensed is not what senses.

4.   In this way he [Aristotle] gives an analogy of intellect; for when the soul makes a connection with the intellect—I mean the forms [356] that are neither material nor imagined—[the intellect as these forms] becomes the same thing as the soul—I mean that it exists in actuality in the soul, whereas before, it did not exist in actuality in the soul actually, but rather potentially. This form that is neither material nor imagined is the intellect acquired for the soul from the first intellect, which is the specificity of things that is always actual. [The first intellect] is what bestows and the soul is what receives precisely because the soul in potentiality is something that [can] intellect, whereas the first intellect is [such] actually.

5.   [With respect] to anything that bestows something on its own, whatever receives [that thing from it] has that thing in potentiality; it does not have it in actuality. Whatever has something in potentiality cannot bring itself into actuality, because if it were [to do so] on its own, then it would be in actuality always, because it would always have what belongs to itself. Thus, anything that is in potentiality is brought into actuality only through something else that is that thing in actuality. Therefore, the soul is something that intellects[e] in potentiality and comes [into actuality] through the first intellect when [the soul] makes a connection with it to the point that it intellects actually.

6.   When the form of the intellect becomes the same thing as [the soul], it and the form of the intellect are not different from one another, because [the two] are not divided and thus distinct from one another. When the form of the intellect becomes one with it, then it and the intellect are one thing. So it intellects and is intellected. Thus, the intellect and what is intellected are a single thing with respect to the soul.

7.   As for the intellect that is actual always and brings the soul to the point that it becomes an actual intellect after it was a potential intellect, [357] it and [the soul as] intellect[f] are not a single thing. Thus, from the perspective of the first intellect, what is intellected in the soul and the first intellect are not a single thing, whereas from the perspective of the soul, the intellect and what is intellected are a single thing, where [what is intellected] in the intellect is, in terms of being simple, more similar to the soul and much stronger than it is in the object of sensory perception.

8.   Thus, the intellect is either a cause and a first principle of all intelligibles and secondary intellects, or it is a second [intellect] and potentially belongs to the soul as long as the soul is not intellecting actually. The third is that which belongs to the soul

---

[16] In other words, there comes to be an identity between the sensory power and the object of sense; see Aristotle, *De anima* II 5, 418a3–6.

actually [358] once [the soul] has obtained it; it belongs to the soul [in that] whenever [the soul] wants, it uses it. [The soul] makes it apparent so that it will exist for others as something that comes from it. [This is] like writing in the writer; it belongs to [the writer] as a possible disposition that he has obtained and that is established in his soul, after which he brings it into action and uses it whenever he wants. The fourth is the intellect that appears from the soul whenever it brings it into action, at which point it is something that exists for others as something coming from it actually.

9.   The distinction between the third and the fourth is that the third is a possession belonging to the soul—the time from which it first possesses it having passed—which [the soul] can bring into action whenever it wants, whereas [in the case of] the fourth, whether it is the time that it possesses it first or the time that it appears next, it is[g] whenever the soul uses it. Thus, the third is what belongs to the soul as a possession that previously has been obtained and whenever [the soul] wants, it is in it, and the fourth is what appears in the soul whenever it actually appears.

10.   As much praise belongs to God as He merits. These are the opinions of the first philosophers on the intellect, and this—may God be your guide!—is the amount [we will] say about it, since it is sufficient for the epistolary and explanatory statement that you requested. Be happy with it.

III.   ON DIVINE UNITY AND THE FINITUDE OF THE WORLD'S BODY[a]

1.   [137] O praiseworthy brother, may God's benefit encompass you; may His guidance direct you.[17] May His constant protection preserve you from all error; may His favor allow you always to accomplish the most virtuous deed. May knowing Him lead you to gain His eternal satisfaction and to deserve His good estimation.

2.   I understood your request that I set down what you heard me explain orally—namely God's unity (exalted is His mention!), the finitude of the world's body, the impossibility of something's actually being infinite, and that the infinite exists only potentially, not actually—in a book that will preserve the form of the account for you to think about until comprehension takes root, and that I make the account of that concise, lest it preclude comprehension or impede memorization. I implore the Bestower of goods and the Receiver of merits to make this match what you seek, and thereby graciously lead you to the path of the rightly guided, far from the horrors of the hereafter. I swear, [one cannot] discuss this topic without prolixity and verbosity except with someone who has reached your rank in scientific investigation and is held in such high esteem, who is backed with the likes of your ability to understand, and is safe from sliding into fanciful notions by the likes of your determination. Therefore, I have outlined [what you requested] to the extent that I was able to adhere to your

---

[17] The addressee seems to have been the poet ʿAlī ibn al-Jahm (d. 863).

stipulations, but I also spared no effort to make it clear to you. So be happy with it and find it favorable. May God grant you happiness in this life and the next and adorn you with all that you produce. The following is the beginning of what we have to say as a result of your request. [139]

3.   The premises that are first, evident, true, and immediately intelligible are the following.

3.1   All bodies, none of which is greater than the other, are equal.

3.2   Equal things are those whose dimensions between their limits are the same, both actually and potentially.

3.3   The finite is not infinite.

3.4   When any one of equal bodies is increased by the addition of another body, it becomes the greatest of them and greater than what it was before that body was added to it.

3.5   When any two bodies of finite size are joined, then the body that comes from them is of finite size, and this must be the case for any size and anything possessing a size.

3.6   Of any two homogeneous things, the smaller measures the greater or a part of it.

4.   If there is an infinite body, and a body of finite size is separated from it, what remains is either a finite or infinite size. If what remains is a finite size, then when the finite size that was separated from it is added to it, the body that comes to be from them is a finite size [from (3.5)], but the body that came to be from them before something was separated from it was an infinite size. Thus, it would be finite and infinite [contra (3.3)], and this is a contradiction.

5.   If what remains is an infinite size, and then what was taken from it is added [back] to it, it becomes either greater than it was before the addition or equal to it. If it is greater than it was, then an infinite has become greater than an infinite. Now, the smaller of two homogeneous things measures the greater of the two or a part of it [from (3.6)], so the smaller of two infinite bodies must measure the greater of the two or a part of it. If it measures it, undoubtedly it measures a part of it, and so the smaller of the two is equal to a part of the greater of the two bodies. Next, two equal things are two things that have the same dimensions between their limits [from (3.2)]. Therefore, the two must possess limits, and so they are finite (because equal bodies that are not similar are those that a single body measures as one and the same measure, but whose limits differ in quantity [141], quality, or both).[18] Thus, the smaller infinite

---

[18] This aside appears to be nothing more than the proverbial adage that one cannot compare apples and oranges, even if they are of equal size. A more sophisticated example involves a small piece of green fruit that is both increasing in size (a quantitative change) and ripening, i.e., going from green to red (a qualitative change). The time it takes the fruit to grow to its full size and ripeness will be the same, and so the two processes are equal, but nonetheless one cannot compare ripening with increasing in size.

is finite [contra (3.3)]. This is a contradiction, and so neither of the two is greater than the other.

6.   If it is not greater than it was before the readdition, then a body has been added to a body without any increase [contra (3.4)], and the whole of that has now become equal to [what it was] on its own—but on its own it is a part of [the whole]—as well as equal to the two parts that were combined. So the part becomes like the whole. This is a contradiction, and so it has been made clear that a body cannot be infinite.

7.   Moreover, the things predicated of the finite are also necessarily finite. Everything predicated of the body—whether it be quantity, place, motion, time (which is what divides motion), as well as the sum of everything predicated of the body—is then also finite, since the body is finite. Thus, the body of the universe, as well as everything predicated of it, is finite.

8.   Since the body of the universe can be increased without end in the imagination, in that one can imagine it as greater than it is, and then again greater than that without end, it can be increased infinitely in terms of possibility. So it is potentially infinite, since potentiality is nothing but the possibility of the existence of the thing said to be in potentiality. Everything [predicated] of something that is potentially infinite is also potentially infinite, including motion and time. Therefore, anything infinite is so only potentially, whereas nothing can be infinite actually, because of what we said above.

9.   Now, since that is necessary, it has been made clear that time cannot be infinite actually. Time is the time of the body of the universe, I mean its duration. So, if time is finite, then the existence unique to the body [of the universe] is finite, since time is not itself something that exists. Nor is there a body without a time, because time is nothing but the measure of motion—I mean that [time] is a duration that motion measures. Thus, if there is motion, there is time, and if there is no motion, there is no time. Next, motion is nothing but the motion of body, and so if there is a body, there is motion, and if there is no body, there is no motion. Motion is the change of states. The change of place of all the parts of the body and its center, or all the parts of bodies alone, is locomotion. The change of place of [a body's] limits, whether towards its center or away from it [143], is augmentation and diminution. The change of just its predicated qualities is alteration. The change of its substance is generation and corruption. Every change is something that measures the duration of what is changed, that is, the body, and so each change belongs to something that has a time.

10.   Change includes being composed and composition, because it is the ordering and collecting together of things. Now, the body is a substance possessing three dimensions—I mean length, breadth, and depth. Thus, [the body] is a composite of the substance (which is its genus) and the dimensions (which are its differences), and a composite of matter and form. The act of composition is the change of the state, [in] that there is no composition, and so the act of composition is a motion; if there is no motion, there is no composition. The body, as we have made clear, is a

composite. If there is no motion, there is no body, and so neither body nor motion precedes the other.

11.   Time is by means of motion, because motion is a certain change, and change is what measures the duration of what changes. So motion measures the duration of what changes, and time is the duration that motion measures. Every body has a duration, which is the state during which [the body] is, I mean the state during which it is what it is; and, as we made clear, the body does not precede motion, nor does the body precede a duration that motion measures. Hence, body, motion, and time do not precede one another in existence, but are together in existence.

12.   Every change occurs by means of something that partitions some duration,[b] and the partitioned duration is the time. Before every partition of time [for example, a day] there is a partition [such as an earlier day] until one arrives at a partition before which there is no partition, that is to say, a partitioned duration before which there is no partitioned duration. No other option is possible, since otherwise every partition of time would be preceded by another partition infinitely, and then it would never be possible to reach any posited time, because the duration from an infinite past up to the posited time would be equal to a duration ascending backward in times from the posited time [145] to the infinite. However, if the time going from an infinite up to a determinate time is something that can be marked off,[19] then [so too] from that marked-off time back through the infinite time is something that can be marked off, and then the infinite will be something finite, which is an absolutely impossible contradiction. Moreover, if one cannot reach some determinate time unless a time before it is reached and so on infinitely, and neither the distance of what is infinite can be traversed nor its end can be reached, then one cannot traverse the temporal infinite to reach any determinate time whatsoever. But a determinate time *is* reached. So time is not some infinite continuum but instead is finite necessarily.[20] So the duration of the body is not infinite, and there is no body without a duration. So, the body's existence is not infinite but rather is finite, in which case it is impossible for any body to have existed always.

13.   [Since this is the case], the body must be something temporally created. Something created in time is the creation of a Creator, since Creator and created are correlated. Thus, the universe necessarily has a Creator who creates from nothing. Next, the Creator must be either one or many. If they are many, then they are composites, because they all share one state in common, that is, they are all agents. Anything that has one thing in common is multiple only by virtue of some being separated from others by means of a given state. So if they are many, then there are multiple differences in them, and so they are composites made up of what is common to them and what is specific to them—I mean [specific to] each one *to the exclusion of* the other.[c] Composites, however, have a composer, because composite and composer fall

---

[19] That is, marked off by limits, because of the commensurability noted in the preceding sentence.

[20] Literally, "time is not something approaching from no limit, but instead from some limit necessarily."

under the heading of correlatives. The agent, then, must have an agent. If that is one, then it is the First Agent. If it is many, and if the agent of the many is many always and this goes on infinitely [147], then there is something [that is, the sequence of agents] that is actually infinite—but the falsity of this has been explained—so it has no agent. Therefore, there are not many agents, but One without any multiplicity whatsoever (glorious and exalted is He above the descriptions of the heretics!). He is unlike His creation, because there is multiplicity in all creation, but none whatsoever in Him, and because He is the Creator and they are creatures, and because He is eternal and they are not, since the states of whatever is in motion change, and whatever changes is not eternal.

14.   Examine these conclusions through the penetrating eye of your intellect, O praiseworthy brother, instill them in your chaste soul, and be patient with your soul as it pursues their hidden tracks, since these are what will lead you to the vast home-lands of knowledge, the gentle repose of your resting place, and the merciful shade of the Creator of mercy—Him I beseech to illuminate your understanding, expand your knowledge, and make your final outcome a happy one. The treatise is complete. Praise God, Lord of the worlds. Blessings on His messenger, Muḥammad, and all his family.

IV.   THE ONE TRUE AND COMPLETE AGENT AND THE INCOMPLETE METAPHORICAL "AGENT"[a]

1.   [169] We should explain what action is and how many ways action is said. The first true action is bringing beings into existence from nonbeing. Clearly this action is proper to God, who is the final end of every cause; for bringing beings into existence from nonbeing belongs to Him alone. The term "creation" properly applies to this action.

2.   The second true action that follows this action is the effect of the agent on what is affected. The true agent is what causes the effect without itself being affected by any kind of effect. Thus, the true agent acts upon what is affected without itself being acted upon in any way. The one acted upon is the one affected by the effect of the agent, I mean what is acted upon by the agent. Thus, the true agent, who is not acted upon in any way, is the Creator, the Agent of the universe (exalted be His praise!).

3.   As for whatever is below Him—I mean everything that He creates—they are called "agents" metaphorically, not in the true sense—I mean that all of them in fact are acted upon. The first of them proceeds from its Creator, and each one then pro-ceeds [171] from another. The first of them is acted upon, and as a result of its being acted upon another is acted upon, and as a result of that one's being acted upon another is acted upon, and so on until one reaches the final one that is acted upon. So the first that is acted upon is metaphorically called an "agent" of the one acted upon that proceeds from it, since it is the proximate cause of the [second one's] being acted upon, and so too for the second, since it is the proximate cause of [the third one's] being acted upon, until one reaches the last of the things acted upon.

4.   As for the Creator, He is truly the First Cause of everything acted upon, both mediately and immediately, because He is an agent, not acted upon in any way. Nevertheless, He is a proximate cause of the first thing acted upon, and a cause, through mediation, of the effects after the first thing acted upon.

5.   This latter species of action—I mean the metaphorical, not real, action of the things that are acted upon—is sometimes divided into two divisions, since there is no genuine agent among the things acted upon, but there is genuinely something acted upon whose being acted upon is a cause of another thing's being acted upon. This general term—I mean "action"—applies to one of the two divisions whenever the effect passes away with the passing away of its agent's being acted upon. An example is the walking of someone who is walking; for when he stops walking, the walking passes away by virtue of the passing away of the walker's being acted upon, without leaving any perceptible effect.

6.   The second division is [that] the effect on the one being acted upon persists after the one causing the effect by being acted upon ceases to be acted upon,[21] for example, the piece of sculpture, the building, and all such manufactured products; for the piece of sculpture, the building, and all manufactured products are [the craftsman's] effect, I mean that one who is acted upon who was a cause of their being affected. The term "production" properly applies to this species of action. This is sufficient to answer your question. The treatise is complete. Praise God, Lord of the worlds. Blessings be on His messenger, Muḥammad, and all his family.

V.   ON THE MEANS OF DISPELLING SORROWS[a]

1.   [31] O, praiseworthy brother, may God preserve you from every depravity, protect you against every harm, and make you successful in the paths that will end at His satisfaction and ample reward. I understood your request for a description of arguments that will combat sorrows; put one in mind of any weaknesses; and provide protection against any pains you have.[b] The likes of your superior soul and balanced temperament has scorned the acquisition of vices and sought to protect [itself] against their harms and the persecution of their rule. I have described for you what I hope will be sufficient for you; may God protect you from all anxieties!

2.   The cure will not be found for any pain whose causes are not known. Thus we should make clear what sorrow and its causes are so that its cures will be clear and easily administered. So we say that sorrow is a psychological pain that appears owing to the loss of loved things or the failure to obtain the things one desires. Thus, from what was said, the causes of sorrow also have become clear, since [sorrow] appears owing to the loss of something loved or the failure to obtain something desired.

---

[21] That is to say, the one producing the effect ceases to act because it itself is no longer being acted upon.

3.   Now we should investigate whether anyone can be free of these causes; for it is impossible for anyone to obtain all of [32] his desires and to be safe from losing all the things he loves, because in the world of generation and corruption in which we find ourselves nothing exists permanently and perpetually. The permanent and perpetual necessarily exist only in the world of the intellect, which we can experience. So if we want neither to lose the things we love nor to fail to obtain what we desire, we should look to the world of the intellect and make what we love, own, and desire [come] from it. If we do that, we will be safe from someone forcibly taking our possessions or some power lording them over us; we shall [be safe against] losing what we loved of them since neither does misfortunes reach them nor does death cling to them. Since the objects of the intellect's inquiry attach to one another steadfastly, neither changing nor ceasing, [once] grasped, they do not escape.

4.   As for sensible possessions and cherished and desired things, everyone briefly has them, and they are attainable[c] by every hand. It is impossible to preserve them and safeguard against their corruption, disappearance, and change. So <all of that>, after having been a source of comfort by its closeness, becomes a source of loneliness, after trusting that something will be of service, it becomes intractable, and after its embrace, it turns its back, since it is not natural that it be what it is not naturally. If we want to be uniquely ours one of the common states and dispositions that does not uniquely belong to one person to the exclusion of others but is a possession of everyone, and if we want one of the corruptible things to be incorruptible, and if we want only to be embraced by what both embraces and turns its back, and if we want what always passes away to be always permanent, then we have wanted something that is not natural of nature. Whoever wants what is not natural desires what does not exist, and whoever wants what does not exist seeks in vain, and the one who seeks in vain will be unhappy. So whoever desires things that briefly remain and desires that his possessions and cherished objects to be made up of [sensible things] will be unhappy, whereas he who has his desire fulfilled will be happy.

5.   Therefore, we should strive to be happy and be on guard against being unhappy. Indeed, our desires and the things we love should be what we can attain. We should neither grieve over things that slip away nor seek unattainable sensible things. Instead, when we experience the things that people enjoy, such as the desirable things of the intellect—I mean in the measure that the soul needs to bring about permanence in its form during the allotted days of its duration [33] and to produce their like, as well as to drive pain from [the soul] and to provide it rest—then we shall have taken hold of [the things we desire] in the most befitting way in the measure of the need. Neither shall we desire them before we have laid eyes and hand on them, nor shall we make ourselves regretful and anxious after they leave us. Indeed, this belongs to the manners of the greatest kings, for they neither set out to meet anyone arriving nor escort anyone departing. Quite the contrary, they enjoy whatever they experience with the calmest action and most obvious indifference. The contrary of that belongs to the manners of the low-born masses and those of ill-natured base ways and stinginess; for they will greet anything that arrives and call out to anything that

departs. It is fitting of those possessed of intellects not to prefer the manners of the low-born masses and their base ways over the manners of the greatest kings.

6.   Similarly, we say that when what we want does not exist, then we should want what does exist. We should not prefer perpetual sorrow over perpetual delight. Truly he who is unhappy about the disappearance of transitory things and the lack of the things that do not [in fact] exist, his sorrow will never wane because in every situation in his life he will lose a loved one or what [he] seeks will pass him by. Now sorrow and delight are contraries that do not remain in the soul together. So when one is sad, he is not delighted, and when he is delighted, he is not sad. Thus we should not be sad about what passes us by and the loss of cherished things, and through proper habit, we should make ourselves content in every situation so that we are always delighted.

7.   We can see that [the role habit plays in what makes someone happy] clearly existing in the habits [of people], and we can see a clear indication of that from the various states and differences of people with respect to what they want and seek. Thus we see that the aesthete who takes joy in food, wine, women, clothes, and similar sensual delights and by these is blissfully delighted, sees whatever is contrary to those as deprivation and afflictions. We see that the obsessive gambler is blissfully delighted in his [life] despite the looting of his money, the idle lolling away of his days, and the vicissitude of becoming rich and poor through what he has gambled away, but in his opinion whatever is contrary to that and keeps him away from it are afflictions and deprivations. Again, we see that the highwayman is [set] in his evil ways and rough treatment—and because of [his evil ways he suffers] the atrocious and monstrous injuries resulting from flogging, dismemberment of limbs, and many painful wounds, while ceaselessly continuing to wage war until [his evil ways] ultimately result in his due reward: crucifixion. Yet he joyously considers all of these injuries marks of glory and honor, while considering the healthy things that oppose them as deprivation and afflictions. We also find that the transvestite is joyous, gay, and flamboyant with [his] infamous [34] depravities and disgraceful characteristics from which everyone [else] recoils and tries not to think about: the disfigurement of [their] appearance by tweezing [their] beards and affecting the appearance of women. By that [behavior] they see themselves as having surpassed everyone [else], and that [everyone else] has been deprived in what they have failed to obtain of that most generous good fortune. [The transvestite sees himself] as having been made special to the exclusion of [everyone else] by a most special delight and a most splendid delicate life, and he sees whatever is contrary to that as deprivation and afflictions.

8.   Therefore, clearly the sensible things that one hates and loves are not something necessary by nature, but rather are [loved and hated] as a result of habits and regular practice. Hence, if the way to produce delight is through what we have experienced, and the consolation for our lost things is clearly facilitated through habit as we have described, then we should apply ourselves to winning over our souls to that and educating [our souls] until that becomes an intrinsic habit for us and an acquired disposition. I mean that in order that life will be pleasant for us during the

days of our appointed time, we [should] mold ourselves to a certain disposition, since that [disposition] does not actually belong to us by nature (I mean at the beginning of our habituation).

9.   Sorrow results only from pains of the soul. Now it is necessary for us to dispel our bodily pains by means of bitter medicines, cauterization, amputation, the application of salves and dressing wounds, abstaining from certain foods and similar things that cure bodies, and for that we are willing to pay significant sums of money to whomever cures these ailments. The well-being of the soul and curing it from pains, however, take precedence over the well-being of the body and curing [the body] from its pains, just as the soul takes precedence over the body since the soul rules, whereas the body is ruled and the soul remains while the body expires. Also, the well-being of what remains and the concern for putting it into right order and keeping it well-balanced is more appropriate and takes precedence over maintaining the well-being and balance of what expires [and] inevitably is corruptible by nature.

10.   [If all this is the case], then maintaining the soul and curing it from illness is more required of us than maintaining our bodies; for it is not by means of our bodies, but by means of our souls that we are what we are, because corporeality is something common to every body, whereas every living things' [state of] being alive is by means of its soul. Our souls are essential to us, and the welfare of our being is more required of us than the welfare of the things extraneous to us. Now our bodies are instruments for our souls by mean of which [the souls'] actions are made apparent, and so the maintenance of our being is more fitting to us than the maintenance of our instruments. So we should persevere in maintaining our souls through the unpleasantness and difficulty of therapy and enduring the pains involved in it many times [more than] what we endure of that in maintaining our bodies, along with the fact that maintaining our souls is less unpleasant and a much lighter burden than what is associated with that in the maintenance of bodies. [35] [That is] because maintaining our souls is only through our power of resolving to bring about our welfare, not by drinking medicine or the pains of iron and fire or paying [doctors'] fees. Quite the contrary, it is by forcing the soul into praiseworthy habits in the smallest affair in which forcing it is easy for it, and indeed from that one progresses to forcing [the soul] in greater [affairs]. When [the soul] is habituated to that by its being led in continuous degrees to what is greater than the former until the habit sticks with it in the most significant affair just as the habit sticks with it in the most trivial affair, then by means of what we have described, the habit comes easily and, by that, patience in the face of the loss of things and the consolation of things lacking comes easily.

11.   One of the simple remedies for that is to reflect on sorrow and divide it into its classes. So we say: What gives rise to sorrow must either be our action or the action of another. If it is our action, then we should not do what makes us sad; for if we do what makes us sad, but refraining from doing it is up to us—since our acting and refraining from [acting] are up to us—then we have done either what we want to do or what we do not want to do. If we did what we wanted to do, but we never want to be sad, then we want what we do not want, and this is characteristic of one who

has lost his mind, and thus we have lost our minds. If what makes us sad is the action of someone else, then dispelling it is either up to us or not. If dispelling it is up to us, we should dispel it and not be sad. If dispelling it is not up to us, then we should not be sad before the cause of sorrow occurs—perhaps the one who can dispel it will do so before it befalls us, and perhaps the one who can bring about sorrow will not bring about sorrow and will not do what we feared. If we are sad before the cause of the sorrow occurs, then we have acquired for ourselves a sorrow that perhaps will not occur, either because the cause of the sorrow refrains from causing the sorrow or because the one who can dispel it from us dispels [it]. In that case, we would have acquired for ourselves a sorrow that someone else had not imparted to us. Now whoever makes his soul sad has harmed it, and whoever harms his soul is stupid, uncouth, and acting in the worst way, since he has brought harm to his soul. [That is] because if he were to do that to someone else, he would be stupid and acting wrongly, but his doing that to his own soul is all the more so. In that case, we should not consent to being the stupidest, the most uncouth, and the most wrong of all. [Even] if sorrow were something necessary, then what happens at the time of its cause's occurrence would be sufficient, which we ought not[d] anticipate before the occurrence [36] of its cause, where acting upon it before the occurrence of its cause is a kind of evil and is contemptible. Moreover, acting upon it at the time of the cause of sorrow requires that it is not to be acted upon before it is resisted, since there is in it one of the harms similar to what we have mentioned previously, [namely, doing a type of violence to one's own soul]. Therefore, resisting it is necessary at the time of its occurrence. Consolation necessarily dispels every cause of sorrow over a given amount of time—if the sad person is not overcome with sorrow or near the source of the sorrow. If[e] overcoming sorrow is a part of nature (since all of what is subject to generation does not last and is not perpetual in the particular instances of things), we should direct our efforts towards the strategy to facilitate the shortening of the time of the sorrow; for if we are remiss in that,[f] then we will be remiss in something else as well, [namely,] dispelling the misfortune that we can dispel from our souls. This is the sign of the unjust, uncouth, miserable, and stupid man, because the unjust man is one who drags out misfortune, and the most miserable man is one who does not try to dispel misfortune from his soul by means of whatever he can. So we should not be content with being miserable when we can be happy.

12.   Part of a fine strategy for that is remembering the causes of our sorrow from which we have long since been consoled, and the causes of other peoples' sorrows whose sorrow we have witnessed and whom we have consoled, and comparing our current cause of sorrow with our past causes of sorrow and those we have witnessed and the solace to which they eventually led; for by this we will gain a great power to console like that by which Alexander, son of Philip, the Macedonian king, consoled his mother when his death was approaching. He wrote to her, among other things: "Think, O Mother of Alexander, about the fact that all of what is subject to generation and corruption is fleeting, and that your son is not satisfied with having the character of a petty king! At his death, do not be content with having the character

of the petty mothers of kings: order the construction of a magnificent city when you receive news [of the death] of Alexander! Send orders to the effect that the people in all the countries of Africa, Europe, and Asia will be assembled on a certain day in that city for food, drink, and festivities. Order that it be announced to them that anyone who has been struck by misfortune should not come to you, so that the funeral of Alexander [37] will be delightful, unlike other, sad, funerals." When she had commanded that, not a single person showed up at the time she had decreed. She said: "Why did the people disobey us, in spite of what we offered?" It was said to her: "You commanded that anyone who has been struck by misfortune [should] not come to you, but all the people have been struck by misfortune; so no one obeyed us." She said: "O, Alexander! How much your end resembles your beginning! You had wanted to console me in a perfect way for the misfortune [of your death], since I am neither the first nor the only person to suffer misfortune."

13. We also [have] to remember that everything we have missed or lost has been missed or lost by a great many people, and all of them came to terms with its loss, exhibiting joy and removed from sorrow; for someone whose child has died or doesn't have any children has many people like him in that, for instance, someone who doesn't have a child but is joyful, or someone whose child has died, but he has been consoled and is joyful. A similar thing happens with money, and all the sensible possessions of the world, and all the desires of the human soul. Therefore, sorrow is solely by convention, not by nature, because when we find a man who is stripped of a possession, he is sad, whereas many don't have that possession and are not sad. Therefore, he has devised that sorrow for himself in place of what he was stripped of or lost. So we should not devise for ourselves anything bad (since sorrow is something bad, as we said); for anyone who invents something bad for himself has lost his mind. We should not lose our minds because it is the height of contemptibility, because there is no difference between someone who has lost his mind and the rest of the nonrational animals. In fact, those are superior to him, because each of them has a timed, inherent, ongoing property like the law at its beginning, and [that] leads it in every situation, whereas the person who has lost his mind has neither order nor regularity in his actions; rather, they [are performed] according to the confusion and the imagination of the intellect. We should be ashamed to be in this miserable state, the object of pity by the rational, the object of laughter by the insolent.

14. We should also keep in mind that if we want not to suffer misfortune, what we really want is not to be at all, because misfortunes come about precisely through the corruption of things subject to corruption. If there were no corruption, [38] there would be no generated thing. Therefore, if we want there to be no misfortunes, we have also wanted there to be no generation and corruption in nature. If we want what is natural not to be, we have wanted the impossible. Whoever desires the impossible is deprived of what he wants, and whoever is deprived of what he wants is miserable. We should be ashamed of this characteristic and disdain this rank—I mean stupidity and misery; for one of them (I mean stupidity) produces contemptibility, and the other (I mean misery) produces debasement and maliciousness.

15.   We should keep in mind that all the things that hands can reach are common to all people. They are merely near us, [but] we have no more right to possess them than do others. They are the possessions of the one who possesses them [only for] as long as he possesses them. As for the things that we have but are not common to others, others' hands cannot reach them and possess them. [They are] the soul's virtues that our souls possess; these are the ones about which we can be excused for feeling sad if our souls are bereft of them. It is not seemly for us to feel sad over what we have only through the exigencies of change, because anyone who feels sad over the fact that he does not naturally possess what [other] people have is envious. We should not teach our souls envy, since it is the worst evil, because anyone who wants evil for his enemies loves evil [itself], and anyone who wants evil is [himself] evil. More evil than this is anyone who wants evil for his friends. Anyone who wants to prevent his friend from [obtaining] what he wants to possess, possessing it being a good in his [friend's] view, has wanted for his friend a situation that he believes is evil. So he has wanted evil for his friends. Anyone who wants that no one else possesses what they have the right to obtain has wanted neither enemies nor friends to possess it. So, anyone who feels sad at someone else's obtaining it is envious. We should not accept this baseness.

16.   We should also keep in mind that the common possessions that we have are a loan from a Lender, who is the Creator of the possessions (great is His praise), [Who] can retrieve His loan whenever He wants and give it to whomever He wants; for, if He had not given it to whomever He wants, it would not have come to us at all. Sometimes, we suppose that when He takes it from us by means of the hands of [our] enemies, He does it to harm us. We should bear in mind [in this instance] that the Lender [39] has the right to take back what He loaned and to do so by the hand of whomever He wants. Consequently, there is neither shame nor disgrace in this for us; rather, the shame and disgrace for us is to feel sad whenever the loans are taken back from us. These are part of the character traits of those who are greedy, stingy, of bad discernment, and of anyone who, once he is loaned something, assumes that he owns it. This is beyond the pale of gratefulness, because the least thing required of grateful-ness on the part of the one loaned something is to return the loan whenever the lender wants it back, with a pleasant spirit and a joy to hasten to meet the desire of the lender for [the item] to be returned. Therefore, anyone who is sad at returning what has been loaned to him is ungrateful. We should be ashamed at ourselves for this character trait that departs from justice. We should also be ashamed of giving idiotic, childish excuses for our sadness at repaying the lender, not saying we are sad precisely because the Lender took His loan back by the hands of our enemies; for the messenger of the lender is not required, in taking back the loan, to be the way we desire in terms of his bearing, disposition, love of us, and timeliness. Since that is not required of him, it *is* required of us not to be sad that the messenger's configuration differs from our [expectations]; for this is one of the characteristics of children and anyone who lacks discernment.

17.   We should keep in mind that, since the Lender does not take back the most costly of what He has loaned us but rather the meanest of it, then He has done to us

the utmost good. We will be most joyous through the lasting beauty of the noble gift [He has given] us and not be sad at the loss of what He has taken back from us, since, were He to reclaim everything He loaned us, we must not be sad but joyous, since our joy at that is part of gratitude to Him and consonant with His desire, as He has left behind the most superior [loan], I mean what no hand can reach and in which no one can share. [Moreover, we should] consult our souls, and if we want what has been reclaimed to stay with us, we [should] say that the meanest and the least has been taken back, while the superior and the most has remained as long as our souls remain.

18.   We should bear in mind that if we must be sad for things that are lost and pass us by, we must be sad always, and [yet] we must *not* be sad at all. This is an egregious contradiction. [That is] because if [40] the cause of sorrow is the loss and passing of possessions that are external to us, and it is hateful that sorrow get to us (where its cause is what we have just mentioned), then if we neither have nor seek a possession external to us, then we shall not suffer the loss or passing [of an external possession]. So we must not have possessions at all lest we be sad. If we must not have possessions, and despite our lacking the possession there is sorrow, then sorrow is forever necessary if we do not have possessions. Therefore, there must always be sorrow, whether we have or do not have possessions. Therefore, if we must be sad always, we must not be sad at all, whether we have or do not have possessions. All of this is an absurd contradiction.

19.   Thus, it is not necessary that we be sad, and whatever is not necessary, the rational person should neither think about nor act on, especially if it is harmful or painful. On the contrary, we must reduce possessions, since their absence or loss, being beyond our control, are a cause for sorrows; for [they] come from that alone. It is related about Socrates, the Athenian, that it was asked of him: "Why do you not get sad?" He responded: "Because I do not possess anything for which I would get sad at its loss." It is also reported about Nero, the Roman king, that someone gave him a gift of a wonderfully crafted, precious crystal dome, and it was presented to him while he was receiving a group of people, among whom was a philosopher of his time. His joy at [the gift] was great, and those present described its virtues at length. So he turned to the philosopher and asked: "What do you say about this dome?" He said: "I say that it shows a poverty about you and indicates a great misfortune that you will experience." [Nero] said: "How is that?" He said: "Because if it is lost, it is hopeless for you to own its like [again]. So it reveals your poverty in its like. If any damage happens to it that deprives you of it, a great misfortune will have been foisted upon you . . . ," and he went on in a similar vein. It was reported that what happened was exactly as the philosopher said. According to the report, one Spring day, the king went out to some nearby islands for amusement and ordered that the dome be brought along in what carried it in order that it be set up during his amusement, but then the boat in which it was sank, and [41] it could not be recovered. So a great misfortune, recognized as such by all his courtiers, befell the king, and although he tried to get something similar to it [right] until his death, he did not. Consequently we say:

"Anyone who wants to lessen his misfortunes, let him lessen his external possessions." In fact, it has been reported about the wise Socrates that for days he was taking shelter in a broken jar in the army camp, and he said one day when one of the youths was having a discussion with him: "We should not possess [anything] so as not to get sad." The youth said to him: "[What] if your jar breaks?" Socrates said to him: "The jar may break, but the place will not." The philosopher spoke truthfully, because there is a replacement for everything lost.

20.   Consequently we say that the Creator of the universe (great is His praise!) did not create anything that is cut off from nature but rather is provided for; for we see the magnificent whale and the wondrously formed elephant, each of them in need of sustenance, shelter, habitat, and all the requirements necessary for them both, and all the creatures under them are provided for with the measure of their need for subsistence prepared for them. Nothing considered to be missing is missing from their good life. All of them have a pleasant life as long as they touch nothing harmful, with the exception of humans; for, despite being increased by the virtue through which he came to have dominion over all the animals, governing and managing them all, he is stupid about managing his own soul. This is a sign of the absence of intellect. We should be ashamed of anyone lacking an intellect;[g] for, despite being increased by rational discernment, he wants to possess many things for which he has no need in sustaining himself and the improvement of his life, such as the garnishing of foods, pictures of animals and other things, sculpting and ornamenting what he sees, as well as things he hears and smells that distract him from things of genuine benefit to him and distance him from his worldly ease. All of these will gain him [only] hardship in his search for them, pain at his losing them, and distress at their passing him by; for with every desired thing that is lost, there is misfortune, and with everything that passes him by, there is distress and sadness, and with the anticipation of every absent thing, there is sorrow and anxiety, and after every hope, there is fear, because the fearful one is distracted and worried. [42] Consequently we say that anyone who occupies himself with increasing[h] his external possessions will miss out on his eternal life, his temporal life will be dreary, his illnesses will increase, and his pains will not cease.

21.   In their passage through this ephemeral world—its fading[i] states, its deceitful images, its ends crying lie to its beginnings (forsaken is the one who trusts it! pitiable is the one who is misled by it!)—people resemble a group traveling by boat to a destination they intend to be their homeland.[22] The captain brought them to a headland to get some provisions. The boat anchored and anyone in the boat needing provisions disembarked. Some, having concluded what they had disembarked for, returned to the boat without dallying for anything. So they got the roomiest berths and the most comfortable seats without any competitors or rivals preventing that.

---

22 The parable of the ship, which follows, appears to be taken from the Stoic philosopher Epictetus (c. 55–135), *Enchiridion*, 7.

22.   Some, however, stopped to see the meadows blooming with all kinds of flowers; to smell all the different kinds of scents of those flowering meadows and the stands of trim trees bearing wondrous kinds of fruit; to hear the pleasant songs of the hidden birds; to pick out, in the earth of that land, different colored stones and pretty shells with strange shapes and wondrous markings. [They did all of this] without leaving their landing site in which their needs were met. They then returned to their places on the boat, the best, most spacious places with the softest seats having already been taken before [them].

23.   Others eagerly devoted themselves to gathering up those shells and stones and nearby fruits and flowers, without leaving the place where they had met their needs. So they returned, burdened by their loads, servants of the stones of the earth, and its shells and flowers that were perishing, changing from what shortly before had deceived them, and the fruits that would soon become spoiled and disgusting to those nearby. They then discovered that others had already taken the roomiest spaces on the boat; and they had to sit in the cramped, rough, and uneven ones. The stones, shells, flowers, and fruit that they had valued earlier became a burden in those cramped, rough, and uneven places, preventing them from the rest that came to the others who had preceded them to the roomiest places and who did not have stones nearby that further cramped their spaces and required them to guard and protect them and ward off damages to them. [43] Most of their relaxation time was broken up into [fretting over] the stones not being there, and worries about it, many fears about it, and the intense devotion of [their] souls to their being nearby. The legacy of the stones bequeathed regret, sorrow, and worries every time they or even one of them was missing.

24.   Some [of the passengers] had[j] penetrated far into those fields and stands of trees, forgetting about the boat and the place that they had intended to be their homeland, being preoccupied with collecting those stones, shells, and flowers, distracted by eating that fruit from recollecting their homeland and the grief to which they would come at the boat. In that [foray], they were not free of successive fears, continuous calamities, and the anxiety of harm from a fleeing wild beast, a poisonous snake, a frightening noise, and a hanging branch that would scratch and wound their faces and the rest of their bodies, or a thorn sticking to a foot requiring a long time to heal, or mud holding them back, soiling and destroying their clothes that covered their private parts, or a piercing branch tearing their cloaks, or a hanging vine preventing their progress.[k]

25.   When the captain of the boat called to them that he was weighing anchor, some of them returned, burdened with what they had collected, and so suffered the harms we have described. No sooner had they arrived at the boat than they found no place except for cramped, uncomfortable ones that allowed for no rest and led them to contract fatal diseases. For some, the captain's call did not reach them, because they had gone so far into the stands of trees and tramping through the muddy fields. So the boat left, and they were in the place, cut off from their homelands, exposed to its deadly, vicious dangers and horrific injuries. Some became the prey of savage beasts; some became caught up in diversions and distractions. Some became soiled in

the muddy places; still others were bitten by the poisonous snakes. They became deserted, disgusting, and putrid [corpses] with their limbs torn away, and their conditions horrific, as [objects of] pity for whomever did not know them and a lesson to whomever knew them as cut off from their homelands to which they had intended to go.

26. As for those who reached the boat burdened with what they considered valuable of what they had gathered (and which deceived their minds, shackled their freedom, did away with their rest, cramped their berths, and caused them anxiety), [they found that] it did not take long before those flowers wilted and the colors on those stones faded (since the freshening moisture they and their color had was gone). The shells, in their brackish [water] and with their horrible stink, [also] changed and became a burden and a harmful companion for them. There was nothing to do with them besides throw them into [44] the sea. Whatever prevented their hastening [back to the boat], spoiled their lives, made them sad at their places, and robbed their freedom, became a burden and left them empty-handed. No sooner had they reached the place [on board the boat] than their illnesses had multiplied because of [the effects] of the putrid smells on them and the exhaustion of strength through the hardship affecting them from the cramped quarters and the serious attention to [their illnesses and exhaustion], which brought them ruin and harm. Some perished before reaching their berths. Some arrived at theirs weak and ill. As for those who stayed behind and whose preoccupation was to the extent of sightseeing and breathing in the fresh air, they missed only the spacious and comfortable berths. As for those who returned to the boat without being preoccupied by any of what their senses took in except for whatever their eyes saw while they were going to meet their needs, then they got back early to the most spacious and comfortable berths, and would reach their homeland relaxed.

27. This parable is like our passage through this world to the true world and the simile of the conditions of the travelers in this world. How wretched it is for us to be deceived by the pebbles of the earth, the shells of the sea, the flowers of trees, and the chaff of plants, [all] of which is paltry [and yet] a burden to us! To our mind, we have no cure from their horribleness besides burying them in some part of the ground, in the depths of the sea, or in the flames of a fire, while we block our noses to their putrid stench, avert our eyes from them because they are repulsive, and seek distance from them because we are repelled when they are close and our souls are adverse to experiencing them; for these are the causes of our sorrow that occupy this place for us. If we are sad, we should rightly be sad at being cut off from our true place and coming to a wide expanse of sea [from which] the boat cannot deliver us to our true homelands, in which there are no misfortunes because there is no lack nor anxieties in it, because there are no things that pass us by, because there is nothing that is not rightful [for us] in that place. There, one does not want anything that he should not want. As for what should be wanted, there is with the one who wants neither anything that is kept separate nor anything that produces harm. We should be sad precisely at being deprived of not being sad; for this is a property of reason. As for sorrow at being deprived of being sad, this is a property of stupidity.

28.   We ought to keep in mind that we should not hate what is not evil. It is precisely what is evil that we should hate. If that is firmly fixed in our memory, its attention to dispelling the sensible causes of sorrow is thereby strengthened. We do not suppose that anything is more evil than death, but death is not evil; the fear of death is only what is evil. Death is no more than the perfection of our nature. If there were no death, there would certainly be no man, because the definition of man is [45] is a living, rational, *mortal* being. The definition is thus based on the nature, I mean the nature of man is that he is a living, rational, *mortal* being. So, if there is no death, there is no man, because if someone did not die, he would not be a man. Therefore, it is not evil to be what we are; what is evil is precisely to be what we are not. Thus, the evil thing would be that there would be no death, because if there were no [death], there would be no man. Therefore, death is not evil. Consequently, if what is thought by all to be the most evil thing is not evil, then anything less evil, such as lost and lacking sensory things, is not evil.

29.   Therefore, the cause of the opinion that death is evil—since it has been proved that it is *not* evil—ought to have its origin in ignorance about the state of life and death. For instance, I might say that if food were possessed of an intellect and it was in the liver, and yet it had not experienced anything else, and then it is broken down in order to be transported from [the liver], that would sadden it, even though it is being transported from [the liver] to a physical constitution of a form and reaching something closer to being perfect. So if it goes into the testicles and changes into sperm, where it is [again] broken down in order to be transported to the womb, which is more spacious than the testicles, that would cause it great sorrow. If it were said to it after it had come to the womb that it would be returned to the testicles, that would cause it to be even sadder than it was originally, because of its recollection of the cramped space of the testicles and its distance from the perfection of the human form when its condition in them is compared to its condition in the womb. Also, if it were going to be roused from the womb into the spaciousness and wideness of this world, that would make it very sad. Then, when it had come out to this spaciousness and perfection, and next it was said to it that it would be returned to the womb, when it possessed all the earth and everything in it, it would relinquish it [all] not to return to the womb. Similarly, while it is in this place that is the world, it is very apprehensive about departing from it. So, when it comes to the place of the intellect—[a place that] lacks sensory pains and the sensory possessions that are the sources[l] of all sensory and psychological pains <. . .>[m] of which neither hands nor harm can take hold, and so its possessor is never separated from his possession—if [at that time] it were told "you will be returned to this [earthly] world that you were in," then its anxiety would be many times greater than the anxiety [it felt when] it was said to it, "you will be returned from this worldly expanse to within the womb." [46]

30.   It has been explained, therefore, how souls that are weak in their discernment and partial to the senses have misconstrued death and have assumed it is a horrible thing when it is not. Thus, being deprived of all the things, like sensible possessions, on this side of earthly life is not evil; but rather feeling sad about them

is evil, because [then] they are unnecessary pains we foist upon our souls. When we are like that, we have an evil nature and an evil life; for anyone who has consented to that has made evil choices and is devoid of intellect, because the intellect puts things in their rightful places, whereas to be devoid of intellect is to put things elsewhere than in their rightful places and to suppose that they are the direct opposite of what they [really] are.

31. With every thing that passes us by and that we lack, we should keep in mind to be concerned about remembering every possession of the senses or the intellect that we continue to have and counting them off from past ones; for remembering what we continue to have is a solace in the face of misfortunes. Moreover, with every cause of sorrow due to lost or spoiled[n] sensible possessions, we [can] keep in mind that the anticipation of misfortune after [the loss of] our sensible possessions has been eliminated, reducing some of the causes of sorrow; for, if that is fixed in our memory, it transforms the causes of sorrow from [having] the nature of misfortunes to [having] the nature of blessings. Every time a misfortune overcomes us, it will be a blessing for us, because, if such misfortunes reduce our misfortunes, they are blessings. [This is so] because, if the misfortune is a cause of sorrow in our opinion, then everything that reduces the cause of sorrow is a blessing. So, every time we lose a sensible possession, we acquire a misfortune that, for our souls, is a blessing.

32. Therefore, we say that whoever does not [desire to] possess the things that are outside his control *does* control the things that make slaves of kings, I mean the anger and desire that are the sources of vices and pains. The greatest illness, then, is the illness of the soul, more so than [any] illness of the body, as we said before, because anyone who is not influenced deleteriously by anger and desire does not have them as ruler over himself. Whoever is so influenced has them as ruler and king over himself, making him act when they want. So, it is true that anyone who does not possess the things that are outside his control *does* control the things that make slaves of kings. He conquers most of the enemies that are with him in his fortress, [enemies] the sharp deceits of whose weapons cannot be guarded against by the protection of iron; in their dwellings, one is not safe from the most abominable sins and the most monstrous ruin. [47]

33. So, praiseworthy brother, make these counsels fixed models in your soul, by which you will save yourself from the damages of sorrow and reach the most virtuous homeland of the abode of permanence and the dwelling place of the righteous. May God bring your happiness to perfection in your two abodes, give you a surfeit of virtues in both. [May He] make you one of the guided and blessed by reaping the harvest of reason, and keep you far from the contemptible lowliness of ignorance. [The treatise] is sufficient for what you requested, even though the kinds of discourse about [the topic] are many. When the sought-after goal is reached, the end of what was wanted has been obtained, even if the paths to the goal are so many as to be virtually infinite. May God give you such protection in your present life and the hereafter that by it you can reach the most perfect ease and the best life!

AR-RĀZĪ

Abū Bakr Muhammad ibn Zakariyā ar-Rāzī was born in Rayy near present-day Tehran in Iran around 864, and he died there as well in either 925 or 932. In the Arabic intellectual tradition ar-Rāzī was famous as a doctor—he was called "the unsurpassed physician in Islam"—and infamous as a philosopher, labeled a "freethinker," "schismatic," and even an "infidel." A polymath and voluminous in his writings, ar-Rāzī composed approximately two hundred books covering virtually the whole gamut of scientific and philosophical topics; most of these works dealt with issues in medicine, but still more than a third were dedicated to philosophy. From what is available of his writings it is clear that ar-Rāzī was a nonconformist who refused to accept things solely on the basis of authority, no matter who or what that authority might be. Thus, in medicine he readily challenged such illustrious ancient authorities as Hippocrates and Galen, correcting and emending their claims on the basis of his own observations and medical experience; he developed his own metaphysical system—a medley of Greek and perhaps Sabean influences—at odds with many of the features of Neoplatonized Aristotelianism, which was already gaining prominence among Arabic-speaking philosophers; and most notoriously, he denied the need for revelation and prophecy, arguing that at best they are superfluous, since we have reason, and at worst, morally repugnant, since they lead to schisms and bloodshed.

The influence of ar-Rāzī's thoughts on medicine was not limited to the Islamic world but also extended into Latin Europe, where as early as the twelfth century some of his medical works were being translated. Indeed, ar-Rāzī's works were still being read in Europe as late as the sixteenth century. His philosophical writings, however, did not fare as well. We thus have to glean our understanding of his philosophical thought from short extant works, fragments, and *testimonia*, which most frequently are drawn from hostile sources. The loss of the greater part of his philosophical corpus is no doubt due in large measure to the repugnance later thinkers had for the heterodox aspects of his thought, with its rejection of important features of both Aristotelianism and Islam itself.

I. THE PHILOSOPHER'S WAY OF LIFE[a]

1. [99] Abū Bakr Muhammad ibn Zakariyā ar-Rāzī (may God augment his soul with refreshment and repose!) said the following.

2. When scholars of reflection, discernment, and intellectual achievement see us mixing with the people and pursuing various ways to earn a living, they chastise and disdain us. They argue that we have abandoned the life of philosophy, not to mention the model of our leader Socrates, about whom it is related that he would not

associate with kings and scorned them if they sought him out; that he did not eat delicious food or wear luxurious clothes; that he did not build a home or acquire possessions or have children; that he did not eat meat or drink wine or attend any public entertainment. Rather, [they say], he confined himself to eating dry herbage, wrapping himself in a threadbare robe, and taking shelter in a barrel in the wilderness.[1] Furthermore, he did not conceal his thoughts before commoner or king, but answered their questions with what he deemed the truth, in the clearest and most straightforward manner of speech. They say that we are the complete opposite of that. Then, however, they talk about the evils of this way of life that Socrates pursued, saying that it is against the natural way of things and the preservation of civilization, and that it encourages the ruination of the world and the destruction of human life. We will respond to them here with what we think about that, God willing.

3.   They speak the truth about the reports they record concerning Socrates. That was certainly part of what he was. However, they ignore many other things about him, and they intentionally neglect to mention these things in order to bolster their argument against us. These things reported about Socrates were applicable to him from the beginning and for a long period of his life. But then he gave up many of them, so much so that eventually he died leaving behind daughters, fighting enemies, attending entertainment, eating tasty food (with the exception of any meat), and even imbibing a little. This is common, received knowledge to anyone who has bothered to look into the reports about this man. His behavior [100] in the beginning was the result of his strong fascination with and love for philosophy; his intense desire to spend his time on it instead of on bodily desires and the pursuit of pleasure; his natural propensity to do that; and his scorn and disdain for anyone who does not examine philosophy with the keen eye that it deserves and who chooses instead anything less.

4.   At the outset of any pursuit that is desired and loved, one cannot but long for it, love it excessively, persevere in it, and hate anyone opposed to it, until, after he has immersed himself in it and [his activity] has brought him close to achieving it, he stops overdoing it and returns to moderation. There is a proverb for this: "Every novelty has its appeal."

5.   This was Socrates' condition at that time in his life, and it is this aspect of what is reported about him that is best known and widespread, because it is the strangest and most amazing and furthest from people's usual behavior—and because people love to spread the rare and odd report and avoid the mundane and customary ones.

6.   So we do not object to the most praiseworthy aspect of Socrates' way of life, though we ourselves mostly fall short of his [standards] and acknowledge our short-

---

[1] For this apparent confusion with the Diogenes of Greek wisdom literature, see generally Ilai Alon's study *Socrates in Mediaeval Arabic Literature,* esp. p. 49.

comings in applying the just way of life, in taming our whims, in the love of knowledge and the passion for it. Our dispute with Socrates, then, lies not in the quality of his way of life, but rather in the quantity. And we are not diminished by admitting to our deficiency, since it is the truth, and acknowledging the truth is nobler and more honorable. So that is what we have to say on that topic.

7.   With regard to what they condemn about Socrates' two ways of life, we say the following. The blameworthy aspect rightly lies again in quantity, not quality, since, clearly, obsessive attention to bodily desires and their pursuit is not more noble and honorable, as we have explained in our book *On Spiritual Medicine*. Rather, for each need, it is nobler to take the necessary measure or a measure that does not invite a pain that exceeds the pleasure derived from it. And, in fact, Socrates ultimately did turn away from the excessive behavior that is truly reprehensible and that leads to the ruination of the world and the destruction of human life, since he returned to fathering children and fighting [101] enemies and attending entertaining gatherings. Anyone who does that has stopped working for the ruination of the world and the destruction of human life, but one does not have to be different from that to be awash nonetheless in desires. We ourselves, though unworthy of the title of philosopher in relation to Socrates, are entitled to it in relation to those people who do not want to pursue philosophy.

8.   Having come this far, let us now make as thorough a statement about the philosophical way of life as will be of benefit to those who love and honor knowledge.

9.   We need to lay the foundations of our aim in this treatise on some basic principles that we have already explained in other books, the aid of which must be sought if the contents of this treatise are to be lightened. These books include our *On Metaphysics*, our *On Spiritual Medicine*, our *On Censuring the Philosophasters for Their Obsession with the Minutiae of Geometry*, our book entitled *The Noble Discipline of Chemistry*—especially our book known as *Spiritual Medicine*, for it is indispensable in seeking to complete the aim of this treatise.

10.   Now, the basic principles on which we base the practical elements of the philosophical way of life and which we use here in abridged form are the following. We have a state after death that is either praiseworthy or blameworthy, depending on the way we lived during the time our souls were with our bodies. The noblest thing for which we were created and to which we are directed is not the pursuit of bodily pleasures but rather the acquisition of knowledge and the application of justice, both of which lead to our liberation from this world in the world in which there is neither pain nor death. Both nature and whim led us to prefer the pleasure of the present, while the intellect often calls on us to give up present pleasure in favor of things that *it* prefers. The Lord of us all, from whom we anticipate reward and fear punishment, watches over us, is merciful with us, does not seek to harm us, loathes our injustice and ignorance, and loves our justice and knowledge. For this Lord [102] will punish in fair measure those of us who cause harm and those who deserve to suffer pain. We are not required to suffer pain in place of a pleasure that is preferable to that pain in quantity and quality. The Creator (mighty and high is He) has placed in our trust

things particular to our needs, such as the cultivation of land, the craft of weaving cloth, and other such things that allow for the maintenance of the world and our livelihood. Let us accept these principles as valid so that we may build upon them.

11.   Inasmuch as the pleasures and pains of this world are brought to abrupt conclusion with the end of life, while the pleasures of the world where there is no death are eternal, unceasing, and infinite, the idiot is one who purchases a perishable, transitory, and limited pleasure in exchange for one that is eternal, perpetual, unending, and infinite. This being the case, it necessarily follows that we should not seek out a pleasure the attainment of which requires the perpetration of something that prevents our liberation in the eternal world of the soul or that imposes on us in this world a harm greater and more intense in quantity and quality than the pleasure we chose. Any other pleasure is permitted us. But the philosopher will often forgo many of these permitted pleasures for the sake of training and conditioning his soul to resistance, so that when it becomes necessary he will find that easier and more effortless, as we wrote in our *Spiritual Medicine*.[2] For habit, as the ancient philosophers said, is a second nature that can make what is difficult seem easy and inure one to it, whether it be in matters of the soul or the body. Thus we see couriers more capable of walking long distances and soldiers more courageous in battle and other such unremarkable examples of the way in which habits ease things that were burdensome and difficult before one was accustomed to them.

12.   While this statement is condensed and summarized (I mean what we said about circumscribed pleasure), it covers many specific examples, as we have explained in *Spiritual Medicine*. For, if the principle [103] that we have set down is correct and true in itself or derivative of such, that is, the principle that the thinking person should not yield to any pleasure that is accompanied by his fear of a pain that will outweigh the pain he experiences by suffering to forgo the pleasure and restrain the desire, then it necessarily follows that were we, at some given point, capable of possessing the whole Earth for the duration of our lives by perpetrating against people an act that does not please God, that is, an act that prevents us from attaining eternal good and permanent blessing, then we should neither do that nor want to do that. Furthermore, were it our lot, or all but certain, that if we ate a plate of ripe dates our eyes would be inflamed for ten days, we obviously would not want to eat them. The result is the same for anything that falls between these two examples we mentioned, in terms of the relative extremes of great and small, for each case is small in relation to the greater and big in relation to the smaller, but the discourse cannot encompass them all because of the plethora of specific individual examples that fall under this general summary.

13.   Now that what we wanted to explain on this topic is clear, allow us to try to elucidate another one of our aims consequent to that one. Since the principle that we set down—that is, that our Lord and Master takes a concern in us, watches over us, and has compassion for us—also entails that He abhors any harm that befalls us,

---

2 See *Spiritual Medicine*, ch. 11.

and that every such thing that is not the result of our action and choice but is rather a part of nature is a necessary thing, that is, its occurrence is unavoidable, then, on that account, we must not harm any sentient creature whatsoever unless it is absolutely necessary to inflict that harm or by doing so we avert a greater harm. [104] Under this summary statement there is, again, much detailed division of examples, including acts of injustice as a whole; the pleasure rulers derive from hunting animals; and people's extreme overwork of the beasts of burden they use. All of that must accord with a reasoned and just aim, behavior, method, and doctrine that cannot be transgressed nor violated, so that pain is inflicted only when it will deflect a greater harm, as in such cases as lancing an abscess, cauterizing an infected limb, taking a foul-tasting medicine, and avoiding tasty food as precaution against seriously harmful illnesses. Beasts of burden may be overworked for a specific purpose that does not involve excessive force, unless such is deemed absolutely necessary by reason and justice. For instance, spurring on a horse to arrive at safety from an enemy: in such a case justice deems it necessary to spur it on and even destroy it if the person hopes to be saved, especially if that person is learned and virtuous or is rich in some other way that will be of benefit to all people, since the largesse of such a man and his survival in this world is of greater good to the people than preserving the horse. Another example is that of two men stranded in a waterless wasteland, one of whom has enough water to save himself but not his companion. In such a situation, the water should go to the man who is of most benefit to the welfare of society. This is the logical conclusion applicable in such examples.

14.   With regard to hunting and chasing, exterminating and destroying, this should be reserved for animals like lions, leopards, and jackals, which feed only on meat, and those like serpents and scorpions, which cause the greatest harm, which people have no interest in taming, and for which there is no need to otherwise use. This is the logical conclusion applicable in such examples. There are two reasons why it is fitting to exterminate these animals. The first is that if they are not exterminated, they will eradicate many other animals; [105] this is a case unique to solely carnivorous animals. The other reason is that souls are liberated only from human bodies. Since this is the case, liberating souls from animal bodies is akin to paving the way to and facilitating that liberation. Since both reasons are combined in the case of solely carnivorous animals, it is obligatory to exterminate them when possible, because doing so both minimizes harm to other animals and allows for the hope that their souls will then inhabit more suitable bodies. In the case of serpents, scorpions, and hornets, etc., the fact that they both harm animals and are of no use to humans, the way beasts of burden are, combine to permit their destruction and extermination.

15.   However, animals used by humans and fed on herbage must not be destroyed and exterminated. Rather they should be worked gently, in the manner we have stated, their use as food should be kept as far as possible to a minimum, and they should not be bred to such a great number as would require their inordinate slaughter—rather slaughtering them should follow an aim and accord with need. If it were not for the benefit to be had from releasing souls from nonhuman bodies, reason would deem it

right that they not be slaughtered at all. In fact, those who pursue the way of philosophy have different opinions about this, some judging it good for people to eat meat, while others, including Socrates, do not.

16.   Since neither reason nor justice grants people the right to harm others, it follows that neither should they harm themselves. Many examples fall under the general notion of self-harm that reason rejects, like the Hindus who, in seeking to be near God, set fire to themselves and fling themselves on sharp nails, or like the Manis[3] who castrate themselves to resist the urge for sex, weaken themselves through hunger and thirst, and allow themselves to get filthy by avoiding water, using urine instead. Also falling under this heading, though to a much lesser degree, are Christians [106] who practice monasticism and withdrawal from the world in cloisters, as well as many Muslims who spend all their time in mosques, give up daily affairs, and limit themselves to a small amount of unpalatable food, and to wearing painful and uncomfortable clothes. All such behavior is just a form of self-oppression and self-harm that does not help one avoid a more preferable pain. Yes, Socrates used to follow this path at the beginning of his life, but he gave it up at the end, as we already said (see par. 3).

17.   Now, people hold vastly divergent but inarticulate views on this subject [of self-denial], so we should offer an accessible statement on it so that there will be some examples [with which to work]. Since people differ in their circumstances—some accustomed to prosperity, some to hardship, and some seeking gratification of one desire more than another (such as those passionate about women, or wine, or power, or any other thing in which people show great diversity)—the pain they experience by restraining their desires varies greatly according to their differing circumstances. Consider, for instance, someone born to a king and raised in prosperity: his skin cannot bear rough clothes and his stomach will not accept bad food in comparison to what will satisfy someone born to a commoner; rather he will experience great pain as a result. Or those accustomed to a particular pleasure will experience pain when denied it, and the suffering they endure will be multiplied and all the more grave and intense than for someone not accustomed to that pleasure. For this reason people cannot be burdened in the same manner but rather differently, according to their different circumstances. So the king's son who seeks the way of philosophy cannot be made to bear what the commoner's son can in terms of food and drink, except by slow degrees if necessity calls.

18.   But the limit that cannot be transgressed is that they must refrain from a source of pleasure that they could not attain but [107] by perpetrating oppression and murder and, in sum, anything that invites divine displeasure and is not necessary by

---

3 "Manis" refers to the Manicheans, who believed that two principles governed the world: one was light and associated with the soul, the other was dark and associated with matter. In order to limit the amount of matter in the universe, certain Manicheans avoided procreation, since they believed that it trapped the soul within matter.

judgment of reason and justice. Anything below that is permissible. This is the upper limit, by which I mean the upper limit in terms of freely pursuing the enjoyable life. The lower limit, by which I mean the lower limit in terms of self-denial and self-restraint, is that a person eats what does not cause him harm or makes him ill, and does not go beyond that to desire and pursue what brings him the most pleasure, so that his aim becomes the pleasure and the desire and not the appeasement of hunger; that he dresses in clothes that his skin can bear without pain, but does not incline to sumptuous embroidered wear; and that he dwells in a home that affords him shelter from extreme heat and cold, and does not exceed that by dwelling in a magnificently ornamented and appointed palace—unless of course he is sufficiently wealthy to afford such luxurious things without recourse to oppression, injustice, and self-destruction in the pursuit of money. In this sense, then, those born to poor fathers and raised in straitened circumstances are superior, because self-restraint and self-denial are easier for such people, just as they were easier for Socrates than for Plato.

19.   Whatever falls between these two limits is permissible and does not divest one who does such of the title of philosopher; rather, it is fitting that he be called by it, though superiority lies in preferring the lower and not the higher limit, while virtuous souls accompanying bodies born to prosperity can bring their bodies by degrees to the lower level. But to go beyond the lower limit is to go beyond philosophy to a state similar to those we mentioned with regard to the Hindus, Manis, monks, and ascetics, in other words, to depart from the moderate way of life, to provoke divine displeasure, to engage in a futile form of self-harm, and to merit [108] losing the title of philosopher. This is also the case with going beyond the upper limit. We ask God, Who bestows intellect, drives away anxiety, and discloses the goal to grant us success, to guide us and to help us achieve what is most pleasing and favorable to Him.

20.   We say summarily that, since the Creator is the Knower Who is not ignorant, the Just Who does no wrong; since knowledge, justice, and compassion exist absolutely; since we do have a Creator and Lord; since we are to Him servants to be ruled; and since the servants most beloved of their masters are those who carry out their way of living and pursue their code of behavior, then the servant closest to God (mighty and exalted is He!) is the most learned, most just, most compassionate and merciful. The whole of this statement is what is meant by the philosophers' saying, "Philosophy is imitating God (mighty and exalted is He!) to the degree that humans are able." This is a summary statement of the way of philosophy, the details of which are found in On Spiritual Medicine,[4] for there we have set down how to remove vices from the human soul, and how much effort the one who loves philosophy should apply in terms of pursuing, amassing, and spending wealth, and seeking out ranks of leadership.

21.   Now that we have explained what we wanted to on this topic, let us turn back to explain ourselves, to take note of those who slander us, and to declare that

---

[4] See Spiritual Medicine, ch. 19.

no particular way of living that we have followed to this day (with God's bestowal of success and aid) would merit our being denied the title of philosopher. For the one who deserves to be stricken from the roster of philosophers is someone who has an inadequate grasp of both parts of philosophy—I mean the theoretical and the practical—because he does not know what a philosopher should know or follows a path that a philosopher should not. But we are innocent of that (with all due praise to God, His bestowal of success, and His guidance).

22. In the category of theoretical philosophy, even if we had only the ability to compose a book like this one, that alone would prevent the erasure of the title of philosopher from our name, not to mention the likes of our books *On the Demonstrative Syllogism, On Metaphysics,* [109] *On Spiritual Medicine*; our book *Introduction to Natural Science,* commonly called *Auscultatio physica*; our discourses *On Time and Place, Extension, Eternity, and the Void, On the Shape of the Universe, The Cause for the Earth's Fixed Location in the Middle of the Sphere, The Cause of the Sphere's Circular Motion, On Compositeness, On the Essential Motion of the Body and its Determination*; our books *On the Soul* and *On Prime Matter*; our books on medicine, such as *The Mansuri, For Anyone Lacking an Attending Physician, On Current Drugs,* the one known as *Medicine for Kings,* and the book known as *The Compendium,* the likes of which no one in this kingdom had composed before me and no one since has imitated in quite the same way; our book *On the Discipline of the Philosophy Known to Commoners as Alchemy*; in sum, close to two hundred books, discourses, and treatises produced by me up to the time of my work on this discourse, on the branches of philosophy including natural science and metaphysics. With regard to mathematics, however, I admit that I have given it slight attention, but only inasmuch as I have no pressing need for it and have not given over my time to mastering it with a particular aim in mind, not because I am incapable of it. I will set forth an account of that to anyone who wishes by arguing that the correct thing in that is what I have done, not what those who call themselves "philosophers" have done, who spend their lives obsessing over the minutiae of geometry. So if my achievement in theoretical philosophy is not enough to merit being called a philosopher, I'd like to meet the person in our time who does.

23. In terms of the practical part of philosophy (with the help of God and His bestowal of success), I have not exceeded in my way of living either of the two limits I defined above, and nothing observed in my actions would merit its being said that my way of life is not that of the philosopher. I have attended the ruler not as one who bears arms nor as one entrusted with doing his work, but rather as a physician and confidant who has independence of action in one of two cases: either in time of illness, to cure him [110] and improve the condition of his body, or in time of health, to keep him company or to advise him—God knows this of me!—to do all that I hope will lead to his welfare and that of his subjects. None of the evil he perpetrates arises from me, such as hoarding and wasting money and fighting people, arguing against them and oppressing them. In fact, the exact opposite of all that and the relinquishing of much of what is in my rights are well known about me. As for how I behave with

food, drink, and entertainment, anyone who has frequently observed me would know that I do not go to extremes, and the same applies to all my other observable circumstances, in dress or riding mount or servant or slave girl.

24.   When it comes to my love of knowledge, my intense desire for it, and my hard work in pursuing it, it is common knowledge to anyone who has spent time with me or observed me that from the days of my youth to the present that I have been so devoted to it that whenever I come upon a book I have not read or a man I have not encountered, I pay no mind to any task (even if that be greatly detrimental to me) without finishing the book or learning what the man knows. My endurance and effort has reached the degree that in one year I wrote more than twenty thousand pages in the minute script used for talismans. I persevered in composing the huge *Compendium* for fifteen years, working day and night, to the point that my eyesight grew weak and the tendon in my hand tore, preventing me now from reading and writing. Despite my condition I still pursue these two things to the best of my ability while regularly employing someone to read and write for me.

25.   If this group finds that the measure [of my achievements] in these things causes me to fall below the rank of philosophy in practice, and they deem the goal of following the philosophers' way of life to be different from what we have described, then let them substantiate that, whether in person or in writing, so that we can yield it to them if they show superior knowledge, or refute them if we establish a point of error or deficiency in what they say. But suppose I indulge them and admit to shortcoming in the practical part of philosophy, what might they say about the theoretical part? If they were [111] to find me deficient in it, then let them present what they say about that to me so that we can investigate it and afterward give them what they are due or refute their error. If they do not find me deficient in the theoretical part, then they had best learn from my knowledge and pay no heed to my way of living, that they may follow the proverb of the poet: "Act according to my knowledge so that if I fall short in my action, my knowledge will aid you and my shortcoming will not harm you."

26.   This is what we wanted to explain in this discourse. To the Bestower of intellect goes praise without end, as is His merit and desert. God bless His chaste bondsmen and His virtuous bondswomen.

II.   ON THE FIVE ETERNALS[a]

I. Bīrūnī on ar-Rāzī

1.   [195] Muhammad ibn Zakariyā ar-Rāzī related on the authority of the ancient Greeks that there are five eternal things: (1) the Creator (glory to Him!); (2) the universal Soul; (3) Prime Matter; (4) absolute time; and (5) absolute space. On this he based his own derivative doctrine. He distinguished between time and duration by applying number to one of them and not the other, by reason of the fact that finitude is a consequence of being numbered, just as the philosophers made time a dura-

tion of what has a first and a last but made eternity a duration of what does not. He stated that the five in terms of this [eternal] existence are what exist necessarily. What is sensibly perceived in [this existence] is Prime Matter informed by composition, which is localized, and so necessarily there is place. The difference in states [in the sensibly perceived] are the result of the necessities of time—for some precede and some follow, and it is by time that one knows old and new, older and newer, and simultaneity—and so necessarily there is time. Next, living things exist, and so necessarily there is Soul. Finally, in living things there are intellects and the most perfect craftsmanship, and so necessarily there is the Creator Who is wise and knowing, Who perfects and rectifies (to the greatest extent possible), and Who causes the power of the intellect to flow down for the purposes of purification.

2. Al-Marzūqī against ar-Rāzī

1.   [196] Know that those who maintain that time is something other than day and night, is other than the rotations of the celestial sphere, and is neither a body nor an accident, thereupon say: It is not possible except at a given time that God creates anything, and time does not perish such that actions would occur not at set times. This follows because if time were to perish, one thing could not come before or after another, but that is not observed among things. So this is an absurdity.

2.   Their doctrine is the same as those maintained by people who say that absolute time and place (or correctly in Arabic, "eternity" and "void") are eternal substances that subsist through themselves. The refutation of this will come after differentiating their sects and explaining their methods.

3.   [197] So we [al-Marzūqī] say: through God is strength and power. There are four sects who maintain that the eternal is more than one: (1) those who say there are only two, the agent and matter (that is, Prime Matter); (2) those who teach that there are three eternals, the agent, matter, and void; (3) those who teach that there is the agent, matter, void, and duration; and (4) the group for which ar-Rāzī the physician is the spokesman, who adds by his blather the rational Soul, bringing the number of eternals to five.

4.   The explanation of their [ar-Rāzī's] doctrine is that five things never cease: two of which are living agents (the Creator and Soul); one of which is unalive and acted upon and from which is generated all existing bodies (Prime Matter); and two of which are neither alive nor agent nor acted upon (Void and Duration)—leading to other such drivel that the hand cannot bear to write, the tongue to utter, or the heart to imagine. He also maintains that the Creator is the perfection of wisdom to Whom neither neglect nor oversight attach and from Whom life emanates like the light from the Sun's orb. This life is the Perfect Pure Intellect.[5] From the Soul life emanates like light, but it swings between ignorance and intelligence like a man who

---

5 Compare this account to that given by Fakhr ad-Dīn ar-Rāzī II. 3, par. I.

sometimes forgets and sometimes recalls, because when it turns its gaze to the Creator, Who is Pure Intellect, it intellects and reaches for the heights, but when it turns its gaze to Prime Matter, which is Pure Ignorance, it falls back oblivious. [. . .]

5.   [198] One of them (that is, one of the heretics) states on the authority of the ancients that [the ideas of] eternity and void are innate to intellects without the need for inference. For there is no one possessed of reason but that he finds and conceptualizes in his intellect that bodies have something like a receptacle and a container; and that there is something that flags the concepts of before and after; and that not only is there our time which is past and future but also something between them; and that this thing has an interval and is extended.

6.   He said: People have imagined that the void is place and eternity is time, but this is not the case absolutely. Instead, void is the interval lacking body but in which body could be. Place is the surface common to what contains and what is contained. Time is whatever motion measures of the time that has immeasurable duration [that is, eternity]. So they turn the sense of relative time and motion into two absolutes and suppose that [relative time and motion] are [absolute time and motion]. But the difference between them is quite significant. For *relative place* is the place of this situated thing; if there is no situated thing, there is no place. And *time measured by motion* both ceases with the cessation of what is in motion and is found with its presence, since [time] is what is measured by its motion. *Absolute place*, however, is the place in which body would be even if it is not. And *absolute time* is duration, whether measured or not. It is neither the case that motion makes duration (rather it is what measures it), nor is it the case that the situated thing makes place (rather it is what settles in it).

7.   He said: It is now clear that [void and time] are not accidents; rather they are substances, because void does not subsist by body. If that were the case, void would cease with body's cessation in the way that being square ceases with the cessation of the square. [199] If someone said that *place* does cease with the cessation of the situated thing, it would be said: with *relative* place this is the case, because it is nothing but the place of this situated thing. This is not so, however, with *absolute* place. Do you not see that were we to imagine the celestial sphere as nonexistent, with its nonexistence, we would be unable to imagine the place in which it is nonexistent? Equally, were there something that measured the duration of a given Saturday, but not the duration of a Sunday, in the absence of that measurement it would not be the duration of that unmeasured day that would be eliminated, but the very measurement itself. Equally, in neither the cessation of the celestial sphere nor its coming to rest is there anything that would eliminate true time, which is duration and eternity. It ought to [be clear] that [void and time] are substances and not accidents, since neither needs a place or a subject, and so they are neither through body nor an accident. All that remains is that they are substances.

8.   In addition to this approach is what one of them told us. He said: The nature of time is of such certain existence in itself and by force of the stability in its substance that its nonexistence is immediately inconceivable, there being no way it could ever

have been nonexistent. It has neither beginning nor end and is, in point of fact, permanent and eternal. Do you not see that there is no way one could imagine the nonexistence of time without affirming a duration in which there is no time?! But duration is time itself! So how can one imagine the nonexistence of something the necessity of whose substance is certain, when the sound intellect refuses to conceptualize its nonexistence and annihilation? How could one tolerate making its nonexistence a possibility when its necessity is one of the eternal necessities?

9.   This is what was reported on the authority of the ancients. Ar-Rāzī the physician, with his nonsensical talk when he argues, hovers around what we recorded about them, but he neither throws light on their explanations nor achieves their rank. For that reason he was made but a follower of them.

3. Fakhr ad-Dīn ar-Rāzī on ar-Rāzī, Part I

1.   [203] [. . .] Then [there are] those who maintain that the source of the world is not a body. There are two such groups. One is the Harranians [followed by ar-Rāzī], who established five eternals: the Creator, Soul, Prime Matter, eternity, and void. They said that the Creator (exalted is He!) is the perfection of knowledge and wisdom to Whom neither neglect nor oversight happens and from Whom [204] the intellect emanates like the light from the orb; He (may He be exalted!) knows things perfectly. Next, from the Soul life emanates like light from the orb, but it is ignorant, not knowing [205] things as long as it has not applied itself to them. The Creator (may He be exalted!) knew that the Soul is inclined toward cleaving to matter, to desiring it passionately, to seeking bodily pleasures, to loathing separation from bodies, and to forgetting its true self. Since perfect wisdom is characteristic of the Creator (may He be exalted!), He directed Himself to Prime Matter after the Soul had cleaved to it, and He combined it in a variety of combinations, like the heavens and the elements, and combined the bodies of the animals [206] in the most perfect way, though the corruption that remains in them cannot be eliminated. Next, He (sublime and exalted is He!) caused intellect and perception to flow down on the Soul, which became the reason for the Soul's recollection of its world and for its understanding that as long as it remained in the material world, it would never be unfettered from pain. When the Soul realizes that and understands that in its own world it would have pleasures free from pain, it will yearn for [207] that world, and rise up after its separation [from its world] and remain there forever and ever in utmost joy and happiness.

2.   They said: In this way, the puzzles circulating among those who hold either the world's eternity or temporal creation are removed. For the adherents of the world's eternity say: Had the world come about in time, why would God (exalted is He!) bring it about at this specific time and not either before or after that? Also, if the Creator of the world [208] is wise, why is the world full of suffering? The adherents of creation say: Had the world been eternal, it would have no need for a maker; but this is patently false, because we see the traces of wisdom manifest in the world. Both of the groups are confused about [these issues].

3. Now, according to this way, the problems raised are removed. For, since we believe in a wise Maker and not a body [as the source of the world], we maintain the world's creation. And whenever it is said: But why did He create the world at this specific time? We say: It was precisely at that time that the Soul cleaved to Prime Matter, and the Creator (exalted is He!) knew that that cleaving is the cause of corruption, but that after the occurrence of that misfortune, [209] He would redirect it to the most beneficial course possible. Any other evils remain simply because it is impossible to separate this composition from them.

4. Two questions remain. One is: Why did the Soul cleave to matter after not cleaving to it? If that cleaving came about for no reason, then the creation of the world as a whole could have come about [210] for no reason. The second is: Why wouldn't the Creator prevent the Soul from cleaving to matter?

5. They respond to the first by saying: This question is unacceptable to the theologians, because they hold that the One Who has the power to act and to choose may give preference to one of the things He can do over the other without any selectively determining factor; [211] so why wouldn't they permit that in the case of the Soul? It is equally unacceptable to the philosophers, because they allow what comes before to be a cause that prepares what will follow, so why wouldn't they allow one to say that the Soul is eternal and has an infinite number of new ideas, but everything that comes before has not ceased to be a cause for what follows to the point that the Soul arrives at the one that makes the cleaving necessary?

6. They respond to the second question by saying that the Creator knew that the best corrective for the Soul is that it comes to know what is harmful about this cleaving until on its own it gives up that [212] commingling. Furthermore, it is on account of that commingling with Prime Matter that the Soul acquires the virtues of the intellect that it did not have before. For the sake of these two goods, the Creator did not prevent the Soul from cleaving to Prime Matter.

4. Fakhr ad-Dīn ar-Rāzī on ar-Rāzī, Part II

1. [213] The Harranians established five eternals: two living agents, that is, the Creator and Soul—and what they mean by Soul is a principle of life, that is, human and celestial spirits; one that is passive and nonliving, that is, Prime Matter; two that are neither living, agent, nor passive (that is, Eternity and Space). Now the proof of the eternity of the Creator is commonly known. [214] The eternity of the Soul is based on the fact that every created being is preceded by matter. So they said that, had the Soul been created, it would be material; and if its matter is created, then it needs another matter, ad infinitum. If it is eternal, however, that is what was sought. With matter, if it is created, an infinite regress necessarily ensues. If it is eternal, however, that is what was sought. As for eternity, it is time and not susceptible to nonexistence, because with everything that is in fact subject to nonexistence, its nonexistence comes *temporally* after its existence. But then time would exist right when it was posited not to exist. This is a contradiction. If positing the nonexistence of time necessarily entails [215]

something absurd in itself, then it is something necessary in itself. Next, space is also something necessary in itself, because one's innate sense immediately rejects its elimination. Space is like that because, if it were eliminated, directions could not be distinguished by pointing at them, and that is unintelligible.

III.   SELECTIONS FROM *DOUBTS AGAINST GALEN*[a]

1.   [1] I know that many people will consider me an ignoramus for writing this book, and many will criticize me harshly, or it will all come down to stereotyping me as someone who, simply because he happens to find it an amusing diversion [to write such a book], sets out to be at odds with a man like Galen. [This is solely] on account of the reverence in which [Galen] is held, and his learning, precedence, and status in all parts of philosophy. God knows I find some resistance in myself to that, since I have been tried sorely in contradicting someone who has benefited me more amply and more often than anyone else (this is someone to whom I have looked for guidance, someone in whose path I have followed, and someone from whose ocean of knowledge I have sought to quench my thirst!), [especially when such contradiction] has been by means of [the very thing] with which the slave would not contradict his master, the student his teacher, and the benefited his benefactor.

2.   As God is my witness, I would prefer that the doubts I record in this book were not applicable to the books of this illustrious and learned authority whose status is so awesome, whose rank is so majestic, whose legacy is so universal, and whose memory is revered so eternally. That said, however, the discipline of medicine and philosophy does not allow us to submit blindly to prominent leaders or to comply with them, or to avoid thoroughly investigating [their views], and no philosopher would want his readers and students to do that. Galen himself said that in his book *On the Usefulness of the Parts of the Body*,[b] wherein he lambasted those who force their disciples and partisans to accept their teachings without demonstrative proof. What encouraged and aided me the most was the thought that if this great man were alive today, he would not rebuke me for writing this book, and it would not weigh upon him nearly as heavily as the truth does, and the love of investigating topics of research and arriving at conclusions about them. On the contrary, he would happily [2] and eagerly want to get started examining and studying it, either in order to solve all the puzzles in it and praise me for serving as a cause on account of which his discussion concerning those problematic points received additional clarification as well as protection from the challenges leveled against it as it was before, or for the purposes of retracting the problematic points entirely, in which case he would heap great praise on me for having alerted him to the habitual negligence and obliviousness conferred upon humankind, or so that he could solve some of the problems and retract others, as long as the two activities came together in a manner that pleased me.

3.   As for the person who criticizes me and calls me an ignoramus for excerpting these puzzles [from Galen's books] and talking about them, I will neither heed him nor indeed count him a philosopher. [By criticizing this], he has tossed the practice

of philosophy over his shoulder and held fast to the behavior of the great mass of idiots who blindly obey their masters and avoid challenging them; for the practice of those who wish to be philosophers has always entailed competing against one's leaders, arguing intensely with them, and renouncing deference to them. Here is Aristotle, saying "The truth and Plato contradict one another, and while both are dear to us, the truth is dearer to us than Plato," when raising objections against [Plato] and contradicting him on the most important of his doctrines.[6] And here is Theophrastus contradicting Aristotle [even] in the clearest part of philosophy after geometry, that is, logic. And here is Themistius explaining [Aristotle's] errors on many topics, to the point that often he is left dumbfounded and says, "I just cannot understand how the Philosopher overlooked this, when it cannot be any more self-evident!"

4.   In the case of Galen, there is certainly no need for me to recount his many refutations of both the ancient philosophers as well as the revered authorities of his time, the fortitude and stamina he had for [such refutation], and the lengths to which he could go in talking about it, since there are more than I could count, and since it is clear to anyone who reads his books that [such refutation] was of greatest concern to him. I do not think any of the philosophers or physicians got away from him without being crushed to pieces, but most of what he said against them is true. In fact, if I had the mind to, I would say that all of it is true. That just shows [you] the great extent of his knowledge, the natural acuity of his intellect, and the vast amount of learning he obtained.

5.   If I were asked the reason why later scholars [have to] make such corrections to past illustrious authorities, I would say there are a number of reasons. One reason is the habitual negligence and obliviousness conferred upon humankind. Another reason is that bias in a man prevails over judgment [3] on a particular issue to such an extent that he says something that is just wrong about it, whether knowingly or unknowingly, but when another man—who is sharp but unencumbered by that particular bias—examines what the first man said, he does not overlook what the first man missed, and no bias provokes him to make the error the first man made. Another reason is that the scientific disciplines continually increase and grow closer to perfection with each passing day, and they give what it takes the ancient philosopher a long time to discover to the later philosopher in a shorter period time, allowing the latter to evaluate it and make it a means whereby he can easily discover something else. In such a circumstance, the ancient philosophers are the ones who acquire with effort, and those coming after them are their heirs, whose inheritance makes it easy for them to acquire more and more by their own efforts. Now, if someone said to me that this [theory] makes the claim that later scientists are superior to the ancients, I would say that is not absolutely the case unless one qualifies the description of the later scholar by saying "as long as he is someone who perfects what the ancient scholar produced."

---

[6] That is, Plato's doctrine of the Forms; this is a paraphrase of Aristotle's *Nicomachean Ethics* (hereafter "NE") I 6, 1096a16–17.

6. Let us now take up the aim we seek by beginning with [Galen's] book *On Demonstration*,[c] since, in my opinion, it is the most important and most useful book ever, after the books of divine revelation. We will discuss not only [instances] in which he is incorrect, but also [instances] in which he abandons his customary procedure and the method that he follows almost always, since [in the case of the latter instances], even if his view were correct, nevertheless he was negligent about proving it, or he used it without establishing its credentials, or he rushed into the traditional approach to it and did not change his view, or he contradicted himself about it.

7. Galen had earlier denied but then concluded, in the fourth chapter of *On Demonstration*, that the universe does not corrupt. He said, "If the universe were corruptible, then the [celestial] bodies, the distances between them, their magnitudes, and their motions would not persist in one and the same state, and, moreover, the waters of the oceans, which preceded us, would have to cease existing. But not a single one of these ever departs from its state or changes, as the astronomers have observed for thousands of years. Therefore, it necessarily follows that, since the universe does not age, it is not susceptible to corruption."

8. I note first that this contradicts what he said both in his *On My Own Opinions*[7] [ch. 2] and in his book called *On Medicine*;[8] for there he sought to provide a demonstration [4] for the impossibility of knowing whether the universe is eternal or originated, whereas [here] in the fourth chapter of *On Demonstration* he has avowed—and elsewhere he has stated unequivocally—that anything that does not corrupt is not generated. Now, any reader of Galen knows that he composed his book *On My Own Opinions* only after he had settled himself and his opinions had become unshakable, and that it was the last of his books and compilations. So, if what he said in *On Demonstration* is his real view, then there is no rationale[d] for why he would stop maintaining unequivocally the eternity of the universe,[9] since the conclusion of the two premises—I mean, "the universe does not corrupt" and "anything that does not corrupt is not generated"—is that "the universe is not generated," whence he has contradicted his statement that "it is impossible to know if the universe is eternal or temporally created."

9. Next, I note that he has violated the injunction that he always orders us to obey, namely, to be careful to use and acquire premises from the positions that are *necessarily* consequential to the object of investigation.[10] The [premise] that the mag-

---

[7] See the edition and translation of Vivian Nutton in *Corpus Medicorum Graecorum*, vol. 3, no. 2, 57–59.

[8] This is *Kitāb al-Ṣināʿa al-Ṭibbīya* = *Kitāb al-Ṣināʿa al-ṣaghīr*, Muhammad S. Sālim, ed., *Technē iatrikē* Muhammad, Karl Kühn, ed., vol. I, 305–412. See Sezgin, *Geschichte*, vol. 3, no. 4, 80–81.

[9] That is, why he would revise his view, in his "final" book *Opinions*, to maintain that it is impossible to know whether the universe is eternal or originated.

[10] That is, to use the premises appropriate to the object of inquiry; the "object of investigation" here is "whether or not the universe corrupts."

nitudes of the planets and the earth and the measurement of the water in the oceans and of the rest of the parts of the universe always remain the same, does not entail the impossibility of the corruption of the world. The corruptibility of things is not just by way of deterioration and degeneration, but also such that something can corrupt when it is the most complete and perfect it can be, like a building erected on a support once the support is removed from under it, or a tree once it is uprooted, or a fire once it is doused, and so on. So, he should not have established his conclusion by means of [the premise] he used without explaining that the universe is one of the things that corrupt only by degrading. Not only did he not pay attention to this at all, he also added to this antecedent, that is, "If the universe were corruptible," this consequent, namely, "then the [celestial] bodies . . . would not persist in one and the same state," as though [the universe] could corrupt as a result of this only. This consequent would conclude necessarily for this antecedent only if one adds either a stipulation to it, such that it becomes, "If the universe were corruptible through deterioration [of its parts], then the [celestial] bodies . . . would not persist in one and the same state," or a premise to explain that corruption does not happen to anything whatsoever except by way of deterioration alone. That, however, is not a possibility [in this case], because things may "doff" their forms not just by simple disintegration but also such that the form in substances that disintegrate and dissipate very slowly will barely corrupt at all, except through their immediate degeneration when they are the most perfect and complete that they can be, like a glass vessel when smashed with a rock, or a cliff-top fortress [5] when the ground below it gives way after a jolt. Similarly, then, the universe may corrupt in this way, even if its form stays in the same state right up to the moment of its corruption. It is in this manner that the world corrupts according to those religious scholars who maintain that it corrupts—I mean, by immediate degeneration, not by deterioration.

10.   Moreover, there are very great distinctions among bodies with respect to disintegration and deterioration. The disintegration and deterioration that will not happen to gold, gems, and glass in a thousand, no a hundred thousand, days will happen to vegetables, fruits, and spices in but a single day, despite the fact that both are subject to generation and corruption. Similarly, in terms of being less susceptible to corruption, the ratio of the substance of the celestial sphere to the substance of gems is equal to the ratio of gems to vegetables, or rather so much greater that I do not want it to increase still further lest it can increase infinitely. Consequently, the corruption of the celestial sphere can go on for thousands of year, and the degradation that takes place in it over the period of time in which the epochs of one people give way to others is so minuscule as to be immeasurable by astronomical observation, since the astronomer can only approximate a measurement of this magnitude. Any degradation that might be perceptible by astronomical observation takes place only over a period of time that is so lengthy and continuous as to make it impossible for the epochs, histories, and observations of one people to pass to another because of some catastrophic devastation, like a flood or plague or something along those lines. How much of a ruby would be likely to degrade between the time of the astronomer

Hipparchus[11] and the time of Galen? By our time, I would estimate that not even the amount that might be discernible by the most precise scale possible would have degraded from deterioration, and this is based on the possibility that the ratio of deterioration between [the ruby] and the celestial sphere might be equal to the ratio of herbs to [the ruby], if not a great deal more than that. However, while we can look at an object placed in our hands and measure it, we are completely incapable of getting at the measurements of the planets' sizes and distances, except by means of the various types of measuring strategies such as visual appearances and ratios, which never provide complete accuracy but rather approximations only. So, if the substance of the Sun were to increase or decrease by as much as the size of the biggest mountain, our observations would get at nothing more than the very same thing it got at before such an increase or decrease.

11. By way of summary, then, the doctrine that the universe is incorruptible cannot be verified by any of the premises that he advanced in this part of the book, nor are these [premises] even first principles, the way he requires them to be and the way he uses them as such. [6] Moreover, the conclusion that the universe is incorruptible is incorrect unless it can be verified that it is finite or that there is nothing else other than it, since he should know that the [same] thing[12] can be said about the substances that are not bodies. Either [the universe] is finite or something besides it *does* exist. So the conclusion that the universe is incorruptible is definitely incorrect unless it can be verified that this other thing cannot cause the corruption [of the universe], or that no part of its substance whatsoever is susceptible to alteration or disintegration.

12. If someone argues in defense [of Galen] by saying that in this passage [from *On Demonstration*] he was unable to verify that the universe is incorruptible so instead he showed from where one should take the premises, I say the following. My criticism and questioning of him on this is all the more extreme since such an example is intended to serve simply as representative of the rest of the premises [he employs]. He uses first principles that are not, in fact, first principles, and consequents that do not follow necessarily from their antecedent. It does not seem worth it to me to lengthen overly my book by listing each and every one of them, since anyone who reads this passage of his book methodically, consciously, and with the aim of arriving at its ultimate implications will grasp them, and shortly thereafter come to that [conclusion] and proceed with caution.

---

11 Hipparchus flourished throughout 190–120 B.C.E., while Galen's approximate dates are 131–201 C.E., so there is a difference of about three hundred years.

12 That is, "it is incorruptible."

AL-FĀRĀBĪ

Although it would be difficult to overstate the significance of al-Fārābī's work on the development of philosophy undertaken in Islamic lands, the number of details with which we can feel confident about the man's life are few. The most reliable sources agree that his name was Abū Naṣr Muhammad ibn Muhammad ibn Tarkhān ibn Awzalagh (or perhaps Uzlugh) al-Fārābī, but even here there is room for doubt since his familial origins are given as both in Fārāb, Khurāsān and in Faryāb, Turkistān. He was born probably around 870, if we accept that he died in his eighties. Part of the circle of Baghdad Peripatetics, he studied Aristotelian logic with Yuḥannā ibn Ḥaylān (d. 910) and Abū Bishr Mattá (d. 940), and was himself the teacher of Yaḥyā ibn ʿAdī. Al-Fārābī left Baghdad in 942 and traveled to Damascus, Aleppo, and Egypt. He died in Damascus in 950 or 951. Beyond this bare skeleton of an outline, little else can be said with assurance about the personal circumstances of al-Fārābī's life.

Al-Fārābī has been credited with writing over one hundred works; however, if this number is correct, then very little of his philosophical corpus is still extant. Broadly speaking, al-Fārābī's works can be classified under three headings: (1) introductions or prolegomena to the study of philosophy; (2) commentaries primarily on the Aristotelian logical corpus (although a commentary on Aristotle's *Nicomachean Ethics* should also be included under this rubric); and (3) original works, in which al-Fārābī presents his own syncretistic philosophical system. The greater outflow of his works are dedicated to logic, and indeed his renown as a logician earned him the moniker "Second Master" or "Second Teacher'" (*al-muʿallim ath-thānī*) — second, that is, to Aristotle himself. His significance for the history of Arabic philosophy, though, arguably comes as much if not more from his penchant for system-building rather than from his logical works. Al-Fārābī was the first great systematic philosopher in the Arab-speaking world, followed in this respect a generation later by Ibn Sīnā (ca. 980–1037). Al-Fārābī's works show the mark of a man driven to rehabilitate and then reinvent the Neoplatonized Aristotelianism of the late Greek world, while adapting it to fit the new cultural matrix of the Near East. The best examples of his system-building are *The Principles of the Opinions of the Inhabitants of the Virtuous City* and *The Principles of Beings* (also titled *Governance of Cities*).

Like earlier philosophers, al-Fārābī distinguished between theoretical and practical philosophy, the former terminating in understanding, the latter in action. As for theoretical philosophy, al-Fārābī synthesizes an Aristotelian metaphysics of causation with a highly developed Neoplatonic emanationist scheme that incorporates the Ptolemaic planetary system. He in turn integrates a sophisticated theory of the intellect into this metaphysical framework, which develops the notion that the Active Intellect of

54

Aristotle's *De anima* III 5 is a self-subsisting substance, one that plays a role not only in human cognition, but also in generation and corruption in the sublunar realm. Although in practical philosophy al-Fārābī treats various ethical issues, his main focus is on the ideal or virtuous state and its ruler, which on the whole is reminiscent of ideas found in Plato's *Republic*.

I. THE *EISAGŌGĒ*—THE INTRODUCTION[a]

1.   [118] Our aim in this book is to enumerate the things from which propositions are composed and into which they are divided, that is, each one of the parts of the premises used generally in all of the syllogistic disciplines. So we say: Every proposition is either categorical or conditional. Every conditional proposition is made up of two categorical propositions connected by a conditional particle. Every categorical proposition is composed of and divided into a predicate and a subject. [119] Every predicate and every subject is either a term indicating a meaning (*ma'nā*) or a meaning that a given term indicates. Every meaning that a given term indicates is either universal or individual.

2.   The universal is that to which two or more things can be similar, while the individual is something for which even among two there can be no shared similarity. Furthermore, the universal is something that can be predicated of more than one, whereas the individual cannot be predicated of more than one.

3.   The two parts of a proposition may be both universal, as when we say, "Man is an animal," and other such propositions that are used in the sciences, in dialectic, in sophistics, and in many of the other disciplines. Its two parts may both be individual, as when we say, "Zayd is the one standing," or "The one standing is Zayd," though this [type] is rarely used. A proposition's subject may be individual and its predicate universal, as when we say, "Zayd is a man"; this is used often in rhetoric and poetry and in the practical disciplines. A proposition's subject may be universal and its predicate individual or individuals, as when we say, "Man is Zayd" and "Man is Zayd, 'Amr, and Khalid." These two are used in analogy and induction when they are reducible to the syllogism. When the subject is a single individual, it is used in analogy; when the subject is many individuals, it is used in induction.

4.   The universal meanings that are treated as parts of the categorical propositions include (a) those that are single to which single terms refer; and (b) those that are combined to which combined terms refer—albeit restrictive and conditional combinations, not assertoric ones—as when we say "the white man" and "the rational animal"; for "animal" is restricted by "rational" and conditional upon it, and so too "man" is restricted by and conditional upon "white." Universal meanings combined in this manner clearly can also be divided into single ones.

5.   According to the enumeration of many ancient philosophers, there are five simple universal meanings: genus, species, difference, property, and accident.

6. *Genus and species.* Universals that are predicated of a single individual can vary generally and specifically, like "man" and "animal" predicated of "Zayd." For "man" is more specific than "animal." Since there are simple universals varying generally and specifically, each is a proper response to the question "What is this individual?" Among [these universals] there is one above which there is none more general and one below which there is none more specific; those that fall between these two ascend in order from the more specific to the more general and so on until they stop at the most general of them. The more general of any two of them is a genus and the more specific a species. The more general above which there is none more general is the highest genus, and the more specific below which there is none more specific is the final species.

7. Each of those that fall [120] in between is at once a genus and a species: a genus in relation to the more specific one below it; and a species in relation to the more general one above it. All of them are said to be genera, one below another. For example, the individual thing one is looking at is a palm. We did not know that it is a palm, so we ask, "What is this thing we see?" to which the proper response is, "It is a palm," and "It is a tree," and "It is a plant," and "It is a body." These responses vary with respect to the general and the specific, and whichever two of them you take, the more general is a genus and the more specific a species. For example, "plant" is a species and "body" is a genus; so too "tree" is a species and "plant" is a genus; and so too "palm" is a species and "tree" is a genus. The most general of them all is "body," so let it be the highest genus. The most specific of them is "palm," so let it be the final species. "Tree" and "plant" fall in between "palm" and "body," and each of them is both a species and a genus. "Tree" is a genus of "palm" and a species of "plant"; and "plant" is a genus of "tree" and a species of "body." "Tree," "plant," and "body" are genera arranged one under the other in descent from the highest genus in order from the more general to the more specific, and so on. So the highest genus is a genus that is not a species, being the genus of all the genera under it. The final species is not a genus, being a species of all the species above it. In sum, the genus is the more general and the species the more specific of any two universals that serve as a proper response to the question, "What is this individual?"

8. Every universal predicate is a proper response to the question, "What is it?" For it is the predicate for the "What is it?" question. Now, since every genus is more general than the species that is below it, it is predicated of more than a single species. Similarly, every final species is predicated of more than one individual. The individuals whose final species is one and the same are those that differ in number, like Zayd and an individual horse, and an individual ox. Now since every genus is predicated of more than one species *and* of the individuals of each of [the species], it is predicated of the individuals differing in number in the "What is it?" method. It is certainly not inconceivable that there are many individuals, each one of which is under a final species different from the one that another is under, and every final species of them is under a genus different from the one that another is under, and every genus of them is under another more general genus different from the one that another is under,

until every genus of them in this order will stop at a highest genus different from the one that another ascends to, so that [all of] these are so many highest genera.

9. When there are [multiple] species under one genus and there is no inter-mediate genus between them, that genus is the proximate genus of [121] those species, and those species are cognate species. Every genus above that proximate [genus] is the remote genus of those species. The species that are under differing genera are non-cognate species. The genera that are not one under another are four. They are: the highest genera; the intermediate genera, each one of which is under a different highest genus; the genera that are cognate species; and the intermediate genera that are species under different intermediate genera, all of which ascend ultimately to one highest genus. The question "What is it?" is thus not solely about the individual but also may be about a final species and an intermediate species. So responding with either a proximate or remote genus is like responding to our question, "What is the palm?" with "It is a tree and a plant," or asking "What is a tree?" and getting in response "It is a plant" or "It is a body." The same holds for the rest of the species.

10. *Difference.* The difference is a simple universal that allows one to distinguish each of the cognate species in a substance from the species that shares its genus. For a thing may be distinguished from another thing not in its substance but in one of its characteristics, like distinguishing one garment from another in that one is white and the other is red. A thing may also be distinguished from another thing in its substance, like distinguishing felt from palm fiber, and distinguishing one garment from another in that one is of linen and the other of cotton or wool. So the simple universal by means of which one distinguishes the substance of one species from another that shares its proximate genus is the difference. It is obvious that when [a species] is distinguished in its substance from its cognate species, it is distinguished from every species other than it. Other names should be used when one species is distinguished from another not in its substance [but by a characteristic].

11. Genus and difference are common in that each one of them indicates the very being and substance of the species. However, while the genus indicates the sub-stance that the species has in common with another or what makes its substance similar to another, the difference indicates the substance by which the species is distinct from another or what makes its substance distinct and separate from another. Or, [expressed differently], the genus indicates each of the species under it [but not] what is unique to each, whereas the difference indicates what is unique to the substance of each one. Thus, when we ask about a given species "What is it?" and we are informed about its genus, we are not satisfied without seeking to learn what distinguishes it from the other [species] that share that genus. [We do this] by adding the specifying question "What kind?"[1] to the genus of that species. We do not think we yet know the species

---

[1] Here in Arabic, the discussion concerns the particle *ayy*, which does not have an immediate equivalent in English, and reducing it to the simple question word "Which?" does not seem to satisfy the requirements of logical division being discussed here.

sufficiently when [122] we know what is common to it and another species, but only if in addition to that we also know what is proper to it alone. For example, we ask, "What is the palm?" and the response is "It is a tree." We are not satisfied without asking "What kind of a tree?," thereby seeking to learn what distinguishes the palm, in its substance and very being, from the other species common to the genus that encompasses it and others.

12.   By way of summary, it is only ever to a universal by which we know the species in a nonspecific way that we add the query "What kind?" Sometimes that universal is the most general one to describe that species, like "What kind of a *thing* is the palm?" or "What kind of a *being* is the palm?" For "thing" and "being" are the most general things possible for describing an individual or a species. Sometimes [that universal] is the closest genus in proximity; other times it is very close in proximity, for example, "What kind of a *body* is the palm?" or "What kind of a *plant* is the palm?" or "What kind of a *tree* is the palm?" The proper response to these questions is the difference.

13.   When the genus connected to the "What kind?" query is near to the species we want to know about, it is then proper to respond with a difference that belongs to that species and that distinguishes it in substance from its cognate species. Usually the proper response to this question in most things is not just the difference but also the genus of that species as restricted by its difference. For example, we ask "What is the palm? and we are told "It is a tree," and we ask next "What kind of a tree?" and the response is "It is a tree that bears dates." Or we say, "What kind of a garment is the cloak?" and the response is, "It is a garment made of wool"; so "cloak" is its genus and "made of wool" is its difference, its genus having been restricted by it. So we make the response to the query "What kind?" the genus of that species as restricted by its difference. With that, we deem we have learned a sufficient and thorough amount about that species in itself, as the genus restricted by the difference is the definition of the species about which we asked first "What is it?" and second "What kind?"

14.   The first part of the definition of every species is its genus and the second part is its difference, which is what completes its definition and what constitutes it, since it provides knowledge of it by means of what is proper to it in its substance. The difference is related to the species; so it is said to be a difference belonging to the species that constitutes its definition. The difference is also related to the genus of that species; so it is said to be a difference belonging to that genus because it restricts and complements it. The genus is complemented by differences in one of two ways. Either (1) it is restricted by contrary and contradictory differences in a sentence to which the disjunctive particle is added. For instance, we say, "The garment is made either of wool *or* of linen *or* of cotton," and "The body either takes nourishment *or* does not take nourishment." This is division of genus by differences. Or (2) it is complemented by a series of differences with neither contradiction nor the disjunctive particle. For instance, we say, "A garment of wool, a garment of cotton, and a garment of linen," and "A body that takes nourishment, and a body that does not take nourishment."

This type of complement is the response to the question "What kind?" and by means of it definitions of species that are under that genus are acquired.

15. In most cases the genus complemented by the difference [123] has a name that is equivalent to it for the purposes of signifying. They both point to one thing and one meaning, so that thing is a species that has a definition and a name. But it is not inconceivable for there to be a genus accompanied by a difference, but there is no name whatsoever in that particular language to serve as its equivalent for signifying, in which case that is a definition of the species with no name, for example, "the body that takes nourishment; for that has no name to serve as its equivalent for signifying. So the definition of that species serves instead of its name in all places that the name would be used.

16. The very differences by which the genus is divided complete the definitions of the species under it. This is why the division of the genus by differences ends ultimately at the species that are under it, since once the disjunctive particles are removed, the definitions of the species appear. Every intermediate genus contains a difference that constitutes it and another difference that divides it. For example, "animal" is an intermediate genus constituting "sentient," since it is the last part of its definition, because the definition of "animal" is "a body that seeks nourishment and is sentient," and it is divided into "rational" and "nonrational" when the disjunctive particle is added to it. Every difference constituting a given species divides the genus of that species, and whatever divides a given genus constitutes a species under that genus. Now clearly the highest genus cannot have a difference constituting it but only differences that divide it, while the final species cannot have differences dividing it but only differences that constitute it, and finally each one of the intermediary species has one difference that constitutes it and other differences that divide it.

17. Now when the genus combined with the query "What kind" is remote from the species about which we seek information, the proper response should be a difference that constitutes the species closest to that genus, and so is complemented by it and so produces a definition of a proximate genus below the first genus to which we had connected the query "What kind?" Then the query should also be added to this second genus, the response then being a difference constituting the species closest to this second genus, thereby also producing a definition. If that genus is the same as the species about which we seek information, then we have ended at what we sought. But if that definition is more general than the species sought, then that also is one intermediary species closer in proximity to the species sought, and the query "What kind?" is added to it, and the response is a difference complementing that third genus. You continue in this sequence until the combination of the difference now serving as response and all that came before it is equivalent to and coextensive with the species for which information was sought.

18. For example, we ask "What is man?," and it is said "Man is a certain body"; so we ask "What kind of a body?" to which the proper response is, "He is a body that seeks nourishment." From that is produced "a body that seeks nourishment." Now that is a definition of a species more proximate to body but still more general

than man; so we ask, "What kind of a body that seeks nourishment?" and the response is [124] "One that is sentient." So the response produces "He is a body that seeks nourishment and is sentient." Now this is the definition of animal, since it is the same as [saying "animal"], and had we been seeking the meaning of animal, then we would have arrived at our goal and been finished with the questioning. However, since animal is more general than man, which is our goal, we need to add again the query "What kind?" and so we say, "What kind of a body that seeks nourishment and is sentient is he?" and the response is, "He is rational." Now we have "He is a body that seeks nourishment and is sentient and is rational," which we find coextensive with and the same as "Man." One arrives at what was sought by following this order and sequence, that is, the sequence proper to the "What kind?" questioner and his respondent.

19. In response to the question "What kind?" we arrive at an intermediary species that has no name, in other words, when we find a genus complemented by a difference but we don't find a name that, for signifying, is equivalent to the genus-difference combination, the questioner should use that definition in place of a name, then add to it the question "What kind?" and ask again. For example, after the response to "What is man?," namely, "He is a body," the questioner says "What kind of a body?" and the response is, "He is a body that seeks nourishment": this is a genus complemented by a difference, but in Arabic there is no name that is equivalent for signifying, so that definition of the species has no name.

20. This definition should be used in place of the name. So it is said, "What kind of a body that seeks nourishment is he?" If the respondent ends at a definition of a species that has a name, the respondent, if he so wishes, can use the name of that species and add "What kind?" to it and ask his question, or he can use the definition itself. For example, to the query about man, "What kind of a body that seeks nourishment is he?" the response is, "He is a body that seeks nourishment and is sentient," which is the definition of "animal." After this, if the questioner wants, he can say, "What kind of an animal is he?" or he can say "What kind of a body that seeks nourishment and is sentient is he?" Often the questioner will aim at brevity and add the "What kind?" question to the final difference, saying "What kind of a sentient being is he?" which has the force of the whole definition.

21. The thing that a respondent to a "What kind?" query should preserve in terms of order and sequence is what is preserved by the one who divides the genus by its differences until he arrives at the species whose definition he sought. In other words, when he knows its highest genus, he should divide it by the differences that constitute the species most proximate to it, and he should continue to do that *in that sequence* until he arrives at the species he sought to know. When by his method he arrives at a species that has no name, he uses its definition in place of the name and then divides. When he arrives at an intermediary that has a name, he may either divide by using its name or its definition, as long as he does not pass by an intermediary species between the species he seeks [125] to know and its highest genus without

stopping at it and using its constitutive difference, until he arrives at the species he sought.

22. *Property.* The property is the simple universal belonging to a particular species alone, to all of it and always, but without indicating its very being or substance. For example, "neighing" for horse and "barking" for dog: these are used only in distinguishing one species from another, not for identifying its substance. Properties are similar to the difference in distinguishing one species from another but different in that they do not serve as a distinction for its substance. Obviously, the property is equivalent to the species of which it is a property and converts with it in predication, for example, when we say "every horse neighs" and "everything that neighs is a horse."

23. *Accident.* The accident is a simple universal belonging to a genus or a species, whether it be more general or more specific, but it does not indicate the very being or substance in any. For example: white, black, standing, sitting, moving, resting, hot and cold. There are two types of accident. (1) A permanent accident, which is never separate from the thing it is in or from some of the things it is in. For example "black," which is never separate from tar, and "hot," which is never separate from fire. (2) A separable accident, present sometimes, absent at others, though its subject remains. For example: standing and sitting, both of which belong to human. The accident includes that which while present in only one species, belongs to but some of the individuals of that species, like "snub" in nose; for it is present only in nose but is not found in every nose, or "blue" in eye. It also includes that which is present in more than one species, like white, black, moving, resting.

24. The accident also may be used to distinguish one genus from another, one species from another, and one individual from another, but for none of them in which it is an accident does it distinguish the very being or substance. So it is like the difference in that it distinguishes one species from another, but it is not like it in that it does not distinguish the substance. This is why accidents may be called differences, not unconditionally, but "accidental differences."

25. The accident may also be common with the property in distinguishing one species from another but not in terms of its substance. However, it differs from property in that the latter distinguishes the entire species from anything else and that always, whereas the accident distinguishes the species, but not the entire species, just some individuals, and only at some times. This is why accident may be called a "relative property," because the accident's distinguishing of a thing is only in relation to a precisely delimited thing and at a precisely delimited time. So when we ask "Which one is Zayd in this group?" we are told "He is the speaker," when he happens to be the only one in the group speaking at that time. He is distinguished from the others only in that group and only at that time since it may very well be the case that at that time among others there is a speaker, or that in Zayd's group there is someone else who is a speaker at another time. [126] This is why "the

speaker" becomes a property of Zayd relative to anyone else in that group and at that time only.

26. The inseparable accident distinguishes most completely. Next in rank, among the separable accidents, the one that is present only in one species, but not all of it, [distinguishes more completely]. Finally the remaining separable accidents distinguish least [completely] and, as we said, only relative to a precise thing and at a precise time. Porphyry of Tyre, in his book *Eisagōgē*, called the separable accidents used for distinguishing "general differences," and the inseparable accidents "proper differences." He called the absolute differences, that is those that distinguish among species in their substances, "most proper differences," though they are sometimes also called "substantive differences" and "essential differences."

27. The genus is divided by difference. Sometimes they are also divided by properties of their species, as when we say, "Animal includes what neighs and what barks," and sometimes also by accidents, as when we say "Animal is white and black." The division used in the sciences and of benefit in definitions is the division of the genus by differences; for it leads to definitions of species and to species necessarily. Division of the genus by properties is also sometimes of benefit, for it leads to species necessarily, but does not provide their definitions. In contrast, division by accidents does not necessarily lead to the species sought, as when we say "Animal includes white and not-white, capable of writing and not-capable of writing." For that reason it is of little help in the sciences.

28. *Composite universals.* The composite meanings used as predicates and subjects in propositions are combined from certain simple universals of the sort we have enumerated. Their combination—which is conditional and restrictive, but not assertoric—is (1) the definition, (2) the description, and (3) a statement that is neither.

29. The definition is a composite universal made up of a genus and a difference, as when we say about man, "He is a rational animal." When it so happens in a given definition that there is a genus and the differences are more than one, like the definition of animal that "It is a body that seeks nourishment and is sentient," you should know that the constitutive difference of that species is the last difference. Now, any preceding differences connected to the genus are a definition of the genus of that species whose definition either stands in for a name or which has a name but its definition is used instead of its name. This is not objectionable, for our saying "body that seeks nourishment" is the genus of "animal." Equally, were it to happen that there were three, four, or more differences, the intermediary genera whose definitions are used instead of their names would be the number of differences. For example, in defining man we say, "He is a body that seeks nourishment, that is sentient, that is rational," where "body that seeks nourishment" is the genus; "body that seeks nourishment and is sentient" is another [127] genus below it; and, as long as the whole combination is more general than the final species, anything that takes another difference thereafter is a genus below the first, until it ends at the final species. So every intermediary genus adds a difference to what is above it, just as every species adds a

difference to the genus above it. This becomes clear only when the definition of the genus takes the place of its name and is complemented by the difference that constitutes the species. This is why one group said that the difference is that by which the species exceeds the genus.[2]

30.   The description is made up either (1) of a genus and a property, as when we say of man, "He is an animal capable of laughing," or (2) a genus and an accident or accidents, as when we say, "He is an animal capable of writing" and "an animal that buys and sells."

31.   The statement that is neither a definition nor a description may consist either (1) of a species and an accident, as when we say, "Zayd is a white man"; or (2) of many accidents, as when we say, "Zayd is an excellent writer." It need not be impossible for the one made up of many accidents to be the same in predication as the species to which it belongs, and so it may also be called a property of it, as when we say about the triangle, "Its three angles equal two right angles"; for that is said to be a property of the triangle, so too when we say about man, "capable of learning," etc., following Aristotle who, in his *Topics*, calls descriptions "properties."[3]

32.   The definition is the same as the thing defined in terms of predication, as when we say, "Every man is a rational animal," and "Every rational animal is a man," so too in the case of the description and what is described. For every meaning that has a name and a definition, its definition is equivalent to its name in signifying, and both indicate the essence of the thing. However, the name indicates the meaning of the thing and its essence in concise form without being detailed or precise, whereas the definition indicates its meaning and essence precisely and in detail by including things that make it subsist. This is also the case with a description and a name, for they are equal to one another in signifying; however, the description indicates that by which the thing is distinguished from something else by means of things that do not make the thing subsist. Finally, for whatever does not have a name, its definition or description is used in place of its name.

The Introduction is complete. Due praise to God.

II.   SELECTIONS FROM *BOOK OF DEMONSTRATION*[a]

On Assent and Conceptualization

1.   [20] Perfect assent is certainty. Perfect conceptualization is to conceptualize something by means of a concise account of what it is in a manner proper to it, because

---

[2] Porphyry attributes this to "our predecessors"; see *Porphyrii Isagoge*, 10.25 (Edward Warren, trans., *Porphyry the Phoenician, Isagoge*, 46; Arabic: al-Ahwani, ed., 79).

[3] *Topics*, I 5, 102a18. Al-Fārābī has made a connection between Aristotle's discussion of property in the *Topics* and his own account of description.

conceptualizing something by means of what signifies it is to define the thing. We will begin [discussing] these two [activities] with a precise account of what is proper to perfect assent. By way of summary, assent is for someone to have a conviction about something to which a judgment can apply, by judging that what the thing is outside the mind accords with the object of conviction in one's mind, where the truth is that the thing outside the mind does in fact accord with the object of conviction in the mind. Assent may apply both to what is true as well as to what is false. Assent may be certain, it may be approximately certain, it may be the assent that is called "the acquiescence of the soul" with respect to something (which is the one most removed from certainty), and [finally], there is nothing certain whatsoever in false assent. In fact, only the assent to something that is true can be certain.

2.   Certainty means that we are convinced, with respect to the thing to which assent has been granted, that the existence of what we are convinced about with respect to that thing cannot possibly be different from our conviction. Moreover, we are convinced that this conviction about it cannot be otherwise, to the point that when one reaches a given conviction concerning his initial conviction, he maintains that it [also] cannot be otherwise, and so on indefinitely.

3.   Uncertainty means that we are convinced, with respect to the thing to which assent has been granted, that it is possible, or not impossible, that it is different, in terms of its existence, from the conviction we have about it. As for approximate certainty, it means either that one is not aware of anything opposing it, or one is aware of it, but what one is aware of is so thoroughly obscure that neither it nor anything that would explain its opposition can be articulated.

4.   The "acquiescence of the soul" means that one assents to something despite the fact that he is aware of something opposing it and can articulate it. There are varying degrees to the acquiescence of the soul depending on the strength and weakness of the opposing thing.

5.   Assent that approximates certainty is dialectic assent. The acquiescence of the soul to something is assent based on oratory. The things to which approximate certainty grants assent are either commonly held views and anything like them, or the necessary conclusion of syllogisms composed of commonly held premises, or the necessary conclusion of the form of induction, [21] in which one cannot be certain that there has been a thorough review of the particular instances. The things to which the soul acquiesces are either views accepted on trust, or the necessary conclusion of a syllogism composed of premises accepted on trust, or the necessary conclusion of a syllogism composed of possible premises, and that may be the result of other things (we have enumerated these where we explained rhetorical premises).

6.   Assent to both commonly held views and views accepted on trust occurs only, in sum, as a result of testimony, with the difference that the commonly held view is based on the testimony of all or most people, or of whomever functions in that capacity, whereas the view accepted on trust is based on the testimony of one person, or of a group that is accepted by one person or one group only. Neither of these produces certainty, although confidence in a view on which the testimony of all or most people

agree is stronger and more widespread than a view based on the testimony of one person or a smaller group. Now, it may so happen, however, that in a view based on such testimonies there is something that is in fact true, in which case it happens accidentally to be certain. As a result of that, many people suppose that the testimonies themselves produce certainty nonaccidentally, while with another group it is as though they are aware that the testimonies do not produce certainty, but they suppose that any [testimony] through which certainty occurs is the result of divine command, especially in the case of anything that produces the acquiescence of the soul.

7.   Now let us discuss certainty and [the constituent factors] that result in certainty. There is both necessary certainty and nonnecessary certainty. Necessary certainty means that, with respect to something whose existence cannot be different from what it is, one is convinced that it is not possible for it to be different from one's conviction in any way at any time. Nonnecessary certainty is certainty at a particular time only. Necessary certainty cannot alter and so become false, but rather is always in accord with what is present in the mind that results from either a negation or an affirmation. In the case of nonnecessary certainty, it can alter and so become false without any contradiction occurring in the mind.

8.   Necessary certainty can apply only to permanently existing things, for example, that the whole is greater than the part, for such a thing cannot alter. Nonnecessary certainty applies only to things whose existence shifts and alters, like the certainty that you are standing up, that Zayd is in the house, and other such things. [22] The necessary is something for which it is impossible that its opposite exists; consequently, [that opposite] is an impossible falsehood. The nonnecessary is something whose opposite is not impossible. So the opposite of the nonnecessary certainty is a possible falsehood, whereas the opposite of the necessary certainty is an impossible falsehood. Thus, falsehood includes both what is impossible and what is not impossible. Necessary certainty and necessary existence convert with one another in terms of entailment; for anything that is a necessary certainty necessarily exists, and in the case of anything that necessarily exists, complete certainty about it is a necessary certainty. At this point we will stop investigating nonnecessary certainty.

9.   Necessary certainty may result from a syllogism or from something that is not a syllogism. The former results either essentially or accidentally, but we will also leave off investigating what produces necessary certainty accidentally. An example of [the former] is, "Man is a biped; anything that is a biped is an animal, therefore man is an animal."[4] The necessary certainty that results from a syllogism nonaccidentally is the result of two premises that have also been ascertained to be certain necessarily. That [ascertainment of their certainty] is either not initially the result of a syllogism, or it can be reduced analytically to premises through which necessary certainty is present not as a result of a syllogism.

---

[4] The example comes from Aristotle, *Metaphysics* VII 12, and is also found in Porphyry's *Eisagōgē*, under "proprium," 12.

10.   The premises by means of which this certainty is ascertained are either universal or particular, but we will focus our investigation of these on universal premises alone, because they are employed in [this] science most often and because the investigation of universal premises may include[b] [examples of] particular premises.

Universal Premises

1.   [23] There are two types of universal premises by means of which necessary certainty is present but not as a result of a syllogism. One type occurs naturally; the other type occurs through methodic experience. The type that occurs naturally provides us with a certainty without our knowing whence or how it occurred, and without our being aware at any time that we were ever ignorant of it, or that we ever had the desire to discover it, or that we ever considered it an object of scientific investigation. Instead, we find that we seem to have it in us from the very beginning of our existence, as though it were a connate property[c] of ours that we have never been without. Such premises are called "first premises naturally belonging to man," or "first principles." We have absolutely no need in this book to discover how or whence they come about, because our ignorance of the manner in which they come about in no way obviates or contradicts [their] certainty or prevents us from using them to construct a syllogism that provides us with the certainty that necessarily concludes from them. The manner in which these primary instances of knowledge come about is one of the objects of investigation in science and philosophy [and not logic].[5]

2.   It is obvious that we arrive at certainty about the manner in which [these first premises] come about through syllogisms constructed only from instances of such premises. If these [first premises] are incorrect, or it cannot be known whence or how knowledge of them occurs [24], we cannot use them to explain anything at all. If the ways in which [the first premises] come about cannot be known except by means of [instances of such first premises], but these [instances] cannot be used to explain these [first premises], it necessarily follows that we cannot arrive at knowledge of anything at all. The result of this is the error committed by anyone who would require logic to investigate the ways in which these premises come about. Instead, learning about these premises in logic should extend only to characterizing them, describing them, enumerating their classes, determining the way to use them as parts of syllogistic statements, and explaining how it is that all other knowledge goes back to them. While there is no doubt that the opinions of people differ on the ways of their occurrence, we do not need to know how and whence they occur in order for us to use them—with the following exception. On the basis of the majority of these universal premises, it appears that the actual individual instances of them are perceived by the senses. This is why one group maintains that they in fact derive from the senses. It is possible to clarify this here: even if they derive from the senses, the senses alone are not capable of producing them completely. The reason for this is that, if we restricted ourselves

---

5 See al-Farabi, *On the Intellect*, par. 6, p. 70.

to how much of them we perceived through our senses, and we ourselves perceived only a limited number of their individual instances, it necessarily follows that we would derive only particular premises from them, not universal ones. Now we ourselves find them to be universal premises, so much so that we have arrived at universal judgments about the subjects of these premises that encompass both what we have perceived with our senses and what we have not perceived with our senses.

3.   It should be clear from this that the soul performs an activity with respect to the objects of the senses that goes beyond our sensory perception of them. Now, since explaining that here in this [science] is difficult, we may turn our attention away from it and limit ourselves to the amount of [discussion] about them that was stated concisely. Then we need not concern ourselves with how [the universal premises] are perceived and whether the soul's perception of them is an activity specific to it without our sensory perception of their particular instances, or[d] whether we obtain knowledge of them only once we have had prior sensory perception of their particular instances.

4.   Methodic experience results in universal premises that have this level of certainty as a result of a direct intention on our part to use our senses to perceive their particular instances, whether a little or a lot. [This is the case since] methodic experience means that we examine the particular instances of universal premises [to determine] whether [a given universal] is predicable of each one of [the particular instances], and we follow this up with all or most of them until we obtain necessary certainty, in which case that predication applies to the whole of that species. Methodic experience [25] resembles induction, except the difference between methodic experience and induction is that induction does not produce necessary certainty by means of universal predication, whereas methodic experience does. Many people use these two terms interchangeably, but for our part we have no interest in the customary way of expressing these two things. We [should] also clarify here that the soul does not limit itself in methodic experience to just the scope of [particular instances] that it has examined, but rather after its examination it forms a general judgment that encompasses both what it has examined and what it has not examined. As for the question of how it comes to this general judgment as an immediate consequence of its examination, that, as we say, should be postponed here, since knowing that is not itself sufficient [to produce] the resulting certainty, and not knowing it does not obviate or contradict the certainty of the premises or prevent us from using them. So let us call these premises the first principles of certainty.

5.   Let us now discuss the types of knowledge that result from the first premises that have this kind of certainty. The term "knowing" occurs in a sentence with two meanings—one is "assenting"; the other is "conceptualizing." There is both a certain and an uncertain assent, and there is both a necessary certainty and a nonnecessary certainty. Clearly, the term "knowledge" is more applicable to what is necessarily certain than to what is uncertain or to what is certain but not necessarily so. [What is necessarily certain], then, should be termed "certain knowledge."

6.   There are three types of certain knowledge. One is certainty about only the existence of a thing, that is, knowing that something exists, which one group calls

knowing *that* a thing is.[6] The second type is certainty about only the *cause* for the existence of a thing, which one group calls knowing *why* something is. The third type is the first two types together. It is precisely by means of one of these three types of investigation that one seeks to understand the things that are investigated through certain principles. [26] Clearly, when we seek to discover just the cause of something, we must necessarily already know *that* the thing exists, and [so] the type of knowledge that is most properly termed "certain knowledge" is the one that is a combined certainty about both existence and cause.

7.　Syllogistic statements that are constructed out of premises that are necessarily certain in this manner are thus divided into three types. One on its own provides knowledge only *that* a thing is. The second on its own provides knowledge only of the cause. The third on its own provides both of these. The syllogism designed to discover only the cause for something's existence is constructed only for something that is already known to exist, either by virtue of first premises or on the basis of a syllogism that provides only the knowledge *that* the thing is. The syllogism that is constructed out of premises that are certain necessarily and that provided one of these three types of knowledge is called a "demonstration." There are three types of demonstration. One is the demonstration of existence, which is called the demonstration *that* a thing is. The second is the demonstration *why* a thing is. The third is the demonstration that combines both of these, namely, the absolute demonstration. Certain knowledge about existence and cause is called, in an absolute sense, "demonstrative knowledge." So, the absolute demonstration is the certain syllogism that, on its own and nonaccidentally, provides knowledge of the existence and cause of something. Every demonstration is a cause for the knowledge derived from it, although not all of them provide the knowledge of the cause of the existence of something.

III.　*ON THE INTELLECT*[a]

1.　[3] The term "intellect" is used in many ways for the following. The first is the thing by virtue of which most people say that man is rational. The second is the "intellect" that the theologians constantly have on their tongues, saying *x* is something the intellect requires or rejects. The third is the intellect to which the master Aristotle refers in *Posterior Analytics*.[7] [4] The fourth is the intellect to which he refers in Book Six of [*Nicomachean*] *Ethics*.[8] The fifth is the intellect to which he refers in *De anima*.[9] The sixth is the intellect to which he refers in *Metaphysics*.[10]

---

[6]　The group indicated here and immediately following is the Aristotelian logicians with reference to the various types of scientific questions that Aristotle enumerated in *Posterior Analytics* II, 1–2.

[7]　See *Posterior Analytics* II 19.

[8]　See *Nicomachean Ethics* VI 6.

[9]　See *De anima* III 4ff.

[10]　See *Metaphysics* XI 7.

2. What most people refer to by "intellect" and on account of which they say man is intelligent, is discernment,[b] sometimes saying about the likes of Muʿawīya[11] that he was "intelligent,"[12] and sometimes refusing to call him "intelligent" by saying that the intelligent person should have religion (religion being something that they believe is *the* virtue). By "intelligent person," then, these people mean only someone who is virtuous and deliberates well when deducing [5] any good to be preferred and any evil to be avoided. They avoid applying this term to anyone who deliberates well [only] when deducing anything evil; instead, they call [that person] "shrewd" and "clever" and similar names. Excellent deliberation in deducing what is in fact good in order to do [that good], and in deducing what is evil in order to avoid [that evil], is discernment.

3. By "intellect" in the universal sense, then, these people mean no more than what Aristotle meant by discernment.[13] So anyone who calls Muʿawīya "intelligent" means [that he displayed] excellent deliberation in deducing what should be preferred and what should be avoided, without restriction. Whenever such people fight over Muʿawīya or someone similar by raising the [question of] who, in their opinion, is "intelligent," and asking whether or not to apply this term to someone who [6] was evil and who used to use his excellent deliberation for what they deem evil, they hesitate or refuse to call him "intelligent," whereas when they are asked whether someone who uses his excellent deliberation to do evil is called "clever" or "shrewd" or something similar, they do not deny him this name.

4. It also necessarily follows from these people's opinion that, beyond possessing excellent deliberation, the "intelligent" person is intelligent only in as much as he is a virtuous person who uses his excellent deliberation to perform virtuous deeds and to avoid evil ones. This, in fact, is the *discerning* person. The majority of people are divided into two parties on whom they mean by this term ["intelligent"]. One party grants on their own behalf that the intelligent person is definitely not intelligent as long as he has no religion, and they will not call the evil person "intelligent" regardless of what he might arrive at as a result of his excellent deliberation [7] in deducing evil. The other party summarily calls a man "intelligent" because he deliberates well on what he should do; for when they are again asked [the question of whether] a person is to be called "intelligent" who is evil but who has excellent deliberation concerning whatever evil he should do, they hesitate or refuse [to answer]. What both parties mean by "intelligent" is "discerning." According to Aristotle, someone who is "discerning" is someone who deliberates well when deducing the *virtuous* acts he should perform at the moment he acts, in one situation after another, when that person also has a virtuous disposition.[14]

---

11 The first caliph of the ʿUmayyad Dynasty, r. 661–680.

12 Al-Fārābī uses the term ʿāqil here, which is used to translate "rational" elsewhere.

13 See *Nicomachean Ethics* (hereafter "NE") VI 5, on *phronesis*, practical wisdom, here called "discernment."

14 See NE, II 6, 1106b21–22; VI 7, 1141a25–26, 1141b14–16.

5.   What the theologians mean by the term "intellect" that they constantly have on their tongues—saying about *x* that this is something the intellect affirms or denies, accepts or [8] does not accept—is no more than what is commonly accepted on first sight by all people; for the immediate point of view common to all or most people is what they mean by "intellect." You will notice this once you collect each one of their statements on ["intellect"] by means of which they address one another for rhetorical purposes, or which they write in their books when using this expression for it.

6.   When Aristotle uses the term "intellect" in *Posterior Analytics*,[15] he means precisely the faculty of the soul by means of which man gains certainty about the necessary, true, and universal premises. [Man does not arrive at these premises] as a result of any syllogism at all, nor from discursive thought, but rather by means of his natural disposition and nature, or in his youth, or without being conscious of whence or how they come about. This faculty is a certain part of the soul by means of which [man] [9] possesses primary instance of knowledge—not at all through discursive thought or reflection—and certainty about the premises we have described, such being the first principles of the theoretical sciences.

7.   When Aristotle uses the term "intellect" in Book Six of the [*Nicomachean*] *Ethics*,[16] he means the part of the soul in which there occurs, by the assiduous habituation to one thing after another in each genus of things and by long experience of one thing after another in each genus over a lengthy period of time, certainty about any propositions and premises concerning the things pertaining to human volition that should be preferred or avoided; for it is that part of the soul he calls "intellect" in Book Six of the [*Nicomachean*] *Ethics*. The propositions that come to man in this way and in that part [10] of the soul are the discerning and clever man's principles for whatever can be deduced about the things pertaining to volition whose character is to be preferred or avoided. The relation of the propositions to whatever is deduced by discernment is the same as that of the first propositions mentioned in *Posterior Analytics* to whatever is deduced by means of them. So, just as [those propositions] are principles by means of which scholars of the theoretical sciences deduce the theoretical things that can be known but not done, these [propositions] are principles of the discerning man and the clever man for the practical things pertaining to volition and action that can be deduced.

8.   This intellect referred to in Book Six of the [*Nicomachean*] *Ethics* increases in the course of man's life, since those propositions become firmly established in him and, [11] at each point in his life, he adds to them propositions that he did not have before. People are of varying degrees of superiority with regard to this part of the soul that [Aristotle] calls "intellect." The man in whom these propositions have reached perfection in a given genus of things becomes a man of opinion with regard to that genus. The meaning of "man of opinion" is someone who, when he offers counsel on

---

[15] See *Posterior Analytics* II 19, 100b15–17.

[16] See NE VI 6.

something, his opinion is [immediately] accepted. This happens without recourse or reference to its demonstrative proof, his counsels being accepted even though he did not establish a demonstrative proof for any of them. In light of this, rarely is a man described thus without having reached old age, by reason of the fact that this part of the soul requires the long experience that can occur only over a lengthy period of time, and because these propositions [must] become firmly established in him.

9. The theologians suppose that the term "intellect" they constantly employ with one another is the [same] "intellect" that Aristotle uses in *Posterior Analytics,* and they make a general reference in its direction, but when you [12] collect instances of the first principles they use, you find that all of them without exception are principles derived from the first thing that comes to the mind [of most people]. The result of this is that they vaguely mean one thing but use something else.

10. Aristotle established four aspects to the term "intellect" that he uses in *De anima*: (i) the potential intellect, (ii) the actual intellect, (iii) the acquired intellect, and (iv) the Active Intellect.

11. The (i) potential intellect is a certain soul, or a part of a soul, or one of the faculties of the soul, or a certain thing whose being is prepared or disposed to extract the essential definitions and forms of all existing things from their matters and to make them all a form or forms for itself. Those forms extracted from matter do not become extracted [13] from the matter in which they exist unless they have become forms for the potential intellect. Those forms that are extracted from their matters and become forms in this intellect are the intelligibles (this term is etymologically derived from the term for this intellect that extracts the forms of existing things, whereby they become forms for it).

12. The potential intellect is comparable to matter in which forms come to be. When you imagine a particular corporeal matter to be like a piece of wax on which an impression is stamped, and that impression and form that comes to be in its surface and depth, and that form so encompasses the entire matter that the matter as a whole comes to be like that form in its entirety by the form's having spread through it, your imagination comes close to understanding what is meant when the forms of things come to be in [14] that [intellect] that resembles a matter and a subject for that form but which differs from other corporeal matters in as much as corporeal matters receive forms only on their surfaces, not in their depths. Moreover, this intellect does not itself remain so distinct from the forms of the intelligibles that it and the forms stand removed in themselves from one another; rather, this intellect itself *becomes* those forms. It is as though you were to imagine the impression and mold through which a piece of wax takes on the form of a cube or sphere, and that form sinks into it, spreads throughout it, and entirely engulfs its length, breadth, and depth, then that piece of wax will have become that very form, with no distinction between what it is and what that form is. [15] It is by way of this example that you should understand the coming to be of the forms of existing things in that thing that Aristotle in *De anima* calls the "potential intellect."

13. As long as none of the forms of existing things is in it, it is potential intellect. Then, when the forms of existing things come to be in it as in the example we

have provided, that thing itself becomes (ii) an actual intellect. This then is the meaning of "actual intellect." When the intelligibles that it extracts from matters come to be in [the intellect], those intelligibles become actual intelligibles, having been potential intelligibles before they were extracted. Once extracted, they become actual intelligibles by virtue of becoming forms for that intellect, and it is precisely by those things that are [now] actual intelligibles that the intellect becomes an actual intellect. Their being actual intelligibles and its being an actual intellect is, then, one and the same thing. [16] What we mean when we say that it "intellects" is nothing other than that the intelligibles become forms for it, in the sense that it itself becomes those forms. Thus, what is meant by the intellect's actually intellecting, of being an actual intellect, and of being an actual intelligible, is one and the same thing and [is used] for one and the same account.

14.   The intelligibles that are *potentially* intelligibles are those things that, before they become actual intelligibles, are forms in matters outside the soul.[17] When they become actual intelligibles, their existence as actual intelligibles is not the same as their existence as forms in matters, and their existence in themselves [as forms in matters] is not the same as their existence as actual intelligibles. Their existence in themselves is a consequence of whatever else is connected to them, whether that is place, time, [17] position, quantity, being qualified by corporeal qualities, acting, or being affected. When they become actual intelligibles, many of those other categories are removed from them, in which case their existence becomes another existence that is not the former existence. Moreover, what is meant by these categories, or much about them, in relation to [the actual intelligibles], comes to be understood in ways different from the former ways. For example, when you consider the meaning of place as understood in relation to [the actual intelligibles], you find either that none of the meanings of place apply to them at all, or you give the term "place" as understood by you in relation to them another meaning, one that is different from the former meaning.[18]

15.   Once the actual intelligibles come to be [in the intellect], they come to be among the existing things [18] of the world and are counted, as intelligibles, among the totality of existing things. All existing things can be intellected and become forms for that intellect. Consequently, it is not impossible that they are intelligibles insofar as they are actual intelligibles, and [insofar as] they are an actual intellect, [it is not impossible] that they also intellect. In that case, what is intellected is not something different from what is actually an intellect, but what is actually an intellect—due to the fact that a particular intelligible has become a form for it—may be an actual

---

[17] Al-Fārābī is here focusing on just one of the two types of intelligibles: those that were forms in matter, and those that were never in matter, which he treats in par. 17.

[18] According to Aristotelian physics, a thing's place in the strict sense is the innermost limit of the containing or contacting body. Since the actual intelligible is immaterial, it does not have a limit that is either contained by or in contact with a body, and so it cannot have a place in the strict sense, and yet in some sense intelligibles do have a place, inasmuch as they are in the soul.

intellect in relation to that form only, and a potential intellect in relation to some other intelligible that has not yet actually come to be in it. When the second intelligible comes to be in it, it becomes an actual intellect through the first and the second intelligible. Now, when it becomes an actual intellect in relation to all intelligibles and becomes one of the existing things by becoming the actual intelligibles, then, whenever it intellects the thing that is an actual intellect, it does not intellect anything [19] outside of itself but rather it intellects its very own self.

16.   It is clear that when it intellects itself, inasmuch as it is itself an actual intellect, there does not come to be in it from whatever it intellects of itself any existing thing whose existence in itself would be different from its existence as an actual intelligible. Instead, it will have intellected of itself an existing thing whose existence as an intelligible is its very own existence as such. Thus, this intellect becomes an actual intelligible, even though prior to being intellected it was not a potential intelligible but was in fact an actual intelligible. Nevertheless, it is intellected actually due to its being in itself both an actual intellect and an actual intelligible. [This] is different from the way in which these things themselves were intellected initially; for they were intellected initially due to being extracted from the matters in which they existed and as potential intelligibles. They are next intellected—when their existence is not that prior existence but rather is separate from their matters—as forms that are no longer in their matters and [20] as actual intelligibles. So, once the actual intellect intellects the intelligibles that are forms for it as actual intelligibles, the intellect, which we first called the actual intellect, now becomes (iii) the acquired intellect.

17.   In the case of existing things that are forms that neither *are* in matters nor *were ever* in matters, when those things are intellected, they are intelligibles whose existence is the same one they had before being intellected; for our saying "The thing is intellected initially"[19] means that the forms that are in matters are extracted from their matters and acquire another existence different from their initial existence. In the case of things that are forms that have no matters, however, the intellect does not need to extract them from matters at all; rather, it encounters them as abstracted. So it intellects them as intelligibles that are not in their matters in the same manner that it encounters itself when it is an actual intellect. Then it intellects them [as an acquired intellect], [21] and their existence as something intellected a second time is the same existence they had before this [acquired] intellect [began to] intellect.[c] This is the same thing that ought to be understood with regard to those things that are forms that are not in matters. When they are intellected, their existence in themselves is the same existence they have as intelligible objects for us. So the account concerning what is actually an intellect as [a constituent] part of us and actually an intellect in us is the very same account concerning the forms that are not in matters and never were in them; for just as we say that the [constituent] part of us that is an actual intellect is

---

[19] See the sentence beginning "[This] is different from the way in which these things themselves were intellected initially" in par. 16.

"in us," so too it ought to be said that those things are "in the world"—although those forms can be intellected [by us] completely only after all or most of the intelligibles become actually intelligible [22] and the acquired intellect comes about, at which point those forms become intelligible and so become like forms for the intellect as an acquired intellect.

18.   The acquired intellect is like a subject for those [forms], whereas it is like the form for the actual intellect. The actual intellect is like a subject and matter for the acquired intellect, whereas it is like a form for that [potential intellect]. That [potential intellect] is like matter. At this level, forms begin to reduce to corporeal, material forms, and whatever they were before that gradually proceeds to break away from matter, each one in a different way and at a different level. [23]

19.   If the forms that are not, never were, and never will be in matter are of varying degrees of perfection and immateriality and have a particular order in terms of existence, and their circumstances are considered, then the more perfect of them in this ranking is a form for the less perfect, until it comes to the least perfect, which is the acquired intellect. Then they continue to decline until one arrives at [the potential intellect] and the faculties of the soul below it and then, after that, at the nature. Then they continue to decline until one arrives at the forms of the elements, which are the lowest forms in terms of existence and whose subject is the lowest of the subjects, which is prime matter. Then if one ascends by degrees from prime matter to the nature that is [24] the corporeal forms in prime matter, then up to [the potential intellect] and above that to the acquired intellect, one will have reached something like the outermost boundary and limit to which the things related to prime matter and matter reach. When one ascends from [that], it is to the first level of immaterial beings, that of (iv) the Active Intellect.

20.   What Aristotle calls the "Active Intellect" in Book III of *De anima* is a separate form that has never been and never will be in matter in any way. In its species it is an actual intellect very similar to the acquired [25] intellect. It is what makes the potential intellect an actual intellect, and it is what makes the potential intelligibles actual intelligibles.

21.   The relation [of the Active Intellect] to the potential intellect is like the relation of the Sun to the eye, which is potentially vision as long as it is in darkness, for vision is potentially vision simply as long as it is in darkness. The meaning of darkness is potential transparency and the privation of actual transparency. The meaning of transparency is to be lit by something opposite that is luminous. So, when light comes about in vision and in the air and anything similar, vision becomes actual vision by the light that comes about in it, and colors become actually visible. [26] In fact, we say that vision becomes actual vision not solely by light and actual transparency coming about in it, but also because when actual transparency comes about in it, the forms of visible things come about in it. Through the occurrence of the forms of visible things in vision, it becomes actual vision, and because [vision] was prepared beforehand by the rays of the Sun or something else to become actually transparent, and the air in contact with it also becomes actually transparent, anything potentially

visible now becomes actually visible. So, the principle by which vision becomes actual vision after having been potential vision, and by which visible things that had been potentially visible become actually visible, is the transparency that comes about in vision from the Sun. In a similar manner, there comes about in [27] the potential intellect a certain thing whose relation to it is like that of actual transparency to vision. The Active Intellect gives that thing to [the potential intellect], whereby it becomes a principle through which the potential intelligibles become actual intelligibles for [the intellect]. In the same way that the Sun is what gives the eye actual vision and makes [potentially] visible things actually visible by the light it gives, so too the Active Intellect is what makes the potential intellect an actual intellect by the principle it gives it, and by that same [principle] the intelligibles become actual intelligibles.

22.   The Active Intellect belongs to the same species as the acquired intellect. The forms of the immaterial beings above it have always been and always will be in it, although their existence in it follows an order different from the order in which they exist in the actual intellect. [28] The reason for this is that what is lesser in the actual intellect is often ordered to be prior to what is more excellent on account of the fact that *our* ascent to things that are more perfect in their existence is often from things that are less so (as explained in *Posterior Analytics*),[20] since we proceed from what is better known to us precisely to what is unknown, and that which is more perfect in its existence in itself is more unknown to us (I mean that our ignorance of it is greater). For this reason, the order of existents in the actual intellect has to be the reverse of their order in the Active Intellect, given that the Active Intellect first intellects the most perfect existent and then the next more perfect; for the forms that are now forms in matters are extracted forms in the Active Intellect not by virtue of having once existed in matters and then having been extracted. On the contrary, [29] those forms [in the Active Intellect] have always been actual, whereas it is precisely by actually being given these forms that are in the Active Intellect that [the actual intellect] imitates prime matter and other matter. Furthermore, the existents whose origination was primarily intended for this world are those forms [in the Active Intellect], except that since they could be created here only in matters, these matters were generated. These forms are indivisible in the Active Intellect but divisible in matter. It is absolutely undeniable that the Active Intellect, which is indivisible or which is itself indivisible things, gives matter the semblances [30] of what is in its substance, but matter receives it only as something divisible. This is something Aristotle also explained in his *De anima*.[21]

23.   There is a topic of investigation in what preceded, namely, that if these forms can exist without matters, what is the need to put them in matters, and how do they descend from the most perfect existence to the less perfect? There might be someone who says that this is done just so that matters may attain a more perfect existence, from which it would necessarily follow that those forms are generated just

---

20 See *Posterior Analytics* II 2.

21 See *De anima*, III 6.

for the sake of matter. That, however, is contrary to Aristotle's opinion. Or we might say that all of these forms are in the Active Intellect potentially, but when we say "potentially" here, one should not understand it in the sense that the Active Intellect [31] has the potentiality to receive these forms so that they would be in it in the future. We mean instead that it has a potentiality to put them in matter as forms, where this is the potentiality to act upon something else; for after all it is the Active Intellect that puts them in matter as forms.

24.　Next, [the Active Intellect] aims to bring [those forms in matter] closer and closer to the immaterial forms until the acquired intellect comes to be, at which point the substance of man, or man by virtue of what constitutes his substance, becomes the closest thing possible to the Active Intellect. This is the ultimate happiness and the afterlife, which is that the ultimate thing by which man becomes a substance comes about for him, and he attains his final perfection, which is that the final thing through which he becomes a substance performs the final action by virtue of which he becomes a substance. This is what is meant by the afterlife. When [the acquired intellect] does not act on some other thing outside of itself, where to act is to cause itself to exist, then it itself, its action, and the fact that it acts are one and the same thing. At that point, it has absolutely no need for the body to be a matter for it in order to subsist, and it has absolutely no need in any of its actions to seek the help of a faculty of a soul in a body, [32] or to use any corporeal instrument whatsoever. The least perfect existence belonging to it is when it requires the body to be a matter for it in order to subsist as an existent, and when it is a form in a body or a corporeal matter as a whole. Above that, it does not require the body to be a matter for it in order to subsist, but in order to perform its actions, or many of them, it needs to use a corporeal faculty and to seek the aid of its action, for example, sensory perception and imagination. Its most perfect existence, though, is to reach the state we just mentioned.

25.　Now, it has been explained in De anima[22] that the Active Intellect exists. Furthermore, it is clear that the Active Intellect does not always act but rather sometimes acts and sometimes does not. It necessarily follows, then, that this is the result either of the action it performs or the thing on which it acts according to different relations, in which case it would change from one relation to another. If it does not always exist according to its ultimate perfection, then it would change not just from one relation to another but also in its very being, since its ultimate perfection is with respect to its substance. Then, in its very substance it would at one time be in potentiality and at another time in actuality, in which case what belongs to its [essence] in potentiality would be the matter [33] of what belongs to it in actuality—except that we have posited[d] that it is separate from every kind of matter. This being the case, it is always at its ultimate perfection, changing necessarily [only] from one relation to another. Therefore, the imperfection is not in itself, but rather either in as much as it does not always encounter the thing on which it acts, because it does not find ready

---

[22] See De anima III 5.

the matter and subject on which it acts, or there is an external obstacle [that] later disappears, or both of these things together. It is clear from this that [the Active Intellect] is not sufficient itself to be the First Principle of all existents, since it needs to be given some matter on which to act and needs the obstacle to be removed. As it is insufficient in itself and in its substance to produce all things, there is thus in its substance an inability to produce many of the existent things. Anything that is deficient in its substance is not sufficient enough to have its existence be by virtue of itself without being by virtue of something else. It necessarily follows that there is another principle for its existence and that there is another cause that aids it in producing the matter on which it acts. It is clear that the subjects on which the Active Intellect acts are either bodies or powers in bodies that are generated and corrupt. In fact, it has been explained in [34] *De generatione et corruptione*[23] that the celestial bodies are the first efficient causes[e] of those bodies. It is these [celestial] bodies, then, that provide the Active Intellect with the matters and subjects on which it acts.

26. Every celestial body is set in motion only by a mover that is neither a body nor in a body in any way. [This mover] is the cause of [the celestial body's] existence, inasmuch as it is that by virtue of which [the celestial body] is a substance, but its level, in terms of the existence that is [the celestial body's] substance, is the same as that body. The mover of the more perfect of [the celestial bodies] is the more perfect in terms of existence, and the more perfect in terms of existence is the first heaven. So the more perfect in terms of existence is the mover of the first heaven. However, the mover of the first heaven is a principle by virtue of which two distinct things exist. One is what constitutes the substance of the first heaven, namely, a corporeal substance or something corporeal. The other is the mover of the sphere of fixed stars, namely, that which itself is neither a body nor in a body. [Now, since the mover of the first heaven is a principle of two distinct things], it cannot produce both things in a single way and by a single thing in itself by virtue of which it is a substance. On the contrary, it [must produce them] by two natures [35], one of which is more perfect than the other, since the nature by which it produces the more perfect thing—that is, the one that is not a body nor in a body—is more perfect than the nature by which it produces a corporeal thing, that is, the one that is less perfect. Therefore, it is a substance through two natures, only through both of which does it exist. Therefore, its existence has a principle, since whatever is divisible has a cause that makes it a substance. Therefore, the mover of the first heaven certainly cannot be the First Principle for all existing things; rather, it must [itself] have a principle, and that principle undoubtedly has a more perfect existence than it. Now, since the mover of the first heaven is neither matter nor in matter, it necessarily follows that it is an intellect in its substance, in which case it intellects itself and the very thing that is the principle of its existence. Clearly, of its two natures, the nature it has that intellects something about the principle of its existence is the more perfect, whereas

---

23 See Aristotle, *De generatione et corruptione* II 10, 336a15.

the nature it has by which it intellects itself is the less perfect of them. Nothing more than these two is required to divide its essence into two natures.

27.   The Principle of the mover of the first heaven—that is, the Principle by virtue of which it is a substance—is necessarily one in all respects. It is absolutely impossible for there to be an existent more perfect than It or for It to have any principle. Therefore, It is the Principle of all the principles and the First Principle of all existing things. This is the Principle that Aristotle discusses in [36] Book *Lambda* of *Metaphysics*. While each one of those other [principles] is also an intellect, this One is the First Intellect, the First Existent, the First One, and the First Truth; it is only in an ordered succession from It that these others become intellects. Further investigation into these things lies outside our aim here.

IV.   *THE AIMS OF ARISTOTLE'S* METAPHYSICS [a]

1.   [34] Our intention in this treatise is to point out the aim and primary divisions of the book by Aristotle known as the *Metaphysics,* since many people have the preconceived notion that the point and purpose of this book is to discuss the Creator (may He be glorified and exalted!), the intellect, the soul, and other related topics, and that the science of metaphysics and the science of theology are one and the same thing. Consequently, we find that most people who study it are perplexed and misguided by it, since we find that most of the talk in it is devoid of any such aim, or rather, we find that the only talk specifically related to this aim is that in the eleventh chapter, that is, the one designated by the letter *Lambda*.[24] Moreover, none of the ancient philosophers has commented on this book in the correct manner, as they have for the rest of his books. To be more specific, there is an incomplete commentary on *Lambda* by Alexander of Aphrodisias and a complete commentary by Themistius, but as for the rest of the chapters, either there was no commentary, or none has survived to our times—since upon examining the books of the later Peripatetics, it may be assumed that Alexander did in fact comment on the entire book.

2.   For our part, we want to point out the aim of the book and the contents of each chapter. So we say that the sciences are concerned either with the particular or with the universal. The particular sciences have as their subjects certain existing beings or certain objects of the estimative faculty and their investigation is specifically concerned with the proper accidents [35] belonging to them. For example, natural science investigates one existent, namely body, in terms of whatever is subject to motion, alteration, and rest, and whatever has the principles and consequential accidents of such. Geometry investigates magnitudes in terms of whatever is susceptible to the qualities proper to [magnitudes] and the ratios that arise in [those qualities] with regard to its principles and consequential accidents, and whatever else is like that.

---

24 For the confusion over the order of the books of the *Metaphysics,* see Amos Bertolacci, "On the Arabic Translations of Aristotle's *Metaphysics,*" 241–75.

Arithmetic does the same with respect to number, medicine with respect to human bodies, in terms of being healthy or sick, and so too the rest of the particular sciences. Not one of them investigates whatever is common to all existing beings.

3. The universal science is the one that investigates something common to all existing beings (like existence and unity), its species, its consequential accidents, as well as accidents that are not specific to any one subject of those treated by the particular sciences (such as priority, posteriority, potentiality, actuality, perfection, imperfection, and similar accidents), and [finally] the principle common to all existing beings, namely, the thing that should be called God. It is appropriate that there is only one universal science; for if there were two universal sciences, each one would have a specific subject; but the science that has a specific subject and does not address any subject of another science is a particular science; so both sciences would be particular, and this is a contradiction. Thus, there is only one universal science. [Now, since there is only one universal science], theology should fall under this science, because God is a principle of the existent in the absolute sense, not of one existent to the exclusion of another, and the part of [the universal science] that provides the principle of the existent [absolutely] should itself be theology.

4. Next,[b] since these accounts are not specific to natural beings but are higher in universality than natural beings, this science is higher than natural science and comes after natural science. Therefore, it should be called the science of *meta*physics.[25] Although mathematics is higher than natural science—since its subjects are abstracted from matter—it most certainly should not be called the science of *meta*physics because its subjects are abstracted from matter [36] only by human imagination, not actually. In terms of actual existence, they exist only in natural things. Now as for the subjects of this science, there are two.[26] One has absolutely no existence in natural things at all, whether imaginary or actually, and it is not simply that the human estimative faculty abstracts them from natural things,[27] but even more so that their very being and nature are wholly abstract. Another exists in natural things, although one can imagine them as abstracted from them. However, while they do not exist in [natural things] *essentially*—such that they could not exist independently of natural things and would subsist [only] by virtue of them—they nonetheless do belong to natural things, as well as to other things, namely, the things that are separate [from matter] in reality, and the things that are separated [from matter] by the human estimative faculty. Thus, the science that deserves to be called by this name is this science, and therefore it alone, to the exclusion of all other sciences, is the science of metaphysics.

5. The primary subject of this science is absolute existence and what is equivalent to it in universality, namely, the one. However, since the knowledge of contraries

---

25 I.e., "the science of what comes after physics."

26 Here al-Fārābī aims to contrast the subjects of metaphysics with the subjects of mathematics to determine which of the two sciences most deserves to be considered *the* universal science.

27 I.e., the way that the subjects of mathematics are abstracted from matter *only* by human imagination.

is one, this science also investigates privation and multiplicity. After [investigating] and verifying these subjects, it investigates things that are akin to species for [these subjects], like the ten categories of the existent, the species of the one (like the individual one, the specific one, the generic one, the relative one, and the subdivisions of each of these), and, in a similar way, the species of privation and multiplicity. Then [it investigates] the consequential accidents of the existent (like potentiality, actuality, perfection and imperfection, cause and effect), the consequential accidents of oneness (like identity, similarity, equality, coincidence, parallelism,[28] and comparison, etc.), the consequential accidents of privation and multiplicity, and then the principles of each one of these. Then it divides and subdivides [all of] this until it reaches the subjects of the particular sciences. Once the principles of all of the particular sciences and the definitions of their subjects are expounded, this science then concludes. So these are all of the things investigated[c] in this science.

6.   [The aims of the individual chapters of Aristotle's *Metaphysics*.]

6.1.   The first chapter [α][29] is a kind of preface and preamble to the book, in explaining that all kinds of causes terminate at a primary cause in their class.[d]

6.2.   [37] The second chapter [B] enumerates difficult problems[30] related to these subjects (*ma'ná*), explains what aspect makes them difficult, and sets out the opposing arguments for them to alert[e] one's mind to the method and structure[f] of the inquiry.

6.3.   The third chapter [Γ] enumerates the subjects of this science, that is, the concepts (*ma'ná*) that, together with their[g] proper accidents (which we enumerated [par.3]), are what is investigated.

6.4.   The fourth chapter [Δ] differentiates what is signified by each of the terms that signify the subjects of this science, their species and their consequential accidents, [these terms being] either synonyms, amphibolous terms, or true homonyms.

6.5.   The fifth chapter [E] explains the essential differences of the three sciences, namely, natural science, mathematics, and theology, and that these sciences are only three in number. It clarifies the fact that theology falls under this science [of metaphysics], or rather is this science in a certain respect.[h] It explains that it can

---

[28] Cf. *Metaphysics* 1016b25–30.

[29] Al-Fārābī refers here to alpha minor [α]; the first book [A] is absent from his account, as is the final book, N. These omissions alone would suggest that al-Fārābī was aware of only the ninth-century translation of the *Metaphysics* by an individual named al-Ustāth (Eustathius). For the rather complicated history of the various translations of the *Metaphysics*, see Bertolacci, "On the Arabic Translations of Aristotle's *Metaphysics*," 241–75. In light of al-Fārābī's omission of Book A, note that the enumeration of "chapters" here—first, second, etc.—should be increased by one to correspond with the text as we know it.

[30] I.e., the *aporiai*, or puzzles and problems.

investigate essential identity not accidental identity. It explains how [metaphysics] is associated with dialectic and the discipline of sophistry.

6.6.   The sixth chapter [Z] verifies the definition of the identity that is predicated essentially, especially with respect to its substance.[i] It classifies the divisions of substance as matter, form, and the composite. [It explains] that, if real definition belongs to existents, then to which existents it belongs, that is, if it belongs to substance, then to which substances it belongs. [It explains] how to define composite beings,[j] and which parts are in definitions, and which forms are separable and which are not. And [it verifies] that[k] the [Platonic] Paradigms do not exist.

6.7.   The seventh chapter [H] summarizes the [preceding] chapter and completes the doctrine concerning the Platonic Forms[31] and [the doctrine] that generated things have no need of [Platonic Forms] in order to be generated. It verifies the doctrine concerning the definitions of the separable forms when they exist, and that their definitions are the same as their essences.

6.8.   The eighth chapter [Θ] concerns potentiality and actuality and their priority and posteriority.

6.9.   The ninth chapter [I] concerns the one, the multiple, otherness, difference, and contrariety. [38]

6.10.   The tenth chapter [K] makes distinctions about the principles and accidents of this science.

6.11.   The eleventh chapter [Λ] concerns the Principle of substance and of all existence. It establishes Its identity and establishes that It knows Itself as Itself.[l] [This chapter also concerns] the separate existents that come after [the Principle] and how their existence is ordered from [the Principle].

6.12.   The twelfth chapter [M] concerns the principles of natural and mathematical things.

This, then, explains the aim and the parts of this book.

V.   THE PRINCIPLES OF EXISTING THINGS[a]

[Part One]

1.   [31] The principles by which the six types of bodies and accidents subsist are divided into six major levels, each one comprising a single kind. The First Cause is in the first level. The secondary causes are in the second. The Active Intellect is in the third. The soul is in the fourth. Form is in the fifth. Matter is in the sixth. In the first level there cannot be many but rather only a single one. In each of the other grades,

---

31 See the last sentence of par. 6.6.

there are many. The first three levels (namely, the First Cause, the secondary causes, and the Active Intellect) are neither bodies nor are they in bodies. The second three levels (namely, soul, form, and matter) are in bodies, although they themselves are not bodies. There are six genera of bodies: celestial bodies, rational animals, non-rational animals, plants, minerals, and the four elements. The composite whole of these six genera of bodies is the universe.

2.   With regard to the First, one should be convinced that it is the divinity and the proximate cause of the existence of the secondary causes and the Active Intellect. The secondary causes are the causes of the existence of the celestial bodies, since it is out of them [32] that the substances of these bodies come, and the existence of each one of the celestial bodies is a necessary consequence of them. The highest level of the secondary causes necessarily entails the existence of the first heaven; and the lowest level of the secondary causes necessarily entails the existence of the orbit containing the Moon. The secondary causes in between these two necessarily entail the existence of each of the spheres in between these two spheres. The number of secondary causes equals the number of celestial bodies. One ought to call the secondary causes "spiritual beings," "angels," and similar names.

3.   The function of the Active Intellect is to watch over the rational animal and endeavor to have him reach the highest level of perfection that man can reach, namely, ultimate happiness, which is for man to arrive at the level of the Active Intellect. The way that occurs is by attaining separation from bodies, without needing anything below in order to subsist (whether it be body or matter or accident), and by remaining in that state of perfection forever. Although the Active Intellect itself is singular, its rank nonetheless accommodates whatever part of the rational animal is freed of matter and attains happiness. The Active Intellect ought to be called the "protective spirit" and the "holy spirit"—since it is given names similar to these two—and its rank ought to be called "the heavenly kingdom" and other such names.

4.   At the level of the soul, the principles are many. Some are the souls of celestial bodies, some are the souls of rational animals, and some are the souls of nonrational animals. The rational animal possesses the faculties of reason, appetite, imagination, and sensory perception.

5.   The faculty of reason is what [33] enables man to acquire the sciences and technical disciplines, to discern the difference between virtuous and vicious actions and ethical dispositions, to deliberate on what he should and should not do, and moreover to perceive what is beneficial and what harmful, what is pleasurable and what painful. The faculty of reason is divided into the theoretical and the practical [faculties], and the practical [faculty] is divided into vocational and deliberative [faculties]. The theoretical faculty is what allows man to gain knowledge of anything that he does not act upon in any way, whereas the practical faculty is what allows man to gain knowledge of anything that man does act upon through his volition. The vocational faculty is what allows man to acquire crafts and vocations, while the deliberative faculty is what allows him to think and reflect on any of the things that he should or should not do. The faculty of appetite allows man to seek out or flee from something,

to desire something or be repulsed by it, and to prefer something or avoid it; it is also the faculty that occasions hatred, love, amity, enmity, fear, security, anger, satisfaction, cruelty, mercy, and all the other accidental affections of the soul.

6.   The faculty of the imagination stores impressions of the objects of the senses once they are no longer present to sensory perception. It combines and separates [the impressions] while one is awake and asleep such that some are true and others false. It also perceives what is beneficial and what is harmful, what is pleasurable and what is painful, but not what are virtuous and vicious actions and dispositions.

7.   What the faculty of sensory perception does is obvious. It perceives the objects of the five senses (as commonly accepted by all) and what is pleasurable and what is painful, but it does not discern the difference between what is harmful and what is pleasurable, nor what is virtuous and what vicious.

8.   The nonrational animal includes those that have the three faculties other than that of reason, with the faculty of imagination in [those animals] functioning in place of the faculty of reason in rational animals. Others have the faculties of sense perception and appetite only.

9.   The souls of the celestial bodies belong to a species different from the souls [of rational and nonrational animals] [34], entirely separate from them in their substances. The celestial souls have substance by virtue of [this difference in species], and they move in circular fashion by virtue of their [souls]. In terms of their existence they are nobler, more perfect, and more excellent than the souls of the species of animal that we have. [This is] because they are in no way and at no time in potentiality. On the contrary, they are always in actuality, due to the fact that the objects of their intellect are present in them from the very beginning, and they are always intellecting what they intellect. Our souls, on the other hand, are at first in potentiality and then later in actuality. [This is] because, at first, they are [simply] configured to receive and prepared to intellect the intelligibles, and [only] later do the intelligibles come to be in them, at which point they become actual. The celestial souls have neither sensory perception nor imagination; rather, they have only the soul that intellects, which in some sense is congeneric with the rational soul [in humans]. It is by virtue of their substances that the celestial souls intellect the intelligibles, which substances are separate from matter. Each of their souls intellects the First, and itself, and whichever secondary cause that gave it its substance.

10.   The celestial souls definitely do not intellect the majority of the intelligibles that humans intellect from things in matter because, they are far too high in rank by virtue of their substance to intellect the intelligibles that are below them. The First intellects Itself, which, in a certain way, is all of the existents; for when It intellects Itself, It intellects, in a certain way, all of the existents, because it is only out of Its existence that every other existent receives its existence. Each of the secondary causes intellects itself and the First.

11.   The Active Intellect both intellects the First, all of the secondary causes, and itself, as well as makes intelligibles of things that are not in themselves intelligibles. Things that are intelligibles in themselves are separate from material bodies and do

not subsist in any matter whatsoever. These are the intelligibles by virtue of their substances. These substances both intellect *and* are intellected, for they intellect on account of the fact that they are intellected, what is intelligible about them being the very thing that intellects. The other intelligibles are not like that, because neither the stone nor the plant, for example, is an intelligible, and it is certainly not the case [35] that whatever is intellected of them is also what intellects. Nothing that is a body or that is in a body is an intelligible by virtue of its substance, and the substance of none of them is at the rank of an actual intellect. The Active Intellect is what makes them actual intelligibles and makes some of them actual intellects by raising them from their level of existence to a level higher than the one given them by nature. For example, the rational faculty, by virtue of which man is man, is not in its substance an actual intellect and was not given by nature to be an actual intellect; instead, the Active Intellect causes it to become an actual intellect and makes everything else an actual intelligible for the rational faculty. Once the rational faculty becomes an actual intellect, that intellect (which is now actual) comes to resemble the separate things, by intellecting itself as actually an intellect, and what is intellected of it is the very thing that is intellecting, at which point it is a substance that intellects by virtue of being an intelligible, which in turn is due to the fact that it is intellecting. At that point, the thing that intellects, the thing that is intellected, and the act of intellecting is one and the same thing. It is as a result of this that it arrives at the rank of the Active Intellect. Once man arrives at this rank, his happiness is perfect.

12.   The relation of the Active Intellect to man is like that of the Sun to vision. The Sun gives light to vision, and by the light acquired from the Sun, vision actually sees, when before it had only the potential to see. By that light, vision sees the Sun itself, which is the cause of its actually seeing, and furthermore actually sees the colors that previously were [only] potentially the objects of vision. The vision that was potential thereby becomes actual. In the same manner, the Active Intellect provides man with something that it imprints in his rational faculty. The relation of that thing to the rational soul is like that of light to vision. It is by reason of this thing that the rational soul intellects [36] the Active Intellect, that the things that are potentially intelligible become actually intelligible, and that man, who was potentially an intellect, becomes actually and perfectly an intellect, until he all but reaches the rank of the Active Intellect. So [man] becomes an intellect *per se* after he was not, and an intelligible *per se* after he was not, and a divine [substance] after being a material one. This is what the Active Intellect does, and this is why it is called the Active Intellect.

13.   Form is in the corporeal substance the way the shape of the bed is in the bed, matter being like the wood of the bed. The form is that by virtue of which the substance that can be corporeal becomes an actual substance. The matter is that by virtue of which it is potentially a substance. For the bed is potentially a bed due to the fact that it is wood, whereas it becomes an actual bed once its shape occurs in the wood. Form subsists through matter, and matter is a subject for bearing forms. Forms do not subsist by themselves, as they need a subject in order to exist,[b] and their subject is matter, whereas matter exists only for the sake of forms. It would seem that the

existence of forms is the primary aim, but since they subsist only in a given subject, matter was made a subject to bear forms. For this reason, as long as forms do not exist, the existence of matter is in vain. But none of the natural beings is in vain.[32] Therefore, prime matter cannot exist devoid of a given form. Matter, then, is a principle and cause solely by way of being the subject for bearing the form; it is not an agent, nor an end, nor something that can exist independently of some form. Matter and form are both called [37] "nature," although form is more aptly named such. By way of example, vision is a substance, the body of the eye is its matter, the potentiality by which it sees is its form, and by virtue of them both combined, vision is vision in actuality. This is the same for all other natural bodies.

14.   In the case of souls,[33] as long as they do not seek perfection and undertake activities to that end, they remain but potentialities and configurations, in a state of preparation to receive the imprints of things. Examples of this are vision before it sees and receives the imprints of visible objects, and the faculty of imagination before it receives the imprints of objects of the imagination, and reason before it receives the imprints of the intelligibles (that is, forms). Once the imprints are actually in them—I mean the imprints of objects of the senses in the faculty of sensory perception, the objects of the imagination in the faculty of imagination, and the imprints of the intelligibles in the faculty of reason—the forms become distinct from what they were. Now, while the imprints present in the prior configurations are like forms in matters, they are definitely not called forms, unless equivocally. Those most unlike forms are the imprints of the intelligibles present in the rational, for they are almost completely separate from matter, and their manner of existing in the faculty is extremely unlike the existence of forms in matter. In the case of the actual intellect's becoming like the Active Intellect, the intellect is not a form nor even *like* a form. Despite this fact, one group calls all noncorporeal substances "forms" equally by homonymity, and divides them into those that are separate from matter by not needing it and by being free of it, and those that are not [38] separate from matter (which are the forms we discussed), but the latter is a category of forms only by homonymity.

15.   There are different orders of forms that require matter to subsist. The lowest order contains the forms of the four elements, that is, four different forms in different matters, though the species of the four matters is one and the same; for the matter of fire can itself bear the form of air and the other elements. The remaining orders, arrayed in ascending rank, contain the forms of bodies that come to be out of the blend and mixture of the elements. The forms of mineral bodies are above the order of elemental forms. The forms of plants in all their differences are above the order of mineral forms. The forms of the species of nonrational animals in all their differences

---

32 Nature does nothing in vain; compare Ibn Sīnā's articulation of this Aristotelian axiom in Ibn Sīnā, "Selections on Psychology from *The Cure*, "The Soul," V.4, par. 4, p. 196.

33 I.e., in the case of souls considered as forms.

are above the plant forms. Finally, the forms of the rational animals—that is, the natural configurations that rational animals have by virtue of being rational animals— are above the forms of nonrational animals.

16.   Form and prime matter are the most deficient of the principles in terms of existence, because in order to exist and subsist they each need the other. Form can subsist only in matter; and matter, in substance and nature, exists for the sake of form, and *that*ᶜ it exists is that it bears forms. As long as form does not exist, matter does not exist, since *this* particular matter does not in fact have a form in itself at all. Therefore, for it to exist devoid of form is vain, and no natural thing can be vain. Equally, as long as matter does not exist [39], form does not exist, on account of the fact that form requires a subject in order to subsist. Next, both form and matter have a deficiency and a perfection that are proper to it and not the other, as follows. It is by virtue of its form that the body has its more perfect state of being, that is to say, its actual existence, whereas it is by virtue of its matter that the body has its more deficient state of being, that is to say, its potential existence. The form exists neither because through it the matter exists, nor because it was created for the sake of matter, whereas matter exists for the sake of the form (I mean in order that the form subsist by it). This is how form is superior to matter. Matter is superior to form by virtue of the fact that it does not require a subject in order for it to exist, whereas form does. Matter has neither a contrary to it nor a privation that would be its opposite, whereas form does have a privation or a contrary. Anything that has a privation or a contrary cannot exist forever. Forms are similar to accidents in that they both need a subject in order to subsist, but forms are different from accidents by the fact that the subjects of accidents are not made so that accidents would exist or in order to bear the accidents, whereas the subjects of forms (that is, matters) were made solely for the purpose of bearing forms. Matter is a subject for contrary forms, that is, it is receptive to the form and to the contrary, or privation, of that form. Matter transfers from one form to another, always without lagging and without any one form being more appropriate than its contrary; rather, matter receives all contraries equally.

17.   In the case of the noncorporeal substances, none of the deficiency characteristic of form and matter attaches to them. Each one of them exists not in a subject. The existence of each one of them is not for the sake of something else, whether that be as matter, or as the instrument of something else, or as something that serves something else, or by needing to be replenished by an existence it would receive in the future by its action on something else, or by being acted upon by something else. Moreover, there is no contrary to any one of them, nor any privation opposing any one of them. These more properly deserve to be [called] substances [40] than form and matter. Now, even though none of these deficiencies attach to the secondary causes and Active Intellect below the First, they are nonetheless not entirely free of another type of deficiency. [This is] because their substances derive from something else, and their existence is consequential to the existence of something else. The perfection of their substances does not extend so far that in themselves they do not need

to receive existence from something else; it is rather the case that their existence is bestowed on them by something more perfect in existence than they are. This is a deficiency common to all existents other than the First.

18.   In addition to this, none of the secondary causes or the Active Intellect is capable of acquiring the splendor and adornment of existence, not to mention the joy, pleasure, and beauty of such only by intellecting itself alone; instead, it needs to intellect, in addition to itself, another being more perfect and magnificent than itself. In this respect then, there is a certain multiplicity in the very being of each of them, since anything that intellects some other given thing does itself, in a certain manner, become that other thing while simultaneously being its own proper self. It is as though the excellence of its being is completed only through the support of a certain multiplicity, but it is also that very multiplicity in what makes the thing a substance that is a deficiency in terms of that thing's existence. However, it is no part of their nature to gain the splendor, beauty, and adornment of existence by intellecting anything existing below them, or anything that comes to be out of each one of them, or anything that is consequential to the existence of each of the existing beings; none of that is associated with any one of them or inheres in any one of them. Furthermore, in order to come to be out of something else, none of them stands in need of any instrument [41] or other circumstance, except its very being and substance. In point of fact, on its own it is capable of bringing something *else* into being without seeking the help of any instrument or circumstance beyond its own substance.

19.   The souls of the celestial bodies are completely free from the aspects of the deficiency found in form and matter, except that they are [also] in subjects. In this respect they resemble the forms, although their subjects are not matters; instead, each of them is proper to one subject that cannot be a subject of any else. In this respect, [the souls of the celestial bodies] are different from form. Although they have all aspects of the deficiency found in the secondary causes, the multiplicity whereby they are substances is significantly greater than the multiplicity whereby the secondary causes are substances; for they attain the beauty and joy [of existence] only in as much as they intellect themselves, the secondary causes, and the First. Next, a consequence of the existence whereby they are substances is that they bring into existence other beings[d] external to their substances, though they are also incapable of bestowing existence on something else without an instrument or any other circumstance belonging to them.[e] In both cases, then, [the souls of the celestial bodies] need other things external to themselves (by "both cases" I mean their subsistence and their providing other things with existence), whereas the secondary causes are entirely free of the need for anything external to themselves in both cases. Nevertheless, [the souls of the celestial bodies] certainly do not receive the splendor and beauty of existence either by intellecting the beings below them or by virtue of their existence being limited to them without any existence issuing from it to another.

20.   [42] In the case of the souls that are in animals, once their faculties of sensory perception and imagination reach a perfection through the appearance in them of the imprints of sensible and imaginable objects, a certain resemblance to the separate

things comes about in them. When the rational part of the soul is perfected and it then becomes an actual intellect, it very much resembles the separate things, except that it receives perfection, actuality, and the splendor, adornment, and beauty of existence only by intellecting not just the things above it in rank but also the things below it in rank, making the multiplicity in what affords its substance very great. Moreover, its existence is limited to itself alone and is not bestowed on anything other than it when it achieves complete separation from all other parts of the soul. Once it separates from the appetitive, imaginative, and sensing faculties, it receives existence from something else. It would appear that anything something else might acquire from it serves the sole purpose of making it itself more perfect in existence by virtue of doing that, so once it separates from the corporeal instrument, it can have no effect on anything else and continues to be restricted in its existence. Apparently, it is not a part of its substance to bestow existence on something else; instead, it suffices that its existence in its substance be preserved forever and that it be a cause among the causes—a final cause, that is, *not* an efficient one.

21.   In the First there is no deficiency in any way whatsoever. There can be no existence more perfect and superior than Its existence. There can be no existence prior to It nor at a rank equivalent to It that is not Its own [43] existence exclusively. Therefore, the bestowal of existence [on It] from anything other than and prior to It is as equally unlikely as the possibility that such bestowal would come from anything less perfect than It. Thus, It is also completely different in Its substance from everything other than it. The existence that It has cannot belong to more than one, because there cannot be a difference between whatever has this existence and something else that has the very same existence. If there is a difference, then that difference would itself be something other than what they have in common, in which case what makes the one different from the other would be one part of what sustains both of their existences, <and what they share in common would be another part>.[f] Then, each of them would be divisible in definition, in which case each one of the two parts that each of them has would be a cause for its subsistence. Then it would not be First; instead, there would be an existent that is prior to it that sustains it. That is an absurdity, since *It* is First. And, as long as there is no difference between the two, they cannot be multiple, neither two, nor more.[34]

22.   Moreover, if it were possible for something other than the [First] to have the very same existence [It has], then it would be possible for there to be an existence outside of Its existence, which It would not possess alone and which would be at the same rank. Then Its existence would be less than whatever had both existences together, and then there would be a deficiency in Its existence, because the complete is that outside of which nothing exists that it could have. Then, Its existence cannot belong to anything else outside of Itself, and therefore It cannot have any contrary whatsoever, because the existence of the contrary of something is at the same rank as

---

[34] For a fuller version of this argument, see *Opinions*, ed. Walzer, Ch. I, §2.

its existence. But there can be no existence at the same rank that It does not possess alone, as otherwise, Its existence would be deficient.

23.   [44] Moreover, the perfection of the existence of anything that has a contrary is through the absence of that contrary, because something that has a contrary can exist at the same time as its contrary only if it is preserved by things outside and things external to its being and substance; for there is no way that the substance of one of the two contraries is sufficient to preserve itself against its contrary. It necessarily follows from this that the First would have some cause by which It exists. Therefore, [that cause] could not be at the same rank as [the First]; instead, [the cause] alone would be unique. So [the First] is one in this regard.[35]

24.   Next, It cannot be divided essentially in definition—I mean, it cannot be divided into things through which It would subsist—because each part of the definition that would explain what it is could not designate each part of what makes it subsist. [The reason for this is] that in such cases, the parts by which something subsists are the causes of its existence, in the sense that the factors designated by the parts of the definition are causes for the existence of the defined thing, the way that matter and form are causes for the existence of the thing constituted of them. That is not possible for It, since It is First. Since It cannot be divided in this manner, it is even less likely that It could be divided by quantity and the other manners of division. So It is also one in this other respect.[36]

25.   In light of this, Its existence, by which it is distinguished from all other beings, also cannot be other than that by which It is an existent in Itself. Therefore, Its distinction from everything else is through a unity that is Its being. One of the meanings of "unity" is [45] the proper existence by which every existent is distinguished from another, and it is by virtue of this that each existent is called "one," in the sense that it has an existence proper to it alone, and this particular connotation [of the term "unity"] goes along with existence.[g] In this respect, the First is also One, and more deserving of that name and connotation than anything else.[37]

26.   Because [the First] does not have matter nor is <in matter>[h] in any way, It is an intellect[i] in Its substance, because it is matter that prevents something[j] from being an intellect and from actually intellecting. It is [also] an intelligible by virtue of being an intellect; for the one whose identity is intellect is likewise an intelligible to that one whose identity is intellect.[k] It has absolutely no need for anything outside of itself to intellect It in order to be an intelligible. On the contrary, It Itself intellects Itself and, by intellecting Itself, It is an intellect and, by Its intellecting Itself, It is an intelligible. Thus, in order to be an intellect and something that intellects, It has absolutely no need to receive any other being or thing outside of Itself. On the

---

[35] For a somewhat different version of this argument, see *Opinions*, Ch. I, §3.

[36] For another version of this argument, see *Opinions*, Ch. I, §4.

[37] For a variant of this argument, see *Opinions*, Ch. I, §5.

contrary, It is an intellect and something that intellects by virtue of intellecting Itself;
for the thing that intellects is the very thing that is intellected.[38]

27. This is equally the case with [the First's] being a "knower." To be a knower,
It has absolutely no need outside of Itself for any other thing from which It would
receive excellence by knowing it; nor does It need to know any other being in order
to be known. On the contrary, It is sufficient in Its substance to be knower and known.
Its knowing Itself is not different from Its substance; for knower, known, and knowing
are one being and one substance.[39]

28. The same is the case with [the First's] being "wise," for wisdom is intellecting the perfect thing by the perfect knowledge. [46] By virtue of intellecting and
knowing Itself, It knows the perfect thing by the perfect knowledge. Perfect knowledge
is the complete knowledge that always belongs to what is always eternal. Likewise,[l]
[the First] is wise not by a knowledge that It receives through knowing something
outside of Itself. On the contrary, It is sufficient in Itself to be wise in knowing
Itself.[40]

29. The beauty, splendor, and adornment of every being is to exist as perfect
and to reach its final perfection. Now, since the existence of the First is the most
perfect existence, Its beauty surpasses that of every beautiful being, as does the adornment and splendor[m] It has in Its substance and being. [All of] that It has in Itself and
by virtue of intellecting Itself.[41]

30. Now, since pleasure, happiness, delight, and joy result all the more by
perceiving the most beautiful by means of the most accurate perception, and since
[the First] is the most beautiful absolutely and the most splendid and most adorned,
and Its perception of Itself is the most accurate perception and perfect knowledge, the
pleasure that the First enjoys is a pleasure the real nature of which we cannot understand and the massive extent of which we cannot grasp but by reference and in relation
to the minuscule pleasure we have when we suppose that we have perceived what we
take to be most beautiful and splendid by means of some accurate act of perception,
whether that be through sensory perception, imagination, or the intellect. Since in
this state we experience a pleasure that we suppose surpasses all others in sheer extent,
and we experience the ultimate degree of happiness in ourselves as a result, then to
compare the knowledge and perception [that the First has] of what is most perfect
and beautiful to our knowledge and perception of what [we take to be] the most
perfect and most splendid, is to compare Its delight, [47] pleasure, and joy in Itself
to the pleasure, delight, and joy we have in ourselves. But since there is no way to
relate our perception to Its perception, nor our knowledge to Its knowledge—though
if there is some relation, it is minuscule—there is then no way to relate our pleasure,

---

[38] Cf. *Opinions*, Ch. I, §6.

[39] Ibid., Ch. I, §7.

[40] Ibid., Ch. I, §8.

[41] Ibid., Ch. I, §13.

delight, and joy in ourselves to that of the First.[42] Even if there is some relation, it is incredibly minuscule; for how could there be any relation between a minuscule part and something that has no temporal measure, between something deficient in so many ways to something of the utmost perfection? Since It takes greater pleasure, joy, and happiness in Itself, and so loves and desires Itself all the more, it is obvious that the relation between the First's necessary desire, love, and adoration of Itself to our own desire and pleasure of the perfection of ourselves is like the relation of Its excellence and perfection to our own excellence and the perfection we adore of ourselves.[43] [In the case of the First], lover and beloved are one and the same, and what desires and what is desired are one and the same, so It is the First Beloved and the First Desired.[44]

31.   Since the existence that belongs to the First is due to Itself,[n] it necessarily follows that naturally existing things—that is, those things not due to human choice—derive from It whatever existence they have (some types of which are available to sensory perception, while others are knowable through demonstration). The existence of anything derived from It is by way of a bestowal that comes to be for the sake of the existence[o] of something else and by the existence of something else being bestowed from Its existence. In this respect, the existence of anything derived from It [48] is not a cause for It in any way whatsoever, nor is it a final cause for Its existence,[45] nor does it provide It some sort of perfection, the way that such does with the majority of things that we bring about; for in our case we are disposed to bring many things into being where those things are final causes for the sake of which we exist, and many of those final causes afford us some perfection that we did not have before.

32.   The aim of the existence of the First is not the existence of the other things, such that those would be the final causes of Its existence, since then there would be a cause apart from Itself for Its existence. It is also not the case that in providing existence It gains another perfection apart from what It is or Its own Perfection the way that one who gives money or something else to another gains pleasure, honor, status, or some other good or perfection as recompense, in which case the existence of the other is a cause of some good he acquires and a [state of] being he did not have. It is absurd for any of these things to apply to the First, because they would preclude Its being the First and necessarily entail the priority of something other than It and make that a cause of Its existence. On the contrary, it is on account of It and as a consequence and result of Its substance that anything other than It derives existence from It. Therefore, the existence It has through which It bestows existence on

---

[42] Cf. *Opinions*, Ch. I, §14.

[43] In other words, since the First's perfection is greater than the perfection of humans, and one loves the perfection in a thing, the love It has for Itself is greater than the love humans have of themselves.

[44] Cf. *Opinions*, Ch. I, §15.

[45] In the *Opinions*, Fārābī provides as an example of this the son *qua* son's being a final cause of the parent's *qua* such; cf. Opinions, ch. 2 §1.

[everything] else is in Its substance. The existence It has through which It is in Itself a substance is that very existence that It has through which everything else derives existence from It. [The First] is not divisible into two things, one through which Its essence is substance, and another through which something else comes to exist from It. [The First] also does not need anything other than Its very being and substance to bestow the existence of something else from Its existence, the way that we and many other agents do. Its existence through which It bestows the existence of something else is not more perfect than the existence It has through which It is substance. Therefore, although the existence of what derives existence from It is not temporally posterior to It, it is certainly so in every other way.[46] [49]

33.   The terms that should be employed for [the First] are the terms that designate those existents among us that are perfect and excellent without, however, any of those terms designating the excellence and perfection that the First has in the way that those terms customarily designate such existents among us. On the contrary, they should designate the perfection that is specific to It in Its substance. Moreover, the types of perfections that different terms customarily designate are multiple, but one absolutely should not thereby suppose that the types of perfection that It has that are so designated by multiple terms are multiple species into which It could be divided and through the aggregate total of which It would have substance. On the contrary, those terms, though multiple, should designate a single substance, a single absolutely indivisible existence. Finally, whenever such a term is conventionally agreed to designate an excellence and perfection outside of the substance of such an existent among us, that term when employed for the First ought to be made to designate an excellence and perfection in Its very substance. For example, "beautiful" is used to designate a perfection of color, shape, or position *pertaining to* many a thing but not *in the substance* of that thing.[47]

34.   The terms that designate the perfection and excellence pertaining to things among us include the following. There are terms that designate what belongs to something in itself, not as something relating to something else, like "existent," "one," and other such terms. There are terms that designate what belongs to something in relation to something external to it, like "just" and "generous." With respect to the things among us, these terms designate an excellence and a perfection of a part of the thing that is the relation it has to another thing apart from it, such that this relation constitutes a part of the whole of what [50] that term designates, and in that excellence and that perfection subsisting through something being related to something else. Now, whenever these terms are made to apply to the First and intended to designate the relation that It has to something else through the existence bestowed from It, the relation should not be thought to constitute a part of Its perfection as designated by that term, nor in the sense that the perfection subsists through that

---

[46] For pars. 31–32, cf. *Opinions*, Ch. 2, §1.

[47] Cf. *Opinions*, Ch. 2, §4.

relation. Instead, that term should be thought of as designating Its substance and Its perfection, whereas the relation should be viewed as a result and consequence of that perfection, in the sense that the relation subsists by virtue of Its substance and the perfection belonging to It, where the relation is viewed as necessarily resulting from and consequential to what has the substance so described.[48]

35.   Homonymous terms that apply to the First and something else include those that apply generally to all existing beings and those that are homonyms for some of them. In the case of many homonyms applied to It and something else, such a term designates *Its* perfection primarily and something else secondarily, according to its order of existence from the First. For example, the terms "existent" and "one" primarily designate that by virtue of which the First is substance, and then secondarily anything else on the strength of the fact that its substance derives from the First, that its existence is acquired and received from the First.

36.   In the case of many homonyms that designate the substance and existence of the First, [51] if they designate something else, they designate whatever one imagines to be similar, whether very much so or just a little, to the First Existence. Now, these terms are applied to the First in the most prior and true manner and to anything else only by posteriority, but it is not unacceptable if our application of these terms to the First came after our application of them to something else—for clearly our application of many of them to the First is only by way of transferring them from something else to It and after we had applied them to something else for a time— because it is impossible for what is prior by nature and existence to be posterior in time and for any deficiency to be associated with what is prior.

37.   Now, since we have numerous terms that designate particular perfections commonly accepted by us, and many of them we use simply to designate those perfections as particular perfections and not as species of perfection, clearly the most excellent perfection of them all is necessarily most deserving of that term. Every perfection among existing beings that we perceive to be more complete we consider more worthy of the term [perfection], until we arrive at the knowledge of what constitutes the upper limit of that perfection and we naturally call It, that is, the First, by that term, and we then rank all other beings according to their relation to that term from the First. Examples of [such terms] are "existent" and "one." [We also have] other terms that designate one species of perfection to the exclusion of another. Such species include whatever is in the substance of the First in the most excellent manner that the species can be, and is so elevated in the estimation to the highest level of perfection of that species that absolutely no deficiency remains. Examples of such terms are "knowledge," "intellect," [52] and "wisdom." With such terms, it necessarily follows that the term for that species is most appropriately and truly applied to [the First]. In the case of any species of perfection that is associated with a deficiency and a certain diminution of existence, and whose separation from what is associated with it would eliminate

---

[48] Cf. *Opinions*, Ch. 2, §5.

its substance completely, the term for that species of perfection should not be applied [to the First]. Since this is the case, it is as inappropriate as applying terms that designate diminished existence [to the First].

38. After the First Cause, there are the secondary causes and the Active Intellect. The secondary causes are ranked in order of existence, besides which each of them not only has an existence through which it is a substance in itself but also an existence proper to it that is the very same existence from which it bestows the existence of another thing. They do not require anything else apart from themselves in order for something else to exist from them or to bestow the existence of something else from their existence, whereas all of them derive their existence from the First. Each one of them intellects the First and itself, since none of them is capable in itself of finding joy in itself by itself alone; instead, it finds joy in itself by intellecting the First while intellecting itself. The relation of the excellence of the First to the excellence of [a given secondary cause, x] is commensurate with the joy that x takes in intellecting the First in relation to the joy x takes in intellecting itself. Equally, the comparison of the pleasure it finds in itself by intellecting the First to the pleasure it finds in itself through intellecting itself is commensurate with the additional excellence of the First in relation to the excellence of itself. So too in the case of its delight through itself and its desire of itself where the object of love and the object of delight it has initially is what it intellects of the First and secondarily what it intellects of itself. The First, then, in relation to these is again the First Beloved and the First Desired. [53]

39. All of these [secondary causes] are divisible in a certain way. The perfection and deficiency in each of them, and [consequently] what each of them should be called, is easy following this model, when we apply that to what was said about the First. Each of these secondary causes has received from the outset the complete measure of the existence it has, and there is no remaining existence due it that might come to it in the future and toward which it would strive, besides what was provided it at the outset. Consequently, they have not been set in motion and do not strive toward anything whatsoever, but each one does bestow the existence of each heaven from its existence. So there follows from the first of them the existence of the first heaven all the way down to the last heaven containing the Moon. The substance of each heaven is composed of two things: of a subject and of a soul. Despite the fact that the soul that is in each of them is something existing in a subject, it is the parts of the soul that is an actual intellect in that it intellects itself, intellects the other [secondary cause] from which it derives its existence, and intellects the First.

40. The substances of the celestial bodies are divided, in as much as they are substances, into many things. They are in the first rank of the ranks of beings that are deficient, due to the fact that the thing[49] by virtue of which they are actually substances requires a certain subject. Thus they resemble the substances that are composed of matter and form. Moreover, they are insufficient in their substances for anything

---

49 I.e., the soul.

else to come about from them. The degree of their perfection and excellence certainly does not reach the point that any effect on another would issue from them unless something external to their substances and to the things that constitute their substances comes about for them. The thing external to what constitutes their substances [and] part of the existents is quantity or quality [54] or other such categories. As a result of that each of these substances possesses determinate size, shape, other determinate qualities, and the rest of the categories that necessarily result from these. Each of them, however, possesses only the most excellent of these [categories]. Subsequent to that, they possess the place most excellent for them, since it follows necessarily that every body is delimited by a determinate place. These substances have also received already nearly all of their existence, with but a little of it remaining, since they are not such as to receive it entirely all at once from the outset; rather, there is always a little more for them in the future. Thus they strive to acquire it, and they acquire it only by eternal motion. Therefore, they are in motion eternally and without interruption. They are in motion toward and strive for the best of their existence. As regards what is most noble and what most approximates the most noble in terms of their existence, that is what they have received in full from the outset. The subject of each one cannot receive another form different from the one present in it from the very outset. Consequently, their substances have no contraries.

41.   The existents below the celestial bodies are at the lowest degree of deficiency in terms of existence, because they did not receive fully at the outset all of what constitutes their substance. Instead, the substances that they received are merely in a state of remote potentiality, not actuality, since they received only their prime matter. Consequently, they forever move toward the form that will give them substance. Prime matter can potentially be all of the substances under heaven. In a certain respect, then, they are substances in potentiality that are always in motion toward becoming substance in actuality. Their posteriority and diminished existence is of such a degree that they are incapable of even undertaking on their own behalf any effort to acquire their self-perfection in the absence of an external mover. What sets them in motion from without is [55] the celestial body and its parts and then the Active Intellect; for both of these together perfect the existence of things below the celestial body.

42.   The substance, nature, and activity of the celestial body is such that there immediately follows from it the existence of prime matter. It then gives prime matter whichsoever of the forms that is in its nature, possibility, and predisposition to receive. The Active Intellect is disposed in its nature and substance to examine everything that the celestial body prepares and gives, and whatever is receptive in one way to being freed and separated from matter, it frees from matter and privation, as a result of which [that thing] comes to be closest in rank to it. [This means] that the intelligibles that are potential become actual intelligibles, and, as a result of that, the intellect that was a potential intellect becomes an actual intellect. Humans alone can become like that, and this is the ultimate happiness, that is, the most excellent perfection that humans can reach. It is as a result of the agency of [the celestial body and the active

intellect] that the existence of the things that came after[50] is rendered perfect, and their emergence into existence is made requisite by virtue of the ways through which they are brought into existence as well as by virtue of the ways through which they can have eternal existence.

43. The celestial bodies are numerous. They move variously in circular fashion around the Earth. All are connected to the power of the first heaven, which is one, and consequently they all move by virtue of the motion of the first heaven. They have other powers by virtue of which they are distinct from one another and because of which their motions differ. A necessary result of the power common to the whole celestial body is the existence of the prime matter common to everything below the heaven, and a necessary result of the things by virtue of which [the celestial bodies] are distinct from one another is the existence of many different forms in prime matter. As a consequence of their different positions in relation to one another and to the Earth, they are made [56] to approach something sometimes and recede from it at others, to be in conjunction with one another sometimes and to be in opposition at others, to be visible sometimes and occluded at others, to happen to speed up sometimes and to slow down at others. These contrary features are not attributable to their substances but to their positions relative to one another, to the Earth, or to both.

44. It is a necessary result of these contrary features that are a consequence of their relative positions, that contrary forms come to be in prime matter, and contrary accidents and alterations come to be in the bodies below the celestial body. This is the first cause for the contraries found in prime matter and in the bodies below the heaven. [This is so] because contrary things exist in matter either on account of contrary things, or on account of one thing that has no contrary in its essence and substance. Matter can be in contrary states and relations, and while the celestial bodies are not themselves subject to contrariety in their substances, their relations to prime matter are contrary relations, since they are in contrary states relative to it. So it is through prime matter and the contrary forms necessarily existing that possibly existing things come together.

45. Possibly existing things are the latterly existing things that are most deficient in terms of existence. They are a mix of existence and nonexistence because, between what cannot not exist and what cannot exist—which two are the absolute extremes—there is something for which the opposite of both holds true, that is, the thing that can exist and can not exist. This is what is a mix of existence and nonexistence, namely, the existent to which nonexistence is opposed but with which a certain privation is associated, privation being the nonexistence of what can exist.

46. [57] Now, since the "possibly existent" is one of the two modes of the existent, and "possible existence" is one of the two modes of existence, the First Cause, whose existence in Its substance bestows the existence not only of what cannot not

---

[50] I.e., the existence of the human souls, which came after the existence of the celestial bodies and the Active Intellect.

exist but also of what can not exist, is such that there is no mode of existence but that It gives it. The nature of the possibly existent is such that it simply cannot have a single determinate existence; rather, it can exist as F and not, and it can exist as x and its opposite. Its actuality with respect to both of the opposing existences is one and the same, and its being *this* existent is no more likely than its being the opposite of *this* existent—"opposite" here is either a privation or a contrary or both of them together. Therefore, it necessarily follows that existents opposing one another can exist. This can happen in only three ways: either at two different times; or at one time from two different perspectives; or there are two things each one of which exists as an opposite of the other. A single thing can be two mutually opposing existents only in two ways: either at two different times, or from two different perspectives.

47. It is only through contrary forms that there are mutually opposing existents. The occurrence of something as one of two contraries is its settled existence. What allows for the two contrary existences is matter. So it is through matter that the exis-tence the thing will have is unsettled, whereas it is through form that its existence will be settled. [The thing], then, has two existences: a settled existence through one thing and an unsettled existence through another thing. Therefore, its existence by virtue of its matter is to be at one time *this* and at another time not-*this*, and its existence by virtue of its form is to be *this* only and not its opposite. It necessarily follows, then, that it is given two existences, one when considered with respect to *this* at one time, and one with respect to not-*this* at another.

48. [58] The "possible" can be viewed in two ways. One is what is possible to be x and to be not-x—this is matter. The other is what is possible to exist *per se* and to not exist—this is the composite of matter and form. The possibly existing things have the following orders. The lowest order comprises what has not had any settled existence, not even through one of two contraries—this is prime matter. The second order comprises those things that have settled existence by virtue of contraries occur-ring in prime matter—these are the elements. When these come to have particular forms, they thereby acquire the possibility of being other equally contrary existences, in which case they become matters for additional forms, until, when they come to have those secondary forms also, they thereby come to have the possibility of being again still other contrary existences by virtue of still other contrary forms, in which case those also become matters for still other forms until, when they come to have those forms also, they thereby come to have the possibility of being again still other contrary existences, in which case they become matters for still other forms. It con-tinues like this until it reaches forms by virtue of which the existents that are becoming settled *cannot* become matters for still other forms. The forms of those existents, then, are those of each form that preceded. These last existents are the most noble of the possibly existing things, while prime matter is the lowest of the possibly existing things.

49. The existents falling between these two also have an order. Everything closer to prime matter is more debased and everything closer to the form of the forms is nobler. Prime matter exists to belong [59] to something else, having absolutely no

existence on its own. Consequently, when that for the sake of which it was brought into being does not exist, neither does it. For this reason, when one of these forms does not exist, it does not exist. Thus, it is impossible for prime matter to exist separate from a given form at any time at all. In the case of the existents whose form is the form of the forms, they exist always for the sake of themselves, and it is impossible that through their forms they would be brought into being for the sake of anything else—I mean so that something else could have substance through them and that they would be matters for something else.

50.   In the case of the intermediate existents, they are brought into being sometimes for their own sake and sometimes for the sake of something else. Next, each one of them has adaptive and reticent [qualities] through its matter, and adaptive and reticent [qualities] through its form.[51] What it has by virtue of its matter is that it will become something else contrary to the existence that it has; what it has by virtue of its form is that it remain in the existence it has and not cease. When there are two contrary reticent [qualities], the state of equilibrium is that [the existent] receive each of its two measures in full, existing for a time as one particular thing, then being finished, and existing for a time as something contrary to the first existence, remaining that way for a time and then being finished, and existing as something else contrary to the former, and so on forever. Furthermore, the matter of each of these contrary existents is the matter of its opposite, so with each of them there is something that belongs to another and something that belongs to itself, since they share in common their primary matters. Thus, it is almost as though, from this perspective, each one has an adaptive [quality] each of which ought to go to one [60] from the other. The state of equilibrium in that is clear: what each one has should belong to the other so that both receive their full measure.

51.   Now, since the possible existents are not sufficient in themselves to strive on their own behalf for their remaining existence—not only have they received just prime matter, but also once they come to be they are incapable of maintaining their existences for themselves and, moreover, when the fair measure of their existence is with their opposite they cannot on their own strive to claim their full worth—it necessarily follows that each has an external agent that sets it in motion and directs it toward what it is due and to what will maintain the existence it has. The primary agent that directs them toward their forms, and maintains it for them once they have it, is the celestial body and its parts. It does that in the following ways. One, it sets each one

---

51 We speculate that *ḥaqq wa-istiḥāl* translates the Greek *euorizon kai dusorizon* ("easily determined and difficultly determined") from Aristotle's *Meteorology* (IV 1, 378b24, and IV 3 and 4), whose context loosely follows the context that al-Fārābī presents in our text. In the *Meteorology* Aristotle distinguished between active powers, hot and cold, and passive powers, moist and dry. The active powers are associated with the form and the passive powers with the matter. He further divides these powers into powers that are determined easily, hot and moist, and powers that are determined with difficulty, which by implication (but left unstated by Aristotle) would be cold and dry.

of them in motion, without intermediary or instrument, toward the form by virtue of which each exists. Two, it gives matter the potential whereby on its own it can undertake to move toward the form by virtue of which it exists. Three, it provides a certain thing with a potential whereby that thing can set something else in motion toward the form by virtue of which that other thing exists. Four, it gives a certain thing a potential whereby that thing can provide something else with a potential through which it sets in motion that other as a particular matter moving toward the form whose nature is to exist in the matter. In this, it will have set matter in motion by means of two things. Equally, it may set matter in motion through three things and more in this sequence.

52.   Likewise, it gives each possible existent the means to maintain its existence, either by providing, along with the form by virtue of which [61] it exists, some other potential, or by putting the means for maintaining its existence in another body apart from it, in which case its existence is maintained by that other body that was made for this one. That other body is the servant of this one in maintaining its existence for it. The maintenance of its existence is either through one body serving it or through the help of numerous bodies disposed to facilitate the maintenance of its existence. In addition to that, many bodies have associated with them another potential through which they can make out of matter things similar to themselves by giving them forms similar to their own.

53.   Often the agent finds these matters to contain forms that are contrary to the forms toward which the agent is accustomed to set them in motion, in which case another potential is needed to eliminate those contrary forms. Also, since it is certainly not impossible for something else to act on it the way it acts on something else in order to try to eradicate it the way it eradicates something else, it follows that there is another potential in these [matters] to resist the contrary that seeks to destroy it. The thing by which it eliminates something else and detaches it from the form through which it exists may be a potential in itself connected to the form through which it exists, but often that potential is in another body apart from it, in which case that potential is either an instrument or servant for it in extracting the matter disposed to it from the contraries of that body. An example of this is vipers, for this species is an instrument or servant of the elements in extracting from other animals the matters for the elements.[52] Likewise, the potential through which it produces out of matters something similar to itself in species may be connected to its form in one body, or it may be in another body apart from itself, like the sperm of the male animal, for it serves as its instrument. These potentials are also forms in the bodies to which these potentials belong, but there are things similar to these belonging to others—I mean that they are brought into being as [62] instruments or servants for something else. When these instruments are connected to the forms in a single body, they are inseparable instruments, and when they are in other bodies they are separate instruments.

---

52 See par. 64 for further details.

54.   Each of these existents has a reticent quality by virtue of its matter and a reticent quality by virtue of its form. The reticent quality that is through its matter is an existence contrary to the one it has. The reticent quality through its forms is the existence it has either on its own account, or on account of something else, or the reticent quality it has through its form is that it have something else—I mean to have something else brought into being for it—or that it have a type of unity that combines both, that is, that it be for its own sake for the sake of something else, in which case part of it will be for its own sake and part will be used for the sake of something else. That which is for the sake of something else by virtue of its form is either its matter, or an instrument or servant for it. That which has something else brought into being for it has it brought into being for it either as matter or an instrument or servant of it.

55.   The first thing to come into existence from the celestial bodies and the differences in their motions is the elements, then the minerals, then the plants, then the nonrational animals, and finally the rational animal, with the individuals of each species coming into being with modes of the powers too numerous to count. Now these powers that are put in each species are not sufficient in themselves to act and maintain the existence [of their species], unless the celestial bodies, again through the types of their motions, aid one another and prevent one another from acting in such an alternate and sequential fashion that when one aids another against its contrary for a time, it then prevents it at another time by aiding its contrary [63], for example, by a certain increase in heat or coldness or a decrease of one or the other in something that acts or is affected by heat or coldness, for they sometimes increase one and sometimes decrease it. As for the bodies below [the celestial bodies], due to the fact that they share in common prime matter and much of their proximate matters and because some have forms similar to some and contrary to others, some of them aid one another and hinder others, whether for the most part, or rarely, or equally, depending on the similarity or contrariety of their powers; for the contrary one hinders and the similar one aids, and these actions come together and combine in the possible existents, and from them diverse mixtures come to be.[53]

56.   Once [the mixtures] combine, however, they move into a combination, a harmonious balance, and a just distribution through which each existent receives the fair measure of existence naturally allotted to it, commensurate with either its matter, or its form, or both. The measure commensurate with its form is either for the sake of itself, or something else, or both. With the rational animal, however, the measure it receives according to its form is not for the sake of any other species, neither as matter, nor as instrument, nor servant. [In general, however], each of the existents [below the celestial bodies receives a measure] by virtue of its form, either for the sake of something else only, or through a combination of existence for its own sake and existence for the sake of something else, although it would be just that it receive each

---

[53] Cf. *Opinions*, Ch. 8, §5.

of its two measures in full. All of these things occur either equally, or for the most part, or but rarely. Whatever is generated but rarely is a necessarily unavoidable feature of the nature of the possible existent and introduces nothing strange. [64] In this manner and by this process, the possible existents are so equitably regulated and ordered that each one receives the measure of existence commensurate with its reticent quality.

57.   The activities of the celestial bodies are sometimes contrary to the powers of acting and maintaining that the possible existents have received, in which case the possible existents are not affected by those actions. Equally, however, the celestial bodies may prevent one possible existent from acting on another, when one is weaker than the other. Thus, the possible existents that have such powers of action may not act, either because of their weakness, or because contrary actions prevent them, or because the power of their contraries is too great, or because their contraries are aided by something external to them but with similar forms, or because another contrary thing opposes the action of the agent from another direction. In the case of the celestial bodies, they sometimes do not have an effect on [the sublunar world], and no action of theirs that is directed at the subjects below them may result, but not on account of any feebleness in them, but rather because their subjects are prevented from receiving their actions, or because one of the possible existents acts as an agent to help and strengthen their subjects [against the action]; for the possible existents are able to produce actions both contrary or similar to the celestial beings—whether or not the celestial beings, after giving them those powers, aid or oppose them—as long as they received their powers at the outset and refrained from acting on others.

58.   These bodies that are possible existents by nature include the following categories: what exists for its own sake and is not employed in any other thing, not even for a given action to issue from it; what is prepared to produce a given action, either in itself or in something else; and what is prepared to receive the action of something else. The type that is brought into being for its own sake and for nothing else [65] whatsoever may produce a particular action as a bestowal of its existence on something else. For all of these, once they exist in such a way that there can issue from them whatever can issue from them without anything of their own opposing it, that state of their being is their final perfection. (An example of this is the state of vision when it sees.) When they are in a certain state of existence such that nothing more can issue from them as a result of that state without their being moved to an existence more perfect than what they have now, then that state is their first perfection. An example of this is the relation between the sleeping writer in terms of writing and his state when awake, or like the relation between his state with regard to writing when he is exhausted and resting and his state with regard to it when he is actually writing. Whenever something is at its final perfection and that thing is such that a given action can issue from it, its action is not delayed and comes out of it instantaneously. The action of something at its final perfection is delayed only by something apart from itself hindering it, like, for instance, sunlight being blocked from something hidden by a wall. Things that are separate from matter are in their substances at their

final perfection from the very beginning and cannot be divided into two states, one in which it would be at its first perfection, the other in which it would be at its final perfection. Because they have neither contraries nor subjects, there is nothing to hinder them in any way. Therefore, their actions are not delayed.

59. The celestial bodies are, in their substances, always in a state of final perfection. What first issues from them is their actual sizes, magnitudes, the configurations of their relative distances from one another, and everything else they possess that is not subject to change. What next issues from them is their motions, which come out of their final perfections and in which they have no contraries and no external opposites. Therefore, their motions are never interrupted, not even for an instant. [66]

60. The possibly existing bodies are sometimes in their first perfections and sometimes in their final perfections. Because there is a contrary to each one of them, their actions can be delayed for both of these reasons or for one; for the writer does not produce an action either because he is sleeping, or engaged in something else, or because the various elements involved in writing are not called to his attention at that time, or because everything involved is completely present but there is an external obstacle. The aim of the existence of all these is to be in their final perfections. The final perfection of anything that is in its first perfection by nature and not by force is obtained from [nature] only because there is either an unimpeded way to [the final perfection] or because there is something to aid it, for instance, the animal sleeps or rests from action after being exhausted, whereby it recovers the power to act.

61. Moreover, the deficiency of these [possibly existing bodies] is of such a degree that they are incapable of achieving their [final] perfections through their substances alone, without other [modes of existence] from the rest of the categories external to their substances, and that is by having size, shape, position, and the rest of the categories, such as being hard or soft, hot or cold, etc. Now, the individuals arrayed under many of these species subsist on the basis of similar parts, but their shapes are indeterminate, for example, the elements and the mineral bodies, whose shapes depend on the chance action of their efficient cause or on the shapes of things that contain them. Equally, the magnitudes of their sizes are indeterminate, though they do not have an infinite [variety of] sizes. Their parts are sometimes combined and sometimes separated; there are some that become continuous [bodies] when [their parts] are combined in one place, and others whose [parts] come into contact only and do not become continuous. The separation and combination [of their parts] does not occur in a set order but in a chance manner depending on the agent that combines and separates them. Consequently, the individuals under each of these species are distinct from one another not by necessity but rather [67] by chance, because their perfections result regardless of whatever state these accidents in them happen to be. So these things [all] have equal possibility.

62. In the case of plants and animals, however, the individuals under each species are distinct from one another by nature, and each is singular through an existence that does not belong to another. Thus, their individuals have number by nature.

Each one of them is a composite of dissimilar parts of determinate number, and each part has determined size, shape, quality, position, and level. As we have stated, the genera of possibly existing things have different levels of existence, the lowest helping the highest in the possible existence of each one. The elements aid the others through all of their parts in three ways: as matter, and by being servants and instruments. The mineral bodies aid the remainder, but not in every one of their species nor through every manner of help; rather one species [aids] as matter, another species by being servant to it (for example, mountains with respect to the generation of water's trickling down from springs), and another species by being instruments. The species of plants often aid animals in these three ways, and so too the nonrational animals aid the rational animal in these three ways; for some of them help as matter, some by being servants, and others by being instruments.

63. With the rational animal, however, since there is no species of possible beings more noble than it, [68] it provides none of the three types of help to anything nobler than it. [This is so] because, by virtue of reason[54] it does not serve as matter for anything whatsoever, whether above or below it, nor as instrument for anything other than it at all, nor by virtue of nature is it servant to anything else. As for whether it aids anything else in as much as it is rational, then it is by virtue of reason and volition, not by virtue of nature, that it aids other possible beings, and the individuals of its species aid one another (let us postpone talk of that now); for the actions of [the rational animal] might accidentally serve the purposes of many other natural things— namely, directing the flow of water, cultivating trees, planting seeds, breeding and herding animals—but it is not by virtue of nature that [any rational animal] serves a species other than its own, nor does it possess by nature anything through which another species may be served, nor are any of them by nature an instrument for another species. In the category of help from the noblest genera of possible things to the lowest, however, as we said, no rational animal serves or aids any lesser species, where that would be by virtue of its form. This is what should be understood when we talk about species helping other species.

64. With the nonrational animal, in as much as it is an animal, it is not matter for anything lesser than it; for none of them, by virtue of its form, is matter for plants. It is not impossible, however, for it to help by being a servant or instrument. In fact, some animals are brought into being by nature to serve the elements by dissolving things distantly removed from them [in composition] into [the elements]; for example, poisonous animals that by nature are enemies of other species of animal, like the viper that serves the elements through its poison by breaking down species of animals into [the elements]. A similar example is the poison in plants and, [in this case], they are poisons relatively, so that species aids two things. One should know that predatory animals are not like vipers, because the poison of vipers is not fit to be nutritious to other animals; on the contrary, [vipers] are hostile [69] by nature to all species of

---

[54] *Nuṭq* (lit. the power of speech).

animals in as much as they seek to destroy them. Predatory animals, on the other hand, instinctively kill not because of a natural enmity but because they seek nutrition. Vipers are not like that. [Finally], in the case of mineral bodies, in as much as they are such, they are not matter for the elements, but they do aid them by being their instrument, the way the mountain aids in the generation of water.

65.   [For the purposes of survival], the species of plants and animals include the following types. There are those species that cannot obtain what they need to survive unless they all come together as a group of individuals. There are other species in which each individual might achieve what is necessary for survival even if some individuals remain apart, but they will not collectively arrive at what is best for them unless they all come together as a group. In other species, every individual might achieve in full both what is necessary for survival as well as what is best, even if some individuals remain apart from the others, although if they do come together as a group, no individual prevents another from having what it has. In other species, if they come together as a group, they do hinder one another from obtaining either what is necessary to survival or what is best, and consequently in some species of animals the individuals always stay away from one another even for procreation (for instance, many species of sea animals). In other species, the individuals do not keep apart from one another except for procreation. Finally, with other species the individuals never keep apart in anything, like ants and bees and many others, like the birds that feed and fly together in flocks.

VI.   *DIRECTING ATTENTION TO THE WAY TO HAPPINESS*[a]

1.   [47] Happiness is an end that everyone desires, and everyone who strives to direct himself toward it does so precisely because it is a known perfection. This requires no explanation since it is so completely well known. Man desires every perfection and every end precisely because it is a certain good, which is unquestionably something preferred. Now, while there are many ends that are desired because they are preferred goods, happiness is the most advantageous of the preferred goods. It is thus clear that of all goods, happiness is the greatest, [48] and of all preferred things, happiness is the most perfect end that man has ever desired.

2.   Some goods are preferred in order to obtain by them some other end, like physical exercise or taking medicine, while other goods are preferred for their own sake. It is obvious that those that are preferred for their own sake are more preferable and more perfect than those that are preferred for the sake of something else. More-over, some of those preferred for their own sake are also sometimes preferred for the sake of something else. An example of this is knowledge; for sometimes we might prefer it for its own sake [and] not in order thereby to obtain something else, and sometimes we might prefer it in order to obtain wealth or something else that can be obtained by leadership or knowledge. Other [goods], by their very nature, are always preferred for their own sake and at no time are preferred on account of something

else.b These are more preferable, more perfect, and of greater good than [those goods] that are sometimes preferred for the sake of something else.55

3. Since we deem it correct that, once we obtain happiness, we have absolutely no need thereafter to strive to obtain some other end, it is apparent that happiness is preferred for its own sake and never [49] for the sake of something else.56 Consequently, it is clear that happiness is the most preferred, the most perfect, and the greatest good. We also deem it correct that, once we obtain happiness, we are in need of nothing else to accompany it. Anything like this is most suitably considered to be sufficient in itself. This statement may be supported by the conviction each person has concerning what alone is happiness, whether this has been explained to him or he supposes it to be so. Some think that wealth is happiness; others think that the enjoyment of sensible pleasures is happiness; some think that the power to rule is happiness; others think that knowledge is happiness; still others think that happiness resides in other things.57 Each one is convinced that what he considers to be absolute happiness is the most preferable, the greatest, and the most perfect good—such is the rank happiness holds among the goods! Now, since happiness is of such a rank, and since it is the highest degree of human perfection, anyone who chooses to obtain it for himself surely must have a path and the means that allow him to arrive at it.

4. We begin by saying that the states belonging to a person in his life include some that entail neither grounds for praise nor grounds for blame, and others that, when he has them, [50] do entail grounds for praise or blame. Now a person certainly does *not* obtain happiness by means of those of his states that do not result in praise or blame. On the contrary, the states through which he obtains happiness are (in summary here) those that do entail praise or blame of him. Those states of his that entail his praise or blame are three. Onec is the actions for which he requires the use of the organic parts of his body, such as standing, sitting, riding, seeing, and hearing. The second is the accidents of the soul, such as appetite, pleasure, joy, anger, fear, desire, mercy, jealousy, etc. The third is discernment by use of the mind.58 A person has these three, or some combination of them, at any given point in his life, and for each one a person is either praised or blamed. Grounds for blame attach to him when his actions are ignoble; grounds for praise attach to him when they are noble. Grounds for blame attach to him through the accidents of the soul whenever they are not what they should be; grounds for praise [attach to him] whenever they are what they should be. Grounds for blame attach to him on account of his discernment whenever it is poor. [51] Excellent discernment is either when he has a true conviction, or when he is capable of distinguishing with regard to what he receives [from others]. Poor

---

55 Cf. NE I 1–2094a4–22.

56 Ibid., I 7, 1097b1.

57 Ibid., I 4, 1095a23; I 5, 1095b16ff.; X7, 1177a12–1178a8; X8, 1178a22–1179a32.

58 Cf. NE II 5, 105b19–1106a12.

discernment is when man has neither a true nor a false conviction about what he would like to pursue. So we have to explain how we come to possess the means to make our actions noble and the accidents of our souls what they should be, and which path leads to our obtaining excellent discernment.

5.   We should know first that a person's actions can be noble (1) by chance, or his performance of them is (2) without will and choice. But happiness is definitely not obtained through noble actions when they come from the person in this manner. [The person obtains happiness] when he has undertaken them (3) willingly and by choice—and not when he does them by choice in just some things and just some of the time, but rather when he chooses the noble for every action and for the entire duration of his life.[59] These very same conditions must also be present in the noble accidents of the soul. Excellent discernment also sometimes comes to a person by chance, for sometimes man has a true conviction neither by intention nor skill. But happiness is definitely not obtained [52] through excellent discernment as long as it is not by intention and skill but such that the person is aware of *how* he discerns what he discerns. Sometimes it may be possible for a person to possess [excellent discernment] and be aware of it, but in just a very few things and only some of the time, and it is not by this amount of excellent discernment that happiness is obtained. Happiness is obtained only in as much as man has excellent discernment while being aware of how he discerns what he discerns and at every moment of his life. [Finally], misery attaches to a person when his actions, the accidents of his soul, and his discernment are all the opposite of what has been said, namely, that he performs ignoble actions willingly and chooses them in everything he does for as long as he lives—and so too with the accidents of the soul—and that he has poor discernment at every point of his life about all things discernible to people.

6.   We should speak now of the circumstances in which a person's actions, the accidents of the soul, and his discernment inevitably yield happiness or inevitably do not yield happiness. Then we can bypass the latter and devote our attention to the former.

7.   Every person, from the moment he exists, is endowed with a potentiality through which his actions, the accidents of his soul, and his discernment are the way they should be, and it is through the very same potentiality [53] that these three are not the way they should be. It is through this potentiality that he performs noble actions, and it is by the very same potentiality that he performs ignoble ones. Consequently, it is equally as possible for a person to do what is ignoble as it is for him to do what is noble. Through [this potentiality] he can have excellent discernment; through the same he can have poor discernment. This is also the state of the potentiality[d] with regard to the accidents of the soul; for it is equally as possible for them to be ignoble as it is for them to be noble. After that, the person comes to have another state in which these three follow only one of two possibilities, I mean, in terms of

---

[59] Cf. the discussion of these three types of actions in NE III 1–3.

what should be, they are either only noble, or only ignoble. However, *doing* what one should do remains equally as possible as doing what one should not do; but in [the second state] one is more likely than the other.

8.   A person does not acquire the potentiality he is endowed with, but rather he has it from the moment he exists. The other state, however, comes about only by the person's acquisition of it. This state has two divisions. In one, his discernment is either only excellent or only poor. In the other, the actions and the accidents of the soul are either only noble or only ignoble. The one in which discernment is either excellent or poor has two further divisions. In one, there is excellent discernment; this is called the powerful [54] mind. In the other, there is poor discernment; this is called the weak mind, or stupidity. The division in which one's actions and the accidents of one's soul are either noble or ignoble is called *disposition*. Disposition is what leads to a person's ignoble and noble actions.

9.   Now, since the actions and discernment through which happiness is obtained require the conditions enumerated, and since one of those conditions is that [these actions and discernment are undertaken] in everything and always, it necessarily follows that the thing through which these actions and discernment issue from the person with these conditions is a state that accords with only one of the two possibilities[60] if the person is to sustain noble action and excellent discernment in everything always. Moreover, since the person's endowed potentiality is not such that only one of the two possibilities issues from it without the other, but the acquired state that comes about after is such that only one of the two possibilities issues from it, the following necessarily holds true. First, it necessarily follows that the actions and accidents of the soul can come from us in such a way that happiness inevitably results only when we have a noble disposition. Second, it necessarily follows that we can have excellent discernment in such a way that happiness inevitably results only when the powerful mind becomes a habit that is either impossible or very difficult to lose.

10.   Thus, the noble disposition and the powerful mind together constitute human excellence, in the sense that anything's excellence is what imparts to it goodness and perfection in its being and goodness in its actions. [55] When both [the noble disposition and the powerful mind] are present, we have goodness and perfection in our being and action. It is through them, then, that we become noble, good, and virtuous, that the way we behave in our lives becomes virtuous, and that our modes of comportment become praiseworthy.

11.   Now we will begin discussing how we may arrive at the stage in which the noble dispositions are a habit. Then we will proceed to discuss how the potentiality to perceive what is correct becomes a habit. By "habit" I mean that it is such that the loss of it is impossible or very difficult.[e] So, we say that all of the ethical dispositions, noble and ignoble, are acquired. Whenever a person does not have a disposition

---

[60] I.e., only noble and only ignoble; see the end of par. 7.

actually present [in him], he can obtain it for himself, and whenever he finds that he
has a given disposition, whether noble or ignoble, with respect to a given thing, he
can convey himself by means of his volition to the opposite of that [56] disposition.[61]
What enables a person to acquire a disposition or to move away from a disposition
he finds in himself is habituation.[62] By "habituation" I mean the repetition of doing
one thing many times over a long span of successive periods. Now, because the noble
disposition is also acquired by habituation, we should speak of the habitual actions
by means of which we acquire a noble disposition, and the habitual actions by means
of which we acquire an ignoble disposition.[63]

   12.   I say that the things through which we acquire the noble disposition when
we do them habitually are the actions characteristic of those who have noble dispositions. [The things] that impart to us the ignoble disposition are the actions that come
from those who have ignoble dispositions. The state in which one acquires the dispositions is like the state in which skills are acquired; for proficiency in writing is obtained
only once a person habitually performs the actions of the proficient writer, and so too
with all other skills. Being good in the act [57] of writing comes from man only
through proficiency in writing, and proficiency in writing is obtained only when man
has previously habituated himself to the act of writing. Before attaining proficiency
in writing, excellence in terms of the act of writing is a possibility for a person on
account of the potentiality with which he is endowed, whereas afterwards it is because
of the skill. In the same way, before obtaining the noble disposition, the noble action
is a possibility for man on account of the potentiality with which he is endowed,[64]
whereas afterwards it is because of the [noble] action. When these actions that come
from the dispositions are present, they are the very same actions that, as long as the
person has habitually performed them before obtaining the dispositions, the dispositions will be present.[65] What shows that it is only through habit that the dispositions
come about is what we observe occurring in cities: the legislators of governing policy
make the inhabitants noble only through the noble actions they habituate them to
doing.[66] We will now describe which actions are the noble ones, that is, those actions
that, when we do them habitually, result in the noble disposition.[67]

   13.   A person's perfection with regard to his disposition is the perfection of that
disposition. The point about the actions through which a person attains perfection in
terms of his disposition is identical to that for the actions through which a person
obtains perfection with respect to his body, [58] the perfection in terms of the person's

---

[61] Cf. the translation of Ibn Sīnā's On Governance, par. 16, pp. 229–30.

[62] See NE VII 10, 1152a32–3.

[63] See NE III 5, 1114a6.

[64] See par. 7.

[65] I.e., a person can obtain a disposition by habitually performing its corresponding action.

[66] Cf. II 1, NE 1103b4.

[67] For this paragraph as a whole, see NE II 6, and III 7, 1113b21–1114a4.

body being healthiness. So just as it is the case that whenever healthiness is present it should be preserved and whenever it is not it should be acquired, and just as healthiness is produced by the requisite actions only when those actions are in a median state—for whenever eating [follows] the median, healthiness is produced, and whenever exercise is steady, strength is produced—so too is it the case that whenever those actions accord with the median, the noble disposition is produced. Just as it is the case that whenever those things that produce healthiness are absent, healthiness [itself] is absent, so too is it the case that whenever actions are habitually imbalanced, no noble disposition results from them.[f] [The habitual actions] are imbalanced either toward an excess of what should be or toward a deficiency of what should be; for whenever there is more food or less food than there should be, healthiness does not result. Whenever physical exercise is steady, it makes [59] bodies strong, but whenever it exceeds what should be or is less than what should be, it undoes strength or perpetuates weakness. Equally, whenever those actions fall away from the median, by either exceeding what they should be or by being less than what they should be, they impart or perpetuate ignoble dispositions and undo noble dispositions.

14.   Now, just as it is the case that the median state in whatever imparts healthiness involves the frequency and rarity of its occurrence, its intensity and weakness, the length or brevity of the period of its occurrence, and the excess or deficiency [of the contrary states], so too is it the case[g] that proportion in actions involves the frequency and rarity of their occurrence, their intensity and weakness, and the length and brevity of the period of their occurrence.[68] Since a median state is present in anything whenever the degrees of its frequency or infrequency and its intensity or weakness are in precise accord with a given amount, and the production of anything in accordance with a given amount is effected only when assessed by a standard gauge, we must discuss the gauge by which we assess actions so that they will be apportioned equally.[69]

15.   I say that the gauge by which we assess actions is patterned on the gauge by which we assess whatever imparts healthiness, and the gauge of what imparts healthiness is [relative to] the conditions of the body for which we seek healthiness; for the median in what imparts healthiness can be grasped only when brought into relation with bodies and assessed by reference to environmental[h] conditions. Equally, the gauge of actions is [relative to] the conditions surrounding[i] the actions, and the median state in the actions can be achieved only [60] when compared and assessed by reference to their surrounding[j] conditions. [By way of analogy], whenever a doctor seeks to determine the measure that is a proportion with respect to what imparts healthiness, he proceeds by identifying the temperament of the body that he aims to make healthy, the times [of illness], the occupation of the patient, and the rest of the things that medicine delimits and makes the measure of what imparts healthiness by measuring

---

68 Cf. NE II 6, 1106a25–1106b23.
69 Cf. Aristotle's "right rule," NE III 5, 114b26–8.

what the temperament of the body will endure and what is appropriate to the period of treatment.[70] It is equally the case that whenever we want to determine the measure that is a median with respect to actions, we proceed by identifying the time and place of the action, who performs the action, who suffers it, what the action consists of, the means of the action, the aim of the action, and what the action belongs to, and we take measure of the action in relation to each one of these. At that point we will have spotted correctly what is the median action. Whenever the action is measured in all of these factors, it is the median; whenever it is not measured in all of these factors, it is either excessive or insufficient. Since the measures of these things are not always one and the same in terms of frequency and infrequency, it necessarily follows that the measures of the balanced actions are themselves not always one and the same.

16.   It may be appropriate now for us to present some examples of what is commonly accepted as being the noble dispositions and the median actions [61] that result from and are produced by them, so that the mind might find a way to correlate what I summarize here with the various types of dispositions and the actions that result from them.

16.1.   So we say that courage is a noble disposition and is produced by a median state between attacking and fleeing frightening things. Being too willing to attack leads to temerity, while too little [willingness to attack] leads to timidity, which is an ignoble disposition.[71] Whenever these dispositions are present, the very same actions result.

16.2.   Generosity is produced by a median state between saving and spending wealth. Too much saving and too little spending produce stinginess, which is ignoble, whereas too much spending and too little saving produce profligacy.[72] Whenever these dispositions are present, the very same actions result.

16.3.   Self-control is produced by a median state in the pursuit of the pleasures that come from eating or sex. Too much pleasure produces avidity, whereas too little produces insensitivity to pleasure, which is censurable.[73] Whenever these dispositions are present, the very same actions result.

16.4.   Urbanity, which is a noble disposition, is produced by a median state in the use of humor. People are in need of relaxation in their lives, and relaxation always only tends toward anything that, even when done excessively, is a source of pleasure, or at least not a source of pain, and humor is one of those things that, even when engaged in often, is a source of pleasure, or at least not a source of pain. [62] However, a median use of humor produces urbanity, whereas too much

---

[70] Cf. NE 1138b30.

[71] Cf. NE 1107a33–1107b3 and NE 3.6–9.

[72] This is, essentially, Aristotle's discussion of wealth, NE, 1107b8–14; IV 4, 1125b 5–6, and esp. IV 1–2.

[73] Cf. NE II 7, 1107b3–5 and NE III 2.

humor produces buffoonery, while too little produces boorishness.[74] Humor includes whatever a person says, does, and uses. A median use of it is appropriate for a noble, free, and unburdened man to say and hear. This book will by no means take on the task of defining these things thoroughly, since they have been treated fully elsewhere.[75]

16.5. A person's honesty about himself comes about only once he has become habituated to describing himself with the virtues he has where it is appropriate. Whenever he has become habituated to describing himself with virtues that he does not have, he gains dissimulation, lying, and hypocrisy. Whenever he has become habituated to describing himself as having less than what he does, he gains false modesty.[76]

16.6. Displaying affection,[77] which is a noble disposition, comes about in a person's interactions with another through a median state with respect to whatever words or actions please the other. Too much of it results in sycophancy, whereas too little results in churlishness—even worse, if it has also caused the other pain, the person has become [63] antisocial.[k] We could apply the same model of a median state, excess, and deficiency to other actions.[78]

17.   Now it is appropriate for us to discuss the means by which we can acquire the noble dispositions. I say that we must first enumerate the dispositions one by one, as well as the actions that result from each disposition. After that we ought to reflect and investigate which disposition we find in ourselves. Is the disposition that we happen to have since the beginning of our life noble or ignoble? The method for determining this is to reflect and investigate which action gives us pleasure whenever we perform it, and which action harms us whenever we perform it. Once we determine this, we consider that action: Is it an action that comes from a noble or ignoble disposition? If it has come from a noble disposition, we say that we have a noble disposition; if it has come from an ignoble disposition, we say that we have an ignoble disposition. In this way, we identify which disposition it is that we find in ourselves. [By way of analogy], the doctor ascertains the condition of a body through the [symptoms] that follow from the conditions of the body. If the state in which he finds the body is a healthy one, he comes up with means to preserve it for the body. If the state in which he finds the body [64] is an unhealthy one, he employs means to eradicate that sickness. So too is it the case that when we find ourselves to have a

---

[74] Cf. NE II 7, 1108a10–26 and NE IV 8.

[75] The reference is probably to al-Fārābī's no longer extant commentary on *Nicomachean Ethics.*

[76] Cf. NE IV 7.

[77] Aristotle says of this noble disposition, "no name is assigned it though it most resembles friendship" (NE IV 6, 1126b20).

[78] It is significant that al-Fārābī, in his ethical enquiry, does not reproduce Aristotle's discussion of justice.

noble disposition, we come up with means to preserve it, and when we find ourselves to have an ignoble disposition, we employ means to eradicate it. For the ignoble disposition is a disease of the soul, and in order to eradicate the diseases of the soul, we should copy the doctor's procedure for eradicating the diseases of the body.

18.   We next investigate the ignoble disposition we find ourselves to have: Is it [ignoble] because of excess or deficiency? Just as it is the case that whenever the doctor finds the temperature of the body to be too high or too low, he returns it to the median temperature according to the mean determined by medicine, so too is it the case that whenever we find ourselves to have an excess or deficiency in our dispositions, we return ourselves to the mean defined in this book. Now, since identifying the mean initially proves very difficult, a way is sought to allow a person to bring his disposition into accord with it, or as close as possible, just as it is the case that, since identifying the median body temperature initially proves very difficult, a way is sought to bring the body into accord with it, or as close as possible. The way to bring the disposition into accord with the mean is to investigate the disposition we currently have. If it is excessive, we habituate ourselves to the actions that come from [65] its contrary, that is, from the direction of deficiency. If we find it to be deficient, we habituate ourselves to the actions that come from its contrary, that is, from the direction of excess. We continue this for a period, and then we reflect and investigate which disposition is present. It can admit only of three states: either it is the mean, or it inclines away from the mean, or it inclines toward the mean. If it is close to the mean, without our having gone beyond it toward the other contrary, we continue with the very same actions for another period until we have reached the mean.[79] If we have gone beyond the mean toward the other extreme, we perform the actions of the initial disposition and continue with them[l] for a period. Then we reflect on [our] condition. By way of summary, whenever we find ourselves leaning to one side, we habituate ourselves to the actions of the other side, and continue that until we arrive at the mean or as close as possible.

19.   How can we know that we have brought our dispositions into accord with the mean? We know by considering the ease of the action coming, [for instance], from deficiency: Is it performed with ease or not? If both[m] are performed with equal ease, or closely approximate one another, we know that we have brought ourselves into accord with the mean. The test of their ease is to consider both actions together. If [66] we are not harmed by either one of them, or if each brings us pleasure, or if one brings us pleasure and the other does not harm us (or at least the pain from it is minimal), we know that they are equally easy and approximate one another. However, since the mean lies between two extremes, and there could be something resembling the mean in the extremes, we must be wary of falling into the extreme that resembles the mean. Examples of this are impetuousness, since it resembles courage: [similarly], profligacy resembles generosity, buffoonery resembles urbanity, sycophancy resembles

---

[79] Cf. NE II 9, 1109a24–30, 1109b4.

affection, false modesty resembles modesty, and dissimulation resembles man's honesty about himself. Moreover, since these extremes are [dispositions] to which we are more inclined by nature, we must be wary of falling into them. For example, being deficient [when it comes] to attacking something frightening is something to which we are naturally more inclined. We are also more inclined to stinginess. That which is most properly to be guarded against is that to which we are more inclined, despite the fact that it resembles the mean.[n] An example of this is buffoonery; for in as much as it is pleasurable, or at least not a source of pain, excessive use of humor is an easy thing to do, and so we become inclined to it. It remains now for us to identify what we should use as an instrument [67] that will allow us easily to draw ourselves away from one extreme toward another, or toward the mean; for deliberation is often insufficient on its own without this instrument.

20. We say that it is easy for us to perform the ignoble action simply because of the pleasure we experience in doing it, whereas we acquire the noble whenever it seems to us to bring us pain, but only because we assume that pleasure is the ultimate end of every action, and so this alone we seek in everything we do. Now, pleasures include some that result from sensory perception, like the pleasures consequential to something heard, seen, tasted, touched, or smelled, and others that are consequential to the conceptual, like the pleasures resulting from leadership, authority, domination, and knowledge. We always prefer most of the pleasures consequential to what is sensed, and we suppose that they are the ultimate end of life and [that] the perfection of life comes from our indulging in [those pleasures] from the beginning of our existence. Moreover, [the latter pleasures] include those that are a means to things necessary for survival, whether our own or with respect to the world as a whole. Eating, whereby we stay alive, is [a necessity] for us, whereas reproduction is a necessity for the world.[80] We suppose by virtue of this that [such pleasures] are the ultimate end of life, and we suppose that they are happiness.[81] In addition to this, the objects of our senses constitute what is best known to us, since we perceive them most strongly [68] and can attain them most readily. Through investigation and reflection, however, it has become clear that [such pleasures] present us with an obstacle to most of the virtues and an impediment to our greatest means of attaining happiness. For whenever we see that a sensory pleasure will cause us to neglect a noble action, we are inclined to eschew the noble, whereas whenever a person becomes strong enough to forsake these pleasures, or to partake of them in an appropriate measure, he comes closest to the praiseworthy dispositions.

21. The pleasures and pains that follow the actions, whether of the senses or understanding, are either immediate or delayed. For each pleasure there are actions that follow one of two courses: either the action is such that a pleasure or a pain always follows it—like the pain that follows being burned (since for the animal, the nature

---

[80] Cf. NE VII 4, 1147b24–30.

[81] Ibid., VII 13, 1153b34–5.

of being burned is such that harm or pain always follows) and the pleasure that follows sex, or the pain that follows the action is inflicted by virtue of the law, while the nature of the action is not such that pain necessarily follows [69] (for instance, the state of the adulterer, or killing a murderer). The noble actions that immediately result in pain are undoubtedly followed later by pleasure, whereas the ignoble actions that immediately result in pleasure are undoubtedly followed later by pain. [Thus], we ought to take stock of the pleasures and pains that follow each action and discriminate which among them has an immediate pleasure and a delayed pain. Then, whenever we incline toward an ignoble action by reason of some pleasure we suppose will follow it immediately, we compare that immediate pleasure to the pain that later results, and through [thought of the later pain], we thwart the immediate pleasure that incites us to commit the ignoble action, thereby making it easy for us to refrain from it. Whenever we are inclined to refrain from the noble action by reason of a pain that would immediately follow it, we compare that pain to the pleasure that later results, and through [thought of the later pleasure], we thwart the pain that dissuades us from the noble action, thereby making it easy for us to do it. Moreover, whenever we are inclined to the ignoble action by reason of an immediate pleasure, we compare that pleasure to any [70] immediate ignominy it may entail.

22.   Some people have excellent skills in deliberation and powerful determination to do whatever deliberation enjoins them to do; such people we customarily call "free by merit."[82] Others have neither of these; we customarily call them brutes. Others have excellent skills in deliberation only, without powerful determination; these we call slaves to their nature. This [last state] has befallen a group[83] who are described as learned or who like to think they are philosophers, but they have degenerated to the rank of someone who possesses [excellence in deliberation] but is in a state of slavery, and what they ascribe [to that person] is, in fact, their own defect and a source of their own shame, since it is an error from which they learn nothing. Still others have the power of determination but not the excellent skills of deliberation. Anyone like this has someone else who deliberates for him, and he either obeys him or he does not. If he does not, he is also a brute; if he does, he successfully performs most of his actions, and by virtue of that reason he has emerged from slavery and is associated with the free.

23.   Some of the pleasures that follow actions are better known—since we have a better perception of them—while others are more obscure. The better known is what immediately follows and [71] derives from the senses. Pain is also like this, since when it is immediate and derives from the senses, it is more apparent to us, especially if it is also a pain inflicted by law. The more obscure pleasures and pains are different. The most obscure of these is what occurs by nature, is delayed, and moreover, is not

---

82 *Istiḥāl,* "by merit," may be a later scribal alteration (perhaps on religious grounds) of *istiʿlāh,* "[by being] god-like"; cf. NE VII 7, 1145a15ff., where Aristotle contrasts the god-like man and the brutish man.
83 Cf. NE II 4, 1105b14ff.

understood. The less obscure is what occurs immediately and by nature, and so too in the case of what occurs in the future and is not perceived by the senses.

24.   Now, whenever the free people want to make it easy for themselves to do the noble and refrain from the ignoble by comparing pleasure and pain, they consider the most obscure and the most apparent to have the same value. [In this way], the pleasures that incite them to the ignoble are thwarted by the [thought of] the pain, and even if that pain is one of the more obscure, it is thwarted in the same way as the more apparent, on account of the fact that their excellent skills at deliberation make whatever is more obscure the same as whatever is more apparent.

25.   For other people [comparing pleasure and pain] is insufficient unless their pleasures are thwarted by a pain of the most apparent sort. Such people might perhaps [72] include someone who, when inclining toward an ignoble action for the sake of immediate pleasure, can be curbed by a pleasure set down as an obstacle, so that he will refrain from [the ignoble] or do° its opposite. It is also by this method that the young should be trained. If, however, a young person is one of those people for whom this is insufficient, then the pain that follows the ignoble action should be intensified and made as apparent as possible to him. The brutish people and anyone incapable of the first method[84] should be educated by means of this latter method. The most apparent pleasures and pains are those that affect the senses, whereas those that do not [so affect the senses] include, for instance, fear, distress, anxiety, etc.

26.   The brutish people include those for whom [nonsensible] pain alone is enough [to prevent them from doing the ignoble], and others for whom that is not enough or to whom sensible pain has to occur [to prevent them from doing the ignoble]. The most effective[P] means of causing harm to a person's senses is through the sense of touch, then smell, then taste, and then the remaining senses. In this way, a person can make it easy for himself and others to do good and avoid evil.[q] This amount of discussion is sufficient here; [73] a thorough discussion for anyone interested in investigating governing policy can be found elsewhere.[85]

27.   It is appropriate now for us to discuss excellent discernment, so we will first discuss excellent discernment and then the means whereby we obtain it. I say that excellent discernment allows us to come into possession of the knowledge of everything people can know. It is of two types. One type of knowledge can be known [but] not acted upon by people. It is simply an object of knowledge, like our knowledge that the world is created and that God is One, and our knowledge of all the things available to sensory perception. The other type of knowledge can be known and acted upon, like our knowledge that honoring our parents is good, that disloyalty is bad,

---

84 I.e., the method of thwarting by means of an obstacle.

85 He is probably referring to his concise presentation of Plato's *Laws*, but maybe also to the second parts of his *Opinions* and *Principles*.

and that justice is a virtue. It is also like the knowledge [imparted by] medicine of what produces healthiness.

28.   The perfection of what can be known and acted upon is that it be acted upon. Whenever knowledge of these things comes about and is not immediately followed by action, it is purposeless knowledge lacking [74] benefit. The perfection of what can be known but *not* acted upon by people is simply that it be known. For both types of knowledge, there are disciplines for mastering them. Learning the type of knowledge that can be known but not acted upon is acquired only through disciplines that impart knowledge of what is known and not acted upon. The knowledge that can be known and acted upon is imparted by other disciplines. Thus, there are two types of disciplines: in one type we acquire knowledge of what can be known only; in the other type we acquire knowledge of what can be acted upon as well as the ability to do it. The disciplines that afford us whatever knowledge can be acted upon as well as the capability to do it are of two types. By means of one type people learn to comport themselves in cities; such disciplines include, for example, medicine, commerce, navigation,ʳ etc. By means of the other type people learn to comport themselves in ways of individual behavior—namely, whichever is the most excellent way—and how to discern pious and good actions, as well as the ability to undertake them.

29.   [75] Each of these three [types of] disciplines has a human aim, by which I mean the aim that is specific to people.ˢ There are three human aims: the pleasurable, the beneficial, and the noble, where the beneficial is so either in terms of the pleasurable or the noble. The aim of the disciplines with which people comport themselves in social groups is the beneficial—as alsoᵗ [in the discipline] that discerns the ways of personal behavior—and through them [people] acquire the ability to do what is good for them. The aim of these disciplines is also the noble, due to the fact that they produce certainty of the truth, knowledge of the truth and certainty being undeniably noble. It thus results that the aim of all disciplines is either the noble or the beneficial, and therefore there are in fact two types of disciplines: one in which the aim is to obtain the noble, another in which the aim is to obtain the beneficial. The discipline that has the noble as its sole aim is called philosophy or, generally, wisdom. None of the disciplines that have the beneficial as their aim are called philosophy, though some of them might be given this name in the sense that they [76] imitate philosophy.

30.   Now since the noble is of two types—one that is knowledge only, the other that is knowledge and action—the discipline of philosophy is of two types. With one type, [people] obtain knowledge of existing things, which people do not act upon; this is called theoretical philosophy.[86] With the second type, [people] obtain knowledge of the things that can be acted upon as well as the ability to do that which is noble of [those things]; this is called practical philosophy and social philosophy.[87] Theoretical

---

[86] I.e., scientific knowledge.

[87] "Social philosophy," lit. philosophy pertaining to cities, *falsafa madaniya*.

philosophy comprises three types of sciences: mathematics, the natural sciences, and metaphysics. Each of these sciences treats one type of the existing things, the nature of which is that they be known only; but there is no need for us here to acquire knowledge of each type of the existing things that the three sciences contain. Mathematics includes arithmetic, geometry, and optics. Social philosophy is of two types. The first produces knowledge of the noble actions and the dispositions that produce them, as well as power over their causes, whereby we come to possess the noble [dispositions]; this is called the discipline of ethics. The second type comprises knowledge of the factors [77] that produce noble dispositions for city-dwelling people, as well as the ability to acquire and preserve them; this is called the philosophy of governance. These, then, are the divisions of the disciplines of philosophy.

31.   Since we attain happiness only when we come to possess the noble disposi-tions, and since the noble dispositions become our property only through the disci-pline of philosophy, it necessarily follows that philosophy is the means by which we attain happiness. This is what we acquire through excellent discernment. Since phi-losophy comes about only through excellent discernment, and excellent discernment comes about only by the potentiality of the mind to perceive what is correct, the potentiality of the mind belongs to us prior to all of this. The potentiality of the mind belongs to us precisely in as much as we have a faculty through which we perceive with certainty that the truth is the truth and thereby adhere to it with conviction, and that the false is the false and thereby avoid it, as well as that through which we perceive the false [conviction] that resembles the truth and thereby do not err with regard to it, and perceive that which is in itself the truth—even if it has been made to resemble the false—and thereby neither err in it nor are deceived about it. The discipline through which we make use of this faculty is called logic.

32.   This discipline [of logic] is the means to understanding what is true convic-tion and what is false conviction; what [78] the things are that lead a person to the truth, and what the things are that lead a person to depart from the truth; what the things are that lead a person to suppose that the true conviction is a false conviction; and what the things are that lead a person to imagine[u] the false conviction in the form of the true conviction, thereby causing the mind to fall into the false conviction without realizing it. [It is also] the means by which a person can eliminate the false conviction from his mind whenever he happens to have a false conviction without realizing it, and by which he can eliminate the false conviction from [the mind of] someone else if that person has fallen into it without realizing it. As a result [of this], if a person wants to discover information about any object of scientific investigation, he employs the things that allow him to hit upon what is correct about his object of investigation, and whenever he holds a conviction about something the correctness of which he might doubt, he can examine it in order to become certain as to whether it is correct or not, and in the course of that [examination], whenever he falls into an error without realizing it, he can immediately eliminate the error from his mind. Now, since this discipline is as we have described, it necessarily follows that attention to it must precede attention to the other disciplines.

33.   Since some of the virtues that man has are more specific to him and others less so, and since the virtue most specific to man is his act of intellecting—given that the thing that makes man man is intellect—and since that virtue that the discipline of logic teaches man is the act of intellecting, this discipline provides man the virtue most specific to him.

34.   [79] The term "intellect" is sometimes applied to man's act of perceiving something by means of his mind, and other times it is applied to the thing through which man perceives. The thing through which man perceives—which is called "intellect"—was customarily called "*logos*" by the ancient philosophers. The term "*logos*" may also denote "organized expression with the tongue" [that is, speech] and it is in this sense that most people understand the term "*logos*"—in other words, this is the commonly accepted sense of the term. According to the ancient scholars of this science, this term has both meanings, and it is perhaps true of man that he is *logikos* in both senses, by which I mean that he expresses himself, and that he has something by which he perceives. However, what the ancient scholars meant when they said that man is *logikos* is that he has something by means of which he perceives that which he aims to discover.

35.   Since this discipline gives *logos* its perfection, it is called logic, and that by which man perceives what he aims to discover is^v also sometimes called the "*logikos*" part of the soul, and so logic is that by which the *logikos* part of the soul obtains its perfection. Since the term "logic" is sometimes used to mean "expressing with the tongue,"^w many people assume that the aim of this discipline is to give man knowledge about correct expression, but this is not the case.[88] It is rather the case that the discipline that imparts knowledge of correct expression and the ability to do so is grammar. [80] The reason for this error is the simple homonymy in the aim of grammar and the aim of this discipline, since both are called "*manṭiq*." However, of the two meanings signified by the term *manṭiq*, what is meant with respect to this discipline is one of them and not the other. Now there is indeed a certain similarity between grammar and logic, in that grammar imparts knowledge of the correct way to speak and the ability to do so according to the custom of those who speak a given language, and logic imparts knowledge of the correct way to think and the ability to come into possession of what is correct with respect to the objects of thought. Just as grammar correctly orders the tongue so that it utters only that which is correct according to the habits of those who speak a given language, so too logic orders the mind so that it thinks only that which is correct about everything. By way of summary, then, the relation of grammar to utterances is like the relation of logic to intelligibles, and so

---

[88] The most notable instance of this assumption is the famous debate between Abū Bishr Mattā and Abū Saʿīd as-Sīrāfī concerning the usefulness of Greek logic; for an English translation of the transcription of that debate, see David S. Margoliouth, "The Discussion between Abū Bishr Mattā and Abū Saʿīd as-Sīrāfī on the Merits of Logic and Grammar," 79–129.

this constitutes a certain similarity between them. But as for whether each of them *is* the other, or whether each one includes the other, [the answer is]: No.

36.   The path to happiness, the way to pursue that path, and the steps in what one should pursue [on that path] have been made clear by this discussion. Thus, the first step is to obtain logic. Now, since this is the first of all the scientific disciplines that one should pursue, and since [81] any discipline can be pursued only when, in addition to one actually studying it, there are certain things that can be used to expose what that discipline contains, we perhaps should first learn about the things that must be employed to expose what that discipline comprises, that is, the things that one will have to possess prior to embarking upon the discipline—which is why they are sometimes called first principles with which one sets out in a discipline. The things that a person knows include those that, no one can take away from him his knowledge of them (as long as he is of sound mind); for example, that the whole of something is more and greater than its parts, and that "man" is not "horse." These are called common knowledge and accepted principles and are such that even if a person denied them with his tongue, he could not deny them in his mind, since assenting to their opposites[x] simply could not occur to him. [Things that a person can know] also include what only some people know[y] and not others, and these include some that can easily be understood. Still others are such that the majority of people do not know them; rather, they are learned only by discursive thinking, but we can come to know them through those principles of which no one can be deprived.

37.   Since logic is the first thing one pursues [82] in a scientific manner, it necessarily follows that the principles pursued are knowable things that man knows beforehand and that no one can take away from him. There are many such things, but not just any random thing can be employed in any given discipline. On the contrary, one specific type is used in one discipline, and another specific type is used in another discipline. Therefore, the type of those things that is best suited to logic alone should be present, and the rest should be left for the other disciplines.

38.   All of these things the knowledge of which no one can take away are connate to man's mind from the beginning of his existence. While he is sometimes unaware of what is in his mind, once he hears the term that signifies it, he immediately becomes aware that it has been in his mind all along. Equally, sometimes these things are not distinctly separated from one another in his mind in such a way that he sees each of them in his mind independently of one another, but then the minute he hears the congeneric terms that signify them, he sees them distinctly separated from one another in his mind. Consequently, for any of [the principles] that he may not be aware of or may not perceive independently of one another, the terms signifying them should be enumerated so that then he will be aware of them and see each of them independently. Most of [83] the things with which one can begin to study logic are not perceived according to their logical differences, although they are in man's mind. Thus, in as much as our aim is to direct attention to them, we should list the types of terms that signify the types of intelligibles, so that when one becomes aware of these intelligibles

and sees each of them separately, he can then extract the intelligibles that can be employed in the exposition of this discipline.[89]

39.   Since it is the discipline of grammar that contains the types of signifying terms, it must be sufficient on its own to determine and direct attention to the principles of [logic]. Therefore, we should take from grammar an amount sufficient to direct attention to the principles of [logic], or take upon ourselves a proper enumeration of the types of terms that the speakers of the language customarily use to signify the things [logic] contains, if it should so happen that the speakers of that language do not themselves have a discipline that enumerates the types of terms in their language. This explains the [84] task of anyone who prefaces the introduction to logic with things taken in sufficient amount from grammar. As a matter of fact, the truth is that he employs whatever is necessary to make the task of teaching easy. Anyone who proceeds differently has been remiss or has neglected the discipline's order of presentation.

40.   Since we intend to adhere to the order of presentation required by the discipline, we should preface one of the books of the ancients[90] that facilitates introduction to this discipline with an enumeration of the types of signifying terms. We should begin with [this enumeration], making it follow[z] this book.[91]

---

[89] This is a reference to al-Fārābī's work, M. Mahdi, ed., *The Terms Employed in Logic* (*al-Alfāẓ al-mustaʿmala fī l-Manṭiq*).

[90] Al-Fārābī refers here to Porphyry's *Eisagōgē*; see our translation of al-Fārābī's version of this work, 55–63.

[91] Thus, the order of works al-Fārābī envisions here is: his own *Terms Employed in Logic*; his own version of Porphyry's *Eisagōgē*; and then *Categories*, the first book of the Aristotelian *Organon*.

BAGHDAD PERIPATETICS

The Baghdad Peripatetics included among their numbers such figures as Abū Bishr Mattá, Abū Naṣr al-Fārābī, Yaḥyá ibn ʿAdī, Abū Sulaymān as-Sijistānī, Ibn as-Samḥ, and Abū Ḥayyān at-Tawḥidī, as well as, with certain reservations, Abū l-Ḥasan al-ʿĀmiri. As one might expect, they were centered in Baghdad, then the capital of the ʿAbbasid Caliphate, and the period of their activity extends approximately between 870 and 1023. As a general rule, their work focused on aspects of Aristotelian logic, yet all of them also wrote treatises on subjects other than logic, although usually from an Aristotelian perspective, as is witnessed in the selections included here. These readings are taken from Abū Bishr Mattá's commentary on Aristotle's *Physics*; selections from Yaḥyá ibn ʿAdī's treatise on the nature of possibles (parts of which, though not included here, are in fact a commentary on Aristotle's *On Interpretation* 9); and finally, Abū Sulaymān as-Sijistānī's treatise *On the Proper Perfection of the Human Species*, which is a work of philosophical psychology very much in an Aristotelian vein.

The "founder" of the Baghdad Peripatetics was the Nestorian Christian Abū Bishr Mattá (d. 940), who was of Syriac origin. He was both a logician and translator of some of Aristotle's logical works, as well as the teacher of al-Fārābī, Yaḥyá ibn ʿAdī, and Abū Sulaymān as-Sijistānī. Abū Bishr Mattá is perhaps best known for his famous debate with the Arabic grammarian Abū Saʿīd as-Sīrāfī concerning the value of "Greek" logic within an Arabic milieu. The debate took place in Baghdad in 932, and by all accounts as-Sīrāfī took the day. Abū Bishr Mattá had argued that logic is a "tool" that is universal in its scope and application. As such, logic can be used to judge the correctness of a discourse regardless of the specific grammar, such as Arabic grammar, used to convey the ideas. As-Sīrāfī responded that there is no "universal logic" that is distinct from the rules of a particular language. As such, Greek logic is really nothing more than Greek grammar dressed up in philosophical clothing. Arabic speakers, concluded as-Sīrāfī, would be better served by appealing to the highly sophisticated linguistic theories of the Arabic grammarians rather than Greek linguistic intrusions. In addition to interests in logic, Abū Bishr Mattá also wrote on aspects of Aristotle's *Physics* and *On the Heavens*, and seems to have had a part in the translation of Aristotle's *Metaphysics*. The readings here concern the issue of material necessity as it is found in Abū Bishr's commentary of Aristotle's *Physics*.

Abū Zakariyā Yaḥyá ibn ʿAdī (d. 974), like Abū Bishr Mattá, was a Syriac Christian, although of the Jacobite persuasion, and a translator of Aristotle's *Sophistical Refutations*. He was a student of both Abū Bishr and al-Fārābī, and like both of his teachers he had a particular interest in the relation among logic, language, and grammar. In addition to logical issues, he was interested in epistemology and wrote as well on Christian theological questions and ethics. He in his turn was the teacher for nearly all the subsequent Baghdad philosophers active at the beginning of the eleventh century. His students included such figures as Abū Sulaymān as-Sijistānī, at-Tawḥīdī, Ibn as-Samḥ, ʿĪsā ibn ʿAlī, Ibn Zurʿah, Ibn Suwār and Ibn Abī Saʿīd. The treatise, *Establishing the Nature of the Possible*, part of which is translated here, shows Yaḥyá ibn ʿAdī combining his interests in logic and theological questions.

The Muslim philosopher Abū Sulaymān Muhammad ibn Ṭāhir ibn Bahrām as-Sijistānī, known as "the Logician" (al-Manṭiqī). (ca. 912–985) had been a student of both Yaḥyá ibn ʿAdī and Abū Bishr Mattá. With the death of Yaḥyá ibn ʿAdī, the leadership of the Baghdad Peripatetics, it would seem, fell to as-Sijistānī who, unlike either Abū Bishr Mattá or Yaḥyá ibn ʿAdī, set aside the task of editing and commenting on the works of Aristotle and instead took up the project of introducing Aristotelian modes of thought to a wider audience, which would include theologians, grammarians, lawyers, and humanists. The treatise *On the Proper Perfection of the Human Species* is a case in point. Addressed to the Būyid ruler ʿAḍud ad-Dawla (r. 949–983), the work ostensibly is a discussion of the traits of the perfect human and the claim that in his time ʿAḍud ad-Dawla is the individual in whom all these perfections appear, but the work is also equally a piece of Aristotelian psychology.

I. ABŪ BISHR MATTÁ

Selections from *Commentary on Aristotle's* Physics II 7–9[a]

AD II 7, 198A14FF. THE FOUR CAUSES

1. [137] Matter, for example, [accounts for] why the body of the animal is subject to corruption: because it is a composite of the four elements. Now in mathematics, [the explanation for] why this line is straight is because it is a subject according to which any one of the points along it lies evenly with another, where this is the definition and form of [a straight line].[1] Also, when it is asked, "Why are two lines that extend from the center [of a circle] to the circumference equal?" it is said, "Because they extend from the center to the circumference, [which is the form and definition of a circle]."[2] So in mathematics, one answers by mentioning the form, where the "why" has occurred as a result of it, because mathematics is what is conceptualized in the soul free of matter. So [in mathematics] the why-question occurs as a result of [a form], while not being directed towards a final [cause] owing to its lack of motion. As for natural things, they include [both] matter and form and have a final and efficient cause, and so the why-question is frequently directed towards all of these [that is, the material, formal, efficient, and final causes].

---

[1] See Euclid's *Elements*, Book I, definition 4.

[2] Euclid defines a *circle* as "a plane figure contained by one line such that all the straight lines falling upon it from one point among those lying within the figure equal one another" (*Elements*, Book I, definition 15).

2. [138] Natural science concerns knowing these causes and reducing the answer to the why-question to them. So sometimes [the answer] reduces to the proximate matter, and then those [matters] that are subsequent to it until they terminate at [prime] matter. When it reduces to the form, let it reduce to the material form, not the absolute [form], and to some given end (because the first principle in a certain way is a final cause), and to the moved efficient cause (because the discussion concerning the unmoved efficient cause does not belong to natural science).

3. [139] Concerning natural [causes], three of them ultimately reduce to one; for the motion of the semen, [for instance], ultimately reduces to the soul, when [the soul] and the form of the agent's organs are one in definition, and likewise it is an end, namely, the form of human. These three, then, have reduced to one. Abū ʿAmr asked Abū Bishr, "Why does [Aristotle] say that they [reduce to one] "for the most part" [instead of "always"]?" He said, "It may be [for example] that hair is not made for the sake of the form, as in the case of whiskers, but instead is for the sake of being embellished by them, and the same holds in the case of eyebrows, whereas pubic hair is necessary through a cause of necessity, namely, because it provides covering. [Again] the Sun and man are equally one and the same with respect to the form of body [that is, inasmuch as they are bodies], but the Sun is bereft of all other causes, because it is unaffected by whatever it affects since it has no matter; however, it has something like matter—where 'matter' is that which is susceptible to affectation—and so it might receive the transmitted form that is simple."

4. [140] Whoever has scientific knowledge about the universal things subject to corruption [knows] (1) whichever form it is [that came to be] before any [other] form; for example, the vegetative form[b] that came to be in the semen and thereafter some other form came to be. [He also knows] (2) whatever matter is before any matter, since the natural [philosopher] answers with the proximate material and then the next proximate [material] until he reaches prime matter. [Finally], (3) with respect to the efficient causes, [he knows] the first of them, and then that which is before it until he reaches the first efficient cause.

5. [141] In most natural things the form is the final [cause], but in some of them there is another final [cause]. [For example], the reason why there is a human is because he is a rational animal, whereas the reason why he is created with reason is in order that the First Principle is intellected. The form of a thing is its essence, because the thing is what it is through its form, whereas the matter only is attached to it. Because [Aristotle] wanted to explain that nature acts only for the sake of something, we should also know the final [cause] of the form.

6. The Heavens' rotation results from the efficient cause always [and] without exception, while human's coming from semen is for the most part.[3] Premises are matter for the syllogism, and because of this the production of the conclusion from them is deemed to be something like what is due to matter. The final [cause] and

---

3 While things in the heavens happen always (and so necessarily), things here on Earth happen only with a high degree of probability or "for the most part."

form of something are not the absolute best but are the best for that thing, and the same holds for every material form.

AD II 8, 198B10FF. THE FINAL CAUSE IN NATURE

7. [143] [Here, Aristotle] is investigating the necessary: whether (1) it is the matter, while the form is conditional [on the matter], so that when the matter is in such and such a state the existence of the form is necessary, [or whether] (2) the necessary is the form while the matter is conditional, so that when the form is something that invariably is, then necessarily the matter is in such and such a state. The ancient natural philosophers make the necessary the material's being in such and such a state, so they say, [for example], that there was the form of human precisely because the elements were in such and such a state, and that the front teeth were sharp because the material from which they were formed was thin. Although Anaxagoras mentioned Intellect along with the matter, he did not give it its full due, because when he was asked, "Why is the man sad and happy?" he responded with the matter, saying, "Because the homeomerous parts are in such and such a state."[4] Democritus made the cause of existing things the form of the matter and its being in a certain state, and so he said that the cause of fire is the elements' spherical form and the cause of earth is the elements' cuboidal form. Aristotle deemed [that] the necessity of the form required that the matter be in such and such a state, so he said that since [the form] requires that [the matter] comes to be[c] with, [for example], the human form's coming to be, the elements will be in such and such a state. Also, since the teeth are invariably sharp in order to eat with them, the matter is in such and such a state, because given that the matter is in such and such a state, that is, thin, the front teeth must be thin, and moreover, that turns out to have been useful for cutting up food. He likewise says that given that the form of the house is invariable, the matter must exist. If the form were reducible to the matter so that owing to the necessity of the matter the form must exist, then when the matter of the house exists, it would be necessary that its form exists, because its matter exists in such a state. As it is, however, since according to his account the form's necessity is in the form of [the house], demanding the necessity of the matter, when the form of the house comes to be, its matter must come to be in such and such a state.

8. [144] Empedocles said that to act for the sake of something is neither in nature's being nor in nature's nature, whereas Aristotle believes that [nature] does act for the sake of something; for it is directed towards it and so makes the thing in accordance with the matter. So when the matter of the teeth is thin, the teeth are thin, which is useful for cutting up food, and the nature [of the teeth] acts for the sake of cutting up the food. Also, [nature] makes vapor rise and descend not in order to make the crops grow but in order to balance the air and so help animals reproduce. Sometimes [nature] makes something have more than is needed, like the second hand

---

4 Cf. Plato, *Phaedo* 97D–98D.

to use in lifting and in order to be a replacement for the loss of the other hand. Also, [nature] adapts the [extra] phlegm and fat in order that the body is nourished by them when food is absent, and so [the body] is maintained.

9. [146] Whatever is always or for the most part is not by chance, and whatever is not by chance is for the sake of something; hence, whatever is always or for the most part is for the sake of something. Now the front teeth are always or for the most part sharp, and so they are for the sake of something. [148] When you attentively consider the stars and their rotations, you find [that] that is something well-defined [and] perpetual, and [similarly] you know that spring, winter, fall, and summer in their times are not by chance, but that they have a moving cause, [which] is either external or in fact a nature and a predisposition in the thing itself. Nature, then, acts in accordance with that predisposition to a given end. Aristotle said that since these things are infinite, it necessarily follows that there is a power without a limit, that is, an infinite [power]. Now the whole of the cosmos is finite, whereas what is infinite cannot be in the finite, thus the nature of the infinite power must be distinct from these natures.

10. Just as the animate thing acts, so does what is by nature, and this is without exception. [That is] because when the form is posited, then inevitably [both] the matter and the predisposition existing in [the matter] exist, whereas the converse is not the case. In other words, there might be the predisposition of the matter when the form does not exist, since some obstacle impeded it. Thus in crafts, the bed is made from the wood, because [the wood] is predisposed to that, whereas it need not be the case that by the existence of the predisposition, the bed occurs. [Also] boats continue their voyage until they reach the shore and then stop, in which case we know that their voyage is for the sake of this end. Artificial things [then] are only for the sake of something, such as the house. Now if the nature were something external like a craft, and craft [were something internal like] nature, then the two would act just as they currently act. So since a craft acts only for the sake of something, nature does as well. In other words, the craft [of building, for example], makes heavy things the foundation of the house and puts the light things on top, and were a house [to come to be] by nature, it would likewise [come to be] in this way.

11. [149] A bed comes from wood only because [the wood] is naturally disposed to that, and likewise a human comes from semen only because it is naturally disposed to receive the soul. Medicine completes nature's shortcoming and is for the sake of health, and so the nature that medicine completes is also for the sake of health. Craft draws upon nature in making hexagons, [150] such as the hexagons of bees[d] and [other] hexagons that come to be from nature for the sake of something, and so what it draws upon is such. The beginnings of a craft are for the sake of the outcomes, namely, the end, and so likewise[e] the beginnings of nature are like the semen's changing in order to receive the soul.

12. [151] I do not mean by "active nature" either matter or form, but rather the nature that is disseminated into the generated things that bring about generation. That is because, by the generable and corruptible body's coming into contact with

the heavenly body, [the heavenly body] affects it through this nature, and that [heavenly] body [is affected by] another body and the other by the motion of the Creator, like the excellent action of the excellent individual. Now this nature is in the semen that is emitted, and when it is present in the womb it receives a form and then another form (in which case that other form, I mean the first, passes away), and again another form, until the time when the soul comes to be present, [and] then this nature ceases to produce motion. After that [the soul] exists as an organizing and generative principle. This [active] nature does not act by assimilating, that is to say, bone is not from bone. As for the nature that does assimilate, it is the nature that is in the human body, digesting food by breaking it up into blood, flesh, and bone. So all of these forms[f] that [exist] between the beginning of the semen up to the time that the soul comes to be are like the matter for the soul's coming to be, because they are necessary for the soul's existence and they are generated for its sake. The sense of my argument that the nature's being is to act for the sake of something is that [the nature] is naturally disposed to do whatever it does for the sake of something.

13.   [152] The end is predicated of the form, which is the nature, and is predicated of the form's action and what is affected and brought about by it. Aristotle's discussion here concerns the end that is the nature, where the nature is the form, not the form's act.

14.   [153] Error occurs in a craft in two ways: one of them is from a slip of the hand and the incompetent individual. [For example], the hand of the shoemaker may slip and cut the leather at a place where he should not cut it, and so a shoe is not produced from what was made; or he erroneously thinks that he has cut the leather at the place where he should, but that place is not where he should cut it. [The second way] that error occurs is from the matter's lack of suitability. The leather can be unsuitable, [for example], since it droops from excessive weight when [the shoemaker] cuts it, and so it does not cut straight, or [again] the fibers are extremely hard and so the knife does not penetrate it. The mistake that occurs in nature is from the unsuitability of the material, not from the first option, because [nature] does not deliberate.

15.   [155] Imperfection in plants is more frequent than in animals, owing to the recalcitrance of the matter. Thus, it is not as clear that they are generated for the sake of something as that is in the case of animals. Now when plants are for the sake of something, and it is not allowed that they occur by chance ([for example], there are no grape-headed olive trees!), then animals will be all the more suited to that, owing to the fact that the generation of the animal is from a determinate starting point to a determinate end point, since not [just] any animal comes to be from [just] any matter. Quite the contrary, the donkey comes to be from a determinate matter, namely, donkey semen, not from any semen as chance has it; nor does [the semen of the donkey] arrive at [just] any form as chance has it, but at the form of the donkey.

16.   [156] The man's going to the market and meeting the debtor who settles his debt with him is by luck, because even if he did not intend to meet the debtor, he could have intended to do so, because were it not possible to intend to do so, it

would not be by luck. Now what is by luck is rare, whereas what is by nature is always or for the most part, and so is not by luck.

AD II 9, 199B34FF. THE NECESSARY IN NATURE

17.   [159] It has become clear that the form was not for the sake of the necessity of the matter, which is the sense of [Aristotle's] saying "hypothetical," that is, on the hypothesis of the necessity of matter. An example [of where the form would have been for the sake of the matter would be if] the human body were in such and such a state because the hot and cold are in such and such a state, and the front teeth were sharp because the bone from which they were composed is thin, which is what the ancients had thought. [Aristotle, conversely,] believes that the matter was in such and such a state precisely because the form is in such and such a state, which is the sense of his saying "absolutely," that is, the form was absolutely, not on the hypothesis of the matter. So because the front teeth *are* sharp, the thinness of the bones[5] from which they are composed must have preceded them; and because the human body is in such and such a state, the hot and cold must be in such and such a state. Owing to this, [namely], when the teeth are sharp, that, [namely, thinness] must be in the bones, whereas it is not the case that whenever the bones are thin, the sharpness of the teeth inevitably exists. It is just as when the house exists in such and such a state, then the heavier material must be lower and the lighter material higher up, while it is not the case that when the heavy and light materials exist—both of which are the matter— the house must exist. If the form were for the sake of the necessity of the matter, then, when the matter exists, it would be necessary that the form exists. Still, upon my life, the matter's existing in such and such a state is a cause, but a material [cause], whereas the form is a final cause. The existence of the end is not made necessary by the existence of the matter; rather, when the end exists, then inevitably there is the earlier existence of the matter. In [Aristotle's] opinion, the efficient cause is the nature belonging to the sharpness of the teeth, where [the nature] belonging to the bone is for the sake of the teeth's sharpness. [160] So the necessity of the form of sharpness is for the sake of that act which is so described, namely, that for the sake of which there is the form of sharpness.

18.   [161] Between mathematics and the natural sciences there is a similarity, but it is just the reverse. That is because the premises are the matter of the [mathematical] proof and the conclusion is the end, where the existence of the premises necessitates the existence of the conclusion, whereas the existence of the conclusion does not necessitate the existence of the premises, because one can conclude from different premises. Still, he means by "premises" the premises that produce [the conclusion], and that whenever the conclusion is not, those are not. In mathematics it is inevitable that the middle [term] is the same, but the two extremes are different if they produce the conclusion by different premises. [The case is different in the natural sciences, as

---

[5] By "thinness of the bones" Abū Bishr means the matter.

for example,] in proving that human is an animal, we have argued that by means of two middle terms: sometimes through "having senses" and sometimes through "having reason." In the natural sciences, then, the end is that which necessitates that the existence of the matter had preceded it, and [yet] the existence of the matter does not necessitate the occurrence of the end.

19.   [162] Whatever the end is in the crafts is a starting point for discursive thought. In other words, [for example], what thought initially begins with is [the idea of] shelter and [only] thereafter with the [idea of] the form of the house, whereas production [begins] with the last thing thought, namely, the foundation.[6]

20.   [164] Because the form is material the matter is taken into account in its definition, when the definition is complete, whereas the dialectical [definitions] do not take into account the matter in the definition. I [Abū ʿAmr?] asked Abū Bishr, "Is the act that issues from the form always taken into account in the definitions [used in] natural science?" He said: "Perhaps it is taken into account because the act is a form in a certain way. So when the act is taken into account, the form from which that act comes to be as well as its matter are taken into account, since it is material. For example, it is taken into account in defining the act of sawing, which is to saw, and so the teeth, that is, a matter, are taken into account in the definition of the act of the saw." Then it was asked of him, "and so we define the act in all of the natural sciences?" and he said that it seems so.

II.   YAḤYÁ IBN ʿADĪ[a]

Selection from *Establishing the Nature of the Possible*

1.   [65] *I.1: Enumerating the kinds of claims made by those investigating the object of inquiry concerning [the nature of the possible].* Theorists differ concerning the possible. Some of them asserted its existence and admitted that there are things whose existence and nonexistence is possible. Others denied its existence and said that everything is necessary, and concerning [the necessary], there is nothing in it whose existence and nonexistence is possible. Despite their difference concerning this, they agreed that everything judged to exist or not exist at either some past or present time does not have the nature of the possible existing in it. The difference between them only concerns the nature of the possible in what is judged to exist or not exist at some future time, such as, for example, so-and-so or Zayd's walking tomorrow.

2.   [66] *I.2: The refutation of [the nature of the possible] from the proofs of those opposing its reality.* In order to validate its claim the latter group presented several proofs; the stronger of them get at the heart of the matter, whereas the more obscure of them are sophistry. There are two proofs: the first of them has its origin and source in the Creator's foreknowledge (great and exalted is His name beyond whatever the

---

[6] See S. M. Stern, "The First in Thought Is the Last in Action: The History of a Saying Attributed to Aristotle," 234–52.

misguided say). The other is taken from the necessary truth of one of two contradictories and the necessary falsity of the other. Thus, we shall refute the proof taken from [divine] foreknowledge . . .

3. *II. The strongest of the proofs for establishing and confirming the claim of those rejecting the truth.* They said that it is undoubtedly affirmed that the Creator (praised and exalted!) knows everything that exists and comes to be. It is not the case that He does not know and then later knows; rather, He eternally knows. Now one who knows truly knows only when he knows the things as they are. Thus, it necessarily follows that the state of the objects of knowledge must agree with the state of the one who knows them insofar as he knows them. The state of this knower [that is, God], insofar as He knows, is a necessary state since [His state of knowing] exists invariably and neither changes nor is changeable, and so the state of what He knows necessarily neither changes nor is changeable.

4. So, on the one hand, whatever He knows to exist, because He cannot change into one who knows its nonexistence, must exist necessarily, because it cannot change into something nonexisting. On the other hand, whatever He knows not to exist, because He cannot change into one who knows its existing, must necessarily not exist, because it cannot change into something existing. On account of the fact that He knows everything without exception and everything is known to Him, everything known to Him seemingly being necessary according to our explanation that the state of its existence or nonexistence cannot change, nothing can change the state of its existence or nonexistence. Whatever cannot change its state of existing or not existing, however, is not possible, and thus none of them is [67] possible. Therefore, there is nothing possible.

5. When there is nothing that is possible, then the nature of possibility [itself] does not exist, since should the nature of possibility exist, its existence would require certain things existing in which it exists, in which case certain things would exist as possible, but the impossibility of this has already been explained. [Whenever] something impossible necessarily follows upon some supposition, [the supposition itself] is impossible. Now this impossible thing necessarily followed precisely on the supposition of the existence of the nature of possibility. So the existence of possibility, then, is something impossible. This, which we have just explained, is the strongest of this group's proofs. We have strengthened it and made it convincing as much as was "possible" for us.

6. *III. The explanation of the basis of this proof and its refutation, which is divided into seven sections; III.1. The basis [of this proof] and an enumeration of the causes of everything that comes to be.* We shall pursue this by pointing out the basis upon which it was founded and the principle from which it arose. We say: Their presumption is precisely that [divine] foreknowledge is a necessary cause of the necessity of things. So, if it becomes clear that [divine foreknowledge] is not a cause of [necessity], then by undermining [the proof's] basis, its foundation collapses and is without its support owing to the deceitfulness of its principle. The explanation of that is to say that there are six causes: (1) a material cause, such as the gold of a golden signet ring; (2) a

formal cause, such as the roundness and [the ring's] hollowness; (3) an efficient cause, such as the one who crafts it; (4) a final cause, which is of two types: one of which is (4a) [the state of the ring's perfection] where the craftsman ceases working when he completes it, and this is the form itself in the subject (I mean the hollowness and roundness, albeit in the sense of it as a perfection, not the sense of it as the form); and the other (4b) is the beneficial use intended by matter's acquiring a form, like signing with [a signet ring]; (5) a paradigmatic cause, such as a form in the craftsman's soul by virtue of which there is his craft; and (6) an instrumental cause, such as the hammer used in his craft.

7.   *III.2. Repudiating that foreknowledge is a material cause of the necessity of things.* It is impossible that [God's foreknowledge] is a material cause. First, [this] is because the matter is only matter for something composed from it and from a certain form, but nothing exists that is a composite of this knowledge. Furthermore, [68] the matter exists in the very being of the composite thing, like the part's existing in the whole, but we do not find foreknowledge as a part of the necessity of things. Also, the form of every composite is nobler than its matter, but it belongs to the vilest calumny to say that the necessity of things is nobler than [divine] foreknowledge! So it has been explained that foreknowledge is not a material cause of the necessity <of things>.[b]

8.   *III.3. That it is not their formal cause.* It is also impossible that [divine foreknowledge] is a formal cause of [necessity], because the material form requires the matter for its subsistence and existence, just as the form of wine made from grapes requires the juice in order to exist. It is vile, however, to say that the necessity of things is prior to the foreknowledge.

9.   *III.4. That it is not their efficient cause.* [Divine foreknowledge] is also not the efficient cause, on the one hand, <because the efficient cause>[c] must do what it does by its nature, such as fire's activity is to heat nearby bodies that are disposed to its heating, and similarly the influence of sunlight on the air over which it rises.[d] [God's] knowledge cannot be an efficient cause in this way, because in this way the efficient cause and its effect are simultaneous, whereas this knowledge is prior to its effects.

10.   On the other hand, [efficient causes] acting by choice are only efficient causes that have the power to act and to refrain from acting on one and the same thing. This requires the possibility of existing, that is,[e] the power to make [some one thing] exist and not exist. This, however, refutes the necessity of things, because it is patently obvious that, on the one hand, the power is only to make whatever necessarily exists exist (not to make it not exist), and, on the other hand, the power is only to make whatever necessarily does not exist not exist (not to make it exist). In other words, whatever necessarily does not exist cannot exist, just as whatever necessarily exists cannot not exist. [69] So if this group requires an existing power that makes one and the same thing exist and not exist, then they must affirm what they had denied about the existence of the nature of the possible, since whatever falls within the scope of [the efficient cause's power] to make it exist or not exist is possible. In other words, the possible is nothing other than what might and might not exist in a given state.

11. Also, the state of the necessity of things vis-à-vis [divine] foreknowledge is contrary to the state of the effect vis-à-vis its efficient cause. That is because when in the imagination the existence of every efficient cause is eliminated before and simultaneous with the existence of its effect, then the existence of the effect must inevitably be eliminated. Now it is possible to imagine the elimination of the existence of foreknowledge before and simultaneously with the existence of necessary things, but the elimination of the necessity of necessary things need not be inevitable. The conclusion of these two premises in the second mood of the second figure [that is, Camestres], is that foreknowledge is not an efficient cause of the necessity of things.[7]

12. *III.5. That [divine foreknowledge] is not their final cause.* The knowledge cannot be a final cause of the necessity of things as well. That is because perfection, as we said, is of two kinds: a first and a second. The first of them is the form itself, which is like the first perfection belonging to writing, namely, when a form producing writing is complete and perfect, for instance, in the soul of Zayd, and so by it he becomes a writer. Foreknowledge cannot be perfection in this way, because every form requires its matter for its existence, and it is exceedingly deplorable to say about this knowledge that it requires the necessity of things for its existence.

13. Furthermore, the existence of this kind of perfection and what has a perfection are simultaneous, neither one of which is prior to the other, but to say that the necessity of things and this knowledge are simultaneous is odious. Despite this, the defenders of this doctrine recognize the priority of [divine] knowledge and its precedence over the necessity of things. So then clearly knowledge <is not>[f] in this way a final cause.

14. The second perfection, namely, the usefulness occurring in the one possessing the first perfection, is like the usefulness [70] occurring from the skill of writing, that is, the preservation of words and ideas and communicating with people at a distance from one another. Now it is impossible that this knowledge is a final cause in this way because this perfection temporally follows what has a given perfection. For example, the usefulness gained by the skill of writing, namely, the preservation of words and ideas and communicating with those at a distance, temporally follows the skill of writing that has become firmly established in the writer's soul. This knowledge, however, temporally precedes the necessity of things. So then the knowledge is not a final cause of the necessity of things.

15. *III.6. That it is not their instrumental cause.* It is also clear that [divine foreknowledge] is not an instrumental cause of [the necessity of things] from the fact that the nature of the instrument differs from the nature of the thing produced by it. In other words, if the nature of the two were one and the same, then it would be a formal[g]

---

7 Today, we would consider this argument an example of *modus tollens*: if x is an efficient cause of y, then the elimination of x entails the elimination of y; the elimination of God's foreknowledge does not entail the elimination of the necessity of things; therefore, God's foreknowledge is not an efficient cause of the necessity of things.

cause, not an instrumental cause. For example, concerning the instruments used in a craft, such as, for instance, the carpenter's adze, the nature differs from the nature of the door carved by it. As for natural instrumental causes, transparent air is an instrument for vision, but it is different in its nature from the nature of colors, which are the primary objects of vision.

16.   The form of the intelligible object is itself the knowledge, because knowledge is nothing but the form of the intelligible object in the soul of the knower. The distinction between them is only in that the soul of the knower is the subject in which the knowledge exists, whereas the matter is the subject of the form of the material intelligible object, just as we explained in the treatise that we composed to make clear what knowledge is.[8]

17.   Again, the instrument is of two kinds. One of them is that without which that which is produced would not be able to be produced. An example taken from natural instruments is the lung and respiration; for without [the lung], respiration, I mean inhaling and exhaling air, cannot exist. An example taken from artificial instruments is the lute, for without it the sound that is produced by it cannot come to be. Clearly, the necessity of things does not need knowledge about them in order to exist; for if they were imagined to be unknown, eliminating the knowledge of them would not necessarily eliminate them themselves. I certainly do not mean that the knowledge of them can be dispensed [71] with insofar as they are known; rather, I mean only that they do not need [to be known] in order to exist. Thus, knowledge is not an instrumental cause of the necessity of things according to this kind of instrument.

18.   The other kind of instrument is the sort that what is done by it can be done by another instrument; nevertheless, when one does the operation particular to it, [the instrument in question] is better and more efficient than when performed by another [instrument]. An example would be the scalpel and blood-letting; for it is possible to open veins with something other than the scalpel, as for example a dagger or a piece of glass. Still one opens them better with [the scalpel].

19.   Knowing the necessity of things adds nothing to them by its belonging to them as a judgment, and eliminating [the knowledge] that they have an instrument neither diminishes nor destroys them. We have made an exception in our claim that "they have an instrument" only to distinguish between knowledge's being an instrument and its being their paradigmatic cause. That is because when it is a paradigmatic cause in the soul of the knower, there is a useful definition for judging whatever action one intends to do; nevertheless, it is not like an instrument, but instead is a paradigmatic cause and is within the scope of the agent. So knowledge is not an instrumental cause of the necessity of things in this way.

20.   *III.7. That it is not a paradigmatic cause of the necessity of the possible things among them.* Once it is demonstrated that among existing things there is what exists as possible, it becomes clear that the knowledge is not a paradigmatic cause of the

---

[8] See *On the Attribution of Knowledge* in *Maqālāt Yaḥyá bin ʿAdī al-falsafīya*, Saḥbān Kalīfāt, ed., 185–87.

necessity of things that are in themselves possible. That is because when knowledge is only the form of the intelligible object in the knower and the form of these possibly existing things, as possible, is the possibility, then true possibility is something incompatible with necessity's two modes, [that is, necessity of existence and necessity of nonexistence]. That is because whatever is possible in this [sense of] "true possibility" is subject to existence, and so because of that it is incompatible with necessarily not existing; and whatever is subject to nonexistence is also consequently incompatible with necessarily existing. In no way whatsoever, then, is the form of necessity in possible things. Thus, it cannot be known as a necessity.

21.   That there are some possible things among existing things becomes clear, first, by describing the sense that is signified by the term "possible," and then by examining existing things. So if this sense is found among them, its existence will become clear,[h] and clear in such a way that [72] this knowledge plainly is not a paradigmatic cause of the necessity of possible things. By God's aid and the expedience of His help, we resolve to explain the existence of the possible after completing the refutation of this argument and explaining its source and method and pointing out the ways to be on guard against the errors in the investigation of [this issue].[9] So here let it be granted that it has been made clear, and by granting that it is plain that this knowledge is not a paradigmatic cause of the necessity of possible things, even if it is a paradigmatic cause of the necessity of things that are necessary among them.[i]

22.   By explaining this, then, this knowledge as causally necessitating all things is completely repudiated [and is done so] by a syllogism of the following form: any cause of the necessity of all things is either a material, formal, efficient, final, paradigmatic, or instrumental cause, but this knowledge is not a cause of the necessity of all things either materially, formally, efficiently, finally, paradigmatically, or instrumentally, and so this knowledge is not a cause of the necessity of things, which is what we wanted to make clear.

23.   *IV. As for the method of this error and the way of this sophistry, each one of the two* relata *are intertwined, connected with, and enter into the meaning of one another in a similar sense to the point that they cannot be distinguished in existence nor understood.* It is difficult to distinguish between (1) when the concomitants of things are taken in abstraction from the thing itself without an addition of a description, condition, or relation to something—in sum, when considered in themselves in abstraction on their own—and (2) when their concomitants are taken with a condition or the addition of a description or relation to something. Frequently, the concomitants of one and the same thing are different. In fact, when [one and the same thing] is taken according to one of the two situations, its concomitants are contradictory when [the thing] is taken according to the other situation. Still, even if they are hard to distinguish inasmuch as the distinction between them is hard to make owing to their extreme similarity as well as the obscurity and the intertwined nature of their differences, they are distinct in themselves and differ with respect to the properties of their descriptions.

---

[9] See pars. 41–44.

24.   [73] Whoever wants to explain their true natures needs sophistication and a trained eye for spotting hidden factors, an acute perception that goes to the heart of the problems, and a great strength for picking out sophistries. In seeking to lay hold of them, one also needs to investigate repeatedly, focus one's thought, have wolf-like patience in pursuing them, free oneself from fancy when pondering them, have intellectually sound judgment on one's path to them, and an ease of being bound to one's judgment about them.ʲ Perhaps by organizing this disorder that belongs to the two [types of concomitants], they would fulfill their functions and achieve that for which they are intended.

25.   Our discussion in this treatise only concerns this knowledge, and our goal is to distinguish between concomitants of [this knowledge] itself [considered] abstractly, and its concomitants [considered] along with the addition of descriptions, conditions, relations, and the knowledge of the nature of related things. It is difficult to distinguish the concomitants of things that possess certain relations from those of things that possess other relations, since they are not distinct in understanding or existence. Thus, we need to organize the described disorder before touching on the knowledge of them.

26.   Iᵏ shall speak about them as briefly as one can about that, that is, I, lest I use up my energy, shall reserve it to make their meanings more nearly understandable. I shall not turn aside from any path that seems to me to facilitate making them understandable, but shall follow it trusting God in that; for should I reach the intended goal, then praise to God and the success He has granted. Should I be incapable of it, then it is owing to my own weakness and limitations. I hope not to deprive myself of the reward of those who strive in conveying good and removing wrong, for there is no good more virtuous than knowing a truth nor a wrong more foul than believing a falsity. Even if failure hampers the power of the one who strives in reaching a good, his ardor is rewarded if he is of use and excused when he gives little.

27.   We say that this proof [for the necessity of things from divine foreknowl-edge] is based upon some premises that are false when taken universally, for example, the premise stating that it necessarily follows that the state of existence of the object of knowledge agrees in this state with the state of the knower, insofar as he is a knower; for when this premise is taken absolutely, it is false. That is because it is definitely not necessary that the existence of the object of knowledge agrees in all states of [agreement] with the one knowing it, insofar as he is a knower, [74]; for it is agreed that this eternal Knower's state of existence is everlasting,ˡ whereas the state of existence of the objects of knowledge is not such. If [the premise] is understood in some other applicable way of understanding it, then its advocate has taken what is initially sought concerning which there is a disagreement; for if one understands from it that the state of existence of the object of knowledge must be necessary just as the state of the knower is necessary, insofar as he is a knower, then this is false in the opinion of the one who demands possibility and is not granted. It is [the very issue] that is being examined and about which there is dispute! The sense according to which this premise is eter-

nally true requires that the states of the existence of the objects of knowledge agree in their form with what the knower [knows] of them paradigmatically. So it has become clear that this premise is false.

28.   The premise stating, "The state of the knower, insofar as he is a knower, is necessary since it is unchangeably fixed," is also false, when taken absolutely without condition. That is because "necessary" is not entailed of [the state] in every way, for that would be only if none of its descriptions change. This does not belong to [the state of the knower], since the relation of the knower to the object of knowledge, which exists in one state and not in another, is something that changes by the change of the state of what is known to exist and not exist. Even if the knower in himself does not change, the relation of the one knowing, for example, Zayd in the case of his existence, is a relation to his existence that is different from the relation of [the knower] to Zayd in the case of his nonexistence. The evidence of that is that the essence and being of each one of two related things, insofar as it is related, subsists only with its correlative, insofar as it is related to it. An example is that the essence and particular being of, for instance, Zayd, insofar as he is the father of, for instance, ʿAmr, subsists with ʿAmr insofar as he is his son. Whenever ʿAmr's filial relation is lost, then Zayd's paternal relation is lost, since Zayd does not exist as a father if ʿAmr does not exist as a son, nor is ʿAmr a son if Zayd does not exist as a father. One should know that we have substituted the example of *Zayd* for any father, and ʿ*Amr* for any son.

29.   Thus, the fact that the subject that has certain varying states is numerically one is definitely not enough in order [to show] that the knower, insofar as he is knower, is numerically one and unchanging [75] in every way. In other words, to know the existence of Zayd is numerically different from knowing the nonexistence of Zayd, even if the two, insofar as they are knowledge, are entirely one and the same thing, and even if the subject of the existence and nonexistence, Zayd, is numerically one. That is because knowledge is related to the object of knowledge, and the essence and particular existence of each one of the two related things, insofar as it is something related, subsist through the other; the existence of one can be only by the existence of the other as something related. Now the knowledge of Zayd's existence has no need, in its essence and particular being, for Zayd's nonexistence. Hence, to know Zayd's existence is not to know his nonexistence. Likewise, knowing merely the essence itself of Zayd is different from knowing the essence itself of the existent Zayd, because knowing the essence itself of Zayd abstracted from the description ["existent"] does not need, in its essence and particular being, "existent," whereas knowing the essence itself of the existent Zayd does need, in its essence and particular being, "existent." Thus, knowing the very essence of Zayd is not to know the very essence of the existent Zayd himself.

30.   It has become obvious that the relation of the knower to the object of knowledge, insofar as he is a knower, might change through the change of states of the object of knowledge, even if the knower himself does not change. Hence, when the claim "The knower does not change, insofar as he is a knower" is taken absolutely,

as it is in this proof, it is not true. So this example of ours makes it clear that this premise is false.

31. Also those advancing this proof must concede the falsity of the premise claiming that the state of the knower, as knower, agrees with the object of knowledge with respect to necessity and remaining in a single state. [They must do this] as a result of the very thing that they judged in this proof concerning the eternity of this Knower, insofar as It is a knower and that He did not become a knower after not being a knower. That is to say, since [God] never has nor will cease knowing the essence and particular being of Zayd, for instance, the permanence and everlasting continuation of [Zayd] as [God] knows him and the impossibility of [Zayd's] undergoing change is a necessary result of [God's] knowing him. Through the change of existing and not existing, the essence of Zayd as an existent is different from his essence as a nonexistent. That is something required owing to the change of the two essences, since Zayd might change from not existing to existing and from existing to not existing. So Zayd, that is, the object of knowledge, clearly must undergo change, but the state of the One knowing him does not change in Its particular being. This contradicts what they affirmed, while making necessary the very thing to which they consented in this proof.

32. [76] As long as the claim is not true that the state of the object of knowledge with respect to necessarily existing or not existing is like the state of the knower as [one who] understands, inasmuch as he is a knower, then what they hoped to conclude by it does not necessarily follow. Thus, we have fulfilled our promise to explain the weakness of this proof and to make obvious what leads to its error and the sophistical method resulting from it.

33. *V. Pointing out ways to be on guard and to defend oneself against error in investigating the true nature of what is sought.* Next, we shall point out ways to be on guard against the errors and pitfalls into which the investigators may slip and fall and be driven from the truth in this issue. They say that one of the ways to do that is neither to assume nor to grant that all of the states of the existence of the knower agree with all of the states of the object of knowledge, which is proven to be so by what we have already said.

34. A second way also is to point out that not every state from among the states of existence and nonexistence entailing Zayd's walking tomorrow[10] (when [Zayd's walking tomorrow] is considered in abstraction from every description) must belong to it permanently (when the description is any description whatsoever). In other words, when Zayd's walking tomorrow is not at all qualified by anything, it is something whose existing or not existing is possible according to what we shall explain. If a given description is added to it, as for example, his being chained to a column, the existence of this walk becomes impossible and necessarily does not exist. If another description is added to it, as for example, nothing hinders his walking, which he desires

---

10 Lit. "the determinate being (*dhāt*) of Zayd's walking tomorrow."

to do, then the existence of this walking becomes necessary, and it is impossible not to exist. Likewise, if Zayd's walking tomorrow is said to exist, then by the addition of this description it is outside[m] the scope of being possible and must be necessary. That is because the existent, when it is an existing thing, precludes not existing in that state, whereas when only Zayd's walking tomorrow is taken without adding what exists, it must be possible.

35.   A third way should also not be neglected and should be present in the mind of the one arguing for the existence [77] of the possible. It is [this]: saying that the objects of knowledge exist or do not exist is the same as saying that the things [themselves] exist or do not exist. In other words, when knowledge grasps the true natures of existing things inasmuch as they exist, which is the form in the soul of the knower, and the form of existence is as the existent thing is in the state with respect to which it exists, then saying of it that it is an object of knowledge is to say that it is some existing thing, and all the things truly said of it to exist cannot not exist with respect to that state.

36.   The same holds for nonexistence, for nonexisting things are nonexistents. Thus, saying that objects of knowledge agree with what is, [namely, the nonexistent in this case], is the same as saying that they do not exist, because what is is that they not exist. For this reason, possible existence is not truly said of them because the existence of the nonexistent thing is not possible from the fact that saying that the thing is something whose existence is possible is *not* the same as saying that the nonexistent thing is something whose existence is possible. [This is] because when the thing is described by nonexistence and the description is true of it, its existence is impossible.

37.   It should also be pointed out that those who submit that the necessity of Zayd's walking necessarily follows from the premise claiming, "The foreknowledge of all things accords with what is," have lumped together several numerically distinct pieces of knowledge under the term "knowing." That is because we cannot count the accidents of Zayd, who is one of many things. In fact it would not be far from the truth if we said that [Zayd's accidents] are virtually infinite. So how much more so would it be in the case of the accidents of all things?! The response that the respondent must give to the question is that the sense of a single thing is the sense of a single thing.

38.   If they are particular in saying that the foreknowledge of the state of Zayd's walking tomorrow, for example, is with respect to existence and nonexistence, we will point out that two different senses underlie this claim, because the sense of knowing Zayd's walking tomorrow, if "tomorrow" is understood as the time of the walk, is different from the sense of it if it is understood as the time of the knowledge. In other words, the senses of those things in abstraction are not their senses in their concrete particulars as qualified things, even if all the pieces of knowledge had been foreknown.

39.   [78] The way to approach the question that contains varying senses is not to answer it with a single response, but to separate out each one of the senses as a

single question. In addition, let us here point out that many pieces of knowledge have been lumped together in the term "knowing," because knowing the state of Zayd's walking tomorrow is not a single thing, if, setting aside the knowledge, the reckoning of the time of the walk is understood. Quite the contrary, the number of multiple pieces of knowledge is as many as the number of things known about the existing and nonexisting states of Zayd's walking; for knowing Zayd's walking tomorrow before tomorrow arrives is different from knowing it when it is present and different again from knowing it after tomorrow passes. The truth of this claim becomes clear on account of the fact that the existence or nonexistence of the state of Zayd's walking tomorrow before tomorrow is either necessary existence, [and so] would preclude nonexistence, or necessary nonexistence, [and so] would preclude existence, and each of these senses is different from the other. We have made it clear that the number of pieces of knowledge is equal to the number of objects of knowledge, and so knowing the states of Zayd's walking tomorrow is not numerically one piece of knowledge but is several pieces of knowledge. Thus, one should not answer with a single response to [a question containing] more than one [sense], even if it is true for each one of them to say that it is something foreknown; for when the question concerning knowledge is separated from these pieces of knowledge and in answering it the truth is hit upon, then neither the respondent will err nor the questioner be able to mislead [him].

40.   This ends what we shall say about the sophistry foisted on the investigator of this issue because of this proof, which is the strongest proof that we know of those opposing the truth.

41.   *VI. Establishing the true belief.* [. . .] This part concerns the intended goal of this treatise, namely, to explain the existence of the nature of the possible [79] and that possible things might exist. In fact, the time has come for us to explain the true nature of it, namely, among existing things there is what is possible.

42.   We say that the first thing one must begin with concerning the existence or nonexistence of any subject of inquiry <is>[n] to present concisely what the term signifies; for when that is presented concisely and followed by the examination of the things, then its investigation will be complete. So if its account is found among things, then it is necessarily established, whereas if it is not found, then its denial is entailed and its nonexistence is established. Therefore, we shall follow this method in this, the object of our investigation, namely, "Does the possible exist?"

43.   We call "possible" precisely what neither exists necessarily nor necessarily does not exist. Since in this description we have mentioned "necessary existence" and "necessary nonexistence," let us explain what we mean by each one in turn. We say that "necessary existence" is that whose existence is perpetual and simply does not not exist. "Necessary nonexistence" is that whose nonexistence is perpetual and simply does not exist. So, because the possible does not exist necessarily, and necessary existence is perpetual existence, the possible does not exist perpetually. In addition to the fact that the possible does not exist necessarily, because the possible also does not necessarily not exist, and necessary nonexistence is perpetual nonexistence, [the

possible] must not perpetually not exist. So combining these two syllogisms what becomes clear to us about the possible is that it neither exists perpetually nor does it not exist perpetually. This is the description of the possible and so we have concisely presented it.

44. Thus, let our investigation of it be complete by the examination of things; for if we find among them what neither exists perpetually nor does not exist perpetually, then we shall have found what we sought and have reached our intended goal. So we say that walking with respect to the human, for instance, does not exist perpetually, since a human might be found who is not walking, and this cannot be proven since it is self-evident. Likewise, [walking with respect to the human] does not perpetually not exist, because a human might be found who is walking, and this also is self-evident. Hence, it has been found that the walking of the human neither perpetually exists nor does it perpetually not exist, but whatever neither perpetually exists nor perpetually does not exist is possible. [80] So then the walking of the human is possible, and we have attained what we sought.

> The soundness of our belief has been validated by God's
> aid and the excellence of the success He grants.

III.   ABŪ SULAYMĀN AS-SIJISTĀNĪ

Selection from *On the Proper Perfection of the Human Species*[a]

1. [377] Praise God, Who creates the dawn [in] the gloom of nonexistence by the generous light of existence; Who establishes proofs of divinity and demonstrations of unity; Who refutes the sophistry of agnosticism and unbelief; Who brings to completion signs of the worlds' origination and the wonders of creation as evidence for the minds' eyes and external senses to see; that One Who gives everything its natural disposition, whether rational or dumb. He endowed with intellect the worthy among those who knelt and prostrated themselves and designated them Seraphim, Cherubim, and the Angelic choir standing in ranks as a testament for individuals of the human species—not for all, but rather for those whose vision is clear. He put [them] at the extreme limits and ordered things according to their rank from the beginning of body to the termination of the line belonging to surface, as well as quantity and what is numbered, and so something settled in a place did not exceed its place and nothing moving overcame[b] its contrary. If it does exceed its proper bounds, then to its station it returns. Every effect depends upon [378] its cause, and whatever has an end is led to its end. So the lower things are bound to the higher things, and potentialities enter one after another into the higher region [above] them. The universe is brought together by divine wisdom in a clearly discernible order that conserves the proper and general perfections of existing things. Among them, humans were conferred with the most beautiful form and most excellent shape, and so He properly balanced their humoral and elemental mixtures. From the overflow of His goodness and the light of His substantiality, He poured onto [humans] that by which their souls are illuminated

and from which their bodies are sustained. Then their power spread to all the kinds existing beneath them until through might and main they subjugated them. [God] provided them with knowledge of Himself that included the accounts and causes [of existing things]—from which they result, to which they go, that which is in them, and the manner in which they are, [that is, the efficient, final, material, and formal causes]—making clear the substance and essence of each one of them. By virtue of their knowledge and intellect [humans] express clearly His hidden reality.

2.   Since the goal of this treatise is to explain the perfection proper to the human species and to describe the individual that has appeared at this time in whom all the elements of that perfection are brought together, let our patron, the king, pay heed (may God prolong his dynasty, elevate his grandeur, and strengthen his reign!).[11] Concerning that [goal], one must indicate the account I mentioned, that is, the power originating from the Ultimate Principle: a power that flows over the faculties and souls until it reaches, with all of the excellence in it that can appear in this world, a pure soul, a chaste nature, and an intellect free from the taint of opinions and teachings that deviate from the truth. [Such a ruler] will then be entrusted with directing the world and governing its inhabitants through just practices. He will free them from the hands of rulers who have negated the influences of lawful opinions; who have done away with the regulations of civic authorities; who have allowed the bloodshed of citizens through the rivalry of important men; and who have sparked a fire in the souls of firebrands such that the contemptible among them rise up against the noble ones and the lowly of them against the prominent. He will then arrange them according to their rank and sort them in such a way that every person recognizes his station and stops at the proper place set before him, obediently recognizing the authority of whomever is above him and not tending to criticize whomever is superior to him in standing and leadership. So affairs will flow towards their ends, which have been set down by divine wisdom [379] and rational law. He will be a safeguard against misfortune and will preserve long-held possessions. All leaders will be brought into submission under a single leadership and single leader, since human leadership comes about solely by virtue of the faculty that rules over [all] faculties, whose inner workings are known to the [World] Soul that uses all that is in this world, manifesting its activities in the kinds of animals and providing each of their species with its proper perfection according to each of its faculties to the degree assigned to them in proportion to [their] excess, moderation, and deficiency. The [faculties] are assimilation, inclination, desire, sensation, imagination, estimation, conceptualization, discursive reasoning, opinion, intention, intuition, acumen, understanding, memory, recollection, enlightenment, conjecturing, knowing, and intellecting.

3.   Their cause has been divided into two divisions. So (1) some [animals] were equitably assigned a part [of sensation], namely touch, to which there is joined the powers of desire, inclination, and assimilation, and only through all of these being

---

11 The ruler mentioned is ʿAḍud ad-Dawla (r. 949–983).

present together can there be an animal. (A share of imagination was not assigned to them, since imagination only belongs to animals that have the perfect senses. In other words, [imagination] is also associated with the sense of sight in particular, and whatever lacks this sense, then in virtue of its lacking [this sense] it also lacks imagination.) Under this kind of animal there falls the snail, worm, and many insects. (2) Other [animals] were assigned all of the senses along with imagination, like the horse, ox, ass, etc. Some of [these animals] have, in addition to these [external senses], the estimative faculty and a hint of the faculty of conceptualization and discursive reasoning, like animals such as the so-called "monoped"[12] and the lion.[c] One of them, that is the human, has in addition to these, the faculties of conceptualization, discursive reasoning, memory, and recollection, and, included together with these, the remaining faculties of intuition, understanding, acumen, resolution,[13] determination, opinion, conjecturing, knowing, and intellecting.

4.   Some, namely the celestial bodies, have the faculties of knowing and intellecting, which are firmly incorporated in them in an incorporeal way such that they need not encounter things that are external to themselves in order to comprehend sensible objects. [That is], because they are not composed of that which the other sensibles are composed, namely, fire, air, water, and earth; for what has sensation apprehends its sensible objects precisely because the common matter is affected by the contrary qualities of these bodies (I mean the hot by the cold, the wet by the dry, and, in sum, according to the subject's predisposition to receive the kinds of contraries), whereas [the celestial bodies] are not composed of [these elements]. I said that [knowing and intellecting] are firmly incorporated in them precisely because they can in one way act on and influence [380] this world of generation and corruption, without [themselves] being acted upon and affected, both of which concern the fluctuating substance that alternates one state after another; for every agent acts on its patient according to the paradigm that is in [the agent] as is appropriate to that subject. Hence, celestial bodies perform their activities, [namely, knowing and intellecting], according to the universal[d] forms in each species of existing things in the world of generation and corruption just as they are in sensible existence, which includes particulars, potentialities, qualities, quantities, and accidents; however, [the forms] are in [the celestial bodies] through an incorporeal species, unified by their souls. Next, by means of their particular corporeal motions in this world, they transmit [the forms] to the matter that is susceptible to them, thereby receiving them. As a result of [those celestial bodies] there are temporally created the particular individuals, which resemble the paradigm of their universals. <They come to be perfect on the part of the agent and the universal forms, while they are imperfect on the part of their subject>[e] by virtue of a fluctuation of a substance; the variations of its parts; its motions increasing,

---

12 Nasnās, which was a purportedly ape-like creature that has a single leg and moves by leaps and bounds.

13 "Resolution" was not included in the original list mentioned in par. 2.

decreasing, and being uniform; the many concomitant changes and alterations; as well as its proximity to the bodies that move [the individuals] by their motions.

5.   Let us now describe how the present case stands concerning that Being to which various descriptions and significations are applied according to different opinions and schools indicated by past peoples.

6.   Some of them maintained that that Being conjoins with things themselves, which, they maintained, become one with It. More precisely, the adherents of ancient religions said that [the things to which It conjoins and unites] are the celestial bodies, and they maintained that It manifests Itself in them and performs Its functions through them. They called [the celestial bodies to which It conjoins and unites] "secondary gods."

7.   Others said that It unites with human substances. Among them some said that from all of the [human] substances there is [only] one substance with which It unites, namely, the substance of the human nature of the Messiah. These are the Christians, despite their differing opinions concerning that. The Jacobites [or Monophysites] maintain that from two substances (I mean the human and divine substances) there comes to be a single substance and a single hypostasis. <The Nestorians said that the unity is only through will,[14] and the two substances remain two and two hypostases. The Melkites said that from two substances, two substances and one hypostasis.>[f]

8.   Of those who advocated unity [namely, Muslims], some maintained that It united with more than one individual, namely, the Shī'ī extremists,[15] and those who advocate incarnation, as well as a sect [381] of Sufis who advocate substantial union.

9.   Others [namely, the Zoroastrians and Manicheans] said that the world is entirely composed of that substance and another substance, which is its contrary. They advocated two principles: light and darkness.

10.   Most of the Muslim[16] speculative theologians have indicated that Being by means of descriptions that correspond with the relation of Its effects to It and by means of that Being's obvious influences on [Its effects]. Among all of [those descriptions], they held in high regard the foundations and principles of what immediately follows below It and called them "attributes of the essence," namely, life, power, knowledge and their like. Concerning [these attributes], It cannot be described by [one of them] *and* its contrary or even the potentiality for its contrary. So some of [the speculative theologians] made a distinction between "attributes of the essence" and "attributes of action" in that attributes of action are those by which [both] they and their contrary as well as the potentiality for their contrary can describe It, whereas

---

[14] Kraemer suggests that *mashī'a*, translated as "will" here, might reflect the Greek *eudokia*, "good pleasure"; see *Philosophy in the Renaissance of Islam*, p. 297, n. 76.

[15] *Ghulāh*, an extreme Shi'ite sect who venerated 'Ali, the fourth Muslim caliph, almost like God.

[16] Literally, "adherents of the Laws."

the attributes of the essence are those signs of that Being that cannot do that. So they judged It by means of those signs that were apparent to them.

11. Each sect taught in accordance with what was most evident to it and in accordance with its ability to reason and to acquire knowledge of It. The Christians described the Being by the sign attributed to that which was apparent from the characteristics of perfection in the person of the Messiah. The adherents of light and dark described the sign attributed to the Being itself [namely, light]. The eminent philosophers say that the Being that created existing things is beyond being encompassed by any of its creations (lest the attributes attached to It should limit It to existing in this world), since that which transcends and encompasses the universe cannot be encompassed by it nor is it within the power of any of the particulars in the universe to have an effect on it. The reason is that attributes are certain names by which the human intellect designates, in an incorporeal way through inner speech, those very existing things that it apprehends below itself by means of the signs of the activity and passivity that proceed from them and are present in them. Thereafter, the soul makes [those internal signs] public, and gives voice to them corporeally by means of outward speech according the various languages of people. The intellect has this activity by way of what is specific to it in its very substance and it is according to the order of existing things and the harmony between them, [which is] by virtue of the well-suited relation [382] that results from the intellect's giving to each of them their proper perfection. [That] is because no perfected existent, as something whose being brought into existence is directed by wisdom, results from anything that just happened by chance; rather, [the harmony] among any given things is by virtue of determinate relations.

12. The intellect has two other activities. One of them concerns it as a first and simple actualized effect of the First Cause. The First Agent (praised and exalted is He!) is the One who gives to each existing thing, for example, an intellect, a soul and whatever is below them, the existence general to them all; for it distributes that existence among existing things themselves by virtue of the proper forms it gives to each one of them. <It orders [existence] according to whatever benefit the existence of the specific thing derived from It in order to preserve order, and makes the soul appear in bodily things endowed with life, and brings to fruition in them the power called "nature." It preserves them and pervades them, and so gives to them the natural disposition and form peculiar to each one of them>g whether animate or not. The second activityh is that which it performs through the intermediacy of the soul, namely, to provide life to each thing prepared to receive it. This activity belongs to the soul in itself and to [the intellect] through [the soul's] intermediacy, since the soul is the form that makes the animate thing, while it is the intellect that gives [the soul].

13. Hence, [intellect] is what deserves being called "complete," "whole," "perfect," and "what perfects others." Or, it is complete from the First Agent inasmuch as It made [intellect] a cause of the existence of each existing thing by its providing the order in the harmonious relations in existing things, and [the First Agent] did not make anything else a cause of [intellect's] existence. [Intellect] also is complete from

the fact that, by providing existence according to the manner that was described, it is the *beginning*, whereas it is the *end* in ascending and conceptualizing by virtue of [being] the first form of all powers. In other words, it is the mean between the First Principle and all other existing things. [Intellect] properly, truly, and by nature has this [activity of] ordering, whereas everything else has it conditionally. Furthermore, there is in it the causal factors (*maʿná*): (1) by which something is what it is, and (2) from which [the thing proceeds], and (3) to which [it returns]. It is on account of its having this tripartite form that Christians came to profess three hypostases.

14.   In fact, philosophers have virtually venerated being tripartite and revered God by virtue of it. The philosopher, Aristotle, mentioned that in his work *De caelo et mundi*, as well as the commentator of this work.[17] I believe that he meant to indicate by that the intellect universal to the three modes of existing, namely: (1) the divine existence that embraces all existing things; (2) the orderly existence resulting from [intellect]; and (3) the natural existence that is divided among sensible existents, specifically [383] and generally, through the soul's transmitting nature to them. Furthermore, the account of the universe belongs to [intellect], since it is by means of [intellect] by virtue of the universal forms that there are all the causal factors of things below it, that is to say, [their] perfection. [That is] because it is the final end at which the potentialities terminate when being informed, regardless of whether [they are] informed incorporeally like the faculties of the soul, namely, discernment, comprehending, and perception what is in the intellect itself, or informed corporeally commensurate with the faculties of the body that acquire their existence from [the intellect] by means of their ordered relations as divisions that are determined for them. [The intellect], however, does not need to be informed by any other form, for it is <the form of forms and the power of powers.>[i]

15.   <[Intellect's] awareness of the First Agent, its Creator and the Creator of> the universe (blessed is His mention!), can neither encompass nor apprehend Him, since it is not possible as we described above.[18] However, because [the intellect] needs what will conserve its continuation and provide it with existence in order that it will continue to provide order, it is aware in virtue of its continuation and existence that it is the result of a Being [Who is the First Agent]. So [intellect] submits to It, needing It to supply it with life, which is the first power that is transmitted from It to [the intellect], where "life" here means to tend toward the most excellent thing in order that it be perpetuated by It. This submission is divine reverence.

16.   That [the intellect] is what perfects everything else has become obvious from what we have described, namely that every existing thing, whether animate or not, acquire its existence and form by which it is what it is from that form, [that is, the

---

[17] See Aristotle, *De caelo* I 1, 268a10–15; the commentator in question may be either Alexander of Aphrodisias, part of whose commentary on the first book of *De caelo* was available in Arabic translation, or Themistius, whose commentary on the entire *De caelo* was available in Arabic.

[18] See par. 11, p. 143

intellect], in accordance with the well-suited relations, both incorporeal and corporeal, commensurate with souls and bodies.

17.   When the case is as described, then it is man, among everything else in the world, in whom there are combined all the faculties scattered among the rest of existing things and distributed among the varying kinds, both the powers of the celestial bodies and earthly bodies as well as the animate and inanimate bodies. So [man] is the multiple one containing the dispersed units, just as the First Agent (may He be praised and exalted!) is the Pure One in all respects and in no way multiple, from Whom is transmitted all the units and powers that spread into this world until they reach [384] in their entirety the human form. The particular individual obtains [those powers] in accordance with his predisposition to receive them as well as his measure of moderation, excess, and deficiency of composition in accordance with the motions of the celestial bodies and according to their varying influence vis-à-vis their occultation, opposition, rotations, their superior, quasi-, and inferior conjunctions, and their progression through the Zodiac from one trine to another. What appears as a result of them will vary in strength and weakness as well as the portent and degree of significance and insignificance. Prodigious events and the appearance of perfect individuals able to receive fully the powers of the First Principle and to take charge and possession of managing the world take place precisely with the change of these rotations and the transition of these conjunctions from one trine to another.

18.   When the time is right that, through the agreement of the celestial sphere's configurations, the divine individual can appear, that one will appear in the land most suited to him to manage and through [the celestial sphere's configurations] to influence. [This will occur] by there being made to appear the excellence transmitted from the First Principle by which [that divine individual] is distinguished in administering peoples, managing empires, and sustaining sanctioned practices. [These sanctioned practices] will preserve for mankind their best interests through the sorts of policies that proceed in accordance with what the legal requirements of that time demand in order to convey the benefits to [that land's] people, to repel harmful influences from them, and to acquaint them with everything else that will bring together for them worldly prosperity and a beautiful afterlife.[j]

[In the remainder of the treatise, which is not translated here, as-Sijistānī casts a horoscope for ʿAḍud ad-Dawla, to whom the treatise is addressed. He claims that the celestial configuration is such that ʿAḍud ad-Dawla himself can take up this role as the perfect ruler described both here and at the beginning of the treatise.]

IBN SĪNĀ

Together with al-Fārābī, Ibn Sīnā, known in the Latin West as Avicenna, was one of the most significant thinkers and original system-builders in the history of Arabic philosophy. Indeed, his renown in the Islamic world brought him the title "the leading eminent scholar" (*ash-Shaykh ar-Raʾīs*). Unlike al-Fārābī, however, we are on much surer grounds concerning the details of Ibn Sīnā's personal life, since, in an uncustomary fashion, he wrote an autobiography detailing his early education. Moreover, al-Jūzjānī, his student and secretary, chronicled the later part of his life.

Abū ʿAlī l-Ḥusayn ibn ʿAbdallāh ibn Sīnā was born in the year 980 in the small village of Afshana in what is now part of Uzbekistan and then part of the Sāmānid dynasty. His father was the governor of Kharmaythan, an important village in northern Persia outside of Buhkārā, the seat of Sāmānid rule. Ibn Sīnā by all accounts was a prodigy; at the age of ten he claims to have completed the study of the Qurʾān and a major part of belle lettres and already surpassed his teacher of logic, Abū ʿAbdallāh an-Nātilī. He continued his own education thereafter, and it is claimed that by the age of eighteen he had taught himself, and in fact mastered, all the sciences, including Islamic law, astronomy, medicine, and of course philosophy. It was his knowledge of medicine that provided him an introduction to the Sāmānid Sultān, Nūḥ ibn Manṣūr who was suffering from an ailment that baffled the court physicians. Ibn Sīnā, whose skill as a doctor even at an early age was recognized, was called in, and he cured the Sultan who enrolled him into his service. The rest of Ibn Sīnā's career was a series of often short-lived associations with such lords. In 1037 Ibn Sīnā died on his way to Hamadan in modern Iran at the age of fifty-eight, after apparently overdosing himself in an attempt to cure himself of colic.

Ibn Sīnā's literary outpourings were voluminous, with the better part of three hundred works being ascribed to him. His "The Cure" appears to be the first philosophical compendium in Islam. He also wrote several other compendia, such as "The Salvation," "Pointers and Reminders," "The Book of Science for ʿAlāʾ ad-Dawla," and a compendium of medicine, "The Canon of Medicine," which was the major reference work on medicine in both the Islamic East and Christian West for centuries to come. Among his compendia one should also mention his "Eastern Philosophy" and "Fair Treatment," only parts of which are still extant, which purport to give Ibn Sīnā's own judgment and philosophical system rather than following the presentation of earlier thinkers.

Like few others in the history of philosophy, Ibn Sīnā's knowledge embraced all the known sciences of his day as well as going beyond that knowledge in ways that would fundamentally alter the course of philosophical study. In virtually every area of scientific and philosophical discourse Ibn Sīnā made novel and creative advancements. (The one exception appears to be mathematics, where he contented himself with the existing mathematical knowledge, although he integrated the newly created algebra into his discussions of mathematics, and so his account of mathematics went beyond earlier Greek mathematical works.) It is not an overstatement to claim that virtually all subsequent medieval philosophers—whether Muslims, Jews, or Christians—either adopted or modified or in some sense reacted to the thought of Ibn Sīnā.

I. *THE CURE,* "BOOK OF DEMONSTRATION," I.9ᵃ

On Induction and Methodic Experience and What Makes It Necessary[1]

1. [43] One may rightly ask, "When no cause actually exists between predicate and subject, how is the relation between them made obvious?" [44] We say the following. On the one hand, when that [cause] is obvious in itself without requiring explanation, and certainty about it is established on account of the fact that the relation of the predicate to the subject belongs to the very being of the subject, then the connection of the subject to the predicate is necessary (you have already learned about connection and its necessity, insofar as it is necessary), and so the resulting knowledge is certain. On the other hand, if [the cause] is not obvious, then it simply cannot result in certain, intransitory knowledge. This follows because when we take the connection[2] to be something that is not a cause, it cannot be through it that one seeks this certain knowledge. If, however, we do take it to be a cause, we have made a cause the middle [term]; but this is a contradiction, since we posited that it is not a cause.

2. So it would appear that all such causes are either obvious in themselves, or explained through induction.[3] When explained by induction, however, one of two cases must obtain: either the fact that there is a relation between the predicate and the particulars of the subject is itself obvious without a cause [being obvious] (since it is precisely in this manner that induction seeks explanation), or the fact that there is a relation between the predicate and the particulars of the subject is itself through a cause.

3. Now if it is obvious in itself in each case, the explanation is either through sensory perception alone or through the intellect. It is not through sensory perception, because sensory perception ensures neither something that holds always nor the

---

[1] A close analysis of this selection is available in Jon McGinnis, "Scientific Methodologies in Medieval Islam," 307–27; and Jules L. Janssens, "Experience (*tajriba*) in Classical Arabic Philosophy (al-Fārābī–Avicenna)," 45–62.

[2] That is, the connection between subject and predicate, and more generally, the middle term that allows such connection.

[3] For Aristotle's account of induction see *Prior Analytics* II 23, where the conception of induction presented there seems to be the object of criticism here, and *Posterior Analytics* II 19.

elimination of something that could be transitory. So no certainty comes from premises based on sensory perception. The option through the intellect also is not likely,
because the predicate [belonging to the particulars of the subject] cannot be something
essential in the sense of something constitutive (for we will explain later that what
is essential, in the sense of something constitutive, is not a real object of scientific
investigation), but rather its existence is obviously owing to that to which it essentially
belongs.

4. As for [the predicate of the particulars] being accidental—in which case it
is undoubtedly one of the concomitant accidents of a universal said of a species of
particulars as long as predicating it of the universal is valid—this accident would be
a concomitant of one of the essential accounts of the particulars, for this is the character of the accident so described. Consequently, predicating it of each particular is
because of an essential account belonging to it and others, and then that (I mean the
essential account) would be a common cause for this accident's being in the particulars. But we posited a lack of cause [for the relation between the predicate and the
particulars]. And when [the relation of predicate to subject] is known from some
perspective other than that cause, it is neither necessary knowledge nor certain knowledge—never mind obvious in itself.

5. It cannot be an accident belonging to the common account if it is to be a
valid object of scientific investigation; rather it must be something essential to each
and every one of the particulars. For what is essential to all the particulars cannot be
accidental to the universal account that is equivalent to them, because that predication
is not accidental to any of the subjects of that universal, whether in negating or affirming it. If it is not an accident of any one of them, how could it be an accident [45] of
all of them?! Whatever is accidental to the nature of the universal is an accident
of the whole; for since volitional movement is a concomitant accident of the genus
human, it is an accident of human and every species with human [under a common
account].

6. It is clear that the relation of the predicate in cases like the ones we discussed
is accidental in a common way and needs to be made apparent in each one of the
particulars by means of its cause. Thus, it is invalid to argue that an inductive examination of any particulars is reason for our assent on the grounds of certainty to anything lacking a connection,[4] and it is invalid to argue that that [connecting cause] is
obvious in itself with respect to the particulars.

7. Now if the case of predication with respect to the particular instances of the
subject is not obvious in itself but can be made obvious by an explanation, then either
(1) that explanation will not ensure, with respect to every one of them, the real certainty that is our aim (and then how could something that does not allow for certain
knowledge produce the further real certainty about the universal?); or (2) it is an
explanation by way of the cause, in order to ensure real certainty about each of them
(and then it must happen with respect to the cause—as[b] we just said).

---

[4] That is, the middle term that connects the predicate with the subject.

8. The existence of the cause for the universal account comes first. When the cause is of no help with respect to the universal account, it will equally be of no help with respect to the particular. When it is of help with respect to the universal, the help is the syllogism accompanying it, not the induction. As for the cases in which there is no cause at all, either it is obvious in itself—and that has already been refuted—or there is some other induction, in which case this would go on without stopping. So it is now clear that anything lacking a cause for the relation between its predicate and its subject is either obvious in itself or simply cannot be made obvious by means of an explanation leading to certainty by way of a syllogism.

9. Methodic experience is not induction, and we will explain that later. For now, methodic experience is like our judging that the scammony plant is a purgative for bile; for since this is repeated many times, it stops being a case of something that occurs by chance, and the mind then judges and grants that it is characteristic of scammony to purge bile. Purging bile is a concomitant accident of scammony.

10. Now one might ask: "This is not something whose cause is known, so how are we certain that the scammony cannot be sound of nature, and yet not purge bile?" [46] I say: Since it is verified that purging bile so happens to belong to scammony, and that becomes evident by way of much repetition, one knows that it is not by chance, for chance is not always or for the most part. Then one knows that this is something scammony necessarily brings about by nature, since there is no way it can be an act of choice on the part of [scammony]. Had it been known that the body [of scammony], as a body, does not make this thing necessary, then it would have to make it necessary by means of an associated power in it, or as a property belonging to it, or [as part of] some relation linked to it.

11. It is by means of this kind of explanation that one can know that in scammony, whether by nature or accompaniment, there is a cause that purges bile. When the power to purge bile is sound and the patient is suitably disposed, the activity [of purging] and the affection [of being purged] occur, and then it is valid to maintain that the scammony in our country always purges bile, when it is sound. Hence, we recognized that the major term belongs to the minor term through the connection of the middle term, which is the purgative power, that is, the cause. When you analyze the remainder of the syllogism, you find that every explanation is an explanation only by means of a connection that is a cause for the presence of the major term in the middle term, even if there is no cause for knowledge by means of the major term. Thus, it is again by the cause that we acquire this kind of certainty.

12. One could ask: "Why is it that methodic experience provides humans with knowledge that scammony purges bile in a manner that is different from that by which induction provides it?" [I say:] Induction either provides an exhaustive account of the divisions,[5] or it occasions merely probable belief. Methodic experience is not like that.

---

5 That is, the divisions of genera into species through difference.

13.   Then he raises doubts again by saying: "Why is it that methodic experience produces a judgment that is certain about things? Were we to imagine that there were no people but Sudanese, and that only black people were repeatedly perceived, then would not that necessarily produce a conviction that all people are black? On the one hand, if it does not, then why does one repetition produce [such a belief] and another repetition does not? On the other hand, if the one [instance of methodic experience] *does* produce [the belief that there are only black people], it has in fact produced an error and falsehood. If methodic experience produces so much as one error and falsehood, it is unreliable and unusable for acquiring the principles of demonstrations."

14.   We say in response that methodic experience does not provide knowledge solely on account of the frequency of what is observed on the basis of that judgment, but rather because a syllogism is connected with it, as we have already mentioned. Nonetheless, it does not provide universal, syllogistic, and absolute knowledge, but rather conditional universal knowledge, which is to say that the character of this thing that is repeatedly perceived is necessarily joined to something that holds always in the domain in which the thing is repeatedly perceived, unless there is an obstacle. So [the knowledge] is universal with this condition, not absolutely universal. For when something happens that necessarily requires a cause, and, moreover, it repeatedly happens in conjunction with the occurrence of some other thing, then it is known [47] that a cause has been repeated. That latter thing is either the cause or something naturally joined to the cause or it is not. If it is not the cause or something naturally joined to the cause, then the occurrence of the latter thing is not for the most part in conjunction with the former thing's happening, but it was known that the cause is something that happens in conjunction—in fact, then, there is no doubt that one has to know that the latter thing is the cause or something that happens naturally in conjunction with the cause.

15.   Know that methodic experience is useful only with regard to occurrences like this and to this extent. When you consider this basic rule that we have presented, you can easily resolve the puzzle that arose concerning the Sudanese and their procreation of black children. In summary form, when procreation is taken to be procreation by black people, or people of one such country, then methodic experience will be valid. If procreation is taken to be that of any given people, then methodic experience will not end with the aforementioned particular instances; for that methodic experience concerned a black people, but people absolutely speaking are not limited to black people.

16.   Methodic experience is also often in error for the following reason. When we treat what is accidental as essential, it produces an assumption that is not certain. Certainty results from [methodic experience] only as long as it happens that, with regard to a given methodic experience, what is subject to methodic experience is the thing itself. When one takes something other than [the thing itself], such as what is more general or more specific than it, then methodic experience does not provide certainty.

17.   We certainly do not maintain that methodic experience is a safeguard against error and that it always produces certainty. How could it, when not even the syllogism does that? Instead, we say that frequently we do happen to have certainty as a result of methodic experience, and so we want to know how it produces certainty. It happens when we safeguard against taking something accidentally. When we know the properties of x and furthermore y is always or for the most part found together when x exists, and when y itself does not exist x does not exist, then (1) if y is from a general property, then x is connected to the specific property through its general property, and the specific property [of x] is connected also with the judgment. Likewise, (2) if y is something coextensive with x, then its specific coextensive property is connected with the judgment. Also, (3) if something belongs to a specific property, indeed is more specific than x's nature, then it might be that the specific property is what is repeated for us during our examination and found in more things around us than x.

18.   So this is the sort of thing that undermines the [48] absolute universal and makes it a universal more specific than the thing's absolute universal. Neglecting this causes us to make errors in methodic experience with respect to our universal judgments. For in such cases, even if we are certain that x is such and does y, we are not certain that whatever is described by the property x does y. We also do not preclude that in some country, some temperament and special property is connected with or absent from the scammony such that it does not purge. Nonetheless, the judgment based on methodic experience that we possess must be that the scammony commonplace among and perceived by us purges bile, whether owing to its essence or a nature in it, unless opposed by some obstacle. The same holds in the case of the emerald in blinding the viper.[6]

19.   If methodic experience accompanied by its syllogism had not prevented the thing investigated by it from being more specific, then methodic experience on its own would produce certainty about the absolute universal and not solely about the restricted universal. For [methodic experience] alone does not ensure [that what is too specific is not taken], unless it is accompanied by an investigation and a syllogism other than the one that forms part of the methodic experience. It is fitting to say that methodic experience as such does *not* provide that. This is the truth. Anyone who says otherwise is either biased or incapable of discernment, not distinguishing between what is difficult to doubt because of the plethora of its indications and particulars and what is in fact certain. For there are beliefs that seem to be certain but in fact are not certain.

20.   In short, methodic experience considers things that happen according to a condition other than the one that we stipulated for considering their causes only. If, following some type of methodic experience, there is any universal certainty that

---

[6] It was a widely held belief in the ancient and medieval world that the emerald, in addition to curing most eye diseases, was also capable of blinding snakes; cf. Theophrastus (372–287 B.C.E.), *De lapidus,* "On Stones," § IV.

imposes a condition other than the unassailable one we stipulated, the occurrence of that certainty does not seem to come from the methodic experience as such (in the sense that it is something necessarily resulting from it) but rather from the separate cause that provides the first principles of certainty (an account[c] of which is found in sciences other than logic).[7] In this case, it would seem that methodic experience is like the preparatory thing—but it is not the necessary preparatory thing, that is, the syllogism. It is simply a preparatory thing.

21.   In conclusion, the difference between what is acquired by perception and what is acquired by induction and methodic experience is that what is acquired by perception in no way provides a universal concept, whereas the latter two might. The difference between what is acquired by induction and what is acquired by methodic experience is that what is acquired by induction does not ensure a universal, whether conditionally or not, but produces probable belief, unless it leads to methodic experience; and what is acquired by methodic experience ensures a universal with the aforementioned condition.

II.   *THE CURE,* "BOOK OF DEMONSTRATION," III.5[a]

The Manner in which the Soul Uses Sensory Perception with Respect to the Intelligibles; Simple Universals and How They Are Acquired; the First Order of These; and How Syllogistic Analysis Arrives at Them.

1.   [158] It is said, "Whoever loses a certain sense necessarily loses a certain knowledge,"[8] which is to say that, one cannot arrive at the knowledge to which that sense leads the soul. That is because the starting points[b] from which one arrives at certain knowledge are demonstration and induction, that is, induction of the essential. [Of these two], induction necessarily relies on sense perception, and, while the premises of the demonstration are universal, their principles are acquired only by sense perception and, by means of that, by acquiring the images of the simple terms so that the faculty of the intellect can readily act on them in such a way that it leads to acquiring the universals as simple terms and combining them into the form of a statement.

2.   Now if one wants to explain the principles to someone who is heedless of them (and there is no more suitable way to draw attention to them), it can be only through an induction that relies on sensory perception, because such principles are primary and cannot be demonstrated—for example, the premises of mathematics used to explain that the Earth is at the center of the universe, and the premises of the natural sciences used to explain that earth is heavy and fire light. This is why it is through sensory perception that the primary principles of the essential accidents [159]

---

[7]   That is, the Active Intellect, discussed in psychology and metaphysics. See for instance "The Soul," V.5, pars. 1–2., pp. 199–200.

[8]   Aristotle, *Posterior Analytics* I 18, 81a38–39.

of every subject are first learned. Then, from what was sensed, some other intelligible is acquired—for example, the triangle, the plane, and so on in geometry, regardless of whether [such intelligibles] are separable or inseparable, for the ways to arrive at them are first through sensory perception.

3. This is a summary statement set out in the first teaching [of Aristotle]. While we have already matched that in our own discussion, we will further provide you with details. So we say, you must know that nothing of the intelligible object is sensible, and nothing of the sensible object, in as much as it is something presenting itself to sensory perception, is intelligible, that is, something presenting itself to[c] the intellect's perception of it, even though sensory perception is a starting point for acquiring much of the intelligible object. Let us first give as an example of this concerning the sensible and intelligible human. Sensory perception, in addition to taking hold of any human present to it in virtue of a given measure of magnitude, a given qualitative configuration, a given determinate position in the parts of his limbs, and a position with respect to his place, also takes hold of these states in each one of its members. Now either what the senses perceive is the intelligible human, or the intelligible is something other than what is perceived by the senses, albeit concomitant with it.

4. Next, it is obvious that the human as the object of the intellect is something common equally, so Zayd, just like 'Amr, is a human to the intellect, and that by absolute univocity. But the human as the object of the senses is *not* common, since his magnitude, quality, and position are not, and he cannot be an object of the senses in any way but that. Thus, the human as the object of the intellect is not the form of the human in the imagery [faculty][9] that is derived from the object of the senses. In short, the thing that sensory perception encounters is neither the true nature of the common human nor [the true nature] that the intellect encounters, except accidentally.

5. So let us investigate how [to conceptualize] the human as an object of the intellect. It must be something abstracted from any condition attaching to it externally, like measurement by a given determinate magnitude, qualification by a given determinate quality, delimitation by a given determinate position and place.[10] On the contrary, it is an intelligible nature configured to receive all the measurements, qualities, positions, and places that an actual human can naturally receive. If conceptualizing the human in the intellect by defining him were at all connected with any measurement, position, or anything similar, every human would have to share in [those things]. But this magnitude that is observable by the senses, this position, place, etc., all attach to the human only on account of his matter that is particular to him. [160] So, obviously, insofar as "human" is conceptualized in the intellect by means

---

9 For this "faculty" of the human soul, see the translation of "The Soul," I.5, par. 8, p. 182.

10 For a discussion of Ibn Sīnā's theory of "abstraction" *(tajrīd)* see Dag N. Hasse, "Avicenna on Abstraction" in *Aspects of Avicenna*, Robert Wisnovsky, ed., 39–72.

of the definition [of "human"], it is something abstracted by the intellect from matter and its consequential accidents and, as such, it is not something that can be arrived at by sensory perception. Rather, when sensory perception takes in the human, it takes in something that is obscured by extraneous consequential accidents.

6.   Next, existing things are divided into two classes: essences intelligible in existence and essences perceptible in existence. Essences intelligible in existence are those that have neither matter nor any consequential accidents of matter. They are intelligible in themselves precisely because no operation is needed to make them intelligible, and because they cannot be perceived by the senses in any way. Essences perceptible in existence are those that are not in themselves intelligible but rather perceptible by the senses. However, the intellect makes them such that they become intelligible, because it abstracts their true nature from the consequential accidents of matter.

7.   Now, conceptualizing the intelligibles is effected by means of the senses precisely in one way: sensory perception takes the forms of its objects and delivers them to the imagery [faculty], and then those forms are subject to the action of our theoretical intellect.[11] There are there [in the imagery faculty] many forms taken from actual humans as perceived by the senses, which the intellect finds all mixed up with material accidents. For example, it finds Zayd having a particular color, complexion, shape of limbs, etc., and it finds 'Amr having other such particular things. So the intellect turns to these material accidents and extracts them, as though it were peeling away those material accidents and setting them to one side until it arrives at the core account (*ma'nā*) common [to all individuals perceived by the senses] without difference, and thereby acquiring knowledge about it and conceptualizing it. From the first moment that the intellect inspects the confused mix in the imagery [faculty], it finds accidental and essential things, and, of the accidental, those that are consequential and those that are not. It separates out one by one the many accounts mixed together in the imagery [faculty] and keeps them for itself. This is not the place to find out how this works and what the faculty is that does this and which one helps it; rather that belongs to psychology.[12] But what we will say here is that sensory perception conveys to the soul things that are mixed up and unintelligible, and the intellect makes them intelligible. Once the intellect separates them out as intelligibles, it can then combine them in all manner of ways, some in the order proper to a statement that explains the account of a thing, like definition and description, others in the order of the [syllogistic] proposition [161].[13]

---

[11] That is, as opposed to the action of the practical intellect. For both the imagery faculty and the theoretical intellect, see the translation of "The Soul," I.5, pp. 182, 184–85.

[12] See the translation of "The Soul," I.5 pars. 6–9, pp. 181–82; V.3, pars. 1–2, pp. 192–93; V.5, pp. 199–202.

[13] See the translation of "The Soul," V.6, par. 4, (4.1–3), pp. 203–4, for the various ways that the intellect combines intelligibles.

8. [To be] specific now, assent to the intelligibles is effected by means of the senses in four ways: (1) accidentally; (2) through the syllogism treating the particular; (3) through induction; and (4) through methodic experience.

8.1. The one by (1) accident is to acquire from the senses, in the manner we said, individual intelligible accounts that are abstracted from the confused mix of the senses and the imagery [faculty], after which the intellect engages in separating them one from another and combining them together, following which the intellect is bolstered by its natural disposition in some cases, while it proceeds[d] to demonstration in others. (1a) The first of these occurs by the intellect's coming into contact with a light flowing upon the souls and nature from the agent called the "Active Intellect,"[14] which is what brings the intellect from potency to actuality. But even though this is the case, sensory perception is a starting point for [the intellect] accidentally not essentially. (1b) For the second of these [the intellect] applies itself wholly[e] to the middle term. When the middle term is obtained, the intelligible to which there is assent is acquired in the manner that the first principles themselves are acquired and on the strength of that starting point. This is one of the four ways.

8.2. The one (2) through the syllogism treating the particular is when the intellect has a given universal generic judgment, and then the individuals of a species belonging to that are sensibly perceived. So the form of the species is conceptualized from[f] [the genus], and then that judgment is applied to the species. An intelligible not previously possessed is then acquired.

8.3. The one through (3) induction is that many of the first principles will not have appeared and become clear to the intellect by way of the method mentioned first. So when the particular instances [of the first principles] are sought inductively, the intellect is alerted to become convinced about the universal; however, the induction that is based on perceiving particulars through the senses does not require at all that one be convinced about a universal but rather alerts one to it. For example, when two things both touch a third thing but not each other, they require that that thing be divisible.[15] Frequently this is not rooted firmly in the soul,[g] so whenever particular instances of it are observed by the senses, the intellect is alerted to it and becomes convinced about it.

8.4. The one through (4) methodic experience is almost a blend of syllogism and induction, but it is more convincing than induction, and its utility does not concern pure first principles, but rather whatever is acquired through the senses. It is not like induction, for induction, insofar as it collects particulars, does not

---

[14] The Active Intellect is called "the agent" here with reference to its activity of informing the material world.

[15] The thing will be divisible in that it has sides touching the two things. Cf. the use of this example to the treatment of the soul in the translation of "The Soul," V.2, par. 3, p. 189, and "Physics," III.4, par. 4, pp. 167–68.

occasion certain universal knowledge, though it may well alert [the intellect to such], whereas methodic experience does. Or rather, methodic experience is like someone seeing or sensing certain things [162] of one species followed by a particular act or affection, and when that is repeated a great many times, the intellect judges that this is essential to that thing and is not the result of chance, for chance occurrences are not consistent. An example of this is our judgment that magnets attract iron, and that scammony purges bile. Also under this heading is something's changing from its natural state because of something joining it and connecting with it, and the intellect does not admit that its change is through itself, and so judges that the cause of the change is the thing connecting with it, especially when this occurs again and again.

9.   These are the ways by which we acquire many of the sciences and their principles from sensory perception. And methodic experience is in fact one of them; for methodic experience is almost a blend of induction based on sense and a syllogism founded on the difference between what is essential and what is accidental, since the accidental does not hold always. We have already pointed to the explanation of this remark in what preceded.[16]

III.   THE CURE, "PHYSICS," I.2[a]

Enumerating the Principles of Physics by Postulate and Thesis[17]

1.   [13] Natural things have principles. We will enumerate these principles by positing a thesis about which of them are necessary and by providing their essential definitions. So we say that the natural body is a substance in which one can posit an extension and another extension crossing it perpendicularly and a third extension crossing both of them perpendicularly. Its having this description is the form by which it becomes a body. The body is not a body in as much as it possesses any three posited extensions. The body is something existing as a body and something fixed, even if the extensions actually existing in it change; for certain actual dimensions (that is, length, breadth, and depth), might be present at one time in a piece of wax or a portion of water as delimited by the extremities [of the wax or water], and then, when it is replaced by another shape, each one of those observed determinate dimensions ceases to be and other extensions and dimensions occur. Yet the body remains in its corporeality, neither corrupting nor being replaced, and the form that we made it have (namely, that it is such that one can posit those extensions in it), remains fixed and does not cease to be.

2.   This was pointed out to you elsewhere when you learned that these assignable extensions are the quantity of its sides and that they can be attached to it and replaced,

---

[16] See the translation of "Book of Demonstration," I.9, 147–152.

[17] Most of this section is commentary on and occasionally criticism of Aristotle, *Physics* I, 7–9.

whereas its form and substance cannot be replaced. This quantity often follows an exchange of accidents or forms in it, as when water is heated and then increases in bulk. This natural body, however, as a natural body, has certain principles; but it has additional principles inasmuch as it is something subject to generation and corruption and in general undergoes change. The principles that occasion its corporeality include whatever are parts of its existence as present in its very being. In the view of [the natural philosophers] these most deserve to be called "principles." They are two. The first is like the wood of the bed, and the other is the form and shape of bedness in the bed. What is like the wood of the bed is called "prime matter," [14] "subject," "matter," "constituent," and "element" according to various considerations. What is like the form of bedness is called "form."

3.   Now, the form of corporeality is either something prior to the rest of the forms that belong to natural bodies and their genera and species, or it is something joined to them and not separate from them. This [principle] that belongs to the body the way wood belongs to the bed also belongs to everything else that possesses these forms in this way,[b] [i.e., the way that natural bodies possess those forms], since each of them has determinate existence together with the [form of] corporeality in it. [Matter] is a substance that, when investigated without relation to anything else, is found actually to be devoid of these forms, while nonetheless having the character of receiving this form [of corporeality] or joining with it. [This receptivity] is a result either of [matter's] universal absolute nature, as though [its universal absolute nature] were a genus with two species, the nature of the prior [matter] and the nature of the associated [matter], and each one of them specifically receives some forms and not others after [receiving] the form of corporeality. Or [the receptivity] is the result of a nature that is itself common to all [the forms], in which case, through its universality, [matter] receives each of these forms, succeeding one another in combination or individually, in which case its nature contains a certain correspondence with the forms on account of the fact that [the substance] is something that receives them, where that correspondence is like an impression in [its nature] and a dim semblance of the form, while the form itself is what actually perfects this substance.

4.   Let it be posited as a thesis that the body has a "that with which," namely, matter, as well as a principle, namely, a form—whether you mean an absolute corporeal form or a species form that is one of the forms of the body, or an accidental form (such as when you take the body as being white, or strong, or healthy). Let it also be posited as a thesis that the former, that is, prime matter, is not in any way separable from form as something subsisting by itself, nor is it something actually existing except when the form is present, in which case it exists actually through the form. If it were not the case that the form departs from it only with the arrival of another form that substitutes for it and takes its place, then prime matter would actually cease to be. This matter, inasmuch as it potentially receives a form or forms, is called its "prime matter"; and, inasmuch as it is actually bearing a form, it is called in this [book] its "subject." (The sense of "subject" here is not the sense of "subject" we used in logic, namely, as part of the description of substance; for prime matter [15] is not a subject

in that sense at all.) Next, inasmuch as it is common to all forms, it is called "matter" and "stuff."[18] It is also called an "element" because it is resolved into [elements] through a process of analysis, and so it is the simple part receptive of the form as part of the whole composite, and likewise for whatever is analogous. It is also called a "constituent," because the composition begins from it in this very sense, and likewise for whatever is analogous. It is as though when one begins from it, it is called a "constituent," whereas when one begins from the composite and ends at it, then it is called an "element," since the element is the simplest part of the composite.

5.   These are the internal principles of the subsistence of the body, but the body also has an efficient and final cause. The efficient cause is what imprinted the form belonging to bodies into their matter. So it is through the form that the matter came to subsist, and from the two of them there came to subsist the composite that acts through its form and is affected through its matter. The final cause is that for the sake of which these forms were imprinted into matters.

6.   Since our discussion here concerns the common principles, the term "agent" used here and the term "final cause" applied here are both common. Here, what is common is understood in two ways. (1) One is that the agent is something common on the grounds that it performs the first action according to which the rest of the actions are ordered, like what bestows the first corporeal form on the first matter—if there is something like that (according to what we will learn in its proper place)—in which case it bestows the initial foundation subsequent to which what comes next reaches completion. The final cause is common [in this sense], in that it is the end to which all natural things are directed—if there is an end for that (according to what we will learn in its proper place). This is one way [we understand "common"]. Another way something is common is (2) by way of universality, like the universal "agent" said of each one of the particular agents of particular things, and the universal "end" is said of each one of the particular ends of particular things. [16] The difference between the two is the following. What is common in the first sense is a determinately existing being one in number to which the intellect makes reference by reason that it is such, without its being able to be said of many. What is common in the second sense is not a single determinately existing being; rather, it is an intelligible thing that encompasses many determinate beings, which, for the intellect, are common in that they are an agent or an end, in which case this common thing is said of many.

7.   If it is in the first way that the common efficient principle of the whole is an efficient principle for things possessing natures, then it does not itself possess a nature, since all of the things that possess a nature come after this principle, and it is related to all of them in that it is their principle because they possesses a nature. So if the principle were to possess a nature, it would then either be a principle of itself—but this is absurd—or something other than it is the efficient principle—and this is a contradiction. When this is the case, the natural philosopher has no way to investigate it, since it is not in any way mixed with natures. Moreover, it may be a principle of

---

18   Ṭīna, literally, "clay."

both things possessing natures as well as things existing without natures, in which case its causality is of a more general existence than the causality of anything that is a cause of natural things specifically, and also more general than things that have a specific relation to things possessing natures (if there is such a thing).

8.   In fact, for all causal relations in nature, it may be the case that what is an efficient principle for all natural things other than itself is not an efficient principle of them in an absolute sense, but the common efficient principle in the latter way.[19] It would be unremarkable, then, if the natural philosopher were to investigate the state of [the common efficient principle in the latter way], where the method of the investigation would be to discover the state of each thing that is an efficient principle of any one of the causal relations in nature, how it has its power, how it is related to its effect in terms of proximity, remoteness, when in direct contact and not in direct contact,[20] etc., and to demonstrate it. When one does that, one has learned the nature of the general agent common to natural bodies in this latter way, since one will know the state that is specific to being an agent with respect to natural bodies, and then, on the basis of this reasoning, the state of the final principle itself will be better known. That the principles are these four (and we[c] will differentiate them later) is something posited for physics and demonstrated in First Philosophy [i.e., metaphysics].[21]

9.   The body has an additional principle due to the fact that [17] it undergoes change, or is perfected, or comes to be and is generated. Its undergoing change is different from its being perfected, and what is understood by something's temporal creation and being generated is different from what is understood by either [undergoing change or being perfected].

10.   What is understood by its being subject to change is that it had one attribute that ceased to be and another attribute came to belong to it. In that case there are [three things]: (1) something that endures, namely, what undergoes change, (2) a state that was existing and then did not exist, and (3) a state that did not exist and then did exist. Clearly, then, in as much as it is something undergoing change, it must have something receptive to what it changes from and what it changes into, as well as a current form and its privation, which accompanied the form that departs, for example, the garment that blackens, the white and the black, the black's having been absent when the white was present.

11.   What is understood by something's being perfected is that it comes to have something that was not in it without anything departing from it. An example is something that was at rest being moved; for at the moment it was at rest, it was deprived only of the motion that may belong to it possibly and potentially, and whenever it is moved, it is only the privation that ceases. Another example is the blank

---

[19] See par. 6, no. (2).

[20] Lit. "parallel," "in correspondence with," but neither captures the example Ibn Sīnā has in mind, that is, magnetism.

[21] For the account of causes in Ibn Sīnā's metaphysics, see our translation here of *The Salvation*, "Metaphysics," I.12, 209–11.

slate on which one writes. What is perfected must also involve [three things]: (1) a determinate being that was imperfect and then perfected, (2) something that took place in it, and (3) a privation that preceded it.

12.　Privation is a condition for the thing to be subject to change or perfection; for if there had been no privation, it would be impossible for the thing to be subject to perfection or change; instead, the perfection and form would always belong to it. So, to the extent that something truly is either subject to change or to perfection, it requires a preceding privation, whereas privation, to be a privation, does not require any change or perfection to occur. In that case, eliminating privation eliminates what is subject to change or perfection as such, whereas eliminating what is subject to change and perfection need not eliminate the privation. From this perspective, privation is prior and so it is a principle—if a principle is whatever must be present, no matter how so, in order that some other thing exist but not conversely. If that is not sufficient for something to be a principle, and a principle is not whatever must be present in whatever manner but is instead whatever must be present at the same time as the thing of which it is a principle without being prior or posterior, then privation is not a principle. We gain nothing by quibbling over terminology, so instead of "principle" [in the statement "a principle is whatever must be present . . . but not conversely"] let us use "whatever is required . . . but not conversely." Thus, we find that the thing receptive to change and perfection, the privation, and the form are all required for the body to be something subject to change and perfection. This is clear to us upon the most rudimentary consideration.

13.　What is understood by a body's being generated and temporally created requires us to affirm something that has come to be as well as a preceding privation. It is not easy to prove that the generation and temporal creation of this thing that comes to be and is generated requires a prior existing substance that was connected to the privation of the generated form [18] and then separated from it when the privation ceased [and the form came to be]. In fact we must simply posit it for the natural philosopher as a thesis and persuade him by means of induction, but demonstrate it in First Philosophy.[22] (Sometimes the discipline of dialectic furnishes some useful bit of information to quiet the soul of the student, but the demonstrative disciplines are not mixed with dialectic.)

14.　So the body has certain principles that cannot be separated from it and whatever is in it by way of subsistence—for these we reserve the term "principles." Inasmuch as it is a body in the absolute sense, [these principles] are the aforementioned matter and corporeal form, adhering to which are either the accidental quantities or the species form that gives it a perfection. Inasmuch as it is something subject to change, perfection, or generation, it had, prior to its generation, the additional relation of the privation joined to prime matter—this being a "principle," based on what was said.[23]

---

[22] See our translation here of *The Cure*, "Metaphysics," IV.2, 219–23.

[23] See par. 12.

15.   Next, if we take what is general about the changing, perfecting, and generated thing, then the principles are matter, configuration,[24] and privation. If we single
out what is subject to change, then the principles are matter and a contrary; for the
thing that changes away from and toward the intermediate does so only inasmuch as
it contains a certain contrariness—the distinction in the contrariety, [that is] between
configuration and privation,[d] seems to be part of what you have learned, now that it
comes to you on the basis of what you learned. The substance, inasmuch as it is a
substance, is a configuration of a form—you have learned the difference between the
form and the accident. As for things that are subject to nonsubstantial change and
perfection, their configurations are an accident, but the convention in this discipline
has been to call every configuration a "form." So let us call every configuration a form
and mean by it everything that comes to be in a recipient on account of which it is
described by some specific attribute. The prime matter is different from either of these
in that it exists together with both of them in its current condition.[25]

16.   The form is different from the privation in that the form is in itself an
essence that adds to the existence belonging to prime matter, whereas the privation
does not add to the existence that belongs to prime matter. Instead prime matter is
associated with [privation] as its state of being correlated with this form, when [that
form] does not exist, but the potentiality to receive it does. This privation is not
absolute privation but rather a privation that has some manner of existing. It is a privation of something concurrent with a configuration and a disposition for [that thing]
in a determinate matter; for human does not come out of what is wholly not-human;
rather it comes out of what is not-human in something that is receptive to human.
So generation is by way of the form, not the privation, whereas corruption is by way
of the privation, not the form.

17.   It may be said [19] that the thing was "out of" ('an) the matter and privation, but it is not said that it is "out of" the form; for it is said that the bed was out
of the matter, that is, out of the wood, and out of the not-bed. In many situations it
is correct to say that it was out of prime matter, whereas in many others it is not
correct; however, it is always said that it was out of the privation. For a writer is not
out of a human; rather, it is said that a human was a writer, and it is said that a human
was out of the sperm and a bed was out of the wood. The reason for that in the case
of the sperm is because the form of sperm was cast off, and so in that case the expression "out of" indicates the sense of "after," in the way what is indicated in "it *was* out
of the privation" is like saying that a human is out of not-human, that is, after the
not-human. As for wood, inasmuch as it is also said that the bed was out of the wood,
then it *was* wood, even if the wood had not been devoid of the form of wood, it was
devoid of a certain form, since as long as the wood did not change with respect to a

---

[24] That is, the form.

[25] By its having x configuration it is deprived of a not-x configuration. See the definition of "privation"
in par. 16.

given description and was not given a shape through woodworking and carving, the bed is not "out of" it, and it does not receive its shape. The sperm is similar in a way—since both [the sperm and the wood] had changed out of a certain state—and so with reference to it one also uses the expression "out of."

18.   With reference to these two kinds of subject and matter, "out of" is said in the sense of "after," whereas for another kind of subject one uses the expression "out of" and "from" (min) in a different sense. An illustration of this is that when a given form is attributed to certain subjects only by reason of mixture and composition, it could be said that what is generated is "out of" them, where one indicates with the expressions "out of" and "from" that what is generated comes to subsist from them, as we say that the ink was "out of" the vitriol and gall. Moreover, with the first kind [namely, the case of the sperm and the wood], the expression "out of" seems to be said in a sense that is compounded of afterness and this latter sense; for what was out of the sperm and the wood was in the sense that it was after they were in some state and then something was drawn from them and what was generated, which was said to have been out of them, is made to subsist. So, for whatever is like the sperm and the vitriol, it is not said that the thing was what is generated, and so it is not said that the sperm was a human or the vitriol was ink (in the manner that one says the human was a writer), except by some kind of metaphor and in the sense of "to become," that is, "to change."[e] In the case of whatever is like the wood, it might be said in both ways, and so it is said that the bed was out of the wood and the wood was a bed. That is because the wood, insofar as it is wood, does not corrupt the way that sperm corrupts, and likewise for the human inasmuch as he receives the [form of] writing. Whatever is not devoid of a shape, however, does not receive the shape of the bed and likewise for the sperm, [20] inasmuch as it undergoes alteration into humanness. Now any instance in which it is incorrect to say "out of" becomes correct once privation is related to it, the way one says "the writer was out of the nonwriting human," but the privation itself cannot be expressed at all correctly except in conjunction with the expression "out of"; for it is not said that the nonwriter *was* a writer, otherwise he would be a nonwriter writer. Certainly, if one does not mean by "nonwriter" the nonwriter himself, but rather the subject described as a nonwriter, then that could be said, but it is always correct to use the expression "out of."

19.   Still, I will not be an extremist in this or anything like it. Languages can differ in the license of such usage and its import. I say instead that when one means by the expression "out of" the two senses that we mentioned, they are permitted wherever we permit them [i.e., as licensed by the Arabic language] and not permitted wherever we do not permit them.

20.   In the place corresponding with this one [here],[26] there is sometimes mentioned the desire of prime matter for the form and the imitation of [prime matter]

---

[26] That is, Aristotle's *Physics* I.9.

by the female and form by the male, but this is something I just do not understand [for the following reasons]. (1) No one would dispute denying psychological desire of matter. (2) Equally improbable [as simile] is the natural, compulsory desire that sets [matter] in motion, as for example [the inclination] the stone has to move downwards in order to be perfected after having a defect with respect to its natural place. (1) It could have been conceivable that matter would be something desiring form if (1a) there had been an absolute absence of all forms, or (1b) a weariness with an adjoined form, or (1c) a dissatisfaction with one of the perfecting forms that causes [the matter] to be of a given species, and if it could set itself in motion to acquire the form the way the stone does in acquiring its place—if it contained a motive power. [Matter], however, is not (1a) wholly devoid of all forms. It is ill-suited to [matter] to be weary with the present form (16) such that it would effect [the form's] destruction and abandonment; for if the presence of this form is something that necessarily causes weariness with [the form's] very presence, then [the matter] must not desire it. If [the weariness] is due to the length of time, then the desire happens accidentally to [the matter] after a time—it is not something in its substance—and in that case there will be a cause that imposes [that weariness]. It is also inconceivable that (1c) [matter] can be dissatisfied with [the form that is] present and in fact desire to gather contraries into itself. This is absurd—and the real absurdity would be to suppose that [matter] desires the way the soul desires. (2) The compelled [natural] desire is only towards some perfecting end in the perfected nature, and natural ends are not impossible. In light of this, how could the matter be moved to the form when the new form comes to it only as a result of a cause that eliminates its existing form [21] and not by its acquiring it through its own motion? If they had not made this the desire for the forms that cause [the matter] to subsist, that is, those that are first perfections, but rather for the second consequential perfections, then conceiving what is meant by this desire would have been somehow understandable. How can that be, however, when they have made that a desire of [the matter] for the forms that cause subsistence?!

21.   As a result of these things, it is difficult for me to understand this talk—which is more like the talk of mystics than the talk of philosophers. I only hope that someone else will be able to understand this language, as he should, so that one might refer to him in this matter. If one were to replace [in the thesis] the prime matter understood as an absolute with some certain matter that receives perfection from the natural form in such a way that, from the natural form, it comes to have an incitement toward the perfections of that form (like earth for descending and fire for ascending), then there would be a way to understand this talk, although it will attribute that desire to the efficient form. [Prime matter's having desire] in an absolute sense, however, I definitely do not understand.

IV. SELECTIONS ON ATOMISM FROM *THE CURE*, "PHYSICS"[27]

I. From "Physics," III.3[a]

THE STATE OF BODIES WITH RESPECT TO THEIR DIVISION AND A REPORT OF THE VARIOUS ARGUMENTS ON WHICH THE DETRACTORS RELY

1. [184] People have different opinions concerning these perceptible bodies. (1) Some give them a composition from parts that are absolutely indivisible and make each body something comprised of a finite number of [these parts]. (2) Others make the body something composed of an infinite [number] of parts. (3) Still others either make each body have a finite number of parts actually existing in it, or something lacking actual parts initially, and when it actually possesses parts, then each one of its separate parts is also a body lacking actual parts. So in opinion (3) the body is either a body lacking parts, or it is composed of bodies lacking parts. The meaning of "lacking parts" is that at that moment [the body] has no part that one can posit as distinct, but instead [the body] is one by way of continuity. That does not mean it cannot be divided. It is rather the case, in their opinion, that it is always receptive to division, and whenever it is divided, what results from the division is itself a body that can be divided [further]. Sometimes, however, there is no division, because of the absence of what facilitates dividing it, or it is beyond the power of what divides it, or owing to [the body's] hardness, or the impossibility of its being broken up, though in itself a mid-point can be posited in it. Before division, then, every body lacks parts entirely; instead, what affects the parts is the occurrence of division, whether that division happens by a disruption of the continuity, or by an accident which, with its arrival, distinguishes one part from another (whether it be a [non]relational accident, such as white, or a relational accident, such as being opposite and parallel), or by imagining and positing [a division]. Those who say that bodies terminate at indivisible parts include (1a) some who make those parts bodies themselves, (1b) others who make them indivisible lines, and (1c) still others who make them neither bodies, nor lines, nor anything that has in itself sides or dimensions.

2. Proponents of the first of the former two doctrines,[28] namely, the followers of Democritus (1a), Proclus[29] (1b), and Epicurus (1c), differ from the true doctrine in that [185] they say that combining these bodies occurs by way of contiguity alone;

---

[27] A translation of Ibn Sīnā's entire discussion of atomism, along with commentary, is available in Paul Lettinck, "Ibn Sīnā on Atomism," in *al-Shajarah* 4 (1999): 1–51.

[28] By "these two doctrines" Ibn Sīnā means (1) and (2) in the main division, par. I, nos. (1) and (2)

[29] Although it is odd to see Proclus (*Ubrūqilūs*) alongside Democritus and Epicurus, Proclus was an atomist of sorts, even if not a corpuscularian. He followed Plato's *Timaeus* in holding that the ultimate building blocks of the physical world were atomic triangles, and, moreover, his *Commentary on Plato's Timaeus* had been translated into Arabic. Perhaps Ibn Sīnā is extending Proclus' line of thought and reasoning that if these basic triangles are atomic, then likewise there must be atomic or indivisible lines from which these triangles, as it were, are constructed, and so Proclus in Ibn Sīnā's mind may very well correspond with (1b).

that nothing continuous comes to be from them at all; that perceptible bodies are not in fact continuous (for these primary bodies in perceptible bodies are actually distinct one from another); and that [the primary bodies] are not receptive to further division, unless it is imagined division—though nonetheless some are smaller and others larger. Proponents of the truth [i.e., opinion (3)] allow that a large perceptible body cannot have actual parts, and when parts actually happen to be separate, they can be rejoined as a single thing, but then the specific property of each one of the [separate] parts ceases, and so it itself does not remain. [. . .]

3.   [The proponents of indivisible parts that are not bodies (1c)] say that if the parts of the body were not finite, then they would be infinite, but then a body would be divisible into half and again into half and so on infinitely.[30] When something in motion wanted to cross a given distance, it would need to cross half, but before that, half of half of it, and in a finite time it would need to cross an infinite number of halves. So it necessarily would not cross the distance at all. The swift Achilles also necessarily would never catch up to the creeping [186] tortoise, and the ant would never completely cross a sandal over which it travels (the first example is from the ancients, the second is from the moderns). But motion exists. So the body's divisions are finite. [. . .]

4.   Those who make these parts terminate at a body (1a), namely, the followers of Democritus, say that the body must either be completely divisible until nothing remains of it that is not divided or it is not completely divisible. If it is in its nature to be divided, then the occurrence [of such division] is not impossible. When the not-impossible is posited as existing, no absurdity arises from it—a nonabsurd falsity might result, but a nonabsurd falsity does not entail an absurdity. So let us posit that every possible division in the body has actually resulted, at which time either nothing exists, or points exist, or indivisible bodies exist. It would be absurd, however, for them to terminate at nothing [187] or at points. If it breaks down into nothing, then its composition is from nothing, which is absurd. If it breaks down into points, then its composition is also from points, which is also absurd. (The consensus among the learned is that (i) no matter how many points are joined together, they do not exceed the bulk of a single point; (ii) [the points] meet *completely*, not with some of them hindering others from meeting; (iii) they do not undergo combination so as to become something occupying a place; and (iv) something continuous does not come to be from them). So the only other option is that [the body] breaks down into bodies whose nature is not to be separated and divided [further], except by imagining and positing [such division].

5.   As for (2), those who maintain that the body has an infinite number of existing parts, they were driven to that by the impossibility of combining bodies out of

---

[30] This argument and the ones presented below rely heavily on Zeno's paradoxes; see Aristotle, *Physics* VI 9 for the classical understanding of Zeno's paradoxes and G. E. L. Owen, "Zeno and the Mathematicians," in *Logic, Science, and Dialectic: Collected Papers in Greek Philosophy*, 45–61 for a contemporary discussion.

indivisible parts and bodies. They said: Since bodies in themselves also possess divisions even if they are not actually separated, if it is stipulated and posited that they
are divided into parts, then each one of [those parts] is some of and a part of the body,
even if it is not separated at all. They say: It remains, then, that the parts of the body
are infinite, and, because of that, the body is infinitely divisible. [This is so] since the
divisions, whether suppositional or involving actual separation, arrive only at parts
adjacent to one another in the body, in which case the parts of the body are commensurate with the capacity for the divisions. So if the capacity for divisions is infinite,
the [body] possesses an infinite number of parts.

6.   Since the atomists harassed those [advocating that the body has an infinite
number of parts] and forced their hand with the problem of the sandal and the ant
as well as the tortoise and Achilles and, in sum, that motion will proceed over an
infinite number of halves and so the final end will never be reached, [those advocating
that the body has an infinite number of parts] took refuge with Epicurus, and so
advocated the leap.[31] In other words, the body might cross a given distance in order
to arrive at an intended terminal point from a point of departure without touching
or passing directly over what is in the middle.

7.   The first foreign imitators of Epicurus produced an example of that from the
rotations of two circles: one near the edge of a spinning millstone and the other near
the center. They noted that if the motion of the part at the edge were equal to the
motion of the part that is near the center, then the two together would cross an identical distance. Next, it is absurd that the part at the center would be at rest, because
the [whole millstone] is continuous, with each part adhering to another. So, clearly
the part at the center is moved, but its leaps are few, and equally clear is that the part
at the edge is moved, but it leaps more frequently in order to cover a larger interval
than the interval of the part at the center.

8.   Since the first of the aforementioned foreigners needed this argument but
considered the leap repulsive, and further did not allow that one continuous motion
is faster than another motion without the intermediacy of a rest, they were forced to
make the part near the center rest more frequently than the part at the edge and forced
into the possibility of [188] intermedial rest. They were also forced to decide that the
millstone fragments while moving, with one of its parts breaking away from another
such that one of them does not need to be moved together with the other, but instead
one of them rests while the other is moved. Thus, one of them stuck with the repulsive
leap, and the other with the repulsive fragmentation.

2. From "Physics," III.4[b]

ESTABLISHING THE TRUE OPINION AND REFUTING THE FALSE

1.   [188] Since we have made reference to the different doctrines concerning this
question of ours, let us begin by indicating the soundness of the true doctrine, then

---

[31] For an explanation of the "leap," see the Introduction, xxx–xxxi.

take on the doubts produced by its detractors, and then solve them. The doctrine that maintains that there is an actually infinite number of parts in the body is obviously false due to the impossibility of crossing an infinite number of things in a finite period of time, and because the assertion of the leap is clearly false in itself. It is also false in that any given multiple consists only of its units, and when one unit does not actually exist, then neither does a multiple. So when a unit part does not exist, then [a given multiple] will not have an infinite number of parts, where the unit part, insofar as it is a unit, is indivisible. Also, when units like it are added to [the multiple], then the addition must be either by contiguity, interpenetration, or continuity. If it is by continuity, then something continuous comes to be from magnitudes consisting of discrete limiting points, so the opinion is falsified. If it is by interpenetration, then no measure comes to be from it whatsoever, even if it reached an actually infinite number of multiplications. If it is by contact [i.e., contiguity], then each one of two parts requires a unique position, since it must have a corporeal magnitude in itself (as we will explain later), in which case it is a body. Now, when one body is joined with a finite number of bodies like it, [189] then the combination of that undoubtedly results in a body, x, that will have a certain proportion to the body, y, [made up of] infinite parts, where the proportion is of one determinate thing to another determinate thing with respect to its size. So when that proportion is increased with respect to the parts, then x, which is composed of finite parts, will ultimately reach the level of y. So x is a body consisting of a finite number of parts that is equal to y, but then y, likewise, consists of a finite number of parts. . . .

2.   We must clearly refute the doctrine of those who compose bodies from [indivisible] nonbodies [i.e., opinion 1c]. We say that when these parts are aggregated and a body made up of them results, then they are aggregated either by means of (1) succession only, (2) contiguity, (3) interpenetration, or (4) continuity. Next, there either is or is not an interval between things that are aggregated. If there is not an interval between them, then either they are in contact with one another completely or not. If they are [in contact with one another] completely, then they interpenetrate, as we explained.[32] If they are not completely [in contact with one another], then either there is something unique to each of them by which it contacts the other or that thing is something common. If it is unique, then there is contiguity, whereas if it is common there is continuity. Thus, when these parts are aggregated, their aggregation must be in one of these ways.

3.   If (1) they are aggregated according to succession only, then no perceptibly continuous bodies result; but our discussion is about [just such bodies].

4.   When they are aggregated according to either (4) continuity or (2) contiguity, then each one of them is divisible into what is occupied and what is unoccupied, what is being touched and what is not being touched, according to what we explained in the preceding chapters. If (3) they do not interpenetrate, then when one of them, x,

---

[32] See the parenthetical observation in III.3, par. 4, p. 165.

contacts another, *y*, and then a third one, *z*, comes into contact with one of the two, [e.g., *y*,], then necessarily *z* is hindered from contacting *x* by the intermediacy of *y*'s contact, in which case each [i.e., *x* and *z*] will have obtained by the contact what the other has not [i.e., one of the two sides of *y*]—this is self-explanatory. So the intermediate object, *y*, is divisible.

5.   If they are in contact completely, then they interpenetrate, [190] and so a magnitude is not increased by their aggregation, in which case, whenever they are aggregated they will be like the unit, which has neither length nor breadth nor depth. Since these indivisible parts do not aggregate in such a way that thereby a body is composed of them, the body, then, is not reducible to them. Thus, the division of bodies does not terminate at parts that cannot be divided by any type of division, and the same holds for all other magnitudes (I mean surfaces and lines).

6.   Also, what rational person would allow us to say that a sheet of atoms that the Sun illuminates on one side, or any other state that happens to it on one side, must be such that the other side is in that state as well?! Or who would allow us to say the following. The sheet itself does not have two sides. Instead the light falls on one side of the sheet, and the side that does not face the Sun is that very same side; for when one sees *this* side, one has already seen *that* side, since this one and that one are the same when there is no this and that, in which case anyone standing on one side of the sheet sees the sheet illuminated from the other side.

7.   In fact, the existence of indivisible parts would necessarily entail that there be no circles, nor right triangles, nor many other [geometrical] figures. [This follows in the first case] since the circle requires that the outside circumference be larger than any inside circumference that is contiguous with it, but what is contiguous is equal to that with which it is contiguous, not larger. [In the second case], when two sides of a right triangle are each ten units, then the hypotenuse is the square root of two hundred, which [according to the present view] would either be an absurdity that does not exist or it is true, but parts would be broken up, which [according to the present view] they are not.

8.   They say, however, that vision errs with respect to the circle and right triangle, and they are, strictly speaking, figures made up of successively indented layers. They nonetheless do not deny the existence, for instance, of a square having the following description. Let one construct a straight line from four atoms as well as three other lines like it, where one of the lines is AD, and let us superimpose it on another line EH such that there is no space whatsoever between them, and in like manner IL is after EH, and MP is after IL until a surface AP is produced according to their doctrine.

A	B	C	D
E	F	G	H
I	J	K	L
M	N	O	P

Now it is commonly accepted [according to their doctrine] that there is no space left between these atoms in the surface to accommodate another atom, so four atoms—

namely the first, A (from line AD), the second, F (from line EH), the third, K (from line IL), and the fourth [191], P (from line MP)—are the diagonal. There are only two possibilities. One possibility is that these atoms must be touching one another along a line projected between atoms A and P, in which case there is a straight line composed from them, namely the diagonal, but it will be equal to the two equal sides. This, however, is far from acceptable, for it is known from observations that the diagonal in a case like this is longer than the side. The other possibility is that these atoms must be separated from one another. In this case, there is either an empty space between them or not. If there is an empty space between them, then the lines were not superimposed on one another with no empty space between them, but that is what was done—this is a contradiction. If there is no empty space between them, then there must be something between them, whether an atom or more or less than [an atom]. If it is less than an atom, then the atom has been divided. If it is a whole atom contiguous with them or is two atoms, then the length of the diagonal must always either not fall short of the two sides together, or it falls short of the combined length of the two sides by a single imperceptible atom. But the diagonal always falls short of the combined length of the two sides, and [the length by which it falls short] is perceptible and a significant magnitude. [. . .]

9. [195] Another abomination entailed by [the doctrine] of the atoms is the following. We are absolutely certain that when a moving object is moved from right to left and another is moved from left to right along two parallel, straight lines, the two get closer and closer to one another until they meet opposite one other, and then they depart from one another. So let us posit one set of four atoms and another set of four, and construct from each set two lines positioned next to one another, just as we did for the square built of atoms:

A   B   C   D
E   F   G   H

[196] Now we posit an atom on the right extreme of one of them and an atom on the left extreme of the other. We set the two atoms in motion until the one that was on the right arrives at its other extreme and the one that was on the left arrives at its other extreme. We also imagine that their velocity is equal. So the two will be opposite one another and then they will depart from one another. Now the two must be opposite one another either along the [first] half or after the half. If being opposite occurs precisely when the latter is at the second atom from the extreme from which it is moved and the former is at the second atom from the extreme from which it is moved, then the two are not yet opposite, because the second atom from both of [the points of departure] is the third from the other according to what was laid down.

A   <u>B</u>   C   D
E   F   <u>G</u>   H

If they are opposite one another by each one being at the third atom, then the two departed from one another at the very moment of being opposite.

A   B   C   D
E   F   G   H

If they are opposite when one is at the second atom on its line and the other is at the third atom of its line, then their motions were not equal. [. . .]

3. From "Physics," III.5ᶜ

THE RESOLUTION OF THE PUZZLES OF THOSE WHO REFUTE THE PART

1.   [198] Let us now begin the solution of their puzzles and complete what is appropriate to this discussion with respect to the potentially infinite divisions pertaining to moved objects, motion, and time . . . [199] There would be something to their argument based upon halving only if we were to say that the body has parts as long as they are not divided into halves, thirds, fourths, or the like, such that it would appear to have an infinite number of parts. We ourselves, however, in no way require that the body have parts until it is [actually] parted, but it is not possible for a body to have been divided already into an infinite number of halves. Thus, what they say does not follow. Most of what they say here is "You see that . . ."—when nothing is indicated and no part marked off from another, and this one and that one are not distinct! They fail to recognize that this one and that become [distinct] only by indicating, but if there is no [indicating], then neither is there a this one and a that one. Now when there is neither this one nor that one, then how can this one and that one be distinct? And [all of this] despite the fact that the distance covered is covered in a time like itself, that is, its limits are finite, being infinitely divisible into halves by imagination and supposition, but it has no actually existing divisions. [. . .]

2.   [202] Democritus erred in his argumentation by granting himself one premise—namely, that the whole body is divisible—since this has two meanings. One is that [the body] is divided simultaneously in its entirety. The other is that [the body] is not divisible in any manner unless it leads to parts that are themselves divisible without end. The first is not admissible, nor is its true opposite that the body terminates in the division at what is indivisible; rather, its opposite is [that the whole of it is not actually divided simultaneously]. As for the whole of its not being actually divided simultaneously, this does not preclude its being divided one division after another infinitely. Moreover, neither is it the case that when each one of them taken separately is separately possible, then the whole is something whose occurrence is possible. For instance, any numerical doubling can apply to number, but not every numerical doubling can apply simultaneously. The truth, rather, is that there can occur in the body, potentially without end, any division you want, where each one successively is some type of division, but we in no way grant that they all occur [simultaneously], because the very first thing that that would require is that the things effecting the division are themselves actually infinite, and this is impossible. In short, this is one of the errors that occurs as a result of equating the two expressions "the whole" and "each one."

V. SELECTIONS ON "INCLINATION" (*MAYL*) AND PROJECTILE MOTION

I. From *The Book of Definitions*[a]

[34] Tendency and inclination are a quantity by which the body offers resistance to whatever opposes [the body] from moving toward a given direction.

2. From "Physics," IV.8[b]

1. [298] Every motion in the proper sense proceeds from an inclination that is independently verified by either the repulsion of the thing standing in the way of the mobile or the power needed [by the thing standing in the way] to oppose [the mobile]. This inclination in itself is one of the causal factors (*maʿnā*) by which [the mobile] continues to the motions' limiting points, namely, by repelling a given thing, which the resistance to whatever is in the path of the motion entails, and by advancing towards a given thing. Now it is absurd that what reaches a given limiting point do so without a continuously existing cause, and it is also absurd that this cause is not that which departed[c] from the initial resting place. This cause is proportional to what causes the departure and what resists.[33] That proportion designates inclination; for this thing, as something continuous, does not designate inclination, even if the subject is one [and the same], whereas this thing that is called "inclination" sometimes exists at a single instant.[34] Now motion is precisely that which might require for its existence a continuous time, and as long as the inclination is neither constrained and repressed nor corrupted, the motion that necessarily results from it will exist. When the inclination is corrupted, its corruption will not itself be the existence of another inclination, but rather that [inclination] is another causal factor that might connect with [the inclination that was corrupted]. Now when two motions come to be, the result is from two inclinations, and when there exists a later inclination toward a different direction, then [the inclination] is not itself this continuous thing such that simultaneously it would be a cause of the attainment and separation. Rather, some other inclination inevitably comes to be that has a first [instant] of coming to be, that is, it exists at that first [instant]; for its existence is not dependent upon a time that is not, such as motion and rest, which do not have a first [instant] of coming to be, since neither of them exist in any way save during a time or after a time given that [that motion] requires an instant[d] before which and after which the body is not at it, and so requires a temporal priority and posteriority. Quite the contrary, [the later inclination] is like the nonmotion that is at each instant. So likewise it is permissible that that instant

---

[33] That is, inclination will be proportional to the force causing the body to be displaced and the force resisting what is in the body's way.

[34] Ibn Sīnā's point seems to be that inclination can be assigned a fixed quantity without reference to time, inasmuch as there can be a determinate quantity of inclination at an instant, which in turn is to be contrasted to motion, which can only be assigned a determinate quantity after a given period of time.

that might mark off the limit of the motion is itself a limiting point for the nonmotion, to the extent that a nonmotion as something existing at an instant is a limit of the motion continuing to exist after it. So between the motion and the nonmotion there is no need for one instant and another instant; rather a single instant is enough. No absurdity arises, because motion and rest are not simultaneous at that instant; rather only one of them is.

2.   [299] The instant at which there is the first existence of the second inclination is not the instant at which there is the last existence of the first inclination, since it is the last existence of the first inclination at which—we have explained—it exists when there is something continuous. So if it exists as something continuing for a time, then in fact there is rest, whereas if it does not exist as something continuous but at an instant, then that instant is not the last, yet what has a last [instant] is something existing at it, since what has a last [instant] is something continuous. Now the continuous thing is not something continuous, while it is not occurring, and the two instants were not a single thing precisely because what simultaneously requires the occurrence and nonoccurrence is not in the nature of the thing, such that its natures require that there is and is not a certain actual requirement in it. Hence, the last instant of the first inclination is not the first instant of the second inclination.

3.   Do not pay attention to whoever says that the two inclinations are conjoined; for how could there be something in which there is a resistance or clinging to a given region as well as a withdrawal from it? For it is not supposed that in a stone that is thrown upward there is a positively downward inclination. Quite the contrary, there is a principle whose character is to produce that inclination, when the obstacle is withdrawn or overcome, just as in water there is a power and principle to produce coldness in the water's substance, when the obstacle is withdrawn or overcome, as you have learned. So it has become evident that the two instants are distinct, and between every two instants there is a time, and it is more likely that the juncture remains a temporal juncture; however, we took it as an instantaneous juncture. Let it be closer to what is required owing to the absence of rest.

3. From "Physics," IV.12ᵉ

1.   [314] Bodies found possessing inclination are like the heavy and the light: the heavy is what inclines downward, whereas the light inclines upward. Whenever [bodies possessing inclination] undergo an increase in inclination, they undergo displacement more slowly;ᶠ for lifting or dragging a large heavy stone is not like lifting or dragging a small little one, and pushing a little air [e.g., a partially inflated balloon] under water is not like pushing a lot of air [e.g., a fully inflated balloon]. The reason that small bodies are overwhelmed—for example, when a single mustard seed, a piece of straw, or a splinter of wood are thrown and do not pass through the air the way the heavy body does—is not that the heavier thing is more susceptible to being thrown and dragged, but because some of these, owing to their smallness, do not receive from what throws them a power that would move both them as well as what is adjacent to

them [i.e., the medium] sufficiently to make them capable of cutting the air. Moreover, the quick depletion of that [power] [315] is due to the cause that depletes the acquired, accidental, and motive powers. For example, a single spark would be extinguished by the cause that depletes an acquired heat before a large fire would be so depleted. Also, some rarified things are not able to cut the air, but instead the air through which they pass commingles with them, thus becoming a cause for the depletion of their acquired power.

2.   You will learn that whatever opposes what passes through it is the thing that depletes the power of the motion. This is like rarefied fire and water, for they are more susceptible to alteration [i.e., depletion]. Now if [a projectile's] largeness and increased weight were the reason for its susceptibility to being thrown farther, then whenever the projectile's size and weight were increased, its susceptibility to being thrown farther would be greater, which is contrary to fact. Instead, when the heavy and light object are considered, and no other causes are considered, then the smaller magnitude is more susceptible to forced motion and a faster velocity. So the ratio of the distances and times covered by the mobiles—both those moved by force and those having a natural inclination—is proportional to the relation between one inclination and another. The times, however, are inversely proportional to the distances, that is, in the case of distances, the more intense the inclination, the greater the distance covered, whereas in the case of time, the greater the inclination, the shorter the time.

3.   Now if there is absolutely no inclination, and the forcibly moved object is moved for a period of time, and that period of time is proportional to a given time of a motion possessing a forced inclination—in which case it is proportional to a given ratio of one inclination (should it exist) to an inclination possessing the inclination of the forcibly moved object—then what has absolutely no inclination in it would be just as susceptible to the force as what does have a given inclination (should it exist). In that case, however, what meets no opposition would be proportional to what meets some opposition (were it to exist), thus resulting in a contradiction exactly like the one we addressed in the case of the void and for the very same reason.[35]

---

35 See "Physics," II.8, p. 175 for the case of the void. Roughly the same argument is also found in al-Ishārāt wa-t-tanbīhāt, Jacques Forget, ed., 109–10. "Indication: the body in which there is neither a potential nor actual inclination is not susceptible [110] to a forcible inclination by which it is moved, and in general it will not be forcibly moved. If this were not the case, then let x be forcibly moved in a given time $[t_1]$ [and] given distance $[d_1]$ and let y, for example, in which there is a given inclination and resistance, $[i_1]$ be moved. Clearly, then, y will be moved $[d_1]$ in a longer time. Now let z [have] an inclination $[i_2]$ weaker than that inclination $[i_1]$ which as a result of the same mover covers a [greater] distance $[d_2]$ in the same time $[t_1]$ whose ratio to the first distance $[d_1]$ is the ratio of the time of the one possessing the first inclination $[t_2]$ and the time of the one lacking the inclination $[t_1]$ such that it is forcibly moved the same distance in the same time of the one lacking the inclination. Thus, there will be two forced motions $[x$ and $z]$, z having a resistance in it and x not having a resistance in it, that are of comparable states with respect to fastness and slowness, which is absurd. Note: you must note here that there is not some indivisible time [i.e., 0 amount of time] such that during it a certain motion having no inclination might occur and would have no ratio to a given time of a motion possessing an inclination."

4. From "Physics," IV.14g

PROJECTILE MOTION IN A MEDIUM

1. [326] When we independently verify the issue [of projectile motion], we find the most correct doctrine is the doctrine of those who think that the moved object acquires an inclination from the mover, where the inclination is what one perceives through the senses when one attempts to bring to rest either [something moving] naturally or forcibly by means of another force. In this case one perceives the power to resist that admits of intensification and weakening, that is, at one time it is more intense and at another time weaker than what is undoubtedly present in the body, even if the body is brought to rest by a force.

2. Moreover, the doctrine of those who think that the air is driven forward and in turn drives [the projectile] forward has missed the mark.[36] How could it have hit the mark, when the discussion concerning the air is the same as the discussion concerning the projectile?! [That follows] because this air that is driven forward either continues to be in motion at the same time that the mover comes to rest or it does not. If it does not continue to be in motion, then how does it cause the projectile to be moved forward? If it continues to be moved, then the discussion concerning [how it stays in motion] still remains.

3. Next, if [something] moves faster and so must penetrate a wall more intensely than the arrow's penetration—for in their opinion the arrow penetrates only through the power of what causes it to penetrate,[h] that is, from the motion of the air, which is faster—but the air is obstructed and deflected by those things that stand in its way, then why is the arrow not obstructed and deflected? If the reason is that the air near the tip of the arrow is obstructed, while the air near to the notch of the arrow still retains its power, then the arrow has to have arrived before the air, but they maintain that the air arrives first. If the arrow does arrive first, then the air adjacent to the arrow cannot have, as part of the propulsive power, what would cause the arrow to penetrate the wall that blocks it, were its propulsion not from behind. Indeed, the arrow's penetrating the wall cannot be likened to its penetrating the air; for in their opinion the air bears [the arrow] along and drives it forward by reason of the fact that it itself is driven forward. If [the air is driven forward] because the arrow attracts the air behind it in such a way that the air responds by driving forward what attracted it, then what is attracted [i.e., the air] is more intensely attracted than the thing necessarily attracting it [i.e., the arrow].[37] If this intensity is a power or inclination, [327] then the claim in favor of that has been achieved. If [the intensity] is a mere consequence [of its cause], then it ceases when its cause ceases. If the intensity remains [in the thing], then the cause is the power and the inclination.

---

[36] See Aristotle, *Physics* VIII.

[37] The reasoning seems to be that from the arrow's purported attraction the air must have a sufficient power to move both itself and the arrow, which the air supposedly is driving forward.

5. From "Physics," II.8[i]

PROJECTILE MOTION IN A VOID

1. [133] If there is forced motion in the projectile as a result of some power in the void, then [the motion] must continue without ever abating or being interrupted. [That follows] because when the power is in the body, it must either remain or cease. If it remains, then the motion would continue perpetually. If it ceases, or even weakens, its cessation or weakening must either be from a cause or owing to itself. The discussion concerning cessation will provide you the way to proceed with respect to weakening.

2. We say that it is impossible for [the power] to cease owing to itself; for whatever necessarily ceases owing to itself cannot exist at any time. If it ceases by a cause, then that cause is either in the moved body or in something else. If [the cause of the motion's ceasing] is in the moved body, and at the beginning of the motion it had not actually been causing that [cessation] but in fact had been overpowered, and then later became a cause and dominated, then there is another cause for its being such, in which case an infinite regress results.

3. If the cause is either external to the body or cooperates with the cause that is in the body, then the agent or cooperative cause act either by direct contact or not. If it acts by direct contact, then it is a body that is directly contacting the mobile, but this cause would not be in a pure void, and so the forced motion would neither abate nor stop in the pure void. If it does not act by direct contact, but is something or other that acts at a distance, then why did it not act initially? The counterargument is just like the argument concerning the cause if it were in the body.[38] It is most appropriate, instead, that the continuous succession of opposing things is what causes this power to decrease and corrupt [134], but this is not possible unless the motion is not in the pure void.

VI. SELECTIONS ON PSYCHOLOGY FROM *THE CURE*, "THE SOUL"[39]

I. From "The Soul," I.I[a]

ESTABLISHING THE EXISTENCE OF THE SOUL AND DEFINING IT AS SOUL

1. [4] We must first direct our discussion to establishing the existence of the thing we call a soul, and next to whatever follows from that. We say: We commonly

---

38 That is, it leads to an infinite regress of causes.

39 For a general overview of Ibn Sīnā's psychology see Herbert Davidson, *Alfarabi, Avicenna, and Averroes on Intellect*; for its subsequent influence on medieval Latin philosophy, see Dag N. Hasse, *Avicenna's De Anima in the Latin West*. For more specific studies see Micheal E. Marmura, "Avicenna's 'Flying Man' in Context," 181–95; Thérèse-Anne Druart, "The Human Soul's Individuation and Its Survival after the Body's Death: Avicenna on the Causal Relation between Body and Soul," 259–73; Dimitri Gutas, "Intuition and Thinking," 1–38.

observe certain bodies perceiving by the senses and being moved by volition; in fact, we observe certain bodies taking in nutrients, growing, and reproducing their like. That does not belong to them on account of their corporeality; so the remaining option is that in themselves there are principles for that other than their corporeality. The thing out of which these actions issue and, in short, anything that is a principle for the issuance of any actions that do not follow a uniform course devoid of volition, we call "soul." This expression is a term for this thing not on account of its substance but on account of a certain relation it has, that is, in the sense that it is a principle of these actions.[40] We will seek to identify its substance and the category to which it belongs later. For now, we have established the existence of something that is a principle only of what we stated, and we have established the existence of something in the sense that it has a particular accident. [5] We need to move from this accidental thing it has to a point at which we can verify the thing itself, if we are to discover what it is, as though we had already come to know that there is a mover for something set in motion but we do not thereby know what this mover is itself.

2.   So we say: Since we think that the things to which the soul belongs are bodies, and since it is only through this thing belonging to them that their existence as plant and animal is complete, then this thing is a part of their subsistence. As you have learned in a number of places, there are two parts to subsistence: a part through which the thing is what it is actually, and a part through which the thing is what it is potentially, that is, what is like the subject.[41] If the soul belongs to the second division—and there is no doubt that the body belongs to that division—then the animal and the plant will not be complete as animal or plant by the body or by the soul. So we will need another perfection that is the actual principle of what we said, in which case that would be the soul, but that is the very thing we are discussing. In fact, the soul rightly should be that through which the plant and the animal actually are a plant and an animal. So if it is also a body, then the form of the body is what we said. Now if it is a certain body through a certain form, then that body is not that principle, inasmuch as it is a body; rather [that body's] being a principle will be due to that form, and the issuance of those states [i.e., sensation, motion, etc.] will be from that form itself, albeit through the medium of this body. So the first principle is that form, and its first actuality is through the intermediacy of this body, where this body is a part of the body of the animal; but there is a primary part [i.e., the form] associated with it that is the principle, and [that] is not a body as such except as part of the whole subject. Clearly, then, the soul itself is not a body; rather it is a part of the animal [6] and the plant: it is a form, or like a form, or like a perfection.

---

[40] That is, actions such as perceiving and being moved by volition, taking in nutrients, growing, reproducing, and the like.

[41] Ibn Sīnā refers here to form and matter, respectively; cf. the translation of "Physics," I.2, par. 2 and 4, pp. 157–58.

3. We say now that the soul can be called a "faculty" (*qūwa*), in relation to the actions that issue from it. In another sense it can be called a "potentiality" (*qūwa*) in relation to the forms of the sensible and intelligible objects that it receives. It also can be called a "form" in relation to the matter it occupies, in which case a material plant or animal substance is a combination of the two. It also can be called a "perfection" in relation to the genus being perfected by it as a fully determinate species among the higher and lower species. [This is so] because the nature of the genus is imperfect and indeterminate as long as the nature of the simple or nonsimple difference is not added to it; once it is added to it, the species is perfected. So the difference is a perfection of the species inasmuch as it is a species. There is not a simple difference for every species (as you have learned), but only for species compounded of a matter and a form, where the form is the simple difference because it is the perfection [of such species].

4. Now every form is a perfection, but not every perfection is a form. For the ruler is a perfection of the city, and the captain is a perfection of the ship, but they are not respectively a form of the city and a form of the ship. So whatever perfection that is itself separate is not in fact the form belonging to matter and in the matter, since the form that is in the matter is the form imprinted in it and subsisting through it, unless perhaps one says in a technical sense that the perfection of the species is the form of the species. Strictly speaking, however, the technical language has settled on [7] "form" when [talking about] something in relation to matter; "end" and "perfection" when it is something in relation to the whole; and "efficient principle" and "motive faculty" when it is something in relation to causing motion. Consequently, the form requires a relation to something at a remove from the substance itself resulting from [the form], and to something through which the actual substance is what it is potentially, and finally to something to which the actions cannot be attributed—that is, the matter—because [the form] is a form with respect to its belonging to the matter. The perfection also requires a relation to the complete thing out of which the actions issue, because it is a perfection on account of its being said of the species.

5. It is clear from this, then, that when we define the soul as a perfection, this most properly denotes its meaning and likewise includes all species of the soul in all respects, not excluding the soul that is separate from matter. Furthermore, when we say that the soul is a perfection, it is more fitting than saying "potentiality," because some of the things that issue from the soul fall under motion and some fall under sensation and perception. Now, properly speaking, perception belongs to them not inasmuch as they have a potentiality that is a principle of action but rather a principle of reception; whereas moving belongs to them not inasmuch as they have a potentiality of reception but rather a principle of action, and neither one deserves more than the other to be related to the soul by reason of its being a potentiality. So, if [the soul] is said to be a potentiality, and both things are meant,[42] this is by way of homonymy.

---

[42] That is, the potentiality of reception and the potentiality of action.

[8] If [the soul] is said to be a potentiality and [potentiality] is limited to one of the two things, then both what we said results as well as something else, namely, it does not include an indication of what the soul is as a soul absolutely; rather, it indicates one of the things and not the other, and we have already explained in the logic books that that is neither good nor correct. When we say "perfection," however, it includes both meanings; for the soul is a perfection due to the potentiality by which the animal's perception is brought to perfection, and it is also a perfection due to the potentiality out of which the actions of the animal issue. Also, both the separate soul and the inseparable soul will be a perfection. [. . .]

6. [11] Perfection has two modes: first perfection and second perfection. The first perfection is that by which the species actually becomes a species, like the shape that belongs to the sword. The second perfection is whatever comes after the species of the thing, such as its actions and passions, like the act of cutting that belongs to the sword, and the acts of discernment, deliberation, sensation, and motion that belong to the human. Certainly these latter perfections belong to the species, but not initially; in order for the species to become what it is actually, it does not need these things to belong to it actually. It is rather the case that, when the principle of these things actually exists, such that these things belong to it in potentiality after having not been in potentiality (save in remote potentiality, [in which case] they need something to be present before them in order really to be in potentiality), it is then that the living thing becomes a living thing actually. Now the soul is the first perfection and, because perfection is a perfection *of* something, the soul is a perfection of something. This thing is the body, where body must be taken in the sense [12] of the genus not the matter (as you learned in "Demonstration").⁴³ This body of which the soul is its perfection is not just any body, for [the soul] is not the perfection of an artificial body, such as the bed, the chair or the like. On the contrary, it is the perfection of a natural body, but not just any natural body—for the soul is not the perfection of fire or earth—rather, in the [sublunar] world, it is a perfection of a natural body out of which issue its second perfections by means of organs that aid in the activities of life, the first of which are nutrition and growth. Thus, the soul—the one that we are defining here—is a first perfection of a natural body possessed of organs that performs the activities of life. [. . .]

7. [15] . . . For the purposes of establishing the existence of the soul belonging to us, here we have to provide a pointer that serves [both] as alert and reminder [16] by hitting the mark with anyone who is at all capable of catching sight of the truth on his own, and also does not require straightening out his way of thinking, or hitting him over the head with it, or steering him away from sophisms. So we say that it has to be imagined as though one of us were created whole in an instant but his sight is veiled from directly observing the things of the external world. He is created as though floating in air or in a void but without the air supporting him in such a way that he

---

⁴³ "Book of Demonstration," I.8; for a parallel passage, also see Ibn Sīnā's "Metaphysics" V.3. Neither text is translated here.

would have to feel it, and the limbs of his body are stretched out and away from one another, so they do not come into contact or touch. Then he considers whether he can assert the existence of his self. He has no doubts about asserting his self as something that exists without also [having to] assert the existence of any of his exterior or interior parts, his heart, his brain, or anything external. He will, in fact, be asserting the existence of his self without asserting that it has length, breadth, or depth, and, if it were even possible for him in such a state to imagine a hand or some other extremity, he would not imagine it as a part of his self or as a necessary condition of his self—and you know that what can be asserted as existing is not the same as what cannot be so asserted and that what is stipulated is not the same as what is not stipulated.[b] Thus, the self whose existence he asserted is his unique characteristic, in the sense that it is he himself, not his body and its parts, which he did not so assert. Thus, what [the reader] has been alerted to is a way to be made alert to the existence of the soul as something that is not the body—nor in fact *any* body—to recognize it and be aware of it, if it is in fact the case that he has been disregarding it and needed to be hit over the head with it.

2. From "The Soul," I.5[c]

CLASSIFICATION OF THE FACULTIES OF THE SOUL

1.   [39] Let us now enumerate the faculties of the soul according to convention and then direct our attention to explaining the nature of each faculty. We say that the faculties of the soul have three primary divisions. The first is the vegetative soul, which is the first perfection of a natural body possessed of organs in terms of its reproducing, growing, and taking nourishment. (The nourishment is a body characterized as similar to the nature of the body of which it is said to be its nourishment, and to which it adds the amount spent, or more or less.) The second is the animal soul, which is the first perfection of a natural body [40] possessed of organs in terms of it perceiving particulars and moving by volition. The third is the human soul, which is the first perfection for a natural body possessed of organs in terms of attributing to it the performance of actions occurring by choice based on thinking and the ascertainment of opinion, and in the sense that it perceives universals.

2.   Were it not for convention, it would be best to make each initial [perfection] an explicit condition in describing the second [perfection], if we wanted to describe the soul and not the faculty of the soul belonging to it by reason of that actuality. For "perfection" is used to define the soul not a faculty of the soul. You will learn the difference between the animal soul and the faculties of perception and motion, and the difference between the rational soul and the faculty for the things mentioned, such as discrimination, etc. If you want a thorough account, the correct thing to do would be to make the vegetative soul a genus of the animal, and the animal a genus of the human, using the more general in the definition of the more specific; but if you consider the souls in terms of the faculties peculiar to them as animal and human [souls], you may be satisfied with what we have mentioned.

3.   The vegetative soul possesses [the following] three faculties. (1) The nutritive, which is a faculty that makes a body other than the one it is in to resemble the body in which it is, and binds it to it as replacement for what has dissipated from it. (2) The faculty of growth, which causes the body it is in to increase in size to a commensurate body, relative to its dimensions in length, width, and depth, so that the perfection of growth will be reached. (3) The faculty of reproduction is [41] that which takes from the body that it is in a part that is potentially similar to it, and, by drawing on other bodies similar to it in constitution and elemental mixture, makes in it what will become actually similar to it.

4.   The animal soul, in its primary division, possesses two faculties, that of motion and that of perception. The motor faculty itself has two divisions: a faculty that causes motion by inciting [other faculties] to move, and a faculty that produces the motion. The faculty that causes motion by inciting is the faculty of appetite, which, when there is formed in the imagination—which we have yet to discuss—an image [of something] that is to be sought or avoided, the faculty incites other motor faculties—which we will discuss—to move. It has two branches. One is called the appetitive faculty, which incites a motion by which [the animal] draws close to something imagined to be necessary or beneficial when seeking pleasure. The other is called the irascible faculty, which incites a motion by which [the animal] repels something imagined to be harmful or damaging when seeking to prevail. The motor faculty, in the sense of what produces the motion, is a faculty dispersed in the nerves and muscles whose job is to contract the muscles and draw the tendons and ligaments attached to the organs to their starting point, or to loosen them or stretch them out, in which case the tendons and ligaments will be at the opposite end of their starting point.

5.   The faculty of perception has two divisions: that of external perception and that of internal perception. The faculty of external perception comprises the five, or eight, senses. These include *sight*, which is a faculty arrayed in the concave nerve that perceives the form of what is imprinted on the vitreous humor, that is, the images of bodies possessing color that are transmitted through the actually transparent bodies to the surfaces of smooth bodies. [42] Another sense is *hearing*, which is a faculty arrayed in the nerve dispersed on the surface of the ear canal that perceives the form of what is transmitted to it from the oscillation of the air that is compressed between what causes the disturbance [of the air] and what, with resistance, receives the disturbance, the air being compressed by a disruption that produces a sound. In this case the oscillation of the air is transmitted to the still air enclosed in the chamber of the ear canal, and makes it move in the pattern of its motion, and the vibrations of that motion touch the nerve, and one hears. Another sense is *smell*, which is a faculty arrayed in the two appendages in the anterior part of the brain resembling two nipples, and which perceives what is transmitted to it by the air in the nasal passages, such as the odor present in the vapor mingled with [the air] or the odor imprinted in it through alteration by an odiferous body. Another sense is *taste*, which is a faculty arrayed in the nerves spread out on the tongue that perceives the tastes that dissipate from substances in contact with them and mingle with the salivatory fluids that mingle

and alter on [the tongue]. Another sense is *touch*, which is a faculty arrayed in the nerves of the skin and flesh of the entire body, and which perceives what comes into contact with [the body] and causes an opposition in it that alters the temperament or that changes the configuration of the elemental composition. According to one group,[44] this faculty is apparently not a final species but rather a genus of four or more faculties dispersed as a group throughout all of the skin. The first faculty judges the contrast between hot and cold; the second judges the contrast between wet and dry; the third judges the contrast between hard and soft; and the fourth judges the contrast between coarse and smooth. [43] Combining them in a single organ, however, makes them appear to be one in essence.

6. As for the faculties of internal perception, some of them are faculties that perceive the forms of sensibles and some the connotational attributes (*maʿná*) of sensibles. The faculties of perception include those that both perceive and act; those that perceive but do not act; those that perceive in a primary way; and those that perceive in a secondary way. What distinguishes perceiving forms from perceiving connotational attributes is the following. Form is something that both the internal and external senses perceive, but the external sense perceives it first and relays it to the internal sense. For example, the sheep perceives the form of the wolf—I mean its shape, pattern, and color. The internal senses of the sheep *do* perceive it, but it is the external senses that perceive it first. The connotational attribute is something that the soul perceives from the sensible without the external senses first perceiving it, for example, the sheep's perceiving the connotational attribute of enmity in the wolf or the connotational attribute of having to fear it and flee from it, without the external senses perceiving it at all. So, what perceives something about the wolf first is the external senses, and then the internal senses. [What the external senses perceive] should here be restricted to the term "form," whereas what the internal faculties—not the senses—perceive should here be restricted to the term "connotational attribute." What distinguishes perceiving with action from perceiving without action is the following. The actions of some internal faculties include combining certain perceived forms and connotational attributes with others and separating certain of them from others, and so they will have perceived and also acted on what they perceived. Perceiving without action is when the form or connotational attribute simply takes shape in [the animal], without [the animal] having the freedom to act on it. Finally, what distinguishes the first perception from the second perception is that the first perception [44] is acquiring in some manner the form that belonged to the thing itself, whereas second perception is acquiring the form of the thing from another thing that conveys it to the first thing.

7. The faculties of internal perception include "*fantasiya*," that is, the common sense, which is the faculty arrayed in the anterior ventricle of the brain that

---

[44] It is not clear to whom Ibn Sīnā is referring, although something like the position put forth is suggested in Aristotle's *De anima* II 11.

receives in itself all the forms imprinted on the external senses that are then conveyed to it.

8. Next, the imagery and form-bearing faculty, which [are two names for] a faculty arrayed behind the anterior ventricle of the brain that retains [the forms that] the common sense receives from the five external senses, where [those forms] remain in it after the departure of those sensibles. Know that the receptivity of any faculty other than the faculty used for memory is akin to water, for while water can receive ephemeral representations and, in general terms, shapes, it cannot retain them. However, we will give you still further verification of this. When you want to know the difference between the action of the external sense generally speaking, that of the common sense, and that of the imagery, then consider the drop of rain that falls in such a way that you see a straight line, or the straight thing that revolves such that its edge is thought to be circular. The thing cannot be perceived as straight or circular unless it is considered many times, but the external sense cannot see it twice, or rather sees it as it is; but when it takes shape in the common sense and [the thing itself] disappears before the form vanishes from the common sense, the external sense does see it as it is, and the common sense perceives it as something where it was and where it came to be, and then it sees a circular or [45] straight extension. That cannot be attributed in any way to the external sense. As for the imagery, it perceives the two aspects and forms images of them both, even if the thing itself vanishes and disappears.

9. Next is the faculty called the imaginative faculty in relation to the animal soul and the cogitative faculty in relation to the human soul. It is a faculty arrayed in the medial ventricle of the brain at the *cerebellar vermis*,[45] whose function is to combine and divide at will any [forms] in the imagery.

10. Thereafter, there is the estimative faculty, being arrayed at the back of the medial ventricle. It perceives the connotational attributes not perceptible to the senses but that are nonetheless in particular sensible objects, like the faculty in the sheep that judges that this wolf is something to flee and that this lamb is something to love. It would seem to operate also on objects of the imagination by combining and dividing them.

11. Next, the faculty of memory, arrayed in the posterior ventricle, retains the insensible connotational attributes in particular objects that are perceived by the estimative faculty. The relation of the faculty of memory to that of the estimative faculty is like the relation of the faculty called the imagery to the senses; and the relation of the former faculty [of memory] to the connotational attributes is like the relation of the latter faculty [i.e., the imagery] to the forms of sensibles. These are the faculties of the animal soul.

12. The faculties of the human soul are divided into the practical and the theoretical. Both are called "intellect" as homonyms by similarity. The practical is a faculty

---

[45] The *vermiform epiphysis*, or "worm-like outgrowth" (*skolēkoeidēs epiphysis*), of Galenic anatomy; cf. Galen's *De anatomicis administrationibus*, IX.3–5 and *De usu partium*, VIII.6.

that is a principle that moves the human body to perform particular actions determined by reflecting on what is required by customary opinions specific to [those actions]. There [46] are ways of regarding it in relation to the appetitive faculty of the animal soul, in relation to the imaginative and estimative faculties of the animal soul, and in relation to itself. In relation to the appetitive faculty of the animal soul, it is the aspect as a result of which certain configurations specific to man come about in it by which he is quickly disposed to act or to be affected, for example, shame, timidity, laughing, weeping, etc. In relation to the imaginative and estimative faculties of the animal soul, it is the aspect that joins with those when they become engrossed in discovering ways to manage the natural world of generation and corruption and in devising the crafts of human society. In relation to itself, it is the aspect in which the combination of the practical intellect and the theoretical intellect engenders the opinions that are related to human actions and that are spread around as commonly held, though not as established by the demonstrative method. Examples are that lying is bad, oppression is evil, and other such premises defined as distinct from the purely scientific first principles in the logic books, albeit when they are demonstrated, they also become scientific, as you have learned in the logic books.

13.   This [practical] faculty should rule over the other faculties of the body in accordance with the judgments enforced by the other faculty we will discuss [i.e., the theoretical faculty], so that it is not affected by [the other faculties] but rather they by it, and so that they are kept in check below it lest there come to be in it from the body certain tendencies of acquiescence learned from natural circumstances, that is, what are called vices. Instead, [this faculty] must be unaffected [47] and unyielding in every way—in fact, it must rule if it is to possess moral excellence. Now, one's moral temperaments may be attributable to the faculties of the body also, and if these are in control, they are configured to act, while [the practical intellect] is configured to be affected. But you are not configured as a whole with one moral temperament, so one thing produces one moral temperament in this and another moral temperament in that. If the [bodily faculties] are controlled, they will be configured to be affected, and it will be the [practical intellect] that is configured to act regularly, in which case there will also be two configurations and two dispositions—or one disposition with two relative aspects. Now, the moral temperaments that are in us are attributable only to this faculty, because the human soul, though one substance (as will become apparent), has a relation and reference to two sides, one below it and one above it, and for each side there is a faculty through which the connection between it and that side is ordered. So this practical faculty is the one the soul possesses for the connection with the side below it, that is, the body and its maintenance. The theoretical faculty is the one that the soul possesses for the connection with the side above it, to be affected by it, learn from it, and receive from it. So it is as though our soul has two faces, one directed to the body—and this is the one that must not endure any effect of a type entailed by the body's nature—and another one directed to the lofty principles—and this is the one that must always be receptive to and affected by what is there. It is from the lower side that the moral temperaments are produced, whereas it is from the higher side that the sciences are produced. This, then, is the practical intellect.

14. [48] The theoretical faculty is a faculty whose role is to be imprinted with the universal forms that are separate from matter. If the form is separate essentially, then it is easier for the faculty to take it into itself; if it is not, then it becomes separate by the [theoretical faculty's] abstracting it until not a single material connection remains in it—we will explain how this happens below.[46] This theoretical faculty bears different relations to these forms; for the thing that can receive something may at one time be something potentially receiving it and at another time actually receiving it. The potentiality has three different senses ordered by prior and posterior. (1) "Potentiality" is said of the absolute disposition, in which case not only has nothing actually come to be, but also it has not even acquired that by which it will come to be, just like the potentiality of the infant for writing. (2) "Potentiality" is said of this disposition when the only thing it has acquired is that by which it can acquire the actuality without an intermediary, just like the potentiality of the youth who is coming into his own and is familiar with pen and ink and simple words for the purpose of writing. (3) "Potentiality" is said of this disposition when the perfection of the disposition is completed by the instrument and comes to be with the instrument, such that it can act whenever it wants with no need for acquisition, rather it is enough to formulate the aim only, like the potentiality of the writer perfect in his craft when not writing. The first potentiality is called (1) "absolute" and "material" potentiality; the second is called (2) "possible" potentiality; and the third is called (3) "perfect" potentiality.

15. The relation of the theoretical faculty to the abstracted forms we mentioned, then, is sometimes (1) that of "absolute" potentiality, which is when [49] this faculty belonging to the soul has not yet received any part of the perfection that comes through its body, at which time it is called a material intellect. This faculty that is called a material intellect is present in every individual of the species and is called "material" simply because of its similarity to the disposition of prime matter, which in itself has no particular form being a subject for any form. (2) Sometimes it is a relation of "possible" potentiality, which is when there is now in the material potentiality [i.e., the material intellect] the primary intelligibles from which and by which it arrives at the secondary intelligibles. By "primary intelligibles" I mean the premises to which assent is given without any act of acquisition and without the one assenting to them being aware that he could ever be free of assenting to them at any time, like our belief that the whole is greater than the part and that things equal to one thing are equal to one another. As long as there is still only this degree of a given concept (ma'nā) actually in [the material intellect], [the material intellect] is called a dispositional intellect, although it can be called an actual intellect in comparison to the first potentiality, because the first potentiality cannot intellect anything actually whereas this one can intellect when it actually starts investigating. (3) Sometimes it is a relation of potentiality as "perfect," which is when there are also intelligible forms in it that were acquired

[46] See "The Soul," V.2, par. 9, p. 191; cf. his discussion in the translation of "Book of Demonstration," III.5, pars. 5–7, pp. 153–54.

after the primary intelligible, but it is not actually reviewing and referring to them; rather, it is as though they are stored with it. So, whenever it wants, it actually reviews those forms and intellects them, and intellects that it is intellecting them. It is called an actual intellect [50] because it is an intellect that intellects whenever it wants, without the burden of acquiring [it], although it can be called a potential intellect in comparison to what comes after it. [4] Sometimes the relation is one of actuality absolutely, which is when the intelligible forms are present in it, and it is actually reviewing them. So it intellects them, and intellects that it is actually intellecting them. What it has then is an acquired intellect. It is called an acquired intellect precisely because, as will become clear to us,[47] the potential intellect is brought into act only by an intellect that is always actual, and when the potential intellect makes some kind of contact with that intellect that is actual, there is imprinted in it a species of the forms acquired from outside. These, then, are also the degrees of the faculties that are called theoretical intellects and, with the acquired intellect the genus animal and the part of it that is the species human are complete, and there the human faculty [i.e., the theo-retical intellect] will have made itself similar to the first principles of all existence.

16.   Learn a lesson now by considering how some of these faculties rule while others serve; for you will find the acquired intellect, that is, the ultimate goal, leading while all serve it. Next is the actual intellect served by the dispositional intellect, with the material intellect, inasmuch as it contains some disposition, serving the dis-positional intellect. Then the practical intellect serves all of this, because, as will be explained, the connection with the body is for the sake of perfecting, purifying, and cleansing the theoretical intellect, and the practical intellect manages that connection. Then the practical intellect is served by the estimative faculty. The estimative faculty is served by two other faculties: one in front of it and one behind it [in the body]. The faculty behind it is the one that retains what the estimative faculty relays to it, that is, the memory; [51] and the faculty in front of it is the whole group of animal faculties. Next, imagination is served by two faculties with two different approaches: the appetite serves it through counsel, because it incites it in a specific way to generate motion; and the imagery [faculty] serves it by displaying to it the forms stored in it that are ready for combining and dividing. Then, these two faculties are leaders of two groups. The imagery [faculty] is served by the *fantasiya*, and the *fantasiya* is served by the five external senses. The appetite is served by the appetitive and irascible facul-ties. These two in turn are served by the motive faculty in the muscles. There ends the faculties of the animal soul.

17.   Next, the faculties of the animal soul are served by the faculties of the vegeta-tive soul. The first of them, and their leader, is the faculty of generation. The faculty of growth serves the faculty of generation, and the nutritive faculty serves them both. Then the four natural faculties serve these, namely, the faculty of digestion is served by the faculty of retention from one direction and the faculty of attraction from another

---

[47] See "The Soul," V.5, 199–202.

direction, and the faculty of expulsion serves them all. Finally, the four qualities serve all of this, but cold serves heat, for it either prepares matter for heating or preserves what heat has readied (there being no place for cold in the potentialities entering into natural accidents except as a useful result of a subsequent consequence), and the dry and wet qualities serve them both together. Here ends the ranks of the faculties.

3. From "The Soul," V.I^d

THE PRACTICAL AND THEORETICAL FACULTIES OF THE HUMAN SOUL

1.   [206] The property most specific to the human is to conceptualize the universal connotational attributes (ma'nā) belonging to the intellect that are abstracted completely of all matter—as we have reported and explained—and to arrive at knowledge of things that are unknown by assenting to them when conceptualizing things that are known to the intellect. These aforementioned actions and states are part of what belongs to the human, and the majority of them belong to him alone. Although some of them are bodily, they belong to the human body by reason of the soul that belongs to the human, not to the other animals.

2.   Put another way, we say that man acts freely on particular things and on universal things. With respect to universal things, however, there is only conviction, even if it were to apply to an action. For a universal conviction about how one should build a house does not on its own initially result in the building of a specific house; i.e., for [207] actions deal with particular things and result from particular opinions because the universal, as a universal, does not apply uniquely to one [particular] to the exclusion of another. Let us postpone commentary on this, with the promise to repay you in the philosophical discipline in the final section [i.e., "Metaphysics"].

3.   The human, then, has (1) a faculty that is properly related to universal opinions, and (2) another faculty properly related to reflecting on particular things with regard to what he should do, what he should avoid, what is beneficial and harmful, what is right and wrong, and what is good and evil. That is, by one kind of syllogism and consideration, whether valid or invalid, whose end is that we apply an opinion about some future particular contingent—because one cannot deliberate about whether the inevitable or the impossible will be or not, nor can one deliberate about making what has passed occur, inasmuch as it has happened already.[48]

4.   Then, when this faculty [i.e., the practical intellect] has arrived at a decision, that decision is followed by the motion of the faculty of resolve to set the body in motion just as it does after the judgments of other faculties in animals. This faculty [of resolve] extends out of the faculty for the universals, applying the major premises [of the syllogism] from there to what was considered and forms a conclusion about the particulars.

---

[48] Cf. Aristotle, NE III.3.

5.   The first of the two aforementioned faculties belonging to the human soul is a faculty related to scientific investigation and so is called the theoretical intellect. This second is a faculty related to action and so is called the practical intellect. The former [is employed] for truth and falsehood whereas the latter is for good and evil in particular things. The former [is employed] for [determining] what is necessary, possible, and impossible, whereas the latter is for [determining] what is right, wrong, and permissible. The principles of the former include the primary premises [of deductive reasoning], whereas the principles of the latter include commonly held premises, commonly accepted premises, premises based on assumptions, and tenuous results of methodic experience that consist of those assumptions and that are different from the results of substantiated methodic experience.

6.   Each of these two faculties [produces] opinion and assumption. Opinion is [208] conclusive conviction, whereas assumption is biased conviction [for one side of a thesis] despite the conceivability of the other side. Anyone with an assumption has not been convinced, just as anyone employing the senses has not intellected, or anyone engaged in imagining has neither an assumption nor a conviction nor an opinion.[49] In the human, then, is something that judges on the basis of sensory perception, something belonging to the imagination that judges based on estimation, something that judges through the theoretical intellect, and something that judges through the practical intellect. The principles that incite one's faculty of resolve to set the bodily organs in motion are an estimation based on the imagery; the practical intellect; and desire and anger, the last of which [i.e., desire and anger] belong also to the other animals.

7.   The practical intellect needs the body and its faculties for all of its actions. The theoretical intellect, however, has a certain need for the body and its faculties, but not constantly nor in every way; rather, it is sometimes self-sufficient. Neither one of these is the human soul; rather the soul is something that possesses these faculties, being (as explained) an independent substance with an aptitude for certain actions. Some of [these actions] it completes only by means of [bodily] instruments and by attending to [such actions] by means of the universal; for other actions it has a certain need for [bodily] instruments; and for others it has no such need whatsoever—we will explain all of this later.[50]

8.   The substance of the human soul is predisposed to perfect itself in a specific way on its own and, in that, what is at its uppermost level has no need for what is below it. It has this predisposition through the thing called the theoretical intellect. It is [also] predisposed to be on guard against any harm that may happen to it by associating [with the bodily faculties] (as we will explain in its place) and, when engaged in that association, to act in a manner [209] proper to it. It has this predisposition through a faculty called the practical intellect, that is, the master of the

---

[49] Cf. Aristotle, *De anima* III.2.

[50] See "The Soul," V.3, pars. 1–2, pp. 192–93.

faculties it has in regard to the body. The faculties below that are dispersed from it on account of the body's predisposition to receive them and make use of them. The moral temperaments belong to the soul from the direction of this faculty [i.e., the practical intellect], as we pointed out.[51] Each one of the two faculties has a predisposition and a perfection. The simple predisposition of both is called the material intellect, whether taken to be theoretical or practical. After that, it is only through the principles that happen to come to each of them, by which its actions are perfected. In the case of the theoretical intellect, [these principles are] the primary premises and whatever follows from them; in the case of the practical intellect, they are the commonly held premises and other formulations. At that point, each one of them is a dispositional intellect. Then each one of them has an acquired perfection, which we have explained before. The first thing we must explain [now] is that this soul, predisposed as it is to receive intelligibles by way of the material intellect, is neither a body nor something that subsists as a form in any body.

4. From "The Soul," V.2[c]

ESTABLISHING THAT THE RATIONAL SOUL DOES NOT SUBSIST AS SOMETHING IMPRINTED IN CORPOREAL MATTER

1. [209] One thing about which there can be no doubt is that in the human is a thing and a certain substance that encounters the intelligibles through reception. We say next that the substance, which is the receptacle of the intelligibles, [210] is neither a body nor something that subsists in a body in the sense of being a faculty in it or a form belonging to it in some way. If the receptacle of the intelligibles is a body or a particular magnitude, then the part of it that the intelligible form inheres in is either (1) a single, indivisible thing, or (2) a divisible thing, where the indivisible part of the body is unquestionably a limit akin to a point.

2. Let us first examine whether (1) it is possible for the receptacle [of the intelligible forms] to be an indivisible limit. We say that this is absurd, because the point is a certain terminus that is not distinct from the line with respect to position nor from the magnitude terminating at it, such that the point would belong to it as something in which something could reside without being in some part of that magnitude. Quite the contrary, just as the point is not essentially independent, but is an essential limit precisely of what is itself a magnitude, so too one can say in a certain way only that a limit of something inheres in [the point] as something inhering in the magnitude of which [the point] is its limit, and so [the inhering thing] accidentally possesses a magnitude by that magnitude. Just as [the inhering thing] accidentally possesses a magnitude by [that magnitude], so too it accidentally has a terminus with the [magnitude's essential] point. Thus, its being an accidental terminus

---

[51] See "The Soul," V.3, pars. 1–2, pp. 192–93. I.5, par. 13, p. 183.

with an essential terminus is just like its being an accidental extension [i.e., a magnitude] together with an essential extension.[52]

3. If the point were some independent thing that could receive any given thing, it would be a distinct individual and so the point would possess two sides. One side would be the part touching the line from which it is distinguished, and one side would be the part that is different from and opposite it. In that case, [the point] would subsist by itself as something separate from the line, and the line that is separate from [the point, x], would inevitably have a terminus, y, other than x, which touches x. Thus, point y would be the terminus of the line, not x. But the discussion about x and y is identical. [211] This would lead to points that could be attachable to one another in the line, whether finitely or infinitely—the impossibility of this became clear to us in other places.[53] It is also clear that no body is composed by points being attachable to one another. It is clear also that no particular position can be distinguished for the point.

4. A gesture in the direction of a little bit of these arguments wouldn't hurt.[54] So we say that [if] two points touch one point on its two sides, then either the middle point separates them and so they do not touch, in which case it would follow that the middle point would be divisible, according to the axioms you have learned, and this is absurd. Or the middle point does not keep the sides of the two points from touching. In that case, the intelligible form would be present in all the points, and all the points would be like one single point, but we have posited that *this one point* is separate from the line. So, the line, due to its being separate from [the point], has a limit other than the point by which it is separate from the point; and so that [first] point is distinct from this [other point that is the line's limit] in terms of position. It has also been posited, however, that all points are the same in terms of position. This is a contradiction. It is therefore invalid to argue that the receptacle of the intelligibles is an indivisible part of the body.

5. The remaining option is (2) that their receptacle in the body[55] is a divisible thing—if in fact their receptacle is in the body. So let us posit an intelligible form in a divisible thing. When we posit an intelligible form in something that is divisible in some way, the form is then accidentally divisible. In that case, the result must be either (2a) that the two parts [of the form] are similar, or (2b) they are dissimilar.

6. If (2a) they are similar, then how is the combination of the two different from them [212]—given that the whole, as a whole, is not the part—unless the whole

---

52 Cf. "Physics," III.3, par. 1, position (3), p. 164, and "Physics," III.4, all, pp. 166–70.

53 Cf. the arguments of "Physics," III.4, pars. 2–5, pp. 167–68, where Ibn Sīnā refutes the idea that magnitudes can be composed of indivisibles.

54 Ibn Sīnā's use of "little bit" (*ṭaraf*) is a pun on the Arabic for "limit," (*ṭaraf*) which he has been using.

55 The second of the two options was enumerated at the beginning of this chapter (par. 1).

resulting from the two is not due to the form but to an increase in magnitude or number? In that case, the intelligible form would be a particular shape or number; but no intelligible form is a shape or number, since then the form would be a form represented in the imagery [faculty] not an intelligible form. Next, you know it cannot be argued that each of the two parts is itself the whole. How could this be, given that the second one is included in what is meant by the whole while extraneous to what is meant by the other part, when it is more than obvious that one of them alone cannot indicate the same thing as what is meant by the complete whole?

7.   If (2b) the two parts are dissimilar, let us investigate how that could be and how the intelligible form could have dissimilar parts. There cannot be dissimilar parts unless they are parts of a definition, namely, the genera and the differences, but a number of absurdities result from this.

7.1.   Each part of the body would also be subject to potentially infinite division, and then the genera and the differences would have to be subject to potentially infinite division. This is absurd. It is an established fact that the essential genera and differences of one thing are not *potentially* infinite.

7.2.   And [another absurdity is] because it is absolutely impossible that imagining the division would separate the genus and the difference; rather, there is no question that, when there is a genus and difference that can be made distinct in the receptacle, such distinction need not stop at the imagined division; so the genera and differences must also *actually* be infinite. [213] But it is an established fact that the genera and differences and the parts of the definition of one thing are finite in every way. If the genera and differences could have been actually infinite, they could not have been combined in the body in this form, for that would require that one body be divided actually into infinite parts.

7.3.   Furthermore, suppose that the division had been something that happened in some way, and it separated a genus on one side and a difference on another side. If we were [again] to subdivide the division, it would have to result in either a half-genus on one side and a half-difference on the other, or it would require the transfer of the genus and the difference to one of the two divisions, but the genus and the difference are both equally inclined to any part of the division. Thus, [from] our imagined supposition, or our posited division, the genus and the difference run around in circles, and either one of them could be put on any side, at the whim of any external individual. Even that is not enough, for we could subdivide [ad infinitum].

7.4.   Finally, not every intelligible can be divided into simpler intelligibles. There are intelligibles that are the simplest, and they are the principles for the composition of the rest of the intelligibles; and they neither have genera or differences nor can they be divided by quantity or account.

8.   Therefore, the posited parts can neither be similar—each one of them being included in what is meant by the whole, when the whole results only by combination—nor can they be dissimilar. So the intelligible form cannot be divided.

9. [214] Since the intelligible form cannot be divided nor can it inhere in some indivisible limit of magnitude, but there must be something in us that receives it, we have to conclude that the receptacle of the intelligibles is a substance that is not a body, nor is whatever that is in us that encounters them a faculty in a body. For then all of the divisions that attach to the body would attach to it, with all the attendant absurdities. Rather, that part of us that encounters the intelligible form must be an incorporeal substance.

10. Let us provide another demonstration of this by stating first that the intellecting faculty is that [incorporeal substance] that abstracts the intelligibles from delimited quantity, place, position, and everything else said before. Then we have to investigate this form itself that is abstracted from position: How is it something abstracted? Is it in comparison to the thing from which it was taken or to the thing that does the taking? I mean: Does the existence of this truly intelligible thing that was abstracted from position exist externally or does it exist conceptually in the intellecting substance? It would be absurd of us to say that it is like the external existence, so our remaining option is to say that it is separate from place and position only when it exists in the intellect. When it exists in the intellect, it does not possess any position, where it would be such that pointing, being particular, divisible and other similar things would apply to it. So it cannot be in a body.

11. Furthermore, when the singular, indivisible form that belongs to certain conceptually indivisible things is impressed in a divisible matter possessing sides, then either (1) none [215] of the parts posited as in [the matter] due to its sides has a relation to the singular indivisible intelligible thing as abstracted from the matter; or (2) each one of those posited parts does; or (3) some do and some do not. If (1) none do, then neither does the whole; for anything made up of discrete parts is itself discrete. If (3) some do and some do not, then those having no relation are not a part of its account at all. If (2) each posited part has a given relation, then every posited part either (2a) has a relation to the thing as it is, or (2b) to a part of the thing. If (2a) each posited part has a relation to the thing as it is, then the parts are not parts of the account of the intelligible; rather each of them is itself an intelligible as something independent. If each part has a relation different from the other part's relation to the thing, then it is known that the thing is divisible in terms of the intelligible, but we posited that it is indivisible. This is a contradiction. If (2b) the relation of each part is to a part of the thing that is different from the other, then the division of the thing is even more obvious. It is clear from this that the forms imprinted in corporeal matter are merely exterior shapes of the particular divisible parts, where each part has a relation, potentially or actually, to any other part.

12. Moreover, the thing that has multiple parts in its definition is nonetheless an indivisible single thing from the perspective of the entirety [of the parts]. So we may investigate how that singular existence, as some one thing, [216] is impressed in something divisible. But what can be said about it is the same as what was said about what is indivisible in definition as a singular thing.

13.   It is also correct for us to state that the posited intelligibles, each one of which the rational faculty can actually intellect, are potentially infinite. Moreover, it is correct for us to state that something that has a capability for a potential infinity of things cannot be a body nor a faculty in a body. We have demonstrated this in the preceding sections. Therefore, it is impossible for the thing itself that forms concepts of the intelligibles to subsist in a body in any way, or for its action to be generated out of a body or by means of a body. [. . .]

5. From "The Soul," V.3[f]

Two Issues: (1) How the Human Soul Makes Use of the Senses; (2) Establishing the Temporal Origination of the Soul

1.   [221] The faculties of the animal soul aid the rational soul in some things. For example, from them as a whole the senses convey to it the particulars [of the external world]. Four things happen to it as a result of the particulars. (1) One is that the mind extracts the simple universals from the particulars [222] by abstracting their connotational attributes (ma'nā) from matter and its associative and consequential accidents, and noting what is common and what different, what is essential and what accidental. As a result of this, principles of conceptualization are produced for the soul, and that [takes place] with the aid of the imagery and estimative [faculties]. (2) The second is that the soul occasions certain relationships among these simple universals through, for example, negation and affirmation. Any combination through negation or affirmation that is primary and evident in itself, the soul takes; and anything that is not like that, it leaves alone until it comes across a middle term. (3) The third is the acquisition of premises derived from methodic experience. This is identifying by sensory perception a predicate that must be applied to a given subject, affirmatively or negatively, or a consequential property necessarily connected to the predicate (or its denial) or necessarily opposed to the predicate (or its denial), where that does not apply to just some instances and not others, nor half of the time but rather always. [In that case] the soul is confident that there is such a relationship between the nature of this predicate and this subject, and that the nature of this consequence necessarily entailing or precluding that this [predicate] belongs to [the predicate] essentially and not accidentally. Thus, that is a conviction resulting from sensory perception and a syllogism, as is explained in the "logic" sections.[56] (4) The fourth is the assent resulting from reports because they are so widespread.

2.   So the soul seeks the aid of the body to obtain these basic principles for the purpose of conceptualization and assent. Once it obtains them, it turns back to itself. If one of the faculties below it happens to distract it with one of its [bodily] associated states that distracted it [223] from its activity, the soul abandons what it was doing. If [a faculty] does not distract it, then [the soul] does not subsequently need it for any

---

[56] "Book of Demonstration," III.5, pars. 8.2–4, pp. 155–56.

of its own activities, unless it concerns something for which it has a specific need to consult the imagery faculties another time. That would be for the purpose of acquiring a principle other than the one obtained, or to seek the help of the imagery [faculty] in forming an image of the goal [of its activity], so that with its help the version in the intellect is reinforced. This is something that happens in the beginning but less often thereafter. When the soul reaches a certain perfection and is strong, however, it performs its activities completely on its own, while the senses, the imagery, and the other bodily faculties distract it from its task the way that, for example, a person may need a mount and other aids to arrive at some destination, but when he arrives and one of the means of his arrival happens to hinder his setting them aside, the means of his arrival themselves become a hindrance.

3. We say that the human souls did not subsist separately from their bodies and then arrived in their bodies, because the human souls are of the same species and account. If one posits that they have an existence that does not originate temporally in conjunction with the origination of their bodies, but rather [they have] a separate existence, then in that existence the soul cannot be many. [This is so] because things are many either because of the essence and form or because of the relation to the constituent and matter. [The constituent and the matter] are themselves made many by the places that contain each matter in a given area as well as the times specific to the origination of each thing and the causes that divide them. Now, [souls] are not distinct from one another by essence [224] and form, because their form is one. Therefore, they could be distinct from one another only on account of what receives the essence or that to which the essence is properly related, and this is the body. If the soul could exist without any body, then one soul could not be distinct in number from another soul. This is an absolute fact in every case: multiplying things that are themselves purely formal, even when the fact of their being species has been made many by their individuals, occurs only through the things that bear them, receive them, and are affected by them, or through a certain relation to [those things] or to their times. Since, however, [the souls] are absolutely separate and are not divided in the ways we said, it is impossible for there to be any mutual distinction and multiplicity among them. So, it is false to maintain that before arriving in bodies the souls are numerically many things.

4. I say it is also impossible for them to be numerically one, because when two bodies come into existence, two souls come into existence in the two bodies. Either these two souls are two parts of that one soul, in which case the single thing that has neither bulk nor volume is potentially divisible, but this is patently false according to the principles established in natural philosophy and elsewhere. Or the numerically one soul is in two bodies, but this also does not require much effort to refute.

5. To express it differently, we say that these souls would be identified as one individual soul out of the whole of their species only through certain conditions associated with them but not essential to them as a soul (since otherwise they would be common to all of them) and through the consequential accidents associated with

them from some beginning that has to be temporal (because they come after some cause that happened to some of them but not others). [If this is the case], then the individual identification of these souls is also something that originates temporally. So they are not pre-eternal and their temporal origination occurs together with a body.

6.   It is therefore true [225] that the souls originate in the same manner that a bodily matter suited for its use originates. The originated body is the domain and instrument of the soul, when the substance of the soul that is originated with a given body, [that is], the body suitable for the soul's origination from the first principles is configured with a natural inclination to take an interest in it, to make use of it, to concern itself with its conditions, and to be attracted to it, such configuration being specific to it and turning it away from all other bodies. When it comes into existence as individuated, (1) the principle of its individuation attaches to it the configurations that are indispensable to singling it out as an individual; and (2) those configurations must be what determine its sole possession of that body and establish the relationship of mutual benefit [of the soul and body] (even if that exclusive condition and relationship is obscure to us); and (3) the principles of its self-perfection are occasioned by means of [the body] once there is its body.

7.   Someone could say, however, that this problem forces you to address the issue of the souls when they separate from the body. Either (1) [the souls] pass away—but you do not maintain this; or (2) they become one—but this is the very thing you found repugnant; or (3) they continue to be many individual souls when they are separated from their matter, as you think—but then how could they continue to be many? We say that after the souls are separated from the bodies, there is no question that each one will have existed as a singular thing by reason of the difference of the matters they were in, by reason of the difference of the times of their origination, and by reason of the difference of the configurations belonging to them as a result of their different bodies. Next, we are certain that what makes the universal account exist as an identifiable individual cannot make it exist as an individual unless it adds[g] to it (over and above what species it is) one of the individual factors (ma'ná) that attaches to it at its origination by [226] which it becomes an individual and which our knowledge of it requires or we do not know.

8.   We do know, however, that the soul is not a singular thing that is in all bodies. For if it were singular but many relatively, [the soul] would have the same knowledge or ignorance in all [the individuals], and what is in the soul of 'Amr would not be unknown to Zayd. [This is so] because, while a singular thing related to many may be different by consideration of the relation, it cannot be different in terms of the things it possesses in itself such that if there is a father of many sons and he is young, he is only young all things considered, since his being young belongs to him in himself and then subsequently he enters into each relation. Equally, knowledge, ignorance, assumption, etc., are precisely in the soul itself, and it is with the soul that they enter into each relation.

9.   Therefore the soul is not singular, so it is many in number—but its species is singular—and is temporally originated, as we explained. There is no doubt that it

is through something that they are individuated and that this thing with respect to the human soul is not its being imprinted in matter—the falsehood of that doctrine has been learned—rather that thing belonging to the soul[h] is a certain configuration, or a certain potentiality, or a certain accidental incorporeal quality, or the sum of them together [that] collectively individuates the soul, even if we do not know what it is.

10. After its individuation as a single thing, it and another soul cannot be numerically one thing—we have already argued the impossibility of this in a number of places. We are certain, however, that (1) when the soul comes into existence in conjunction with the origination of a certain humoral temperament, it next may come to have a certain configuration of rational actions and affections that, collectively, is distinct from the comparable configuration it would have in another, [227] the way that two humoral temperaments in two different bodies are distinct from one another. We are also certain that (2) the acquired configuration, called an actual intellect, is, to a certain degree, also something by which it is distinct from another soul. Finally, we are certain that (3) an awareness of its particular self occurs to the soul, where that awareness is also a certain configuration in it and is also unique to it alone.

11. It may also be the case that it has another unique configuration due to the bodily faculties. That configuration is related to the configurations of its moral temperaments, or those *are* that configuration. There may still be other unique attributes unknown to us that adhere to the souls when it comes into existence and afterwards in the way that, just as some such [unique attributes] adhere to the individuals of the corporeal species and make them distinct from one another as long as they perdure, so too the souls are made distinct by the things in them that make them particular in the bodies, whether the bodies exist or no bodies exist, whether we know about those states or not, or know but some of them.

6. From "The Soul," V.4[i]

HUMAN SOULS DO NOT SUFFER CORRUPTION

1. [227] The soul does not die with the death of the body; for anything that corrupts by virtue of something else's corrupting has some type of connection with it. Either (1) it is connected with it as something posterior to it in existence, or (2) as something prior to it in existence (that is, it precedes it essentially, not temporally), or (3) as something coexistent with it.

2. If (3) the soul is connected with the body in the manner of something coexistent with it, and (3a) that [coexistence] is essential, not accidental, to it, then each one would be related essentially to the other, and neither the soul nor the body would be a substance, but they *are* both substances. If (3b) that [coexistence] is [228] accidental, not essential, then if one of them is corrupted, the other accidental thing would be removed from the relation, but the thing itself would not be corrupted through the corruption [of the other], inasmuch as this is the connection.

3. If (1) it is connected with it as something posterior to it in existence, then the body would be a cause for the soul with respect to existence. Now there are four

causes. Either the body would be (a) an efficient cause of the soul, giving it existence; or (b) it would be a receptive cause[57] of it, whether by means of composition, like the elements for bodies, or by means of simplicity, like copper for a statue; or (c) it would be a formal cause; or (d) it would be a perfecting cause.[58] It is absurd that [the body] would be (a) an efficient cause; for the body, as body, does not act on anything—it acts only through a faculty. Were it to act by itself and not by a faculty, then every body would do that action, and then all of the faculties of the body would be either accidents or material forms, but it is impossible for accidents or forms subsisting through matter to provide the very existence of something subsisting through itself, not in matter, [as it is] an existence of an absolute substance. It is also impossible for it to be (b) a receptive cause, since we have already demonstratively explained that the soul is not imprinted in the body in any way.[59] So the body, then, does not bear the form of the soul—according to either simplicity or combination—where the parts of the body would combine and mix in a certain combination and mixture and then the soul would be imprinted in them. Finally, it is absurd for the body to be either (c) a formal or (d) a perfecting cause of the body, for the opposite is more appropriate. The connection of the soul to the body, then, is not that of an effect to an essential cause.

4.   Now, if the humoral temperament and the body are [jointly] an accidental cause of the soul, then when there comes into existence the matter of a body suitable to be an instrument and a domain of the soul, then [either] the separate causes originate [229] a particular soul, or [the soul] originates "out of" [the matter].[60] Otherwise, originating [the soul] without a reason that specifies one such act over another is absurd. That notwithstanding, [if the soul were to come to be without matter], the occurrence of numerically many souls would be prevented, because of what we have already explained.[61] Also, [matter must be an accidental cause for the soul's coming to be], because anything that is generated after not existing must be preceded by a matter that is configured to receive it or is configured to bear some relation to it, as is explained in the other sciences.[62] Again, [matter must be an accidental cause of the soul], because if it were possible for a particular soul to come into existence without there also coming into existence an instrument through which it perfects itself and performs its actions, then [the soul's] existence would be vain, but "nature does nothing in vain,"[j] and when that [instrument] is prevented [from existing, then the

---

[57] That is, a material cause.

[58] That is, a final cause.

[59] See "The Soul," V.2, all, pp. 188–92.

[60] The position that the soul originates out of the matter seems to be that of Alexander of Aphrodisias, De anima I.14–19, 8.13–11.5. Also see Ibn Sīnā's discussion of "out of" and "from" in "Physics," I.2, pars. 17–19, pp. 161–62.

[61] See "The Soul," V.3, pars. 3–11, pp. 193–95.

[62] See "Metaphysics," IV.2, pars. 1–10, pp. 219–22.

soul] is incapable of [perfecting itself and performing its actions]. When being configured for the relation and being disposed to serve as instrument come into being,
however, then it necessarily follows that something, that is, the soul, comes into existence from the separate causes. This is not the case with the soul only. It also applies
to any form that comes into existence after not existing. So it is precisely the disposition of the matter for [the soul] and its becoming suitable for [the soul] that makes
the soul's existence more likely than its nonexistence.

5.   Now, just because one thing must come into existence at the same time as
another thing does not mean that it must perish when the other perishes. That is the
case only when the being of the former subsists through and in the latter. There are
various things, however, that come into existence from other things and survive the
demise of the latter when their being does not subsist in them. [This is] especially the
case when what bestows their existence is something different from the very thing in
conjunction with whose existence there is prepared the bestowal of their existence.
What bestows the existence of the soul is something that is neither a body nor a faculty
in a body; rather, it is unquestionably a being that subsists free of all matter and
magnitudes. So, since the existence of the soul is from that thing, while from the body
there comes only the moment [230] suited to the existence of [the soul], then the soul
has no connection, in its own existence, with the body, nor is the body a cause of it,
except accidentally. Thus, one cannot say that the connection between the two is
of a kind that requires the body to precede the soul in the way that an [essential]
cause would.

6.   The third type of connection we enumerated at the beginning is (2) that the
connection of the soul with the body is as something prior in existence. Such priority
is either (2a) temporal, but in that case the soul's existence cannot be connected with
[the body]—it *preceded* it in time—or the priority is (2b) essential but not temporal.
This second kind of priority means that just as soon as the prior thing exists, it necessarily follows that the posterior thing receives existence from it, and in that case, the
thing that is prior in existence also does not exist when the posterior thing is posited
as not having existed—not that positing the nonexistence of the posterior thing entails
the nonexistence of the prior thing. Quite the contrary, the posterior thing cannot be
nonexistent unless there has first naturally occurred in the prior thing something to
make *it* nonexistent, and then the posterior thing will be nonexistent. So, positing the
nonexistence of the posterior thing is not what entails the nonexistence of the prior
thing, but rather positing the nonexistence of the prior thing itself. [This is so] because
one cannot posit the posterior thing as not existing until after the posterior thing itself
happens to be nonexistent. Consequently, (i) the cause of nonexistence must occur in
the substance of the soul—and so together with [the substance of the soul] the body
is corrupted—and (ii) the body must in no way be corrupted through a cause proper
to it alone. But the body *is* corrupted by a cause proper to it alone, such as the change
of the humoral temperament or composition. So it is simply incoherent to maintain
that the soul is connected with the body as something essentially prior *and* that the
body is corrupted by a cause unique to it. Therefore, this is not the connection

between the two. Now that this is the case, all the ways of connection are invalidated, [231] and all that remains is that the soul has no connection, with respect to existence, with the body; rather, it is connected with other principles that neither change nor cease.

7. I also say there is another reason that the soul does not pass into nonexistence in any way. Anything that can corrupt, due to whatever cause, has in it the potential to corrupt and, before corrupting, has the actuality of persisting, and its being configured to corrupt is not its actuality of persisting; for what is meant by "potentiality" is different from what is meant by "actuality," and the relation of this potentiality is different from the relation of this actuality. [This is so] because the relation of the former is to corrupting and the relation of the latter is to persisting. Thus, these two meanings apply to two different states in the thing. So we say that in composite things, as well as in the simple things that subsist in the composite things, there can combine an actuality to persist and a potentiality to corrupt; but in the simple things that are essentially separate these two states cannot be combined.

8. I say categorically that these two states cannot be combined in something that is essentially one, because anything that persists and has the potentiality to corrupt has equally the potentiality to persist, because its persisting is not necessary and inevitable. If it is not necessary, it is possible, and the possibility that encompasses both sides is the very nature of potentiality. Thus, it has in its substance the potentiality of persisting as well as the actuality of persisting. Now, we have explained that its actuality of persisting is by no means the same as its potentiality to exist. This is obvious. So its actuality of persisting is a state that happens accidentally to the thing that has the potentiality of persisting. That potentiality does not belong to any given essence actually, but rather to the thing whose essence just so happens actually to persist. In other words, that does not belong to the real account of its essence. From this it follows that its essence is composed of something that, when *it* is, then *through* it [232] [the composite] itself actually exists—this is the form in anything—and something *out of* which this actuality occurs but that in itself is its potentiality—this is the matter. So, if the soul is absolutely simple, it is not divided into matter and form, whereas if it is composite—but let us set aside the composite and investigate the substance that is its matter with explicit reference to just that.

9. We say that either matter is divisible in this way perpetually, and the discussion then goes on perpetually (and this is absurd),[63] or the thing that is the substance and root does not perish. Our discussion is about this thing that is the root and foundation, that is what we call the soul; it is not about something that is a combination of it and some other thing. So, it is clear that anything that is simple and not composite, or is the foundation and root of something composite, in relation to itself does not combine in itself the actuality of persisting and the potentiality of not

---

[63] In other words, Ibn Sīnā has eliminated this option on the grounds of the impossibility of an infinite regress, here in the case of dividing matter.

existing. If there is the actuality of not existing in it, then it would be absurd for there to be the actuality of persisting in it, but when the actuality of persisting is in it, and it does in fact exist, the potentiality of not existing is not in it. It is clear, then, that the potentiality to corrupt is not in the substance of the soul. As for the generated things that do corrupt, that part of them that undergoes corruption is the composite combination. Now the potentiality to corrupt or to persist is not in the causal factor (*ma'nā*) whereby the composite thing is one [i.e., the form], but rather in the matter that potentially receives both contraries. Thus, there is not a potentiality to persist and to corrupt in [the form] of the composite corruptible thing, and so they are not combined in it. As for matter, it may be something that persists not by way of a potentiality through which it is disposed to persist, as one group assumes. Or it may be something that persists by way of a potentiality through which it persists, while not having the potentiality to corrupt; rather, the potentiality to corrupt is something else that comes about in it. With the simple things that are in matter, the potentiality to corrupt is in the substance of the matter, [233] not in their own substance. Now the demonstration that requires that every generated thing is corruptible due to the finitude of the two potentialities of subsistence and perishing applies in fact only to anything that is generated from matter and form, where it is with respect to its matter that there is simultaneously the potentiality for that form to persist and the potentiality for it to corrupt, as you have learned. It is then clear that the human soul does not corrupt at all, and it is to this [conclusion] that our discussion has led us.

7. From "The Soul," V.5[k]

CONCERNING THE INTELLECT THAT ACTS UPON OUR SOULS AND THE INTELLECT IN OUR SOULS THAT IS AFFECTED

1. [234] We say that the human soul is at one time something intellecting potentially and thereafter becomes something actually intellecting. Now whatever is brought from potency to act does so only on account of a cause in act that brings it out. So there is a cause that brings our souls from potency to act with regard to the intelligibles. Since it is the cause with respect to providing the intelligible forms, it is precisely but an actual intellect in whom the principles of the intellectual forms are separate (*mujarrada*) [from matter], and whose relation to our souls is the relation of the Sun to our vision. Just as the Sun is actually visible in itself [235] and through its light it makes actually visible what is not actually visible, so likewise is the state of this intellect vis-à-vis our souls; for when the intellecting faculty reviews the particulars that are in the imagery [faculty], and the Active Intellect sheds light onto us upon them (which we discussed), the things abstracted from matter and its associations are altered and impressed upon the rational soul. ["Being altered" is] not in the sense that [the particulars] themselves are transferred from the imagery to our intellect, nor [is "being impressed"] in the sense that the connotational attribute (*ma'nā*) immersed in the [material] associations (which in itself and with regard to its very being is separate (*mujarrada*) [from matter]) makes something like itself. Quite the contrary, [the

alteration and being impressed] is in the sense that reviewing [the things abstracted from matter and its associations] prepares the soul in order that the thing separate from matter [coming] from the Active Intellect [i.e., the intellectual forms] flows down upon them; for discursive thought and selective attention are certain motions that prepare the soul in a way to receive what flows down just as middle terms prepare [the soul] to receive the conclusion in the most convincing way, although the first is according to one way and the second according to another, as you will come to know.

2.   So when a certain relation to this form happens to the rational soul by means of the light shed by the Active Intellect, then from [the relation to the form] there comes to be in [the soul] something that in one way is of its genus and in another way is not, just as when light falls on colored objects, in the seeing of them it produces an effect that is not in every way [reduced] to their sum. So the things in the imagery [faculty], which are potentially intelligible, become actually intelligible— not themselves but what is acquired from them. In fact, just as the effect resulting from the sensible forms by means of the light is not itself those forms, but rather something related to them that is engendered by means of the light in the recipient facing [the light], so likewise when the rational soul reviews those forms in the imagery [faculty] and the light of the Active Intellect comes into a type of conjunction with them, then they are prepared [236] so that from the light of the Active Intellect they come to be within [the rational soul] the abstract version of those forms [free] from [material] taints.

3.   As soon as the essential aspects of [those forms] are distinguished from their accidental aspects on the part of the human intellect, and what makes them similar to the forms of the imagery is distinguished from what makes them different, the connotational attributes that show no difference from those become one in the intellect itself by comparison of similarity, but those connotational attributes that bear comparison to what is different become many connotational attributes and so the intellect has the ability both to consider one of the connotational attributes to be many and to consider the multiple connotational attributes to be one. There are two ways that the many can be considered one. The first is in that when the numerically many differing connotations related to the forms of the imagery do not differ in definition, they become a single connotational attribute. The second way is by combining the many different connotations of genera and differences into a connotational attribute that is singular in the definition. The way to make one connotational attribute many is the reverse of these two processes.

4.   This is one of the properties of the human intellect. It does not belong to any of the other faculties; for they perceive the many as a many as it is and the one as one as it is, whereas they cannot perceive the simple one, but rather the one inasmuch as it is a whole combined of things and their accidents. Also they cannot separate out the accidental aspects and extract them from the essential aspects. So, when the senses present a given form to the imagery [faculty] and the imagery [faculty] presents it to the intellect, the intellect takes a single connotational attribute from it. Then if

another form of the same species is presented to it—"another" only in number—the intellect by no means takes any form different from what was taken, unless it is due to the accident that is particular to this inasmuch as it is that accident such that it takes it one time as separate [of all accidents] and another time with that accident. This is why it is said [237] that Zayd and ʿAmr have one connotational attribute in terms of "humanness," not on the basis of the fact that the humanness associated with the particular properties of ʿAmr is the very same humanness associated with the particular properties of Zayd, as though there were a single thing belonging to Zayd and ʿAmr, as is the case with friendship or property. Instead, "humanness" in terms of existence is many, and there is no existence belonging to some one common humanness in external reality unless it is that very humanness of Zayd and ʿAmr. We will endeavor to explain this in the discipline of philosophy [i.e., metaphysics]. What is intended [here] is that since the first of [the two forms, e.g., Zayd's form of humanness] provided the soul with the form of "humanness," the second [form, e.g., ʿAmr's form of humanness] does not provide anything at all. Instead, the connotational attribute imprinted in the soul by both is a single one, that is, the one from the first presentation of the imagery, while the second presentation has no influence, for either one of them could have preceded and left this very same imprint in the soul, not like the two individuals of a man and a horse.[64]

5. This [is one point]. Next, it is characteristic of the intellect that, when it perceives things that have an earlier and later association with it, it intellects the time with them necessarily—but that is not over a period of time but in an instant, where the intellect intellects the time in an instant. Its construction of the syllogism and the definition is unquestionably in a period of time; however, its conception of the conclusion and the thing defined is instantaneous.

6. The inability of the intellect to conceptualize things that are at the upper limit of being intelligible and abstracted from matter is not on account of something in those things themselves, nor on account of something innate to the intellect, but rather on account of the fact that the soul is distracted while in the body by the body. It needs the body for many things, but the body keeps it at a remove from the most noble of its perfections. The eye cannot bear to gaze at the Sun, certainly not on account of something [238] in the Sun nor that it is not clearly visible, but rather on account of something about the natural makeup of the body [of the eye]. When this state of being immersed and impeded are removed from the soul we have, it will intellect these [extreme intelligibles] in the noblest, clearest, and most pleasurable ways. Our discussion here, however, concerns the soul only inasmuch as it is a soul, and that only inasmuch as it is associated with this matter. So we should not discuss the return of the soul when we are discussing nature, until we move on to the discipline of philosophy [i.e., metaphysics] and there investigate the things that are separate [from matter]. The investigation in the natural philosophy, however, is restricted to

---

64 That is, the forms of two different species.

what is appropriate to natural things, and they are the things that bear relation to matter and motion.

7.   So we say instead that the intellect conceptualizes differently depending upon the existence of things. So with very strong things, the intellect may not be able to perceive them because they overwhelm it, and with very weakly existing things, like motion, time, and matter, the soul may find it difficult to conceptualize them because of their weak existence. As for privations, the intellect does not conceptualize them when it is actual in an absolute sense, because privation is perceived insofar as possession is not perceived, so whatever is perceived of privation as a privation and evil as an evil is something potential and an absence of a perfection. Any intellect that perceives it does so only because it bears some relation to it potentially. So the intellects in which nothing potential is mixed do not intellect nor conceptualize privation and evil as a privation and an evil, given there is nothing in existence that is an absolute evil.

8. From "The Soul," V.6[1]

THE LEVELS OF THE INTELLECT'S ACTIONS

1.   [239] We say that the soul intellects by taking into itself the form of the intelligibles as abstracted from matter. The form is so abstracted either by the intellect's abstraction of it or because that form is in itself abstracted from matter, in which case the soul is spared the trouble of abstracting it.

2.   The soul conceptualizes itself and in doing so makes itself an intellect, something that intellects, and something that is intellected. Its conceptualization of these [intelligible] forms, however, does not make it such; for its substance in the body is always potentially an intellect, even though in some cases it is brought into act. What is said about the soul itself *becoming* the intelligible objects is one of those [statements] that to my mind is impossible;[65] for I do not understand their statement that something becomes something else, nor do I know how that would take place. If it is through "doffing" one form and "donning" another form, where [the soul's substance] is one thing with the first form and another thing with the other form, then in point of fact the first thing does *not* become the other thing.[66] Rather, the first thing had perished and all that remained was its [material] subject or part of that. If it does not happen like that, then we should investigate how it would. We say: when the first thing, x, becomes another thing, y, then—since it had been that first thing—x either exists or does not exist. If x exists, then the second thing, y, either exists also or does

---

65 Cf. Aristotle, *De anima* III 4, 429a16, 430a14; and III 7, 431a1. Al-Fārābī makes this point as well, albeit in terms of the intellects' becoming the intelligible object; cf. al-Fārābī, *On the Intellect*, par. 12, pp. 71–72, and *The Principles of Existing Things*, par.18, p. 87.

66 The "doffing" metaphor is a reference to the metaphor of Plotinus of the soul leaving the body behind, as it was translated into Arabic as part of the Pseudo-Aristotelian *Theology*.

not exist. If *y* exists, then *x* and *y* are two existing things, not one. If *y* does not exist, then [since *x* has become *y*], *x* has become something that does not exist, not some other existing thing [240]—and this is unintelligible. If *x* was nonexistent, then it did not become *another* thing; rather, it is nonexistent and some other thing comes to be. So how does the soul become the forms of things?

3.   The one who wrote the *Eisagōgē* [i.e., Porphyry] caused people the most confusion on this issue. He was so intent to maintain imaginative,[m] poetic, and mystic[67] doctrines that he confined himself, and others, to the imagination—something that is obvious to discriminating people on the basis of his books *On the Intellect and the Intelligibles* and *On the Soul*.[68] To be sure, the forms do settle in the soul, "adorning" and "ornamenting" it, with the soul becoming like a place for them by means of the material intellect. Nevertheless, if the soul were actually to *become* a form of some existing thing, where the form is the actuality—since in itself it *is* an actuality and [thus] does not itself have any potentiality to receive anything (since any potentiality to receive is only in what receives something)—then the soul necessarily cannot have any potentiality to receive another form, or anything else for that matter. In point of fact, however, we do observe [that the soul] receives another form, that is, other than that form [by which it is an actuality]. Now, if that other form is also no different from this form [by which it is an actuality], this would be a strange situation indeed, since receiving and not receiving would be one and the same thing. If it is different, then there is no doubt that the soul, if it is now the intelligible form, has become something other than itself. But this is nonsense! It is rather the case that the soul is what is intellecting, and what is meant by the "intellect" is either [the soul's] faculty through which it intellects, or the forms of the intelligibles in themselves. Now, it is because [the intelligible forms] are *in* the soul that they are intelligible, so the intellect, intellecting, and what is intellected are *not* one and the same thing in our souls. (Certainly in something else this may be the case, [241] as you will catch sight of elsewhere.) Similarly, if "material intellect" means the absolute disposition belonging to the soul, then it is always in us as long we are in the body. If it means [a disposition to receive the form] of any given thing, however, then that ceases with the onset of actuality.

4.   Now that this has been established, we say that there are three ways of conceptualizing intelligibles.

4.1.   The first is the conceptualization that is actually [in the process of] differentiating and arranging [the forms] in the soul. Such manner of differentiating and arrangement need not be obligatory; in fact, it can be rearranged. For example, in your soul when you divide the meanings (*maʿnā*) of the terms indicated by your statement, "Every man is an animal," you find that the meaning of each term

---

[67] Ibn Sīnā uses the term *ṣūfīya* here, an adjective for mystical thought in the Islamic tradition.

[68] For a brief discussion of these works, see Peter Adamson, "*Porphyrius Arabus* on Nature and Art: 463F Smith in Context" in *Studies in Porphyry*, George Karamanolis and Anne Sheppard, eds., Appendix I.

is a universal that can be conceptualized only in an incorporeal substance, and you find that the conceptualization of them in it puts one thing first and another last. If you rearrange that in such a way that the order of the conceptualized meanings is the opposite order of your statement, "Animal is predicated of every man," you have no doubt that this order, as an order of universal connotational attributes (*ma'nā*), can be so ordered only with regard to an incorporeal substance. While it is also ordered in a certain way in the imagery, there it is as something heard, not as something intellected. While the two acts of ordering are different, the simple intelligible is single.

4.2. The second is when conceptualizing [the intelligible] has taken place and [the intelligible] has been acquired, but the soul is turned away from it. It is no longer paying attention to that intelligible, but rather has been moved away from it to another intelligible, for example. For it is not within the capacity of our souls to intellect things together at one time.

4.3. Another type of conceptualization is like something [242] you have with regard to a question you are asked concerning something you learned or all but learned, and the response comes to you at the time and you are certain that you are responding to it on the basis of what you learned, without differentiating [out the intelligibles]. In fact, however, you start differentiating and ordering [them] in your soul just as you begin the response that arises from some certainty you have about knowing it before the differentiating and ordering.

5. The difference between the first and second conceptualizations is obvious; for the first is like something you took out of storage and put to use, whereas the second is like something that is stored for you [and] whenever you want, you put it to use. The third differs from the first by not being something ordered in the discursive thought process at all; rather, it is like some principle of that, given its close connection to certainty. [The third] differs from the second in that it is not overlooked; rather, it is actually being investigated as something that is certain, since with it there is a particular connection to something that verges on being like the stored [intelligible]. [. . .]

THE "SACRED" INTELLECT

6.[n] [248] The acquisition of knowledge, whether from someone else or on one's own, varies in degrees. Some people who acquire knowledge more readily conceptualize because the disposition they have[69] that precedes the disposition we have mentioned[70] is more powerful. If that is the case for the person on his own, this powerful disposition is called "intuition." In some people this disposition may be so intense that they need neither much effort, nor training, nor instruction to conjoin with the Active Intellect; rather, the disposition for that may be so intense that it is almost as

---

[69] That is, the material intellect.

[70] That is, the dispositional intellect; see "The Soul," I.5, pars. 14–15, pp. 184–85.

though they actually possessed the second disposition—in fact, it is as though they know everything on their own. This is the highest degree of this disposition. In this state the material intellect has to be called a "sacred intellect," and, though a part of the genus of dispositional intellect, it is so lofty that it is not common to everyone. It is not inconceivable [249] that some of these actions, which are attributed to the sacred spirit because of their powerful and overwhelming nature, deluge the imagination, which then reproduces imitations of them that can be perceived by the senses and heard as speech, in the manner we have previously indicated.

7.   Something that verifies this is the obvious fact that the intelligible matters that can be acquired are acquired only by obtaining the middle term of a syllogism. This middle term may be acquired in two ways. Sometimes through intuition, which is an act whereby the mind discovers the middle term on its own (acumen being the power of intuition). Sometimes through instruction, the origins of which are intuition; for there is no doubt that things go back ultimately to acts of intuition discovered by those who had the intuitions and subsequently passed them on to their students.

8.   Therefore, it is conceivable that intuition could occur to a person on his own and that he could construct the syllogism in his mind without a teacher. This is something that varies in quantity and quality: in quantity because some people have more intuitions of the middle terms; in quality because some people intuit faster. Now since this variation is not restricted to one particular level but rather is always susceptible to increase and decrease, and since at the lowest extreme it ends at someone who has no intuition whatsoever, its highest extreme must end at someone who has intuition about all or most objects of scientific investigation and who intuits in the quickest and least amount of time. It is possible, then, for there to be an individual whose soul is strengthened by such intense purity and such intense conjunction with the intellectual principles that he blazes with intuition. I mean [that he blazes with intuition] by receiving [the principles]° concerning all matters from the Active Intellect, where the forms that are in the Active Intellect are imprinted in his soul either instantly or almost so. [This] does not occur by [250] blindly accepting them, but rather in an order containing the middle terms; for blindly accepted beliefs about things that are knowable really only through their causes do *not* constitute intellectual certainty. This is a type of prophethood—in fact, it is the highest faculty of prophethood—and it is most appropriate to call this faculty a "sacred" faculty, since it is the highest level of the human faculties.

9. From "The Soul," V.7ᴾ

A VERIFICATION OF THE TRUE ACCOUNT OF THE SOUL

[...]1.   [252] It has become clear from what we have stated[71] that the different actions of the soul are attributable to different faculties, and that each faculty, as such,[72]

---

71 "The Soul," I.5, pp. 179–85.

72 That is, different from another faculty.

is like that only inasmuch as the first action that belongs to it issues from it. So the irascible faculty is not affected by pleasures nor is the appetitive faculty affected by pains. The faculty of perception does not suffer the effects that these two suffer, and nothing about these two, as such,[73] [253] is receptive to the perceptible form and is in-formed by it.[74] This being an established fact, we say that these faculties must have a nexus that joins them all together and to which they are bound as a group, where the relation of that nexus to these faculties is the same as the relation of the common sense to the individual senses that are [like] nurslings. [There must be such a nexus], for we are certain that these faculties distract one another (as you have learned from what preceded).[75] If there were no such nexus employing these [faculties], such that [the nexus] would be distracted by one of them away from another, thus not employing the latter or managing it, then it would not be the case that one prevents another from its activity in some way nor is diverted from [its own activity]. [This is so] because when one faculty has no connection with another faculty, the activity of the first does not prevent the second from performing its own activity since the instrument is not common [to both], the location is not common, and there is nothing else in common to unite them. Now how can this be when we see that the act of sensing excites desire, but the appetitive faculty is not affected by the sensible object as a sensible object? If it is affected but not inasmuch as [the object] is a sensible object, then the affection cannot be attributable to the desire for that sensible object, so it would have to be [attributable to] what is doing the sensing. The two faculties, however, certainly cannot be a single faculty, and so the two faculties clearly belong to one thing. This is why we correctly say: "When we sense, we desire," and "When we saw such-and-such, we became angry."

2.　Now this single thing with respect to which these faculties are joined as a whole is the thing that each of us sees as himself such that he says truly: "When we sense, we desire" [254]. This thing cannot be a body [for the following reasons]. First, it does not necessarily follow from being a body as such that it is a gathering place for these faculties. If that were the case, that would belong to every body rather than to some thing *by means of which* [every body] comes to be such, since that thing is what primarily does the gathering together, that is, it is the perfection of the body inasmuch as it is a gathering place, and it is something other than the body. So the gathering place, then, is something that is not a body, that is, [it is] the soul.

3.　Second, it has already been made clear that these faculties include what cannot be a corporeal thing residing in a body.[76] So this could raise the following doubt: if it is conceivable for these faculties to belong to a single thing despite the

---

[73] That is, different from the perceptible faculty.

[74] See "The Soul," I.5, pars. 8–9, p. 182.

[75] Ibid., V.3, par. 2, pp. 192–93.

[76] See "The Soul," V.2, pp. 188–92.

fact that they are not gathered together in it—since some do not inhere in bodies and others do—and, as corollary to their individual distinctions, they cannot have a single description that can be related to one thing, then why is that not the case now when all of them can be related to a body or a corporeal part? We say in response: Because this thing—the one that is not a body—can be a source of the faculties, and so some of them spread out from it to the instrument [i.e., the body], others are proper to itself, but all of them are traced back to it in a particular manner. The ones gathered together in the [bodily] instrument at a particular originating point are gathered in the instrument by that originating point when it spreads out from the thing [i.e., the soul] that is sufficient in itself without the instrument (. . .).[77] All of these faculties, however, cannot spread out from the body, for the relation of these faculties to the body is not by way of spreading out [from it] but by way of [its] receiving [them]. Spreading out can occur as a departure of the flow from the source, but receiving cannot occur in such a manner.

4.   [255] Third, such a body[78] is either (a) the whole body or (b) it is not the whole body. If (a) it is the whole body, then if it lost some part of itself, what we perceive to be us would not exist. It is not like that, however; for I would be myself even if I did not know that I have a hand or a leg or some other bodily member (as was stated earlier in other places).[79] I suppose instead that they are my appendages, and I believe that they are instruments of mine that I use to fulfill certain needs. Were it not for those needs, I would have no use for them. I would also be myself when they did not exist. Let us return to what was stated earlier on our part. We say: If a human were created in a single instant such that his limbs were separated from one another and he could not see them, and it happened that he could not feel them and they did not touch one another and he could not hear a single sound, he would not know that any of his organs exist, but he would know that he exists as uniquely a single thing[q] despite not knowing everything else. However, what is unknown is not the same as what is known! These bodily members that we have are really only just like clothes that, because they have always been associated with us, we have come to think of as parts of ourselves. When we imagine our selves, we do not imagine them bare; rather, we imagine [our selves] to have enveloping bodies. The reason for that is the permanent association [of the two]. The fact, however, is that we have become accustomed to stripping off and discarding clothes in a way we are not accustomed to doing with the bodily members, and so our belief that these are parts of us is more firmly entrenched than our belief that our garments are parts of us.

5.   If it is (b) that such a body is not the whole body but rather one specific bodily organ, then that organ would be the thing that I believe to be me—unless[r] what is intended in my believing that it is me [256] is not that organ, even if it must

---

[77] Omitted here is a reference to further treatment of this later in the chapter.

[78] That is, the body that is posited as being "the thing that each of us sees as himself," par. 2, p. 206.

[79] See "The Soul," I.1, par. 7, pp. 178–79.

have that organe.[80] If, however, what that organ is, namely, its being a heart, a brain, or some other organ or organs with this description, is identical to it or its totality is identical to the thing that I perceive to be myself, then my perception that I am must be my perception of that thing. But one thing from a single perspective cannot be both what is perceived and other than what is perceived.[81] The situation is not like that anyway; for it is rather by sensing, listening, and experiential knowledge that I know that I have a heart and a brain, not because I know that I am I. Thus, that organ on its own would not be the thing that I perceive to be me essentially but only me accidentally, whereas the aim in knowing about myself that I am me (that is, the aim that I intend when I say "*I* sensed, *I* intellected, *I* acted, and *I*, as something different than these descriptions, joined them together") is what I call "I."

6.   Now, if someone said, "You also do not know that [the 'I'] is a soul," I would say that I *always* know it as the thing intended by what I call the "soul." I might not know it by the term "soul," but once I understand what I mean by soul, I understand that it is that thing and that it is what uses [bodily] instruments such as the motive and perceptive faculties. It is only as long as I do not understand the meaning of "soul" that I do not recognize [that]. That is not the case with the heart or the brain; for I may understand what is meant by "heart" and "brain," but I do not know that [they are the "I"]. When I mean by "soul" that it is the thing that is the principle of these motions and perceptions that I have and is what these [motions and perceptions] are traced back to in this whole, I recognize that either it is in actual fact the "I" or it is the "I" as something using this body. Then, it would be as though I now am unable to distinguish the perception of me as distinct from the mixed perception [257] that there is something that uses the body, and that there is something that is joined with the body.

7.   As for whether it is a body or not a body, in my opinion it is by no means necessary that it be a body, nor that it appear to me in imagined form as any body whatsoever. Instead, its imagined form appears to me to be precisely *without* any corporeality. So I will have understood some part of the aspect of its not being a body when I do *not* understand it to have any corporeality at the very same time that I understand [what it is]. Then, when I undertake an independent verification, the more I add corporeality to this thing that is the principle of these acts, the less conceivable it will be for that thing to be a body. How much more fitting it would be for its first representation in my soul to be something that is different from these exterior aspects, and I am then misled by the association with bodily instruments, the sensory observation of those, and the issuance of actions from them, and I believe that [those exterior aspects] are like parts of me. It is not when an error has been made about something that a judgment must pertain to it, but rather when the judgment pertains to what it

---

[80] If it is the latter, then the organ would be just part, albeit an essential one, of what is identified as the self.

[81] That is, what would be doing the perceiving.

is that has to be intellected. And it is not when I am investigating whether it exists and whether it is not a body that I am wholly ignorant of [these questions], but rather when I neglect [to consider these questions]. It is often the case that knowledge about something is close at hand but one overlooks it, and it becomes the very thing that is unknown and is investigated at the greatest remove. Sometimes knowledge that is close at hand is like the reminder, and despite the least amount of effort it was like something overlooked, and so awareness does not turn to pursue it because it weakly understands it, in which case one needs to take a remote position in relation to it. From [all of] this, it has become clear that these faculties have a gathering place to which all of them can be traced back, and that it is not a body, regardless of whether it is or is not joined with the body.

VII. THE SALVATION, "METAPHYSICS," I.12[a]

I.12 The Division of the Causes and Their States[82]

1. [518] "Principle" is said of anything that already has a completed existence in itself (whether from itself or another) and from which the existence of another thing occurs and subsists by it.

2. Next, the principle is either like part of its effect or it is not like a part. If it is like a part, then either one of two things must be the case. (1) It may be a part from whose actual occurrence its effect need not actually exist: this is matter. So you can imagine matter existing, but from its actual existence alone something [else] need not actually occur but rather may be potential. Or (2) it may be that from its actual existence the existence of its effect must be actual: [519] this is form. An example of the first is the wood of the bed; an example of the second is the shape and composition of the bed.[83]

3. If it is not like the part, then it is something either extrinsic or intrinsic to the effect itself. If it is intrinsic, then either the effect is characterized by it—and this is like the form of the matter—or it is characterized by the effect—and this is like the subject of the accident. If it is extrinsic, then it is either that *from which* there is existence, but the existence is not *for the sake of* it—this is the agent; or the existence is not *from* it, but the existence is *for the sake* of it—this is the end. Thus, the causes are matter belonging to the composite, form belonging to the composite, a subject for the accident, a form for the matter, an agent, and an end.

4. The matter of the composite and the subject of the accident collapse together in that they are the thing in which there is the potentiality of something's existence.

---

82 For discussions of Ibn Sīna's theory of causality see Amos Bertolacci, "The Doctrine of Material and Formal Causality in the *Ilāhiyyāt* of Avicenna's *Kitāb al-Shifāʾ*," 125–54; and Robert Wisnovsky, "Final and Deficient Causality in Avicenna's Cosmology and Theology," 97–123.

83 Cf. the translation of "Physics," I.2, par. 2, pp. 156–57.

The form of the composite and the form of the matter collapse together in that [the form] is that nonextrinsic thing by which the effect actually exists.

5.   The end comes to exist later than the effect, whereas it is prior to the rest of the causes in thingness.[84] There is a difference between the thingness and the existence in concrete particulars [520]; for the account [of what something is] has an existence in concrete particulars and in the soul and is something common [to both]. That common thing, then, is the thingness. The end, insofar as it is a thing, is prior to the rest of the causes and is the cause of the causes inasmuch as they are causes, while insofar as it is something existing in concrete particulars, it is frequently posterior.

6.   When the efficient cause is not itself the final cause, then the agent comes after the end in terms of thingness. That follows because the rest of the causes actually come to be causes only for the sake of the end, not for the sake of something else, since [the end] exists first as a species of existence and then makes the causes actually become causes.

7.   The result of the distinction [between thingness and existence] appears to be that the first agent and cause of motion with respect to anything is the end. For the doctor acts for the sake of health, and the form of health is the medical knowledge that is in the soul and is a cause of motion owing to his will to act. When the agent is higher than the will, then the very thing that is an end is itself an agent and cause of motion without the intermediacy of the will, which comes about as a result of the end's causing motion.

8.   As for the rest of the causes, both the agent and what receives the act may be prior to the effect in time, whereas form is never prior [to the effect] in time. What receives the act is always of a lesser rank than the composite while the agent is nobler, because what receives the act is what is benefited not what imparts the benefit, whereas the agent is what imparts the benefit not what is benefited.

9.   [521] The cause is a cause of something essentially, for example, the doctor is [essentially a cause] of medical treatment. The cause might also be accidental, either because, on the one hand, for some reason other than the one actually set down, it happens to be a cause; for example, if it is said that the writer cures. That follows because he cures not insofar as he is a writer but because of another reason different from [being a writer], namely, that he is a doctor.

10.   On the other hand, a cause might be accidental because one produces an action essentially, but another action might follow upon [the first] action. For example, scammony cools accidentally because it purges bile essentially, where a decrease of the irritating heat accompanies [the purging of bile]. Again, an example is one who removes the support from a wall; for he is an accidental cause of the wall's collapsing, since after he removes the impediment, a natural action, namely, the natural downward inclination of the heavy, is entailed by his action.

---

[84] For a discussion of Ibn Sīnā's notion of "thingness" see Robert Wisnovsky, "Notes on Avicenna's Concept of Thingness (Shay'iyya)," 181–221.

11.   The cause is sometimes in potentiality, like the carpenter before he works the wood. Sometimes it is in actuality, like the carpenter when he is working the wood. The cause might also be proximate, like putrefaction for fever. It also might be remote, the way congestion together with bloating is [a cause of fever].

12.   The cause might also be particular, like our saying that *this* act of building is a cause of *this* building, but it might also be universal, just as we say that the act of building is a cause of building.

13.   The cause might also be specific, just as we say that the act of building is a cause of the house, and the cause might be general, just as we say that the builder is a cause of the house.

14.   [522] Know that matter and form are the proximate causes with no intermediary between them and the natural bodies. As for the agent, it is either a cause of the form alone or of the form and the matter, and thereupon it becomes a cause of the composite through the mediation of whatever of the two [i.e., the form or matter] is its cause. The final cause is a cause of the agent's being a cause of the generation, which itself is a cause of the form's existence, which itself is a cause of the composite's existence.

VIII.   *THE SALVATION,* "METAPHYSICS," II.1–5[a]

II.I: Explaining the Senses of Necessary and Possible[85]

1.   [546] The necessarily existent is the existent,[b] which when posited as not existing, an absurdity results. The possibly existent is the one that, when posited as either existing or not existing, no absurdity results. The necessarily existent is the existence that *must be,* whereas the possibly existent is the one that has no "must" about it in any way, whether in terms of its existence or nonexistence. (This is what we mean by "possibly existent" in this context, although "possibly existent" sometimes means "in potency," and "possible" is sometimes said of anything that in fact exists, as has been detailed in logic.)

2.   Next, the necessarily existent may exist through itself or not through itself. What is necessarily existent through itself is that which is owing to itself not to any other thing, that is, [not to another] thing that, positing its nonexistence, results in an absurdity. [547] The necessarily existent not through itself is that which becomes necessarily existent if something other than it is set down. For example, four exists necessarily not through itself but only when positing two plus two; and burning exists necessarily not through itself but only when positing contact between the natural active power and the natural passive power, I mean what causes burning and what is burned.

---

85 For a discussion of the historical context of Ibn Sīnā's modal metaphysics see Robert Wisnovsky, *Avicenna's Metaphysics in Context,* especially part II.

II.2: The Necessary through Itself Cannot Be Necessary through Another, and the Necessary through Another Is What Is Possible

1. [547] One thing cannot exist simultaneously as necessary through itself and necessary through another. For if the other is removed or its existence not considered, it must be the case that either the necessity of its existence remains unchanged, and so the necessity of its existence is not through another, or the necessity of its existence does not remain, and so the necessity of its existence is not through itself.

2. Whatever exists necessarily through another exists possibly in itself. [This is] because the necessity of the existence of whatever exists necessarily through another is a consequence of a given association and relation, but consideration of the association and relation is different from consideration of the thing itself that has an association and relation. Thus, it is only by considering this association that the necessity of the existence can be determined.

3. In terms of the thing itself on its own, it is something that must exist necessarily, possibly or impossibly. [548] Now it cannot be something that must exist impossibly, because anything whose existence is impossible through itself is neither through itself nor through another. Nor is it something that must exist necessarily, for we have already said that whatever exists necessarily through itself simply cannot have the necessity of its existence through another. So it remains that with respect to the thing itself, it exists possibly; with respect to introducing the association with that other, it exists necessarily; and with respect to disrupting the association with that other, it exists impossibly. It itself, however—in itself without condition—exists possibly.

II.3: Whatever Is Not Necessary Does Not Exist

1. [548] It is now clear that what exists necessarily through another exists possibly through itself. This is convertible. Thus, everything existing possibly in itself—if indeed its existence has occurred—exists necessarily through another. [This follows] because either it in fact has actual existence or it does not. It is absurd, however, that it not in fact have actual existence [when it indeed exists], otherwise its existence would be impossible. So it remains that it in fact has actual existence. In that case, its existence is either necessary or not necessary. If its existence is not necessary, and so it is still possible existence, then its existence is not distinguished from its nonexistence and there is no difference between this state in it and the first state. [This follows] because before existing it was possible existence, and its present state is the same as it was. If one posits [549] that a new state comes to be, then concerning that state the question stands, namely, does it exist possibly or necessarily?

2. If it is possible, and that state before was itself also possible, then nothing new came to be, whereas if the existence [of the new state] is necessary and it is made necessary for the first [possible existent], then the existence of a state has been made necessary for this first. But that [new] state is nothing other than the emergence [of the thing] into existence, so [it is] its emergence into existence that is necessary.

3. Finally, the existence of whatever exists possibly is either through itself or through some given cause. If it is through itself, then it itself exists necessarily not possibly. If it is through a cause, then either its existence is necessary together with the existence of the cause, or it would stay the way it was before the existence of the cause, which is absurd. It must be the case, then, that its existence is together with the existence of the cause. So, whatever exists possibly through itself exists necessarily through another.

II.4: The Necessary Existent's Perfection and Unity and That Two Things Inseparable with Respect to Existence Are Equivalent with Respect to It and so Both Have an External Cause

1. [549] A single necessary existent can neither come to be from two nor is there multiplicity in the necessary existent in any way. There cannot [550] be two things, where this one is not that one, and that one is not this one, and each one is necessary through itself and through the other. [This is so since] (1) it has already been made clear that the necessary existent through itself is not through another. [This also follows since] (2) neither one of them can exist necessarily through the other, such that x exists necessarily through y and not through itself, and y exists necessarily through x and not through itself, and yet their totality is a single necessary existent. [That is so] because considering them as two entities is different from considering them as two *relata*. [In the latter case] each one of them has a necessary existence that is not through itself, and so each one of them exists possibly in itself. Now everything that exists possibly in itself has a cause for its existence that is prior to it, because every cause is prior to the effect with respect to its own existence, even if it is not [prior] with respect to time. Thus, in itself, each one of [the *relata*] has another thing by means of which it subsists, which is prior to it itself; however, according to what we described, neither of them itself is prior to the other. So, then, both have causes external to them and prior to them. Therefore, each one's necessary existence is not derived from the other, but rather from the external cause that occasions the attachment between them.

2. [551] Again, in the case of anything that is necessary through another, its very existence is posterior to the existence of that other and is dependent upon it. It is, then, impossible for one entity, x, to depend for its existence upon another entity, y, where y exists through x. It would be as though it depends for its existence on its very own existence! In summary form, when y is necessary through x, x is prior to [y, which is] prior to [x], and [x] dependent upon [y, which is] dependent upon [x]. So the existence of both is absurd.

3. <So, on the one hand, if x has its own existence through itself, then it has no need for the other, y. On the other hand, if x does not exist until y exists, and y exists only after x exists, then the existence of x is dependent upon something that exists after its very own existence, and so its existence is absurd.>[c]

II.5: On the Simplicity of the Necessary

1. [551] We also say it cannot be the case that the necessary existent has principles that are gathered together and the necessary existent is constituted of them. [In other words], it has neither quantitative parts nor the parts of a definition and account, whether they are like the matter and form, or in any other way as the parts of the account explaining the sense of its name, where each one of them would indicate [552] something that is different essentially from the other with respect to the existence. That is because with anything described thus, each of its parts is neither the same as any other part nor the same as the composite. So either each of its two parts, for instance, can exist independently, but the composite cannot exist apart from them, and so the composite would not exist necessarily. Or one of them can [exist necessarily], but the composite cannot exist apart from it, and then neither the composite nor the other parts can exist independently, and so again [the necessary existent] would not exist necessarily. But it is precisely the necessary existent that can exist necessarily! If those parts cannot exist separately from the whole, and the whole cannot exist separately from the parts, but the existence of each one is attached to another and neither is essentially prior, then none of it exists necessarily. I^d have already explained this, that is, the parts are essentially prior to the whole, and so the cause necessitating existence would first necessitate the parts and then the whole, and none of them would exist necessarily. We cannot say that the whole is essentially prior to the parts, and so it is either later or simultaneous—how could it be?!—since then it would not exist necessarily.

2. From this it has become clear that what exists necessarily is not a body, nor any matter of a body, nor a form of a body, nor an intelligible matter of an intelligible form, nor an intelligible form in an intelligible matter, nor divisible—whether in quantity, principles, or account—and so it is one from these three perspectives.

IX.   THE SALVATION, "METAPHYSICS," II.12–13^a

II.12: The Proof of the Necessarily Existent

1. [566] Undoubtedly there is existence, and all existence is either necessary or possible. [567] If it is necessary, then in fact there is a necessarily existent being, which is what is sought. If it is possible, then we will show that the existence of the possible terminates in a necessarily existent being. Before that, however, we will advance some premises.[86]

2. These include that at any one and the same time there cannot be for anything that is possible [in] itself a cause that is itself possible ad infinitum. This is because all of them exist either all together or they do not. If they do not exist all together but rather one after another, there is no infinite at one and the same time—but let

---

[86] Only one is advanced here, but additional ones are advanced in the next chapter, 215–16.

us defer discussion of this for now. As for their existing all together, and none is a necessarily existing being, then either the totality, insofar as it is that totality, whether finite or infinite, exists necessarily through itself or possibly in itself. If, on the one hand, the totality exists necessarily through itself, but each one of its members is something possible, then what exists necessarily subsists by means of things that exist possibly, which is absurd. On the other hand, if the totality is something existing possibly in itself, then the totality needs for existence [568] something that provides existence, which will be either external or internal to the totality.

3. If it is something internal to it, then one of its members is something existing necessarily, but each one of them exists possibly—so this is a contradiction. Or it is something existing possibly and so is a cause of the totality's existence, but a cause of the totality is primarily a cause of the existence of its members, of which it is one. Thus, it would be a cause of its own existence, which is impossible. Despite this impossibility, if it is correct, it is in a certain way the very thing that is sought; for anything that is sufficient to necessitate itself is something existing necessarily, but it was [assumed] not to exist necessarily, so this is a contradiction.

4. The remaining option is that [what gives existence to the totality] is external to it, but it cannot be a possible cause, since we included every cause existing possibly in this totality. So since [the cause] is external to it, it also is something existing necessarily in itself. Thus, things existing possibly terminate in a cause existing necessarily, in which case not every [effect] that exists as something possible will have simultaneously with it a cause that exists as something possible, and so an infinite number of causes existing at a single time is impossible.

II.13: That Possibly Existents Cannot Be Causes of One Another in a Circular Fashion at One and the Same Time If They Are Finite

1. [568] Furthermore, the causes cannot be finite in number when [569] each of them exists possibly in itself but is necessary through another to the point that one reaches the other circularly.

2. So let us advance another premise. To set down a finite number of possible existents, each one of which is a cause of the others in a circle, is as absurd and obvious as the first problem. Particular to it, however, is that each one of them would be a cause and an effect of its own existence, where x comes into existence from y only after y itself comes into existence, but anything whose existence depends on the existence of what exists only after its own later existence cannot exist.

3. Any case of two *relata*, however, is not like this. For the two exist simultaneously, and the existence of one of them is not dependent such that it must be after the existence of the other. Rather, the cause productive of them and necessitating them produces them both simultaneously. If one of them has a priority and the other a posteriority, like father and son, and if its priority is not with respect to the relation, then its priority is with respect to existence itself. [570] However, the two are simultaneous with respect to the relation that is present after the occurrence of the thing.

If the father's existence were to depend on the son's existence, and the son's existence were to depend on the father's existence, and moreover the two were not simultaneous, but one of them is essentially after, then neither one of them would exist. The absurdity is not that the existence of what is simultaneous with a thing is a condition for the thing's existence; rather, the absurdity is that it is an existence from and after that thing.

X. *THE SALVATION,* "METAPHYSICS," II.18–19ᵃ

II.18. How the Necessary Existent through Itself Intellects Itself and Things

1.   [246] It is absolutely inconceivable that the Necessary Existent would intellect things by way of things. Otherwise, (1) It would subsist inasmuch as it intellects—and so It would subsist by means of the things; or (2) Its intellecting would be accidental to It—and so It would not exist necessarily in every way. This is absurd, since if there were no external things, [the Necessary Existent] would not exist unless It had a state resulting not from Itself but from another, in which case the other would have an effect on It. The axioms set down earlier invalidate this and anything like it.

2.   Now, because [the Necessary Existent] is a principle of all existence (as we will explain), It intellects by way of Itself anything of which it is a principle, and It is a principle of both existents that are complete in themselves, as well as those things that are subject to generation and corruption, as species first, and, by way of that, as individuals.

3.   [247] In another way, however, It cannot be something intellecting, at a given time and at the level of the individual, these things that change, as they are changing, inasmuch as they are things changing; instead, It intellects them in another manner that we will explain. For It could not be the case that at one time It intellects one of them as an existing, not a nonexistent thing, and at another time intellects it as a nonexistent thing, where each of these is a unique form for the intellect and neither form remains with the other, [since] then the Necessary Existent would Itself be subject to change.

4.   Moreover, if the things subject to corruption can be intellected as abstracted essence and as an unindividuated thing following from that, then they cannot be intellected as corruptible. If they can be perceived as something joined to matter and material accidents, and a given moment, and individuated, then they are not objects of the intellect but rather of the senses and the imaginative faculty. We have already explained in other books[87] that we perceive any form derived from the senses as an object of the senses, and we imagine any form derived from the imagery only through a particular organ.

---

[87] See translations of "Book of Demonstration," III.5, pars. 1–7, pp. 152–54, "The Soul," I.5, pars. 6–9, pp. 181–82, pars. 14–15, pp. 184–85; V.3, pars. 1–2, pp. 192–93; V.5, all, pp. 199–202.

5. The assertion that the Necessary Existent has multiple acts of intellecting is just as faulty as the assertion that It has multiple acts. In point of fact, the Necessary Existent intellects everything only universally, but nevertheless no individual thing escapes Its notice, "not even the weight of a dust speck, whether in the heavens or on Earth, escapes His notice."[88] This is one of those wonders that requires a subtle genius to understand.

II.19. How the Necessary Existent Intellects Things

1. [247] In answer to how this is possible, it is because when [the Necessary Existent] intellects Itself, and It intellects that It is the principle of everything that exists, It intellects the first principles of existent things as well as whatever is engendered out of them. Now nothing comes to exist unless it has already become in one respect necessary by reason of some cause—we have already explained this[89]—and then these causes interact with one another until particular things come to exist as a result.

2. The First [i.e., the Necessary Existent] knows the causes and the things coinciding with them and so necessarily knows what they result in, the times between them, and their recurrences. Since It cannot know *this* or *that*,[90] It is aware of particular things insofar as they are universal—I mean inasmuch as they have attributes. If [those attributes] are unique to [one particular thing] as an individual, and so bear relation to an individual time or an individual state, then, if that state were to be understood as those attributes, it would be on par with [those attributes];[91] however, since [the state] is attributable to principles, the species of each one of which is confined to its one individual, the [species] would be attributable to an individual thing.

3. Now we have already said that as a result of such attribution, we can provide the individuals with a description and a characterization limited to them. So if that [248] individual is one of those things that, in the intellect, is also individual, then the intellect has a way of arriving at that described thing, that is, the individual alone in its species, unique of its kind, like the sphere of the Sun, for example, or Jupiter. When its [species] is distributed among individuals, however, the intellect has no way to describe that thing until it has been pointed out.

4. To begin with what you have learned, which we will reiterate, we say this is similar to the fact that, since you know all the heavenly motions, you know each eclipse and each particular conjunction and opposition, but in a universal way. [That follows] because you say about a given eclipse that there will be an eclipse after the time of such and such a planet's northerly motion from such and such a place by such

---

[88] A quotation from the Qur'ān, 10:61 and 37:11.

[89] *The Salvation*, "Metaphysics," II.3, 212–13.

[90] That is, the things to which one can physically point.

[91] That is, it would be an individual state, or a state belonging to an individual.

and such a degree, when part of the Moon comes to be in opposition to such and such a planet, when such and such a period of time elapses between [this eclipse] and a similar eclipse previous or later to it, and that account is so similar for those two other eclipses[92] that not a single accidental aspect of those eclipses remains unknown to you. However, you know it as a universal due to the fact that this account can apply to many eclipses, each one of which is the same as that one, but arguably it is only that single eclipse itself that you know. This does not dispel the universality, however, if you recall what we said before.

5.   Despite all of this, however, you may not be able to judge that this eclipse exists or does not exist *at this instant*, unless you recognize the particulars of the motions by sensory observation and you know the period of time between this observed eclipse and that eclipse. This is not the same as your recognizing that among motions there is one particular motion matching the description of what you observed, and that there is such and such a difference between it and the other eclipse. You may be able to know that according to this kind of knowledge [i.e., universally], but not know it in relation to a given moment, and so you ask whether it exists [at that given moment]. Instead, you have to have obtained by sensory observation something physically identifiable [in space and time] in order for you to know the present occurrence of that eclipse.

6.   If there is something that prevents calling this a recognition of the particular from its universal, [we] will not fight it, since our present aim concerns something else, namely, indicating how you know and perceive particular things in a way that changes [249] the knower, and how you know and perceive in a way that does not change the knower. For when (1) you know eclipses as something understood as a universal, or as existing always, or (2) your knowledge is not of eclipses taken absolutely but of every eclipse that comes to be and then whether that eclipse exists or not, neither introduces any change in you. For in the two states[93] your knowledge is the same, namely, that there is an eclipse with certain characteristics after such and such an eclipse or after the Sun is in such and such a house of the zodiac and at such and such an alignment,[b] where such and such is after it, and after it is such and such. This act of intellecting on your part is consistent, before that eclipse, while it is occurring, and afterwards. If you introduce time into that, however, then at one given moment you know that this eclipse does not exist, and then at another given moment you know that it does exist, in which case your knowledge of the former [state, i.e., the eclipse's nonexistence] does not remain when the eclipse exists; rather, a different knowledge comes about after the change we just indicated. At the moment the [eclipse] passes, you cannot be what you were before the passing. This is because you are temporal and exist at a present moment.

92 That is, the one before and the one after it.

93 Not the two states of existing or not existing, but of knowing eclipses absolutely or in terms of *every* eclipse (with the additional conditions listed).

7. As for the First [i.e., the Necessary Existent], Who does not enter into any time and its status, it is completely inconceivable to apply to Him any status concerning this time or that time, as being in it or as a new temporal status or temporal knowledge being applied to it. Know that you came to perceive particular eclipses only because you fully comprehended its causes and everything concerning the heavens. When full comprehension takes place about all of the causes in things and their existence, there is a transference [of that full comprehension] from those to all of the effects.

8. We will explain this further through an investigation added to our earlier explanation, so that you will know how we know what is unseen. From these two explanations, you will know how the First knows everything from Itself on account of the fact that It is a principle of a thing that in turn is a principle of one or more things that have a state and motion that are such and such, and that what results from them is such, down to the very last difference after which one cannot differentiate further, and then according to the combination that follows that differentiation with the inevitability of corruption following generation. These things are the keys[c] to what is unseen.

XI.   THE CURE, "METAPHYSICS," IV.2[a]

On Potentiality, Actuality, Power, and Impotence; Establishing That Everything That Comes to Be Has Matter

1. [178] The possibility of the existence of the body that comes to be, such as fire's coming to be, is precisely that it comes to be from matter and form. So, in a certain way, there is a receptacle for the possibility of its existence, which is its matter, and then the part of it that comes to be primarily, namely the form, comes to be in the matter, and the body comes to be because of the combination, that is, of matter in one way and form in another way. For it is precisely through the existence of a bodily subject that the soul comes to be. In that case, the possibility of the soul's existence in that [subject] as something subsisting with [the subject] is because that matter is proper to it; for the possibility of its existence is only after it was not. [179] In other words, [the matter proper to it] is the possibility of its coming to be at the moment that there are certain bodies existing in a certain kind of mixture that are appropriate for use as an instrument of [the soul] and are that by which the soul's suitability to come to be from the first principles is distinguished from its unsuitability. So when the possibility of this mixture is in [those bodies], it is the possibility of the soul's existence.

2. When there comes out of any body an actuality that is neither accidental nor forced, then [the body] acts by means of a certain potentiality in it. In the case of [the actuality] through will or choice, that is obvious. When it is not by will and choice, the actuality comes either out of [the body] itself or out of either a corporeal or an incorporeal thing distinct from it. If it comes out of [the body] itself, where [the body] has in common with other bodies the very fact of its being a body, but it is different

from them in that the actuality comes out of it, then there is in it a causal factor (*maʿnā*) additional to its being a body that is the principle of the actuality coming out of it. That is called a potentiality. If that actuality comes out of another body, then this actuality comes out of [the former] body either by force or accidentally, but it was posited to come out of another body neither by force nor accidentally. If [the actuality comes out] of something separate [i.e., an incorporeal being], then the separate thing specifies this body as the intermediary because the body is a body, or because of a potentiality in [the body], or because of a potentiality in that separate thing. If it is due to the fact that it is a body, then it would be common to every body, but it is not. If it is because of a potentiality in [the body], then that potentiality is the principle of that actuality's coming out of it; and this holds whether [the actuality] proceeds from the separate thing along with the intermediacy of [the body], or because [the separate thing] is the primary principle [for the actuality].

3.   [180] If [the separate thing specifies this body as the intermediary] because of a potentiality in that separate thing, then what makes it necessary is either that potentiality itself or a specific act of willing. If the potentiality itself makes that necessary, then either the necessitation of that is from this very body on account of the things mentioned—then there is a vicious circle—or it is by way of will. Now, either that will conferred distinction on this body by a specific property by which it is distinguished from the rest of the bodies, or it distinguished this body from the others haphazardly and by chance. If it is haphazardly and by chance, then it will not always and for the most part continue according to this order; for chance things are not those that are always and for the most part, whereas natural things are always and for the most part. Thus, it is not by chance.

4.   So all that is left is that it is by some specific property through which [the body] is distinguished from the rest of the bodies, and that specific property is something willed from which that actuality comes. Next, that is something's willed because that specific property either necessitates that actuality, or it belongs to [the body] for the most part, or it neither necessitates nor belongs to it for the most part. If it necessitates it, then it is the principle of that. If it is for the most part, and that which is for the most part is the same as that which necessitates, but it has an obstacle—because as you learned in the "Physics,"[94] it is the specific property of that which is for the most part that it be directed toward whatever pertains to it by an inclination from its nature, and so if it is not so directed, it is because of an obstacle—then its being for the most part is also something that necessitates if there is no obstacle. But that which necessitates was conceded to be something without an obstacle. If that specific property neither necessitates nor belongs to it for the most part, then [the actuality's] coming from it or from something else is identical, and so its being a specific property of it is haphazard, but it was said not to be haphazard.

5.   [181] Similarly, if it said that it is more fitting to maintain that it accompanies that particular property, this means it is even more apt that it comes out of it. For

---

[94] The reference is to Ibn Sīnā's *Physics* I.13, which is not translated here.

either it is something necessitating it, or it is something facilitating its necessity. A facilitating thing is either an essential cause or an accidental cause, and when another essential cause is not different from it, then it will not be accidental, because that which is accidental follows one of the two ways previously mentioned [i.e., by force or haphazardly]. So all that is left is for that specific property itself to be something that necessitates, and the necessitating specific property that necessitates is called "potentiality." It is out of this potentiality that the bodily actualities come, even if it is with the assistance of a more remote principle.

6. Let us reiterate emphatically the explanation that every thing that comes to be has a material principle. We say by way of summary that whatever comes to be does so after it was not, and so it must have matter, because before being generated every generable needs to be a possible existent in itself. If it is an impossible existent in itself, it simply is not at all.

7. The possibility of its existence is not that the agent has the power to do it. Rather, the agent has no power over it if it is not something possible in itself. Do you not realize what we are saying? There is no power over the impossible; the power is over what has the possibility to be. For, if the possibility of something's being were simply the power to do it, it would be as though we were saying that power is only over what there is power over; as though we were saying that there is no power over the impossible, because there is no power over it.

8. It is not by our investigation into the thing itself that we learn whether it is or is not an object of power, but rather through our investigation into the nature of the power belonging to the one who has power over it. Thus, if our uncertainty has to do with whether x is or is not an object of power, [182] then we simply could not learn that, because if we were to learn that from the perspective of the thing's being impossible or possible—where the sense of "impossible" is that it is not an object of power, and the sense of "possible" is that it is an object of power—then we would have learned the unknown by means of the unknown. So it is plainly clear that the sense of something's being possible in itself is not the sense of its being an object of power, even if the two are identical in the subject, where it being an object of power is a necessary result of its being possible in itself. Its being possible in itself is through a consideration of it itself, whereas its being an object of power is through a consideration of its relation to what causes it to exist.

9. Now that this is resolved, we say that before any created thing comes to be, its existence is either possible in itself or impossible. The "impossible-to-exist" will not exist, whereas the "possible-to-exist" has been preceded by the possibility of its existence. The possibility of its existence is a causal factor that either does not exist or does exist. It would be absurd for the causal factor not to exist, as otherwise the possibility of [the possible existent's] existing would not precede [the possible existent]. Thus, it is a causal factor that exists. Every existing causal factor either subsists in a subject or does not subsist in a subject. Anything that subsists not in a subject has a proper existence that does not require some correlative thing; but it is precisely in relation to that of which it is the possibility of existence that it is the possibility of existence. So the possibility of existence is not a substance

that is not in a subject. Hence, it is a causal factor *in* a subject and an accident of a subject.

10. We ourselves call the possibility of existence the potentiality of existence, and we call what bears the potentiality of existence in which there is the potentiality of the existence of the thing, "subject," "prime matter," "matter," and the like, on account of many different considerations.[95] Thus, whatever comes into existence is preceded by matter.

11. Now we note that these differentiations we have enumerated [183] lead one to imagine that potentiality is before actuality and prior to it absolutely, not merely in time. This is something to which a majority of the ancients were inclined. Some of them made prime matter exist before form and [said] that afterward the agent, initially either of its own accord or because something motivated it, clothed [prime matter] with form, as [1] one of the poets supposed about what did not concern him and for the likes of which he lacked any method of investigation. [2] [Another] said that something, like Soul, all of a sudden busily applied itself to arranging and informing prime matter; for the arrangement was not in a proper state, nor was the proper state of the formation perfect, and so the august Creator ordered it and set it aright. [3] Some of them said that in eternity these things were moving by their natures in a chaotic manner, and then the most high Creator aided their nature and set them in order. [4] One of them said that the eternal is either darkness, or the abyss, or something infinite that was always at rest and then was moved, or it was the mixture, which Anaxagoras maintained. That was because they said that potentiality precedes actuality, just as is in seeds, semen, and everything produced by craft. So it is fitting for us to consider this and discuss it.

12. The issue concerning particular, generable, and corruptible things accords with what they said, for the potentiality in them is temporally before the actuality. With regard to the universal or everlasting things that do not corrupt, even if they are particulars, potentiality is not prior to them in any way. Moreover, apart from these conditions, potentiality is posterior in every respect. [That follows], because since potentiality does not subsist essentially, it has to subsist in a substance that needs to be actual. So if [the substance] happened not to be actual, there would be nothing prepared to receive anything; for whatever absolutely is not *cannot* receive anything. [184] Now, something might be actual and not need something in potentiality, such as the eternal things, since they are always actual. So from this perspective there is some actual reality preceding the reality of potentiality in itself. From yet another perspective, since potentiality needs to emerge into act by something actually existing at the moment the thing is in potentiality, that thing does not come to be at the exact same time as the actuality. For that also would require something else to bring it into actuality, leading back to something actually existing that does not come to be.

---

[95] See the translation of Ibn Sīnā's "Physics," I.2, par. 4, pp. 157–58.

13.   For the most part, the only thing that can emerge from potentiality into actuality is something generically like the actuality that exists before the actuality is actual, for example, what is hot heats and what is cold cools. Moreover, frequently, the potential, as something bearing potentiality, results in the thing that is actual, such that the actuality temporally preceding the potentiality is not simultaneous with it; for semen has its origin in the human and the seed has its origin in the tree, until from the former there is a person and from the latter there is a tree. Thus, with respect to these things it is no more fitting to posit the actuality as preceding the potentiality than to posit the potentiality as preceding the actuality.

14.   Furthermore, in conceptualizing and defining, actuality precedes potentiality, because you cannot define potentiality unless it has actuality, whereas actuality does not need to have potentiality for the purposes of defining and conceptualizing it. For you define and intellect the square without for a second thinking about the potentiality to receive ["squareness"], but you cannot define the potentiality to be a square unless you make reference to "square" verbally or in the intellect and make it part of its definition.

15.   Moreover, actuality is before potentiality in perfection and finality; for the potentiality is a deficiency, whereas actuality is a perfection. Also, the good in every thing accompanies only the actual, and where evil is, there is in a way a potentiality. When something is evil [185], it is either essentially evil and in every respect—but this is absurd; for if it is something existing, then, inasmuch as it is an existing thing, it is not evil, but is so only insofar as there is a privation of a perfection in it, for example, the ignorance in the ignorant person. Or something might be evil because that is required with respect to something else, for instance, the injustice of the tyrant; for the injustice is an evil only because in it there is a deficiency of the natural good, and a deficiency of what the injustice opposes, such as peace, wealth, or the like. So, as evil, it is something contaminated by a privation or something potential. If what is in potentiality had neither accompanied it nor resulted from it, the perfections that necessarily belong to things would be present, and so it would not be evil in any respect. So, it is made clear that what is actual is good, insofar as it is such, while what is potential is evil—or it includes the evil. Also, know that the potential for evil is a certain good of the actuality, and actually being good is a certain good of the potentiality for good, whereas viciousness is not a certain viciousness in potentiality to do evil but the habit to do evil.

16.   Let us return to our initial concern by saying that you have learned the priority of potentiality in an absolute sense. In the case of particular potentiality, it is prior to the actuality for which there is a potentiality, when an actuality may precede it, like its actuality as far as the potentiality is a part of it, and when it need not, but some other thing may accompany it through which the potentiality emerges into actuality. Otherwise no actuality whatsoever would exist, since potentiality alone is not sufficient for there to be an actuality; rather, it requires something to cause the potentiality to emerge into actuality. Thus, you have learned that actuality really is prior to potentiality, and that it is something prior in excellence and completeness.

XII. ON GOVERNANCE[a]

[Introduction]

1.   [27] Praise be to God Who directed His servants to the path of gratitude by pointing out to them the praise He is due, Who opened the doors to His magnificence by means of the gratitude for which He had prepared them, Who bestowed on them the intellect that He made a safeguard for their spiritual life and a buttress and bulwark for their worldly life, Who gave them the power to reason by means of language, which marks their separation from the savage beasts and mute domesticated animals. Much praise is due to God for the very fact that His excellent design and subtle assignation is so comprehensive that every kind of creature He made has its share of well-being, and every species can seek to fill its allotment of possessions and goods. Nor did He overlook beauty in His creation, whether large or small; rather, He bestowed on them all from the abundance of His blessings and the plethora of His rewards those favors and gifts that best suited their conditions, that made whole their deficiencies and strengthened their frailties. Then He singled out humans for His most special blessings, thereby making them superior to many of His creatures. He gave them the best disposition, the most perfect nature, the most balanced composition, the most comfortable manner of living, the path to their transformation that is most attributable to their intellects that readily aid them, to their convincing insights that give them their superiority, to the proper manners whose beauty adorns them, to the noble virtues with whose eminence they are embellished, in addition to the discernment that allows them to see the difference between what is good and evil, the distinction between temptation and correct conduct, and the disjunction[b] between maker [28] and made, leader and led, manager and managed, so much so that this would become a method for them to recognize the difference between Creator and created and a means to corroborate the Eternal Maker were it not for [their] obstinate opposition and arrogant contrariety.

2.   Then He favored them with the gift of His compassion by instituting a way for them to vie with one another for superiority in what they achieve through their intellects and judgments the way that He made them seek to surpass one another in their political, social, and religious ranks—since they share the same status and worth in terms of the corruption that draws them on to their deaths—on account of the rivalry and envy found among them that arises from the wrongs and injustices they commit against one another. Rational people already know that if everyone were a king, they would seek to destroy each other to the very last person, and, if everyone were a subject, they would just as surely all perish. If everyone were equally wealthy, none could work for another, nor could close friends aid one another. If everyone were equally poor, they would all die of harm and perish from misery. Now, since jealousy is part of human nature and outdoing one another is part of their temper and at the very core of their being, then difference of ability and disparity of circumstance is the very reason of their survival and cause of their satisfaction. The man of

wealth who pays no heed to achievements of the intellect, who is lacking in all culture, and who attained his lot in life with the least amount of effort, when he considers the state of the deprived scholar and the miseries attending the artful and shrewd, he supposes—no, he is certain—that the wealth he has come into is fair exchange for the intellect he lacks. When the destitute man of culture takes note of the ignorant rich man, he has no doubt that he is superior to him and that he is to be given precedence over the other. The man with a profession that allows him but bare subsistence does not envy the man of far-reaching power nor the man of long-lasting authority. All of that is indication of wisdom, palpable evidence of subtle design, and token of divine mercy and compassion.

3. The most deserving and worthy of people to contemplate the wisdom on which the organization of the world runs, [29] the precise manner in which its governance is effected and its design is reinforced, are the rulers, in whose hands God (exalted be His mention!) puts the bridles of His servants, under whose rule He places the order of the settled lands, to whom He entrusts the shepherding of the pasturages, and to whom He grants jurisdiction of the flock. [The next most worthy] are the governing peers, who are given the halters of the people and called upon to keep order in the cities and towns, then those to whom they grant rights of power, namely, the titled lords and the leaders of retinues and servants, and then those to whom these grant rights of power, namely, the landowners and those who oversee the people and their offspring. Each one of these is a shepherd of all within the fence of his field and the orbit of his daily herding, to which his command and prohibition are issued and that is under his protection.

4. However, those that are least important and least significant, those that are the most fragile and in the most straightened circumstances, and those that are least in number are just as much in need of everything that the most majestic king needs. They all need to be managed and organized correctly. They all need a great deal of planning and calculation and the least amount of neglect and negligence. Also, they all need to be rebuked, censured, and reprimanded, and then forgiven, reformed, and set aright.

5. On the other hand, someone might say the following. [The most majestic king] is more in need of warnings and alerts; he needs to seek out information and scrutinize it,[c] to conduct research and investigate,[d] to look for answers and discover them; or he needs to be more conscious of fear and dread, to avoid complacency and self-appeasement, to worry about bonds being severed and dams breached. If he were to say this, he will have spoken rightly, because the man who stands alone without peer and who is isolated without someone to help him is in greater need of good providence, and is more entitled to a greater precaution, than the one who can seek the aid of the wholly sufficient and the help of ministers and attendants, and because the destitute and penniless man is more in need of a means of living and upkeep than the comfortable rich man.

6. Perhaps someone would disapprove of our likening the circumstances of subjects to those of kings, or censure the parallel we have drawn between the two

conditions, or revile our equation of the two affairs. Let the one charged with investigating this know [30] that our discussion concerns how close people are to one another in their ethical and moral temperaments, in the needs of their souls, and the requirements they have for body and home, not in terms of their rank, status, and worth.

Family

7. Every man, whether ruler or ruled, needs food to live and keep himself going, and he needs to prepare a surplus of food for when his time of need recurs. Now, the way humans get their food is not the way of any other animal. Other animals set out in search of pasturage and water at the first stirring of hunger and the onset of thirst, and they abandon it when they are sated and quenched, neither taking interest in [finding] anything better, nor storing what they have gathered, nor even knowing that the need will return. Humans, however, need a place to store what they have procured and to preserve it for the time of need. This is why humans need to live in dwellings and lodgings. As soon as they take up the use of a dwelling and find a safe place for their supply, they need to protect their supply therein from anyone else who wants it and to prevent anyone else from taking it. Now, if a man were to stay by the supply to protect it and watch out for anyone who wants it, then he would deplete it before it could be increased. And when he acquires another supply, the need to protect it comes up again. That tiresome practice goes on to the point that his range of activity is just like that of the beast who goes out to his pasturage when the need takes him. At that point, he needs to appoint someone to protect his supply, and the only one suited to stand in his place in that is someone he can trust, and he can trust no one but the wife whom God (exalted be His mention!) made a reassurance for man. That is the reason for starting a family.

8. Since starting a family is shrouded in the mystery that God made reason for the production of offspring and the cause of human survival and progeny, children are produced and the numbers grow, and the need for food and the preparation of its surplus for times of need increases, at which point the man needs aides and supporters, trustees and servants. And suddenly he has become a leader and those under him his charges.

9. [31] The need for these things, then, is the same for the ruler and the ruled, the leader and the led, the servant and the served, because in his life every man needs the following things. He needs food to keep his spirit together and his body upright. He needs a dwelling in which to preserve his possessions and in which to seek shelter after ending his daily effort. He needs a wife to protect his dwelling and watch over his earnings. He needs a son to advance his efforts when he is detained, to stand in for him when he is aged, to establish his progeny, and to keep his memory alive after he is gone. He needs supporters and trustees to aid him and to carry his burden. When these are brought together, he is a herdsman and a shepherd and they a herd and a flock. Now the herdsman is required to furnish things of benefit to his herd, such as

pasturage and water during the day, stables and paddocks during the night. He is required to set up watchmen over the pastures, and to scatter his sheepdogs around the perimeters to protect the herd against predators, accidental injuries, theft, hunting parties, and raids. He is required to seek out warm winter quarters and cool summer quarters for his herd and constantly find fodder and fresh water for them. He is required to set aside times to milk them and to assist in their parturition. In addition to all of that, he is required to herd them toward safe places and away from dangerous areas by calling out to them, whistling at them, shouting and yelling at them. If that is sufficient to make them amenable and tractable, well and good; otherwise he must take his staff to them. Equally, the man who has wife, children, servants, and followers—in addition to being obliged to protect and care for them, and to assume the burden of providing for them and managing their daily sustenance—is also required to govern them well and to keep them in order by cajoling and intimidating, promising and threatening, by drawing them close and pushing them away, by allowing and forbidding, until their channel to him runs straight and true.

10.   These are summary statements concerning why governance is necessary and why there is the need for it. We will follow them with explanatory examples in discrete chapters after an initial chapter on man's governance of his soul; for that will be both best for the sequence and of most benefit [to the reader], God willing.

Man's Governance of His Soul

11.   [32] Of all the varieties of governance, man would do best to begin with the governance of his soul since his soul is the closest thing to him, the most noble of them, and the one most worthy of his attention, and because once he governs his soul well, he will not falter in what comes at the next level, namely, governance of the city. One of the first things that anyone aiming to govern his soul must know is that he has an intellect, that is, the leader, and a soul—prone to evil, imperfect in many ways, and capable of evil deeds by nature and at the core of its being—that is, the led. He must also know that anyone who aims to reform something corrupt has to identify thoroughly the entirety of the corruption if he is not to leave any part of it behind. Then he can start to reform it. Otherwise, whatever he manages to reform will be neither invulnerable nor trustworthy. Equally, anyone aiming to govern and train his soul and reform its corrupt aspect cannot begin that task until he knows every evil aspect of his soul in a comprehensive manner; if he overlooks even one of those evil aspects and thinks that he has reformed it as a whole, he will be like someone whose wound has healed on the surface, but the inside is completely infected. In just the same way that when an infection has grown stronger out of indifference and long neglect, it will crack the scab and push through the skin until it appears in full view, so too as long as the one lurking defect of the soul was overlooked: until its external aspects became visible to him, its hidden aspect appeared to be the most secure thing the man had. Since man's knowledge of his soul is untrustworthy—because it is in his nature to be foolish about his defects, and because he grants his soul great latitude

when assessing it, and because his intellect is not safe from the admixture of passions that happens to it when he investigates the states of his soul—he cannot manage to inquire into its states and survey its good and bad aspects without the help of a caring sensible brother to act as his mirror and show him his good and evil states as they are.

12.   Now those most entitled to and most in need of this are leaders; for whenever these step outside the rule of premeditated action and the dominion of dissimulation they neglect to watch out for miscalculations and chase [33] errors with regrets, and so become accustomed to much laxity and little propriety (except for a few of them whose intellects are sharp, whose powers of discernment are unsurpassed, and whose insights extend to keeping check on their souls, and so their comportment is good and their behavior upright). [With the majority], however, what has added to their monumental misfortune—by keeping their faults secret from them—is that they make anyone dread to point out their shortcomings face-to-face and fear to expose the backbiting, the insulting, the slandering, the baiting, and the nasty insinuations and innuendos that happen behind their backs. So when they are cut off from knowing that, they suppose that vices passed them by and faults overlooked them, not even to take a shortcut through their plots of land or alight for so much as a night in their courtyards.

13.   This is not the case with those below them, the herded and the led. If one of them were to try to hide his vices once a close friend surprises him with them and demands he make amends with him for the most evil of them, he would not be able to do it; for necessarily he mingles with people and is on close terms with them. Now such intermingling produces disputation and opposition, and that is one of the causes of mutual enmity. Mutual enmity leads to charges of defects and slanderous accusations on both sides, at which point, each side is scarcely satisfied to state the true facts about the shortcomings of the other, but rather denounces him as utterly wrong and counterfeits lies against him. People such as these are even spared the trouble of pumping their [opponents'] drinking buddies for information and sending their spies to gather knowledge on the vices of others from their enemies; for it has already been conveyed to them by another channel. A peaceful citizen, on the other hand, does not attack people or inveigle them or defame them, for he always has someone—a close relation, a neighbor, a partner, a drinking buddy, or someone with whom he shares meals—to give him a stern reminder about his vice and counsel him about his soul.

14.   The likelihood of corruption among rulers and leaders is also increased by the deal that the chronic wrongdoers and habitual evildoers offer them. Despite the fact that these people break their oaths of friendship and behave fraudulently and dishonestly by neglecting to tell their friends the truth about themselves and caution them about [34] their faults, if they were only to avoid blinding them with false praise, seducing them with fake acclamation, and deluding them by making their blunders seem like good decisions, they would be the less ignoble, though they do not thereby get out of being the worst friends and meanest companions. One of them might say

the following when trying out different ways to excuse himself and waxing poetic in lessening his crime: "We gave up advising them on their souls and keeping them away from their [evil] states simply out of dread lest we incense them, as a precaution against their proud defiance, and in fear that they would find what we advised too much of a burden; for advice can have a burn to it like a fire and a bite to it like a spear. We feared that if we tried that with them, our sole recompense would be that they would distrust us, break off ties with us, and turn away from us and our friendship. Keeping them along with their deficiencies is better for us and for them than if we set them on fire, in which case neither they would be left for us nor us for them." This is the response when the companion is considered a steadfast friend. When he is a fickle idiot, he might say: "We're not immune from being cast down from our station and being cut out of the mix by the punch of his rage and the stab of his wrath." The following could be said to him. When you build your companionship on the basis of loyalty and honor, you are not enjoined to heed anything but those two in anything you do or don't do. When you are guided by those two things and turn yourself to their light, you do not stray from that companionship. Now it has already been decided for you that your companion is one of two types of men: either a steadfast, resolute friend, or a fickle idiot. As for the steadfast friend, he may be aghast and bewildered, steamed up and doubled over [in rage] when he first takes in your advice, but how mightily will the virtue of it conquer him! Once he considers it carefully, thinks about it and appraises it, he will recognize how good and beneficial are your intentions, and reconcile with you in the best possible manner. As for the fickle idiot, you are never at any time safe from his erratic behavior, whether you take his side or oppose him, and you have no say in keeping him company as a result of this character trait of his, so you may as well guide him.

15.   If there is a way to direct a reasonable man out of his rash behavior, know that it is not for you to ride after him aimlessly and stumble around in the dark after him. You should instead touch the reasonable man with what you are pointing out to him as though you were touching a thorn piercing your side or a wound draining blood from your body, with the lightest touch, the kindest word, and the softest voice, in the most private surroundings and the most confidential circumstances, in which allusion will be more effective than a direct statement, and the use of examples will be better than straightforward explanation. [35] If you see your companion's interest peaked by your very first words and he appears to be well-disposed to them and heeding them, then elaborate without being excessive, profuse, or tedious, and without adding to your one observation; and keep it from festering in his heart and echoing repeatedly in his soul so that he will know that the consequences go no further. If you see that your companion is indifferent to what you say at first, then break it off and change the point of what you said to something other than what you intended, and postpone it to a time when he is lighthearted and free of concerns.

16.   Anyone who means to become aware of his strong points and weak points should make a study of the ethical behaviors of people, take count of their character traits and temperaments, and observe their strong points and weak points, and then

compare them to his own, at which point he will learn that he is like them and they like him; for people are all alike, in fact they are the same as the teeth on a comb. When he observes an admirable strong point, he should know that something similar is in him, whether it be discernible or buried deep. If it is discernible, let him take control of it and keep it active lest it weaken and fade away. If it is buried deep, he should rouse it and bring it to life and constantly summon it up, for it will respond to the least amount of effort and in the least amount of time. When he observes a weak point, an evil habit, a malicious trait, he should know that the proclivity for it is embedded in him, whether it be patent or latent. If it is patent, then let him rein it in, overpower it, and kill it by infrequent use and intense neglect. If it is latent, then let him be on guard lest it gain ascendancy.

17.　It behooves a person to set his soul in order by governing it with reward and punishment. [When] it obeys well and submits easily to its obligation to take on virtues and stay away from vices, and displays a noble character trait or an honorable virtue, he [should] reward it with repeated praise, ensure its happiness, and allow it one of the things it takes pleasure in. When it disobeys and refuses to submit and becomes unruly, and then refuses to be reined in and prefers vices to virtues and displays a malicious character trait or engages in a reprehensible activity, he [should] punish it with repeated criticism, rebuke it, and bring down on it an intense sense of remorse and deny it any pleasure until it yields to him.

Man's Governance of His Comings and Goings

18.　[36] People's need for food motivates each one of them to exert effort to acquire it in the manner that God inspired him to pursue and which occasions his livelihood by way of a variety of pursuits and paths to a variety of profits. Now, since the category of livelihood contains two types of people—one who enjoys an easy livelihood either provided to him by an inheritance or that he collects, and another who has to earn it—God inspired the latter type to secure his daily bread through business and the professions. The professions are more reliable and longer lasting than business because the latter proceeds by means of money, and money is quick to vanish, ready to be damaged, and full of disasters. The honorable professions are of three types. One type comes out of the domain of the intellect, that is, sound judgment, correct deliberation, and good organization; it is the profession of ministers, managers, governing lords, and kings. Another type comes out of the domain of culture, that is, literary and rhetorical skills, knowledge of the stars, and knowledge of medicine; it is the profession of the cultured men. Another type comes out of the domain of strength and bravery; it is the profession of horsemanship and archery. May he who pursues these professions successfully master their precise requirements and advance in them until he is described eloquently as one of their practitioners, not repudiated or cast aside!

19.　He should know that there is nothing that better adorns or suits a man than a comfortable livelihood. Let him pursue his daily sustenance by means of a profession in the most upright, courteous, and forgiving manner, the one most removed from greed and envy, the one most pure of foul craving and rotten gluttony. Let him also know that every mark of distinction bought by combat and conflict, contention and strife, and every gain obtained by sin and dishonor, with malicious gossip and evil rumor, with a weakening sense of shame and at the expense of esteem, with a sullied honor and a stained reputation, will both afford but a paltry return though its bulk be capacious, a pittance though its mass be commodious, an unhealthy collation though ostensibly wholesome, and an indigestible repast though one apparently salubrious. [Know also] that honesty unstained by ulterior motive and forgiveness unmuddied by conscious effort, though both minuscule and light, [37] taste far better, are swallowed more readily, are grown to greater benefit, and produce a more virtuous yield.

20. The just way for man to behave with what he has acquired is to spend some of it on taxes, alms, and those in need of a favor, and to hold back some of it as a savings against the vicissitudes of time and the exigencies of the future. He should surrender the costs of taxes and alms happily, with a pure intention, an open heart, and a sense of surety that they are insurance for a day of want, that the largest portion of them go to the indigent who veils his poverty from people and from whose circumstances the veil of God is not rent, and that the remainder goes to the one whom poverty has overtaken but whose impoverishment is obvious and his misery plain to see. [He should] do that for the sake of God, Lord of splendor and munificence, expecting neither thanks nor recompense.

21. There are a number of conditions attached to doing a favor. One is that it be done quickly, for that is of more lasting benefit for him. The second is that it be done in secret, for that reveals more about him. The third is to belittle it, for that makes him bigger. The fourth is to follow through with it and keep it going, for that expunges memory of its origin and effaces its track. The fifth is choosing its recipient, for when the good deed is not presented to someone happy to assume its burden, to acknowledge it gratefully, to pass the goodness of it on to another, and to repay it with affection and friendship, it is like planting seedlings in a salt marsh that will neither sustain the seeds nor allow the crop to sprout.

22. The proper way to cover expenses and keep them in order lies between extravagance and stinginess, and fluctuates between risking loss and estimating cost, except that in the face of this there is something that requires one to be good at careful evaluation, namely, that whenever a person has met all the demands of his budget and is aware of the conditions required for him to economize, he does not thereby give himself over to the wink and the nudge, that is, judging without discrimination, to include devious [38] misguidance in the same category as the charming story, or thinking corrosive hatred contains any real sense of honor, or that insidious envy contains any magnificent glory and lofty nobility. In light of this, the reasonable person should put part of his expenses toward the reasonings of the common run of people and employ leeway and latitude in situations in which he fears dubious excess and the disgrace of losing money. Those who praise extravagance are more common

than those who praise economy and hold frugality in high esteem, just as the one who praises economy and holds frugality in high esteem is more elite, more perfect in intellect, and more decisive in judgment.

23. As for his savings, the reasonable man should keep them out of his mind whenever he is able; for whenever misfortune surprises him with a need, but he has not prepared for a future contingency, and he is now compelled to seek support from the bundle of provisions he carries, [the misfortune] will sever [his bundle] tie by tie until he is left destitute. God alone bestows sufficiency and is the best defender!

Man's Governance of His Wife

24. The virtuous woman is the partner to a man's property, the guardian of his possessions, and his deputy in his absence.[e] The best woman is intelligent and devout, modest and prudent, affectionate and fertile, reserved in speech and compliant, sincere in her responses, trustworthy when absent, self-possessed in company, dignified in her bearing, noble in her stature, light-hearted and devoted[f] when serving her husband, well-organized, capable of stretching what little her husband has by her economy, dispelling his grief by the beauty of her proportions, diverting him from his cares by the kindness of her compliments.

25. A man's decisive governance of his wife is comprised of the mean of three things: [her] absolute deference, [his] complete esteem, and her single-minded attention to her duties.

26. [39] As for deference, when she does not defer to her husband, he becomes contemptible to her, and when he becomes contemptible to her, she stops listening to his command and paying heed to his prohibition. No sooner is she content with that than she next coerces him to obey her. She becomes the one who commands and forbids, and he becomes the one who obeys; she turns into the manager, and he the one managed. This is reversed and topsy-turvy. Woe to the man, then, for the disgrace and dishonor and the wreck and ruin that is wrought against him by her revolution and rebellion, that is perpetrated against him by her faulty judgment and mismanagement, and into which he is dragged by her misguidance and the wild horse of her concupiscence! Deference stands at the forefront of man's governance of his wife and forms its support. It is the thing by which every fissure is sealed, the completion of which ends every imperfection. It is what serves as deputy for every absent or temporarily indisposed [husband]. Nothing else can substitute for it, and man's relationship with his wife is incomplete without it. The deference of a woman for her husband is no different from man's respect for his soul, the preservation of his piety and honor, and the confirmation of his promises and threats.

27. The benefit of a man's esteem for his wife lies in part in the fact that when the noblewoman asks for demonstration of her husband's esteem, then the virtue of its constant presence around her, the protections it affords her, and the worry she would experience at its loss, prompts her to [consider] many favorable [aspects of the relationship] that her husband could not have shown her except under severe compul-

sion and heavy burden—albeit the more august and exalted her situation, the more that itself is indicative of her husband's nobility, honor, dignity, and august status. A man's esteem for his wife depends on three things: that she keep her outward appearance beautiful, that she strictly keep herself secluded, and that she avoid making her husband jealous.

28. A wife's single-minded attention to her duties means that she occupies herself with governing her children, managing her servants, and attending to the chores of her chamber; for when she has no duties or concerns, she will be interested only in attracting men with her charms and preening herself, and will think only about demanding more [from her husband], and that, in turn, will lead her to belittle his esteem for her, to consider the increased time he spends with her to be insufficient, and what he gives her to be paltry as a whole.

Man's Governance of His Son

29. [40] Parents are obliged to give their son an apt name and to choose a wet nurse for him who is neither foolish nor uncouth nor sickly—for milk transmits, as they say. Once the child is weaned, his education and moral training begins, before any ignoble ethical traits and reprehensible characteristics can take hold of him. For evil traits pounce on the child immediately, and wicked characteristics swarm over him; any that can will overwhelm him, and then he will be unable either to separate himself from them or to keep away from them. For the sake of the child, then, [the father] should direct him away from iniquitous inclinations and deter him from shameful ways of behaving by intimidating and cajoling him, by giving him solace and the cold shoulder, by shunning him and drawing him near, by praising him one time and scolding him another, [all] in sufficient measure. If [the father] has to have recourse to the hand, he must not flinch. The first slap should hurt a little (as philosophers have pointed out before) [and should come] after threatening him seriously and allowing the mediation of others to prepare him; for when the first slap hurts, the child will assume the worst about what comes next, and his fear will thereby increase, whereas when the first slap is light and does not cause pain, the child will assume the best about the rest and therefore pay it no heed.

30. When the child's joints are strong and his speech is smooth and he is ready to learn and able to pay attention, he will start to learn the Qur'ān and form the letters of the alphabet and learn the basic facts of religion. The child should recite [his lessons] in the *rajaz* meter and later in the form of odes; for the *rajaz* is more easily recited and more able to be memorized because it has shorter verses and a simpler meter. With poetry, the child should begin with what is said concerning the excellence of learning, in praise of knowledge and condemnation of ignorance and censure of foolishness, as well as what encourages him to honor his parents, to do what is approved, to be generous to those in need, and other such noble virtues.

31. The person hired to educate the child should be pious, knowledgeable about training the manners of children, skilled in the ways of instructing them, sober and

composed, utterly removed from silliness and foolishness, rarely casual [41] and infor-
mal in the presence of children, but without being inflexible or rigid. [He should] be
pleasant, loyal, well groomed, and respectable. [He should] have served the nobility
and learned the kingly manners in which they take pride as well as the vulgar traits
that they condemn, and [he should] know the ways in which one comports oneself
in courtly gatherings, at the table, in learned exchanges, and at social functions.

32.   In the classroom, the child should keep the company of the aristocrats'
well-bred and well-behaved children; for the child will learn from them, take heed of
them, and become friendly with them. Isolating one child with a teacher is the surest
way to exasperate both. When a teacher can alternate his attention between one child
and another, that is the best way to alleviate boredom, maintain excitement, and keep
the child devoted to learning and instruction; for he can pit the children against one
another one time, praise them another, and chide them for falling short of their goal
still another. Then the children converse with one another, and such conversation
makes figuring something out enjoyable and produces solutions for what is difficult
to understand; for the only thing each of them talks about is the most pleasing thing
he saw or the most remarkable thing he heard, so the amazing aspect of what he says
is reason for astonishment, and the astonishment is reason for remembering it and
incentive to talk about it. Then they become friends and exchange visits with one
another and extend their hospitality to one another and respect each other's rights,
all of which forms the basis for competition and contest, rivalry and imitation, and
in that lies the rectification of their moral temperaments, the stimulation of their
ambitions, and the exercise of their customary habits.

33.   When the young man has completed his primary education and mastered
the principles of language, he then begins to consider what his discipline of learning
is meant to be and turns toward its path. If it is meant to be the secretarial profession,
he complements his study of language with the study of epistolography, speech
writing, the methods of communicating and talking with people, etc.; arithmetic is
subtracted, keeping registers is added, and he concerns himself with his penmanship.
If another [profession] is intended for him, then he is prepared for it—with the provi-
sion that the teacher knows that not just any profession that the young man desires
will be possible or suitable for him, but only the one to which his nature conforms
and accords, and that if it were the case that the literary arts and professions responded
and submitted to want and desire and not to affinity and suitability, then no one
would be ignorant of any art or lacking in any profession, and then everyone would
choose the noblest art and the top-ranking profession. Proof of what we say is to be
found in the ease with which some people take to learning and the difficulty others
experience. That is why we see one person suited to rhetoric, another to grammar,
another to poetry, [42] another to oratory, and still another to genealogy, and this
one is called master of the pen and master of the poem. When you go outside this
rank of the professions, you find that one person chooses arithmetic, another geometry, and another medicine. You find this to be the case with the other ranks when you
examine them one after another until you make the rounds of them all. These types

of choice, suitability, and concord have obscure reasons and unknown causes too subtle for man's understanding and too refined to be explained by syllogism or investigated scientifically. God alone (exalted be His mention!) knows them!

34.   It may also be the case that the character of a man is incompatible with all of the arts and professions, and so he has not formed an attachment to any of them. Proof of that lies in the fact that certain men of reason want to provide their sons with a cultured education, so they work hard to achieve that and spend their money to that end, but they do not get what they sought. Therefore, when the young man wants to choose a profession, his instructor should first examine the young man's character, sound out his disposition, and test his acumen, and then select certain professions for him on that basis. When he chooses one of those professions for him, he takes measure of the young man's partiality and desire for it, and seeks to determine whether [the profession] will conform to any sense of familiarity on the young man's part or not, and whether his skills and abilities will be a help or a disappointment to him in that [profession]. Only then does he make his final decision; for that [procedure] is the most decisive way to manage and the one least likely to waste the young man's life with something unsuitable to him.

35.   Once the young man has developed a certain mastery of his profession, the plan for him involves his seeking a way to earn money and taking on the responsibility of providing for his livelihood from it, for two benefits will accrue to him in that. One is that when he tastes how sweet it is to make a living by his profession and discovers the great wealth and advantage to be had in his profession, he will not rest in his attempt to master it and reach its summit. The second is that before he arrives on safe ground, he will have accustomed himself to the struggle to earn a daily living; for rarely do we see any of the sons of the well-to-do ever free of their dependency on their fathers' money and the amount for which it has prepared them. So as long as he is dependent upon that, he is prevented from seeking out his own daily living and adorning himself with the robes of good breeding. Once the young man makes a living by his profession, the plan for him is that he marries and sets up his own home.

Man's Governance of His Servants

36.   [43] The way that man governs his servants and aides is the way the body governs its limbs. Just as one group has said, "A man's chamberlain is his face, his secretary his pen, and his messenger his tongue," so too do we say that a man's servants are his arms and legs. [This is so] because having them in place of you has saved you the trouble of acting with your own hand, sending them in your stead has saved you the trouble of walking, and having them look out for you has saved your eye the trouble of watching. The relief servants provide you is great, and the help of those who aid you is considerable. Were it not for them, the great doorway to comfort would be barred to you, the broad avenue of ease would be blocked off to you, and you would constantly have to get up and sit down, and go in and go out. That entails a great wear on the body, which is considered one of the marks of a feckless man, one

of the signs of a fickle man, and one of the features of the vulgar and contemptible man. It implies that a man has thrown away his dignity, lost his seriousness and sedateness, given up his sense of pride, and repudiated his sense of steady purpose and conduct—but it is the very presence of these characteristics that distinguishes the master from the servant, the leader from the led.

37.   You should offer praise to God (mighty and high is He!) for those whom He made to serve you and spare you. You should protect them not drive them away, take notice of them not overlook them, treat them kindly not oppress them; for the worst toil and trouble, weariness and exhaustion that can befall man surely befall them, and all the needs and demands of men's bodies that drive them to act surely drive them.

38.   One proceeds to select a servant only after getting to know him and asking him questions, and only after measuring his character and testing his skills. If you are unable to do this, you should form an estimation of him, an appraisal of his physical qualities, an intuition about him, and a general sense of his abilities. You should avoid unusual mannerisms and disorderly appearances; for a person's exterior conforms to his interior. A proverb of the Persians has it that "the best thing an ugly person has is his face." You should steer clear of anyone who has any handicaps, like someone with only one eye or a limp or leprosy. [44] You should not put your trust in any of them that are overly crafty or cunning, for such will be free neither of deception nor artifice. You should give preference to the one who is ingenuous and modest over the one who is too clever and quick-witted.

39.   Once you have selected a servant, consider what task is most suitable for him, what activity he will undertake, and what job he appears to do best. Entrust him with it and let him see if it suffices him. Never move your servant from one job to another, and never change him from one activity to another, for that is the surest means and strongest inducement to his ruination. There is nothing more like this than someone's making a stallion plow a field or a cow run a race. Every man has a certain set of skills and a particular type of activity that his disposition has granted him and his nature has afforded him; this becomes almost a second nature to him that no artifice could remove, or an innate characteristic that no method could detach. Whenever someone moves his servant from whatever task he has mastered, that he feels confident about, that he wears like a second skin or a set of clothes, to which he is habituated and accustomed and chooses for him, on the basis of his own judgment and what he himself wants, another task that is contrary to his nature and opposes his very being, he spoils the regularity of his service and forces the servant to start over in the way he works, and the servant is again like an untrained colt. So, the servant affords him nothing in the new task except to forget the particulars of the old task, and at whatever point he might return the servant to the old task, he will find him now to be worse at that than the new one.

40.   One should not chastise his servant. When he wants to chastise him, he should rather simply let him go; for rebuking one's servant is a sign of irritation, impatience, and intemperance, and because, once one dismisses his servant, he needs

another to take his place, and another servant will be either the same as the first or close enough, and once he gets into this habit, he is almost guaranteed to remain servantless. It would instead be better for him that the hearts of his servants are so settled that not a single one of them would find a way to pack his bags and leave his home and protection. For that is a more perfect form of honor and more indicative of dignity and nobility. Furthermore, the servant will not back him, nor advise him, nor sympathize with him, nor pay attention to him, nor look out for him, nor stand up for him, nor defend him unless he feels so certain and true that he has [45] an equal share in his master's prosperity and his two allotments of inherited property and what fortune brings him that he feels safe from being dismissed and is not on guard against being discharged. When the servant supposes that the foundations of his safety are not sturdy, that the ties of his security are not firmly bound, and that his position will be unfit for him when the slip fits him and his precision slips away from him, then he will behave like a passerby to his master, neither taking heed of what would concern him nor taking an interest in what would befall him, his only concern having been a stash of provisions for the day that his master treats him harshly and any backer to whom he could return when his master takes offense and turns his back on him. Let there be for the master with his servants, instead of dismissal and discharge, rather than discarding and throwing away, room for improvement and correction. Any servant who seeks to have his crookedness straightened out through correction and his lopsided burden balanced by instruction, the master should bolster with a helping hand and broaden his way at the slip with forgiveness. But any servant who commits the offense again after repentance and breaks the pact after contrition, let him taste a bit of punishment and touch him with a little force, but never let him give up all hope of good conduct as long as the knot of his life has not unraveled and he shows his persistence. As for the servant who defies his master with an act of disobedience so bald there is no meeting worse than it, or perpetrates a crime so perfidious there is no abiding it and no stipulation in the governance to overlook it, the decision belongs to the master to get rid of him instantly, lest he corrupt the other servants.

[Conclusion]

41.   So conclude the chapters in which we gave examples of what a man is bound to do in governing himself and all within his home. We discussed but a little of potentially much and provided summary statements without commentary. If we had expounded every chapter with the appropriate anecdotes and examples of poetry, the book would have been better and more complete, but also bigger and longer. So we chose to lighten the burden of the reader and ease the way of the researcher. Many a little thing yields more than a big one, and many a small thing is more complete than a large one. God alone bestows success and prosperity!

AL-GHAZĀLĪ

When we read al-Ghazālī's *Incoherence of the Philosophers* today, we read him as a philosopher, but he certainly did not think of himself in such terms; rather, he considered himself a critic of philosophy (albeit one well-versed in philosophy) and probably would have preferred being described as a theologian, mystic, and jurist. Abū Ḥāmid Muḥammad ibn Muḥammad al-Ghazālī was born in 1058 in the northeastern Persian town of Ṭūs in modern-day Khurasan. He received a traditional Islamic education that emphasized Islamic law in his hometown of Ṭūs and then Jurjān. He subsequently moved to Nīshāpūr, also in northeastern Iran, where he studied *kalām*, or Islamic speculative theology, with the most distinguished theologian of his day, the Ashʿarite Imām al-Ḥaramayn, Abū l-Maʿālī l-Juwaynī (1028–1085). In 1091, Niẓām al-Mulk, the vizier for the Seljuk Turkish Sultan Malikshāh, appointed al-Ghazālī to teach Shāfiʿite law at perhaps the most prestigious teaching institution of the time, the Niẓāmīya college at Baghdad, where al-Ghazālī remained for four years. It was during this period in Baghdad that he undertook his intensive study of philosophy and wrote his most important "philosophical" work, *The Incoherence of the Philosophers*, as well as his most important theological work, *Moderation in Belief*. At around 1095 al-Ghazālī underwent a spiritual crisis, claiming in his autobiography that he had been motivated by worldly success and he now sought a deeper spirituality, which he found in following the path of Sufi mysticism. He spent eleven years away from his teaching, during which time he wrote his magnum opus, *The Revivification of the Religious Sciences*, which attempts to integrate Sufism into a framework of traditional Muslim belief. In 1106 al-Ghazālī was once again persuaded to take up teaching law, now at the Niẓāmīya college in Nīshāpūr. He resigned the post a little over two years later and died in his hometown of Ṭūs in 1111.

Al-Ghazālī's attitude towards philosophy might best be described as a love-hate relationship. On the one hand, he was openly hostile to those philosophical theses that in his mind contradicted the clear teachings of Islam, opposing them not only as heresy but also as bad philosophy. In this respect, al-Ghazālī happily drew on the arguments of earlier philosophers themselves, particularly the Greek-Christian Neoplatonist John Philoponus, in his critique of the philosophers. On the other hand, al-Ghazālī was clearly aware of the value of philosophical reasoning and certain philosophical concepts for the articulation and defense of Islamic theology. In this respect, he frequently recast philosophical ideas of Ibn Sīnā and other philosophers into Qurʾānic language and then employed them in his own philosophical theology. Similarly, his *The Standard of Knowledge* is something of a handbook of Aristotelian and Avicennan logic, which was intended to provide the Muslim jurists and theologians with the basics of discursive and philosophical reasoning.

I. *CONCERNING THAT ON WHICH TRUE DEMONSTRATION IS BASED*[a]

1. [243] Know that true demonstration is what provides necessary, perpetual, and eternal certainty that cannot change, such as your knowing that the world temporally came to be and has a Maker. The examples of that involve what can never vary, since it is impossible that some time should present itself to us when we would judge that the world is eternal or [244] deny the Maker.

2. The changing things about which there is no perpetual certainty are all of particulars that are in the earthly world. Of [changing things] the ones that most closely approximate permanence are mountains. Now when I say:

[major premise]:	every mountain whose elevation is x is F;
[minor premise]:	the elevation of this mountain is x;
(and then I conclude):	this [mountain] whose elevation [is x] is F

no eternal knowledge results. [That] is because the certainty with respect to the minor premise is not perpetual, since a change of the mountain's elevation is conceivable. The same is the case for the depths of the seas and the locations of islands; for these are things that do not remain. So how do you know that Zayd is in the house and similar cases that are dependent on accidental human states? [Accidental human states] are so unlike "human is an animal," "animal is a body," and "the human is not in two places at one and the same time" as well as other examples of that sort (for these are perpetually and eternally known with certainty to which change cannot apply to them), [that it reaches] the point that some of the theologians said that knowledge is a kind of ignorance. They intended this kind of knowledge [i.e., knowledge of accidental human states and changing things] by [this claim]: for when you know through repeated observations, for instance, that Zayd is in the house, then if it were supposed that this belief continues on in your soul but Zayd has left, then this belief itself would have become ignorance. This kind [of knowledge, i.e., concerning changing things], however, is inconceivable with respect to perpetual certainty.

3. So if it is asked, "Is [this kind of knowledge] understood to provide demonstration for what occurs for the most part or by chance?" we say that [when] things that happen for the most part pertain to the major terms, [then] they undoubtedly have causes that are for the most part. So when those causes are made middle terms, then they produce knowledge and an overwhelming probability. By the knowledge's being generally for the most part, when we [for example] recognize as a result of God's customary course (exalted be He!) that the beard grows only owing to the skin's becoming firm around the jaw and the root's becoming hardy, then, if we recognize with one's advancing in years that the skin [245] is becoming firm around the jaw and the root is becoming hardy, then we take the beard's growth as normal, that is, we judge that the growth is generally the case and that that area of the growth is more likely than another area. This is a certainty. For what occurs is generally the case and so is undoubtedly due to being selectively determined; however, [it is] by means of a hidden condition that is not disclosed, but the failure of that condition to obtain is

rare. Thus, we judge as certain that whoever marries a young woman and has inter-course with her will in general have a child; however, the existence of the child in the particular case is an object of probability, whereas generally [a child's] coming to exist is absolute.

4.   Thus, concerning points of legal opinion, we judge that the knowledge is absolutely obligatory [even] when there is apparent opinion [among the jurists]. So the practice is an object of opinion and the judgment exists as an object of opinion; however, the existence of the practice is absolute, since there is a knowledge concerning the truth of the obligation of the practice that is through a decisive proof where the divine law, bordering on certainty, stands in for the certainty. So the judgment's being an object of opinion would not have precluded the absoluteness of what we have determined.

5.   As for chance events, such as a person's discovering a treasure during his walk, neither probability nor knowledge can occur through them, since if they could occa-sion probability, then [the chance event] would become something that is generally for the most part and would go beyond its merely being a chance event.[1] Indeed, it is only possible to demonstrate that it is a chance event, but the logicians have agreed to reserve the term "demonstration" for what produces universal, perpetual, and neces-sary certainty. If you do not agree with them on this technical use, then you can call the whole of true knowledge demonstrative, when the premises are made conditions that [already] have come to pass. If you agree with them on this, then the demonstra-tive sciences are the knowledge of God and His attributes and all of the eternal things that do not change, such as "two is greater than one," for this will always be and has always been true.

6.   Knowledge of the configuration of the heavens and planets, their distances, magnitudes, and the manner of their progression is demonstrative in the opinion of whoever thinks that they are eternally unchanging. They are not demonstrative in the opinion of those who possess the truth who see that the heavens are like earthly things in that change can extend to them.

7.   [246] It is well known that what varies from place to place and region to region, such as the sciences of linguistics and governance (since they differ with [different] ages and creeds), as well as the extension of the lawful and unlawful to legal and religious practices, are not among the demonstrative sciences in this technical sense.

8.   The philosophers maintain that the only sense to be made of the blessedness of the afterlife is that the soul reaches its perfection that it can have and that its per-fection is in knowledge not physical pleasures. Since the soul will remain always, [the philosopher maintains that] its salvation and blessedness is in eternal true knowledge, such as knowing God and His attributes, His angels, the order of existing things, and the chain of causes and effects. If knowledge that is not perpetually certain is sought,

---

[1] Compare Aristotle's detailed discussion of chance and spontaneity in *Physics* II 4–6.

it is not sought for its own sake, but rather for the sake of obtaining something else by means of it. This is a deceit [on the part of the philosophers] that can be uncovered only by a lengthy examination, whose thorough investigation this book cannot undertake; rather, the particular sciences [must undertake] an explanation of this deceit.

II. THE INCOHERENCE OF THE PHILOSOPHERS, "THE FIRST DISCUSSION," ON REFUTING THEIR CLAIM OF THE WORLD'S ETERNITY[a]

1. [12] *Differentiating the Received View.* The philosophers differ concerning the world's eternity, but the opinion upon which the majority of them, modern and ancient, have settled is to claim that it is eternal. It has never ceased existing together with God (exalted is He!) but is His effect and is concurrent with Him, not being temporally posterior to Him but [exists together with God] in the way that the effect is concurrent with the cause, such as light is concurrent with the Sun. Also the Creator is prior to it like the cause is prior to the effect, namely, essentially prior and prior in rank but not in time.

2. That the world is generated and created in time is referenced in Plato.[2] Some of the [philosophers] subsequently interpreted away his [literal] words, denying that he believed in the world's temporal creation.

3. At the end of Galen's life, in the book titled *What Galen Believes to Be Opinion*,[3] he reached a deadlock on this problem, not knowing whether the world is eternal or temporally created. He may have shown that it could not be known—not because of a deficiency on his part, but owing to the inherent difficulty of this problem itself for [human] intellects. This, however, is something of a deviation from the standard view of all of them, which is simply that [the world] is eternal, and in general that it is wholly inconceivable that something temporal should proceed immediately from something eternal.

4. [13] *The Presentation of Their Proofs.* If I were to digress to describe what has been conveyed in order to exhibit their evidence and what has been mentioned in rejecting it, I would fill many pages on this problem; however, there is no good in lengthening the discussion. So let us omit their proofs that are arbitrary or weak fancy, which any one with reason can easily resolve, and limit ourselves to presenting [the

---

2 Al-Ghazālī is referring to the creation account presented in Plato's *Timaeus.* Within the ancient and medieval worlds there was a debate about what Plato's true position was. Speusippus and Xenocrates, Plato's successors at the Academy, thought that Plato's eternal *demiurge,* or God, was causally, but not temporally, prior to creation. The Middle Platonists Plutarch and Atticus in contrast maintained that Plato thought that the world was created at some first moment in time. The great Neoplatonist Proclus criticized this latter interpretation of Plato in a work *On the Eternity of the World,* which was in its turn criticized by the later Neoplatonist John Philoponus in his *Against Proclus.* Both works were available in Arabic translation.

3 See ar-Rāzī's *Doubts against Galen* translated here, pp. 49–53.

proofs] that leave a strong impression on the mind and that can give rise to doubt even for those of outstanding reason; for by the most feeble [of proofs] one can produce doubt in the weak.

5. [. . .] [*Their Strongest Proof.*] They claim that the procession of the temporal from the eternal is absolutely impossible. [That is] because when we posit the eternal but not, for example, the world's proceeding from it, then it does not proceed precisely, because there is no selectively determining factor for the [world's] existence, but rather the world's existence would be a pure possibility. So if [the world] temporally comes to be after that, then a selectively determining factor must either come to be anew or not. On the one hand, if a selectively determining factor does not come to be anew, then the world remains purely possible just as it was before. On the other hand, if a selectively determining factor comes to be anew, then who is the creator of that selectively determining factor, and why did it temporally create now and not earlier? The question concerning the temporal creation of the selectively determining factor still stands.

6. In brief, when the states of the eternal are similar, then either nothing exists from it or [something] exists perpetually, for it is impossible to distinguish the state of refraining from the state of commencing.

7. Its independent verification is to ask, "Why did [the Creator] not temporally create the world before [the moment] of its creation?" It can neither be attributed to His inability to create temporally nor to the impossibility of the temporal creation. Indeed, that would lead either to a change in the Eternal from being unable [to create], to having the power [to create] or to the world's changing from being impossible to being possible, both of which [14] are absurd. It cannot be said that there had been no previous wish and thereafter a wish came to be anew. Also it cannot be attributed to lacking an instrument, which thereafter came to exist. In fact, the nearest one can imagine is to say, "[The Creator] did not will its existence," in which case it must be said, "[The world's] existence came to be because He came to will its existence after not willing [it]." In that case the will would have been temporally created, but its temporal creation in Him is absurd, because He is not that in which temporally occurring things inhere, and [the will's] temporal creation is neither in Him nor makes Him One Who wills.

8. Let us set aside speculating about the substrate of [the will's] creation. Does not the difficulty concerning the origin of [the will's] creation still stand, namely, from whence is it created and why was it created now but not earlier? Was its being created now not due to God? If there can be a temporal event without a creator, then let the world be a temporal event that does not have a Maker, otherwise what is the difference between one temporal event and another? Also, if it is created by a creation of God, then why did He create now and not earlier? Was it because of an absence of an instrument or power or intent or nature? But then why,[b] if that [absence] is replaced with existence, was it created? The very same difficulty returns! Or is it owing to the absence of the will? But then the will would need a will and likewise the first will, [resulting] in an infinite regress.

9. Thus, it has been independently verified by absolute argumentation that the procession of the temporal from the eternal without the change of something pertaining to the eternal, whether a power, instrument, moment, intent, or nature, is absurd. To assign a change of state [to the eternal] is impossible, because that temporal change would be like any other, the whole of which is absurd. Inasmuch as the world exists and its temporal creation is impossible, its eternity is necessarily established.

10. This is the most imaginative of their proofs. In general, their discussion concerning the rest of the metaphysical problems is poorer than their discussion concerning this problem, since here they exploit certain sorts of imagination that they cannot in the others. Because of that we have treated this problem, the strongest of their proofs, first.

11. The refutation comes from two fronts.

12. [15] The first of them is to ask by what means would you [philosophers] censure one who says, "The world is temporally created by means of an eternal will that made necessary [the world's] existence at the moment at which it came to exist; [the world's] nonexistence continued to the limit up to which it continued, and the existence began from whence it began; before the existence it was not something willed and so owing to that was not created, but at the moment at which it was created, it was willed by the eternal will and so owing to that was created"? What precludes this belief and would render it absurd?

13. It might be said that this is self-evidently absurd, because the temporal is something necessitated and caused. Just as it is impossible that there is something temporal without a cause and what necessitates it, [so likewise] it is impossible that what necessitates should exist, having been complete in the conditions, principles, and causes for its necessitating, such that no awaited thing remains at all, but then what is necessitated is delayed. Quite the contrary, the existence of what is necessitated is necessary when there is the realization of what necessitates with the completion of its conditions. The absurdity of its delay is tantamount to the impossibility that the temporally necessitated exists without what necessitates [it].

14. Before the world's existence, the one who wills, the will, and its relation to the one who wills [all] existed, and neither did the one who wills, nor the will, nor some relation that did not belong to the will come to be anew, for all of that is to change. So [the rebuttal continues], how did that which is willed come to be anew, and what prevented [its] coming to be anew earlier? The new state is no different from the previous state with respect to some factor, state of affairs, state or relation. In fact, the states of affairs were just the same as they were [before]. Therefore, what is willed would not have existed but would have remained the same as it was. But [on the present view] the willed object comes to exist! What is this, but the most extreme absurdity?!

15. The impossibility of this type is not only in what necessitates and what is necessitated necessarily and essentially, [continue the philosophers], but also in the customary and conventional; for if a man were to pronounce [the legal declaration] divorcing his wife and the separation were not to occur immediately, then it is

inconceivable that it would occur later, because the pronouncement is made a cause of the [divorced] status by convention [16] and accepted practice. So the delay of the effect is unintelligible unless the divorce is linked with the coming of tomorrow or the entrance into the house, and so it does not occur immediately. It will occur, however, with the coming of tomorrow or the entrance into the house, for he has made it a cause in relation to some awaited thing. So since it, that is, tomorrow or the entrance, is not present at the moment, the occurrence of what is necessitated [must] await the presence of what is not present. So what is necessitated does not occur unless something has come to be anew, namely, the entrance or the presence of tomorrow. Even if he were to want to delay what necessarily results from the [legal] declaration without [making it] conditional on an event that is not [presently] occurring, it would be unintelligible, despite the fact that it is conventional and that he makes the choice with respect to the details of the convention. So if we cannot posit this [delay] by our own desire, nor make it intelligible, then how can we make it intelligible with respect to essential, intellectual, and necessary necessitations?

16.　Concerning customary things, what occurs by means of our intention is not delayed after there is the intention along with the intention to do it, except by some obstacle. So if the intent and power are realized and the obstacles removed, then the delay of what is intended is unintelligible. The former is conceivable only in the case of resolve, because the resolve is insufficient for the action's existence. In fact, the resolve to write does not occasion writing so long as there is not also a renewal of the intention, that is, the renewal of the state to act reemerges in the human [at the time he does write].

17.　If the eternal will has the same status as our intention to act, then, unless there is an obstacle, it is inconceivable that what is intended should be delayed and that the intention should be earlier [than the act]. So an intention today to carry through [with some action] tomorrow is intelligible only by way of resolve. If the eternal will has the same status as our resolve, then that [alone] is insufficient for the occurrence of what is resolved; rather, at the time that [what is resolved] is made to exist, there is inevitably a new intentional reemergence, in which there is an admission that the Eternal changes. Moreover, the very same difficulty remains concerning why that emergence or intention or will (or whatever you want to call it) was created now and not earlier. So it still remains [that] a temporal event is either without a cause or there is an infinite regress.

18.　[17] The gist of the discussion reduces to the necessitating thing's existing with the conditions for [the necessitated effect] completed and no anticipated thing remaining, and yet what is necessitated is delayed, and delayed for a period of time whose beginning the imagination cannot even fathom—indeed, a thousand years would not even be a drop in the bucket—and then all of a sudden the necessitated thing pops up without anything's coming to be anew or some condition being realized. This is simply absurd!

19.　The response is to ask whether it is through the necessity of reason or inference that you [philosophers] know that an eternal will that is related to a certain thing's temporal creation (whatever that thing should be) is impossible? According to your own logical terminology, do you know the connection between these two terms [i.e., "eternal Will" and "temporal creation"] through a middle term or without a middle term? If, on the one hand, you maintain that there is a middle term, which is the way of inference, then it must be made obvious. If, on the other hand, you maintain that that [connection] is known necessarily, then how is it that those at odds with you do not share your view about its being known [necessarily]? [And why is it not the case that] no land contains the school of thought that believes in the world's temporal creation by an eternal will, when [in fact] there are innumerable [lands whose people believe in creation]? Undoubtedly they do not stubbornly disregard [their] intellects while possessing the knowledge. Thus, it is incumbent [upon you] to construct a logical demonstration that shows the impossibility of that, since in all of what you have stated [you have shown] only improbability and analogy with our resolve and will. On the one hand, [the analogy] is imperfect; for the eternal will is not analogous with temporal intentions. On the other hand, probability taken simply is not enough [to show that the world is eternal] without a demonstration.

20.   It might be said, "We do know by the necessity of reason that what necessitates with the completion of its conditions is inconceivable without there being what is necessitated, and the one who allows [otherwise] is showing contempt for the necessity of reason."

21.   We ask what is the difference between you and your opponents when they say to you that we necessarily know the inconsistency of the claim, "A single entity knows all the universals without that [knowledge] requiring multiplicity, and without the knowledge being something additional to the entity, and without the knowledge being made multiple [18] despite the multiplicity of objects known"? This is your position concerning God's reality, but with respect to us and to what we understand, it is inconsistent in the extreme! But you will say, "Eternal knowledge is not to be compared with temporal [knowledge]." Now there is a group among you who was aware of the inconsistency of the above and so said that God only knows Himself, in which case He is what intellects, the intellection and the object of intellection, and the whole is one. What if one should say that the unification of intellection, what intellects, and the object of intellection is necessarily impossible, since it is necessarily absurd to suppose that the world's Maker does not know what He makes? If the Eternal knows only Himself (may He be greatly exalted above your claim and the claim of all those who distort the truth), then He simply will not know what He makes.

22.   In fact, we would not be overstepping the requirements of this question to ask by what means would you censure your opponents should they say that the world's eternity is absurd, because it comes down to affirming an infinite number of rotations of the celestial sphere, whose units are innumerable, while simultaneously [affirming that those units are divisible into] sixths, fourths, and halves? For the sphere of the Sun completes its rotation in one year, whereas it takes the sphere of Saturn thirty years; thus Saturn's rotations are three-tenths those of the Sun. Also Jupiter's rotations

are one-half of one-sixth [i.e., one-twelfth] those of the Sun, for it completes a rotation in twelve years. Moreover, Saturn's number of rotations would be infinite just as is the Sun's; nevertheless, [Saturn's] would be three-tenths [of the Sun's]. In fact, the infinite number of rotations of the sphere of the fixed stars, which takes thirty-six thousand years to complete a single rotation, would be equal to the infinite number of the Sun's eastward motions, which are [completed] in but a day and night. Should one say that this is something whose impossibility is known necessarily, how would you dispose of his claim?

23.   Indeed, one might ask whether the number of these rotations is even, odd, both even and odd, or neither even nor odd. If you say either that they are both even and odd or that they are neither even nor odd, the falsity [of this claim] is known necessarily. If you say that they are even, in which case the even would become odd by one unit, then how could what is infinite be lacking one unit? If you say that they are odd, in which case the odd would become [19] even by one unit, then how could it lack that single unit by which it would become even? Thus, the claim that [the number of rotations] is neither even nor odd becomes incumbent upon you. If it is said that even and odd are attributed only to the finite but are not attributed to the infinite, we reply that a totality composed of units that has a sixth and tenth, as previously mentioned, and yet even and odd is not attributed to it, is known to be false necessarily without reflection. So by what means do you disassociate yourselves from this?

24.   [The philosopher] might say that the locus of the error is in your claim that [the heavenly rotations] are a totality composed of units; for these rotations are non-existents. [They are] either past, and so they no longer exist, or future, and so they do not yet exist, whereas "totality" indicates presently existing things, but in this case there is nothing existing [such as to be a totality].

25.   We say that number divides into the even and odd, and it is impossible that what is numbered should lie outside of [this division], regardless of whether it is something that continues to exist or perishes. So when we posit a number of horses, we must believe that [the number] is either even or odd, regardless of whether we suppose [the horses] to be existing or nonexisting. If they cease to exist after existing, this proposition does not change.

26.   Moreover, we say to them that it is not impossible according your own principles that there are presently existing things that are individuals varying in description and [yet] are infinite, namely, the human souls separated from the body by death, in which case they will exist without even and odd being attributed to them. So by what means do you censure the one who says that the falsity of this is recognized necessarily just as you claimed that the eternal will's association with creating temporally is necessarily false? This opinion concerning the soul is the one that Ibn Sīnā chose and perhaps is Aristotle's position as well.[4]

---

[4] See Aristotle, *De anima* III 5 and Ibn Sīnā, "The Soul," V.4, 195–99.

27. It might be said that the truth lies with Plato's opinion, namely, that the soul is eternal and one and divided only with relation to bodies, but when they are separated from [the bodies], they return to their source and are united.[5] We say that [20] this is most atrocious, most repugnant, and most deserving of being believed to be contrary to the necessity of reason. For we ask: Is Zayd's soul the very same soul as 'Amr's or is it different? If it is the very same one, then it is necessarily false, for everyone is aware of himself and knows that he is not some other individual. If it were the very same, then the two would be the same with respect to the things they know, which are essential attributes of the souls, entering along with the souls into every relation. If you say [Zayd's and 'Amr's souls] are different and divided only by the association with bodies, we say that the division of the individual who has no magnitude with respect to bulk and quantitative magnitude is absurd by the necessity of the intellect. So how will the individual [soul] become two—in fact a thousand—and thereafter return and become one!? Indeed, this is intelligible concerning what has bulk or quantity, such as the water of the sea, which divides into streamlets and rivers and then returns to the sea, but as for what has no quantity, how could it be divided!?[6]

28. The whole of our intention is to make clear that [the philosophers] have neither undermined the belief of those who oppose them concerning the eternal will's relation to creating temporally, except by the pretension of necessity, nor have they disposed of the one who invokes necessity against them in those issues that are opposed to their belief, from which there is no escape.

29. It might be, [the philosopher complains], that this turns against you in that God was able to create the world before He did by a year or several years owing to His infinite power. It is as if He bided His time, not creating, and then created. Is the [temporal] extent of [His] refraining either finite or infinite? If you say, on the one hand, that it is finite, the existence of the Creator goes back to the finite beginning. On the other hand, if you say that it is infinite, then there would have been a period during which an infinite number of possibilities had elapsed.

30. We say that in our opinion duration and time are created, and we shall explain the true nature of the answer to this when we dispose of their second proof.[7]

---

[5] See Plato, *Meno* 81A–E; *Phaedo* 81E-82B; and *Republic* 617D-621D.

[6] Cf. Ibn Sīnā, "The Soul," V.2, pars. 1–8, pp. 188–91.

[7] The philosophers' second argument for the eternity of the world and al-Ghazālī's refutation of it are not translated here; however, the philosophers' argument is much like that outlined in the immediately preceding paragraph, 29, and again in the chapter on Ibn Ṭufayl's *Ḥayy ibn Yaqẓān*, paragraph 20, pp. 290–91. Al-Ghazālī's response was to say that since time is among the things that God creates, it is inappropriate to ask about the time when God was not creating. The philosophers have been misled by the estimative faculty, continued al-Ghazālī, into assuming that since one can imagine something only as existing in time, whatever exists must be in time.

31.   [21] If [the philosopher] asks by what means would you deny one who refrains from invoking necessity and proves [the impossibility of an eternal will's temporally creating the world] in another way, namely, that moments of time are indiscernible with respect to the possibility that the will has a preference for [one of] them [over the others]. So what is it that distinguished one determinate moment of time from what was before or after it, when it is not absurd that what is willed should be earlier and later? In fact, with respect to white and black and motion and rest, you [theologians] yourself say that the white is temporally created by the eternal will, but the substrate is [just as] receptive to black [as] it is to receiving white. So why does the eternal will prefer white over black? What is it that distinguished one of the two possibilities from the other with respect to the will's having a preference for it? We [philosophers] know necessarily that something cannot be distinguished from its like except by some specific property. Now if [some specific property] were possible, then the temporal creation of the world would be possible. [In fact], however, the possibility [of the world's] existing is just like the possibility [of its] not existing, and the aspect of existing, which is like the aspect of not existing with respect to possibility, would be specified without any specific property. If you [theologians] say that it is the will that specifies, then the question arises about the will's specifying: "*Why* did it specify [it]?" If you say that why-questions do not apply to the eternal, then let the world be eternal and do not seek its Maker and cause, because why-questions do not apply to the eternal.

32.   Next, [continues the philosopher's objection], if one allows that it is by chance that the eternal [will] specified one of the two possibilities, then it is at the pinnacle of improbability to say that the world is specified by some specific design when it could have been according to some other design instead of [the one it in fact has], and so its occurring as such would be said to be by chance. Just as you said that the will specified one moment to the exclusion of another, it [would have specified] one design to the exclusion of another by chance. If you say this question is not necessary because it arises for whatever He wills and refers to whatever He has power over, we say, "No! Quite the contrary, this question is necessary because it does refer to any moment and is necessary for whoever differs from us concerning [whether there is] any power over [something]."

33.   We respond [22] that the world came to exist when it did and according to the description [with] which it came to exist and in the place in which it came to exist only by will. The will is an attribute whose character is to distinguish something from its like. If this were not its character, then one would settle content with the power; however, since the power's relation to two contraries is equal, and there must be something that specifies one thing from its like, it is said that, in addition to power, the Eternal has an attribute whose character is to specify one thing from its like. So asking, "Why did the will specify one of two things?" is just like asking, "Why does knowledge require comprehending the object of knowledge as it is?" The answer is because knowledge is equivalent to an attribute whose character is this, and so in

similar fashion the will is equivalent to an attribute whose character is this. In fact, its very essence is to distinguish one thing from its like.

34. [The philosopher] might say that affirming an attribute whose character is to distinguish one thing from its like is unintelligible. Nay, it is outright contradictory; for the sense of one's being like [the other] is that it cannot be distinguished from [the other], whereas the sense of being distinguished is that it is not like [the other]. One should not erroneously suppose that two black things in two locations are like one another in every respect, since this one is in one location while that one is in another location, and this is necessarily the distinction. Nor are two black things at two moments in time in a single location like one another absolutely, since this one is separate from that one with respect to the moment of time. So how can one be indiscernible from [the other] in every respect!? When we say two black things are similar to one another, by [being similar to one another] we mean with respect to the blackness as something related to the two, specifically [as something black] not absolutely. Otherwise, if the location and time were one [and the same] and nothing different remained, then neither *two* black things nor their being two would be intelligible at all. This is independently verified [in] that the expression "will" is a metaphorical expression derived from our will, but it is inconceivable of us that we distinguish one from its like. Quite the contrary, if immediately before a thirsty person there were two glasses of water indiscernible in every respect in relation to his desire, he would not be able to take one of the two; rather, he would take only what seems to him superior or easier to lay hold of or nearer to his right side [23] (if his habit is to move the right hand) or some other such cause, whether hidden or obvious, otherwise distinguishing one thing from its like is all together inconceivable.

35. The response comes from two fronts.

36. The first concerns [the philosopher's] claim that this is inconceivable. Do you recognize it as something necessary or as an inference? It is impossible to invoke either one of these. Also your likening [the eternal will] with our will is an imperfect analogy comparable to the analogy concerning knowledge. God's knowledge is distinct from our knowledge with respect to the issues that we have established. So why would the distinction with respect to [our and the eternal] will be improbable? In fact, it is just like one who says that it is unintelligible that there is a being who exists neither outside the world nor inside of it, nor is connected nor disconnected [from it], [simply] because we do not intellectually grasp it regarding ourselves. [The philosopher] may respond that the former is the work of your estimative faculty, whereas intellectual proof has led those who are intellectually endowed to affirm the latter. So by what means do you [philosophers] deny whoever says that intellectual proof leads to affirming an attribute of God (may He be exalted!) whose character is to distinguish one thing from its like? If the name "will" does not correspond with [this attribute], then give it some other name; for there is no quibble over names, and we have used it only on the sanction of the divine law. Otherwise "will" is something imposed by language in order to designate whatever concerns an object of wish, whereas with

respect to God there is no object of wish. Only the meaning is intended, not the utterance.

37.	Moreover, we do not concede that regarding ourselves that is inconceivable.[8] So [let] us posit two indiscernible dates immediately before someone who is hungrily looking at them but is incapable of taking both. He will take one of them necessarily through an attribute whose character is to specify one thing from its like. Everything you mentioned concerning specifications of superiority, proximity, or facility of access, we determine, by supposition, to be absent, but the possibility of taking remains. You have two options: either (1) to say that the indiscernibility in relation to his desires is wholly inconceivable, which is fatuous given that the supposition [of the date's indiscernibility] is possible; or (2) to say that when the indiscernibility is supposed, the hungrily longing man would always remain undecided, staring at the two [dates] but not taking either of them simply by [24] willing, but choosing to stand aloof from the desire, which is also absurd, whose falsity is known necessarily. Thus, anyone investigating the true nature of voluntary action, whether directly or indirectly, must affirm an attribute whose character is to specify one thing from its like.

38.	The second manner of objection is for us to say that in your own school of thought you do not dispense with specifying one thing from another; for [according to you], the world came to exist from its necessitating cause according some specified design similar to its opposite. So why was it specified with some aspects [and not others], when there is no difference in the impossibility of distinguishing one thing from its like, whether with respect to [voluntary] action or what is entailed naturally or by necessity?

39.	You might say that the world's universal order cannot but be according to the manner that came to exist. If the world were either smaller or bigger than what it presently is, then this order would not be complete, and the same is said of the number of the celestial spheres and planets. You maintain that the large is different from the small, and that the many are distinct from the few concerning what is willed of it, and so they are not alike. Quite the contrary, [the philosopher continues], these are different, except that the human [cognitive] faculty is too weak to grasp the aspects of wisdom concerning their magnitudes and their differentiations. The wisdom is grasped only concerning some of them, such as the wisdom concerning the inclination of the sphere of the Zodiac from the equator, and the wisdom concerning the apogee and the eccentric sphere. Frequently, the underlying reason is not grasped concerning them, but their differing is recognized. It is not unlikely that one thing is distinguished from its opposite because of the thing's relation to the order. Moments of time, however, are absolutely similar vis-à-vis possibility and order, and one cannot claim that if [the world] were created after or before it was by one instant that the order would be inconceivable; for the similarity of the [temporal] states is known necessarily.

---

[8] I.e., it is not inconceivable that the human will can distinguish indiscernibles.

40. We say that [25] even though we could oppose you in a similar way with respect to the [temporal] states—since there are those who said that [God] created [the world] at the moment that was most suitable for its creation—we shall nonetheless not content ourselves with this comparison. Instead, on the basis of your own principle, we shall require you to specify [one thing from its like] in two situations concerning which no difference can be assigned. One is the difference of direction of the motion of the [celestial spheres], and the other is assigning the position of the pole with respect to the motion along the [Zodiacal] belt [i.e., ecliptic motion].

41. The illustration of the pole is that the heaven is a sphere rotating around two poles as if the two remained fixed. The sphere of the heavens is something whose parts are similar (for it is simple) and especially the outermost celestial sphere, which is the ninth (for it is wholly without stars). Also, [these spheres] are moved[9] around a northern and southern pole. Now we say that there are no two points among the points, which in [the philosophers'] opinion are infinite, that cannot be conceived as being the pole. So why have the northern and southern points been assigned to be poles and to remain fixed? Why does the line of the [Zodiacal] belt not pass through the two points [and continue on] until the pole returns to two opposite points on the [Zodiacal] belt? If there is a wisdom concerning the magnitude of the heavens' largeness and its shape, then what is it that distinguishes the location of one pole from another so that the one was assigned to be a pole and not any of the other parts and points, when all the points are alike and all the part of the sphere are indiscernible? From this there is no escape.

42. [The philosopher] might say that perhaps the position that corresponds with the point of the pole is distinct from the others by a special property that accords with its being a location for the pole so that it remains fixed. So it is as if [the position of the pole] does not move from its place, space, position (or whatever names are applied to it), whereas the celestial sphere's remaining positions do exchange their position relative to the Earth and the [other] spheres by rotating. Now the pole's position remains fixed, and so perhaps that position was worthier of remaining the fixed position than the others.

43. [26] We respond that in this there is an open acknowledgment of the natural dissimilarity of the parts of the first sphere, and that [the first sphere] is not something whose parts are similar, which is contrary to your own principle, since one [of the principles] by which you proved that the heavens are necessarily spherically shaped is that the naturally simple is something similar [throughout] without dissimilarity. Now the simplest figure is the sphere (for the quadrangle, hexagon, and the like require projecting angles and their dissimilarities, which only results from something in addition to the simple nature). Even though [your response] is contrary to

---

[9] The text's specific claim that there are *two* things moved probably refers to what has an apparent westward motion, namely, the outermost sphere, and what has an apparent eastward motion, namely, the rest of the spheres.

your own standard view, it still does not ward off the necessary consequences following from it; for the question concerning that special property arises, since [there is still the question of] whether the rest of the parts are susceptible to that special property or not. If, on the one hand, [the philosophers] say, "Yes," then why does the special property specify one from among the similar things? If, on the other hand, they say, "That [special property] is only with respect to that position, and none of the others is susceptible to it," we say that the remaining parts, inasmuch as they are a body receptive to the forms, are necessarily similar. That position [of the pole] is no more deserving of that special property [than the others] by simply being either a body or a heaven. Indeed, this sense is common to all the rest of the parts of the heaven. Inevitably, [God's] specifying it is either by fiat or an attribute whose character is to specify one thing from its like. Otherwise it is just as proper for [the theologians] to claim that the [temporal] states are indiscernible with respect to the susceptibility of the world's occurring at [one of] them as it is for their opponent [to claim] that the parts of the heaven are indiscernible with respect to the susceptibility of the thing (ma'ná), on account of which the position's remaining fixed is more fitting than the position's changing. From this there is no escape.

44.   The second necessity is to assign a direction to the celestial spheres' motion; some of [the spheres] move from east to west, whereas others move in just the opposite direction, despite the indiscernibility of directions. What is their cause, when the indiscernibility of directions is just like the indiscernibility of moments of times and are without difference?

45.   It might be said that [27] if everything were to rotate in one direction, then neither would the relative positions of [the stars and planets] vary, nor would the stars' relations [to one another] as trine, sextine, in conjunction,[10] and the like come to be. Instead, everything would have a single relative position that never varies, but these relations are the principle of coming to be in the world.

46.   We say that we are not clinging to [the position] that the difference of the motion's direction does not exist. Quite the contrary, we say that the outermost celestial sphere is moved from east to west and that which is below it [is moved] in the opposite direction. Now whatever can cause it to happen in this way can cause it to happen in the opposite way, namely, that the outermost celestial [sphere could] be moved from east to west and the opposite for what is below it, in which case there would be the dissimilarities. The motion's direction, setting aside its rotating and being opposite, is indiscernible. So why is one direction distinguished from another that is its like?

47.   If they say, "The two directions are opposites and contrary so how could they be indiscernible?" we say that this is just like one who says that priority and posteriority with respect to the world's existence are contraries, and so how can one invoke their similarity? They allege, however, that one knows the similarities of moments of

_____

[10] That is to say, when the aspect of two bodies is 120°, 60°, or 180° between each other, respectively.

time by relation to possible existence and to any benefit supposedly thought to exist. But in like fashion one knows the indiscernibility of the spaces, positions, places, and directions by the relation to the motion's susceptibility and any benefit that is associated with it. So if they are allowed to invoke difference despite this similarity, their opponents are allowed to invoke difference concerning [temporal] states and design as well.

48. The second objection against the principle of their proof is to say that you [philosophers] regard the temporal creation of a temporal event from an eternal improbable, and yet you [must] inevitably admit it; for there are temporal events in the world and they have causes, but if temporal events were based on temporal events infinitely, there would be an absurdity, which is simply not a belief of an intelligent person. If [an infinite causal chain] were possible, then you could dispense with [28] admitting a Maker and establishing a necessary existence as the basis of the possibles. When temporal events have a limit at which their causal chain terminates such that that limit is the eternal, then, according to [the philosophers' own] principle, the possibility of a temporal event's proceeding from an eternal is inevitable.

49. It might be said, "We do not find a temporal event's proceeding from an eternal improbable. What we in fact find improbable is that a *first* temporal event should proceed from an eternal, since there is no difference between the very moment of the creation and what was before it with respect to selectively determining the aspect of existence, which does not [differ] inasmuch as it is a present moment, an instrument, a condition, a nature, a wish, or any other cause. When the event is not the first, it is permitted that it proceeds from [an eternal] when there is the creation of some other thing, such as the preparedness of the receiving substrate and the presence of the fitting moment, and whatever is analogous to this.

50. We say that the problem concerning the occurrence of the preparedness, the presence of the moment, and whatever is renewed, still stands: either there is an infinite causal regress or it terminates in an eternal from which the first temporal event results.

51. It might be said that the matter's receptivity to forms, accidents, and qualities is not at all something temporally coming to be. The qualities that temporally come to be are the motion of the celestial spheres, I mean the rotation, and the renewal of their relational attributes such as being trine, sextine, and quadrate,[11] that is, the relation of some of the parts of the celestial sphere, stars, and planets to one another, and the relation of some of them to the Earth. Examples are the occurrence of ascending and descending, passing from the highest point of elevation, remoteness from the Earth by the star or planet's being at apogee as well as proximity by its being at perigee, [29] and its inclination away from some celestial or terrestrial zones by their being in the north and south. This relation [of the heavenly bodies] follows necessarily because of the rotation, and so the rotation necessities it. As for the temporal events

---

[11] That is to say, when the aspect of two bodies is 120°, 60°, or 90° between each other, respectively.

encompassed within the sublunar realm, namely, by the appearance of generation and corruption, mixing and separating, as well as the alteration of one attribute for another in the elements, all of those are temporal events depending upon one another in an extended ordering of differences. In the end, however, the principles of their causes terminate at the celestial rotation and the stars and planets' relation to one another and to the Earth.

52.   From all of that, [claims the philosopher], it results that the perpetual, eternal rotation is the reason for all temporal events. The movers of the heavens' rotation are the souls of the heavens; for they are alive in a way comparable to our souls in relation to our bodies, but their souls are eternal. So of course the rotation that they necessitate is also eternal. Since the states of the soul are uniform because [the soul] is eternal, the states of the motions are also uniform, that is, they rotate eternally.

53.   Thus, [continues the philosopher], it is inconceivable that the temporal proceeds from the eternal, except through an intermediate everlasting rotation that is similar to the eternal in one way; for it is perpetually everlasting. In another way, however, [the rotation] is similar to the temporal; for each of its posited parts was temporally created after they were not. So inasmuch as [the rotation] is temporal through its parts and relations, then it is the principle of temporal events, whereas inasmuch as it is everlasting, similar to the states [of the soul], it proceeds from an eternal soul. So, if there are temporal events in the world, there is inevitably rotation, but there are temporal events in the world, and so everlasting rotation is established.

54.   [In response] we say that this lengthy [discourse] does not improve your situation; for the rotation that is the basis [of all temporal events] is either temporal or eternal. If it is eternal, then how does it become a principle for the first [30] temporal events? If it is temporal, then it depends on another temporal event, and there will be an [infinite] causal chain. You maintain that in one respect it is similar to the eternal and in another respect it is similar to the temporal; for it is permanent [and] renewed, that is, it is permanently renewed and renewed permanently. But we ask, "Is it a principle of temporal events insofar as it is permanent or insofar as it is renewed?" If it is insofar as it is permanent, then how is it that something [that exists] at some moments and not others proceeds from something permanent that has similar states? If it is insofar as it is renewed, then what is the cause of its renewal in itself? It would need another cause, and there would be an [infinite] causal chain. This was [our] goal, to establish the necessity [of a temporal event's proceeding from an eternal].

III.   ON POWER[a]

1.   [51] We claim that the world's Creator is powerful, because the world is an act exhibiting wisdom, design, perfection, and order and contains various kinds of marvels and signs that indicate power. Constructing the syllogism, we thus say: Every act that exhibits wisdom proceeds from an agent having power; the world is an act

exhibiting wisdom; thus it proceeds from an agent having power. Concerning which of these principles is there dispute?

2.   If is said, "Why did you say that the world is an act exhibiting wisdom?" we say, we meant by its "exhibiting wisdom" its design, orderliness, and harmony. Whoever considers his own external and internal organs, [the wisdom] is obvious to him from the marvels of the perfection, whose list is long. So this is a principle whose recognition is perceived by the senses and observation and so cannot be gainsaid.

3.   If it is said, "By what means do you recognize the other principle, namely that the agent of every action that exhibits design and wisdom has power?" we say that the intellect is what necessarily perceives this. So the intellect affirms it without proof, but neither can the intellect deny it; however, despite this we shall draw forth a proof that will decisively suppress the doubts and opposition. So we say that we mean by [the agent's] having power that the action proceeding from it must proceed from it either (1) essentially, or (2) owing to something additional to it. Now it is false to say that it proceeded from it essentially, since if that were the case, then [the action] would be eternal along with the essence. So it has been shown that it proceeded from something additional to [52] its essence. That additional attribute by which the existing act was able to be performed we call "power," since "power," in standard parlance, is equivalent to the attribute belonging to the agent to be able to perform the act and by which the action occurs.

4.   If is said, "This turns against you concerning power (for [how] is it eternal, but the action is not eternal?)" we say, its answer will be presented during [the discussion of] the precepts involving the will concerning that by which the action occurs.[12] This attribution is something that the decisive division, which we mentioned, proved [namely, the division between actions that proceed from their agent essentially and those that proceed owing to something additional]. We mean by "power" only this attribute. Having settled this, let us mention the precepts involving [power].

5.   One of the precepts concerning [divine power] is that it is related to all objects of power. By "objects of power" I mean all of the infinite possibles. Now everybody knows that the possibles are infinite, and so the objects of power are infinite. We mean by "the possibles are infinite" that the creation of one temporal event after another never reaches a limit beyond which it is impossible for the intellect [to conceive] of some [further] temporal event's coming to be. So possibility is temporally limitless, and the [divine] power extends to all of that. The demonstration of this claim, namely, the extensiveness of the [divine] power's relation, is that it has already become apparent that the Maker of the entire world is one. So either (1) He has some power corresponding with each object of power but the objects of power are infinite, in which case an infinite number of powers would have been affirmed, which is absurd, just like what preceded in refuting infinite rotations. Or (2) the power is one, in which case, despite its being one, its relation to whatever it is related to among the substances

---

12 Cf. *The Incoherence of the Philosophers*, "The First Discussion," pars. 33–37, pp. 248–50.

and accidents, despite their being different, is due to some thing that [the substances and accidents] share in common. There is, however, nothing in common other than possibility, from which it follows that every possible is necessarily an object of power and occurs by power.[13]

6. In general, when substance and accidents proceed from Him, then it is impossible that their likes not proceed from Him as well. [That is] because the power of something is a power over its like, since numerical multiplicity in the object of power does not preclude [His power over numerically many things], because His relation to all motion and all color is according to a single uniform course. So [the divine power] is suited to always creating one motion after another,[b] and likewise one color after another, and one substance after another, and so on. That is what we meant by saying that His power (exalted be He!) is related to every possible; for possibility is neither limited in number nor is the relation of that power itself specific to a given number to the exclusion of another. Also, one cannot point to some motion and then say that it falls outside of the possibility of the power's relation to it, despite the fact that [the power] was related to [the motion's] like, since you know necessarily that whatever is necessary for something is necessary for its like. There are three subsidiary topics that result from this [account of power].

7. *The First Subsidiary Topic.* If one should ask, "Do you say that something contrary to fact is an object of power?" we say that this is something about which there is dispute, but the dispute over it represents nothing when it is investigated and the gnarl of words is removed. Its proof is that it has already been established that every possible is an object of power, and that the impossible is not an object of power. So consider whether what is contrary to fact is impossible or possible. You will only know that when you know the meaning of "impossible" and "possible" and have undertaken a thorough investigation of them. Otherwise, if you are lax in the inquiry, then perhaps that it is impossible, possible, and not impossible would [seem to] apply to what is contrary to fact, but then that it is impossible and that it is not impossible would [both] apply, but the two are contradictory and the two cannot simultaneously apply.

8. [53] Know that a whole collection [of senses] are subsumed under the expression ["object of power"], which will be revealed to you precisely by what I say, namely, that it applies to the world, for example, that it is (1) necessary, (2) impossible, and (3) possible. (1) It is necessary insofar as when the will of the Eternal is assumed to exist necessarily, then the object of the will also must be necessary and not possible, since the nonexistence of the object of will is impossible [taken] together with the reality of the eternal will. (2) [The world's existence] would have been impossible, if

---

[13] In other words, if the divine power is one, then it must be directed to some one, single feature that all the varying objects of power share in common, but the one and only thing they share in common is possibility, either the possibility to be a substance or accident as well as the difference between them with respect to their substantiality or accidental features.

He were to have decreed the nonexistence of the will's relation to bringing about [the world's] existence, in which case its coming to be would necessarily be impossible, since it would lead to the coming to be of some temporal event without a cause, which has already been discovered to be impossible. (3) It is possible if you focus on it itself and do not consider it together with either the existence or nonexistence of the will, in which case possibility is attributed to it.

9.   Thus, there are three ways to consider [the world as an object of power]. The first is to make the existence of the will and its relation a condition for it, and so by this consideration it is necessary. The second is to consider the absence of the will, and so by this consideration it is impossible. The third is that we avoid taking into account the will and cause and consider neither its existence nor nonexistence, but isolate the investigation to the world itself, and so by this consideration the third thing remains for it, namely, possibility. We mean by ["possibility"] that it is possible in itself, that is, when we do not impose any conditions other than it itself, then it is possible. From which it is obvious that one thing can be possible and impossible; however, it is possible by considering it itself and impossible by considering another. It cannot be possible in itself and impossible in itself; for the two are contradictory.

10.   So let us return to what is contrary to fact. We say that when God (exalted be He!) foreknows that Zayd will be killed Saturday morning, for example, then we [ask], "Would the creation of life for Zayd on Saturday morning be possible or not possible?" The truth is that it is possible and impossible, that is, it is possible by considering it itself if nothing else is taken into account. [The creation of life for Zayd on Saturday morning] is impossible, however, owing to another, not in itself, namely, if in addition to [Zayd considered in himself] one takes into account [his being killed] itself and the knowledge itself, since [God's knowledge] would have been turned into ignorance [if the creation of life for Zayd were to occur on Saturday morning], but it is impossible that [God's knowledge] is turned into ignorance. So it has become evident that it is possible in itself, but impossible owing to a necessary impossibility in relation to another.

11.   So when we say that the life of Zayd at this moment is an object of power, we mean only that the life as life is not impossible, as would be joining black and white. The power of God (exalted be He!) insofar as it is power is neither inconsistent with nor incapable of creating life owing to some abatement, weakness, or some [other] cause with respect to the power itself. These are two things whose denial is impossible, I mean, (1) [one must] disavow impotency of the [divine] power itself, and (2) affirm the possibility in itself of life insofar as it is life only, without taking into account anything else.

12.   When the adversary says that [given God's foreknowledge of Zayd's death, Zayd's life] is not an object of power in the sense that its existence would lead to an impossibility, he speaks the truth concerning this meaning; for we do not deny it, but the inquiry into the expression ["object of power"] remains. Is it appropriate, with respect to the language, to apply this term to [the case of Zayd's life] or not? As everyone knows, the application of the expression is appropriate, for people say, such

and such a person has the power to move and to rest. If he wills, he is moved; if he wills, he rests. They also say that he has the power over the two contraries at every moment. They know that what takes place in God's [fore]knowledge (exalted be He!) occasions one of the two. So the applications [of this term] [54] are direct evidence of what we said, and the sense allotted to it is binding, there being no way to deny it.

13. *The Second Subsidiary Topic.* One might say that when you claim the extensiveness of the [divine] power with respect to its relation to the possibles, then what do you say concerning the objects of power of animals and other created things? Are they objects of God's power (exalted be He!) or not? If you say they are not objects of [divine] power, then you contradict your claim that the [divine] power's relation is extensive. If you say that they are His objects of power, then you have necessarily affirmed an object of power subject to two powers, which is absurd. Now to deny that humans and the other animals have power is to deny the necessary and to reject the demands of religious law, since it is impossible to demand something over which there is no power. It would be impossible for God to say to His servant, "You must undertake what is an object of power for me and over which I alone have exclusive power, whereas you have no power over it."

14. To digress a bit, we say that people have taken up varying sides on this [topic]. So the determinists believed that the servant's power is to be denied, and so they must deny the necessary difference between involuntary and voluntary movements and likewise the entrusting of religious law must be impossible for them. The Mu'tazilites[14] believed that the relation of God's power (exalted be He!) to the actions of the servants from among animals, angels, jinn, humans, and demons is to be denied. They alleged that all that proceeds from [the servants] belongs to the servant's creative act and origination, where [these actions] are not subject to God's power (exalted be He!) neither by way of precluding nor necessitating, and so two great repugnancies follow for them.

15. This first of them is the denial of what the forefathers (may God's peace be upon them!) [all] agreed upon, namely that there is no creator save God nor originator except Him.

16. The second is that [if, as they say, everything that proceeds from created things is owing to their own power alone and is not subject to divine power, then they must] ascribe origination and creation to the power of one who has no knowledge of the movements that he has [purportedly] created. [The reason is that] if [a Mu'tazilite] were asked about the number of motions that proceed from humans and other animals and their difference and scopes, he would be at a loss as to what to say about them. In fact, [the Mu'tazilites cannot explain why] the infant as he leaves his

---

14 The Mu'tazilites were a group of early Muslim speculative theologians who maintained that, in order for God to reward and punish us justly, we must have complete free will, and so our actions cannot be in any way determined by God.

crib crawls to [his mother's] breast and nurses, and the cat just as it was born, while its eyes are still shut, crawls to its mother's breast. [They also cannot explain why] spiders weave webs whose marvelous shapes amaze the geometer in their circularity, the parallelism of their sides, and the regularity of their arrangement, when [the spiders] are necessarily bereft of the knowledge of what geometers are incapable of recognizing. [They also cannot explain why, devoid of any knowledge of geometry], bees shape their hives as hexagons, and so in [a hive] there is no square, circle, septagon, or any other figure; that is because the hexagon is distinguished by a unique property that geometrical demonstrations have proven, which is not found in other [figures] and is based on certain [geometrical] axioms.

17.   One of [the geometrical axioms] is that [among] figures the one that encloses the greatest space and has the greatest area is the circle, which is free of exterior rectilinear angles. The second is that when circular figures are placed together, unoccupied gaps inevitably remain between them. The third is that with respect to enclosing space the closest of the figures with few sides to the circle is the hexagon. [55] The fourth is that when a set of any of the [other] figures approximating the circle, such as the septagon, octagon, and pentagon, are placed adjacent to one another, unoccupied gaps remain between them, and they do not fit together tightly. Although squares do fit together tightly, they are far from enclosing the space of a circle owing to the distance of their angles from their centers.

18.   Since bees need a figure approximating circles in order to contain the individual [bees]—for they [themselves] are approximately circular—and, owing to the limitation of their space and their great numbers, they must not lose any space through gaps interspersed between their cells that are not wide enough for the individual [bees], and [since] among the figures, despite their being infinite, only the hexagon is a figure that is approximately circular and has this special property, namely, when it is placed together it is devoid of remaining gaps within its arrangement,[c] God (exalted be He!) subjected the [bees] to choosing the hexagon in producing their cells. So, really, I would like to know, are the bees more cognizant of these details [than] intellectual humans, most of whom fail to grasp [the details]?! Or does the sole, unique Creator subjugate [the bees] in order to accomplish what is required through omnipotence courses, while they are in the middle as a conduit and so through them and in them God's foreordination flows (exalted be He!), and they neither comprehend it nor have any power to prevent it?

19.   Indeed, among the skills of the animals of this kind there are marvels that should I mention just a fraction of them, the breast would be filled with God's majesty (exalted and sublime is He!). Woe to those who stray from the path of God, those who are deluded by their limited power and weak ability, those who erroneously believe that they take part with God (exalted be He!) in creating, originating, and introducing the like of these marvels and signs. How absurd! How preposterous! The creatures were created low, and the Almighty of heaven and earth was alone without equal in sovereignty and dominion. These, then, are the kinds of repugnancies that follow upon the thought of the Mu'tazilites.

20.   Now consider orthodox Muslims, and how it was that they were guided to what is fitting and prepared for moderation in belief. Thus, they said that advocating determinism is a baseless absurdity, whereas advocating origination is an egregious affront. The truth is precisely to establish two powers over one act and to advocate an object of power correlated to the two powers. So only the improbability of the simultaneous occurrence of two powers over a single act remains, but this is improbable only when the interrelation of the two powers is according to a single perspective. So if the two powers differ and the perspective of their interrelation differs, then the simultaneous occurrence of the two interrelations over a single thing is not absurd, as we shall explain.

21.   If it is said, "What is it that drove you to affirm [one] object of power [shared] between two powers?" we say: [with respect to the creature's power] there is the absolute demonstration that voluntary motion is different from involuntary, even if the convulsion is assumed to belong to the one suffering the convulsion as something willed as well as something he wanted, there will be no difference save by power. Moreover, [with respect to God's power] there is the absolute demonstration that God's power (exalted be He!) is related to every possible, and every temporal event is possible, and the servant's act is a temporal event, so then [the servant's act] is possible; for if the power of God (exalted be He!) is not related to it, then it would be impossible.

22.   Indeed, we say that voluntary motion, as a motion that is a possible temporal event, is like involuntary motion, and so it would be impossible that the power of God (exalted be He!) should be related to one of the two, but fall short of the other, when the two are alike. In fact, another absurdity follows on it, namely, that if God [56] (exalted be He!) were to want to stop the servant's hand when the servant wanted to move it, then either the moving and the not moving exist together or both of them do not exist. In that case, however, it would lead to either the [simultaneous] joining of moving and not moving or to the absence of the two. The absence of the two, in addition to being a contradiction, would require nullifying both powers, since power is that by which the objects of power come to exist when the will and the susceptibility of the receptacle are both realized. So if the opponent erroneously believes that God's object of power (exalted be He!) is selectively determined because His power is greater, then there is an absurdity. [That is] because the relation of [one] power to a single motion does not surpass the relation to it of the other power, since the end result of the two powers is origination, whereas His power is only His having power over the other, but His having power over the other is not what selectively determines the motion, which is under discussion. Since the share of motion from each one of the two powers is that the originated thing comes to be by it, and the origination is similar, then one is neither stronger nor weaker with respect to [the origination] such that there is a selective determination. Thus, the absolute proof affirming two powers drove us to affirm an object of power [shared] between two powers.

23.   If it is said that proof does not lead to an incomprehensible absurdity, whereas what you have related is incomprehensible, we say that we must make it comprehensible. To wit, we say that God's (may He be praised!) origination of the

motion in the servant's hand is intelligible without the motion's being an object of power for the servant. But as long as He creates the motion and creates along with it a power over it, then He is the sole Author of the origination of both the power and the object of power. From [that] it arises that (1) He is unparalleled in originating, and (2) that the motion exists, and (3) that the one that is moved has a power over [the motion], and because he has a power his state is different from the state of the one suffering a convulsion. So all of the difficulties have been dispelled. The main point of [this] is that the one who has a power, which extends to [the creation of] power [itself], has a power over the origination of both power and the object of power. Also since the terms "Creator" and "Originator" apply to whoever brings something into existence through its power, and the power and the object of power are both within the power of God (exalted be He!), He is called "Creator" and "Originator." The object of power was not something originated through the power of the servant, even if it is together with him, and so [the servant] is called neither a creator nor an originator. So it was necessary to seek some other different term for this sort of relation, and so, as good fortune would have it, the term "acquisition" was demanded of it in God's Book [57] (exalted be He!); for the application of that [term] to the works of the servants was found in the Qur'ān.[15] As for the term "act," there has been reluctance to its application, but why quibble over terms after the meanings are understood.

24.   One might say,[16] "The issue concerns comprehending the sense, but what you have related is incomprehensible; for if the temporally created power has no relation to the object of power, then [that power] is incomprehensible, since a power that has no object of power is absurd just as a knowledge that has no object of knowledge is. If [the power] is related to it, then the power's relation to the object of power is intellected only insofar as there is the production of an effect and the bringing into existence and occurrence of the object of power by [that relation]. So the relation between the object of power and the power is the relation of the effect to the cause, namely, its being by means of it. So when it is not by it, then there is no connection and so no power, since whatever has no relation [to an object of power] is not a power, since power is among the attributes involving relations.

25.   We say that [power] is something related, and the relation of will and knowledge falsifies your claim that relation is limited to occasioning [something] by it. If you say that only power's relation is limited to occasioning [the object of power]

---

[15] Cf. Qur'ān 4:112 and 52:21.

[16] Here and in the next paragraph al-Ghazālī is considering the Muʿtazilites thesis that power exists only when the effect of that power exists. The Muʿtazilite argument for that thesis given here is that power is essentially a relative term and so must involve a relation; a power that is not related to anything, i.e., which brings nothing about, is in fact no power at all. Since power essentially involves a relation, and a relation exists only when both of its *relata* exist, then if the power's purported effect does not exist, then neither does the relation exist, in which case the power does not exist. The power then exists only when it occasions, or brings into existence, its correlated effect.

by [the power], it too is false; for in your opinion the power remains when it is assumed before the act. So is [the power that is prior to the act] something related or not? If you say, "No," then [the purported object of power] is impossible. If you say, "Yes," then what is meant by ["power"] is not the occasioning of the object of power by it, since the object of power had not yet been occasioned. So inevitably there is the affirmation of another kind of relation other than being occasioned by it, since the relation *at the moment* there is the temporal coming to be is designated by the expression "the occasioning [of something] by it," whereas the relation before that is different from it and so is some other kind of relation. So your claim that power's relation to [the object of power] is a single kind is mistaken. The same holds for the [divine] eternal power in their view, for it is something related to knowledge in the eternal past but before the creation of the world. So, then, our saying that [the divine eternal power] is something related is true, but our saying that the world is occasioned by it [at any moment God has the power] is false, because it had not yet been occasioned. If the two were to express a single sense, then one would assent to one of them wherever one assents to the other.

26. If it is said, "The sense of 'power's relation before occasioning the object of power' is that the object of power, when it is occasioned, is by [the power]," we say this is not a presently existing relation but an anticipation of a relation. So it ought to be said that the power exists, namely, as an attribute to which there is no relation, but it is expected to have a relation when the occasioning of the object of power by it is occasioned, and likewise for the one having the power. But an absurdity necessarily follows, namely, that the attribute that had nothing to do with related things comes to have something to do with the related things, which is absurd.

27. If it is said, "Its sense is that it is something predisposed to occasioning of the object of power," we say, the sense of being "predisposed" is nothing but the anticipation of the occasioning by it, but that does not require a presently existing relation. So just as in your opinion it is intelligible that a power exists related to the object of power, while the object of power is not occasioned by it, so likewise in our opinion it is intelligible that a power is like that and that the object of power is not occasioned by it, but will be occasioned by God's power (exalted be He!). So there is no difference between our position here and your position, except in our claim that [the power of the servant] was occasioned by God's power (exalted be He!). So when the existence of the object of power is neither from the existence of the power nor its relation to the object of power, from whence is the nonexistence of the occasioning of [the power of the servant] by God's power (exalted be He!) required, when its existence by God's power (exalted be He!) has no priority over its nonexistence insofar as the relation is disassociated from the temporally occurring power? [That question arises] since when the relation is not precluded by the nonexistence of the object of power, then how could it be precluded [58] by the existence of the object of power? So however the object of power is assumed, whether as existing or not existing, there inevitably is some related power that does not have a presently existing object of power.

28. If it is said, "'A power that does not occasion an object of power' and 'impotence' are tantamount to the same thing," we say that if you meant by it that the state [of having power over something] that the human perceives when it exists is like what one perceives when impotent with respect to involuntary motion, then it is to deny the necessary [difference between voluntary and involuntary motion]. If you mean that [the power] is tantamount to impotency in that that object of power was not occasioned by it, then it is true, but your calling it "impotence" is mistaken, even if it is supposed to be like impotency insofar as it is inadequate when compared to God's power (exalted be He!). This is as if one were to say, "The power before the act, according to their principle, is equivalent to impotence insofar as the object of power is not occasioned by it [at the present moment]," then the expression ["impotence"] would be denied inasmuch as [power] is a perceived state whose perception in the soul is different from the perception of impotence. The same holds for this. There is no difference! In summary, affirming two different powers is inevitable: one higher, the other resembling "impotence" as long as it is compared to the higher. You have the option between (1) affirming that the servant has a power, which in a certain way gives the appearance of ascribing impotence of the servant, or (2) affirming that [appearance of "impotence"] of God (may He be exalted and beyond what the deviators say!). Have no misgivings, if you are righteous, in that the ascription of inadequacy and impotence is more fitting of the creatures, but it is not said to be more fitting concerning God (exalted be He!) owing to the impossibility of that. This is the limit of what this brief outline of this issue can bear.

29. *The Third Subsidiary Topic.* One might say, "How can you claim the extensiveness of the [divine] power's relation to the totality of temporal events, when most of the motions and the like in the world are engendered things, some of which are necessarily engendered by others? [59] The motion of the hand, for example, necessarily engenders the motion of the ring, and the motion of the hand in water engenders the motion of the water, which is directly observed. Likewise, the intellect proves it, since if the motion of the water and the ring were by means of God's creation (exalted be He!), then He could create the motion of the hand without the motion of the ring and the motion of the hand without the motion of the water, which is absurd. The same is the case concerning [all] engendered things as well as their being disrupted."

30. We say that one cannot make an unbiased decision about what is not understood, either negatively or affirmatively, for it is after the position is intelligible that it is either rejected or accepted. Now in our opinion what is known concerning the expression "to be engendered" is that some body emerges from inside of another body, as the fetus emerges from the mother's belly and plants from the belly of the Earth. This is absurd with respect to accidents, since the motion of the hand has neither an inside, such that from it the motion of the ring emerges, nor is it something containing things such that from it part of what is in it emerges. So if the motion of the ring is not concealed in the very motion of the hand, then what is the meaning of its being engendered by it? So this must be made understandable. If this is not

understandable, then your claim that it is "directly observed" is fatuous, since the only thing that is directly observed is the temporal coming to be of [the motion of the ring] *together with* [the motion of the hand]. Its being engendered by it is not directly observed.

31.   You claim that if it were by means of God's creation (exalted be He!), then He would be in a position to create the motion of the hand without the [motion of] the ring and the water. This is lunacy akin to one's saying, "If knowledge were not engendered by the will, then [God] would be in a position to create the will without knowledge and knowledge without life." But we say that the impossible is not an object of power, and the existence of something that requires a condition without the condition is unintelligible. Now knowledge is a condition of the will, and life is a condition of knowledge. Likewise a condition of the substance's occupying space is that that space be empty. So when God (exalted be He!) moves the hand, He inevitably makes it occupy a space in proximity to where it was, but as long as [that space to which He moves the hand] is not empty, how could He make it occupy it? The [space's] being empty is a condition of its being occupied by the hand, since if it were moved and the space were not emptied of the water, whether by the loss of the water or [the water's] moving, then two bodies would be joined together in a single space, which is impossible. So being devoid of one of the two was a condition for the other, and so the two [i.e., the hand's moving in the water and the water's moving] were constantly conjoined, but it was erroneously supposed that one of them is engendered by the other, which is a mistake.

32.   As for the constant conjunctions that are not a condition, in our view they can be separated from the association of what is constantly conjoined with them.[17] In fact, its constant conjunction is the result of a conviction driven on by habit, such as the burning of cotton when placed near fire or the occurrence of coldness in the hand when it touches ice; for all of that continues on unabated through God's customary course (exalted be He!). Were it not [for God's custom], then the [divine] power, considered in itself, is not incapable of creating coldness in the ice and there being contact with the hand together with the creation of hotness in the hand instead of coldness.

33.   Thus, what the opponent believes to be [a single class of] engendered things [in fact] has two divisions: the first of them [involves] a condition, in which case only the [necessary] association is conceived with respect to it, whereas the second does not [involve] a condition, in which case no association is conceived with respect to it, when the habitual [course of affairs] is violated.

34.   One might say, "You have not proved the falsity of being engendered, but have denied understanding it, but it is understandable; for we do not intend by ["being engendered"] that the one motion exudes out of the [other] motion by the one's

---

[17] An extended discussion of "constant conjunction" and "habit" can be found in *The Incoherence of the Philosophers*, Discussion 17.

emerging from inside [the other]. Nor is the coldness engendered by the coldness of the ice through the coldness emerging from the ice, whether [by] its transference or emergence from the coldness itself. Instead we mean by ["being engendered"] [60] that an existence of an existing thing, [call it x], immediately follows [another] existing thing, [call it y], and the existence of x and having come to be is by means of y. We call what comes to be "what is engendered" and that by which there is the coming to be "what engenders." This designation of terms is understandable, and so, what proves it false?

35. We say that when you acknowledge that, then whatever proves the falsity of the temporal power's being an existing thing [in the sense you described above, namely, as something by whose existence another thing comes to exist] proves its falsity; for when we absurdly say [that] an object of power has occurred by means of a temporal power, then how could the occurrence not be imagined to be by means of what is not a power? Its impossibility is derived from the extensiveness of the [divine] power's relation: its emerging from the [temporal] power would nullify the extensiveness of the [divine] power, which is absurd. Moreover, it would necessarily render [the divine power] impotent and defeasible, as was previously [argued].

36. Indeed, against the Muʿtazilites who advocate engenderment, there are contradictions in the differentiation of engenderment too great to be numbered. An example is their claim that contemplation engenders knowledge, but recollection does not engender it. There are others as well that we shall not waste time mentioning; for there is no sense in bandying words on that which is dispensable.

37. From the whole of this you have come to recognize that all temporal events, both their substances and accidents [and] of them their coming to be in both animate and inanimate things, are occasioned by God's power (exalted be He!). He alone has control over their origination. It is simply not the case that some created things are occasioned by others; rather, everything is occasioned by [divine] power. That is what we wanted to explain with respect to establishing God's attribute of power (exalted be He!), and the extensiveness of its dominion and what derivative and inseparable attributes are connected with it.

IBN BĀJJA

The first of the great Andalusian philosophers, Abū Bakr Muḥammad ibn Yaḥyá ibn aṣ-Ṣāʾigh [at-Tujībī al-Andalusī as-Saraqusṭī] ibn Bājja, called Avempace in Latin, was born between 1085 and 1090 in Sargossa, Spain, purportedly of Jewish ancestry. He was living in that town when it fell in 1110 to the Almoravids, or al-Murābiṭūn, a dynasty of Berber origin that spread from North Africa to Spain and upheld a strict Malikite interpretation of Islamic law. Apparently on the basis of his ability as a poet, Ibn Bājja, while still a young man in his twenties, was appointed vizier to the Almoravid governor of the province, Abū Bakr ibn Ibrāhīm aṣ-Ṣahrāwī, known as Tīfalwīṭ; however, the appointment was short-lived and ended with the death of Tīfalwīṭ in 1116 or 1117. While serving as vizier Ibn Bājja was sent as part of an embassy to the still independent former ruler of Sargossa, ʿImād ad-Dawla, who had Ibn Bājja imprisoned, apparently on the charge of treason, but then released him after several months. Ibn Bājja shortly thereafter again found himself imprisoned, now on the charge of heresy, this time at the command of the Almoravid ruler Ibrāhīm ibn Tāshfīn, but, so the story goes, through the intervention of Ibn Rushd's father, or more likely grandfather, Ibn Bājja was released.

Ibn Bājja's fortunes were to take a favorable turn when again he was appointed vizier, now in Granada to the Almoravid governor Yaḥyá ibn Yūsuf ibn Tāshufīn, a position in which he served for twenty years. Despite the fact that the Almoravids adhered to a conservative Malikite interpretation of Islamic law and that the prominent legal scholars opposed philosophy, Andalusia at this time appeared to provide a positive environment for philosophy, Ibn Bājja took advantage of this fact, writing commentaries on Aristotle and Arabic-speaking philosophers as well as independent philosophical treatises. While still in the prime of his life he decided to travel to Oran, but died during his journey at Fez in May 1139, purportedly having been poisoned by the servant of one of his enemies.

Some thirty-odd treatises have come down to us by Ibn Bājja. These works may loosely be divided into three categories: (1) writings on music, astronomy, and logic, particularly commentaries on the logic of al-Fārābī; (2) works on aspects of natural philosophy, which would include primarily his commentaries on Aristotle's *Physics* and *De anima*; and (3) treatises representative of Ibn Bājja's own philosophical thought, the most important of which are *The Governance of the Solitary*, the *Epistle of Farewell*, and the *Epistle of Conjunction of the Intellect with Man*. As Ibn Bājja himself sometimes notes, and Ibn Ṭufayl complains one generation later, most of these works are either incomplete or hastily done with little, if any, subsequent polish and development. The result is that

266

much of Ibn Bājja's writings are disjointed and hard to follow; yet despite these short-comings, they are philosophically rich.

I. SELECTION FROM *COMMENTARY ON ARISTOTLE'S* PHYSICS[a]

1. [18] A problem arises since either all natural bodies are subject to generation and corruption (as we directly experience concerning all that we sensibly perceive), or some of them are not like that. Things subject to generation and corruption are like copper when it becomes verdigris or water when it becomes steam. On the one hand, (1) all of the copper might perish with the verdigris replacing it, where nothing of the copper remains. In that case, however, there is not generation but only succession; for if water originally comes from a pipe, but air replaces it, air is not in fact generated. On the other hand, (2) all of the copper might remain and the verdigris comes to be together with it. In that case, however, the verdigris would be [both] copper and verdigris, but that is not the case, unless the verdigris is an accident in the copper, but that also is absurd (for verdigris is a certain natural substance, which may be artificially fabricated). Necessarily, then, (3) something in the copper perishes and something remains, and it is in virtue of that thing that remains that the verdigris is said to be generated from the copper. Moreover, at the time when it was copper, it was not verdigris; nevertheless, if [the coming to be of the verdigris] is impossible, then it would not come to be at all, but since it is something that comes to be, it is possible.

2. So what is this that is said to be possible? Is the possibility a separate thing subsisting by itself, that is, is it a substance, or is it something in a subject? It [must be] in a subject, however, [because] "possible" indicates both a possibility and whatever the possibility is in. So the possibility of the verdigris, namely, the possible verdigris, is in that subject; however, when we find the verdigris [existing], the possibility has disappeared from it, and so the possible [verdigris] and the possibility [of verdigris] are only in the copper. [Recall], however, that it has been explained that the copper has two parts: the part that perishes and the part that remains. So which of them is the possible thing? That which perishes is not the possible thing, for the copper being copper is not verdigris. So the possible [verdigris] is the remaining part, [19] and its possibility is that it becomes verdigris. Now positing it as verdigris is not something absurd. Indeed, in *On Interpretation*, Aristotle defines "possible" as that which when we posit it as something existing, no absurdity necessarily results.[1] However, when the formal factor (*maʿnā*) of verdigris appears, the formal factor of possibility disappears. Hence, the subject of the form of verdigris and the subject of the possibility are numerically one, although their existence is different. Privation necessarily accompanies the possible, while existence accompanies the form (*ṣūra*)—in fact it is the existence. So is possibility the privation, just as the form is the existence, or not?

---

[1] The reference seems to be to *On Interpretation* 13, 23a7–19.

3. Now I maintain that the possible, as possible, does not have privation because of itself; for possibility is the subject's being disposed to the formal factor whenever that subject accidentally happens to have privation. [That is because] not only does the thing not essentially come to be from privation, but [privation] itself and its essence is that it not exist. Now possibility and what is exist in that the thing exists. So privation is something accidental to the possible, not because of what is possible, but rather because of the possibility in it, and there is privation because what is possible is something else, as if you mentioned either copper or a contrary form. Thus, the existence of the form in the possible is completely like alteration, and the alteration of the possible is only because of the privation. When this perfection of the possible takes time to complete, it is "motion" (as will become clear when we examine the account), whereas if it takes place instantaneously, then it has no specific name but is generally called "change."

4. If this possible subject is in itself an existing thing, that is to say it [has] a certain formal factor, then it necessarily follows that it is some actual body, and the first absurdity [(1)], returns, and so the copper and verdigris would be two accidents, which is absurd. Hence, [the subject of the possible] is not something actually existing. An existing thing, however, might be generated from more than one actually existing thing, such as oxymel (for it comes from honey and vinegar), and so when each is separate from the other, [each] is an existing thing, but when they are like that [i.e., separated], there is no oxymel until the two are blended and a single thing comes to be in the whole. Also, as long as we assume that the matter has a form, it necessarily follows that it is something divisible into matter and form, and were that to continue infinitely, then there would be an infinite number of matters in this verdigris, which is not only repugnant but absurd. Thus, one must end at a matter that has no form. Obviously, whatever has this description is "prime matter," where I mean by "prime" that it has no matter. Clearly, it is not subject to generation and corruption, because if it were subject to generation and corruption, it would necessarily have a form, which is absurd. Also obvious is that it is not separate from the form. That is [because], if it is separate [20] from form, then it does not exist at all, and if it exists, then it necessarily follows that it is a certain thing, and the issue returns to its having matter and not being prime.

5. So on the basis of what has been explained, let it be settled that prime matter is that whose existence is essentially without a form, and that indeed privation always accompanies its existence—not a single privation, but privations that replace one another. Moreover, possibility is not its form; for one possibility after another occurs successively in it just like the privations occur successively in it. Here, then, one understands first matter itself. The conception preferred before this investigation was only by way of analogy, and there is no [exact] analogue [for prime matter] that can take place in the analogy;[2] for [prime matter] is conceived as something whose

---

[2] Cf. Aristotle, *Physics* I 7, 191a7–12.

relation to the elements is like the relation of wood to a wardrobe, but this relation is like a relation between two actually existing things, whereas the former relation is between something existing potentially and something existing actually. Thus when the one is substituted for the other, the relation of [prime] matter to the wood is not like the relation of the wardrobe to the <elements>,[b] but perhaps this relation is conceived after there is wood.

6. In summary, every body is something having matter, and [every body] comes to be a matter precisely because this [prime matter] exists in it, but whenever you explain this [prime matter], it cannot be something having matter. Moreover, it is not something possible in a certain way and according to a certain condition. Therefore, it is not subject to motion, but if it is not subject to motion, then it is not subject to rest (except metaphorically, since whatever cannot undergo motion is designated as something at rest, where "being at rest" is said of this privation by way of simile, as we shall defend when we examine the position). In what we have presented we have reached the limit of what can be said concerning this kind of cause, and we have certainty and scientific knowledge about its existence commensurate with what is known about its nature. This is the most that can be known about this cause.

II.   CONJUNCTION OF THE INTELLECT WITH MAN[a]

1. [155] Peace be upon you to a degree suited to your desire to acquire virtues. Since I believe that it would be impractical for us to meet at this time, I thought that I should not delay and send you this piece of knowledge whose demonstration I found and about which I have arranged the account as something written with an eye to natural philosophy according to what I know you understand. Its technical account is too long, and a clearer explanation [would require] both numerous syllogisms and stronger premises. Shortness of time and a constant preoccupation with my obligations have dissuaded me from proving it that way (if I have some free time to prove it in a technical manner, I shall send it to you); for I hurried to send it now wary of losing it given the size and peculiar nature that it is.

2. I say that "one" is said in ways that have been concisely presented in both [Aristotle's] Metaphysics[3] and al-Fārābī's [156] book On Unity.[4] I shall proceed from that to what is required for this discussion. "One" is said specifically, generically, and accidentally, and in summary of what is common in a given universal. The subject of this kind of one is many, for individual horses are one in species, and all of the individual plants are one in genus.

3. "One" is also said numerically, and it is that to which I shall proceed here. The continuous thing is said to be one as long as it is something continuous, but

---

[3] Metaphysic Δ (V), 6.

[4] See Al-Fārābī, Kitāb al-wāḥid wa-l-waḥda, Muhsin Mahdi, ed.

when it is divided, then it becomes many. ["One"] is said of what coalesces when it resembles what is continuous, and is said of what is concentrated when it resembles what coalesces, and is also said of what is connected when it resembles what is concentrated. ["One"] is said of the combined sum that is numbered according to some defined aim, as it is said that Ṭabarī's *History*[5] is a single composition and that this [present] work is one. Also the mixed sum is said to be one, as it is said concerning oxymel, that is, what is composed of vinegar and honey. (Now it is often erroneously believed that this kind [of one, namely, being one numerically], is included in the kinds that were previously enumerated; however, when the issue is carefully considered, it becomes apparent that it is different.)

4.   Likewise, incorporeal[6] forms are said to be one, like a form of a certain imagined city where one with respect to incorporeal forms is like one with respect to material forms. Similarly, being one is said with respect to the object of intellect when it is indicated by a single term and is an intelligible object of some one existing thing. Also, it is said that [the intelligible object] is one when it is an intelligible object of one thing, even if it is indicated by a composite expression such as the definition, the description, and what is like these. "One" is often said of the intelligible object when a singular expression indicates it as well as by a composite expression [consisting of] a qualification, for example, "the white human" or "the writing geometrician." This, however, is not one, because when it is applied to the example, "the writing geometrician is a given human," there is not one proposition but two. [157] Aristotle has already presented all of this concisely in *On Interpretation*.[7] When a single intelligible object is defined, it is broken up into its [intelligible] parts, and whatever is entailed in the initial parts is entailed in the subsequent multiple parts, but one must terminate at parts that are not defined. At that time they are something simple in every way. These are the kinds [of unity] presented concisely elsewhere.

5.   When what is numerically one is a body or of a body (like white, for instance), it is said to belong to an individual. What is numerically one and abstracted from matter, however, is not an individual but is analogous to it in the case where the individual undergoes change. Let us assume an individual man (for the investigation of the present treatise concerns what is specific to the human). He existed as a fetus when he was in the womb, and then exists as an infant immediately after his birth. He next exists as an adolescent, then a young man, a middle-aged man, and finally an old man. Also he may be educated or ignorant, literate or illiterate, yet he is numerically one, not passing away in that respect. Now when he is sensibly observed in one of these states, and then later observed in another much later state, it is not known

---

5 The *History* of Muhammad ibn Jarīr aṭ-Ṭabarī (ca. 838–923 C.E.) is a universal history ostensibly extending from creation to 915 C.E. It is said that aṭ-Ṭabarī limited his history to a mere thirty volumes for the sake of his students.

6 *Rūḥānīya*, lit. "spiritual" or "psychic."

7 *On Interpretations* 2.

whether he is the former one or not (for instance, observing him as an infant and then as a young man). Thus, sensory perception does not reach that by which the human is one, but only some other faculty reaches it. In like manner, if you cut off a person's hands or pluck his eyes out, or in general, if you remove all of the limbs that he does not require for life, he is still said to be one and the same. Again, the teeth of the small child fall out, and then he has different, permanent teeth, but he is one and the same. Similarly, if it were possible for one to have two legs and hands that replaced two damaged legs and hands, that one would be the same. In this case it is like the carpenter who has lost an adz or ruler and then takes up another one; the carpenter with the first tool is no different than the carpenter with the tool that replaced it. Likewise, were it possible that he conversely had additional limbs, he would still be one and the same.

6.   So it is obvious from this discussion that as long as the initial mover remains one and the same, that one existing is [158] one and the same, whether he has lost his bodily instruments or some part (such as the toothless old man), or acquires a part (like the [child] who grows teeth). Since some of those who investigated natural science stopped at this, that led them to the doctrine of transmigration,[8] but it has already been made clear elsewhere that the doctrine of transmigration is impossibly absurd;[9] however, its proponents wanted certain things and were at a standstill without it, and so they took the initial mover in the human as an undifferentiated whole, making numerically one what was not one.

7.   The initial mover in humans is something proper that brings about motion by means of two kinds of instruments. The first is corporeal and the second is incorporeal, where some of the corporeal [instruments] are voluntary and others are involuntary. [In the case of voluntary instruments], they are like the hand, leg, and lung, which [voluntarily] play the flute. The involuntary instruments that have specific extremities are called "organs," like sinew, whereas those that are fluid, like bile, do not have a name from the perspective that they are instruments. Taken as a whole [the instruments] are called "body," and those that are involuntary are prior to the voluntary. Also, it is said about the hand that it is the instrument of instruments.

8.   Some of these involuntary instruments are prior and others posterior, such as sinew, which is prior to muscle, and the innate heat, which is prior to all of them. In reality and priority the innate heat is the instrument of instruments; for certain instruments that are not being used, such as the flute or staff, might beckon the hand, whereas the innate heat cannot deviate from its work, being an involuntary tool not a voluntary one. Each part existing in the body, whether an organ or fluid, is related

---

[8] Ibn Bājja appears to understand *tanāsukh* not in its proper sense of transmigration but in the sense of panpsychism, that is, the position that there is but a single soul for all humans.

[9] In the chapter on sense perception of Ibn Bājja's *Kitāb an-Nafs*, he said that in the section on the rational faculty he would explain the absurdity of assuming that an individual human soul pre-exists the body, which seems close to the traditional view of transmigration. Unfortunately, not all of the section on the rational faculty is extant and there is no discussion of the absurdity in the part that is extant.

to the innate heat, which even exists at the extremity of the body. You can determine this from Aristotle's book *On the Usefulness of the Organs of the Body* in the later treatises of the *Book of Animals*.[10] Innate heat is found in everything possessing blood as well as in bloodless animals, such as insects[b] and what is analogous. The innate heat is called "innate vital spirit," on account of being an instrument of the motive faculty, being [the innate vital spirit's] form and initial mover, whereas "spirit" is said of the soul and according to what we have described. There is something analogous in plants, except that the similarity is far removed from [159] the innate vital spirit that is summarized in the *De anima*.[11] My goal in the present treatise is only what is specific to humans.

9. For a while a certain state might belong to humans by which they are similar to plants, namely, during the time that they are in the womb; for there is an initial formation, and then when their formation is perfected, they take nourishment and grow. These are activities that belong to plants from the beginning of their existence, and they have no others from the beginning of their existence and so on[c] during [their] development. Innate heat might produce these actions. At the moment when the fetus departs from its mother's belly and uses its senses, it is like the animal lacking reason, which moves about and desires. That is due to the presence of an incorporeal form that is imprinted on the common sense and then on the imagery faculty, where the imagined form is what initially moves him. So at that time there are three movers in the human as if at a single rank: the appetitive-nutritive faculty, the faculty for observable growth, and the imagery faculty. All of these faculties are active faculties, that is to say, they are actual with no privation in them. This is the difference between the active and passive faculties; for there is privation in what is acted on, because the incorporeal, perceptible form is the first of the incorporeal ranks, and (as was explained in the *Governance of the Solitary*), because perception is [a passive faculty], and the body in which there are those other forms <neither>[d] perceives by means of them nor perceives them, the [capacity to] recognize, therefore, is not at all associated with plants, whereas it is so associated with animals.[12]

10. Every animal is something that senses, and sensation is an incorporeal form by which the animal perceives that body, and so the animal is never devoid of the capacity to recognize. So when the human is in the womb and resembles plants, he is said to be an animal merely potentially. That is to say, his innate vital spirit is receptive to the incorporeal form and so will be an animal by that reception, whereas [160] the innate vital spirit in the plant cannot have that in it. The cause of why this

---

[10] Although *On the Usefulness of the Parts of the Body* is the title of one of Galen's works, the reference appears to be to Aristotle's *Parts of Animals* II 1 and 4.

[11] Perhaps a reference to *De anima* II 4, 416b28–29.

[12] Ibn Bājja's point is that plants do not perceive because they lack the passive faculty to be acted upon by perceptible forms, even though those perceptible forms exist in them, whereas animals have the required passive faculty to be affected by perceptible forms.

innate vital spirit is receptive of the form, whereas that one is not receptive to it, is the elemental mixtures. (There is another account about this that is often concisely presented as part of natural science, but presenting it concisely in a sufficient way would merit a separate discussion).[13]

11. The individual may be a potential or actual animal. So let us approach it with respect to its condition by which it is an actual animal but a potential human, namely, when it is still a nursing infant and the faculty of discursive thought has not come to it (the treatise *The Governance of the Solitary* has sections treating the conditions of the human); for it is precisely by the faculty of discursive thought that there is at that time a human. The faculty of discursive thought is present only when intelligible objects are present, and so by the presence of intelligible objects there comes to be a desire that moves one to discursive thought and whatever results from it. It is by the latter, not the former, that there is the individual [human].[14] It has been explained elsewhere[15] that the intelligible objects are not forms of the innate vital spirit; for they are not forms of bodies, and they cannot be that [namely, forms of the innate vital spirit] unless they are material. For example, the stone is in matter only when it is an individual stone. The intelligible object, however, is not at all a form belonging to matter, nor is it an incorporeal form belonging to a body in such a way that the existence of that body is through [that form] like images; rather, it is a form whose matter is the incorporeal, intermediary form in the imagery. (What is proper to these incorporeal intermediary forms has been concisely presented in *The Governance of the Solitary*, namely, what kind of existence they have.) So it is not something connected with body, but moves the body only by means of incorporeal forms, which are its instrument (this has been summarized in the *Epistle of Farewell*). Thus, the initial human mover is the actual intellect, that is, the actual intelligible object; for the actual intellect is the actual intelligible, just as someone else has explained in his writings and I have concisely presented in [my] *De anima* concerning the rational faculty (for I had completed the discussion in most of that work). When [161] it is complete, I shall not delay sending it to you, O illustrious vizier, given what I know of your desire for this kind of virtue and your natural receptivity to it, but now I must not delay what I am writing specifically for you on these sciences. It is the most sublime of the sciences in worth, the most desired of them, and the most noble of them to be acquired, because all other sciences exist for the sake of this science, which has been

---

[13] See Ibn Bājja's *Kitāb an-Nafs*, ch. III, "Discourse on the Faculties of Sense Perception."

[14] That is, it is by the possession of the intelligible object in the faculty of discursive reason, not just by having the faculty of or potentiality for discursive reason ("faculty" and "potentiality" both translate *qūwa fikrīya*), that one is a human.

[15] The reference appears to be to part three of Fakhry, ed., *The Governance of the Solitary*, "The doctrine of the incorporeal forms, (*qawl fī ṣ-ṣuwar ar-rūḥānīya*), 37–95, esp. 49–95.

concisely presented in several places. Upon my life, however, you have surpassed your fellow kinsmen, since you were patient and long-suffering in its great toil until you reached the point where you understand what is said about it at first glance and are able to see it to completion properly. That over which you have toiled with long-suffering is that from which the students of this science flee, limiting themselves to what is beneath it.

12.　In an absolute sense, the actual intellect is the human's initial mover. Clearly, the actual intellect is an active faculty—and not only the intellect alone, but also all of the motive forms are active faculties. (The difference between active and passive faculties has been concisely presented in the *Epistle of Farewell* and other places, as well as a sufficient amount of previous oral communication about it.)

13.　So the intellect is an active faculty, and the "rational faculty" refers primarily to the incorporeal form, on account of its receiving the intellect and being said of the actual intellect. It is [the rational faculty] that al-Fārābī means by his doubt whether it is something existing in the infant, which moisture changes, or whether it comes to be through something else.

14.　If this intellect is numerically one in every human, then clearly, from what has been concisely presented before, people who exist (both those who have passed away and those who remain) are numerically one, but this is deplorable and perhaps absurd. If people who exist (both those who have passed away and those who remain) are not numerically one, then this intellect is not one. In sum, if this intellect is numerically one, then all the individuals who have the equivalent of this intellect are numerically one. It is as if you were to take a magnet and roll it around in wax, and then it moved that piece of iron or some other piece of iron, and then you rolled it around in pitch, and then it moved the piece of iron the same way, and then you rolled it around in some other bodies, then all of those moving bodies would be numerically one, [162] just like the case of the captain of a ship. The former case is like the latter case except that with respect to bodies one of them cannot be in [several] individual bodies like there can be with respect to intelligibles. This is what the advocates of transmigration believed, except they stopped short of it.

15.　Clearly, this intellect, which is one, is a reward and blessing of God bestowed upon whomever of His servants with Whom He is well pleased. Thus, [this intellect] is not the one who is rewarded and punished; rather, it is the reward and blessing bestowed upon the whole of the soul's faculties. Now reward and punishment belong only to the appetitive soul, which is sinning or doing right. So whoever obeys God and does what pleases Him will be rewarded with this intellect, and He will make before him a light by which he will be guided. Whoever disobeys Him and does what displeases Him will remain shrouded in the shadows of ignorance until [his soul] separates from the body, being concealed from him and remaining in His displeasure. The latter are the classes of those who do not apprehend by discursive reasoning, and therefore God completes their knowledge through Religious Law. To whomever He gives this intellect, then, when he separates from the body, he remains a light of lights that extols and glorifies God together with the prophets and companions as well as the martyrs and the pious souls, and he is judged an intimate friend by those.

16. As for investigating the actual intelligibles, [one must first ask] whether every one of them is numerically one or not. If not, then whether one of them is more than numerically one. If not, then we have already addressed that on a different occasion, which has been concisely presented in [my] *De anima*.[16] When what I have to say about that is completed, I will send it to you, but I thought it right that I should address that here to the extent that what preceded I know will be a reminder for you.

17. Whenever we posit that every intelligible is numerically one, there necessarily follows an opinion akin to that of those who adhere to transmigration, where having a superior nature does not benefit one, and following the life of nature is greater than much beneficial knowledge. As for the kind of [knowledge], it will belong to every human as part of the natural course, and thus teaching will not provide qualitatively [different knowledge], but only quantitatively [more knowledge]. In addition to which, there will be all the other repugnant things that follow upon this assumption. If we do not [163] assume that [each intelligible] is one, then that assumption also entails absurdities that are no worse than the former. Among other things, the intelligible that you and I possess will have an intelligible, and likewise you and I will possess that intelligible and so it will have another intelligible, and so on infinitely, but an infinite in this respect does not exist.

18. Since each one of the extremes of this disputation has been given its proper due, it becomes clear that the intelligibles of existing things (that is, the categories and their species) are a composite of something that remains and something transient that passes away. In other words, you initially receive [the intelligibles] insofar as they are perceptions of their subjects, and an intelligible results from them that became related to those subjects as subsisting through that relation. Thus we say concerning a horse that it is an intelligible of a certain thing, whereas we say that the monoped[17] and ogre are in no way intelligibles of a certain thing. So, insofar as they have this relation to their subjects, from which they come to be and by which they belong to the mind, they must be related to certain subjects, but those subjects may be different from the subjects from which they are present in the mind of Zayd. For example, the universal concept (*maʿná kullī*) indicated by "horse" is an intelligible concept, as explained in numerous places, and it comes to be an intelligible only from individuals that may be different from the individuals from which "steed" comes to be an intelligible for Zayd, and moreover different from the individuals from which it comes to be an intelligible for you. Thus, we do not have an intelligible of elephant and giraffe, when we have not experienced them; for the concept indicated by these expressions is not an intelligible possessed by whomever has never experienced one of their instances, except by

---

16 The reference appears to be to a non-extant section on the rational faculty in Ibn Bājja's *Kitāb an-Nafs*.

17 *Nasnās*, lit. a mythological species of humanlike creatures having one arm and one leg, who live in woods.

way of simile, but as for the intelligible concept itself, no. As for myself, since I have experienced them, I possess an intelligible of them; however, it is tied to the individual that I have experienced. This is clear in itself, and to extend it is superfluous to the discussion.

19.   The intelligible, insofar as it has this relation, passes away with the passing away of that to which it is related, as was explained in the *Categories*;[18] for two related things exist together simultaneously either potentially or actually. That becomes clear [164] when the two are examined carefully; for whoever has a son is a father, but if the son dies, then he *had been* a father but is not now a father. The individuals to which the intelligible in some particular human are linked might be destroyed, but their incorporeal forms remain, in which case he is related to those incorporeal forms and so intellects only though them and about them. If we assume these incorporeal forms are destroyed together with the human's existence (and that by annihilation), there will be no conjunction with the intelligible for that annihilated person; for the conjunction of the person with the intelligible is only together with the incorporeal form, and that incorporeal form results from the senses, as has been explained in other places. Because of that the intelligibles are present during sleep, and the dreamer is aware of them and so judges that the form of the wild beast that he sees during the dream is a wild beast.

20.   The masses, all of them, know the universals only in this way, because it is the initial way. The same holds for the theorist; for those who try to philosophize either do so about practical matters, and so know the working of these matters in this way, just like carpentry and medicine, or they do so about theoretical matters. If the [theoretical matters] are mathematical, then they are imperfect intelligibles, because they do not exist in the way in which the [theorists] conceptualize them, since their images and intelligible objects are virtually fictional inventions, because part of that through which they exist is unknown. In general, [mathematicians] know a part by means of the sensible objects that they substitute for their particular existing instances, as in geometry. In sum, what mathematics employs is that which is before the eye. The same is true for the natural philosopher; for his condition with respect to the intelligibles is the same as the condition of the masses, since their conjunction with the intelligibles is by one and the same means and on the basis of one and the same practice. [Natural philosophers] are superior only to the extent of the superiority of the conceptualization. Even when the natural philosopher knows the soul, he also conjoins with intelligibles that he acquires from psychology by means of things that substitute for the particular existing instances similar to his state when there is the forming of images by the imagery faculty and common sense; for at that moment he has present an incorporeal form of a given individual, and thereupon he investigates it from the perspective of the way it exists [namely, that it is incorporeal], not from the perspective that it is something perceived from a given material thing. So when

---

18 See Aristotle, *Categories* 7, 7b1ff.

[the natural philosophers] perceive its intelligible, they do so only by virtue of those forms as they are corruptible. So if it were possible for these [forms] to be annihilated, then, [165] as a result of their no longer being conceptualized, their intelligible would cease. That is to say, the material is connected with the intelligible only by means of the incorporeal forms. This again is the initial and natural way and is common to both [the natural philosophers] and the masses.

21.   The various sorts of theorists will differ from [the masses] only by investigating these existents; for the masses and their like are aware of the incorporeal forms only on account of the perceptions of the subjects as they are sensible bodies, not insofar as they have this existence [namely, that they are incorporeal]. So whoever is aware of this existence and investigates the intelligibles resulting from those things existing in this way comes to have this rank. He is separated from the masses as a whole by a mode of existence of which the masses are unaware and nature does not provide. Still, he does have something in common with the masses in a relative way; for his conjunction with the intelligibles of these existing things is like the masses' conjunction with the intelligibles of material things, because the relation of this one to the incorporeal forms is the [same] relation as that one to the corporeal forms.

22.   The natural philosopher, again, progresses further and so investigates intelligibles not as intelligibles, which are termed "material" and "corporeal," but as one of the things existing in the world. So I propose that there is present among [the things existing in the world] a certain intelligible whose relation to the intelligible subject is the relation of that intelligible to its particular instance, such that that species of intelligibles is a mean in the relation, and so only by that third intelligible in rank does the human conjoin with and see the first intelligible.

23.   So the human initially has the incorporeal form according to its ranking, and then by means of it he conjoins with the intelligible, and thereupon by means of this intelligible he conjoins with that other intellect. Hence, the progression from the incorporeal form is like ascending, and, if the case can exist contrarily, it is like descending. So that conjunction with the intelligibles according to the physical perspective is like the intermediate position in the ascent, and because it is in the intermedial position between the two extremes we [166] therefore find that [humans] simultaneously have two conditions: they are material *and* their intellect is a material intellect. By means of that [that is, the materiality] their intellects are many, and so it is assumed that the intellect is many. That is to say, the related thing is related to what is itself a related thing. Since the intelligible concept they possess is a related thing, and the particular instances of its relation are many, the relation of the intelligible "human" to the particular instances of human in the mind of Jarīr[19] is different from the relation of the intelligible "human" to its particular instances in the mind of Imru' al-Qays.[20] Through this relation "human" is an intelligible belonging to both

---

[19] Jarīr ibn ʿAṭīya ibn al-Khaṭafa ibn Badr, post-Islamic poet, fl. 680.

[20] Probably Imru' al-Qays ibn Ḥudr, pre-Islamic poet, fl. 550.

[Jarīr and Imru᾽ al-Qays] and to all of the masses. These relations are infinitely many, and hence the intellects are many from one perspective but one from another. Thus, the majority cannot be in this mode [of existence] but fall into following that which is contained in the previously mentioned problematic account.

24.   The intellect, whose intelligible is itself, does not have an incorporeal form that serves as its subject, and so the intellect understands of itself whatever it understands of the intelligible. Moreover, it is one without being many, since it already is devoid of the relation by which the form is related to the matter. Contemplating this aspect is the Afterlife, namely, the ultimate uniquely human happiness, and at that moment that person having the experience experiences the sublime. Since the contemplation of something and its being intellected are only in that the one contemplating comes to have the concept (*ma῾nā*) of the thing while he is abstracting it from its matter, and [since] the concept that we intend to intellect is a concept and it has no concept, [the following things must be true about this intellect]. (1) This intellect's act is its substance. (2) There can be neither decay nor corruption in it. (3) What moves it is itself what is moved. (4) As Alexander of Aphrodisias says in his book *On the Incorporeal Forms*, it is self-referring. (5) It is numerically one. (6) The first mover is an exemplar,^e and whoever is like it is numerically one but many by means of the instruments, whether incorporeal or corporeal. (This has been outlined in the *Epistle of Farewell*.) So if it were possible for someone to reach the rank, being able to return and descend, that would [involve both] being moved and causing [itself] to be moved; however, that is not possible.[21] Thus some of the Sufi masters say, [167] "Had they arrived, they would not return." In the opinion of Aristotle and those following him, however, there can be the state similar to descent and return. Examples of the meaning that these names indicate are the intellect at those intermediate ranks, namely, insofar as it has the states of ascent.

25.   So it has become clear from what I have said that there are three stages: one of them is the rank of the masses, namely, the physical rank. The intelligible that the masses have is something linked merely with material forms, without knowing [the intelligible] except by, as a result of, as part of, and belonging to [those material forms]. Included in this is all of the practical skills. The second is theoretical knowledge, which is the apex of natural philosophy. However, the masses consider the subjects first, and the intelligible second and for the sake of the subjects, whereas the theoretical natural philosophers consider the intelligible first, and the subjects second and for the sake of <the intelligible as similar>.^f Thus [the theoretical natural philosophers] consider the intelligible first; however, [they also consider] the material forms together with the intelligible. Because of that [namely, the material forms], all logical propositions used in the sciences include a subject and predicate to which one can point, whereas because

---

[21] Stated slightly differently, since "being moved" is an effect, and "causing to be moved" is a cause, one and the same thing would be both the cause and effect of itself, which is absurd.

of that [other] one [namely, what is intelligible], the logical propositions are universal. For it is already clear in "Every human is an animal," that there is a third [element] that Arabs omit in explaining the meaning of this statement, just as they omit the conjunctive particle ["then"]; for "Every human is an animal" indicates the same thing as, "Whatever is a human, *then* it is an animal," as well as, "Anything described as 'human,' *then* that thing is described as 'animal.'" Instances of this expression are either synonymous, or they indicate consequential aspects that mutually entail one another. Obviously the preceding is different from "Human is a species or intelligible," which has been outlined in several places. So the one holding this theoretical rank sees the intelligible but through an intermediary, just as the Sun appears in the water; for the thing visible in the water is its reflection, not it itself. The masses see a reflection of its reflection, just like the reflection of the Sun crossing over the water while it is reflected into a mirror, where one sees in the mirror that which does not belong to an individual. The third is the rank of the happy who see the thing in itself.

26.   [168] Consider now (God give you strength!) and affirm what I say, spending time verifying it until you see it more distinctly than the face of the summer Sun at noontime, because it is the most similar thing to sunlight. So just as when we do not have light, we find ourselves visually blind, and the blindness is a certain evil (where the difference between trying to see in light and in darkness is self-evident), it is the same for the ignorant person and whoever does not know something. "To know something" means that the one who knows has the predicate of [the thing] as his intelligible. Judging that that intelligible applies to certain individual instances at one time and not another is like trying [to see]; and the faculty in which the intelligible is impressed is like the eye; and the intellect is like seeing (that is, the form impressed during seeing). Just as that form is by means of light—for light makes it actual and by it [the form] is impressed in sensation—it is the same for the actual intellect. That intellect, which does not have an individual instance, comes to be a certain thing when it is impressed into the faculty. Also, just as this form causing sight is what leads one on his way, not the separate light, this actual intellect is what leads one on his way and guides. In fact, if the form causing sight were impressed on the eye during darkness, [the eye] would not require light; however, that is not possible, since its subsistence and existence is through the light. The same holds for the state concerning the actual intellect and the Active Intellect. The relation between the two is identical: what the light is with respect to the sensible form, so also [the Active Intellect] (which is a light in a certain way by analogy) is with respect to the intelligibles.

27.   So the state of the masses with respect to the intelligibles is like the states of those who see in a cave where the Sun does not shine on them, and so they see it, but they see all the colors in shadows. So whoever is in the cave's depths sees in a state equivalent to darkness, whereas whoever is at the cave's mouth sees the colors in the shadows. All of the masses see existing things merely in a state equivalent to the shadows. Since they see a portion of that light, then just as it seems to the inhabitants of the cave that the light does not exist separated from colors, so likewise it will seem to the masses, not being aware of that intellect, that it does not exist. The theorists

step outside of the cave and so see light separated from colors and see all the colors according to their true nature. There is no [169] equivalent in [the example of] seeing for the happy, since they themselves become the thing. So, if sight were to alter and so become light, then at that moment, it would arrive at the stage of happiness. The allegory of the state of happiness with the state of whoever views the Sun itself is not comparable to the state of the masses; rather, the allegory of the state of the masses is more comparable and well-connected to this [aspect of reality]. Since Plato posits [separate] Forms, his allegory of the state of happiness with the state of viewing the Sun is comparable with the state of the masses, and so his allegory is comparable [in all of its] elements.

28.   Here one must know that the Form that Plato posits, but Aristotle rejects, is as follows. They are Ideas (*maʿān*) separate from matter that the mind apprehends, just as the senses apprehend the forms of perceptible objects, to the extent that the mind is like the faculty of sensation for the forms or the faculty of reason for the objects of imagination. From that it follows that the intelligible Ideas of those forms are simpler than those forms. So there are three things: (1) the sensible ideas, (2) the forms, and (3) the Ideas of the forms. The refutations leveled against the Forms concern only the following aspect, namely, Plato designated them by the name of the thing and defined them by [the thing's] definition. We say concerning the incorporeal form of man, [or fire], for instance, that they are a form of man or a form of fire, but we do not say that they are a realm. Likewise, we say of our intelligible that whatever it is in is fire, but we do not say about the intelligible that it *is* fire; if it were fire, then it would burn. Socrates says about the Form that he posits that it *is* the Good and it *is* the Beautiful and that the human *is*[g] the Idea of Human. [Consequently], the absurdities that Aristotle mentioned in his *Metaphysics*[22] do follow [from Plato's account of Form]. All of those *aporiai* fall away from the present view. Thus, that which we have advocated—when taken freed of the aforementioned relation—is a single thing remaining, neither passing away nor corrupting.

29.   So suppose that that rank belongs to a certain individual—let it be Aristotle—and so Aristotle [170], for instance, is that intellect that was described before, two ranks being below him. So the masses will see[h] the forms by means of that [intellect], but they will see it as they see light reflected from surfaces possessing colors. So they are guided by it in a way, just as others in the shadows are guided by the Sun. So they are not Aristotle, but Aristotle had been in a state similar to theirs, and they have one or another of Aristotle's [previous] states. The second rank (that is, the vision of the natural philosophers when they achieve the definition)[23] sees this intellect, but as something joined to some other thing by which they see it, just as the disc of the

---

22 For example, Aristotle, *Metaphysics* Z (VII) 14.

23 Ibn Bājja's point is that when the natural philosophers arrive at the definition of a thing, they no longer are considering merely particular material things, like those in the first rank; rather, they have reached something universal, albeit a universal that is linked with particular material things.

Sun is seen in the mirror and in the middle of the water. So they have advanced further, and yet they still see [this intellect] with the third rank [that is, as something associated with matter].

30.   Those, such as Aristotle and the rest of the happy, are numerically one, and there is no distinction between them in any way, except for the difference that I shall use as an example. It as if Rabīʿa ibn Mukarram[24] were to approach us, wearing a breastplate and an iron helmet and gripping a spear and sword, and we saw him in this attire, and then, after he is hidden from our sight, he approaches [again], but wearing a coat of mail and a plumed headpiece and using a javelin and mace, and then [we] instinctively assume that he is someone other than Rabīʿa ibn Mukarram. [This is because] the members of the spiritual body are analogous to the organs of the animal's body. Since they are involuntary, they are one and the same for one and the same thing. Now the incorporeal form in the body serves the members only at first. The incorporeal forms cannot be one and the same; for we have already explained that this is absurd: it is the doctrine of the transmigrationists. This intellect serves them in a number of ways, the most obvious being by means of the intermediary incorporeal form (the account of which has been concisely presented in *The Governance of the Solitary*).

31.   So whoever puts his body ahead[i] of the incorporeal form (howsoever their various kinds were concisely presented in *The Governance of the Solitary*), he and his body will pass away and corrupt. In that case he is like an unpolished surface in which light is obscured only being scattered. In the case of whomever comes to be in the second intermediary rank, he is more like the polished surface, such as the mirror's surface [171], which is itself seen and by which other things are seen as well. He is nearer to being purified than those first while still being in a state of passing away. In the case of whoever belongs to the third rank, he is more like the Sun itself, but in fact he does not resemble material bodies in any way. [That] is because whoever is in the former two ranks has only a material semblance and is material in a certain way, whereas this one is not material in any way. So it is fitting that there does not exist any material things whose relation to him is similar to the relation of the material things in the former two ranks. Only this one is one in every respect and neither passes away nor corrupts.

32.   By this alone the temporally prior and posterior are numerically one. As for all of the ways [of being numerically one] that preceded on first sight[25]—should they be possible—the prior would be different from the posterior. So, for instance, Hermes and Aristotle are not one, but rather they are close together. This is self-evident, which when reflected upon becomes easier. So as a result of this account it has become clear in what way it is said that the posterior and prior are numerically one, and that that

---

24 We have not been able to identify this individual. It is possible that he is wholly a fictional character used for the sake of example.

25 This seems to be a reference to the sense of "numerically one" enumerated at pars. 3–5, pp. 269–71.

manner is more perfect in unity than all the commonly accepted kinds of unity that are immediately sought. The skepticism to which those doctrines gave rise vanished, and that was our intention in this account.

33.   A part of the state that belongs to the faculties of the soul possessing this rank is what belongs to the imagery [faculty], that is to say, something analogous to this intellect comes to be in it, where [that analogous thing] is a light that when mixed with something, what is seen either cannot be articulated in any way or it is difficult to articulate. Owing to the appetitive soul, one comes to have a state resembling awe, which in a certain way resembles the state that appears when sensing something great and frightful. That state is called "wonder." (The Sufis have exaggerated in describing this state, and that is [because] this state appears to them owing to the objects of imagination that they find in their souls according to what they believe, regardless of whether they are true or false; for that unfortunately befalls the appetitive [soul] because it is conjoined only with the estimative soul, whereas truth and falsity are due to another appetitive part, namely, the rationally desiring part.) [172] Moreover, there appears to the one at this rank a state resembling immense joy; since something magnificent overcomes him, he is overcome by contempt for any thing below it. This faculty specifically but also the imagery faculty both preserve their states, whereas the amazement passes from the other appetitive [part], namely, the animal-like one, which returns to something close to its state among the masses.

34.   The length of the discussion and the shortness of time have diverted me from establishing the existence of this and how the many doctrines about this ought to be concerning happiness. In the future (God willing), I shall establish it with a clear explanation and will send it to you. My desire, if you please, is that you read what I have written on it. If any problem about it presents itself to you, send[j] it to me, and I shall respond. May God give you this rank and at that moment deliver to you what I have promised and whatever things that will establish your vision in order that through them (God willing) you will be happy. May you be in most complete peace and continue in a most prevailing good health through God's power.

[Postscript]

35.   May God strengthen you. This doctrine was established during a disjointed period of time, sometimes coming to me and sometimes leaving. After having read it, I observed that it falls short of explaining what I had wanted it to explain; for the idea I had in mind was a demonstration that this account does not provide except after difficulty and much disagreeable [toil]. Still, there is some indication of [the demonstration]. When from the explanation a portion of it is provided and the sense is understood, then from that it is obvious that what is known from the given sciences cannot be in its rank, but the one who comprehends it, once he fully understand that idea, comes to be in a rank in which he himself sees with respect to [the sciences], totally opposed to all preceding beliefs about ultimate things that are not material. They are too sublime to be related to physical life; rather, they are states included

among the states of happiness [173], and so they are purified of the composition of physical life and are aptly said to be divine states, which God (glorious and powerful is He!) gives to whomever of His servants He wishes.

36.   Likewise, I found the arrangement of the explanation in some places less than the perfect method, but the time was not adequate to replace it. I have relied upon you to do that, and this I have witnessed in you. So whatever is found in it of this sort, rearrange the explanation more elegantly. God willing, may you take my place in that role with which I have entrusted you.

IBN ṬUFAYL

Ibn Ṭufayl, the second of the great Andalusian Peripatetics, can be credited as the first author of a popular philosophical novel, *Ḥayy ibn Yaqẓān* ("Alive Son of Awake"). Abū Bakr Muhammad ibn ʿAbd al-Malik ibn Muhammad ibn Muhammad ibn Ṭufayl al-Qaysī, the Latin Abubacer, came from the small town of Guadix, forty miles northeast of Granada. He was born most likely between 1110 and 1116, while the Almoravids were still in power in Andalusia. During the middle part of the twelfth century the Almoravids fell from power and were replaced by the Almohads, or *al-Muwaḥḥidūn*—a reformist movement originating in North Africa among the Berbers that emphasized divine unicity (*tawḥīd*). Ibn Ṭufayl, who most likely never rose to the level of vizier within the Almohad power structure, was nonetheless active in its court circles. He was appointed secretary to the governor of Ceuta and Tangier and later became court physician and friend to the Almohad ruler Abū Yaʿqūb Yūsuf (1168–1184). The two were reported to spend hours, even days, in philosophical discussion. Moreover, Ibn Ṭufayl was responsible for introducing the young Ibn Rushd to the Caliph and was influential in starting Ibn Rushd on his career as Aristotle's commentator for which the latter is so celebrated. Ibn Ṭufayl died at an old age in Marrakech in 1185.

We know that Ibn Ṭufayl wrote at least two works on medicine; one of them, a poem on medicine, is still extant in manuscript form. He also was the author of works on philosophy, natural science, and metaphysics, and an *Epistle on the Soul* is included among these philosophical writings. Unfortunately, with the exception of *Ḥayy ibn Yaqẓān*, none of these philosophical writings is extant. Still, that work, which attempts to reconcile revealed religion, mysticism, and philosophy, provides at least an outline of Ibn Ṭufayl's philosophical thought. Although only part of that text is translated here, there are at least two complete modern English translations of it, and the text is well worth reading for its philosophical content as well as the sheer literary pleasure it provides.

SELECTIONS FROM *ḤAYY IBN YAQẒĀN*[a]

[The story begins with the newborn Ḥayy ibn Yaqẓān (Alive, son of Awake) finding himself on a desert island in the Indian Ocean, appearing there either as a result of spontaneous generation or some less fantastic means. When the child cries from hunger, a deer, which had just lost its own fawn, takes Ḥayy as her own child and raises him. After several years the doe dies, and Ḥayy in grief performs a rudimentary autopsy in order to find out what happened to his adopted mother and thus try to bring her back to life. Seeing that she had not died of a wound, Ḥayy concluded that the death must

284

have been the result of the loss of her innate heat. This discovery set Ḥayy on a road of scientific inquiry that provides in outline the whole of the Graeco-Arabic philosophical curriculum as well as showing the extent of knowledge that unaided human reason can reach.][1]

1.   [81] [Ḥayy] began to examine all the bodies that are in the world of generation and corruption, namely, the various species of animals and plants and minerals and the kinds of stones, soil, water, vapor, snow, cold, smoke, [82] ice, flame, and heat. He saw that they were of several descriptions and had various actions and motions, [some] comparable and [some] contrary. He devoted himself to investigating and carefully considering [these things]. So he saw that in some attributes they are comparable, but in others they differ, and that from the perspective in which they were comparable they are one, whereas from the perspective in which they differ they were diverse and many. Sometimes he would focus on the special properties of things and that by which some are individuated from others, and so it seemed to him they were so many that they were beyond reckoning. Existence spread out for him in a way that defied being ordered. It even seemed to him that he himself was many, since he observed the difference of his organs and that each one of them is individuated by a certain action and attribute that is specific to it. He observed each organ and saw that it could be divided into very many parts, and so he judged that he was himself many, and the same held for everything [else] itself.

2.   Then he would begin again along a second line of speculation, and so see that even though his organs were many, they were all continuous with one another, and there was no discontinuity between them in any way. Thus, for all intents and purposes, they are one. They differed only in accordance with the difference of their actions, but that difference was only because the power of the animal spirit, whose study he had undertaken earlier, is joined with them. Now that spirit is one in itself and is moreover the true nature of the self, whereas all of the other organs are like instruments. So in this way it seemed to him that he himself was one.

3.   Then he moved on to all the species of animals and saw by this kind of speculation that each individual [species] was one. Next he observed one kind of species after another, such as gazelles, horses, asses, and the various kinds of birds, and saw that the individuals of each species resembled one another with respect to the external and internal organs, modes of perception, motions, and appetites. He saw no difference among them, except insignificant things in relation to what was comparable in [the species]. He judged that the spirit that belonged to the whole of that species is one thing, and they do not differ except that[b] [the spirit] is divided among

---

[1]   We have not provided selections from the final sections of *Ḥayy ibn Yaqẓān*, where Ḥayy meets his first human other than himself—thus providing Ibn Ṭufayl with an opportunity to discuss ethics—or Ḥayy's subsequent travel to a city—thus providing Ibn Ṭufayl with an opportunity to discuss politics or statecraft. For an excellent discussion of these final sections see Taneli Kukkonen, "No Man Is an Island: Nature and Neo-Platonic Ethics in *Ḥayy ibn Yaqẓān*."

many hearts. If he could bring together all of that, which was divided among those hearts, and place it in a single vessel, then all of it would be one thing, comparable with dividing a single [quantity] of water or liquid among many containers and then afterwards bringing it back together. [83] So in both the cases of dividing it and bringing it together it is one thing, and the multiplicity accidentally happens to it only in a certain way. So by this line of speculation he saw that every species was one, whereas the multiplicity of its individuals he put on par with the multiplicity of the organs of the single individual, which in fact are not many.

4.   Next, he presented to his mind's eye all the species of animals and considered them closely. Thus, he saw that they are comparable in that they sense, seek nourishment, and move by will to wherever they wish. He had already learned that these activities are the most proper activities of the animal spirit, whereas apart from this comparability, that by which the remaining things differed is not in any strong sense proper to the animal spirit. So through this consideration it became obvious to him that the animal spirit that belongs to the entire genus of animals is in reality one, whereas even if there is an insignificant difference in them by which one species is differentiated from another, it is on par with dividing a single [quantity] of water among many containers, some of which are colder than others, but at its source it is one. Whatever is at the same level of coldness is comparable with specifying that animal spirit by a single species. Moreover, just as all of that water is one, so likewise the animal spirit is one, even if the multiplicity accidentally happens to it in a certain way. So by this kind of speculation he saw that the whole genus of animal is one.

5.   Thereafter, he began again with the various species of plants. He saw that the individuals of all of their species resembled one another with respect to branches, leaves, flowers, fruits, and activities. He then compared them with animals and learned that they too have a single thing in which they are common that is comparable to the animal spirit and by that they are one. In the same way he investigated the whole genus of plant, and determined that it is one in accordance with what he saw, namely, the comparability of its action in that [plants] seek nourishment and grow.

6.   Next he brought together in his mind's eye the genus of animals and the genus of plants and saw that they both are comparable with respect to seeking nourishment and growth, but that animals exceed plants by virtue of sensation, perception, and motion. Still there seemed to be something similar in plants, for example, the faces of flowers turn in the direction of the Sun and their roots move in the direction of nourishment and similar things like that. So by this consideration it became obvious that plants and animals are one thing because of the one thing that is common between them. [This one thing] in one of the two is more complete and perfect, while in the other a certain obstacle has hindered it, [84] and that is on par with dividing a single quantity of water into two parts: one of which is frozen and the other is fluid. Thus, it seemed to [Ḥayy] that plant and animal are one.

7.   Then he investigated the bodies that do not sense, seek nourishment, and grow, namely, rocks, soil, water, air, and flame. He saw that they are bodies having a certain measurable length, breadth, and depth. They differed only in that some of

them have color, while others do not have color, and some of them are hot, while others are cold, and differences of that kind. He also saw that the hot ones become cold and the cold ones hot. He saw that water becomes vapor, and vapor becomes water, and that things that are burned become embers, ashes, flames, and smoke. Also when in its ascent smoke congregates under a stone dome, it is contracted, and becomes comparable to other earthy things. So through this consideration it became obvious to him that all of them are in reality one thing, even if multiplicity is joined to them in a general way, that is, like the multiplicity that is joined to animals and plants.

8. Next he focused on the thing that seemed to him to make plants and animals one. He saw that it was a certain body like the former [inanimate] bodies, having length, breadth, and depth, and which is either hot or cold just like one of the former bodies that lacks sensation and self-nourishment. [The animate body] differed from them only by its activities, which obviously are a result of the animal and plant instruments, nothing else, and perhaps those actions are not essential, but crept into it only from something else, and should they pervade these other [inanimate] bodies, they too would be like [the animate bodies].

9. Then he investigated [the animate body] itself, considered apart from these activities that at first sight appeared to proceed from it, and he saw that it is a body no [different] than the former bodies. So by this consideration it became obvious to him that all bodies are one thing, whether animate or inanimate, in motion or at rest, although some of them obviously have certain activities as a result of instruments. But he did not know whether those actions are essential to them or creep into them from something else. At this state he did not believe that there was anything else other than bodies. So by proceeding in this way he saw that all of existence is a single thing, but by means of the initial speculation he believed that existence is a multiplicity that is irreducible and infinite. [. . .]

10. [89] Then he focused on whether he could find a single description that was general to all bodies, whether animate or inanimate. He found nothing common to all bodies, except the account of extension that exists in all of them with respect to the three dimensions, which are designated by "length," "breadth," and "depth." He knew that this account belonged to body insofar as it is a body; however, he did not readily sense any body existing with this description alone to the point that no more than the previously stated account of extension is in it, being [otherwise] wholly devoid of all the rest of the forms.

11. Next he reasoned about this three-dimensional extension: is it itself the account (maʿnā) of the body without there furthermore being some other account, or is that not the case? He saw that in addition to this extension there is another account in which this extension exists alone; [for the extension] by itself could not subsist, just as the former extended thing could not subsist without an extension. He took as a practical example of that one of these perceptible bodies possessing forms, such as clay, for example. He saw that when he worked it into a certain shape, such as a ball, for instance, it had a certain relative length, breadth, and depth. Thereafter, should

that ball itself be taken up, [and should it] acquire a cube or oval shape, the former length, breadth, and depth would be replaced, and there would come to be other relative [dimensions] different from the ones that it had. The clay, however, is one and the same, not having been replaced, although it inevitably had a certain relative length, breadth, and depth that could not be stripped from it. Still, because [the relative dimensions] followed successively upon it, it became clear to him that they are an account by themselves, but because [the clay] is never wholly stripped of them, it became clear to him that they are part of its true nature.

12.   So by this consideration it dawned on him that the body, insofar as it is a body, is in fact a composite of two causal factors (*ma'nā*): one of them takes the place of the clay belonging to the ball in the above example, and the other takes the place of the ball's length, breadth, and depth or whatever shape [the clay] might have. The body is conceivable only as a composite of these two causal factors, and one of them cannot dispense [90] with the other. However, that which can be replaced and can successively take on many aspects, namely, the account of the extension, is like the form that belongs to the other bodies possessing forms, whereas that which remains in a single state, namely, that which is comparable to the clay above, is like the account of corporeality[c] that belongs to the other bodies possessing forms. This thing that is like the clay in this example is what the theoreticians call "matter" and "prime matter," which is altogether stripped of form.

13.   After his investigation had reached this point, and he had separated himself from the sensible to a certain extent and looked upon the verge of the intellectual world, he began to feel estranged and longed for the world of the senses with which he was familiar. So he withdrew a little and gave up on absolute body, since this thing is neither sensibly perceived nor can one take hold of it. [Instead] he took up the simplest sensible bodies that he immediately experienced, namely, the earlier four, [that is, earth, air, fire, and water], which had been the interest of his [earlier] investigation.

14.   At the onset he observed water and saw that when it is left alone and does what its form requires, a sensible coldness arises from it, and it tries to move downward. When it is initially heated, whether by fire or the heat of the Sun, however, the coldness first disappears, but it still tries to descend. When it is heated excessively, however, it ceases trying to move downward and tries to move upward. So both the attributes that had always arisen out of [both] it and its form disappeared altogether. Now concerning its form, he did not recognize anything more than the emergence of these two activities from it, and so since these two activities had disappeared, the control of the form was nullified. So whenever certain activities appear that characteristically arise as a result of another form, the form of the water disappears from that body and it comes to have another form, which had not existed earlier, and by means of [that new form] there arises out of [the body] activities that had not characteristically arisen from it, that is to say, by means of its initial form. He knew by necessity that every thing that comes to be inevitably has something that brings it about. So by this consideration there came to be in his soul, in a general and indistinct way, the impression of an agent of the form.

15.   Next he pursued the forms one after another that he had previously come to know. He saw [91] that all of them temporally came to be, and that they too inevitably had an agent. Then he observed the things possessing the forms and saw that they were nothing more than a preparedness of the body for that activity arising out of it, like water; for when he heated it excessively, it was predisposed and prepared to move upward. That preparedness is its form, since there is nothing more than a body and certain things that are seen to result from it that had not existed earlier, such as qualities and motions. So the body's being suited to some motions to the exclusion of others is its being preparedness in virtue of its form. It dawned on him that something like that [takes place] in all the forms. So it became evident to him that the activities arising from [the forms] do not in fact belong to them but belong only to an agent who by means of them enacted the activities attributed to them. This idea that dawned on him is a saying of God's Prophet (may God bless and grant him peace!): "I was his hearing by which he hears, and his sight by which he sees," and in authoritative Revelation: "It was not you who killed them, but God who killed them; and it was not you who shot when you shot, but God who shot" [Qur'ān 8:17].

16.   After he had a brief and indistinct glimpse of this Agent, he came to have an avid desire to know It distinctly. He had not yet separated himself from the world of the senses, and so he began to seek this voluntary Agent in the realm of sensible objects. He did not yet know whether It was one or many, and so he examined all the bodies that were at hand, that is to say, those about which he had always been reasoning. He saw that all of them some times are generated and at other times are corrupted. Whatever he did not notice corrupting in its entirety, he did notice that parts of it are corrupted, such as water and earth; for he saw that their parts are corrupted by fire, and likewise he saw that air is corrupted by extreme cold until it comes to be ice and then melts into water, and the same held for the remaining bodies that were at hand. Among them he did not see anything that was not free of coming to be and not need the voluntary Agent. So he discarded all of them and directed his reasoning to the celestial bodies. He reached this level of investigation at the end of four seven-year periods from the time of his birth, namely, at twenty-eight years of age.

17.   He knew that the heavens, as well as the stars and planets in them, are bodies, because they are extended in the three dimensions, length, breadth, and depth. None of them are without this attribute, but everything that is not without this attribute is a body, and so then all of them [92] are bodies. Next he reasoned about whether they are extended infinitely, forever going on in length, breadth, and depth without end, or whether they are finite, bounded by limiting points at which they terminate and beyond which there can be no extension at all. He was at something of a loss about that, but then by the power of his discernment and acute intelligence he saw that an infinite body is an empty notion, something that is impossible and a concept that could not be made intelligible.

18.   In his view this judgment was strengthened by many arguments that inwardly presented themselves to him. To that end he said: This celestial body is finite either on the side near me and the direction of which I am sensibly aware—but concerning this there is no doubt [that it is finite], because I visually perceive it—or the side that

is opposite this side [is finite], and it is about this one that I am uncertain. But I also know that it is absurd that it is infinitely extended because of [the following argument]. (1) Let me imagine that two lines, x and y, begin at this finite side and cover the height of the [purportedly] infinite body commensurate with the extension of the body. (2) Let me imagine that a large part is removed from x along the direction of its finite outermost point. (3) Let me take what remains and superimpose its out-ermost point where the removal was made onto the outermost point of y, which had nothing removed, that is, I superimpose x, which had something removed from it, onto y, which had nothing removed from it. If that is the case and the mind travels along x and y in the direction that was purported to be infinite, we shall find one of two things. On the one hand, both x and y might extend forever infinitely, and neither one is shorter than the other such that x, which had a part removed from it, is equal to y, which had nothing removed from it, which is absurd, just as it is absurd for the whole to be equivalent to the part. On the other hand, x, which is shorter, might not extend forever along with y, but terminate without traveling the full distance of y and fall short of the extension belonging to y. In this case x is finite, but when the amount that had been initially removed, which was also finite, is returned to x, then its whole will also be finite. In that case x [in its restored state] is neither shorter nor greater than y, which had nothing removed from it, and so then, x is equivalent to y, but x is finite, and so y is also finite. So the body with respect to which these lines were postulated is finite, but these lines can be postulated with respect to every body, and so every body is finite. Thus, when we assume that a body is infinite, our assumption is empty and absurd. [. . .]

19.   [94] After [Ḥayy] had reached this level of knowledge, he became aware that the celestial sphere in its entirety, as well as what was included in it, is like a single thing of which each of its parts are continuously joined together, and that all of the bodies on which he had initially focused, such as earth, water, and air, as well as plants and animals and whatever bore a resemblance to them are all within it and not outside of it. Moreover, [he became aware] that it was something wholly resembling some individual animal. The luminous stars and planets are like the animal's senses. The various celestial spheres in it, each one continuously joined with the next, are like the animal's organs. The world of generation and corruption internal to it are like kinds of offal and fluids in the animal's belly, which, just as they are often produced by an animal, so likewise [their analogue is produced] in the macrocosm.

20.   Once it became clear to him that the whole of [the universe] is in reality like a single individual that subsists requiring a volitional Agent, and he believed (as a result of the same kind of investigation by which he thought that the bodies in the world of generation and corruption are one) that the many parts of [the universe] are also one, he reasoned about the universe considered as a whole. Is it something that comes to be after having not been, emerging into existence after nonexistence? Or is it something that has existed throughout all past time, never in any way having been preceded by nonexistence? Now he found himself at loggerheads about that. It seemed to him that neither one of the two positions carried greater weight than the other.

That is [because] when, on the one hand, he resolved to believe in the [world's] pre-eternity, he was confronted by many objections resulting from an impossibility of any infinite [temporal] existence, like the argument by which it seemed that an infinite body is impossible. Likewise, he also saw that the existence of [the universe] is never devoid of things that come to be in time and so it cannot precede them, but whatever cannot precede things that come to be in time is itself something that also comes to be in time. On the other hand, when he resolved to believe in the [world's] temporal creation, he was confronted with another set of objections, because he saw that the account of its coming to be after it was not is intelligible only in the sense that time is prior to it, but time is an integral part of the universe and is not independent of it, and thus the universe's being posterior to [95] time is unintelligible. Likewise he said, if it comes to be in time, then inevitably it has a Creator, but then why did its Creator create it now and not earlier? Was it owing to some new cause that unexpectedly arose? But there was nothing there but [the Creator]. Or was it due to some change that came to be in the [Creator] Itself, and if so, then what was it that brought about that change?

21.   He continued to reason about that for several years, but it seemed to him that the arguments opposed one another, and neither of the two beliefs carried greater weight than the other. Since [finding a decisive argument] defied all his best efforts, he decided to reason about what each one of the two beliefs entailed, and perhaps what they entailed would be identical. He saw that if he believed in the world's temporal creation and its emergence into existence after nonexistence, then that necessarily entails that it could <not>[d] emerge into existence by itself and inevitably has an Agent that makes it emerge into existence. Certainly that Agent could not be something perceived by the senses, because if It were something perceived by the senses, It would just be another body among many. If It were just another body among many, It would be an integral part of the world and [so] would be something coming to be in time and in need of a Creator. Now if that second creator were also a body, it would need a third, and the third a fourth, and that would lead to an infinite causal chain, which is groundless. So the universe inevitably has an Agent, and [that Agent] is not a body. If It is not a body, there would be no way to perceive It by the senses, because the five senses perceive only bodies or what is concomitant with bodies. If It cannot be sensed, then neither can It be imagined, because imagination is nothing but presenting to oneself the forms of sensible objects that are no longer present. If It is not a body, then it is impossible that any of the attributes of bodies apply to It. But the first of the attributes of bodies is to be extended in length, breadth, and depth, and It is high above that and all of the attributes of body that follows upon this attribute. If the universe has an Agent [who temporally creates it], then [that Agent] must have power over it and know it. "Does He not know Who He has created, being Kind and Knowing" [Qur'ān 67:14].

22.   He also saw that if he believed in the world's pre-eternity, and that the world has never been preceded by nonexistence (having always been as it is), then that [belief] would entail that [the universe's] motion is eternal without having a point at which

it began, since it was not preceded by a rest from which it began. Now every motion must inevitably have a mover, and the mover either is a power that pervades one body [96] among many—whether the body of the mover itself or some other body external to it—or it is a power that neither pervades nor spreads through a body. Every power that pervades and spreads[c] through a body is divided and multiplied by [the body's] being divided and multiplied. An example is the weight in a stone, for instance, which moves [the stone] downward, and so if the stone is divided into halves, then its weight is divided into halves, and if another [stone] like it is added to it, then the other one like it increases the weight. If the stone could always be incrementally increased to infinity, then this weight would be incrementally increased to infinity as well, whereas if the stone reaches a certain limiting point in size and stops, the weight also reaches that limiting point. However, it had already been demonstrated that every body necessarily is finite, and hence every power in a body is necessarily finite. So if we find a power that performs an infinite activity, it is not a power in a body, and had we found that the celestial sphere is moved forever, it would be an infinite, uninterrupted motion, since we assumed that it is eternal without having beginning. On the basis of that, then, it is necessary that the power that moves it[f] is neither in the body of [the celestial sphere] nor in a body outside of it. Thus, [the power] belongs to something free from bodies and is not described by any corporeal attributes. During his investigation of the world of generation and corruption, it had dawned upon [Ḥayy] that the true nature of any body's existence is due only to its form, which is its preparedness for the various sorts of motion, while the existence that it has due to its matter is a weak existence that is barely perceivable. Thus, the existence of the whole universe is due to its preparedness for this Mover to move [it]—a Mover that is free of matter and the attributes of bodies and far above any sense's grasping It or any image's reaching It ([God] be praised!). Since It is an Agent of the celestial sphere's motions according to their various kinds, acting continuously and without flagging, then necessarily It has power over it and knows it.

23.　In this way his investigation reached what he had reached in the first way, and he was no worse because of his puzzlement over the pre-eternity or temporal creation of the world. It turned out for him to be true of both viewpoints that there exists an incorporeal Agent, who is neither continuous with nor discontinuous from body, neither internal to nor external from body; [for] continuous, discontinuous, internal, and external are all attributes of bodies, whereas It was beyond [these attributes].

24.　Given that the matter of every body is dependent upon the form, since [matter] only subsists by means of the [form] and would have no fixed true nature without it, while the existence of the form results only from the activity [97] of this volitional Agent, it became evident to him that all existing things in their existence are dependent upon this Agent and that none of them would subsist without It. Thus, It was their cause and they were Its effect, regardless of whether their existence comes to be after having previously not existed, or they had no temporal beginning, never having previously not existed. In both cases, they are an effect. They need the Agent, and their existence is dependent upon It. Were It not to endure, they would not endure; were It not to exist, they would not exist; were It not eternal, they would not be eternal. [That Agent] in Itself, however, can dispense with and is free of them. How could it not be so, when it had been demonstrated that Its strength and power are infinite, whereas all bodies and what is either joined with or related to them (even partially so) are finite [and] demarcated? Thus, the whole universe—including the heavens, Earth, planets, and stars, and whatever is between them, above them, and below them—is the result of Its action and creation. Moreover, [the whole universe] is essentially posterior to It, even if not temporally posterior. It is just as when you grasp a certain body and then move your hand; for that body necessarily is moved as a consequence of your hand's moving, [in which case its] motion is essentially posterior to the movement of your hand, even if it is not temporally posterior to it, but in fact they both move simultaneously. In the same way the whole universe would be an effect and creation of this Agent without a [first moment of] time. "His command, when He wills a thing, is only to say to it 'Be!' and it is" [Qur'ān 36:82].

25.   Once [Ḥayy] saw that all existing things are the result of Its activity, he examined them thereafter as providing a means to considering the power of their Agent and to marvel at the wonder of Its craftsmanship, the brilliance of Its wisdom, the subtlety of Its knowledge. So [the Agent] became evident to him from the traces of wisdom and instances of creative workmanship in the least of things, to say nothing of the greatest of them, which filled him with awe. It seemed to independently verify that [all of] that proceeded only from a voluntary Agent Who is most perfect, even above perfection! "Not the weight of a dust mote escapes His notice, neither in Heaven nor on Earth, nor anything either smaller or greater than that" [Qur'ān 34:3].

26.   Thereafter he considered all kinds of animals, and how It had given each thing its physical constitution and then directed it in its use. Should It not have directed [the animal] in the use of those organs created for it concerning the ways it was intended to benefit from them, then the animal would not have benefited from them and they would have been a burden on it. From that he learned that It is the most Generous and Compassionate. [98] Moreover, whenever he glimpsed any existing thing that had some beauty, magnificence, perfection, power, or any other excellence (whatever that excellence might be), he reasoned and knew that it resulted from the bestowal of that volitional Agent (great is Its splendor!). Part of Its goodness and Its activity is that It in Itself is greater than they, more perfect, more complete, better, more magnificent, more beautiful, and more enduring. [He knew] that, for these are of no comparison with That One. He continued to pursue all the attributes of perfection, and so he saw that they belonged to It and proceeded from It, and he saw that It is worthier of [those attributes] than anything below It that is described by them.

27.   He also pursued all of the attributes of defect and saw that It was free of and beyond them. How could It not be free of them, when "defect" means nothing but pure nonexistence or what is related to nonexistence? But how could nonexistence be related to or sully Whoever is purely Existent, existing necessarily in Itself, giving existence to whatever possesses existence. There is no existence, but It. So It is existence, perfection, completion, excellence, magnificence, power, and knowledge. It is Itself! "Everything shall perish, but His face" [Qur'ān 28:88].

IBN RUSHD

Almost certainly the greatest, or at least the best known, of the Iberian Peripatetics is Abū l-Walīd Muhammad ibn Aḥmad ibn Muhammad ibn Rushd, known in the Latin West as either Averroes or simply "The Commentator." Ibn Rushd was born in 1126 at Cordoba and descended from a long line of legal scholars, and indeed he himself served as the Chief *Qādī* ("Judge") in Cordoba, a post that both his father and grandfather had filled first under Almoravid and then Almohad rule. Ibn Rushd received a traditional education in the Qur'ānic sciences as well as training in medicine and philosophy. We do not know much about his education in these latter two fields. Still we do know that he was associated with Abū Marwān ibn Zuhr (d. 1161), one of the leading medical figures of the time, and Ibn Ṭufayl, the leading philosophical figure of the time, although apparently Ibn Rushd was not a pupil of either. In or around 1169 Ibn Ṭufayl introduced Ibn Rushd to the Caliph Abū Ya'qūb Yūsuf, who straightaway asked Ibn Rushd whether the heavens are an eternal substance or had a beginning, a thorny question regarding which al-Ghazālī had claimed that Muslims who maintained the heavens' eternity were guilty of heresy and should be executed. Not knowing the Caliph's philosophical sympathies, Ibn Rushd remained silent. Apparently recognizing Ibn Rushd's agitation, Abū Ya'qūb Yūsuf began discussing the issue with Ibn Ṭufayl in a very philosophically sophisticated way and was ultimately able to draw Ibn Rushd into the discussion, where the latter amply showed his learning on such matters. The interview can only be deemed a success, for that year Ibn Rushd was appointed judge of Seville and was at around the same time engaged to comment on the corpus of Aristotle, the project for which he was to receive his fame in Europe. In 1182 he was appointed Chief *Qādī* of Cordoba as well as succeeding Ibn Ṭufayl as the court physician. Unfortunately, toward the end of Ibn Rushd's life, he suffered a public humiliation when the new Caliph Abū Yūsuf Ya'qūb al-Manṣūr (ruled 1184–1199) ordered the public burning of Ibn Rushd's books and banished Ibn Rushd with several other scholars to the small village of Lucena south of Cordoba, apparently in an attempt to garner support from the more conservative religious scholars for the Caliph's war against the Christians. Two or three years later Ibn Rushd regained favor and was summoned to Marrakech, where he was to resume his study of philosophy. Ibn Rushd died in Marrakech a few months later on 10 December 1198 at the age of seventy-two.

Just as Ibn Rushd's intellectual pursuits were diverse and far ranging so likewise his writings reflect his multifaceted interests. Thus, his *The Beginning of He Who Shows Zeal and the End of He Who Shows Complacency* is clearly a work of Islamic law; his *Generalities* reflects his medical interest; *The Explanation of the Methods of Proofs* is a religious work. *The Decisive*

Treatise—the work by Ibn Rushd that perhaps is best known to modern readers—is both a religious-philosophical work as well as a legal treatise inasmuch as Ibn Rushd provides a legal defense for the Muslim philosophers who maintain the world's eternity, deny bodily resurrection, and limit God's knowledge to universals, positions that al-Ghazālī claimed were heretical to Islam and as such any Muslim maintaining them could be executed. Similarly, *The Incoherence of the Incoherence* is a religious-philosophical work inasmuch as it is a close commentary of al-Ghazālī's earlier work, *The Incoherence of the Philosophers*. Certainly the genre of writing for which Ibn Rushd is most appreciated in the medieval Latin and Jewish milieus was his commentaries, particularly those on Aristotle, although he wrote a commentary on Plato's *Republic* as well. His commentaries are of three sorts: (1) the short commentary (*jāmiʿ*), which is often no more than an epitome of the work of Aristotle; (2) the middle commentary (*talkhīṣ*), which provides a paraphrase of the Aristotelian text; and (3) his celebrated long commentary (*tafsīr*), which includes the entire text of Aristotle along with a close line-by-line explanation of that text.

I. SELECTIONS FROM *THE INCOHERENCE OF THE INCOHERENCE,* "FIRST DISCUSSION"[a]

[7] Al-Ghazālī says: The refutation [of the argument for the eternity of the world from the impossibility of a temporal event's proceeding from an absolute, unchanging, eternal will] comes from two fronts: The first of them is to ask by what means would you [philosophers] censure one who says, "The world is temporally created by means of an eternal will that made necessary [the world's] existence at the moment at which it came to exist; [the world's] nonexistence continued to the limit up to which it continued, and the existence began from whence it began; before the existence it was not something willed and so owing to that was not created, but at the moment at which it was created, it was willed by the eternal will and so owing to that was created"? What precludes this belief and would render it absurd?[1]

1. I say: This is a sophistical claim, namely, since he cannot maintain that the delay of the effect is possible after the agent's action. When his resolve to act is as a voluntary agent, then one can maintain that the delay of [the act] and the effect is possible after the agent's willing, but its delay is not possible after the action of the agent, and the same holds for the delay of the action after the resolve to act is in the willing agent. So the same problem [8] remains. [Al-Ghazālī] is necessarily faced with only one of two options: either (1) the agent's act does not necessitate a change in the agent, in which case it would require some external cause of the change; or (2) some changes are self-changed, not needing some cause of change that is associated with

---

[1] See Al-Ghazālī, *The Incoherence of the Philosophers*, pars. 11–12, p. 243

them, and that some changes can be associated with the Eternal without a cause of change. In other words, there are two things that the opponents [of al-Ghazālī] firmly hold here, one of which is that change entails the activity of the agent and that every change has a cause of change; the second principle is that the Eternal does not undergo change in any kind of way, all of which is difficult to prove.

2.   That of which the Ashʿarites[2] are not at liberty is either to grant a First Agent *or* to grant that It has a first [temporal] act, because they cannot posit that the Agent's state with respect to the temporal effect at the time of the act is the same state as at the time of the act's absence. So in this case there must be a new state or some relation that had not been. That [new state or previously nonexisting relation] necessarily is either in the agent or in the effect or in both of them. Consequently, when we require that every new state has an agent, then inevitably the agent of that new state is either one or other of the following. It might be (1) another agent, in which case the former agent is neither the first nor sufficient in itself for its act but needs another. Or it might be (2) the agent itself that actualizes that state [9] that is a condition for its acting, in which case the former act, which was assumed to be the first [act] to proceed from it, is not the first, but rather its act of actualizing that state that is a condition for the effect is before its act of actualizing the effect. This, as you see, is what necessarily follows. (The only exception is where one allows that among the temporal states in agents there can be what does not need a temporal creator, which would not even be an option if it were not for those who allow that certain things are temporally created spontaneously—which was a position of the ancients who denied the agent—but that it is baseless is self-evident.)

3.   In this objection there is confusion between "eternal will" and "temporal will," which are equivocal terms, indeed even contrary; for the will that is in personal experience is a power in which there is a possibility to perform one of two opposites equally, and the possibility of [the will's] being susceptible[b] to two objects of will is still equal (for the will is the desire of the agent to act). When it performs its acts, the desire ceases, and the object of desires comes to be. So when it is said here that one of two opposites is willed eternally, then by transferring the nature of willing from possibility to necessity the definition of willing is eliminated, even when it is said that an eternal willing was not eliminated by the presence of the object of will. When [the willing] has no first [moment], then one moment is neither delimited from another nor designated[c] for it to bring about the object of will. Still, we say [10] that demonstration leads to the existence of an Agent with a power that is neither volitional nor natural, but which the Divine Law terms "will," just as demonstration led to things that are intermediary between things that at first sights are supposed to be contradictories but are not contradictories, as for example our saying that there exists something that is neither internal nor external to the world [i.e., God]. [. . .]

---

[2] That is, the theological group to which al-Ghazālī belonged.

4. [18] [The argument that if the world were eternal, then the number of rotations of the planets and stars would be infinite and some infinite rotations would be greater and others smaller],[3] arises when you imagine two motions consisting of rotations between two given extremes of one [and the same] time, and then you imagine at one time a smaller part[d] of each one of the two between two given extremes, so that the proportion of part to part is the proportion of whole to whole. For example, when the rotation of Saturn during a period of time called a year is one-thirteenth of the Sun's rotation in that period, then when you imagine the whole of the Sun's rotations [in proportion] to the whole of Saturn's rotations occurring during one and the same time, inevitably the proportion of all of the rotations of one motion to all of the rotations of the other motion is the proportion of part to part.

5. When there is no proportion between the two motions considered as wholly complete because each of them is potential, that is, they have no beginning but are infinite, whereas there is a proportion between the parts because each one of [the parts] is actual, then it does not necessarily follow that the proportion of whole to whole tracks the proportion of part [19] to part, as their proof concerning the claim supposes. [That] is, because no proportion exists between two magnitudes or extents, each one of which is posited to be infinite. Thus, since the ancients posited, for instance, that the whole of the Sun's motion has no starting point but is infinite, and likewise for Saturn's motion, there simply is no relation between the two, because from [such a relation] it would necessarily follow that the two wholes are finite as must be the case concerning the two parts of the whole. This is clear in itself.

6. [Al-Ghazālī's] account imagines that when the proportion of parts to parts is the proportion of the greater to the lesser, then it is necessary for the two wholes that the proportion of one of the two to the other is the proportion of the greater to the lesser. This is necessary only when the two wholes are finite, but in the case when they are not finite, there is no greater or lesser. When one supposes that here there is a proportion that is the proportion of the greater to the lesser, then one will imagine that some other absurdity necessarily results from that, namely, that what is infinite might be greater than what is infinite. This is an absurdity only when one takes there to be two things that are actually infinite, because in that case the proportion between them would exist, whereas when one takes [them] to be potentially [infinite], there is no proportion. So this is the answer to this puzzle, not the answer provided on behalf of the philosophers by al-Ghazālī. In this way all of their puzzles mentioned in this section are resolved.

7. The most difficult [20] of all of them is the one that they habitually vent, namely, that when the motions that have occurred in the past are infinite, then no motion could exist as a result of them in the present, right here, unless an infinite number of motions before it had already terminated.[4] (This is true and acknowledged

---

[3] Al-Ghazālī, *The Incoherence of the Philosophers*, par. 22, pp. 245–46.

[4] Ibid., par. 48.

by the philosophers, if the prior motion is supposed to be a condition for the existence of the later.) In other words, [the objection runs] whenever one of [the motions] necessarily exists, then an infinite number of causes before it would necessarily exist. Not a single true philosopher, however, allows the existence of an infinite number of causes, as the materialist allows, because a necessary result of [an infinite number of causes] would be an effect's existing without a cause and a moved thing's existing without a mover.

8.   Yet since demonstration has led some people to a principle that is an Eternal Mover Whose existence has neither beginning nor end and Whose action must not be delayed after Its existence, it follows necessarily that Its act, just like the state concerning Its existence, has no beginning. If that were not the case, Its act would be possible not necessary, and so It would not have been a First Principle. So the acts of the Agent Whose existence has no beginning must themselves have no beginning just as the state with respect to Its existence. Consequently, it must necessarily follow that one of Its first acts is not a condition for the second, because no one of them essentially actualizes [another]; that one of them should be before another is [only] accidental.

9.   The [philosophers], however, have allowed a certain accidental, though not essential, infinite. [21] In fact, this kind of infinite is something necessary that is a consequence of a First, Eternal Principle's existence. That is not only the case with respect to successive or continuous motions, but also with respect to things about which it is supposed that the prior is a cause of the posterior, such as the human who reproduces a human like himself. That is to say, that the temporal creation of some determinate human by another human must go back to a First, Eternal Agent Whose existence has no beginning and [likewise] Whose bringing about one human from another has no [beginning]. So one human's resulting from another infinitely is accidental, whereas the beforeness and afterness are essential. In other words, just as there is no beginning for the acts performed without an instrument by the Agent whose existence has no beginning, so likewise there is no beginning for the instrument by which [the agent] performs its acts that are characteristically [performed] by an instrument when those [acts] have no beginning.[5] Since the speculative theologians believe that what was accidental was in fact essential, they reject its existence. The solution to their argument was difficult, and they erroneously supposed that their proof was necessary.

10.   This was evident among the discussion of the philosophers; for their first master, namely Aristotle, had clearly explained that if a motion were [ultimately] owing to motion, then the motion would not exist; and if an element were [ultimately]

---

[5] Although Ibn Rushd's prose is cumbersome, the point is clear. When an Eternal Agent performs an eternal act by means of some tool, then that tool must also be eternal. In the case of the procreation of humans, the Eternal Agent creates a human using an earlier human as its tools for this act. Consequently, since the Agent is eternally creating humans using them as its tools for this act, human as a species must also be eternal.

owing to element, then the element would not exist.[6] This manner of infinite, in their view, neither has a beginning nor is finite. Thus, that [an actual infinite series] has terminated and entered into existence does not apply to anything pertaining to [an accidental infinite], not even past time, because whatever has terminated [22] had a beginning, and whatever did not have a beginning has not terminated. That is also evident from the fact that beginning and ending are related. Thus, whoever claims that the rotations of the celestial spheres are infinite in the future need not suppose they have a beginning, because what has a beginning has an end, and what does not have an end does not have a beginning. The same holds concerning the first and the last: what has a first has a last, and what does not have a first does not have a last. Now what does not have a last, then, in fact neither has a certain part where it terminates nor a certain part where it begins, and what does not have a given part where it begins does not have a termination. Thus, when the speculative theologians ask the philosopher, "Where has the motion that is before the present terminated?" [the philosophers'] response is that it has not terminated, because from the [philosophers'] supposition that it does not have a first, it does not have a termination. So the theologians' delusion that the philosophers concede the termination of [the rotations of the celestial spheres] is not true, because in the [philosophers'] view they would not terminate unless they began. So it has become clear to you concerning the proof cited among the theologians about the temporal creation of the world that it does not sufficiently attain the level of certainty and reach the ranks of demonstration. Also the proof that is introduced and cited from the philosophers in [Al-Ghazālī's *Incoherence*] is not worthy of the ranks of demonstration, which is what we intended to show about this work. The best answer to whomever asks [23] about [the First Agent's] acts going into the past is to say, "Its acts going into [the past] is like Its existence going [into the past]," because neither of them have a beginning.

11.   As for al-Ghazālī's response on behalf of the philosophers to rebut the proof that some of the celestial motions are faster than others and the response to it, here is his text:

[The philosophers] might say that the locus of the error is in your claim that [the heavenly rotations] are a whole composed of units; for these rotations are nonexistents. [They are] either past, and so they no longer exist, or future, and so they do not yet exist. In general, [the whole] indicates presently existing things, but in this case there is nothing existing [such as to be a whole].[7]

Thereafter in opposition to this he said:

We say that number divides into the even and odd, and it is impossible that what is numbered should lie outside of [this division], regardless whether it is something that continues to exist or perishes. So when we posit a number of horses, we must believe that [the

---

[6] See Aristotle, *Physics* VIII 1, 251a23–b10.

[7] See Al-Ghazālī, *The Incoherence of the Philosophers*, par. 24, p. 246.

number] is either even or odd, regardless of whether we suppose [the horses] as existing or nonexisting. If they cease to exist after existing, this proposition does not change.[8]

This is the end of his account.

12. This account applies only to what has a beginning and end, whether outside the soul or in it, I mean that intellects judge it to be even and odd, whether currently existing or not. As for whatever exists potentially, that is, having neither a beginning nor an end, neither being even nor odd, or beginning or terminating, [24] or going into the past or into the future, applies to it. [That] is because what is in potency has the status of something nonexistent, which is what the philosophers intended by saying that the rotations that were in the past and future are nonexistent. The gist of this question is that whatever is described as a delimited whole possessing a beginning and end is so described, as having a beginning and end, whether it is outside of the soul or not. As long as some whole of it is actual and something delimited in the past, it is in the soul and outside of it, and so is necessarily either odd or even. As long as the whole of it is not delimited outside of the soul, then it is not delimited except insofar as it is in the soul (because the soul cannot conceptualize what is infinite in existence), and so from this perspective [namely, within the soul] it also is described as odd or even. Inasmuch as it is outside of the soul, however, it simply is not described as being either odd or even, and the same holds for whatever is in the past. Now it was supposed that it is in potency outside the soul, that is, it has no beginning. So it is not described as being either odd or even, unless it is supposed that it is actual, I mean, that it consists of a beginning and end. A whole or entirety (I mean possessing a beginning and end) belongs to whatever pertains to the motions only insofar as they are in the soul, just like the case concerning time and rotation, but in their nature they necessarily [25] are neither odd nor even, save insofar as they are in the soul.[9]

13. The cause of this error is that when something with a certain description is in the soul, it is imagined that it exists outside of the soul with that very description. Since anything that occurred in the past is only conceptualized in the soul as finite, it is erroneously supposed that the nature of whatever occurred in the past is thus outside of the soul, [namely, that it is finite as well]. Since the conceptualization of whatever will occur in the future is designated as infinite in that one conceptualizes one part after another, Plato and the Ash'arites believed that future celestial rotations could be infinite, but all of this is a judgment based on imagination not demonstration. Thus, whoever supposes that the world has a beginning would have held more

---

[8] See Al-Gazālī, *The Incoherence of the Philosophers,* par. 25, p. 246.

[9] Ibn Rushd's point is that motion considered as a whole or entirety, that is, considered as having a spatial or temporal extension, exists only in the soul. What exists in the world is merely an object at some discrete spatial point at some given moment, not something that exists as actually extending across space and time.

firmly to his principle and better preserved his supposition to suppose that it has an end, as many of the theologians had done. . . .

14. . . . [26] To suppose a numerical multiplicity of immaterial souls is not acknowledged by [the philosophers], because the cause of numerical multiplicity in their view is the matter, while the cause [27] of the similarity in numerically many things is the form. That numerically many things should exist as one in form without matter is absurd. That is [because] an individual is distinguished by some attribute or other only accidentally, since someone else might have that attribute in common with him. Only on the part of the matter is one individual distinct from another. Moreover, the denial of an infinite as something actually existing, regardless of whether they are bodies or not, is a principle universally accepted by [the philosophers]. We do not know anyone who drew a distinction between having a position and not having a position in this sense, except Ibn Sīnā.[10] As for everyone else, I know of no one who has maintained this position. It simply does not fit with any of their principles. So [an actual infinite] is a fiction, because [the philosophers] deny the existence of an actual infinite, whether a body or not, since it would necessarily result that one infinite is greater than another. Perhaps Ibn Sīnā intended it only to satisfy the masses concerning what they regularly hear about the soul. It is, however, hardly a satisfying account; for if things were actually infinite, then the part would be like the whole, I mean when what is infinite is divided into two parts. For example, if a line or number were actually infinite at both of its extremes, and moreover it were divided into two portions, then each one of [28] its portions would be actually infinite, but the whole was also infinite. So the whole and the part would be infinite because each one of them is actual, which is impossible. All of this necessarily follows only when an actual infinite is posited, not a potential.

15. . . . Zayd is numerically different from ʿAmr, but he and ʿAmr are one in form, that is, the soul. So if the soul of Zayd, for instance, were numerically different from the soul of ʿAmr in the same way that Zayd is numerically different from ʿAmr, then Zayd's and ʿAmr's souls would be numerically two [29] [but] one in form, in which case the soul would have a soul. Therefore, it is necessary that Zayd's and ʿAmr's souls are one in form, whereas numerical multiplicity, I mean being divided among the individuals, is associated with what is one in form only by the matters. So if the soul does not perish when the body perishes or there is something in it with this description [i.e., being imperishable], then, when it separated from the bodies, it must be numerically one. There is no way to divulge this knowledge in the place.[11]

16. The account that [al-Ghazālī] used to refute Plato's teaching is sophistical. That is [because] the gist of it is that Zayd's soul is either the very same soul as ʿAmr's soul or it is different from it; however, it is not the very same as ʿAmr's soul, and so it is different from it. "Different" is an equivocal term, just as "he" is said of many

---

10 The reference is to *Najāt*, IV.2.11, "On the Finite and the Infinite," not translated here.

11 Ibn Rushd provides the arguments for this position in his *Long Commentary on the Soul*, 335–60.

things that are said to be different. So the soul of Zayd and ʿAmr are one in one respect but many in another, as if you said "one" with respect to form [and] "many" with respect to what bears [the form].

17.   His claim that divisibility is conceptualized only in what has quantity is partially false. That is because this is true with respect to what is essentially divisible, but not true with respect to what is accidentally divisible, I mean, what is divisible from the fact that it is in what is essentially divisible. What is divisible [30] essentially is, for instance, the body, whereas what is divisible accidentally is like the whiteness that is in bodies, which is divided by the bodies' being divided. Likewise, forms and the soul are accidentally divisible, namely, by their substrate's being divided. The soul is something resembling light, and just as light is divided by the division of the illuminated bodies and then is united when the bodies are absent, so likewise is the case with respect to the soul together with bodies.

18.   His putting forth the likes of these sophistical claims is obscene, for one would think that the above would not escape his notice. He intended that only to dupe the people of his time, but it is incompatible with the character of those striving to reveal the truth. Perhaps the man is to be excused by taking into account his time and place, and that he was testing in his works. [. . .]

Then it was said:

> If [the philosopher] asks by what means would you deny one who refrains from invoking necessity and proves [the impossibility of an eternal will's temporally creating the world] in another way, namely, that moments of time are indiscernible with respect to the possibility that the will has a preference for [one of] them [over the others]. So what is it that distinguished one determinate moment of time from what was before or after it, when it is not absurd that what is willed should be earlier and later?[12]

19.   [34] The main point of what [al-Ghazālī] related in this section on behalf of the philosophers in order to prove that a temporal event cannot result from an Eternal Agent is that in that case there could not be a will. This rebuff would arise against [the philosophers] only by their conceding to their opponent that all opposites are similar in relation to the Eternal Will, whether [the opposites] concern time (such as the prior and posterior) or are found in contrary qualities (such as white and black), and likewise that nonexistence and existence [35] are in their view similar in relation to the First Will. After they concede this premise to their opponent (although they do not accept it), [the opponents] say to them that the will could not selectively determine to do one of two similar things as opposed to the other except by some specific property and cause that exists in one of the two similar things but not in the other. If this is not the case, then the one of the two similar things that occurs as a result [of the will] is by chance. So, it is as if for the sake of argument the philosophers conceded to [their opponent] that if a will *were* to belong to the Eternal, then it *would*

---

12 See Al-Ghazālī, *The Incoherence of the Philosophers*, par. 31, p. 248.

be possible for a temporal event to proceed from an eternal. Since the theologians are unable [36] to answer, they resorted to saying that the Eternal Will is an attribute that can distinguish one thing from its like without there being a specific property that selectively determines doing one of the two similar things from its counterpart, just as heat is an attribute that can warm and knowledge is an attribute that can comprehend the object of knowledge. Their opponents, the philosophers, said to them: This is something absurd whose occurrence is inconceivable, because vis-à-vis the one who wills, his acting will not have a preference for one of the two equally similar things to the exclusion of the other unless it is with respect to whatever it is that is not similar about them, I mean, with respect to an attribute that is in one of them but not in the other. When the two are similar in every respect and there is no specific property at all, then the will prefers both equally. Now when [the will's] preference is equal, where [the will] is the cause of acting, then the preference to do one of them is no more fitting than its preference for the other, and so it prefers to do either two contrary things simultaneously or neither one of them at all, but both cases are impossible.

20.   So for the sake of the initial argument, it is as if [the philosophers] conceded to [their opponents] that all thing are similar in relation to the First Agent, and [their opponents then] foisted on them as a necessary conclusion that there would be a specific property that was prior to [the First Agent], which is absurd. So when the [opponents] respond that the will is an attribute that can distinguish like from its like inasmuch as it is like, [the philosophers] rebutted that this is inconceivable and unintelligible concerning the meaning of "will," and so it is as if [the philosophers] have denied to [their opponents] the principle that they had conceded. This is the sum of what this section contained. It shifts the discussion from the initial question to the discussion of the will, but shifting [the subject of discussion] is a sophistical ploy.

21.   ... [38] The gist of [al-Ghazālī's next] rebuttal consists of two positions. The first is that he concedes that the will in personal experience [i.e., the human will] is that which cannot distinguish something from its like inasmuch as it is like, but that intellectual proof demands the existence of an attribute in the First Agent that can do this. To believe erroneously that an attribute's existing in this condition is impossible is like erroneously believing that nothing exists that is neither internal nor external to the world. On the basis of this, then, the will attributed to the [First] Agent (may He be praised) and to man is an equivocal term, just as is the case concerning the term "knowledge" and the other attributes whose existence in the Eternal is different from their existence in the temporal. It is only by Divine Law that we call [this attribute] "will." This rebuff has obviously sunk to such levels that it is dialectical, because the demonstration that would have led to establishing an attribute with this state, I mean that it specifies that one thing exists instead of another, would posit precisely that the objects of will are similar, but they are not similar. Quite the contrary, they are opposites, since all opposites, every one of them, can be traced back to existence and nonexistence, and these are at the limit of opposition, which is the

contradictory of similarity. So their supposition [39] that the things that the will prefers are similar [i.e., existence over nonexistence] is a false supposition, and the account of it will follow later.

22. If they say: "We claim only that they are similar in relation to the First One Who wills, since It is pure and free of wishes, whereas wishes are what actually specify one thing from its like." We say: The wishes by whose fulfillment the one who wills is himself perfected (such as our own wishes by which our will prefers things) is impossible for God (may He be exalted!). [That] is because the will whose nature is this, then desires completion vis-à-vis the deficiency existing in the very one who wills. As for wishes that are for the sake of the willed thing itself, No! [The First Willer is not free of such wishes], because from the willed thing, the one who wills acquires nothing that it did not have; rather, only the willed thing acquires that. An example would be something's emergence from nonexistence to existence; for undoubtedly existence is more excellent than nonexistence, I mean for the thing emerging. This latter is the state of the First Will in relation to existing things; for it has always chosen for them the most excellent of the two opposites, and that essentially and primarily. This is one of the two sorts of rebuttal to which this account is liable.

23. The second rebuttal [of al-Ghazālī] does not concede the absence of this attribute from the will in personal experience [i.e., the human will] but wants to establish that [even] we have in the presence of similar things a will that distinguishes something from its like. He provides the following example: Assume that immediately in front of [40] a man there are two dates similar in every respect, and suppose that he cannot take both together, and further it is not imagined that in one of the two there is some selectively determining feature. Certainly the man will inevitably distinguish one of the two by taking [it].

24. This is mistaken; for when one assumes a situation with this description and posits one who wills whom necessity has prevailed upon to eat or take the date, then his taking one of the two dates in this case is not to distinguish like from like. It is only to give up the like in exchange for its like. So whichever of the two he took, what he willed was attained and for him his wish was complete. His will, then, preferred only to distinguish between taking one of them and not taking any at all, not between taking one and distinguishing between it and not taking the other (I mean when you assume that the wishes for the two are indiscernible). In this case, he does not have a predilection for taking one of them over the other; he has a predilection only for taking one of them, whichever it happened to be, and selectively determining it over not taking [at all]. This is clear in itself; for to distinguish one of them from the other is to selectively determine one of them over the other, whereas one cannot selectively determine [41] one of two like things from its counterpart *inasmuch as it is like*. Now if the two in their existence as individuals are not alike (because one of any two individuals is different from the other by an attribute proper to it), then if we assume that the will preferred the unique [individuating] factor (*maʿnā*) of one of them, then the will's seizing upon one of them to the exclusion of the other is conceivable owing to the presence of the difference-making [attribute] found in them.

Therefore, the will did not prefer two similar things from the perspective that they are similar.

25. This is the sense of the first way to oppose [the eternity of the world] that [al-Ghazālī] mentioned. [. . .]

26. [56] [Concerning al-Ghazālī's second objection that the philosophers must admit that the temporal proceeds from the eternal otherwise an infinite causal regress would ensue],[13] I say: If the philosophers were to have introduced the Eternal Existent into existence from the temporal existence according to the manner of proof [given by al-Ghazālī], that is, if they *were* to suppose that the temporal as temporal proceeds only from an eternal, then they would have no other alternative but to extricate themselves from the suspicion concerning this problem. However, you should know that the philosophers do allow the existence of one temporal event [to proceed] from another *accidentally* to infinity when that, as something repeated in a limited and finite matter, is on the following model, [namely,] that the corruption of one of two corruptible things [57] is a condition for the existence of the other. For example, in the view of [the philosophers] it is required that the generation of one human from another is conditional on the corruption of the prior human such that he becomes the matter from which the third human is generated. For instance, we imagine two humans of whom the first produced the second from the matter of a human who has suffered corruption, and then after the second himself becomes a human, the first human suffers corruption, and so from the matter of [the first human] the second human produces a third human. Thereafter the second human suffers corruption, and so from his matter the third human produces a fourth human. Indeed, we can imagine the action going on infinitely in two matters without any absurdity appearing in that, provided that the agent continues to remain. So if the existence of this agent has neither beginning nor end, then the existence of this action will have neither beginning nor end, just as was explained above.[14] The same happens concerning two that are imagined in the past, I mean, when there is a human, then before him there was a human who produced him and a human who suffered corruption, and before that human there was a human who produced him and a human who suffered corruption.

27. In other words, when whatever has this characteristic is dependent upon an Eternal Agent, then it is of a cyclical nature in which [all of its potentially infinite members] cannot be [actual]. But if from an infinite number of matters one human were to result from another or could [58] be increased infinitely, then there would be an impossibility. [That is] because it would be possible for an infinite matter to exist, and so it would be possible for an infinite whole to exist, since if a finite whole existed that were increased infinitely without any of it suffering corruption, then it would be

---

[13] Al-Ghazālī, *The Incoherence of the Philosophers*, pars. 48–54, pp. 253–54.

[14] See pars. 9–10, pp. 298–99.

possible for an infinite whole to exist. This is something the Philosopher [i.e., Aristotle] explained in *Physics*.[15]

28.   Thus, the way in which the ancients introduced an unchanging Eternal Existent is not at all in the way that temporal events exist from It inasmuch as they are temporal; rather, they are eternal insofar as they are eternal in genus. The truth in their view is that this infinite process must result from an Eternal Agent. Because the temporal itself necessarily results only from a temporal cause, there are two ways by which the ancients introduced into existence an Eternal Existent, one in number Who is unsusceptible to any sort of change. The first was that they fully understood that this cyclical existence is eternal, namely, they fully understood that the generation of the present individual is a corruption of what was before it. Likewise, they fully understood that the corruption of the one that was corrupted is a generation of what is after it. So necessarily this eternal change results from an Eternal Mover and something eternally moved that does not change with respect to its substance, but only with respect to place through its parts, that is, its proximity and remoteness to some of the generated things. In that case, that [change with respect to place] is a cause of the corruption [59] of what is corruptible from among them and the generation of what is generable. This celestial body exists without changing except with respect to place[16] but not with respect to any other sort of change. So it is a cause of temporal events owing to its temporal actions, whereas owing to its having the continuation of these actions, I mean that they do not have a beginning or an end, it results from a cause that does not have either a beginning or an end.

29.   The second way by which [the ancients] introduced a wholly incorporeal and immaterial Eternal Existent is that they found that all the kinds of motion go back to motion with respect to place,[17] and that motion with respect to place goes back to something that is itself moved by a First Mover that is in no way moved, either essentially or accidentally, otherwise an infinite number of moved movers would exist simultaneously, which is impossible.[18] This First Mover, then, must be eternal, otherwise It would not be first. Consequently, every existing motion goes back to this Mover essentially not accidentally, where [an "essential mover"] is that which exists simultaneous with any moved thing at the time that it is moved. As for one mover's being before another, as for example one human reproduces another, that is accidental not essential. As for the mover who is a condition for the existence of the human from the beginning of [the human's] coming to be to the end—indeed, from the beginning of his existence to the end of his existence—it is this [60] [First] Mover. Likewise, Its existence is a condition for the existence of all existing things, as well as a condition

---

[15] See Aristotle, *Physics* III 5.

[16] *Aina*, lit. "where," i.e., the category of "where" (*pou*) from Aristotle's *Categories*, which is one of the three categories in which motion can occur. The other two are the categories of quantity and quality.

[17] Cf. Aristotle, *Physics* VIII 7, 260a26–b15.

[18] Ibid., VIII 5.

for the conservation of the heavens and Earth and whatever is between them. None of this is explained here demonstratively but by assertions that are akin to [al-Ghazālī's], but are more satisfying than the opponents' assertions for whomever is impartial.

30.   If this is clear to you, then I have dispensed with disentangling that by which al-Ghazālī disentangles the opponents of the philosophers in order to turn the objections against them on this problem; for the ways he disentangles them are feeble. [That] is because when he is not clear on the way by which [the ancients] introduced an Eternal Existent into existence, then he will not be clear on the way they disentangled the existence of the temporal from the eternal. That, as we said, is through the intermediary of what is eternal in its substance, being generated and corrupted with respect to its particular motions, not with respect to the universal rotation; or it is through the intermediary of the actions, being eternal in genus, that is, it does not have either a beginning or an end.

31.   Next al-Ghazālī responds on behalf of the philosophers, saying:

It might be said, "We do not find a temporal event's proceeding from an eternal improbable. What we in fact find improbable is that a *first* temporal event should proceed from an eternal, since there is no difference between the very moment of the creation and what was before it with respect to selectively determining the aspect of [61] existence, which does not [differ] inasmuch as it is a present moment, an instrument, a condition, a nature, a wish, or any other cause. When the event is not the first, it is permitted that it proceeds from [an eternal] when there is the creation of some other thing, such as the preparedness of the receiving substrate and the presence of the fitting moment, and whatever is analogous to this.[19]

After al-Ghazālī conveys this answer on their behalf, he responds to them saying:

We say that the problem concerning the occurrence of the preparedness, the presence of the moment, and whatever is renewed, still stands: either there is an infinite causal regress or it terminates in an eternal from which the first temporal event results.[20]

32.   I say: this question is the one he asked them at the beginning, and this manner of forcing [them to admit] that the temporal proceeds from the eternal is the one that he [already tried] to foist upon them. Since he answers on their behalf with a response that does not correspond with the question, namely, permitting a temporal event that is not a first temporal event to result from an eternal, he turns the question on them a second time. The answer to this question is what was given before, namely, the way that the temporal proceeds from the First Eternal is not by what is temporal; rather, it is it by what is eternal from the perspective that it is eternal in genus, being

---

19 See Al-Ghazālī, *The Incoherence of the Philosophers*, par. 49, p. 253.
20 Ibid., par. 50, p. 253.

temporal through the parts. In other words, in the view of [the philosopher], if some temporal event in itself proceeds from any eternal agent, then [that agent, e.g., the celestial body,] is not the First Eternal in their view, but they believe that its action is dependent on the First Eternal. I mean that the presence of [62] the condition of the action of the eternal, which is not the First [Eternal], depends upon the First Eternal according to the way that what temporally creates depends upon the First Eternal, namely, the dependence that is in the whole [i.e., in genus], not in the parts [i.e., in the individual members of the genus].

33.   Next he offers a response on behalf of the philosophers by representing a partial conception of their position. The sense of which is that the temporal is conceived to result from the eternal only by means of a rotation that is similar to the eternal owing to its having neither beginning nor end, while it is similar to the temporal in that any part of it that is imagined is generated and corrupted. So this motion, through the temporal creation of its parts, is a principle of temporal events, but through the eternity of its totality it is an action of the eternal.

34.   Thereafter he rebuffed this manner by which the temporal proceeds from the First Eternal according to the position of the philosophers, saying to them:

> The rotation that is the basis [of all temporal events] is either temporal or eternal. If it is eternal, then how does it become a principle for the first temporal events? If it is temporal, then it depends on another temporal event, and there will be an [infinite] causal chain. You maintain that in [63] one respect it is similar to the eternal and in another respect it is similar to the temporal; for it is permanent [and] renewed, that is, it is permanently renewed and renewed permanently. But we ask, "Is it a principle of temporal events insofar as it is permanent or insofar as it is renewed?" If it is insofar as it is permanent, then how is it that something [that exists] at some moments and not others proceeds from something permanent that has similar states? If it is insofar as it is renewed, then what is the cause of its renewal in itself? It would need another cause and there would be an [infinite] causal chain.[21]

35.   This is the sense of his account, and it is sophistical; for the temporal does not proceed from [the rotation] from the perspective that it is permanent. [The temporal] proceeds from [the eternal rotation] only inasmuch as [the rotation] is renewed. If it is not [so considered], then from the perspective that [the rotation's] renewal is not something temporally created, it does not need a renewing temporal cause but is only an eternal act, that is, it has neither a beginning nor end. Necessarily, then, the agent of [this eternal act] is an Eternal Agent, because the eternal act is owing to an Eternal Agent, whereas the temporal is owing to a temporal agent. Only from the sense of the eternal in the motion is it understood that it has neither a beginning nor an end, namely, that which is understood concerning its permanence; for motion is not permanent, but is only something that changes.

---

[21] See Al-Ghazālī, *The Incoherence of the Philosophers*, par. 54, p. 254.

II. *THE DECISIVE TREATISE*[a]

What is the attitude of the Law to philosophy?

Thus spoke the lawyer, *imām*, judge, and unique scholar, Abul Walīd Muhammad Ibn Aḥmad Ibn Rushd:

1.   Praise be to God with all due praise, and a prayer for Muḥammad His chosen servant and apostle. The purpose of this treatise is to examine, from the standpoint of the study of the Law, whether the study of philosophy and logic is allowed by the Law, or prohibited, or commanded—either by way of recommendation or as obligatory.

I. The Law Makes Philosophic Studies Obligatory

If teleological study of the world is philosophy, and if the Law commands such a study, then the Law commands philosophy.

2.   We say: If the activity of "philosophy" is nothing more than study of existing beings and reflection on them as indications of the Artisan, that is, inasmuch as they are products of art (for beings only indicate the Artisan through our knowledge of the art in them, and the more perfect this knowledge is, the more perfect the knowledge of the Artisan becomes), and if the Law has encouraged and urged reflection on beings, then it is clear that what this name signifies is either obligatory or recommended by the Law.

The Law commands such a study.

3.   That the Law summons to reflection on beings, and the pursuit of knowledge about them, by the intellect is clear from several verses of the Book of God, Blessed and Exalted, such as the saying of the Exalted, "Reflect, you {who} have vision" (Qur'ān, 59:2): this is textual authority for the obligation to use intellectual reasoning or a combination of intellectual and legal reasoning (7:185). Another example is His saying, "Have they not studied the kingdom of the heavens and the Earth, and whatever things God has created?": this is a text urging the study of the totality of beings. Again, God the Exalted has taught that one of those whom He singularly honored by his knowledge was Abraham, peace on him, for the Exalted said (6:75), "So we made Abraham see the kingdom of the heavens and the Earth, that he might be . . ." [and so on to the end of the verse]. The Exalted also said (88:17–18), "Do they not observe the camels, how they have been created, and the sky, how it has been raised up?" and He said (3:191), "and they give thought to the creation of the heavens and the Earth," and so on in countless other verses.

This study must be conducted in the best manner, by demonstrative reasoning.

4.   Since it has now been established that the Law has rendered obligatory the study of beings by the intellect and reflection on them, and since reflection is nothing more than inference and drawing out of the unknown from the known, and since this is reasoning or at any rate done by reasoning, therefore we are under an obligation to carry on our study of beings by intellectual reasoning. It is further evident that this

manner of study, to which the Law summons and urges, is the most perfect kind of study using the most perfect kind of reasoning; and this is the kind called "demonstration."

To master this instrument the religious thinker must make a preliminary study of logic, just as the lawyer must study legal reasoning. This is no more heretical in the one case than in the other. And logic must be learned from the ancient masters, regardless of the fact that they were not Muslims.

5.   The Law, then, has urged us to have demonstrative knowledge of God the Exalted and all the beings of His creation. But it is preferable and even necessary for anyone, who wants to understand God the Exalted and the other beings demonstratively, to have first understood the kinds of demonstration and their conditions [of validity], and in what respects demonstrative reasoning differs from dialectical, rhetorical, and fallacious reasoning. But this is not possible unless he has previously learned what reasoning as such is, and how many kinds it has, and which of them are valid and which invalid. This in turn is not possible unless he has previously learned the parts of reasoning, of which it is composed, that is, the premises and their kinds. Therefore, he who believes in the Law, and obeys the command to study beings, ought prior to his study to gain a knowledge of these things, which have the same place in theoretical studies as instruments have in practical activities.

6.   For just as the lawyer infers from the Divine command to him to acquire knowledge of the legal categories that he is under obligation to know the various kinds of legal syllogisms, and which are valid and which invalid, in the same way he who would know [God] ought to infer from the command to study beings that he is under obligation to acquire a knowledge of intellectual reasoning and its kinds. Indeed it is more fitting for him to do so, for if the lawyer infers from the saying of the Exalted, "Reflect, you who have vision," the obligation to acquire a knowledge of legal reasoning, how much more fitting and proper that he who would know God should infer from it the obligation to acquire a knowledge of intellectual reasoning!

7.   It cannot be objected: "This kind of study of intellectual reasoning is a heretical innovation since it did not exist among the first believers." For the study of legal reasoning and its kinds is also something that has been discovered since the first believers, yet it is not considered to be a heretical innovation. So the objector should believe the same about the study of intellectual reasoning. (For this there is a reason, which it is not the place to mention here.) But most [masters] of this religion support intellectual reasoning, except a small group of gross literalists who can be refuted by [sacred] texts.

8.   Since it has now been established that there is an obligation of the Law to study intellectual reasoning and its kinds, just as there is an obligation to study legal reasoning, it is clear that, if none of our predecessors had formerly examined intellectual reasoning and its kinds, we should be obliged to undertake such an examination from the beginning, and that each succeeding scholar would have to seek help in that task from his predecessor in order that knowledge of the subject might be completed. For it is difficult or impossible for one man to find out by himself and from the

beginning all that he needs of that subject, as it is difficult for one man to discover all the knowledge that he needs of the kinds of legal reasoning; indeed this is even truer of knowledge of intellectual reasoning.

9. But if someone other than ourselves has already examined that subject, it is clear that we ought to seek help towards our goal from what has been said by such a predecessor on the subject, regardless of whether this other one shares our religion or not. For when a valid sacrifice is performed with a certain instrument, no account is taken, in judging the validity of the sacrifice, of whether the instrument belongs to one who shares our religion or to one who does not, so long as it fulfils the conditions for validity. By "those who do not share our religion," I refer to those ancients who studied these matters before Islam. So if such is the case, and everything that is required in the study of the subject of intellectual syllogisms has already been examined in the most perfect manner by the ancients, presumably we ought to lay hands on their books in order to study what they said about that subject; and if it is all correct we should accept it from them, while if there is anything incorrect in it, we should draw attention to that.

After logic we must proceed to philosophy proper. Here too we have to learn from our predecessors, just as in mathematics and law. Thus, it is wrong to forbid the study of ancient philosophy. Harm from it is accidental, like harm from taking medicine, drinking water, or studying law.

10. When we have finished with this sort of study and acquired the instruments by whose aid we are able to reflect on beings and the indications of art in them (for he who does not understand the art does not understand the product of art, and he who does not understand the product of art does not understand the Artisan, then we ought to begin the examination of beings in the order and manner we have learned from the art of demonstrative syllogisms.

11. And again it is clear that in the study of beings this aim can be fulfilled by us perfectly only through successive examinations of them by one man after another, the later ones seeking the help of the earlier in that task, on the model of what has happened in the mathematical sciences. For if we suppose that the art of geometry did not exist in this age of ours, and likewise the art of astronomy, and a single person wanted to ascertain by himself the sizes of the heavenly bodies, their shapes, and their distances from each other, that would not be possible for him—for example, to know the proportion of the Sun to the Earth or other facts about the sizes of the stars—even though he were the most intelligent of men by nature, unless by a revelation or something resembling revelation. Indeed, if he were told that the Sun is about 150 or 160 times as great as the Earth, he would think this statement madness on the part of the speaker, although this is a fact that has been demonstrated in astronomy so surely that no one who has mastered that science doubts it.

12. But what calls even more strongly for comparison with the art of mathematics in this respect is the art of the principles of law; and the study of law itself was completed only over a long period of time. And if someone today wanted to find out by himself all the arguments that have been discovered by the theorists of the legal

schools on controversial questions, about which debate has taken place between them in most countries of Islam (except the West), he would deserve to be ridiculed, because such a task is impossible for him, apart form the fact that the work has been done already. Moreover, this is a situation that is self-evident not in the scientific arts alone but also in the practical arts; for there is not one of them that a single man can construct by himself. Then how can he do it with the art of arts, philosophy? If this is so, then whenever we find in the works of our predecessors of former nations a theory about beings and a reflection on them conforming to what the conditions of demonstration require, we ought to study what they said about the matter and what they affirmed in their books. And we should accept from them gladly and gratefully whatever in these books accords with the truth, and draw attention to and warn against what does not accord with the truth, at the same time excusing them.

13. From this it is evident that the study of the books of the ancients is obligatory by Law, since their aim and purpose in their books is just the purpose to which the Law has urged us, and that whoever forbids the study of them to anyone who is fit to study them, that is, anyone who unites two qualities, (1) natural intelligence, and (2) religious integrity and moral virtue, is blocking people from the door by which the Law summons them to knowledge of God, the door of theoretical study that leads to the truest knowledge of Him; and such an act is the extreme of ignorance and estrangement from God the Exalted.

14. And if someone errs or stumbles in the study of these books owing to a deficiency in his natural capacity, or bad organization of his study of them, or being dominated by his passions, or not finding a teacher to guide him to an understanding of their contents, or a combination of all or more than one of these causes, it does not follow that one should forbid them to anyone who is qualified to study them. For this manner of harm that arises owing to them is something that is attached to them by accident not by essence; and when a thing is beneficial by its nature and essence, it ought not to be shunned because of something harmful contained in it by accident. This was the thought of the Prophet, peace on him, on the occasion when he ordered a man to give his brother honey to drink for his diarrhea, and the diarrhea increased after he had given him the honey: When the man complained to him about it, he said, "God spoke the truth; it was your brother's stomach that lied." We can even say that a man who prevents a qualified person from studying books of philosophy, because some of the most vicious people may be thought to have gone astray through their study of them, is like a man who prevents a thirsty person from drinking cool, fresh water until he dies of thirst, because some people have choked to death on it. For death from water by choking is an accidental matter, but death by thirst is essential and necessary.

15. Moreover, this accidental effect of this art is a thing that may also occur accidentally from the other arts. To how many lawyers has law been a cause of lack of piety and immersion in this world! Indeed we find most lawyers in this state, although their art by its essence calls for nothing but practical virtue. Thus, it is not

strange if the same thing that occurs accidentally in the art that calls for practical virtue should occur accidentally in the art that calls for intellectual virtue.

For every Muslim the Law has provided a way to truth suitable to his nature, through demonstrative, dialectical, or rhetorical methods.

16.   Since all this is now established, and since we, the Muslim community, hold that this divine religion of ours is true, and that it is this religion that incites and summons us to the happiness that consists in the knowledge of God, Mighty and Majestic, and of His creation, that [end] is appointed for every Muslim by the method of assent that his temperament and nature require. For the natures of men are on different levels with respect to [their paths to] assent. One of them comes to assent through demonstration; another comes to assent through dialectical arguments, just as firmly as the demonstrative man through demonstration, since his nature does not contain any greater capacity; while another comes to assent through rhetorical arguments, again just as firmly as the demonstrative man through demonstrative arguments.

17.   Thus, since this divine religion of ours has summoned people by these three methods, assent to it has extended to everyone, except him who stubbornly denies it with his tongue or him for whom no method of summons to God the Exalted has been appointed in religion owing to his own neglect of such matters. It was for this purpose that the Prophet, peace on him, was sent with a special mission to "the white man and the black man" alike; I mean because his religion embraces all the methods of summons to God the Exalted. This is clearly expressed in the saying of God the Exalted (16:125), "Summon to the way of your Lord by wisdom and by good preaching, and debate with them in the most effective manner."

2. Philosophy Contains Nothing Opposed to Islam

Demonstrative truth and scriptural truth cannot conflict.

18.   Now since this religion is true and summons to the study which leads to knowledge of the Truth, we the Muslim community know definitely that demonstrative study does not lead to [conclusions] conflicting with what Scripture has given us; for truth does not oppose truth but accords with it and bears witness to it.

If the apparent meaning of Scripture conflicts with demonstrative conclusions it must be interpreted allegorically, that is, metaphorically.

19.   This being so, whenever demonstrative study leads to any manner of knowledge about any being, that being is inevitably either unmentioned or mentioned in Scripture. If it is unmentioned there is no contradiction, and it is in the same case as an act whose category is unmentioned, so that the lawyer has to infer it by reasoning from Scripture. If Scripture speaks about it, the apparent meaning of the words inevitably either accords or conflicts with the conclusions of demonstration about it. If this [apparent meaning] accords, there is no argument. If it conflicts, there is a call for allegorical interpretation of it. The meaning of "allegorical interpretation" is: extension of the significance of an expression from real to metaphorical significance, without

forsaking therein the standard metaphorical practices of Arabic, such as calling a thing by the name of something resembling it or a cause or consequence or accompaniment of it, or other things such as are enumerated in accounts of the kinds of metaphorical speech.

If the lawyer can do this, the religious thinker certainly can. Indeed these allegorical interpretations always receive confirmation from the apparent meaning of other passages of Scripture.

20.   Now if the lawyer does this in many decisions of religious law, with how much more right is it done by the possessor of demonstrative knowledge! For the lawyer has at his disposition only reasoning based on opinion, while he who would know [God] [has at his disposition] reasoning based on certainty. So we affirm definitely that whenever the conclusion of a demonstration is in conflict with the apparent meaning of Scripture, that apparent meaning admits of allegorical interpretation according to the rules for such interpretation in Arabic. This proposition is questioned by no Muslim and doubted by no believer. But its certainty is immensely increased for those who have had close dealings with this idea and put it to the test, and made it their aim to reconcile the assertions of intellect and tradition. Indeed, we may say that whenever a statement in Scripture conflicts in its apparent meaning with a conclusion of demonstration, if Scripture is considered carefully, and the rest of its contents searched page by page, there will invariably be found among the expressions of Scripture something that in its apparent meaning bears witness to that allegorical interpretation or comes close to bearing witness.

All Muslims accept the principle of allegorical interpretation; they only disagree about the extent of its application.

21.   In the light of this idea, the Muslims are unanimous in holding that it is not obligatory either to take all the expressions of Scripture in their apparent meaning or to extend them all from their apparent meaning by allegorical interpretation. They disagree [only] over which of them should and which should not be so interpreted: the Ash'arites for instance give an allegorical interpretation to the verse about God's directing Himself and the Tradition about His descent, while the Hanbalites take them in their apparent meaning.

The double meaning has been given to suit people's diverse intelligence. The apparent contradictions are meant to stimulate the learned to deeper study.

22.   The reason why we have received a Scripture with both an apparent and an inner meaning lies in the diversity of people's natural capacities and the difference of their innate dispositions with regard to assent. The reason why we have received in Scripture texts whose apparent meanings contradict each other is in order to draw the attention of those who are well grounded in science to the interpretation that reconciles them. This is the idea referred to in the words received from the Exalted (3:7), "He it is who has sent down to you the Book, containing certain verses clear and definite" [and so on], down to the words, "those who are well grounded in science."

In interpreting texts allegorically, we must never violate Islamic consensus when it is certain. But to establish it with certainty with regard to theoretical texts is impossible, because there have always been scholars who would not divulge their interpretation of such texts.

23. It may be objected: "There are some things in Scripture that the Muslims have unanimously agreed to take in their apparent meaning, others [that they have agreed] to interpret allegorically, and others about which they have disagreed; is it permissible, then, that demonstration should lead to interpreting allegorically what they have agreed to take in its apparent meaning, or to taking in its apparent meaning what they have agreed to interpret allegorically?" We reply: If unanimous agreement is established by a method that is certain, such [a result] is not sound; but if [the existence of] agreement on those things is a matter of opinion, then it may be sound. This is why Abū Hāmid, Abul-Maʿālī, and other leaders of thought said that no one should be definitely called an unbeliever for violating unanimity on a point of interpretation in matters like these.

24. That unanimity on theoretical matters is never determined with certainty, as it can be on practical matters, may be shown to you by the fact that it is not possible for unanimity to be determined on any question at any period unless that period is strictly limited by us, and all the scholars existing in that period are known to us (that is, known as individuals and in their total number), and the doctrine of each of them on the question has been handed down to us on unassailable authority, and, in addition to all this, unless we are sure that the scholars existing at the time were in agreement that there is not both an apparent and an inner meaning in Scripture, that knowledge of any question ought not to be kept secret from anyone, and that there is only one way for people to understand Scripture. But it is recorded in Tradition that many of the first believers used to hold that Scripture has both an apparent and an inner meaning, and that the inner meaning ought not to be learned by anyone who is not a man of learning in this field and who is incapable of understanding it. Thus, for example, Bukhārī reports a saying of ʿAlī Ibn Abī Ṭālib, may God be pleased with him, "Speak to people about what they know. Do you want God and His Prophet to be accused of lying?" Other examples of the same kind are reported about a group of early believers. So how can it possibly be conceived that a unanimous agreement can have been handed down to us about a single theoretical question, when we know definitely that not a single period has been without scholars who held that there are things in Scripture whose true meaning should not be learned by all people?

25. The situation is different in practical matters: everyone holds that the truth about these should be disclosed to all people alike, and to establish the occurrence of unanimity about them we consider it sufficient that the question [at issue] should have been widely discussed and that no report of controversy about it should have been handed down to us. This is enough to establish the occurrence of unanimity on matters of practice, but on matters of doctrine the case is different.

Al-Ghazālī's charge of unbelief against al-Fārābī and Ibn Sīnā, for asserting the world's eternity and God's ignorance of particulars and denying bodily resurrection, is only tentative not definite.

26. You may object: "If we ought not to call a man an unbeliever for violating unanimity in cases of allegorical interpretation, because no unanimity is conceivable

in such cases, what do you say about the Muslim philosophers, like Abū Naṣr and Ibn Sīnā? For Abū Ḥāmid {al-Ghāzālī} called them both definitely unbelievers in the book of his known as *The Disintegration* [*The Incoherence of the Philosophers*], on three counts: their assertions of the pre-eternity of the world,[22] and that God the Exalted does not know particulars" (may He be Exalted far above that [ignorance]!), "and their allegorical interpretation of the passages concerning the resurrection of bodies and states of existence in the next life."

27.   We answer: it is apparent from what he said on the subject that his calling them both unbelievers on these counts was not definite, since he made it clear in *The Book of Distinction* that calling people unbelievers for violating unanimity can only be tentative.

Such a charge cannot be definite, because there has never been a consensus against allegorical interpretation. The *Qurʾān* itself indicates that it has inner meanings that it is the special function of the demonstrative class to understand.

28.   Moreover, it is evident from what we have said that a unanimous agreement cannot be established in questions of this kind, because of the reports that many of the early believers of the first generation, as well as others, have said that there are allegorical interpretations that ought not to be expressed except to those who are qualified to receive allegories. These are "those who are well grounded in science"; for we prefer to place the stop after the words of God the Exalted (3:7) "and those who are well grounded in science," because if the scholars did not understand allegorical interpretation, there would be no superiority in their assent that would oblige them to a belief in Him not found among the unlearned. God has described them as those who believe in Him, and this can only be taken to refer to the belief that is based on demonstration; and this [belief] only occurs together with the science of allegorical interpretation. For the unlearned believers are those whose belief in Him is not based on demonstration; and if this belief that God has attributed to the scholars is peculiar to them, it must come through demonstration, and if it comes through demonstration it only occurs together with the science of allegorical interpretation. For God the Exalted has informed us that those [verses] have an allegorical interpretation that is the truth, and demonstration can only be of the truth. That being the case, it is not possible for general unanimity to be established about allegorical interpretations, which God has made peculiar to scholars. This is self-evident to any fair-minded person.

Besides, al-Ghāzālī was mistaken in ascribing to the Peripatetics the opinion that God does not know particulars. Their view is that His knowledge of both particulars and universals differs from ours in being the cause, not an effect, of the object known. They even hold that God sends premonitions in dreams of particular events.

---

[22] See al-Ghāzālī, *The Incoherence of the Philosophers*, 241–54.

29.   In addition to all this we hold that Abū Ḥāmid was mistaken about the Peripatetic philosophers in ascribing to them the assertion that God, Holy and Exalted, does not know particulars at all. In reality they hold that God the Exalted knows them in a way that is not of the same kind as our way of knowing them. For our knowledge of them is an effect of the object known, originated when it comes into existence and changing when it changes; whereas Glorious God's Knowledge of existence is the opposite of this: it is the cause of the object known, which is existent being. Thus to suppose the two kinds of knowledge similar to each other is to identify the essences and properties of opposite things, and that is the extreme of ignorance. And if the name of "knowledge" is predicated of both originated and eternal knowledge, it is predicated by sheer homonymy, as many names are predicated of opposite things: for example, *jalal* of great and small, *ṣarīm* of light and darkness. Thus there exists no definition embracing both kinds of knowledge at once, as the theologians of our time imagine. We have devoted a separate essay to this question, impelled by one of our friends.[23]

30.   But how can anyone imagine that the Peripatetics say that God the Glorious does not know particulars with His eternal Knowledge, when they hold that true visions include premonitions of particular events due to occur in future time, and that this warning foreknowledge comes to people in their sleep from the eternal Knowledge that orders and rules the universe? Moreover, it is not only particulars that they say God does not know in the manner in which we know them but universals as well; for the universals known to us are also effects of the nature of existent being, while with His Knowledge the reverse is true. Thus the conclusion to which demonstration leads is that His Knowledge transcends qualification as "universal" or "particular." Consequently there is no point in disputing about this question, that is, whether to call them unbelievers or not.

On the question of the world, the ancient philosophers agree with the Ashʿarites that it is originated and coeval with time. The Peripatetics only disagree with the Ashʿarites and the Platonists in holding that past time is infinite. This difference is insufficient to justify a charge of unbelief.

31.   Concerning the question whether the world is pre-eternal or came into existence, the disagreement between the Ashʿarite theologians and the ancient philosophers is in my view almost resolvable into a disagreement about naming, especially in the case of certain of the ancients. For they agree that there are three classes of beings: two extremes and one intermediate between the extremes. They agree also about naming the extremes; but they disagree about the intermediate class.

32.   [1] One extreme is a being that is brought into existence from something other than itself and by something, that is, by an efficient cause and from some matter;

---

[23] That is, *The Epistle of Dedication* (*Risālat al-Ihdāʾ*); an English translation is available in Averroes, *Decisive Treatise and Epistle Dedicatory*, Charles E. Butterworth, trans.

and it, that is its existence, is preceded by time. This is the status of bodies whose generation is apprehended by sense, for example, the generation of water, air, earth, animals, plants, and so on. All alike, ancients and Ash'arites, agree in naming this class of beings "originated." [2] The opposite extreme to this is a being which is not made from or by anything and {is} not preceded by time; and there, too, all members of both schools agree in naming it "pre-eternal." This being is apprehended by demonstration; it is God, Blessed and Exalted, Who is the Maker, Giver of being and Sustainer of the universe; may He be praised and His Power exalted!

33. [3] The class of being that is between these two extremes is that which is not made from anything and not preceded by time, but which is brought into existence by something, that is by an agent. This is the world as a whole. Now they all agree on the presence of these three characters in the world. For the theologians admit that time does not precede it, or rather this is a necessary consequence for them, since time according to them is something that accompanies motion and bodies. They also agree with the ancients in the view that future time is infinite and likewise future being. They only disagree about past time and past being: the theologians hold that it is finite (this is the doctrine of Plato and his followers), while Aristotle and his school hold that it is infinite, as is the case with future time.

34. Thus, it is clear that [3] this last being bears a resemblance both to [1] the being that is really generated and to [2] the pre-eternal Being. So those who are more impressed with its resemblance to the pre-eternal than its resemblance to the originated name it "pre-eternal," while those who are more impressed with its resemblance to the originated name it "originated." But in truth it is neither really originated nor really pre-eternal, since the really originated is necessarily perishable and the really pre-eternal has no cause. Some—Plato and his followers—name it "originated and coeval with time," because time according to them is finite in the past.

35. Thus, the doctrines about the world are not so very far apart from each other that some of them should be called irreligious and others not. For this to happen, opinions must be divergent in the extreme, that is, contraries such as the theologians suppose to exist on this question; that is [they hold] that the names "pre-eternity" and "coming into existence" as applied to the world as a whole are contraries. But it is now clear from what we have said that this is not the case.

Anyhow, the apparent meaning of Scripture is that there was a being and time before God created the present being and time. Thus the theologians' interpretation is allegorical and does not command unanimous agreement.

36. Over and above all this, these opinions about the world do not conform to the apparent meaning of Scripture. For if the apparent meaning of Scripture is searched, it will be evident from the verses that give us information about the bringing into existence of the world that its form really is originated, but that being itself and time extend continuously at both extremes, that is without interruption. Thus, the words of God the Exalted (11:7), "He it is Who created the heavens and the Earth in six days, and His throne was on the water," taken in their apparent meaning imply that there was a being before this present being, namely, the throne and the water,

and a time before this time, that is, the one that is joined to the form of this being before this present being, namely, the number of the movement of the celestial sphere. And the words of the Exalted (14:48), "On the day when the Earth shall be changed into other than Earth, and the heavens as well," also in their apparent meaning imply that there will be a second being after this being. And the words of the Exalted (41:11), "Then He directed Himself towards the sky, and it was smoke," in their apparent meaning imply that the heavens were created from something.

37.   Thus the theologians too in their statements about the world do not conform to the apparent meaning of Scripture but interpret it allegorically. For it is not stated in Scripture that God was existing with absolutely nothing else: a text to this effect is nowhere to be found. Then how is it conceivable that the theologians' allegorical interpretation of these verses could meet with unanimous agreement, when the apparent meaning of Scripture that we have mentioned about the existence of the world has been accepted by a school of philosophers!

On such difficult questions, error committed by a qualified judge of his subject is excused by God, while error by an unqualified person is not excused.

38.   It seems that those who disagree on the interpretation of these difficult questions earn merit if they are in the right and will be excused [by God] if they are in error. For assent to a thing as a result of an indication [of it] arising in the soul is something compulsory not voluntary: that is, it is not for us [to choose] not to assent or to assent as it is to stand up or not to stand up. And since free choice is a condition of obligation, a man who assents to an error as a result of a consideration that has occurred to him is excused, if he is a scholar. This is why the Prophet, peace on him, said, "If the judge after exerting his mind makes a right decision, he will have a double reward; and if he makes a wrong decision, he will [still] have a single reward." And what judge is more important than he who makes judgments about being, that it is thus or not thus? These judges are the scholars, specially chosen by God for [the task of] allegorical interpretation, and this error that is forgivable according to the Law is only such error as proceeds from scholars when they study the difficult matters that the Law obliges them to study.

39.   But error proceeding from any other class of people is sheer sin, equally whether it relates to theoretical or to practical matters. For just as the judge who is ignorant of the [Prophet's] way of life is not excused if he makes an error in judgment, so he who makes judgments about beings without having the proper qualifications for [such] judgments is not excused but is either a sinner or an unbeliever. And if he who would judge what is allowed and forbidden is required to combine in himself the qualifications for exercise of personal judgment, namely, knowledge of the principles [of law] and knowledge of how to draw inferences from those principles by reasoning, how much more properly is he who would make judgments about beings required to be qualified, that is, to know the primary intellectual principle{s} and the way to draw inferences from them!

Texts of Scripture fall into three kinds with respect to the excusability of error. [1] Texts that must be taken in their apparent meaning by everyone. Since the meaning can be understood plainly by demonstrative, dialectical, and rhetorical methods alike, no one is excused for the error of interpreting these texts allegorically. [2] Texts that must be taken in their apparent meaning by the lower classes and interpreted allegorically by the demonstrative class. It is inexcusable for the lower classes to interpret them allegorically or for the demonstrative class to take them in their apparent meaning. [3] Texts whose classification under the previous headings is uncertain. Error in this matter by the demonstrative class is excused.

40.   In general, error about Scripture is of two types: Either error that is excused to one who is a qualified student of that matter in which the error occurs (as the skillful doctor is excused if he commits an error in the art of medicine and the skillful judge if he gives an erroneous judgment), but not excused to one who is not qualified in that subject; or error that is not excused to any person whatever, and that is unbelief if it concerns the principles of religion, or heresy if it concerns something subordinate to the principles.

41.   This [latter] error is that which occurs about [1] matters, knowledge of which is provided by all the different methods of indication, so that knowledge of the matter in question is in this way possible for everyone. Examples are acknowledgment of God, Blessed and Exalted, of the prophetic missions, and of happiness and misery in the next life; for these three principles are attainable by the three classes of indication, by which everyone without exception can come to assent to what he is obliged to know: I mean the rhetorical, dialectical, and demonstrative indications. So whoever denies such a thing, when it is one of the principles of the Law, is an unbeliever who persists in defiance with his tongue though not with his heart, or neglects to expose himself to learning the indication of its truth. For if he belongs to the demonstrative class of men, a way has been provided for him to assent to it, by demonstration; if he belongs to the dialectical class that is convinced by preaching, the way for him is by preaching. With this in view, the Prophet, peace on him, said, "I have been ordered to fight people until they say, 'There is no god but God,' and believe in me"; he means, by any of the three methods of attaining belief that suits them.

42.   [2] With regard to things that by reason of their recondite character are only knowable by demonstration, God has been gracious to those of His servants who have no access to demonstration, on account of their natures, habits, or lack of facilities for education: He has coined for them images and likenesses of these things, and summoned them to assent to those images, since it is possible for assent to those images to come about through the indications common to all men, that is the dialectical and rhetorical indications. This is the reason why Scripture is divided into apparent and inner meanings: the apparent meaning consists of those images that are coined to stand for those ideas, while the inner meaning is those ideas [themselves], which are clear only to the demonstrative class. These are the four or five classes of beings mentioned by Abū Ḥāmid in *The Book of Distinction*.[24]

---

[24] The five classes would appear to be (1) the essential, (2) the sensible, (3) the imaginative, (4) the intellectual and (5) simile; see Butterworth's note in his translation of the *Decisive Treatise*, p. 55, fn. 37.

43.   [1] But when it happens, as we said, that we know the thing itself by the three methods, we do not need to coin images of it, and it remains true in its apparent meaning, not admitting allegorical interpretation. If an apparent text of this kind refers to principles, anyone who interprets it allegorically is an unbeliever, for example, anyone who thinks that there is no happiness or misery in the next life, and that the only purpose of this teaching is that men should be safeguarded from each other in their bodily and sensible lives, that it is but a practical device, and that man has no other goal than his sensible existence.

44.   If this is established, it will have become clear to you from what we have said that there are [1] apparent texts of Scripture that it is not permitted to interpret allegorically; to do so on fundamentals is unbelief, on subordinate matters, heresy. There are also [2] apparent texts that have to be interpreted allegorically by men of the demonstrative class; for such men to take them in their apparent meaning is unbelief, while for those who are not of the demonstrative class to interpret them allegorically and take them out of their apparent meaning is unbelief or heresy on their part.

45.   Of this [latter] class are the verse about God's directing Himself and the Tradition about His descent. That is why the Prophet, peace on him, said in the case of the black woman, when she told him that God was in the sky, "Free her, for she is a believer." This was because she was not of the demonstrative class; and the reason for his decision was that the class of people to whom assent comes only through the imagination, that is, who do not assent to a thing except in so far as they can imagine it, find it difficult to assent to the existence of a being that is unrelated to any imaginable thing. This applies as well to those who understand from the relation stated merely [that God has] a place; these are people who have advanced a little in their thought beyond the position of the first class, [by rejecting] belief in corporeality. Thus, the [proper] answer to them with regard to such passages is that they belong to the ambiguous texts, and that the stop is to be placed after the words of God the Exalted (3:7), "And no one knows the interpretation thereof except God." The demonstrative class, while agreeing unanimously that this class of text must be interpreted allegorically, may disagree about the interpretation, according to the level of each one's knowledge of demonstration.

46.   There is also [3] a third class of Scriptural texts falling uncertainly between the other two classes, on which there is doubt. One group of those who devote themselves to theoretical study attach them to the apparent texts that it is not permitted to interpret allegorically, others attach them to the texts with inner meanings that scholars are not permitted to take in their apparent meanings. This [divergence of opinions] is due to the difficulty and ambiguity of this class of text. Anyone who commits an error about this class is excused, I mean any scholar.

The texts about the future life fall into [3], since demonstrative scholars do not agree whether to take them in their apparent meaning or interpret them allegorically. Either is permissible. But it is inexcusable to deny the fact of a future life altogether.

47.   If it is asked, "Since it is clear that scriptural texts in this respect fall into three grades, to which of these three grades, according to you, do the descriptions of the future life and its states belong?" we reply: The position clearly is that this matter belongs to the class [3] about which there is disagreement. For we find a group of those who claim an affinity with demonstration saying that it is obligatory to take these passages in their apparent meaning, because there is no demonstration leading to the impossibility of the apparent meaning in them—this is the view of the Ashʿarites; while another group of those who devote themselves to demonstration interpret these passages allegorically, and these people give the most diverse interpretations of them. In this class must be counted Abū Ḥāmid and many of the Ṣūfīs; some of them combine the two interpretations of the passages, as Abū Ḥāmid does in some of his books.

48.   So it is likely that a scholar who commits an error in this matter is excused, while one who is correct receives thanks or a reward: that is, if he acknowledges the existence [of a future life] and merely gives a certain sort of allegorical interpretation, that is of the mode of the future life not of its existence. In this matter only the negation of existence is unbelief, because it concerns one of the principles of religion and one of those points to which assent is attainable through the three methods common to "the white man and the black man."

The unlearned classes must take such texts in their apparent meaning. It is unbelief for the learned to set down allegorical interpretations in popular writings. By doing this {al-}Ghazālī caused confusion among the people. Demonstrative books should be banned to the unqualified but not to the learned.

49.   But anyone who is not a man of learning is obliged to take these passages in their apparent meaning, and allegorical interpretation of them is for him unbelief because it *leads* to unbelief. That is why we hold that, for anyone whose duty it is to believe in the apparent meaning, allegorical interpretation is unbelief, because it leads to unbelief. Anyone of the interpretative class who discloses such [an interpretation] to him is summoning him to unbelief, and he who summons to unbelief is an unbeliever.

50.   Therefore, allegorical interpretations ought to be set down only in demonstrative books, because if they are in demonstrative books they are encountered by no one but men of the demonstrative class. But if they are set down in other than demonstrative books and one deals with them by poetical, rhetorical, or dialectical methods, as Abū Ḥāmid does, then he commits an offense against the Law and against philosophy, even though the fellow intended nothing but good. For by this procedure he wanted to increase the number of learned men, but in fact he increased the number of the corrupted not of the learned! As a result, one group came to slander philosophy, another to slander religion, and another to reconcile the [first] two [groups]. It seems that this [last] was one of his objects in his books; an indication that he wanted by this [procedure] to arouse minds is that he adhered to no one doctrine in his books but was an Ashʿarite with the Ashʿarites, a

Ṣūfī with the Ṣūfīs, and a philosopher with the philosophers, so that he was like the man in the verse:

"One day a Yamanī, if I meet a man of Yaman,
And if I meet a Maʿaddī, I'm an ʿAdnānī."

51. The *imāms* of the Muslims ought to forbid those of his books that contain learned matter to all save the learned, just as they ought to forbid demonstrative books to those who are not capable of understanding them. But the damage done to people by demonstrative books is lighter, because for the most part only persons of superior natural intelligence become acquainted with demonstrative books, and this class of persons is only misled through lack of practical virtue, unorganized reading, and tackling them without a teacher. On the other hand, their total prohibition obstructs the purpose to which the Law summons, because it is a wrong to the best class of people and the best class of beings. For to do justice to the best class of beings demands that they should be known profoundly, by persons equipped to know them profoundly, and these are the best class of people; and the greater the value of the being, the greater is the injury towards it, which consists of ignorance of it. Thus, the Exalted has said (31:13), "Associating [other gods] with God is indeed a great wrong."

We have only discussed these questions in a popular work because they were already being publicly discussed.

52. This is as much as we see fit to affirm in this field of study, that is, the correspondence between religion and philosophy and the rules for allegorical interpretation in religion. If it were not for the publicity given to the matter and to these questions that we have discussed, we should not have permitted ourselves to write a word on the subject; and we should not have had to make excuses for doing so to the interpretative scholars, because the proper place to discuss these questions is in demonstrative books. God is the Guide and helps us to follow the right course!

3. Philosophical Interpretations of Scripture Should Not Be Taught to the Majority. The Law Provides Other Methods of Instructing Them

The purpose of Scripture is to teach true theoretical and practical science and right practice and attitudes.

53. You ought to know that the purpose of Scripture is simply to teach true science and right practice. True science is knowledge of God, Blessed and Exalted, and the other beings as they really are, and especially of noble beings, and knowledge of happiness and misery in the next life. Right practice consists in performing the acts that bring happiness and avoiding the acts that bring misery; and it is knowledge of these acts that is called "practical science." They fall into two divisions: (1) outward bodily acts; the science of these is called "jurisprudence"; and (2) acts of the soul such as gratitude, patience, and other moral attitudes that the Law enjoins or forbids; the

science of these is called "asceticism" or "the sciences of the future life." To these Abū Ḥāmid turned his attention in his book: as people had given up this sort [of act] and become immersed in the other sort, and as this sort [2] involves the greater fear of God, which is the cause of happiness, he called his book *The Revival of the Sciences of Religion*. But we have digressed from our subject, so let us return to it.

Scripture teaches concepts both directly and by symbols, and uses demonstrative, dialectical, and rhetorical arguments. Dialectical and rhetorical arguments are prevalent, because the main aim of Scripture is to teach the majority. In these arguments concepts are indicated directly or by symbols, in various combinations in premises and conclusion{s}.

54. We say: The purpose of Scripture is to teach true science and right practice; and teaching is of two classes, [of] concepts and [of] judgments, as the logicians have shown. Now the methods available to men of [arriving at] judgments are three: demonstrative, dialectical, and rhetorical; and the methods of forming concepts are two: either [conceiving] the object itself or [conceiving] a symbol of it. But not everyone has the natural ability to take in demonstrations, or [even] dialectical arguments, let alone demonstrative arguments that are so hard to learn and need so much time [even] for those who are qualified to learn them. Therefore, since it is the purpose of Scriptures simply to teach everyone, Scripture has to contain every method of [bringing about] judgments of assent and every method of forming concepts.

55. Now some of the methods of assent comprehend the majority of people, that is, the occurrence of assent as a result of them [is comprehensive]: these are the rhetorical and the dialectical [methods]—and the rhetorical is more comprehensive than the dialectical. Another method is peculiar to a smaller number of people: this is the demonstrative. Therefore, since the primary purpose of Scripture is to take care of the majority (without neglecting to arouse the elite), the prevailing methods of expression in religion are the common methods by which the majority comes to form concepts and judgments.

56. These [common] methods in religion are of four classes:

56.1. One of them occurs where the method is common yet specialized in two respects: that is, where it is certain in its concepts and judgments, in spite of being rhetorical or dialectical. These syllogisms are those whose premises, in spite of being based on accepted ideas or on opinions, are accidentally certain, and whose conclusions are accidentally to be taken in their direct meaning without symbolization. Scriptural texts of this class have no allegorical interpretations, and anyone who denies them or interprets them allegorically is an unbeliever.

56.2. The second class occurs where the premises, in spite of being based on accepted ideas or on opinions, are certain, and where the conclusions are symbols for the things that it was intended to conclude. [Texts of] this [class], that is their conclusions, admit of allegorical interpretation.

56.3. The third is the reverse of this: it occurs where the conclusions are the very things that it was intended to conclude, while the premises are based on accepted ideas or on opinions without being accidentally certain. [Texts of] this [class] also, that is their conclusions, do not admit of allegorical interpretation, but their premises may do so.

56.4.   The fourth [class] occurs where the premises are based on accepted ideas or opinions, without being accidentally certain, and where the conclusions are symbols for what it was intended to conclude. In these cases the duty of the elite is to interpret them allegorically, while the duty of the masses is to take them in their apparent meaning.

Where symbols are used, each class of men, demonstrative, dialectical, and rhetorical, must try to understand the inner meaning symbolized or rest content with the apparent meaning, according to their capacities.

57.   In general, everything in these [texts] that admits of allegorical interpretation can only be understood by demonstration. The duty of the elite here is to apply such interpretation; while the duty of the masses is to take them in their apparent meaning in both respects, that is, in concept and judgment, since their natural capacity does not allow more than that.

58.   But there may occur to students of Scripture allegorical interpretations due to the superiority of one of the common methods over another in [bringing about] assent, that is, when the indication contained in the allegorical interpretation is more persuasive than the indication contained in the apparent meaning. Such interpretations are popular; and [the making of them] is possibly a duty, for those powers of theoretical understanding have attained the dialectical level. To this sort belong some of the interpretations of the Ashʿarites and Muʿtazilites—though the Muʿtazilites are generally sounder in their statements. The masses, on the other hand, who are incapable of more than rhetorical arguments, have the duty of taking these [texts] in their apparent meaning, and they are not permitted to know such interpretations at all.

59.   Thus, people in relation to Scripture fall into three classes:

59.1.   One class is these who are not people of interpretation at all: these are the rhetorical class. They are the overwhelming mass, for no man of sound intellect is exempted from this kind of assent.

59.2.   Another class is the people of dialectical interpretation: these are the dialecticians, either by nature alone or by nature and habit.

59.3.   Another class is the people of certain interpretation: these are the demonstrative class, by nature and training, that is, in the art of philosophy. This interpretation ought not to be expressed to the dialectical class, let alone to the masses.

To explain the inner meaning to people unable to understand it is to destroy their belief in the apparent meaning without putting anything in its place. The result is unbelief in learners and teachers. It is best for the learned to profess ignorance, quoting the *Qurʾān* on the limitation of man's understanding.

60.   When something of these allegorical interpretations is expressed to anyone unfit to receive them—especially demonstrative interpretations because of their

remoteness from common knowledge—both he who expresses it and he to whom it is expressed are led into unbelief. The reason for that [in the case of the latter] is that allegorical interpretation comprises two things, rejection of the apparent meaning and affirmation of the allegorical one; so that if the apparent meaning is rejected in the mind of someone who can only grasp apparent meanings, without the allegorical meaning being affirmed in his mind, the result is unbelief, if it [the text in question] concerns the principles of religion.

61.   Allegorical interpretations, then, ought not to be expressed to the masses nor set down in rhetorical or dialectical books, that is, books containing arguments of these two sorts, as was done by Abū Ḥāmid. They should [not] be expressed to this class; and with regard to an apparent text, when there is a [self-evident] doubt whether it is apparent to everyone and whether knowledge of its interpretation is impossible for them, they should be told that it is ambiguous and [its meaning] known by no one except God; and that the stop should be put here in the sentence of the Exalted (3:7), "And no one knows the interpretation thereof except God." The same kind of answer should also be given to a question about abstruse matters, which there is no way for the masses to understand; just as the Exalted has answered in His saying (17:85), "And they will ask you about the Spirit. Say, 'The Spirit is by the command of my Lord; you have been given only a little knowledge.'"

Certain people have injured the masses particularly, by giving them allegorical interpretations that are false. These people are exactly analogous to bad medical advisers. The true doctor is related to bodily health in the same way as the Legislator to spiritual health, which the Qur'ān teaches us to pursue. The true allegory is "the deposit" mentioned in the Qur'ān.

62.   As for the man who expresses these allegories to unqualified persons, he is an unbeliever on account of his summoning people to unbelief. This is contrary to the summons of the Legislator, especially when they are false allegories concerning the principles of religion, as has happened in the case of a group of people of our time. For we have seen some of them thinking that they were being philosophic and that they perceived, with their remarkable wisdom, things that conflict with Scripture in every respect, that is [in passages] that do not admit of allegorical interpretation; and that it was obligatory to express these things to the masses. But by expressing those false beliefs to the masses, they have been a cause of perdition to the masses and themselves, in this world and the next.

63.   The relation between the aim of these people and the aim of the Legislator [can be illustrated by] a parable of a man who goes to a skillful doctor. [This doctor's] aim is to preserve the health and cure the diseases of all the people, by prescribing for them rules that can be commonly accepted, about the necessity of using the things that will preserve their health and cure their diseases, and avoiding the opposite things. He is unable to make them all doctors, because a doctor is one who knows by demonstrative methods the things that preserve health and cure disease. Now this [man whom we have mentioned] goes out to the people and tells them, "These methods

prescribed by this doctor for you are not right"; and he sets out to discredit them, so that they are rejected by the people. Or he says, "They have allegorical interpretations"; but the people neither understand these nor assent to them in practice. Well, do you think that people in this condition will do any of the things that are useful for preserving health and curing disease, or that this man who has persuaded them to reject what they formerly believed in will now be able to use those [things] with them, I mean for preserving health? No, he will be unable to use those [things] with them, nor will they use them, and so they will all perish.

64.   This [is what will happen] if he expresses to them true allegories about those matters, because of their inability to understand them; let alone if he expresses to them false allegories, because this will lead them to think that there are no such things as health that ought to be preserved and disease that ought to be cured—let alone that there are things that preserve health and cure disease. It is the same when someone expresses allegories to the masses, and to those who are not qualified to understand them, in the sphere of Scripture; thus he makes it appear false and turns people away from it; and he who turns people away from Scripture is an unbeliever.

65.   Indeed this comparison is certain not poetic, as one might suppose. It presents a true analogy, in that the relation of the doctor to the health of bodies is [the same as] the relation of the Legislator to the health of souls; that is, the doctor is he who seeks to preserve the health of bodies when it exists and to restore it when it is lost, while the Legislator is he who desires this [end] for the health of souls. This health is what is called "fear of God." The precious Book has told us to seek it by acts conformable to the Law, in several verses. Thus, the Exalted has said (2:183), "Fasting has been prescribed for you, as it was prescribed for those who were before you; perhaps you will fear God." Again the Exalted has said (22:37), "Their flesh and their blood shall not touch God, but your fear shall touch him"; (29:45), "Prayer prevents immorality and transgression"; and other verses to the same effect contained in the precious Book. Through knowledge of Scripture and practice according to Scripture the Legislator aims solely at this health; and it is from this health that happiness in the future life follows, just as misery in the future life follows from its opposite.

66.   From this it will be clear to you that true allegories ought not to be set down in popular books, let alone false ones. The true allegory is the deposit that man was charged to hold and that he held, and from which all beings shied away, that is, that which is mentioned in the words of the Exalted (33:72), "We offered the deposit to the heavens, the Earth and the mountains," [and so on to the end of] the verse.

It was due to the wrong use of allegorical interpretation by the Muʿtazilites and Ashʿarites that hostile sects arose in Islam.

67.   It was due to allegorical interpretations—especially the false ones—and the supposition that such interpretations of Scripture ought to be expressed to everyone, that the sects of Islam arose, with the result that each one accused the others of unbelief or heresy. Thus the Muʿtazilites interpreted many verses and Traditions allegorically, and expressed their interpretations to the masses, and the Ashʿarites did the same,

although they used such interpretations less frequently. In consequence they threw people into hatred, mutual detestation, and wars, tore the Scriptures to shreds, and completely divided people.

68. In addition to all this, in the methods that they followed to establish their interpretations, they neither went along with the masses nor with the elite: not with the masses, because their methods were [more] obscure than the methods common to the majority, and not with the elite, because if these methods are inspected they are found deficient in the conditions [required] for demonstrations, as will be understood after the slightest inspection by anyone acquainted with the conditions of demonstration. Further, many of the principles on which the Ashʿarites based their knowledge are sophistical, for they deny many necessary truths such as the permanence of accidents, the action of things on other things, the existence of necessary causes for effects, of substantial forms, and of secondary causes.

69. And their theorists wronged the Muslims in this sense, that a sect of Ashʿarites called an unbeliever anyone who did not attain knowledge of the existence of the Glorious Creator by the methods laid down by them in their books for attaining this knowledge. But in truth it is they who are the unbelievers and in error! From this point they proceeded to disagree, one group saying, "The primary obligation is theoretical study," another group saying, "It is belief"; that is, [this happened] because they did not know which are the methods common to everyone, through whose doors the Law has summoned all people [to enter]; they supposed that there was only one method. Thus they mistook the aim of the Legislator, and were both themselves in error and led others into error.

The proper methods for teaching the people are indicated in the *Qurʾān,* as the early Muslims knew. The popular portions of the Book are miraculous in providing for the needs of every class of mind. We intend to make a study of its teachings at the apparent level, and thus help to remedy the grievous harm done by ignorant partisans of philosophy and religion.

70. It may be asked: "If these methods followed by the Ashʿarites and other theorists are not the common methods by which the Legislator has aimed to teach the masses, and by which alone it is possible to teach them, then what are those [common] methods in this religion of ours"? We reply: They are exclusively the methods set down in the precious Book. For if the precious Book is inspected, there will be found in it the three methods that are available for all the people, [namely], the common methods for the instruction of the majority of the people and the special method. And if their merits are inspected, it becomes apparent that no better common methods for the instruction of the masses can be found than the methods mentioned in it.

71. Thus, whoever tampers with them, by making an allegorical interpretation not apparent in itself, or [at least] not more apparent to everyone than they are (and that [greater apparency] is something nonexistent), is rejecting their wisdom and rejecting their intended effects in procuring human happiness. This is very apparent from [a comparison of] the condition of the first believers with the condition of those

who came after them. For the first believers arrived at perfect virtue and fear of God only by using these sayings [of Scripture] without interpreting them allegorically; and anyone of them who did find out an allegorical interpretation did not think fit to express it [to others]. But when those who came after them used allegorical interpretation, their fear of God grew less, their dissensions increased, their love for one another was removed, and they became divided into sects.

72.   So whoever wishes to remove this heresy from religion should direct his attention to the precious Book, and glean from it the indications present [in it] concerning everything in turn that it obliges us to believe, and exercise his judgment in looking at its apparent meaning as well as he is able, without interpreting any of it allegorically except where the allegorical meaning is apparent in itself, that is, commonly apparent to everyone. For if the sayings set down in Scripture for the instruction of the people are inspected, it seems that in mastering their meaning one arrives at a point, beyond which none but a man of the demonstrative class can extract from their apparent wording a meaning that is not apparent in them. This property is not found in any other sayings.

73.   For those religious sayings in the precious Book that are expressed to everyone have three properties that indicate their miraculous character: (1) There exist none more completely persuasive and convincing to everyone than they. (2) Their meaning admits naturally of mastery, up to a point beyond which their allegorical interpretation (when they are of a kind to have such an interpretation) can only be found out by the demonstrative class. (3) They contain means of drawing the attention of the people of truth to the true allegorical meaning. This [character] is not found in the doctrines of the Ash'arites nor in those of the Mu'tazilites, that is, their interpretations do not admit of mastery nor contain [means of] drawing attention to the truth, nor are they true; and this is why heresies have multiplied.

74.   It is our desire to devote our time to this object and achieve it effectively, and if God grants us a respite of life we shall work steadily towards it in so far as this is made possible for us; and it may be that that work will serve as a starting point for our successors. For our soul is in the utmost sorrow and pain by reason of the evil fancies and perverted beliefs that have infiltrated this religion, and particularly such [afflictions] as have happened to it at the hands of people who claim an affinity with philosophy. For injuries from a friend are more severe than injuries from an enemy. I refer to the fact that philosophy is the friend and milk-sister of religion; thus injuries from people related to philosophy are the severest injuries [to religion]—apart from the enmity, hatred, and quarrels that such [injuries] stir up between the two, which are companions by nature and lovers by essence and instinct. It has also been injured by a host of ignorant friends who claim an affinity with it: these are the sects that exist within it. But God directs all men aright and helps everyone to love Him; He unites their hearts in the fear of Him, and removes from them hatred and loathing by His grace and His mercy!

75.   Indeed, God has already removed many of these ills, ignorant ideas, and misleading practices by means of this triumphant rule. By it He has opened a way to

many benefits, especially to the class of persons who have trodden the path of study and sought to know the truth. This [He has done] by summoning the masses to a middle way of knowing God the Glorious, [a way] that is raised above the low level of the followers of authority but is below the turbulence of the theologians; and by drawing the attention of the elite to their obligation to make a thorough study of the principles of religion. God is the Giver of success and the Guide by His Goodness.

III.   *COMMENTARY ON* METAPHYSICS, ZETA 9[a]

Text 31 (Aristotle's *Metaphysics* Z 9, 1034a31–1034b7).

[878] Hence, as was said, concerning generalizations, substance is a starting point of every thing; in other words, it is precisely from the "what" that generalizations [begin]. The same holds in the case of processes of generation and the things like those that are constituted from natures; for the seed produces just like that which comes from work. That is to say, the form is in it potentially, and that from which the seed comes shares in a certain sense the name (for you should not demand that all things be like the case where a human comes from a human; for the woman comes from the man. That is why the mule does not come from the mule unless it is a certain part). All of the things that come [to be] from themselves, as such, are those things whose matter can be moved as a result of the thing itself in the way that the seed produces this motion, whereas all those things whose matter cannot do that in some other sense are not from [themselves].

1.   *Commentary.* In [Aristotle's] claim, "Hence, as was said, concerning generalizations, substance is a starting point of every thing," he means by "generalizations" the premises and by "substance" the essence of what is made, which is the syllogism. So it is said that just as an essence, which is the [879] syllogism, is the beginning of every thing that is made, so likewise all things generated by nature result from a prior essence. He indicated this by saying, "in other words, it is precisely from the 'what' that generalizations [begin]. The same holds in the case of processes of generation." He means, namely, just as generalizations, that is, the premises from which the things that are made are produced, are precisely the essences of the made things, so likewise the generable things are produced as a result of their essences, whether in the case of art or nature. This is indicated by, "and the things like those that are constituted from natures," which means that the things that are produced as a result of nature are like those that are produced as a result of art. His claim, "for the seed produces just like that which comes from work" means: for the seed makes the generable thing by a power in it similar to work, namely, that it is the essence of what is made. (This is something that he had explained in the sixteenth book of the *Book of Animals*.)[25] When he says, "That is to say, the form is in it potentially," he means, in other words,

---

[25] Aristotle, *Generation of Animals*, I 22, 730b8–732. The Arabic *Book of Animals* was a compilation of Aristotle's *History of Animals* (including the spurious book X), *Parts of Animals* and *Generation of Animals*.

that the form of the generable thing is in the seed potentially, just as the form of what is made is in the artisan potentially. His claim "and that from which the seed comes shares in a certain sense the name" means that that from which there is the seed shares the name and account that results from the seed in a certain sense.

2. Since he has already noted that what is common is not absolute in the case of whatever produces and is produced, but only in the case of production by seeds, he provides the reason for that: "for you should not demand that all things be like the case where a human comes from a human; for the woman comes from [880] the man. That is why the mule does not come from the mule." We said that what is produced is like what produces it only *in a sense,* because what is produced is not found to be absolutely in all cases and in every respect like what produces it, namely, like a male's coming from a male, since a female may come to be from a male. Even more so than that, the mule does not come to be from a mule. Still, what is from a mule is a mule, and that is what he intended by "unless it is a certain part," which means that, nevertheless, some part of the mule is a mule.

3. "All of the things that come [to be] from themselves, as such, are those things whose matter can be moved as a result of the thing itself in the way that the seed produces this motion," means that those things not generated as a result of their like but from themselves are generated in a manner similar to the generation of things in whose matter there is a power from which [the things] are generated similar to the power that is in the seed. He means that the generation of accidents is similar in a way to the generation of substances that come to be from a different kind, where the mode of similarity between the two is that they are not generated from something specifically like them. By "all those things whose matter cannot do that in some other sense are not from [themselves]," he means the animals that neither reproduce nor are produced from their kind; for there is no power to reproduce its like in the matter of these [animals]. Moreover, it also is produced in some other sense different from the sense that the accidents and that which is produced spontaneously are produced as well as different from the sense of that which is produced from seeds. [881] This in general is what [Aristotle] has to say in this place concerning whether there are separate forms, namely, that they have little use in generation, and that generation only concerns things that agree in form but are numerically different.

4. There is a puzzle in what he has said that is not easy but extremely difficult, namely, when it is set down that what is in potency comes to be in actuality only as a result of something belonging to either its genus or species in actuality, whereas we find there are many plants and animals that emerge from potency to actuality without a seed that is produced from something like it in form, then it might erroneously be supposed to imply that there are [separate] substances and forms that give these generated plants and animals the forms by which they are plants and animals. This is what Plato most vigorously argues against Aristotle.

5. Moreover, it might be said that when substantial forms are in an existing thing—existing as something in addition to the forms mixed in the compound things

and in addition to the primary qualities in the four elements (for example, the form of lightness in fire and heaviness in earth), and particularly [when these substantial forms] are souls (for clearly they are something in addition to the mixed forms)—then these forms in addition to the qualities that exist in these things must either (1) be produced of themselves, in which case generation is from the nongenerated, or (2) they come from something external, where that which is external is either (2a) some individual or other of that species or its genus, or (2b) it is a separate form. Since, however, we have found that the forms of the thing that are not produced by seeds are generated from something other than their genus or species, it might be necessary that there are certain [separate] forms that provide the forms of [things not produced by seeds]. This might not only be supposed to be the case with respect to what is not produced by seeds, but also with respect to what is produced by seeds [882]; for a soul is not actually in the seed but is in it only potentially. Now whatever is in potency requires what is in actuality, and the same holds for the thing in the seeds themselves; for a soul is not actualized in the seed such that there is a soul in actuality, nor is it claimed that the soul is something produced as a result of the mixture, except in the opinion of whoever thinks that the soul is a mixture.[26] Owing to the importance of these issues, it might be supposed that separate forms must be introduced here. This is the opinion of the modern philosophers,[27] who call [this separate form] the "Active Intellect" *contra* the philosophy of Aristotle.

6.   It might also be thought that [the Active Intellect] gives not only the forms of souls as well as the substantial forms belonging to similar particulars, but also that it gives the substantial forms that belong to the elements; for obviously the elements act and are acted upon only through their qualities, not through their substantial forms. On the whole, it might appear that there are no active powers except the four qualities [i.e., hot, cold, wet, and dry], which are not substantial forms. Thus, we should not say that light and heavy are either active or passive powers. In general, this puzzle turns on certain premises, one of which is that the thing that is in potency emerges into actuality only as the result of something external to it with respect to its species or genus. Another premise that it turns on is that the substantial material forms are not of themselves active and passive. Finally, another premise is that only the primary qualities are active and passive [powers]. When these premises are posited, the necessary conclusion is that the agent of these forms is certain principles that are immaterial.

7.   Thus, since Ibn Sīnā concedes these premises, he believes that all of the forms are from the Active Intellect, which he calls the "Giver of Forms."[28]

---

[26] Ibn Rushd seems to have Alexander of Aphrodisias in mind here; see the *Long Commentary on the Soul*, Book III, comment 5, pars. 13–16, p. 339.

[27] Ibn Rushd identifies the "modern philosophers" at pars. 7 and 14 respectively as Ibn Sīnā and al-Fārābī.

[28] Cf. Ibn Sīnā, *The Cure*, "The Soul," V.4, par. 4, p. 1993; *The Cure*, "Metaphysics," IV.2, pars. 1–4, pp. 219–20, where he notes that the actuality of potency requires an external agent, although in that text he did not specifically identify this separate agent with the Active Intellect or "Giver of Forms."

8. It might seem that Themistius [883] may also have conceded to this opinion, either with respect to the existing things that are generated without a seed (which is clear from his exposition in his commentary on book *Lambda* in this science) or with respect to all forms, where at the end of his sixth chapter in his commentary on the *De anima*, he says that the soul is not only that in which all the forms are—I mean the objects of intellect and perception—but also that it is what implants all forms in matter and creates them (which comes from his account indicating that he means by this soul the separate forms).

9. Concerning Alexander of Aphrodisias, it is obvious that his opinion is in harmony with the opinion of Aristotle here as well as from what he says in the sixteenth book of the *Book of Animals*; for what is said there concerning the generation of things out of seed from themselves is like what is said here.

10. In addition, one could say that the forms of the elements flow only from the Giver of Forms by indicating that we believe that the motion from which fire actually is produced comes from what is potentially fire, but we are not able to say that motion produces the substantial form belonging to the fire. So the form of the fire coming to be from the motion must exist only as a result of the Giver of Forms. This is a summary of what is advanced on behalf of this opinion, and so let us investigate it.

11. We say: when one reflects upon Aristotle's demonstration in this passage, that is, that material forms produce material forms, it is obvious that the seeds are what provide the forms of produced things resulting from the seeds through the forms that their seed producer provides. As for the things generated from themselves, celestial bodies are what [884] provides this, replacing the seed and the power that is in the seed in what is produced from the seed. All of these are divine natural powers whose likeness is as the arts are to the things made. Thus, what Aristotle says in the *Book of Animals* concerning these powers, namely, that they resemble the intellect, means that they actualize the act of the intellect.[29] In other words, these powers resemble the intellect in that they do not act through a corporeal tool.

12. In this sense these generative powers and [the powers] that the physicians recognize as informing the natural powers in the body of the animal are distinct. That is to say, these [powers recognized by the physicians] actualize the act of the practical intellect; nevertheless, they act through a determinate [bodily] instrument and specific organs, whereas the form-bearing faculty does not act through a specific organ. Thus, Galen had his doubts, saying, "I do not know whether this power creates or does not."[30] In general, however [this power] acts only through the heat that is in the seed,

---

[29] The reference seems to be to *Generation of Animals* I 22, 730b8–32.

[30] Although we have not been able to identify the exact source of this quotation, Galen on numerous occasions denied having knowledge of the nature of the soul and its relation to practical philosophy; cf. Galen, *On My Own Opinions*, chs. 8 and 14.

not like a form in them, such as the soul in the innate heat, but rather as what is confined in them similar to the soul in the celestial bodies. Thus, Aristotle assigns great importance to this power, and he likens it to divine principles not physical ones, but that this power is essentially an intellect, let alone a separate [intellect], is not true.

13. The demonstration that Aristotle uses to support that is that the forms are not generated in themselves, because if they were, then the generation would be without the matter of the enmattered thing. Consequently, what is generated is something informed,[b] but if that [885] is so, then what generates it is that which moves the matter until it receives the form, that is, that which causes [the form] to emerge from potency to act. Now what moves matter must be either a body possessing an active quality or a power of a substance that acts through a body possessing an active quality. If what generates the subject of the form were other than what generates its form, then the subject and its form would be actually two things, which is impossible. Thus, the subject does not exist without the form, unless it is said by homonymy. So because the subject of the form has existence only through the form, the agent's activity is associated with [the subject] only due to [the subject's] association with the form. Since the agent's activity is neither associated with the form alone, nor with the subject without the form, consequently then, the agent's activity is clearly associated with the subject only on the part of its association with the form. So what generates the form's subject is what generates the form; in fact, there would be no subject if it were not for [the agent's] generating the form and generating both of them simultaneously. If the subject of the form were to be generated from one agent and the form from another agent, then a single effect insofar as it is one would be generated from two agents, which is impossible; for it will not be associated with a single act, unless it is an act of a single agent. So one should rely on this [demonstration] in this situation, namely, that on which Aristotle relied.

14. It is only because the earlier group of men [namely, Ibn Sīnā and al-Fārābī] neither understood Aristotle's demonstration nor accepted its truth that they were undone. The conceit does not belong to [886] Ibn Sīnā alone, but also to al-Fārābī; for it is evident in his book on the two philosophers [Plato and Aristotle][31] that he had problems concerning this account. This earlier group of men was inclined toward the thought of Plato only because it was an opinion very much akin to that upon which the theologians of our religion rely in this account, namely, that the agent of all [generated] things is one, and that some of the [generated] things do not bring about an effect in others. In other words, they believed that from some of them creating others they would be committed to the infinite series of actual causes, and so they asserted an incorporeal agent.

---

[31] The reference is to *The Philosophy of Aristotle* (*Falsafat Arisṭuṭālīs*), Mahdi, ed., pp. 129–30; English translation in *Philosophy of Plato and Aristotle*, Muhsin Mahdi, trans., 128. See also, al-Fārābī's *The Principles of Existing Things*, pars. 41–42, p. 95 translated here.

15. One does not arrive at that from this perspective; for if there exists here what is not a body, then it is impossible for it to change the matter except by means of some other unchanging body, namely, the celestial bodies. Thus, what is impossible is that the separate intellects should provide one of the forms mixed with matter.

16. Aristotle was moved to introduce an Active Intellect separate from matter in the coming to be of intellectual powers only because in his opinion the intellectual powers are unmixed with matter, and so he necessarily required that what is not mixed with matter in a certain way be produced from what is absolutely unmixed with matter, just as he required that whatever is mixed with matter be produced from what is mixed with matter.

IV. SELECTIONS FROM *LONG COMMENTARY ON THE SOUL,* BOOK III[32]

I. Book III, Comment 5[a]

Text 5 (De anima III 4, 429a21–24).

[387] Thus, the [material intellect] will have no nature, except that, namely, what is possible. That which is [part] of the soul that is called "intellect" (and I call "intellect" that by means of which we discriminate and think) is not some being in act before it intellects.

1. *Commentary.* Since [Aristotle] has explained that the material intellect does not have some material form, he begins to define it in this way. He said that in light of this it has no nature but the nature of the possibility to receive material intelligible forms. He said, "Thus, [it] . . . will have no nature," which is to say, therefore that [part] of the soul that is called "the material intellect" has no nature and essence by which it is constituted as material but the nature of possibility, since it is stripped of all material and intelligible forms.

2. Next he said, "I call 'intellect' [that by means of which we discriminate and think]." In other words, I mean by "intellect" here the faculty of the soul that is called "intellect" in the true sense, not the faculty that is called "intellect" in the broad sense, namely, the "imaginative faculty" in the Greek language (*ymaginativam* = Arb. *fanṭāsiyā*), but rather the faculty by which we discriminate theoretical things and think about future things to be done. Thereafter he said, it "is not some being in act before it intellects," that is, therefore, the definition of the material intellect is that which is

---

[32] For discussions of many of the topics treated in the following selections see Richard C. Taylor, "Remarks on *Cogitatio* in Averroes' *Commentarium Magnum in Aristotelis* De anima *Libros,*" 217–55, as well as his "Separate Material Intellect in Averroes' Mature Philosophy," 289–309.

potentially all the intentions (*intentio* = *ma'ná*) of the universal material forms, but it is not any of the beings in act before it itself intellects [any of them].

3. Since this is the definition of the material intellect, it obviously differs in [Aristotle's] opinion from prime matter in this respect, that it is potentially all intentions of the [388] material universal forms, whereas prime matter is potentially all of those sensible forms, neither as knowing or comprehending. The reason why this nature discriminates and knows, whereas prime matter neither knows nor discriminates, is because prime matter receives distinct forms, namely, individual and particular [forms], while [the material intellect] receives universal forms. From this it is apparent that this nature is not a particular, neither a body nor a faculty in a body, since if it were, then it would receive the forms as distinct and particular. If this were so, then the forms existing in it would be potentially intelligible, and so [the material intellect] would not discriminate the nature of the forms as forms, in which case it would be a disposition for individual forms, whether incorporeal or corporeal. Thus, if that nature, which is called "intellect," receives forms, necessarily it receives forms by a manner of reception different from that according to which those material things receive forms whose contracting by matter is the determination of the prime matter in them. Thus, it is neither necessary that [the material intellect] belongs to the genus of those material things in which the forms are included nor that it is prime matter itself. Since if it were so, then the reception in these would be generically the same; for a difference of nature in what is received makes for a difference of nature in what is receiving. This, therefore, moved Aristotle to posit that this nature is different from the nature of matter, form, and the nature composed [of matter and form].

4. [389] Thus, this led Theophrastus, Themistius, and many of the commentators to believe that the material intellect is neither a generable nor corruptible substance; for every generable and corruptible thing is a this, but it was just demonstrated that this [nature] is not a this, neither a body nor a form in a body. Accordingly, it led them to believe that this is the view of Aristotle; for this account, namely, that [the material] intellect is such, is quite apparent to those who examine Aristotle's demonstration and his words: concerning the demonstration it is as we explained, and it certainly concerns the words because [Aristotle] said that it is impassive, and said that it is separable and simple. These three words ["impassive," "separable," and "simple"] are frequently used by Aristotle concerning [the material intellect], and it is incorrect—nay, it is not even plausible—that someone use them in a demonstrative doctrine concerning what is generated and corrupted.

5. But they later saw Aristotle say that if there is an intellect in potency, it is necessary that there is also an actual intellect, namely an agent, that is, that which draws what is potential from potency into act, and that there is an intellect drawn from potency into act, that is, that [act] which the Active Intellect places into the material intellect as the art puts the forms of its art into the matter used by the artist. Now when they saw this, they were of the opinion that this third intellect, which is the theoretical intellect and which the Active Intellect puts into the receiving material intellect, must be eternal; for when the recipient and agent are eternal, then the effect

must necessarily be eternal. Since they believed this, it follows [on their view] that in reality [390] [the theoretical intellect] would be neither the Active Intellect nor the effect, since an agent and effect are understood only in connection with generation in time. Or at the very least it turns out that to say [the Active Intellect] is an "agent" and [the theoretical intellect] an "effect" is merely to speak by analogy, and that the theoretical intellect is nothing other than the perfection of the material intellect by the Active Intellect, such that the theoretical intellect [turns out] to be something composed of the material intellect and the actual intellect. That it seems to be the case that the Active Intellect sometimes intellects when it is joined with us and sometimes does not intellect happens because of a mixing, namely, because of [the Active Intellect's] mixing with the material intellect. It was for this reason only [that they supposed] that Aristotle was forced to posit a material intellect, not because the theoretical intelligibles are generated and made.

6. They confirmed this by what Aristotle declared, [namely], that the Active Intellect exists in our soul, when we seem first to strip forms from the matter and then intellects them, but "to strip" is nothing other than to make them actual intelligibles after they were potential [intelligibles], just as to comprehend them is nothing other than to receive them.

7. When they saw that this activity that creates and generates the intelligibles is referred to our will and can be augmented in us as an augmentation of the intellect in us, namely of the theoretical intellect—and it was already declared that the intellect that creates and generates the things that are understandable and intelligible is an Active Intellect—they said that the dispositional intellect is this intellect, but that sometimes a deficiency and sometimes an addition happens to it on account of the mixing. This, therefore, moved Theophrastus, [391] Themistius, and the others to believe this of the theoretical intellect and to say that this was Aristotle's opinion.

8. The problems concerning this [view] are not few. The first of them is that this position contradicts that which Aristotle puts forth, namely that the relation of the actual intelligible to the material intellect is like the relation of the sensible object to the one sensing. It also contradicts the truth in itself; for if the intellect's activity of conceptualizing were eternal, then what is conceptualized by the intellect would have to be eternal, for which reason the sensible forms would necessarily be actually intelligible outside of the soul and not at all material, but this is contrary to what is found in these forms.

9. Also Aristotle openly says in this book that the relation of these rational powers that discriminate the intentions of the imagined forms is like the relation of the senses to the objects of sensation. Thus, the soul intellects nothing without the imagination in the same way that the senses sense nothing without the presence of the sensible.[33] Therefore, if the intentions that the intellect comprehends from the imagined forms were eternal, the intentions of the imaginative powers would be

---

33 Compare Aristotle, *De anima* III 7, 16–17.

eternal. If these were eternal, then sensations would be eternal; for sensations are related to this faculty just as imaginable intentions are related to the rational faculty. If sensations were eternal, then the sensed things would be eternal, or the sensations would be intentions different from the intentions of things existing outside the soul in matter; for it is impossible to posit that they are the same intentions, sometimes eternal, sometimes corruptible, unless it were possible that the corruptible nature is changed and reverts to the eternal. [392] Thus, if these intentions that are in the soul are of generable and corruptible things, necessarily those also are generable and corruptible. Concerning this there was a lengthy discussion in another place.

10. This, therefore, is one of the impossibilities that seems to tell against this opinion, namely, the one that we put forth, that is, that the material intellect is not a power made anew [for each human]. For it is held that it is impossible to imagine in what way the intelligibles will have come into being, while yet this will not have come into being, since whenever the agent and patient are eternal, necessarily the effect is eternal. Also, if we posit that the effect is generated, that is, the dispositional intellect, then how can we say about it that it generates and creates the intelligibles [that are themselves eternal]?

11. There is also a second much more difficult problem. It is that if the material intellect is the first perfection of the human that the definition of the soul makes clear, and the theoretical intellect is the final perfection, but the human is something generable and corruptible and is numerically one by means of his final perfection by the intellect, then he is necessarily such through its first perfection, in other words, through the first perfection of the intellect I am other than you and you are other than me. If not, you would be through my being and I through your being, and in general a human would be a being before he was, and thus a human would not be generable and corruptible in that part that is human, but if at all, it will be in that part that is animal. For it is thought that just as if the first perfection is a particular and as many in number as the number of individuals, it is necessary [393] that the final perfection is of this kind [i.e., it is a particular and as many in number as the number of individuals], so also the converse is necessary, namely that if the final perfection is as many in number as the number of individual humans, necessarily the first perfection is of this manner.[34]

12. Many other impossibilities follow on this position. Since, if the first perfection of all humans were the same and not as many in number as their number, it would follow that when I would have acquired a particular intelligible, you also would have acquired that same one; whenever I should forget a certain intelligible, you would also.[35] Many other impossibilities follow on this position; for it is thought that there is no difference between either position [i.e., whether first or final perfection] concern-

---

[34] Cf. Ibn Bājja, *Conjunction of the Intellect with Man*, par. 17, p. 275.

[35] Cf. Ibn Sīnā, "The Soul," V. 3, par. 8, p. 194 and Ibn Bājja, *Conjunction of the Intellect with Man*, par. 17, p. 275.

ing which the impossibilities follow, namely as a result of our positing that the final and first perfection are of the same kind, that is, not as many in number as the number of the individuals. If we want to avoid all of these impossibilities, it falls to us to posit that the first perfection is a particular, namely, an individual in matter, numerically as many as the number of individual humans and is generable and corruptible. It has now been explained on the basis of the reported demonstration of Aristotle that [the material intellect] is not a particular, neither a body nor a power in the body. Therefore, how can we avoid this error and solve this problem?

13. Alexander relies on this last [line of reasoning]. He says that it belongs more so to physics, namely, the line of reason concluding that the material intellect [394] is a generated power, such that what we think about it is correctly believed about the other faculties of the soul, namely, that they are a preparedness made in the body through itself by mixing and combining. He says this is not unbelievable, namely, that from a mixing of the elements such a noble marvel comes to be from the substance of the elements on account of a maximal mixing, even though it is unusual.

14. He gives as evidence about this that it is possible from this [i.e., a maximal mixing of the elements] that there appears the composition that first occurs in the elements, namely, the composition of the four simple qualities [e.g., hot, cold, wet, and dry], although that composition is minor, it is the cause of maximal mixing, inasmuch as one is fire and the other air.

15. Since that is so, it is not improbable that owing to the high degree of composition that is in the humans and animals, there comes to be in them powers that are different to such a great extent from the substances of the elements.

16. He openly and generally proclaims this at the beginning of his book *De anima,* and he prefaced that one considering the soul at first ought to know in advance the wonders of the human body's composition. He also said in the treatise he wrote, *On the Intellect According to the Opinion of Aristotle,* that the material intellect is a power made from a combination. These are his words: "Therefore, when from the body, at any time something is mixed by means of some mixture, something will be generated from the entire mixture such that it is suited to be an instrument of that intellect that is in this mixture. Since it exists in every [human] body and that instrument is also a body, it is called the 'potential intellect' and it is a power made from the mixture that occurred to the body prepared to receive the actual intellect."[36]

17. [395] This opinion concerning the substance of the material intellect is at odds with the words of Aristotle and his demonstration: with the words where [Aristotle] says that the material intellect is separable and that it has no corporeal instrument, but that it is simple and impassive, that is, it is unchanging, and where [Aristotle] praises Anaxagoras concerning what he said, namely, that it is not mixed

---

[36] *On the Intellect* in *Alexandri Aphrodisiensis, Praeter commentaria scripta minor, Commentariá in Aristotelem Graeca,* ed. I. Bruno supplement, par. I, vol. II, 112.10–16.

with a body;[37] and certainly [far] from the demonstration as it was understood in that which we have written.

18.   Alexander interprets Aristotle's demonstration by which [Aristotle] concludes that the material intellect is not passive and is not a particular, and is neither a body nor a power in a body, such that he meant the preparedness itself, not the subject of the preparedness. [Alexander] thus says in his book De anima that the material intellect is more like the preparedness that is in a tablet on which nothing has been written than a prepared tablet.[38] He says of this preparedness that it can truly be said not to be a particular, neither a body nor a power in a body, and that it is impassive.

19.   There is nothing in what Alexander said; for this is truly said of every preparedness, namely, that it is neither a body nor a particular form in a body. Therefore why did Aristotle take up from among the other instances of preparedness this preparedness that is in the intellect, if he did not intend to demonstrate to us the substance of what is prepared rather than the substance of the preparedness? Quite the contrary, it is impossible to say that preparedness is a substance given what we said, namely, that the subject of the preparedness is neither a body nor a power in a body. That which Aristotle's demonstration concludes concerns a different meaning than that the preparation is neither a body nor a power in the body.

20.   This is obvious from Aristotle's demonstration; [396] for the proposition claiming that in any recipient there must be nothing existing in act of the received nature, is made clear from the fact that the substance of what is prepared and its nature lack this predicate [i.e., the predicate that is to be received] insofar as it is prepared. For the preparedness is not the recipient; rather, the being of the preparedness is through the recipient just as the being of a proper accident is. Thus once there is the reception, there will be no preparedness, but the recipient will remain. This is obvious and understood by all the commentators on the basis of Aristotle's demonstration.

21.   For something that is neither a body nor a power in a body is said in four different ways. One of which is the subject of the intelligibles and is the material intellect of whose being it was demonstrated what it is. The second is the preparedness itself existing in the matter and is close to the way that it is said that privation absolutely is neither a body nor a power in a body. The third is prime matter, whose being was also demonstrated. The fourth is the abstracted forms whose being has also been demonstrated. All of these are different.

22.   Trying to avoid the obvious errors, namely, from the aforementioned problems, led Alexander to this improbable interpretation. Yet we see that Alexander is supported in this because the first perfection of the intellect should be a generated power concerning the general words mentioned in the definition of the soul, namely, because it is the first perfection of an organic natural body.[39] He says that that defini-

---

[37]   See Aristotle, De anima III 4, 429a18–29.

[38]   De anima in Alexandri Aphrodisiensis, Praeter commentaria scripta minor, op. cit., 3.12, 84, 24–85, 5.

[39]   See Aristotle, De anima II 1, 4412a27–28.

tion is true of all the parts of the soul in the same sense. He also gives an additional reason to this: since to say that all the parts of the soul are forms either has one meaning or nearly so, and since the form, inasmuch as it is the end of the one having [397] the form, cannot be separated, necessarily, when the first perfections of the soul are forms, they are not separated. By this it is incoherent that there should be a separate perfection among the first perfections of the soul, as is said of the sailor in connection with the ship,[40] otherwise in general the part that is called a "perfection" in some will have a different meaning than the meaning that is said of others. Whereas this is what [Alexander] imagined was obvious from the general statement concerning the soul, Aristotle clearly said that it was not obvious concerning all parts of the soul; for to speak of "form" and "first perfection" is to speak equivocally of the rational soul and the other parts of the soul.

23.   Abū Bakr [Ibn Bājja] if taken literally, however, seemed to maintain that the material intellect is an imaginative power as what is prepared for this, namely the intentions, which in it are actually intelligibles, and that no other power is the subject for the intelligibles besides that power.[41] Abū Bakr, however, seemed to maintain this in order to avoid the impossible consequences of Alexander, namely, that the subject receiving the intelligible forms is (1) a body made of elements, or (2) a power in a body, since consequently, it would be the case either that the being of the forms in the soul would be their being outside of the soul, and so the soul would not be something that can comprehend, or that the intellect would have a corporeal instrument, [but] if the subject for the intelligibles were a power in the body, it would be just like the senses.

24.   Concerning Alexander's opinion what is more unbelievable is that he said the first [instances of] preparedness for the intelligibles and for the other first perfections of the soul are things made from a combining, not powers made by an extrinsic mover, as is well known from the opinion of Aristotle and all the Peripatetics; for this opinion concerning the comprehending powers of the soul [398], if we have understood him [correctly], is false. For a discriminating, comprehending power cannot come to be from the substance and nature of the elements, since if it were possible that such powers were to come from their nature without an extrinsic mover, it would be possible that the final perfection, which is the [speculative] intellect, would be something that came to be from the substance of their elements, as for example color and flavor came to be. This opinion is similar to the opinion of those denying an efficient cause and who accept only material causes, that is, those who maintain chance. Alexander, however, is well above believing this; however, the problem that confronted him concerning the material intellect drove him to this.

---

40 Compare Aristotle, *De anima* II 1, 413a8–9.

41 Although the reference appears to be to a non-extant section on the rational faculty in Ibn Bājja's *Kitāb an-Nafs*, one gets a hint of his position in *Conjunction of the Intellect with Man*, par. 11, pp. 273–74.

25.   Therefore, let us return to our [opinion] and say that perhaps these problems are what induced Ibn Bājja to say this regarding the material intellect. However, what follows from it is obviously impossible; for the imagined intentions move the intellect and are not moved. For it is explained that these whose relation to the discriminating rational power is like the relation of the object of sensation to the one sensing are not like that of the one sensing, who is sensed, to a state. If it were to receive the intelligibles, then the thing would receive itself and the mover would be the thing moved. It has already been explained that it is impossible that the material intellect has an actual form, since its substance and nature is that it receives forms inasmuch as they are forms.

26.   [399] Therefore,[b] all the things that can be said about the nature of the material intellect seem to be impossible besides what Aristotle said, to which there also occurs a number of problems. One of which is that theoretical intelligibles are eternal. The second is the strongest of them, namely, that the final perfection in the human [i.e., the theoretical intellect] is as many in number as the number of individual humans, while the first perfection is numerically one for all. The third is a puzzle of Theophrastus, namely, it is necessary to posit that this intellect has no form, but [it is necessary to posit that] it is a certain kind of being, otherwise there is nothing in the subject of that for which there is the preparedness and receptivity; for preparedness and receptivity concern that which is not [yet] found in the subject.[42] Since it is a certain kind of being but does not have the nature of a form, all that remains is that it has the nature of prime matter, which is certainly unbelievable; for prime matter is neither something that comprehends nor discriminates. How can it be said about something whose being is such that it is separate [i.e., capable of independent existence]?

27.   Given all of that, then, it seemed good to me to write down what seems to be the case concerning this. If that which appears to me [true] is not complete, it will be a foundation for what remains to be completed. Thus, I ask the brothers seeing this work to write down their questions, and perhaps by this [work] the truth concerning this will be found, if I have not yet found it. If I have found it, as I imagine, then it will be clarified by means of those [previously mentioned] problems; for the truth, as Aristotle says, agrees with and bears witness to itself in every way.[43]

28.   The [first] problem asks how the theoretical intelligibles are generable and corruptible, whereas their agent and [400] recipient are eternal, and what need is there to posit an Active Intellect and recipient intellect if there were not some generated thing there. This problem would not occur if there were not something else here that is the cause of their being generated theoretical intelligibles. [The answer] is simply because those intelligibles are constituted of two things: one of which is generated,

---

[42] That is, a subject's being prepared for or receptive to, for example, the form of heat, entails that the form of heat is not already in the subject.

[43] See *Prior Analytics* I 32, 47a5–6.

the other not generated. What is said about this is according to the course of nature; for since conceptualization through the intellect, as Aristotle says,[44] is like perception through the senses, and perception through the senses is perfected through two subjects—one of which is the subject through which the sense becomes actual, that is, the object of sensation outside the soul, whereas the other is the subject through which the sense is an existing form, that is, the first perfection of what senses—it is also necessary that the actual intelligibles should have two subjects—one of which is the subject by which they are actual, namely, the forms that are actual images, whereas the second is that by which the intelligibles are one of the beings in the world, and that is the material intellect. There is no difference in this respect between the sense and the intellect except that the subject of the sense through which it is actual is outside the soul, while the subject of the intellect by which it is actual is within the soul. This is what was said by Aristotle concerning this intellect, as will be seen later.

29. This subject of the intellect, which in whatever way is that one's mover, is that which Ibn Bājja considered to be the recipient, because he found that sometimes it is a potential intellect and sometimes an actual intellect, where this [disposition] is the disposition of a receiving subject, and he considers [the proposition] convertible.

30. [401] This relationship is found more perfectly between the subject of vision that moves [the faculty of sight] and the subject of the intellect that moves [the intellect]; for just as the subject of vision, which is color, moves [the faculty of sight] only when through the presence of light it was made actual color after it was in potency, so too the imagined intentions move the material intellect only when the intelligibles are made actual after they were in potency. Because of this it was necessary for Aristotle to posit an Active Intellect, as will be seen later,[45] and it is what draws these intentions from potency into act. Therefore, just as the color that is in potency is not the first perfection of the color that is the perceived intention, rather the subject that is perfected by this color is vision, so too the subject that is perfected by the intelligible object is not the imagined intentions that are potential intelligibles but is the material intellect that is perfected by the intelligibles, and [the material intellect's] relation to [the intelligibles] is just like the relation of the intentions of color to the faculty of vision.

31. Since all of this is as we have related, it happens that these actual intelligibles, namely, the theoretical intelligibles, are generable and corruptible only on account of the subject through which they are actual [i.e., the forms that are actual images], not on account of the subject through which they are a kind of being, namely, the material intellect.

---

[44] See Aristotle, *De anima* III.4, 429a13–18.

[45] See *Large Commentary on* De anima, Book III, comment 18, par. 3, p. 351.

32. The second problem—namely, how is the material intellect numerically one in all the individual humans, being neither generable nor corruptible, while the actual intelligibles existing in it, that is, the theoretical intellect, are as many in number as the number of individual humans, being generable [402] and corruptible through the generation and corruption of the individual [humans]—is very difficult and has the greatest ambiguity.

33. For if we posit that this material intellect is as many in number as the number of individual humans, it follows that it is a particular, whether a body or a power within a body. Since it would be a particular, it would be an intention intelligible in potency; however, an intention intelligible in potency is a subject that moves the recipient intellect, not a subject that is moved. Therefore, if the receiving subject were posited to be a particular, it would follow that a thing receives itself, as we said, which is impossible.

34. Besides, if we grant that it does receive itself, it would follow that it receives itself as something distinct, and so the faculty of the intellect would be the same as the faculty of sensation, or there will be no difference between the being of the forms outside and within the soul; for individual, particular matter does not receive the forms except as a this and as individuals. This is one of the things that attests that Aristotle believed that this intellect [i.e., the material intellect] is not an account of an individual.

35. If we posit that [the material intellect] is not as numerous as the number of individuals [i.e., it is one for all humans], it follows that its relation to all the individuals that come to possess their final perfection in generation would be the same, whence if a certain one of those individuals acquires some intelligible object, that [intelligible] would be acquired by all of them. Since if the conjunction of those individuals is on account of the conjunction of the material intellect with them, just as the conjunction of the human with the sensible intention is on account of the conjunction of the first perfection [403] of the faculty of sensation with that which receives sensible intentions—whereas the conjunction of the material intellect with all the humans actually existing at some time in their final perfection ought to be the same conjunction, since there is nothing that brings about a difference of the relation of the conjunction between the two conjoined things—I say if that is so, then when you acquire some intelligible, necessarily I would acquire that intelligible too, which is absurd.

36. Regardless of whether you posit that the final perfection generated in every single individual is a subject of this intellect, namely, [the perfection] through which the material intellect is joined and as a result of which [the material intellect] is like a form separated from its subject with which it is conjoined, supposing there is such a thing, or you posit that it is a perfection that is either one of the faculties of the soul or one of the faculties of the body, the same absurdity follows.

37. Thus it should be believed that if there are things that have souls whose first perfection is a substance separated from their subjects, as is considered concerning the celestial bodies, it is impossible to find more than one individual under each one of their species. Since if under these, namely under each species, there were found more

than one individual, for example [more than] one body moved by the same mover, then the being [of the additional individuals] would be useless and superfluous, since their motion would be due to a numerically identical thing, as for example, more than one ship is useless for one sailor at the same time, and similarly more than one tool of the very same kind is useless for the artisan.

38.   This is the sense of what was said at the beginning of [Aristotle's] *On the Heavens and the World*, namely, that if there were another world, there would be another celestial body, but if there were another celestial body, it would have a numerically different [404] mover from the mover of this celestial body.[46] Thus, the mover of the celestial body would be material and as many in number as the number of the celestial bodies, namely, because it is impossible that a numerically single mover is [the mover] of two numerically distinct bodies. Hence, the artisan does not use more than one tool, when only a single activity is produced by him. It is generally considered that the impossibilities following upon this position follow upon that which we are positing, namely, that the dispositional intellect is numerically one. Ibn Bājja had already enumerated many of them in his *Conjunction of the Intellect with Man*.[47] Consequently, how does one resolve this difficult problem?

39.   Let us say, therefore, that obviously a man does not actually intellect except because of the conjunction of the actually intelligible with him. It is also obvious that matter and form are mutually joined to one another such that what is composed of them is a single thing, and particularly the material intellect and the actual intelligible intention; for what is composed from them is not some third thing different from them, just as is the case with those other things composed of matter and form. Therefore, the conjunction of the intelligible with a human is only possible through a conjunction of one or the other of these two parts with him, namely, the part of it that is like matter and the part of it, namely of the intelligible, that is like form.

40.   Since it has been explained from the aforementioned doubts that it is impossible that the intelligible should be joined with every single human and should be as numerous as their number by means of that part of it that is like matter, namely, the material [405] intellect, it remains that the conjunction of the intelligibles with us humans is through the conjunction of the intelligible intention with us, that is, the imagined intentions, namely, the part of them that is in us in some way like a form. Therefore, to say of the child that he potentially intellects can be understood in two ways: one of which is because the imagined forms that are in him are potentially intelligible, whereas the second is because the material intellect that naturally receives the intelligible of these imagined forms is a potential recipient and potentially conjoined with us.

41.   Therefore, it has been explained that the first perfection of the intellect is different from the other first perfections of the soul's other faculties, and that the term

---

[46] See Aristotle, *On the Heavens* III 8.
[47] See Ibn Bājja, *Conjunction of the Intellect with Man*, par. 17, p. 275.

"perfection" is said of them in an equivocal manner, contrary to what Alexander thought. Thus, Aristotle said regarding the definition of the soul, that is, a first perfection of a natural organic body, that it is not yet clear whether a body is perfected by all faculties in the same way, or among [the faculties] there is a certain one by which the body is not perfected, and if it is perfected, it will be in some other way.[48]

42.   The [instances of] preparedness of the intelligibles that are in the imaginative faculty are similar to the [instances of] preparedness that are in the other powers of the soul, namely, the first perfections of the other faculties of the soul. Accordingly, both types of preparedness are generated and corrupted by the generation and corruption of the individual and, in general, are as numerous as their number.

43.   They differ in this respect, namely that the former, that is, the preparedness that is in the imagined intentions, is the preparedness in a mover, insofar as it is a mover, [406] whereas the latter is the preparedness in the recipient and is the preparedness that is in the first perfection of the other parts of the soul.

44.   On account of this similarity between these two types of preparedness, Ibn Bājja thought that there was no preparedness to bring about the intelligible object except the preparedness existing in the imagined intentions. These two types of preparedness, though, are as different as heaven and Earth; for one is the preparedness in a mover, insofar as it is a mover, whereas the other is a preparedness in what is moved, insofar as it is what is moved and a recipient.

45.   Therefore, it should be believed, as had already been provided to us from Aristotle's discussion, that concerning the soul there are two parts of the intellect: one of which is the recipient, whose being has been explained here, and the other that is the agent, that is, that which makes the intentions that are in the imaginative faculty to be actual movers of the material intellect after they were potential movers, as will later appear from Aristotle's discussion. Also [it should be believed] that these two parts are neither generable nor corruptible, and that the agent [intellect] is to the recipient [intellect] as form is to matter, as will be explained later.

46.   Therefore, Themistius believed that we are the Active Intellect and that the theoretical intellect is nothing other than the conjunction of the Active Intellect with the material intellect. It is not as he thought; rather, it should be believed that in the soul there are three parts of the intellect: one of which is the receiving intellect; the second the efficient intellect; and the third is the caused intellect [i.e., the theoretical intellect]. Two of these three are eternal, namely, the Active and recipient intellects, whereas the third is generable and corruptible in one way but eternal in another.

47.   Since on the basis of this discussion we are of the opinion that the material intellect is one for all humans and also [407] that the human species is eternal, as was explained in another place, it is necessary that the material intellect is not stripped of the natural principles common to the entire human species, namely, the primary propositions and singular concepts common to all; for these intelligibles are one according to the recipient, but many according to the received intention.

---

[48] The reference appears to be to *De anima* II 2, esp. 413b24–414a4.

48. Therefore, according to the way that they are one, they are necessarily eternal, since being does not flee from the receiving subject, namely, from the mover, which is the intention of the imagined forms, and there is no impediment there on the part of the recipient. Thus, generation and corruption happen to them only owing to the multiplicity following upon them, not owing to the way that they are one. Hence, when with respect to some individual one of the first intelligibles is corrupted through the corruption of its subject through which it is conjoined with us and actual, then necessarily that intelligible is not corruptible absolutely; rather, it is corruptible with respect to each individual. In this way we can say that the theoretical intellect is one with respect to all [humans].

49. When these intelligibles are considered as beings absolutely, not with respect to some individual, they are truly said to be eternal, and they are not sometimes intellected sometimes not, but rather they are always intellected. Their being is like a mean between impermanence and permanence; for they are generable and corruptible insofar as they admit of increase and decrease [in number] as a result of their final perfection, but as they are numerically one they are eternal.

50. This will be the case if it is not assumed that the disposition in the final perfection of the human is like a disposition in [408] the intelligibles common to all [humans], namely, that worldly existence is not stripped from such individual existence; for it is not obvious that this is impossible. Nay, one saying this can have a reason that is sufficient and quiets the soul. Since wisdom is in some way proper to humans, just as the arts are in a way proper to humans, it is thought impossible that all habitation should be adverse to philosophy, just as it is believed impossible that it should be adverse to natural arts; for if some part of the [the world], such as the northern quarter, is free of them, namely, the arts, then other quarters would not be without them, since it is clear that habitation is possible in the southern part just as in the northern.

51. Perhaps, therefore, philosophy is found in the greater portion of a place^c [i.e., the world] at all times, just as one human is found [at a distant] from another and a horse from another. Thus the theoretical intellect is neither generable nor corruptible according to this way.

52. In general, just as it is concerning the Active Intellect that creates the intelligibles, so likewise it is concerning the discriminating [and] receiving intellect; for just as the Active intellect absolutely never rests from generating and creating— although it ceases to do this, namely, generate a certain subject—such is it concerning the distinguishing intellect.

53. Aristotle indicated this at the beginning of this book, when he said, "To conceptualize through the intellect and to speculate are different^d such that something else within is corrupted, whereas [the intellect] in itself has no corruption."[49] He intends by "something else" the human imagined forms. By "to conceptualize through the intellect," he intends [409] the receptivity that is always in the material intellect,

---

[49] See *De anima* I 4, 408b24–25.

concerning which he meant to raise doubts in this [book, namely, Book III] and that book [namely, Book I], when he said, "We do not remember because that one is not passive, whereas the passive intellect is corruptible but without this nothing intellects,"[50] where he means by "passive intellect" the imaginative faculty, as explained later. In general, this account appeared improbable, namely that the soul, that is to say the theoretical intellect, is immortal.

54.   Whence Plato said that the universals are neither generable nor corruptible and that they exist outside of the mind. The account is true in this way [that we have explained], but taken literally is false, which is the way Aristotle worked to refute in the *Metaphysics*. In general this account of the soul is the true part in the probable propositions that grant that the soul is both, namely, mortal and immortal; for it is absurd that probable things are wholly false. The ancients defended this, and all laws agree in presenting that.

55.   The third problem, that is, how the material intellect is some kind of being but is neither one of the material forms nor also is prime matter, is resolved thus. It must be believed that this [intellect] is a fourth genus; for just as the sensible is divided into form and matter, thus the intelligible must be divided into the counterparts of these two, namely, into something like the form and something like the matter. This is necessary in every intelligence separate [from matter] that intellects another, otherwise there would be no multiplicity [410] among the separate forms. It has already been explained in First Philosophy[51] that the only form free of potentiality absolutely is the First Form that intellects nothing outside of Itself, and indeed Its existence is Its essence, whereas the other forms are in some way distinguished with respect to essence and existence. If there were not this genus of beings that we know with respect to the science of the soul, we could not intellect the multiplicity among things separate [from matter], just as if we were not to know the nature of the intellect here, we could not intellect that the moving powers separate [from matter] ought to be intellects.

56.   This has escaped many moderns to the point that they have denied what Aristotle says in the eleventh book [i.e., *Lambda*] of the *Metaphysics*, that necessarily the separate forms moving the heavenly bodies are as [many as] the number of the celestial bodies. Thus, a knowledge of the soul is necessary for a knowledge of First Philosophy. That receiving intellect necessarily intellects the actual intellect; for since it intellected the material forms, it is more fitting that it intellects the immaterial forms and that which it intellects of the separate forms, for example of the Active Intellect, does not impede its intellecting the material forms.

57.   The proposition claiming that the recipient ought to have nothing in act of that which it receives, however, is not said absolutely but conditionally, namely, it is not necessary that the recipient be altogether something that is not in act; rather, it

---

[50] See *De anima* I 4, esp. 408b27–30.
[51] Cf. Aristotle, *Metaphysics* Λ (XII) 7.

is not actually something of that which it receives, as we said before. Indeed, you ought to know that the relation of the Active Intellect to this intellect is the relation of light to the transparent, while the relation of the material forms [411] to [the material intellect] is the relation of colors to the transparent; for just as light is the perfection of the transparent, so the Active Intellect is the perfection of the material intellect. Just as the transparent is neither moved by color nor receives it except when it is illuminated, likewise this [material] intellect does not receive the intelligibles that are here unless it is perfected and illuminated by this [Active] Intellect. Just as light makes potential color to be actual such that it can move the transparent, so the Active Intellect makes the intentions in potency actually intelligible such that the material intellect receives them. This, therefore, is what one must understand about the material intellect and the Active Intellect.

58. When the material intellect is joined [with the Active Intellect] as perfected by the Active Intellect, then we are joined with the Active Intellect. This disposition is called "acquisition" and the "acquired intellect," as will be seen later. All the problems entailed by our positing that the intellect is one and many are resolved through the way we have posited the essence of the material intellect. On the one hand, since if the intelligible object in me and in you were one in every way, it would follow that when I know some intelligible that you also know it, as well as many other impossibilities. On the other hand, if we assume that they are many, it follows that the intelligible object in me and in you would be one in species but two in number, and thus the intelligible object will have an intelligible object, and so on to infinity. So it will be impossible that a student learn from the teacher, unless the knowledge that is in the teacher were a power generating and creating the knowledge that is in the student, according to the way that this fire generates another [412] similar to it in species, which is absurd. The fact that what is known is the same in this way in the teacher and in the student made Plato believe that learning was remembering. Thus since we posit that the intelligible object that is in me and in you is many^e with respect to the subject as what is actual, namely the imagined forms, while it is one with respect to the subject through which it is an existing intellect, that is, the material intellect, these problems are solved perfectly.

59. The manner by which Ibn Bājja thought to resolve the puzzles arising about the intellect's being one and many, namely the way he gave in his *Conjunction of the Intellect with Man*, is not a way suited to resolving that problem. For when he worked to resolve this problem, the intellect that he demonstrates in that epistle to be one turns out to be different from the intellect that he also demonstrated there to be many, since the intellect that he demonstrated to be one is the Active Intellect inasmuch as it is necessarily the form of the theoretical intellect, whereas the intellect he demonstrated to be many is the theoretical intellect itself. Here, though, the term, namely "intellect," is used equivocally of the theoretical intellect and the Active Intellect.

60. Thus, if that which is understood concerning the term "intellect" in the two opposing discussions—namely, one concluding that there are many, the other that the intellect is one—is not equivocal in meaning, then that which he gave afterwards

concerning this, namely, that the Active Intellect is one while the theoretical intellect is many, does not resolve this problem. If [413] that which is understood in those two opposing discussions about this term "intellect" equivocates, then the doubt will be sophistical, not a matter of serious dispute, and thus it should be believed that the problems that that man gave in that epistle are not resolved except in this way, if those doubts are not sophistical but matters of serious dispute. In that way [that we have given], the problem about which there is doubt regarding the material intellect, whether it is extrinsic or joined, is resolved. [. . .]

2. Book III, Comments 18–20[f]

Text 18 (De anima III 5, 430a14–17).

[437] Therefore it is necessary that there is an intellect in [the soul] that is an intellect insofar as it becomes every thing, and an intellect that is an intellect insofar as it makes it to intellect every thing, and an intellect insofar as it intellects every thing, like a disposition that is like light; for light in a certain way makes potential colors actual colors.[52]

    1.   *Commentary.* When these three differences are found necessarily in the part of the soul that is called "intellect," there must be in it the part insofar as it is affected by every manner of likeness and receptivity. Also in it is a second part called "intellect" insofar as it makes this potential intellect to intellect every thing; for the cause through which it makes the potential intellect to intellect all things is nothing other than the reason why it is actual, since this, because it is actual, is the cause such that it actually intellects all things. There is also in it a third part called "intellect" insofar as it makes every potential intelligible to be actual.

    2.   He said, "Therefore it is necessary [that there is an intellect in the soul that is an intellect insofar as it becomes every thing]," and meant by that the material intellect. This, therefore, is its aforementioned description. Next he said, "and an intellect that is in an intellect insofar as it makes *it* to intellect every thing," and he meant [438] by that that which comes to be, which is in a positive state. The pronoun "it" can be referred to the material intellect, as we said, as well as to the intellecting human. It should be added to the discussion "insofar as it makes it to intellect every thing *as a result of itself and when it wants*"; for this is the definition of a state, namely, that the one having a state understands by means of it that which is proper to him *as a result of himself and when he wants* without its needing anything extrinsic in relation to this. Thereafter he said, "and an intellect insofar as it intellects [every thing]," meaning by this the Active Intellect. Concerning his claim, "it intellects every thing, [and is] like a certain disposition,"[53] he means that it makes every

---

52 It should be noted that in Aristotle's original Greek he mentions only two aspects: (1) that which becomes all things, and (2) that which makes the other all things.

53 Although *aliquis*, "Certain," appears here, 438.11, it does not appear in Text 18, where the passage is initially cited.

potentially intelligible thing actually intelligible after it was potential, as a state and form do.

3.   Next he said, "like light; [for light in a certain way makes potential colors actual colors]." Now he gives the way according to which one must posit the Active Intellect in the soul. For we cannot say that the relation of the Active Intellect in the soul to the generated intellect is like the relation of art to the artifact in all ways; for art imposes the form on the entire matter without anything existing of the form's account being in the matter before the art makes it. It is not such with respect to the intellect, since if it were such with respect to the intellect, then a human would not need either sense or imagination in grasping intelligibles. Quite the contrary, the intelligibles would come from the Active Intellect to the material intellect without the material intellect needing to observe sensible forms. Nor can we say that the imagined intentions alone move the material intellect and draw it out of potency into act, since if that were so, then there would be no difference between the universal and the individual, and thus the intellect would belong to the genus of the imaginative power. Whence, since, as we have posited, the relation of the imagined [439] intentions to the material intellect is like the relation of the sensibles to the senses (as Aristotle later says),[54] it is necessary to posit that there is another mover, who makes [the imagined intentions] move the material intellect into act, which is nothing other than to make them actual intelligibles by abstracting them from matter.

4.   Because this account, which requires positing an Active Intellect different from the material [intellect] and from the forms of things that the material intellect grasps, is similar to the account by means of which vision needs light; since the agent and recipient are different from light, he was content to make known this manner [by which the Active Intellect is related to the soul] by this example. It is as though, he says, the manner requiring us to posit an Active Intellect is the same as that by which vision needs light. For just as vision is only moved by colors when they are in act—which is only completed by the presence of light, since it is [light] itself that draws them from potency into act—so likewise the imagined intentions only move the material intellect when they become intelligible in act, which is only perfected by the presence of something that is an actual intellect. It was necessary to attribute these two acts to the soul in us, namely, to be receptive to the intelligible and to make it (although the agent and recipient are eternal substances) because these two actions are reduced to our will, namely, to abstract intelligibles and to intellect them. For, on the one hand, "to abstract" is nothing other than to make the imagined intentions actually intelligible after they were potentially [intelligible], while, on the other hand, "to intellect" is nothing other than to receive these intentions. For since we found that the same thing, namely, the imagined intentions, is brought in its very being from one order to another, we said that this must be due to an agent and recipient cause.

---

[54] See *De anima* III 7–8, 431a14–432a14.

Accordingly, the recipient is the material [cause], and the agent is the efficient [cause].

5. When we have found that we act through these two powers of the intellect [440] when we want, and nothing acts except through its form, then it was necessary to attribute to us these two powers of the intellect. The intellect [whose activity] is to abstract and create the intelligible must be prior to the intellect in us [whose activity] is to receive it. Alexander [of Aphrodisias] said that it is more correct to describe the intellect that is in us by its active power not by [its] passive [power], since passivity and receptivity are common to intellects, senses, and discriminating faculties, whereas activity is proper to [the intellect], and it is better that a thing be described by its activity. I say: This would not be necessary in every way unless the term "passivity" were said univocally with respect to them, but in fact it is only said equivocally.

6. All the things said by Aristotle about this are such that the universals have no being outside the soul, which is what Plato maintained, since if they were such, there would be no need to posit an Active Intellect.

Text 19 (De anima III 5, 430a17–20).

This intellect is also separate, neither mixed nor passible, and in its own substance it is activity. For the agent is always nobler than the patient, and the principle is nobler than the matter. Also actual knowledge is always identical with its object.

1. *Commentary.* Having explained that there is a second kind of intellect, that is, the Active Intellect, [Aristotle] begins to make a comparison between it and the material [intellect]. He said, "That intellect is also [separate, neither mixed nor passible]." That is to say, this intellect also is separate, just like the material [intellect], and also is impassible and not mixed, just like that one. When he had related those things that [the Active Intellect] has in common with the material intellect, he gave the disposition proper to the Active Intellect, and said, "in its substance it is activity," that is, in it there is no potency [441] for something like the potency to receive forms that is in the receiving intellect; for the Active Intellect intellects nothing as a result of those things that are here [below]. It was necessary that the Active Intellect be separate and impassible and not mixed insofar as it actualizes all intelligible forms. If therefore it were mixed, it would not make all forms. [We saw that] the material intellect, which insofar as it actualizes all intelligible forms receives all forms, was necessarily separate and not mixed too (since if it were not separate, it would have this particular form and then one of two [possibilities] would be necessary: either (1) it would receive itself, in which case the mover in it would be what is moved, or (2) it would not receive all the species of forms). In the same way, if the Active Intellect were mixed with matter, it would necessarily either intellect and create itself, or it would not create all forms. Thus, what is the difference between these two demonstrations on close inspection of them? They are very similar. It is amazing how everyone concedes that this demonstration is true, namely, the demonstration concerning the Active Intellect, but does not agree with respect to the demonstration concerning the material intellect,

even though they are very similar so that it is necessary for one who concedes the one to concede the other. We can know that the material intellect must be unmixed from its judging and comprehending; for since we judge through [the material intellect] itself an infinite number of things in relation to a universal proposition, but clearly the judging faculties of the soul, that is, individual [faculties] mixed [with the body], judge only a finite [number of] intentions, it follows from the conversion of the opposite that that which does not judge [only] a finite [number] of intentions must not be a faculty of the soul mixed [with body]. When we have added to this that the material intellect judges an infinite [number of] things not acquired by sensation and that it does not judge [only] a finite [number of] intentions, it follows that it is not a power [442] mixed [with body]. Ibn Bājja, however, seems to concede that this proposition is true in the *Epistle of Farewell*, namely, that the faculty through which, by means of a universal judgment, we judge is infinite, but he thought that this power is the Active Intellect, if we take his words there at face value. It is not so; for judgment and discrimination are not attributed to us save on account of the material intellect. Ibn Sīnā certainly used this proposition, and it is true in itself.[55]

2. Having related that the Active Intellect is different from the material intellect in this respect that the agent is always pure activity, whereas the material [intellect] is either [active or passive] because of the things that are here, he gave the final cause with respect to this and said, "For the agent is always nobler than the patient." That is to say, the former in its substance is always activity, whereas the latter is found in either disposition. It has already been explained that the relation of the Active Intellect to the patient intellect is just like the relation of the principle that in some way produces motion to the moved matter. The agent, however, is always nobler than the patient, and the principle is nobler than the matter. Therefore, according to Aristotle it should be believed that the last of the separate intellects in the order is this material intellect; for its activity is less than their activities, since its activity seems to be more a passivity than an activity. It is only in this sense that the [material] intellect differs from the Active Intellect, not because of anything else. Since just as we know that there is a multitude of separate intellects only on account of the diversity of their activities, so also we know the difference between that material intellect and the Active Intellect only on account of the diversity of their activities. Just as it happens to the Active Intellect to sometimes act on things existing here and sometimes not, so also it happens to the [material intellect] to sometimes judge things existing here and sometimes [443] not; but they differ only in this respect, namely, that the judgment is something at the apex of the perfection of the one who judges, whereas the activity is not in that way at the apex of the perfection of the agent. Therefore, consider this: that there is a difference between these two intellects, and if it were not this, there would be no difference between them. (O Alexander, if Aristotle were to believe that the term "material intellect" signifies nothing but a preparedness, then how could he

---

55 See Ibn Sīnā, "The Soul," V.2, par. 13, p. 192.

have made this comparison between it and the Active Intellect, namely, in providing those things with respect to which they agree and those things with respect to which they differ?)

3. Thereafter, [Aristotle] said, "Also actual knowledge is always identical with its object," and indicated, so I think, something proper to the Active Intellect in which it differs from the material [intellect], namely, that in the Active Intellect actual knowledge is the same as the object known, but it is not so in the material intellect, since [the material intellect's] intelligible is not things that are in themselves an intellect. Having explained that [the Active Intellect's] substance is its activity, he gives the cause concerning this, which follows next.

Text 20 (*De anima* III 5, 430a20–25).

What is in potency is temporally prior in the individual; however, absolutely it is not, not even temporally. It is not sometimes intellecting and sometimes not intellecting. When separated, it is what it is alone, and this alone is forever immortal. We do not remember, because this one is impassible, whereas the intellect that is passible is corruptible. Without this nothing is intellected.

1. *Commentary.* This passage can be understood in three ways: one of which is according to the opinion of Alexander [of Aphrodisias]; the second according to the opinion [444] of Themistius and other commentators; and the third according to the opinion that we have related, which is the most literal. According to the opinion of Alexander, it can be understood that [Aristotle] meant the potential intellect to be a preparedness existing in the human composite, namely, that a potential and preparedness in the human to receive the intelligible in respect to every single individual is temporally prior to the Active Intellect; however, absolutely the Active Intellect is prior. When he said, "it is not sometimes intellecting and sometimes not intellecting," he means the Active Intellect. When he said, "When separated, it is what it is alone, not mortal," he means that this Intellect, when it is joined to us and by means of which we intellect other beings insofar as it is a form for us, then this alone among the parts of the intellect is immortal. Next he said, "we do not remember, [because this one is impassible, whereas the intellect that is passible is corruptible. Without this nothing is understood]." This is a problem about the Active Intellect insofar as it is joined with us and by means of it we intellect; for someone can say that when we intellect by means of something eternal, necessarily by means of this we intellect after death just as before. [Alexander] said in response that intellect is joined with us only through the mediation of the being of the generable and corruptible material intellect in us, but since this intellect is corrupted in us, we do not remember. Therefore Alexander might understand this passage in this way, although we have not seen his commentary on this passage.

2. Themistius, on the other hand, understands by "potential intellect" the separate material intellect whose being has been demonstrated. By the intellect of which [445] [Aristotle] made a comparison with this one, [Themistius] intends the Active

Intellect insofar as it is conjoined with the potential intellect, which in fact is the theoretical intellect on [Themistius'] view. When he said, "it is not sometimes intellecting and sometimes not intellecting," he understands the Active Intellect as what does not touch the material intellect. When he said, "When separated, it is what it is alone, not mortal,"g he meant the Active Intellect insofar as it is a form for the material intellect, this is the theoretical intellect in his view. That problem, namely when he said, "We do not remember," concerns the Active Intellect insofar as it touches the material intellect, that is, it [concerns] the theoretical intellect; for he says that it is improbable that this doubt [raised] by Aristotle concerns the intellect except as the Active Intellect is a form for us. For he said that by assuming that the Active Intellect is eternal, whereas the theoretical intellect is not, this question does not follow, namely, why we do not remember after death what we intellect in life. It is just as he said; for to assume that that problem is about the Active Intellect insofar as it is acquired, as Alexander says, is improbable. For the knowledge existing in us in a state of acquisition is said equivocally in connection with knowledge existing by nature and knowledge existing by instruction. Therefore, this question, so it seems, concerns only the knowledge existing by nature; for this question is impossible if it is not about the eternal cognition existing in us, whether by nature, as Themistius says, or by the intellect[56] acquired last. Thus, since Themistius believes that this problem is about the theoretical intellect, but the beginning of Aristotle's discussion concerns the Active Intellect, [Themistius] therefore believed that the theoretical intellect is for Aristotle the Active [Intellect] insofar as it touches the material intellect.

3.   [446] In support of all this there is what [Aristotle] said in the first chapter about the theoretical intellect;[57] for there [Aristotle] raised the same question as here and resolved it with the same answer. He said in the first book: "the intellect appears to be a certain substance existing in itself and does not seem to be corrupted. Since if it were corrupted, then this would be greater with the weariness of old age." Afterwards he gave the way by means of which it is possible that the intellect is incorruptible, while [the activity of] intellecting in itself will be corruptible. He said, "To conceptualize by the intellect and to speculate are different,h such that something else within is corrupted, whereas in itself it has no such occurrence; however, discriminating and loving are not of [the intellect's] being, but of that one which has this, inasmuch as it has it. Thus also, since that one is corrupted, we neither remember nor love."[58] Therefore, Themistius says that [Aristotle's] account in that chapter in which he said, "The intellect, however, seems to be a certain substance existing in the thing and not corrupted," is the same as that about which he spoke here: "when separated, it is what it is alone, forever immortal." What he said here, "We do not remember, because this one is impassible, whereas the intellect that is possible is corruptible and

---

56 *Intellectum* might alternatively be understood as "intelligible."

57 See *De anima* I 4.

58 See *De anima* I 4, 408b24–28.

without this nothing is intellected," is the same as that which he said there, namely, "to conceptualize by the intellect and to speculate are different . . ." Because of this [Themistius] says that here [Aristotle] intended by "passive intellect" a concupiscent part of the soul; for that part seems to have a certain rationality, since it listens to that part that looks to the rational soul.

4.   Since we think that Alexander's and Themistius' opinions are impossible, and we find that Aristotle's literal account is according to our [447] interpretation, we believe that Aristotle's opinion is the one we have stated, and it is true in itself. Since his words in this passage are clear, it is explained thus. When he said, "this intellect is also separate, impassible and not mixed,"[i] he is speaking of the Active Intellect. We cannot say otherwise, but this particle "also" indicates that another intellect is impassible and not mixed. Similarly, the comparison between them is obviously between the Active Intellect and the material intellect inasmuch as the material intellect has in common with the Active [Intellect] many of these dispositions. In this Themistius agrees with us and Alexander differs from us.

5.   When [Aristotle] said, "What is in potency is temporally prior in the individual," it can be understood in the same way by the three opinions. For according to Themistius' and our opinion, the potential intellect is conjoined with us prior to the Active Intellect, while according to Alexander the potential intellect will be prior in us according to being or generation but not conjunction. When he said, "however, absolutely it is not, not even temporally," he speaks of the potential intellect. Since when it is received absolutely, not with respect to an individual, then it will not be prior to the Active Intellect in some manner of priority, but posterior to it in every way. This account agrees with either opinion, namely, saying that the potential intellect is generable or not generable. When he said, "it is not sometimes intellecting and sometimes not," it is impossible that that statement be understood according to its obvious [sense] or according to either Themistius or Alexander, since this phrase "it is," when [448] he said, "*it is* not sometimes intellecting and sometimes not," refers back to the Active Intellect according to them. But Themistius, as we said, is of the opinion that the Active Intellect is the theoretical intellect insofar as it touches the material intellect, whereas Alexander is of the opinion that the dispositional intellect, that is, the theoretical intellect, is different from the Active Intellect. The latter ought to be believed; for the art is different from the thing made by the art, and the agent is different from the activity. According to what appears to us, however, that statement is according to its obvious [sense], that is, the phrase "it is" will be related to the closest antecedent, namely, the material intellect when taken absolutely, not with respect to an individual. For it does not happen to the intellect, which is called "material," according to what we said, that it sometimes intellects and sometimes does not, except in relation to the imagined forms existing in each individual, not in relation to the species; for example, it does not happen to it that it sometimes intellects the intelligible "horse" and sometimes does not, except in relation to Socrates and Plato, whereas absolutely and in relation to the [human] species it always intellects this universal, unless the human species as a whole were to pass away, which is impossible. The

advantage of this account will be that it is according to [the text's] obvious [sense]. When he said, "however, absolutely it is not, not even temporally," he means that the potential intellect—not when it is taken in relation to some individual, but absolutely and in relation to any individual—is not found at certain times intellecting and at certain times not, but it is always found intellecting, just as the Active Intellect—when it was not taken with respect to some individual—is not found sometimes intellecting and sometimes not but is always found intellecting when taken absolutely; for the manner of the [449] two intellects' actions is the same. Accordingly, when he said, "When separated, it is what it is alone, immortal," he means: when it is separated in this way, from this way only is it immortal, not in the [way] it is taken with respect to the individual. [In light of this], his statement in which he says, "We do not remember, etc." will be according to its obvious [sense]; for against this opinion the problem arises perfectly. For he asks: Since the common intelligibles are neither generated nor corrupted on this account, why after death do we not remember the knowledge had in this life? It is answered: Because memory comes through the passive perceiving faculties. There are three faculties that are described in *On Sense and Sensibilia*, namely, imagination, cognition, and memory.[59] Those three faculties are in the human in order to present the form of an imagined thing when the sensation is absent. Thus, it was said there that since these three faculties mutually help one another, they might represent the individual thing as it is in its being, although we are not sensing it. Here he intended by "passive intelligible" the forms of imagination inasmuch as the cognitive faculty proper to the human acts on them; for this faculty is a certain rationality, and its action is nothing other than to place the intention of the form of the imagination with its individual in the memory or to distinguish the [intention] from the [individual] in the form-bearing [faculty] and imagination. Clearly the intellect that is called "material" receives the imagined intentions after this [activity of] distinguishing. Thus, this passive faculty is necessarily in the form-bearing [faculty]. Hence, he correctly said, "We do not remember, because this one is impassible, whereas the intellect that is passible is corruptible. Without this it intellects nothing." That is to say, [450] without the imaginative and cognitive faculty the intellect that is called "material" intellects nothing; for these faculties are like things that prepare the material of the art to receive the activity of the art. This, then, is one interpretation.

6. It can also be interpreted in another way, which is that when he said, "it is not sometimes intellecting and sometimes not," he means: when [the material intellect] is not taken insofar as it intellects and is informed by generable and corruptible material forms, but is taken absolutely and as what intellects separate forms free from matter, then it is not found sometimes intellecting and sometimes not. Instead, it is found in the same form, for example, in the way in which [the material intellect]

---

[59] The reference in fact does not appear to be to Aristotle's *On Sense and Sensibilia*, but to his *On Memory* I.

intellects the Active Intellect, whose relation to it is, as we have said, like that of light to the transparent; for having explained that this potential intellect is eternal and naturally perfected by material forms, it ought to be believed that it is worthier when it is naturally perfected by nonmaterial forms that are in themselves intelligible. However, it is not initially joined with us as a result of this way, but later when the generation of the dispositional intellect is perfected, as we will explain later. According to this interpretation, when he said, "When separated, it is what it is alone," he is indicating the material intellect insofar as it is perfected by the Active Intellect when it is joined with us in this way, and so is separated and perhaps indicates the material intellect in its first conjunction with us, namely, the conjunction that is by nature. [Aristotle] adopts [this view] by [using] this particle "alone," indicating the corruption of the dispositional intellect from the perspective of which it is corruptible.

7. Generally, when someone considers closely the material intellect together with the Active [451] Intellect, they appear to be two in one way but one in another way. They are two through the diversity of their activity—since the activity of the Active Intellect is to generate, whereas the former's is to be informed—whereas they are one because the material intellect is perfected by the Active Intellect and intellects it. For this reason we say that the intellect is conjoined with us, appearing in it two powers, one of which is active while the other belongs to the genus of passive powers. Alexander nicely likened that to fire; for fire naturally alters every body through the power existing in it, yet nonetheless together with this it is acted upon in whatever way by that which it alters, namely, it is likened to it in a certain sense of similarity, that is, it acquires from it a lesser fiery form through the fiery form [causing] the alteration.[60] For this disposition is very similar to the disposition of the Active Intellect in connection with the passive intellect and the intellect that it generates; for it makes these things in one way, but receives them in another way. Accordingly, the statement in which he said, "We do not remember, etc." is a solution to the question that made the ancient commentators believe that the dispositional intellect is eternal, and made Alexander believe that the material intellect is generable and corruptible concerning which it was said: How are the things understood by us not eternal, given that the intellect and recipient are eternal? It is as if he says in response that the cause of this is because the material intellect intellects nothing without the passive intellect, even though there is both the agent and recipient, just as there is no perception of colors, even though there is both light and vision unless there is the colored object. Thus, according to whichever of these interpretations it is said, it will be literal, agreeing with Aristotle's words and his demonstrations without any contradiction or departure from the obvious sense of his discussion.

8. Equivocal terms are thus used correctly in a doctrine [452] only if they, although diverse [in meaning], nonetheless agree in all the things (*intentio* = *maʿnā*)

---

[60] In Alexander's *De intellectu*, III.19ff., he says that fire consumes matter but is also nourished by the matter and so is acted on insofar as it is nourished.

of which they can be said. That to which [Aristotle] referred in another translation in place of his saying, "because this one is impassible, whereas the intellect that is passible is corruptible," demonstrates that here he intended by "passive intellect" the human imaginative faculty; for he says in that [other] translation: "that which led us to say that this intellect neither alters nor is acted upon is that the imagination is a passive intellect and is corrupted, but the intellect does not perceive and understand anything without imagination."ⁱ Therefore, this term "intellect" accordingly is said in this book in four ways: it is said of the material intellect, the dispositional intellect, the Active intellect, and the imaginative faculty. You should know that there is no difference according to the interpretation of Themistius and the ancient commentators and the opinion of Plato in this respect, that the intelligibles existing in us are eternal and that to learn is remembering. Plato says that these intelligibles are sometimes in us, sometimes not, because the subject is sometimes prepared to receive them, sometimes not, but they in themselves are after we receive [them] just as before [we receive them], and just as they are outside the soul so are they also within the soul.

9.   Themistius, however, says that this, namely that [the intelligibles in us] are sometimes joined, sometimes not, happens to them because of the nature of the recipient; for he is of the opinion that the Active Intellect is not naturally conjoined with us at first except insofar as it touches the material intellect. Thus, on the basis of this, deficiency happens to it, since conjunction with the intentions of the imagination is in one way like receptivity and in another way like activity. Thus, the intelligibles are in it in a disposition different from its being in the Active Intellect. The presumption [453] in understanding this opinion is that the reason moving Aristotle to posit that there is a material intellect is not because there is a created intellect here. Quite the contrary, the reason for this is either because (1) when the intellects that are in us are found to be according to dispositions incompatible with simple intellects, it is said that that intellect that is in us is composed of that which is in act, namely, the Active Intellect, and that which is in potency; or because (2) its conjunction, according to this opinion, is similar to generation and, as it were, it is made similar to the agent and the patient, namely in its conjunction with the intentions of the imagination. Therefore, according to this opinion the agent, patient, and effect are the same, and it is indicated by these three states through the diversity that happens to it.

10.   We, however, are of the opinion that [nothing] moved [Aristotle] to posit the Active Intellect except for the fact that the theoretical intelligibles are generated according to the manner that we mentioned. Thus consider this closely, since there is a difference between the three opinions, namely Plato's, Themistius', and our opinion. On Themistius' interpretation there is no need of these intelligibles if not for positing the material intellect alone or the material intellect and the Active Intellect according to the way of similarity; for where there is no true generation, there is no agent. We agree with Alexander in the way of positing the Active Intellect, but we differ from him with respect to the nature of the material intellect. We differ from Themistius with respect to the nature of the dispositional intellect and in the manner of positing the Active Intellect. Also in a certain way we agree with Alexander with

respect to the nature of the dispositional intellect, but in another way we disagree. Therefore, these are the three differences by which the opinions attributed to Aristotle are divided. You ought to know that use and training are the causes of that which appears concerning the power of the Active Intellect that is in [454] us to abstract and the [power of] the material intellect to receive. They are, I say, causes because of the state existing through use and training in the passive and corruptible intellect, which Aristotle calls "passive," and he openly said that it is corrupted. Otherwise, it would happen that the power in us making the intelligibles would be material and likewise a passive power. Thus, on this issue no one can think by this [line of reasoning] that the material intellect is mixed with the body; for what is said by one who believes that [the material intellect] is mixed [with the body] in response to this discussion [of ours] concerning the Active Intellect, we will say in response [to what he says] concerning the material intellect. It is by means of this intellect, which Aristotle calls "passive," that humans differ with respect to the four virtues mentioned in the *Topics*, which al-Fārābī enumerates in the [*Sophistical*] *Refutations*.[61] By means of this intellect man differs from other animals, otherwise it would then be necessary for there to be the conjunction of Active Intellect and the recipient intellect with [other] animals in the same way. Certainly the operative intellect differs from the theoretical [intellect] through the diversity of preparedness existing in this intellect. These things having been shown, let us return to our [text].

V.   *COMMENTARY ON* METAPHYSICS, DELTA 7[a]

Text 13 (*Metaphysics*, Delta 7, 1017a7–22).

[552] Some things are said to be (*huwīya*) in the accidental sense, as we say that one who is just is musical and that the human is musical, and likewise the one who is musical is a human, and likewise our saying that the musical human builds. That is because the builder is accidentally musical, or the one who is musical [accidentally] builds, and so he is accidentally that because of it, and because of that it is accidental to him. Likewise, it is accidental in those things that we mentioned, for example, when we say that the human is musical and that the musical is a human, as well as that the white is musical or the one who is musical is white; for these are said accidentally in one way because both of them are accidental to one and the same being (*huwīya*), and in another way because it is accidental to being that they are those things. So being that is said in the accidental sense actually to be this is said either because both of them belong to one and the same being, or because it is the essence of being, or because it and the thing to which it belongs and is said of are one and the same thing.

1.   [553] *Commentary*. Since both "being" and "existing" are said of whatever the term "one" is said of, and it belongs to the term "one" to be said of that which is essentially and accidentally one, this will be the condition of being. So [Aristotle]

---

[61] The reference appears to be to *Sophistical Refutations*, 2, and al-Fārābī's *al-Amkina al-mughliṭa*.

first introduces the kinds of being that are accidental beings. So he said, "Some things are said to be in the accidental sense, as we say that the one who is just is musical." He intends that it is like our saying, "the one who is just is musical," that is, he is one and the same; for this unity is accidental owing to their being accidental to one another and simultaneously being accidental to a single subject, namely, the bearer of musical and justice, for example. So this is the sense of one of the kinds [of accidental being], an example of which is, "Every musician is just."

2.   A second kind is, for example, "the human is a musician" or "the musician is a human." The sense that we express in this is that he is one accidentally. On the one hand, that might be because being musical belongs accidentally to the human, who is like the genus because [being musical] is accidental to the human in whom being musical is, and it, namely, the human which is like the genus, is one. On the other hand, [the musical human might be one accidentally] because being musical and being human are accidental to one another owing to their being in a single subject, namely, the human in which the musical accidentally exists, as for example in, "Every musician is a human." In this case, however, one of them belongs to the subject common to them accidentally, whereas the other belongs essentially, in contrast to the first kind of [accidental being], [554] I mean, for example, "the musician is white." So his claim, "for these are said accidentally in one way because both of them are accidental to one and the same being, and in another way because it is accidental to the being that they are those things," is an example of "the musical is white" not "the human is musical."

3.   Next he treats the two senses collectively and so said: "So the being that is said in the accidental sense actually to be this is said either because both of them belong to one and the same being or because it is the essence of the being, or because it and the thing to which it belongs and is said of are one and the same thing." He means by this that both of them belong to a single being, for example, the white and the musical that are found belonging to one thing, that is, that in which the white and the musical are by chance joined. So his claim, "or because it and the thing to which it belongs and is said of are one and the same thing," is like our saying, "The one who is musical is a human," because the thing to which being musical accidentally belongs, that is, the human [of whom being musical] is predicated, and the general human, is one and the same. The same holds concerning "the musical human," because its sense is that the human is the human who happens to be musical. Whatever is said of a thing itself essentially, as for example "all humans are animal," is conditionally two in one respect, but is one in another respect; for in one respect human is something different from animal, but in another respect [human] itself is essentially [an animal]. This explains this difference.

Text 14 (*Metaphysics*, Delta 7, 1017a22–b8).

[555] Everything that the types of categories indicate are said to pertain to being essentially, because in whatever number [of ways] these are said, being is also said. So some of the categories indicate what the thing is, others a quality, others a quantity, others a relation,

others action or passion, others where, others when, and each one of these itself indicates a single being; for there is no difference between one's saying that the human is in health and that the human is healthy, or that the human walks or he is in the midst of walking, and likewise with respect to cutting and the rest of the things. Also "being" indicates the particular being of the thing and its reality; for when we say the thing [is], we indicate its reality, whereas when we say that it is not, we indicate that it is not real but rather false. It is similar with respect to affirmation and negation, as in "Socrates is musical," for that is real, and "Socrates is not white," which is not real, and as we say that the diagonal is commensurate with the side is false. Also, some being is potential and some is actual; for some of them are beings with sight and so see, and others see since they have potentials for it. The same holds with respect to knowledge; for in [being] there is what has the potential to use knowledge and what is [556] using it. It is also said of the thing resting in which there is rest as well as that which has the potential to rest. Again the same holds with respect to substance; for we say that the image of Hermes is in the stone, and that half of the line <is in the line>.[b]

4. *Commentary.* Since [Aristotle] explained the kinds of being that are accidental, he starts to explain the number of ways that "being" and "existing" are said essentially. So he said, "Everything that the types of categories indicate are said to pertain to being essentially" and means by "types of categories" either the genera of categories or expressions indicating their genera. Then he said, "because in whatever number [of ways] these are said, being is also said," meaning because being is said according to whatever number [of ways] the categories are said or according to whatever number [of ways] the term "categories" indicates. Next he said, "So some of the categories indicate what the thing is, others a quality, others a quantity, others a relation, others action or passion, others where, others when." He intends that the term "being" indicates whatever the expressions of the categories indicate precisely because when the indication of what the term "being" indicates is studied thoroughly, it is obvious that it is equivalent to whatever the expressions of the categories indicate.

5. [557] Thereafter he made known the number of categories and so said, "some of them [the categories] indicate what the thing is," by which he means the substance indicating the category of substance. He also mentions the categories of quality, quantity, relation, action, and passion as well as the categories of where and when, but omits the categories of position and possession either for the sake of brevity or because they are implicit.

6.[c] You should know that the term "being" (*huwīya*) is not etymologically an Arabic term, and only some of the translators felt obliged to use it. This term was derived from the copulative particle, I mean, that which in Arabic indicates the connection of the predicate to the subject with respect to its substance, namely, the particle *huwa* [i.e., the particle of separation, "it is . . ."] in "Zayd *is* (*huwa*) an animal or human." In other words, the one who says, "The human *is* (*huwa*) an animal," indicates what we indicate by saying, "the substance or very being of the human is that it is an animal." So since they found this particle with this description, they derived this term from it according to the Arabic practice of deriving one term from another, but since [Arabic] does not derive a term from a particle, this term indicated what the thing itself indicates. As we said, some of the translators felt obliged to do that because they saw that to indicate [the Greek, *to einai*] according to what the expression used in Greek indicates would be to substitute in the Arabic [term], "existing." In fact, however, "it is . . ." (*huwa*) indicates more than the term "existing," and that is because in Arabic the term "existing" is one of the derived terms, and derived terms indicate only accidents.[62] [Because of that] were the thing itself indicated by ["existing"] in the sciences, it would be imagined that [existing] indicates an accident in [the thing itself]—which is just what happened to Ibn Sīnā. Thus, some of the translators avoided this expression, [preferring] the expression [558] "being" (*huwīya*), since there is no chance of this happening with respect to it. If the term "existing" were to indicate in Arabic what the thing indicates, then it would be more fitting that it indicate the ten categories rather than "being," since the former is a native Arabic term; however, since the term "existing" does happen to have this sense, some of them preferred the term "being" over it. Thus, when it is used here (I mean the term "existing"), nothing of the derived sense should be understood concerning it, even though its form is a form of a derived term.

7.   He says, "each one of these itself indicates a single being; for there is no difference between one's saying that the human is in health and that the human is healthy." He means that each one of the terms of the nine accidents, together with its indicating that accident, indicates a single category too, namely, the category of substance; for there is no difference between our saying with respect to the category of quality that the human is healthy or that he is in health. If this is the interpretation, then Arabic practice does not follow it and says only the alternate, "health is in the human" [as opposed to "the human is in health"]; however, their analogous statements that "we are in good favor" and "we are in good health" are not too far removed from saying. "we are in health," even if I would not say it in Arabic, particularly with respect to colors, natural dispositions, and passive qualities; for they would not say "Zayd is in white" or "he is in red." By this [Aristotle] intended only to explain that in the proposition whose subject is a substance and whose predicate is a derived term, as for example, "Zayd is white," the derived term does not indicate [559] a substance and accident or an accident in a substance, which is just what Ibn Sīnā supposed. That is [because], since [Ibn Sīnā] thought the expression "white" indicates a thing in which there is whiteness, he imagined that the ["white"] primarily indicates the subject [of white] and secondly of the accident [of white], but the case is just the reverse; rather, it primarily indicates the accident, and it secondarily indicates the subject, owing to the fact that it is characteristic of the accident to exist in a subject. If the case were as

---

62 The Arabic underlying the term "existing" is derived from the verb *wajada, yujidu, wujūd*, which has as its basic meaning "to find"; however, "being found" is something that happens to an already existing thing, and so is accidental to that thing. It is to this possible misunderstanding of *wajada, yujidu, wujūd* that Ibn Rushd is alerting his readers.

Ibn Sīnā says, I mean that "white" primarily indicates a body, then our saying, "Zayd is white" would indicate, "Zayd is a white body"; however, "*white* body" would indicate "a body of a white body," and so on infinitely. [The reason] is because when "white" indicates a white body, and so we say, "white body" and introduce body into the predicate, then another white body different from the body that we introduced must be included. So as a result of our saying "white body" there must be a body of a white body infinitely, because whenever we affirm the expression "white," we must introduce body, but we have already introduced it into the proposition initially, and so the single proposition must include an infinite number of bodies, which is impossible.

8.　Since [Aristotle] mentioned that the term "being" as well as the term "existing" is said of the ten categories, he said, "Also 'being' indicates the particular being of the thing and its reality; for when we say the thing [is], we indicate its reality, whereas when we say that it is not, we indicate that it is not real, but rather false." He means that the term "being" also indicates that what is indicated in our saying of some thing that it exists is true; for when we say of some thing that it is, we indicate [560] by that that it is true, and when we say of it that it is not, we indicate about it that it does not exist, that is, it is false.

9.　Next he said, "It is similar with respect to affirmation and negation, as in 'Socrates is musical,' for that is real, and 'Socrates is not white,' which is not real," meaning by "being" here whatever indicates the truth, whether simple or composite. I mean by the individual or composite object of inquiry[63] either with respect to the composite proposition, as for example, "Zayd is musical" or "Zayd is not musical," or with respect to the simple object of inquiry, as for example "whether Zayd is or is not." The same holds for existential talk with respect to both objects of investigation; I mean [by] the simple, for example, "Is Zayd something existing?" while "Does Zayd exist as musical?" is an example of the composite. In short, in the two situations here the terms "exist" and "is" indicate only the truth not the genus. I mean the copula "is" and "exist" in the first statement indicated only that which is used in the simple proposition and in the second only that which is used in the composite proposition, namely, that which was indicated by [Aristotle's] saying, "It is similar with respect to affirmation and negation, as in 'Socrates is musical,' for that is real." He means that the same holds with respect to affirmation; [for] when we indicate existence by affirming that with respect to which there is a copulative connection, we indicate that it is real, for example, "Socrates is musical." When we indicate by negation, [561] we indicate that it is not real, as for example our indicating of Zayd that he is not white; for that indicates that saying of him that "he is white" is not real. This is what [Aristotle] meant by saying, "and 'Socrates is not white,' which is not real," meaning

---

[63] *Maṭlūb*, "object of inquiry," refers to one of the four basic questions asked in a science, which Aristotle outlined in *Posterior Analytics* II 1–2. The four objects of inquiry are (1) that something is; (2) the reason why something is; (3) whether something is; and (4) what something is.

to say, "Socrates is not white" indicates that to say of him that "he is white" is not real.

10. It should be known in summary, however, that the term "being" that indicates the thing itself is different from the term "being" that indicates the true. Likewise the term "existing" that indicates the thing itself is different from the "existing" that indicates the true. Thus, concerning the second book of [Aristotle's] *Topics*, commentators have varied about the simple object of investigation, namely, "Is the thing something existing?"[64] Does it fall under the objects of investigation of the accident or of the genus? In other words, whoever understands "existing" here as something common to the ten categories, says it falls under the object of investigation of the genus, whereas whoever understands the expression "existing" here as the true, says it falls under the object of investigation of the accident.

11. His claim, "and as we say that the diagonal is commensurate with the side is false," is another example he used in this sense, meaning that when we say, "the diagonal shares no common measure with the side of the square," which is true, then our saying that indicates that its sharing a common measure is false. By this he meant only that there is a difference between the expression "being," which indicates the [562] copula in the mind and "being," which indicates [the being] itself that is external to the mind.

12. Thereafter he said, "Also, some being is potential and some is actual," meaning that the terms "being" and "existing" also are said of what exists external to the soul actually and what exists potentially. He then provided an example of that: "for some of them are beings with sight and so see, and others [are said to] see in that they have a potential for it." He means that possessing vision is said of some things when they actually see, and possessing vision is said of some of them, namely, in their potential to possess vision actually. The same holds for the one who knows: he is said to know at some moment when he is using his knowledge, which is the actual knower. He is also said to know at the moment when he is not using his knowledge, which is the potential but proximate knower. It is also said of whatever does not know yet, however, it is in its nature to know. This is what [Aristotle] intended when he said, "The same holds with respect to knowledge; for in [being] there is what has the potential to use knowledge and what is using it." He means that we say knowing belongs to whoever has a potential to use the knowledge but is not using it, and we say knowing belongs to whoever uses the knowledge at the moment that he is using it. The latter example is one of active potentialities, whereas the first is of passive [potentialities]. That is to say potentiality and actuality are said of both kinds.

13. Next, he said, "It is said also of the thing resting in which there is rest as well as that which has the potential to rest." He means "resting" is likewise said of an actually resting thing, that is, that which [563] has come to rest, as well as of a potentially resting thing, that is, that which has not yet come to rest but has the potential

---

[64] The reference appears to be to *Topics* II 1–2.

to come to rest. Finally, he said, "Again the same holds with respect to substance; for we say that the image of Hermes is in the stone, and that half of the line . . ." where the [rest of the] statement was destroyed. He means only that the being that is potential and that is actual likewise exist in the substance and the form; for we say that the form of Hermes is potentially in the stone, and the actuality either is in potency, because its nature is to receive the form of Hermes, or in actuality, and so in that case has received [the form].

AS-SUHRAWARDĪ

The philosophy of as-Suhrawardī can be claimed to mark the end of the classical period of Arabic philosophy and the beginning of modern, or early modern, Islamic philosophy. Shihāb ad-Dīn Yaḥyá ibn Ḥabash ibn Amīrak Abū l-Futūḥ as-Suhrawardī was born in 1154 in the small town of Suhraward in northwestern Iran. He is frequently referred to as *the eminent scholar of Illumination* after the Illuminationist school of philosophy he founded. As-Suhrawardī lived a good portion of his life as a wandering sage. We first hear of him studying philosophy and theology in Maraghah, a town near his birthplace. Thereafter he traveled to Isfahan (in Iran) or Mardin (in southeastern Anatolia) to continue his studies. In 1183 he traveled to Aleppo in modern Syria, where he remained until his death by execution at the order of Saladin in 1191. Legend has it that when he entered Aleppo he was so shabbily dressed that the director of the *madrasa*—a religious (boarding) school associated with a mosque—where he was staying sent him a gift of clothes. As-Suhrawardī produced a large gem and asked the boy who had brought the gift to have it appraised. The boy returned saying that the gem's value was some 30,000 dirhams. As-Suhrawardī then shattered the gem and said had he wanted he could have had better clothes. Whatever the truth of the story is, we do know that shortly after arriving in Aleppo as-Suhrawardī came to the attention of its governor, al-Malik azh-Zhāhir Ghāzī, son of the Sultan Saladin, who engaged the wandering sage's services as a tutor. As-Suhrawardī's rapid rise to a position of prestige in the court apparently gained him the jealousy of other court figures who complained to Saladin of his control over the young prince. Saladin, who was then facing the threat of the Third Crusade, most likely feared the political teaching of as-Suhrawardī and ordered his son to execute his tutor. This fact has earned as-Suhrawardī the titles "the Murdered" (*al-Maqtūl*) and "the Martyr" (*ash-Shahīd*). As-Suhrawardī was only thirty-six at the time of his death.

We know of some fifty works written by as-Suhrawardī, which were mostly composed over a period of ten years. His four major works are *Intimations, Oppositions, Pathways and Conversations*, and his magnum opus *Philosophy of Illumination.* These works represent an integral corpus and syllabus for the study of Illuminationist philosophy, which critiques the universal validity of Aristotelian scientific methodology and attempts to provide a rational harmonization of immediate experiential knowledge and discursive reasoning. As-Suhrawardī also wrote a number of symbolic narratives. Certainly one of the important features of these works is that many were written in Persian. Indeed, after as-Suhrawardī there is a growing trend towards doing Islamic philosophy in both the Arabic and Persian languages. Finally, among as-Suhrawardī's writings are also many devotional prayers and invocations.

SELECTIONS FROM *THE PHILOSOPHY OF ILLUMINATION*[a]

I.I. Rule Seven: On Defining and Its Conditions

1. [8] When something is defined for someone who does not know [it], the definition should be by means of things specific to it, whether belonging to the specification of the individuals or some portion or to the collection.[1] Inevitably, definition is through something more obvious than the thing, not by (1) what is equally [obvious] as it, or (2) [9] less obvious than it, or (3) something that is known only by what is being defined. So it is incorrect for someone in defining "father" to say, "He is whoever has a son"; for ["father" and "son"] are equivalent in the sense of being known and unknown. Whoever knows one of them knows the other, but it is a condition of that by which something is defined that what is known is [known] before the thing [being defined], not [that it is known] simultaneously with it. Also, [it is incorrect] to say, "Fire is the element resembling the soul," where "soul" is less obvious than "fire." Likewise [it is incorrect] for them to say, "The Sun is a planet that rises daily," where "day" is known only by means of the time of the Sun's rising. To define the true nature is not merely to replace one expression for another; for replacing one expression for another is useful only for whoever knows the true nature, whereas the sense of the [original] expression is obscure to him. Concerning the definitions of correlatives, the cause that brings about the relation should be taken into account, whereas concerning the definition of derived terms, that from which the derivation is made together with some [other] factor should be taken into account in accordance with the proper applications of the derivation.

2. *Section [Concerning the "Essential Definitions"]*. Some people adopt the term "definition" to designate the statement indicating the essence of the thing, where it indicates the essentials and things internal to its true nature, whereas they adopt the term "description" for whatever defines the true nature by means of external accidents. Take note that when, for instance, body is proven to have a part concerning which some people have doubts and others deny outright (as you will understand that part later), then the masses believe that that part does not belong to the concept of the

---

[1] There are at least two ways that Suhrawardī's claim here might be understood. In Walbridge's and Ziai's note (p. 172, n. 15) they argue: "Quṭb al-Dīn, *Sharḥ ḥikmat*, 53–53 [*sic*], explains that something can be identified by a series of attributes, each of which is unique to that thing: 'Man is rational, laughing, etc.' Alternatively, only some part of the definition might be peculiar to that thing: 'Man is a rational animal,' where 'rational' is unique to man but 'animal' is not. Finally, none of the elements may be unique to the thing defined, but in combination they may identify the thing: 'A bat is a flying creature that bears its young alive.'" Alternatively, Ibn Sīnā, in the section on differentiating in his *Introduction*, edited by Maḥmūd al-Hudayrī, Fu'ād al-Ahwānī and George Anawatī, 72–82 says that the differences used for specification might (1) specify a unique individual, such as the differences resulting from the accidents of one's birth, e.g., exact place, time, and parents, (2) specify some portion of a larger whole, e.g., black specifies a certain group of humans such as the Sudanese, or (3) specify a complete whole, e.g., risibility uniquely specifies humans.

designated term; rather, the term only belongs to the composite of things that follow upon conceiving it.

3. Moreover, when it is proven that both water and air, for example, have imperceptible parts, which some people deny, they will believe that none of those parts are included in what they understand about it. [Even] when the body is one of the parts of every true bodily nature (and its state is as what was [explained]), what the people conceive of [those parts] is nothing but certain things that are obvious to them, namely, what both they and the one coining the term mean [in common] by the designation. Now if the state of sensible objects is such, then how much more so is that which is not sensed at all?!

4. Furthermore, [10] it is given that something belongs to humans by which their humanity was realized, and it is unknown to the general populace and even to the specialist among the Peripatetics inasmuch as they make "rational animal" the definition of [human]. Now the preparedness of rationality is something accidental that follows upon the true nature, whereas the soul, which is the principle of these things, is known only through the concomitants and accidents and yet there is nothing closer to the human than his soul.[2] Given that the state of [the human] is such [that it is unknown to both the general populace and the specialist], then— providing that we state what is necessary about it—how much more so the state of anything else?!

5. *An Illuminationist Principle [in Overturning the Peripatetics' Principle Concerning Definitions].* The Peripatetics concede that the general and specific are mentioned in something's essential definition. "Genus" designates the general essential that is not a part of any other general essential belonging to the universal true nature by which the answer to the question "What is it?" changes. They have designated the essential specific to the thing a "difference." (In defining, these two have a classification different than this, which we have mentioned in other places among our works.)[3]

6. They also concede that one arrives at [the knowledge of] something unknown only from something known. In which case, the essential specific belonging to something will be unknown to whoever is ignorant of it in some other context; for if it is known because of something else that is not specific to it (and even when it is something specific to it, but it is not obvious to the senses and is unknown), then [the essential specific] will be something unknown in the eyes of [whoever is ignorant of it]. So when that [essential] specific is also to be defined, if it is defined by general things to the exclusion of what is specific to it, there will be no defining it, and the state of the specific part will be just as what preceded. The regress, however, will not apply to sensible things or things apparent in some other way, if the thing specifies

---

[2] Cf. Ibn Sīnā, "The Soul," I.1, par. 1, pp. 175–76.

[3] Walbridge and Ziai mention *Pathways and Conversations* I.2.1 in their notes; see *Ḥikmat al-ishrāq*, ed. and John Walbridge and Hossein Ziai, trans., 172, n. 22.

the sum of [those sensible things or things apparent in some other way] collectively. You will understand this more fully in what follows.[4]

7.   Furthermore, whoever mentions [only] the essentials that he knows does not provide the assurance that the existence of some other essential has been overlooked, which the one seeking the explanation of or disputing [the purported definition] can demand of him. In this case the one defining the thing cannot say, "If there were another [11] attribute, then I would have been aware of it," since there are many attributes that are not obvious. It is also not enough to say, "If it were to have another essential, we would not have known the essence without it," in which case it is said, "The true nature is known only when all of its essential factors are known," and so when the dispute involves whether there might be some other essential that is not perceived, the knowledge of the true nature will not be certain. So it has become clear that providing the definition as the Peripatetics require of themselves is impossible for humans, and even their master [Aristotle] recognized the difficulty of that.[5] Hence, we believe that there are only definitions as a result of things that are specified collectively.

I.3. Section 3: Concerning Some Judgments with an Illuminationist Coloring

8.   [42] *Preface.* Everything that exists outside of the mind is either (1) a state in another that is diffused throughout it entirely, which we call a "disposition," or (2) or it is not a state in another in a way that it is diffused throughout it entirely, in which case we call it a "substance." In defining "disposition" there is no need to qualify it by saying, "not like a part of it"; for the part is not diffused throughout the whole. Being colored, [43] substantiality, and the like are not parts according to the Illuminationist principle, as we shall mention, and so do not need to be qualified and guarded against. So what is understood by "substance" and "disposition" is a general meaning.

9.   Know that since the disposition is in the substrate, then in itself it needs to diffuse throughout [that substrate], and so the need [to diffuse throughout that substrate] remains as a result of [the disposition's] remaining. So it is inconceivable that [the disposition] in itself primarily brings about its transference [to a new substrate]; for, at the moment of the transfer, it by itself would possess motion, locations, and existence, and so it would necessarily have three dimensions, in which case it would be a body not a disposition. A body, however, is a substance that can be gestured at by pointing, and obviously it is not devoid of a given length, breadth, and depth, whereas nothing of that is in the disposition, and so the two are distinct. Since bodies are common with respect to corporeality and substantiality, while they are different

---

[4] See pars. 33–37, pp. 377–79.

[5] See Aristotle, *Posterior Analytics* II 3, for some of the puzzles associated with definitions, which he mentions.

with respect to blackness and whiteness, they are added to the corporeality and sub-stantiality and so the two are distinct.

10. Know that the thing is divisible into what is necessary and what is possible. Now the existence of what is possible is not selectively determined over its nonexis-tence as a result of itself, and so the selective determination is through something else, in which case the existence of [what is possible] is selectively determined by the pres-ence of its cause, while its nonexistence is selectively determined by the absence of its cause. Thus it is impossible and possible through another, that is, it is possible with respect to its two states of existing and not existing. If existing were to make it neces-sary, as some suppose,[6] then not existing would make it impossible, and so there never would have been anything possible. Moreover, whatever is dependent upon another (and so does not exist when that other does not exist) has something [else] included in its existence, and so [the dependent thing] in itself is possible.

11. Now we mean by "cause" that whose existence the existence of another requires absolutely without conceivable delay. Also included in [our understanding of cause] is the conditions and removal of obstacles; for if the obstacle is not removed, the existence remains something possible in relation to what was posited to be its cause. When its relation to it is one of possibility without selective determination, then there is no cause and effect [relation]. This does not lead to nonexistence's doing something; rather, the sense that nonexistence enters into causality is that when the intellect considers the necessity of the effect, it does not find it as occurring without the nonexistence of the obstacle. The cause is prior to the effect [44] intellectually but not temporally, often being temporally simultaneous, such as breaking and being broken; however, we say, "He broke [it] and so it was broken" not the converse. Concerning what is prior, there is what is temporal as well as what is prior either with respect to place or position, as in [the case of] bodies, or with respect to eminence in accordance with the more eminent attributes. Part of the cause might be [both] tem-porally prior and intellectually prior.

12. Here is another thing upon which you can base what we intend. Know that in every series there is an order, whatever the order might be, and necessarily the col-lective members in [the series] are finite; for if there is an infinite number between every member of the series and any other one that might be, then it follows that [the number] is bounded by two limits of the order, which is absurd. If in [the series] an infinite does not exist between any two [members], then between any one and any other in the series there is nothing but finite numbers, and the whole must be finite. This also applies concerning bodies, and so should we posit among them a series of different aspects or different bodies, then the demonstration [that there cannot be an infinite] also follows concerning them.

13. Also you can posit the elimination of some finite amount from the middle of the [purportedly infinite] series, considering it as it was when its limits were

---

6 Cf. Ibn Sīnā, *The Salvation* "Metaphysics," II.3, pp. 212–13.

sequentially joined to one another [but now without the eliminated amount]. Consider it once like this and then another time together with the amount that was supposed to be removed [added back], as if there are two series. Now in the imagination superimpose one of them upon the other, or in the intellect make the number of each one to correspond exactly with the number of the other (if they are numbers). Inevitably there will be a dissimilarity, but not in the middle since we joined [it]. So it must be at the extremity, and so [one series] falls short at the extremity and the greater exceeds [the smaller] by a finite amount, but [the purportedly infinite series] would not have exceeded the finite by a finite amount. By [this argument] the finite [nature] of dimensions in their entirety as well as causes and effects and the like becomes clear.

14.   [45] *A Judgment [Concerning Intentional Objects]*. "Existence" is applied to blackness, substance, human, and horse with a single sense and a single thing understood, and so it is an intelligible account (*ma'ná*) more general than any one [of these]. The same holds for the concept of "essence" taken absolutely, and "thingness" as well as "true nature" taken absolutely. So we maintain that these predicates are purely intentional; for if existence were equivalent to mere blackness, then [existence] would not apply to whiteness, [blackness], and substance with one sense. When [blackness] is taken in a sense more general than substantiality, then either it is something occurring determinately in the substance, and subsisting through it, or it is something independent in itself. If it is something independent in itself, then it does not describe the substance, since its relation to it and to anything else is the same. If it is in the substance, then undoubtedly it occurs determinately, but to occur determinately is to exist, and so when existence occurs determinately, something exists. If its being an existing thing is taken to be equivalent to existence itself, there would not be a single sense [in the application of] "existing thing" to existence and anything else, since what is meant by ["existing thing"] with respect to things is that something *has* existence, whereas [what is meant by it] with respect to existence itself is that it *is* existence. We ourselves apply [it] to all only in a single sense.

15.   Moreover, we say that if blackness is something that does not exist (and so its existence does not occur), then its existence is something not existing, since its existence is also something that does not exist. When we intellect existence and judge that it is not an existing thing, then what is understood by "existence" is different from what is understood by "existing thing." Furthermore, when we say that the blackness (which we had taken as something nonexisting) exists, but its existence was not something occurring determinately, but thereafter its existence did occur determinately, the determinate occurrence of the existence would be something else. In that case, the existence has an existence, and the discussion returns to the existence of the existence and so on infinitely, but the collection of an infinite number of ordered attributes is absurd.

16.   [46] Another way is the two divergent [views] of those, following the Peripatetics, who understood existence, but doubted whether or not it occurs determinately in concrete particulars just as it is in the original essence, in which case the

existence would have another existence, and the regress follows. As a result of this it has become clear that there is nothing in reality that is itself the essence of existence; for after we conceive what is meant by it, we might doubt whether or not [that purported essence of existence] has an existence, in which case it would have an additional existence and there is a regress.

17. Another way is that when the essence has existence, then [the existence] has a relation to [the essence], and the relation has existence, and moreover the existence of the relation has a relation to it, and again there is an infinite regress.

18. Another way is that when existence is something occurring determinately in concrete particulars, but it is not a substance, it is designated as a disposition in the thing and so does not occur determinately as something independent. Moreover, [when existence is something occurring determinately in concrete particulars], then the substrate of [existence] would come to exist determinately, and so it would exist before its substrate. It is not the case that the substrate occurs determinately with [existence], since [the substrate] would exist *with* the existence [but] not *by* the existence, which is absurd. It is also not the case that [existence] occurs determinately after its substrate, which is obvious. Furthermore, when the existence in the concrete particulars is something additional to the substance, then it subsists by means of the substance, in which case, in the opinion of the Peripatetics, it would be a quality, because, as they state in the definition of "quality," it is a fixed disposition whose conception does not require a consideration of being particular and of a relation to something external.[7] They had judged absolutely that the substrate is prior to the accident of qualities as well as the other [accidents], and so the existing thing [namely, the substrate] would be prior to existence [considered as something additional and so an accident], which is impossible. Moreover, existence would not be more general than things absolutely; rather, being a quality and accidental would be more general than it in a certain way. Also, when [existence] is an accident, then it subsists by means of its substrate, but the sense that it subsists by means of the substrate is that it is something existing by means of the substrate, which it needs for its realization. Undoubtedly, the substrate is something existing by means of existence, and so the subsistence would be circular, which is absurd.

19. One is mistaken who argues that existence is something additional to the concrete particulars by [arguing] that if from the cause something is not joined with the essence, then [the essence] would not exist; for he posits an essence and then joins existence to it. The opponent, however, claims that this particular essence itself is from an agent, that is to say, the discussion returns to the additional existence itself: "Does the agent provide it with something else, or is it the same as it was?"

20. [47] Know that, following the Peripatetics, they said that we intellect "human" without existence, but we do not intellect ["human"] without "animality." How odd! The sense of the relation of "animality" to "humanity" is only that it is

---

7 Cf. Aristotle, *Categories* 8, 11a30ff.

something that exists in [the human], whether in the mind or in the concrete particular. So they have posited two existences in the relation of "animality" to "humanity":
one of which belongs to the animality that is in [the human], and the second of which
is necessary of the existence of humanity in order that something exist with respect
to it. Once more, some who follow the Peripatetics have based the whole of their
metaphysics upon existence.

21.   Existence might be said of the relations to things as it is said, "The thing is
something existing in the house, in the market, in the mind, in the concrete particular,
in time, and in place." The term "existence" together with "in" have a single sense in
each [case]. [Existence] also corresponds with copulas as when it is said, "Zayd exists
as a writer." [Existence] is also frequently said of the true nature and the being as
when it is said, "The being of the thing and its true nature, that is, the existence of
the thing and its concrete instance and its self," and so they are taken as intentional
objects but are related to external essences. This is what people understand concerning
[existence]. If the Peripatetics believe that it has some other sense, then it is incumbent
upon them to explain it in their claims, not [just] taking it as the most obvious of
things and so incapable of defining it by something else.

22.   Also know that in concrete particulars unity is not some thing (maʿnā)
additional to the thing, otherwise the unity would be one thing among many and so
would have a unity. Also "a unit" and "many units" are said just as "a thing" and "many
things" are said. Moreover, when the essence and the unity that belongs to it are taken
as two things, they are two: one of which is the unity, and the other the essence that
itself has [unity], but then each one of them has a unity from which many absurdities
follow. Among which is that when we say they are "two," the essence would have a
unity[b] besides the [initial] unity, and the discussion will regress infinitely. Also among
[the absurdities] the unity would have a unity, and the [same] discussion returns and
so an infinite number of ordered attributes would be together. When the state of the
unity is such, then number also is something intentional; for when number consists of
units and the unit is an intentional attribute, then necessarily number is also.

23.   [48] Another way is that when four is an accident subsisting in human, for
instance, then either the fourness is completely in each one of the individuals, but
that is not the case; or part of the fourness, namely, nothing but the unity, is in each
one, in which case the sum of fourness has no substrate other than the intellect; or
neither the fourness nor any part of it is in each one, and so likewise on this conjecture
it is not in anything other than the intellect. Obviously when the mind joins one in
the east with another in the west, it will observe the duality. When the person sees a
large group, he takes three, four, and five from them collectively according to what
he sees and examines. Concerning numbers he also takes a hundred and sets of a
hundred as well as ten and sets of ten and the like.

24.   Know that something's possibility is in the intellect prior to its existence;[c]
for possible things are possible and thereafter exist, whereas it is incorrect to say that
they exist and thereafter become possible. Possibility applies to different things with
a single sense. Moreover it is something accidental to the essence, but by it the essence

is described. So possibility is neither something subsisting through itself, nor is it something that exists necessarily, since if its existence were essentially necessary, it would subsist through itself, in which case it would not need a relation to a subject. Therefore, [possibility] is something possible, and its possibility is intellected before its existence; for whatever cannot initially not exist is not itself its possibility, and thus the discussion would infinitely return to the possibility of its possibility and so lead to the impossible [infinite] series, because its [infinitely] ordered members are together.[8]

25. The same holds for necessity, for necessity is an attribute of existence. So when it is added to [existence] and does not subsist through itself, it is something possible and so has [both] a necessity and a possibility, and so the numbers of its ordered possibilities and existences go on infinitely. Moreover, the necessity of something is before [the thing], and so it itself is not what [the thing is], since [it is the case that] it is necessary and thereupon exists, not [that] it exists and thereupon is necessary. Again, then, the existence would have a necessity, and the necessity would have an existence. Thus, from the infinite reiteration of necessity to existence and existence to necessity another [infinite] series would follow, which is just as impossible as the earlier one.

26. [49] Know that in concrete particulars blackness' being a color is not being a color and something else, for to make it black is the very same as to make it a color. If being a color were to have one existence and the specification of blackness were to have another existence, [then][d] it would be permissible to unite with [being colored] whatever specification just so happened to be, since none of the specifications is the same as a condition for being colored, and if they are not impossible—despite being contrary and different—the successive combination of the specifications with [being colored] would be permissible. Also, if being colored has an existence independent [of blackness, for example], then it is a disposition, which is either a disposition in the blackness, in which case the blackness exists before it not by means of it; or in the substrate of [blackness], in which case blackness has two accidents—a color and its difference—not one.

27. Relations are also intentional objects; for if being a brother, for example, is a disposition in an individual, then it has a relation to another individual and a relation to its substrate. Each one of the two relations is different from the other, and so necessarily both are different from [the relation of being a brother] itself, since when [the relation of being a brother] itself is supposed to be one and the same existing thing, while the relation of the two is to two different individuals, then how could the two be [the single relation of being a brother]?! Clearly each one of the two

---

[8] The argument seems to be that if possibility were to have some extra-mental existence, then it would exist outside the mind either as something necessary, and so it would subsist on its own, which is false; or the existence of the possible would itself be possible, in which case one can ask whether the possibility of the possible is extra-mental and one is on the road to infinite regress.

relations is a different existing thing. Moreover, this discussion would return to the relation to which the substrate belongs and would involve an [infinite] series in the prohibited way. So then all of these are things perceived as intentional objects.

28.   Privations, such as rest, are something intentional; for when "rest" is equivalent to the absence of motion in that in which there conceivably is motion (where "absence" is not something truly real in concrete particulars, but is an intelligible in the mind and moreover the possibility [of the motion] is something intentional), then it follows that all of the corresponding privations are intentional objects.

29.   Know that substantiality in concrete particulars is also not something in addition to the corporeality; rather, the thing that makes a body is the very same thing that makes it a substance, since in our view substantiality is only the perfection of something's essence in such a way that [the thing] can dispense with the substrate for its subsistence. The Peripatetics define ["substance"] as what does not exist in a subject, but then the denial of the subject is a negation, and being an existing thing is accidental. When the one who defends them says that [50] the substantiality is some other existing thing, then it would be difficult to explain and establish it to one who contests it. Moreover, when [the substantiality] is some other thing existing in the body, and so has an existence that is not in a subject, then it would be something described by substantiality and the discussion returns to the substantiality of the substantiality, and so there is an infinite regress.

30.   Hence, all attributes are divisible into two divisions. [The first] is a concrete particular attribute that has a form in the intellect, such as blackness, whiteness, and motion. [The second] is an attribute whose concrete existence is nothing but its very existence in the mind, having no existence in anything other than the mind, and so its having being in the mind is on the order of the being of other things in concrete particulars. Examples are possibility, substantiality, being colored, existence, and the others we have mentioned. When something has existence outside of the mind, then what is in the mind should correspond with it. That which is only in the mind has no existence outside the mind such that the mental object [needs] to correspond with it.

31.   Now the predicables, insofar as they are predicables, are mental objects. Blackness is a concrete particular, whereas since "being black" is equivalent to a certain thing, the blackness will arise together with it, but neither corporeality nor substantiality will be included in it; rather, if blackness were to subsist by something other than body, then it would be said to be black. So when [blackness] has a certain thing included in being black, it will be only a certain intentional object and no more, even if the blackness has an existence in concrete particulars. As for when one derives a predicable from the intentional attributes and they become a predicable, such as, "Every x is something possible," both what is possible and the possibility are only intentional, unlike being black; for even though [being black] is an intentional predicate, the blackness is a concrete particular, and blackness alone is not predicated of the substance. Now since we say, "x is something impossible in concrete particulars," not meaning that impossibility occurs in the concrete particulars, but rather it is

something intentional that we sometimes join with what is in the mind and at other times with what is in the concrete particular (and the same holds for what is similar to it), then in the case of these things the error arises from taking mental things as occurring independently in concrete particulars. When you know that the case of these things [51] previously mentioned, such as possibility, being colored, substantiality, are intentional predicates, then [you will know that] there are no parts of concrete essences. It is not the case that when something is a mental predicate (such as the generic predicated of something for example) that we can unite it in the intellect with any essence as chance would have it and it be true; rather, [the mental predicable] belongs to what truly belongs to it in virtue of its specification. The same holds for existence and the other intentional objects.

I.3. Section 4: Explaining That Being an Accident Is Outside of the True Nature of Accidents

32. Following the Peripatetics, one says that being an accident is outside of the true nature of accidents, which is correct; for being an accident is also one of the intentional attributes. Some of them justify [this] by [observing] that people frequently intellect something, but have doubts concerning its being an accident. [The Peripatetics], however, have not made the same judgment for being a substance, and have not considered that when people have doubts concerning something's being an accident, they would have had doubts concerning its being a substance as well. Now blackness' being a quality is also something accidental to it, that is, it is an intentional object. What [the Peripatetics] say, namely, "We intellect color and then intellect blackness," is arbitrary, and in fact one could also say, "We first intellect that this is black and thereafter judge that it is a color and that is a quality." (We ourselves do not need this, which is only a dialectical claim, whereas the main point of discussion is what was said above.)

33. *Another Judgment [Explaining That the Peripatetics Have Made It Impossible to Define Anything]*. The Peripatetics have made it impossible to define anything, since substances have unknown differences. Also they have defined "being a substance" by something negative. Moreover, the soul and the separate [Intellects] in their opinion also have unknown differences. They have defined "accident," as for example blackness, as a color that collects sight, but "collecting sight" is accidental, and you have learned about the state of being colored. [52] So bodies and accident are altogether inconceivable. Also for [the Peripatetics] existence is the most obvious of things, but you have already learned about its state. Moreover, if conceptualizing is supposed to be through necessary concomitants, then the necessary concomitants will also have specifications, where a similar discussion will apply to them, which is impermissible since it entails that nothing in existence would be known. The truth is that blackness is a single, simple thing, having been intellected and having no unknown parts. It cannot be defined to someone who has not experienced it as it is, whereas whoever has experienced it can dispense with the definition. Its form in the intellect is just like

its form in sensation, and so in the case of these things they have no definition. Quite the contrary, complex true natures are frequently recognized from simple true natures, just as the one who conceives the simple true natures separately and then recognizes the composite [true nature] by [their] being combined in a given location.

34.   Know that all the categories that they have pinpointed are intentional objects inasmuch as they are categorical and predicable. Some of them are derived, that is, the simple from which the predicate is taken in its specification is also an intentional attribute, such as the member in a relation and numbers in their specification (as was said above), as well as whatever the relation enters into. Some of them are concrete attributes in themselves, in fact, falling under those categories because of some intentional object, as [for example] odor and blackness; for their being a quality is something intentional, which means that there is such and such a fixed disposition, even if in themselves they are attributes realized in concrete particulars. If the thing's being an accident or quality and the like were some other existing thing, then the discussion would regress as before. [. . .]

35.   [58] Furthermore [the Peripatetics] establish other forms and so said that the body must either be incapable or capable of division. In addition to being susceptible to that it is also [susceptible] to being shaped, to saying nothing of whether the susceptibility to these things is with ease or with difficulty. So inevitably any other forms require these things, and the body is specified by them. Now one can claim that these specifications are qualities, whether in the elements, so for example, wet, dry, hot, and cold, or they are in the celestial spheres because of different configurations.

36.   If it is said, "Accidents cannot constitute the substance, whereas what we have mentioned does constitute the substance," I answer that these things that you have called "forms" constitute the substance. If it is because the body is not devoid of some of them, [I say] something's not being devoid of something does not indicate [59] that it is constituted by that thing, since accidents are among the necessary concomitants [that is, things of which the body is never devoid]. If the body is constituted by them because they are what make the body specific, then again, that it is a form and substance has nothing to do with the condition of what specifies; for you have admitted that the individuals of the species are distinguished by accidents, and were there no specific things, then neither the species nor other things would exist. Moreover, you have admitted that specific natures have a more complete existence than the genera, but it is inconceivable to posit their existence without the things that specify. So if the things that make the body specific are forms and substance because the body is inconceivable without some specifying thing, then the things that specify the species would more fittingly be substances, but that is not the case. So it is permissible that what specifies is an accident, and the accident is among the conditions that realize the substance, just as with respect to the species the things that specify are accidents, where the realization of the species in the concrete particulars is conceivable only together with the accidents.

37.   That argument that claims that the specific true nature determinately occurs and thereafter the accidents follow upon it is weak; for if the specific nature, as for

example humanity, determinately occurs first, and thereafter the accidents follow upon it, then absolute, universal humanity would determinately occur and thereafter an individual, which is absurd, since [humanity] determinately occurs only as something individuated, whereas the absolute never determinately occurs in the concrete particulars. If these accidents are not conditions for the realization of the nature, and that by which this individual is distinguished is not a necessary concomitant belonging to the true nature of humanity, then it would be permissible to suppose that one's humanity remains absolutely as it was when it initially came to be, and thereafter without [its being] something distinct the accidents are united to it. [That follows] since these accidents by which the individuals of the species are individuated have nothing to do with the requirements of the specific true nature and its necessary concomitants, otherwise they would happen to be in all [of them], and so therefore they are from an external agent. When the specific nature can dispense with them, we can suppose its existence without them (that is, without these accidents), but this is not the case. From this it turns out to be permissible that the accident is the condition of the substance's existence and is something constituting its existence in this sense. Furthermore, if the occurrence of humanity were allowed to be something absolute and thereafter the things distinguishing [and] specifying [it] follow upon it, then why is not the occurrence of corporeality allowed to be something absolute, and thereafter what specifies it follows upon it? Whatever defense they give here, a similar one will hold concerning the species.

Textual Notes

AL-KINDĪ

I. The Explanation of the Proximate Efficient Cause for Generation and Corruption

a   The translation is based on the edition in *Rasāʾil al-Kindī l-falsafiya*, Abū Rīda, ed., 214–37.

b   The text between acute brackets, < >, 216.10–11, is supplied by Abū Rīda on the basis of parallel passages in al-Kindī's other works (compare, for instance, the translation here of *On Divine Unity*, par. 9) to fill a lacuna in the manuscript.

c   See Edward W. Lane, *An Arabic-English Lexicon.*, s.v. *safar* for this use.

d   Supplying *ghayr*, 218.6, for the lacuna in the manuscript.

e   We supply the conjectural *fī*, 220.10, for a small lacuna in the manuscript, which also helps explain the following accusative *makānan* ("a place"), emended by Abū Rīda for the nominative *makānun*.

f   Conjectural addition of *ḥadīd al-qamr*, 220.13, (cf. *ḥadīd al-falak*, conjectural addition of Abū Rīda).

g   Alternatively, the text's *wāqiʿa*, 220.16, could be *wāqifa*, in which case the sense would be that the Earth as a whole comes to rest at the center of the universe, which would set up a nice contrast with the next line.

h   Reading *wa-ballā*, 226.9, for the text's *wa-bal*.

i   Reading *an-nafsānī*, 226.10, for the text's *an-nafāʾī*(?).

j   Reading *tashbīh*, 227.8, for Abū Rīda's conjectural *nisbatuhu*.

k   Reading *niṣf al-quṭr*, 227.8, for Abū Rīda's conjectural *niṣf buʿd*.

l   Abū Rīda notes that there may be a small lacuna in the text here. Still, the text makes sense as it stands, namely, the magnitude of the Moon is only a small part of the Sun's magnitude.

m   Abū Rīda notes that what he takes to be the number "5" is small in the Arabic; he has in fact mistaken the numeral "0" (•) for a small "5" (○). Thus, in agreement with Ptolemy, the figure given almost certainly should be our "360."

n   On the one hand, the text's *marākiz*, 228.4, (the plural "centers") may perhaps be a reference to both the Sun's geometrical center and the "center" around which it uniformly rotates, or its so-called "equant," which is different than its geometric center. On the other hand, perhaps the text should be corrected to read *markaz* (the singular "center"), in line with al-Kindī's discussion at par. 33 concerning the eccentricity of the Sun.

o   Our conjectural addition, 229.8, to fill a lacuna has evidence in favor of it from the discussion in the paragraphs immediately following.

p   There seems to be a difficulty with the text, noted by the editor. Literally, the text reads "because its remoteness and proximity during each of its two degrees of declination in the north would be a single "declination" (*maylan*) and proximity from the center of the earth, at 230.7–8. We conjecture that the second use of *mayl* ("declination") should be emended to *buʿdan* ("remoteness") to reflect the earlier reference to the Sun's remoteness and proximity.

q   Reading *bihimā*, 230.1, for the text's *bihā*.

r   Conjectural addition, based on the next line, 231.1–2, to fill a lacuna in the manuscript.

s There is a lacuna in the text, 235.11, which the editor conjectures should be filled with *fa-in kānat*. We conjecture that *fa-inna kull* should be supplied, which gives the immediate text a parallel structure with what is below.

t Following Abū Rīda's conjectural *akhlāq*, 235.14, to fill a lacuna.

u We conjecture that the text's *ṭawīla* ("long") 236.8, should be emended to *ṭūlīya* ("longitudinal").

v Emending the text's *mawḍūʿ* ("subject"), 236.11, to *mawḍiʿ* ("region").

II. On the Intellect

a The translation is based on Abū Rīda, 353–57, with comparison to the text and translation of McCarthy in "Al-Kindī's Treatise on the Intellect," 119–49.

b Reading *ath-thānī* with Abū Rīda, 354.1, against McCarthy's conjectural reading *an-nātī*, "the emergent," 122.10.

c Reading *ka-ghayrīya* for *li-ghayrīya*, Abū Rīda, 355.2.

d Reading *ka-ghayr* for *li-ghayr*, Abū Rīda, 355.5.

e Reading *ʿāqila* with Abū Rīda, 356.9, against *ʿāmila*, McCarthy.

f The manuscript has *ʿāqila*, hence "[the soul as] intellect"; both Abū Rīda, 357, n. 1 (on his reading of the Latin translation) and McCarthy, 124, n. 14, suggest *maʿqūla*, "what is intellected," as a possibly preferable reading.

g Adding *huwa* at 358.7, (as copula) with the manuscript.

III. On Divine Unity and the Finitude of the World's Body

a The translation is based on the edition of *Oeuvres philosophiques et scientifiques d'al-Kindī*, Roshdi Rashed and Jean Jolivet, eds., 136–47 (hereafter R/J), with French translation. The English translation, "Al-Kindī's Risala fi Wahdaniya Allah wa Tanahi Jirm al-ʿAlam," F.A. Shamsi, trans., 185–201, has also been consulted.

b Reading *bi-fāṣili muddatin* for the vocalized *bi-fāṣilin muddatun* at 143.15; cf. Shamsi's emendation *yufṣil*, 199, n. 43.

c Reading *aʿnī bi-kull wāḥidin dūna l-ākhar* for the testimony of both manuscripts: *aʿnī bi-l-kull wāḥidin dūna l-ākhar* (see 145.16–17). In none of the asides that al-Kindī introduces with "I mean" does his syntax place the word to be clarified after the preposition *bi-* (cf. *aʿnī l-ḥāla*, "I mean the state . . ." R/J, 143.12), and in most cases, he does not even repeat the word to be glossed, whether implicitly (through use of another similar word) or explicitly. Thus, we treat the preposition *bi-* after *aʿnī* here as belonging to *khawāṣṣ* (from the verb-preposition idiom *khāṣṣa bi-*, special, proper, unique *to* something), thus "what is their specific properties, I mean [what properties are specific] to each one . . ." Cf. the emendation of Abū Rīda, 207.9, implicitly accepted by R/J, 145.16: <lā> *aʿnī bi-l-kulli wāḥidan dūna l-ākhar*, which they translate, 144, "sans comprendre par *tout un un* [*sic*] à l'exclusion d'un autre," and by Shamsi, 194: "and I do not at all mean the one [kind] separately from the other," which is explained at 200, n. 56, as "That is, only the general or the particular properties." The emendation proposed here has the following recommendations: (1) it meddles with the text less than that of Abū Rīda, since it secludes only the definite article *al* of *al-kull*, instead of introducing both a *lā* to negate "I mean" as well as an *alif* to *wāḥid* to denote the accusative "one"; (2) it accords with al-Kindī's usual syntactic style for asides with "I mean"; and (3) it requires less interpretation to make sense than that needed for the emendation of Abū Rīda (cp. the French and English translations given here).

IV. The One True and Complete Agent and the Incomplete Metaphorical "Agent"

a   The translation here is based on R/J, 169–71. Cf. the English translation by Alexander Altmann and Samuel M. Stern in *Isaac Israeli*, 68–69.

V. On the Means of Dispelling Sorrows

a   The translation is based on the edition by Helmut Ritter and Richard Walzer in "Uno scritto morale inedito di al-Kindî," 31–47 (hereafter R/W). We have consulted the English translation by Ghada Jayyusi-Lehn in "The Epistle of Ya'qūb ibn Isḥāq al-Kindī on the Device for Dispelling Sorrows," 121–35, the introduction to which contains a list of editions, translations, and studies. We are also thankful to Peter Adamson and Peter Pormann for allowing us to consult an advance copy of their translation.

b   Reading *ālām tamlikuhā* (see R/W, 31, n. 5a) for the text's *alām bi-mulkihā;* 31.5; Jayyusi-Lehn, 122, translates "the pain of their domination."

c   Following Jayyusi-Lehn, who has silently corrected (?) R/W or has drawn on another edition for the conjectural emendation *mutanāwal <āt>*, 32.8.

d   Reading *lā yanbaghī* for *qabl* (see R/W, 35, n. 15a).

e   Reading, with Jayyusi-Lehn, *fa-idhā* for *fa-idh* at 36.4.

f   Ignoring the lacuna in the text at 36.7.

g   Reading *yakūna adīma l-'aql* for the text's *nakūna 'udamā'a l-'uqūl* at 41.14; Jayyusi-Lehn, 130, translates, "We should be ashamed of being devoid of mind," thus reading with the text.

h   Reading, with Badawi and Jayyusi-Lehn, *bi-tazyīd* for the text's *bi-tazyīn* at 42.1.

i   Reading with the text *al-munqiṣa* at 42.3, Jayyussi-Lehn, 130, reads, with Badawi's edition, *al-munqaḍiya*, and translates "serving."

j   Reading *qad* with Ritter at 43, n. 222, for the manuscript's *mā*.

k   Secluding, with R/W, *qadaman yaṭūlu 'ilājuhu* at 43.10 (see 43.8 where the phrase belongs). Jayyusi-Lehn translates "requiring a long time to cope with it."

l   Reading *yanābī'* for the text's *tatābu'* at 45.18.

m   Ritter conjectures a lacuna here at 45.18. Jayyusi-Lehn, following Badawi's conjectural addition, translates "[the rational place] wherein reside all good things."

n   Reading, with Badawi and Jayyusi-Lehn, *tālif*, for the text's *ta'alluf* ("familiarity").

AR-RĀZĪ

I. The Philosopher's Way of Life

a   This translation is based on the edition in *Opera philosophica fragmentaque quae supersunt*, Paul Kraus, ed., 99–111. Earlier translations consulted include "Raziana I, la conduite du Philosophe, traité ethique de Muhammad b. Zakariyya al-Razi," Paul Kraus, ed., 300–34; and "Apologia pro Vita Sua," A.J. Arberry, trans., 120–30.

II. On the Five Eternals

a   This translation is based on the edition in *Opera*, Paul Kraus, ed., 195–215.

III. Doubts against Galen

a   The translation is based on the edition in *Kitāb ash-Shukūk ʿalā Jālīnūs*, Mahdi Muḥaqqiq, ed., 1–6. There is a partial French translation of the passage presented here by Shlomo Pines in "Rāzī critique de Galien," in *The Collected Works of Shlomo Pines*, Sarah Stroumsa, ed., vol. II, 257–8.

b   Galen, [*Risāla*] *fī manāfiʿ al-aʿḍā, De usu partium*, Georg Helmreich, ed. See *Geschichte des arabischen Schrifttums*, Fuat Sezgin, ed., vol. 3, no. 40, 106–7, for the Arabic translation and epitomes, including references to other citations of the work by ar-Rāzī.

c   In Arabic, *Kitāb al-Burhān; Dubitationes in Galenum*; see *Dictionnaire des philosophes antiques*, Richard Goulet, ed., vol. III, no. 22, 458.

d   Reading *wajhun* for *wajhuhun* [*sic*], 4.4. Unfortunately, there is no explicit mention of the issue of the world's eternity in *On Medicine*, and so it is not clear what passage or even what text ar-Rāzī had in mind here.

AL-FĀRĀBĪ

I. The *Eisagōgē*—The Introduction

a   The Arabic text is found in "Al-Fārābī's *Eisagoge*," Douglas M. Dunlop, ed. and trans., 117–38. The translation here has benefited from Dunlop's, in the same article.

II. Demonstration

a   The translation here is based on the edition in *al-Manṭiq ʿinda l-Fārābī*, Majid Fakhry, ed., 20–26. There is an unreliable English translation by Fakhry in *An Anthology of Philosophy in Persia*, Seyyed H. Nasr and Mehdi Aminrazavi, eds., vol. I, 93–110. See also the study by Deborah L. Black, "Knowledge (ʿilm) and certitude (yaqīn) in al-Fārābī's Epistemology," 11–45.

b   Reading *yataḍammanu* for *yantaẓimu* at 22.16.

c   See Aristotle, *Posterior Analytics* II, 19, 99b35, *dunamin sumphuton kritikēn*; Arabic, ʿAbd ar-Raḥmān Badawī, ed., vol. 2, 483, *qūwa gharīzīya*; English, trans. Jonathan Barnes, "connate."

d   Reading *aw* for *wa-* at 24.17; cf. the construction in Fārābī's *Philosophy of Aristotle*, Muhsin Mahdi, ed., 63.16–9.

III. On the Intellect

a   The translation here follows the edition in *Risāla fī l-ʿaql*, Maurice Bouyges, ed., 3–36. Compare the translation in *Philosophy in the Middle Ages*, A. Hyman, ed., 215–21.

b   Translating Aristotle's *phronesis*.

c   Reading *min qablu an taʿqila hādhā l-ʿaqlu* at 21.2.

d   Reading *wadaʿnā* underlying the Hebrew and Latin translations for *waṣafnā* at 33.1.

e   Reading *asbāb* for *aqsām* at 34.1.

f   Inserting *mā ʿaqala bihi ṭabīʿatihi* (omitted by homoioteleuton) at 35.9, following the Latin translation.

IV. The Aims of Aristotle's *Metaphysics*

a   The translation here is based on the edition in *Alfārābī's philosophische Abhandlungen*, Friedrich Dieterici, ed., 34–38 (hereafter abbreviated as D), and the edition in *Rasāʾil al-Fārābī*, 3–6 (hereafter abbreviated as H), and, where parallel, follows in the main the partial translation of Dimitri Gutas,

Avicenna and the Aristotelian Tradition, 240–42 (hereafter abbreviated as G). We have also consulted the French translation, "Le traité d'al-Fārābī sur les buts de la metaphysique d'Aristote," Thérèse-Anne Druart, trans., 38–43.

b   Reading, with H and G, the manuscript variants *wa-* [or] *fa-li-anna* at 35.19, omitted by D.

c   Reading *yubḥathu* with H (cf. Druart) for *nabḥathu* at 36.20, in D.

d   The phrase "in their class," *fi bābihi* at 36.22, following H (cf. Druart, "en son domaine"), omitted in D.

e   "To alert," *manbaha* at 37.3, (lit. grounds or cause for being alerted) H, *tanbīh* D.

f   Reading *hayʾatihi* at 37.3, with H (cf. Druart, "sa condition"), which is omitted in D.

g   We prefer *bi-hā* at 37.5, with H (cf. Druart, n. 33) for *bi-hi*, in D.

h   For "or rather is this science in a certain respect," cf. Druart, "mais n'est cette science que sous un certain rapport," that is, "but it is this science only in a certain respect."

i   Reading *fi l-jawhar minhu* at 37.15, with H for *fi l-jawharīya*, in D (cf. Druart).

j   Reading *al-murakkabāt* at 37.17, with H (cf. Druart) for *bi-l-murakkabāt*, in D.

k   Reading *wa-annahu* at 37.18, with H for *wa-anna*, in D.

l   Reading *adh-dhāt* at 38.3, with H (cf. Druart) for *bi-dh-dhāt*, in D: "It knows Itself by virtue of being Itself"?

V. The Principles of Existing Things

a   The translation here follows the edition in *As-Siyāsa l-madanīya l-mulaqqab bi-mabādiʾ al-mawjūdāt*, Fauzi Najjār, ed., 31–69.

b   Reading *wa-hiya muḥtājatun fi an takūna mawjūdatan ilá mawḍūʿin* with MS Feyzullah 1279; the editor selected the variant *wa-hiya muḥtājatunan ilá an takūna mawjūdatan fi mawḍūʿin* at 36.10–1, apparently common to the other manuscripts.

c   Reading *innīyatuhu* for *annīyatuhu* at 38.7.

d   Reading *mawjūdāt* with MSS L, ṢI and Ṣ2. for *wujūdāt* at 41.9.

e   Reading *takūnu lahā* at 41.11, with MS Feyzullah 1279, for *takūnu*.

f   The addition here comes from the version of this argument in Fārābī's *Opinions*, Richard Walzer, ed., 60.

g   Reading *al-wujūd*, "existence," instead of *al-mawjūd*, "the existent" at 45.2, following Walzer's choice of variant in the text of *Opinions* at 68, and the variant readings of MSS Ḥ and T of *Principles*.

h   This addition is based on the text of *Opinions* at 70.

i   The text of *Opinions* at 70.2, adds *bi-l-fiʿl*, "an actual intellect."

j   The text of *Opinions* at 70.2, has *ṣūra*, "form," whereas the *Principles* at 45.4, has *ash-shayʾ*, "something."

k   Reading *huwīyatuhu* in both instances, following the text of *Opinions* at 70.8, for *huwa minhu* at 45.5–6, in both instances; and reading *ka-dhālika*, "likewise" at 45.6, with MSS ṢI and Ṣ2 of *Principles* for *li-dhālika*.

l   Reading *fa-ka-dhālika* for *fa-li-dhālika* at 46.2.

m   Deleting *wa-jamāluhu* at 46.6.

n   Reading *lil-awwali al-wujūdu* with the Hyderabad printing in *Rasāʾil al Fārābī*. (Based on MS Salar Jung Falsafa at 113) for *al-awwal al-wujūd*. (*al-wujūda* voc. Najjar) at 47.11); cf. *Opinions*, 88.11.

Walzer opted to follow a marginal gloss in one manuscript for his translation (89): "The First is that from which everything which exists comes into existence." As a protasis, however, this renders the conditional sentence here a tautology.

o Vocalizing *faydin wujūduhu* at 47.13; cf. *Opinions*, 88.15. Alternately, Najjar vocalizes *faydi wujūdihi*, "a bestowal of Its existence."

VI. Directing Attention to the Way to Happiness

a The translation here is based on the edition in *At-Tanbīh ʿalá sabīl as-saʿāda*, Jaʿfar Āl Yāsīn, ed., 47–84 (hereafter abbreviated as AY), with comparison to the Hyderabad 1926 edition (hereafter abbreviated as H).

b Reading *mā shaʾnuhu an yuʾthara* at 48.8, with H, for *mā shaʾnuhā an tuʾthara*.

c Reading *aḥaduhā* for *aḥaduhumā* at 50.4.

d Reading *al-qūwa* for *al-quwá* at 53.5.

e Reading *takūna bi-ḥaythu lā yumkinu zawāluhā aw yaʿsur* (cf. *takūna bi-ḥaythu lā yumkinu zawāluhu aw yaʿsuru* in H) for the editorial conjecture *an yakūna <ṣ-ṣawābu> bi-ḥaythu lā yumkinu zawāluhu aw yaʿsuru* in AY, 55.7–8.

f Reading *wa-<ka-mā> mattá . . . aṣ-ṣiḥḥatu, ka-dhālika mattá* for *wa-mattá . . . aṣ-ṣiḥḥatu kadhālika <wa-> mattá* in AY, 58.7–8.

g Reading *ka-dhālika wa-ʿalá* at 59.7, for *ka-dhālika fa-ʿalá*.

h *al-buldān* ("countries") at 59.16, may be a scribal error for *al-abdān* ("bodies"), but *al-buldān* is the *lectio difficilior* and has support in the medical literature. See also our translation of *The Explanation of the Proximate Efficient Cause for Generation and Corruption*, pars. 20–22, Al-Kindī, p. 8.

i Reading *al-muṭīfa* with H for *al-muṭabbaqa* (?) at 59.17.

j Reading *al-muṭīfa* with H for *al-muṭabbaqa* (?) at 60.1.

k Reading *ʿibra* for the vocalized *ʿushra*, 63.1. See Aristotle, *Nicomachean Ethics* IV 5 1126a21ff.

l Reading *ʿalayhā* at 65.9, for *ʿalayhi*.

m Reading *Fa-in kānā* at 65.15. There is perhaps a lacuna preceding the switch to the dual, e.g., *wa-l-fiʿli l-kāʾini ʿani z-ziyāda*, or the implication is an obvious one; cf. the suggestion of AY (Introduction, 15).

n Conjecturing *Shabīhun <bi->l-wasaṭ* for *shabīhun al-wasaṭ* at 66.13.

o Reading *Li-yatrukahu aw yafʿala* for *li-tarkihi aw tafaʿulihi* at 72.2.

p Reading *Ajrá* for *akhzá* at 72.12.

q Conjecturing *Tarki sh-sharri nafsuhu wa-ghayruhu* for *tarki sh-sharri <ʾan> nafsihi wa- <ʾan> ghayrihi* at 72.15.

r Reading *milāḥa* with MS M for *filāḥa* at 74.10.

s Reading *khāṣṣ al-insān* at 75.2, with MS M.

t Reading the *wa-* at 75.5, secluded by the editor.

u Conjecturing *yukhayyilu <bi-hā> al-bāṭila* for *t.kh.y.l* (?) *al-bāṭil* at 78.3.

v Deleting the editor's inserted *<wa->* "and" at 79.13.

w Deleting *wa-* ("and") at 79.16

x Reading *bi-khilāfihā* for *bi-khilāfihi* at 81.12.

y Reading *yaʿrifuhu* for *yaʿrifuhā* at 81.12.

z   Reading *tāliyan* for the variant *thālithan* found in MSS M and Ḥ. against the possible editorial conjecture *maʾālanā* at 84.8.

BAGHDAD PERIPATETICS

I.   Abū Bishr Mattá

a   This translation is based in the edition of *Aṭ-Ṭabīʿa*, ʿAbd ar-Raḥman Badawī, ed., 137–64.

b   Reading *ṣūrat al-ʿushbī* at 140.7, for the editor's emendation *ṣūrat al-ʿasīy*, which Badawī notes is unclear in the manuscripts.

c   Reading *taḥṣulu* for the text's *yaḥṣulu* at 143.13.

d   Following the suggestion of Paul Lettinck in *Aristotle's Physics and Its Reception in the Arabic World*, p. 190, n. 4, that the text's *ar-rabābin* at 150.1, be emended to *ad-dabābīr*.

e   Reading *ka-dhālika* at 150.3, for the text's *li-dhālika*.

f   Reading the plural *ṣuwar* at 151.13, for the text's singular *ṣūra*.

II.   Yaḥyá ibn ʿAdī

a   Translation based on Carl Ehrig-Eggert, "Yaḥyá Ibn ʿAdī: über den Nachweis der Nature des Möglichen, Edition und Einleitung," 283–297, [Arabic] 63–97.

b   Accepting Ehrig-Eggert's suggested addition of *umūr* at 68.3.

c   Accepting Ehrig-Eggert's suggested addition of *li-anna s-sabab al-fāʿil* at 68.9–10.

d   Excising the first *alladhī* ("which") at 68.11–12, and then changing the text's *ʿalayhā* to *ʿalayhu* to agree with the second *alladhī*.

e   Reading *yūjadu* at 68.15, for the text's *tūjadu*.

f   Accepting Ehrig-Eggert's suggested addition of *laysa huwa* at 69.19.

g   The text has *sababan fāʿilan* ("an efficient cause") at 70.9, but the context clearly indicates that it should be *sababan ṣūriyan*.

h   Reading *tabayyana* for the text's *yatabayyanu* at 71.22.

i   We accept Ehrig-Eggert's suggestion at 72.5, that *al-mumkina* be secluded. Were *al-mumkina* retained, the sense of the text would be "even if it is a paradigmatic cause of the necessity of things that are possible necessary among them."

j   The text's *ʿalayhu* should probably be emended to *ʿalayhā* at 73.4.

k   The vocalized *fa-ammā* at 73.11, should be read *fa-a-mā*.

l   We conjecture that the text's *wa-l-azaliya* at 74.1, be emended to read *hiya azaliya*.

m   The text's *yakhruju* at 76.17, which appears to be the apodosis of an *in*-conditional, should be corrected to *kharaja*.

n   Accepting Ehrig-Eggert's suggested addition of *huwa* at 79.3.

III.   Abū Sulaymān as-Sijistānī

a   From *Muntakhab Ṣiwān al-ḥikma*, ʿAbd ar-Raḥman Badawī, ed., 377–87; we have also consulted MS Iraq Museum Lib. 134, a microfilm copy of which Professor Joel Kraemer graciously provided us.

We have also greatly benefited from Kraemer's translation of this text, *Philosophy in the Renaissance of Islam*, 293–304.

b   We vocalize the text's *d-d-d* as *yaduddu* at 377.9.

c   Reading *farrās* for the text's *ʿirās* (?) at 379.16. Alternatively, Kraemer suggests the text's *ʿirās* might be emended to *ʿirs* (understood as a shortened version of *ibn ʿirs*) and so translated "weasel"; see Kraemer, *Philosophy in the Renaissance of Islam*, p. 295, n. 69.

d   Reading *kullīya* for the text's *kaylīya* at 380.4.

e   We follow the reading of MS Iraq Museum Lib. 134, pp. 155.2–3: *yaṣīru kāmila min ʿinda l-fāʿil wa-ṣ-ṣūra l-kullīya wa nāqiṣa min qibali l-mawḍūʿ lahā* for Badawī's *taṣīru ʿinda l-fāʿil wa-ṣ-ṣūra l-kullīya wa muqaddama* (?) *qibal al-mawḍūʿ lahā.*

f   The sentences in angular brackets are absent from Badawī's edition, but are found in MS Iraq Museum Lib. 134, pp. 155.16–156.1.

g   The sentences in angular brackets are absent from Badawī's edition but are found in MS Iraq Museum Lib. 134, p. 158.1–4.

h   Reading *al-fiʿl ath-thānī* for the text's *al-ʿaql ath-thānī* at 382.7.

i   The phrases in angular brackets are absent from Badawī's edition but are found in MS Iraq Museum Lib. 134, p. 159.10–1.

j   Reading *munqalab* for the text's *maqlab* at 384.14.

IBN SĪNĀ

I. *The Cure*, "Book of Demonstration," I.9

a   The translation is based on the edition in *Ash-Shifāʾ*, *al-Burhan*, ʿAbd ar-Raḥman Badawī, ed., 43–48, with reference to the edition of ed. Abū Ela ʿAffīfī, 93–98.

b   Reading *ka-mā* with ʿAffīfī; *lammā/limā* at 45.9, in Badawī.

c   Reading *khabar* 48.17 ("account") with ʿAffīfī; *ḥayyiz*, in Badawī.

II. *The Cure*, "Book of Demonstration," III.5

a   The translation is based on the edition in *Ash-Shifāʾ*, *al-Burhan*, ʿAbd ar-Rahman Badawī, ed., 158–62, with noted corrections from the edition of Abū Ela ʿAffīfī, ed., 220–27.

b   "Starting points" here translates *mabādiʾ*, which is elsewhere translated as "principles," but that does not convey quite the same sense in this context.

c   Reading *li* with ʿAffīfī for *bi* at 159.5, in Badawī.

d   Reading *yatarraqá* for *yatawaqqafu* at 161.5.

e   *Yafrughu* for *nafzaʿu* at 161.8.

f   Reading *ʿanhu* with ʿAffīfī for *ʿindahu* at 161.12, in Badawī.

g   *Markūzan*, editorial conjecture in ʿAffīfī for *madhkūran* at 161.15, in Badawī.

III. *The Cure*, "Physics," I.2

a   The translation is based on the edition in *Ash-Shifāʾ*, *at-Tabīʿiyāt*, Saʿīd Zāyed, ed., 13–21, with consideration of variants from the edition of Jaʿfar Āl Yāsīn, ed., 89–93.

b   Reading *bi-bādhahi l-manzila* with Āl Yāsīn; *li-bādhihi l-manzila* at 14.3, in Zāyed.

c   Reading *sa-nufaṣṣilu* with Āl Yāsīn, *sa-yufaṣṣalu* (?) at 16.17, in Zāyed.

d   This translation may appear problematic in that the use of *al-farq bayna* at 18.9, normally suggests a contrast between two things and here we find three, but Ibn Sīnā seems to employ a construction involving three elements, the first of which is to be contrasted in some way with the latter two; compare this use in our translation of "Book of Demonstration," I.9, par. 21.

e   Reading *ṣār ay taghayyara* with Āl Yāsīn; *ṣāra an taghayr* at 19.17, in Zāyed.

IV.   Selections on Atomism from *The Cure*, "Physics"

a   The translation is based on the edition of Zāyed at 184.5–185.6; 185.15–186.2; 186.15–188.3.

b   We based the translation on the edition of Zāyed at 188.7–189.3; 189.8–191.8; 195.15–196.8.

c   The translation is based on the edition of Zāyed at 198.4–5; 199.4–10; 202.5–13.

V.   Selections on "Inclination" (*mayl*) and Projectile Motion

a   *Kitab al-ḥudud*, Amélie-Marie Goichon, ed. and French trans., 34 (definition #45).

b   The translation is based on the edition of Zāyed, 298.4–299.13; with consideration of variants from the edition of Āl Yāsīn, 264.

c   Following Āl Yāsīn; Zāyed has *azālat* at 298.7.

d   Following Āl Yāsīn; Zāyed has *li-ayna* ("to where") at 298.15.

e   The translation is based on the edition of Zāyed, 314.13–315.12; Āl Yāsīn, 273–74, with consideration of variants from the edition of Āl Yāsīn.

f   That is, *qabūluha li-t-taḥrīk an-naqlī abṭaʾ* at 314.14, (lit. "their susceptibility to transitional motion is slower").

g   The translation is based on the edition of Zāyed; Āl Yāsīn, 281, with consideration of variants from the edition of Āl Yāsīn at 281.

h   Reading *bi-qūwa munfidha* with Āl Yāsīn, for *bi-qūwa munfidhihi* at 326.12, in Zāyed.

i   The translation is based on the edition of Zāyed, 133.6–134.2 with consideration of variants from the edition of Āl Yāsīn, 162–63.

VI.   Selections on Psychology from *The Cure*, "The Soul"

a   The translation is based on the edition in *Kitāb an-Nafs*, Fazlur Rahman, ed., 4–8, 11–12, 15–16.

b   The text's *al-muqarriba* should be corrected to *al-muqarr bihi*, 16.12.

c   The translation is based on the edition of Rahman, 39–51; cf. *an-Najāt*, Muhammad Dānishpāzhūh, ed., V.1–4, 318–32, and the sections of that text translated in *Avicenna's Psychology*, Fazlur Rahman, ed., 24–33.

d   The translation is based on the edition of Rahman, 206–9; cf. *an-Najāt*, 330–36.

e   We based the translation on the edition of Rahman, 209–16; cf. *an-Najāt*, 356–64, and the translation in *Avicenna's Psychology*, Rahman, ed., 46–50.

f   The translation is based on the edition of Rahman, 221–27; cf. *an-Najāt*, 371–78 and the translation of that section in *Avicenna's Psychology*, Rahman, ed., 54–58.

g   Reading *aw yazīda* at 225.18, [cf. William Wright, *A Grammar of the Arabic Language*, ii. 33A] see a similar use in translation of "The Soul," V.7, par. 5, p. 207.

h   The phrase "belonging to the soul," *lahā* at 226.13, is a conjectural emendation on the part of Rahman; the majority of the manuscripts read *lahu*, in which case the sentence would read "That thing has . . ."

i   The translation is based on the edition of Rahman, 227–33; cf. *An-Najāt* VI.9, 378–87 and the translation of that section in *Avicenna's Psychology*, Rahman, ed., 58–63.

j   Lit. *wa-lā shay' mu'aṭṭal fī ṭ-ṭabī'a* at 229.7, "nothing is vain in nature."

k   The translation is based on the edition of Rahman, 234–8.

l   We based the translation on the edition of Rahman, 239–42, 248–50.

m   The majority of manuscripts used by Rahman for this edition shows *mukhayyila* here at 240.4; MS K has a variant conjectured to read *mukhtalla*, "allusive," by Rahman.

n   Cf. *an-Najāt* VI.1, 339–41, and the translation of that section by F. Rahman in *Avicenna's Psychology*, 33–37. The translation here modifies that of Dimitri Gutas, *Avicenna*, 161–62 (L7).

o   Alternately, "inspiration" (*ilhām*), 249.20i; see the textual emendation suggested by Gutas, 162, n. 37, on the basis of an earlier work by Ibn Sīnā.

p   The translation is based on the edition of Rahman, 252.13–257.17.

q   Lit. *wujūda inniyatihī shay'an wāḥidan* ("the existence of his *that-ness* is a single thing") at 255.9. The correct vocalization of the second word is *inniya* not *anniya*, which apparently is the product of a long history of textual and philosophical misguidance on the part of the first Latin readers of Ibn Sīnā and latterly Western philosophers generally. Although it can be argued that the Latin *annitas* is not derived from the Arabic but rather from the Latin *an* ("whether").

r   Reading *aw yakūna* at 255.17; compare the example in the translation of "The Soul," V.3, par. 7, p. 194.

VII.   *The Salvation*, "Metaphysics," I.12

a   The translation is based on the edition in *An-Najāt*, Muhammad Dānishpāzhūh, ed., 518–22.

VIII.   *The Salvation*, "Metaphysics," II.1–5

a   The translation is based on the edition in *An-Najāt*, Muhammad Dānishpāzhūh, ed., 546–53, with reference to the edition of al-Kurdī, 224–8.

b   Following al-Kurdī, *al-mawjūd*, 546.3.

c   "On the one hand . . . is absurd" is found in only one of the manuscripts that Dānishpāzhūh used for his edition, and it is not found in al-Kurdī. It would appear to be a later explanatory summary of both of the arguments of the chapter that was inserted into the text from the margin at the wrong place, since it interrupts the summary conclusion of the second argument. We have placed it in brackets to suggest that it is not part of Ibn Sīnā's original text, and restored the order of that original text. Nonetheless, it is a correct summary of Ibn Sīnā's two arguments and therefore is perhaps useful to the reader.

d   The first person singular conjugation is found in *An-Najāt*, al-Kurdī ed.; Dānishpāzhūh's edition shows the first person plural, "We have already explained . . ." 552.11.

IX.   *The Salvation*, "Metaphysics," II.12–13

a   The translation follows the text of the edition in *An-Najāt*, Muhammad Dānishpāzhūh, ed., 566–8.

X. *The Salvation,* "Metaphysics," II.18–19

a   The translation is based on the edition in *An-Najāt,* al-Kurdī, ed., 246–9, with noted references to the edition of Dānishpāzhūh, 593–99.

b   *ʿUqda,* 249.5, following the *lectio difficilior* recorded in Dānishpāzhūh; *ʿidda* in al-Kurdī; *mudda* in the parallel passage from *The Cure,* "Metaphysics," VIII.6, not translated here.

c   A reference to Qurʾān 6:59 (*wa-ʿindahū [allāh] mafātiḥ al-ghayb lā yaʿlamuhū illā huwa:* "God has the keys to the unknown that he alone knows"), which confirms Dānishpāzhūh's selection of the variant *mafātiḥ;* cf. al-Kurdī's *mafātīḥ,* 245.19.

XI. *The Cure,* "Metaphysics," IV.2

a   The translation is based on the edition in *Ash-Shifāʾ, al-Ilāhiyāt,* George Anawatī and Saʾīd Zāyed, eds., vol. I, 178–85.

XII. On Governance

a   The translation is based on the edition in *Majallat al-Sharq,* Louis Malouf, ed., 967–973; reprinted in *At-Turāth at-tarbawī l-Islāmī fī khams makhṭūṭāt,* Hisham Nashshaba, ed., 27–45 (hereafter abbreviated as M/N, with reference to the edition of *Al-Madhhab at-tarbawī ʿind Ibn Sīnā min khilāl falsafatihī l-ʿamaliya,* ʿAbd al-Amīr Shams ad-Dīn, ed., 232–60 (hereafter abbreviated SD).

b   Reading *faṣl* for *fḍḍl* at 27.14.

c   Reading *tajassus* with M/N at 29.12, *tajashshush* in SD, 235.

d   Reading *tanqīr* with M/N at 29.12; *tanqīb* in SD, 236.

e   Reading *mulkuhu* and *mālihi* for *malakatin* and *mālatin* in M/N at 38.12; cf. *mulkihi, mālihi* in SD, 250.3.

f   Reading *mubtadhila* with SD, 250.6; *mubidhala [sic voc.]* M/N at 38.15.

AL-GHAZĀLĪ

I. Concerning That on Which True Demonstration Is Based

a   From *Miʿyār al-ʿilm,* Ahmad Shams ad-Dīn, ed., 243–46.

II. *The Incoherence of the Philosophers,* "The First Discussion": On Refuting Their Claim of the World's Eternity

a   The translation is based upon the edition in *The Incoherence of the Philosophers,* Michael E. Marmura, ed., 12–30. Our translation has benefited from Marmura's translation in the same work.

b   Reading *li-mā* for the editor's *lammā* at 14.10.

III. On Power

a   The translation is based upon the edition in *Iqtiṣād fī l-iʿtiqād,* ʿAbdallah Muḥammad al-Khalīlī, ed., 51–60. The translation here has benefited from Michael E. Marmura's "Ghazali's Chapter on Divine Power in the *Iqtiṣād,*" 279–315.

b   Reading *khalq,* 52.19 "to create," for the text's *khilw* "to be devoid or free." If the text's *khilw* is retained, then the sense of the text might be, "So [the divine power] is suitably free [of] one motion's always following another [as the philosophers maintain]." The suggested emendation of *khalq* for *khilw,* however, brings the sense of the present paragraph in line with al-Ghazālī's earlier claim in par. 5 that: "We mean by 'the possibles are infinite' that the creation of one temporal event after another never reaches a limit beyond which it is impossible for the intellect [to conceive] of some [further] temporal event's coming to be," p. 255.

c Reading *iʿdād* for the editor's *aʿdād*, 55.8.

IBN BĀJJA

I. Selection from Commentary on Aristotle's *Physics*

a The translation is based upon the edition in *Sharḥ as-samāʿ aṭ-ṭabīʿī li-Arisṭūṭālis*, Majid Fakhry, ed., 18–20; we have also consulted the edition of *Shurūḥāt as-samāʿ aṭ-ṭabīʿī*, Maʿan Ziyāda, ed., 17–21.

b The manuscript has *al-mādda* ("matter"), 20.9, but is corrected to *usṭuqisāt* in the manuscript's margin, as the analogy requires; see Ziyāda's edition, p. 20, n. 2.

II. Conjunction of the Intellect with Man

a The translation is based upon the edition of *Rasāʾil Ibn Bājja l-Ilāhiya*, Majid Fakhry, ed., 155–73; we have also consulted "Tratado de Avempace sobre la Unión de Intelecto con el Hombre," Miguel Asín Palacios, ed. and trans., 1–47.

b Reading *al-ḥayawān al-muḥazzaz* at 158.21, (lit. "notched animals") for the text's *al-ḥayawān al-muḥazzar*. Cf. Aristotle, *Parts of Animals* II 8, 654a26, corresponding with the Arabic *Kitāb al-Ḥayawān* XII, which was a compilation of Aristotle's *History of Animals* (including the spurious book X), *Parts of Animals* and *Generation of Animals*.

c Following Asín Palacios' text, which has *ka-dhālika* for Fakhry's *dhālika* at 159.7.

d Following Asín Palacios' text, which has *lā*, "not," a variant that neither occurs nor is noted in Fakhry's edition.

e Reading *mithālan* for the text's *mathalan* at 166.18.

f Accepting Fakhry's conjecture at 167.9, to fill a lacuna.

g We accept Fakhry's conjecture that *lā*, "not" at 169.16, which appears in the manuscript, be secluded; however, the text can also make sense if the negation is retained and so be translated thus: ". . . but not that human [i.e., the universal 'human'] is the meaning of 'human.' "

h Deleting Fakhry's inserted <*lā*> ("not") at 170.1.

i We conjecture that the text's *raʾīs* at 170.12, should be emended to *tarʾīs*. The literal translation of the original text is, "Whoever's head of his body is the incorporeal form," which seems inconsistent with Ibn Bājja's whole argument thus far; for the masses and theoreticians in varying ways put the material before the immaterial, with the masses more than anyone else giving preference to the material. That Ibn Bājja has the masses in mind here is clear from his description of this group in the immediately following sentence as akin to "an unpolished surface."

j Reading *infadhta* for the text's *infadta* at 172.9.

IBN ṬUFAYL

Selections from *Ḥayy ibn Yaqẓān*

a The translation is based on the edition in *Ḥayy ibn Yaqẓān*, Ahmad Ameen, ed., 81–84, 89–92, and 94–98, which in turn has been compared with the edition in *Ḥayy Ben Yaqdhân, Roman Philosophique d'Ibn Thofaïl*, Léon Gauthier, ed., 55–61, 69–77, and 80–90. We have consulted the French translation of Gauthier as well as the English translations of Goodman and Khalidi.

b Following Gauthier's *wa-annahu lam yakhtalif illā* for Ameen's *wa-annahu yakhtalifu illā* at 82.12.

c   Following Gauthier, *jismīya* for Ameen's *jinsīya*, "of the generic or genus" at 90.5.

d   Although Ameen's text lacks the required negation, *lā*, needed by the sense of the argument, the negation is found in Gauthier's edition at 82.9.

e   Following Gauthier, whose text does not have the negatives, *laysat* and *lā* at 84.4.

f   Reading with Gauthier *tuḥarrikuhu* for Ameen's *taḥarrakat* at 96.12.

IBN RUSHD

I.   Selections from *The Incoherence of the Incoherence*, "First Discussion"

a   The translation is based on the third edition in *Tahāfut at-tahāfut*, Maurice Bouyges, ed., 7–10, 18–25, 26–30, 34–41 and 56–63.

b   Reading *qubūluhā* at 9.77, with MSS A, B.V for the text's *qubūluhu*.

c   Reading *yataʿayyanu* for the text's *tuʿayyinu* at 9.16.

d   Reading *juzʾ* with MSS. c, q, v, and x for the text's *ḥadd*, "limit" at 18.8.

II.   The Decisive Treatise

a   From *Averroes on the Harmony of Religion and Philosophy*, G. F. Hourani, trans. Reprinted by permission of the E. J. W. Gibb Memorial Trust, with very slight changes in matters of style, spelling, and transliteration, as well as minor corrections. All of the footnotes are by us.

III.   Commentary on *Metaphysics*, Zeta 9

a   From *Tafsīr mā baʿd aṭ-ṭabīʿiyāt*, Maurice Bouyges, ed., 878–86. Parallel passages are found at Ibn Rushd's commentary to Aristotle, *Metaphysics* Λ, texts 13 and 18; for an English translation of those passages see Charles Genequand, *Ibn Rushd's Metaphysics*.

b   Reading *Muṣawwar* at 884.18, the Latin translator vocalized the Arabic as *muṣawwir*, the active participle, and so translated it *formans generans*, "something generating the form," which philosophically seems unlikely; see *Aristotelis opera cum Averrois commentariis*, vol. 8, 181G9–10.

IV.   Selections from the *Long Commentary on the Soul*, Book III

a   The translation is based upon the edition in *Commentarium Magnum in Aristotelis De anima Libros*, F. Stuart Crawford, ed., *Corpus Commentariorum Averrois in Aristotelem*, vol. 6, Book III, comments 5, 387–413.

b   Reading the variant *ideo* with MS B for the text's *cum* at 399.1. *Cum* can be retained if the whole paragraph is read as an unwieldy subordinate clause and the main clause is the first sentence of the next paragraph.

c   The Latin *subjecti*, "subject" at 408.15 is probably due to a misreading of the Arabic *mawḍiʿ*, "place," for *mawḍūʿ*, "subject."

d   There is a textual difficulty here. The Latin has *sunt diversa*, "to be different" at 408.25 which is far removed from Aristotle's *marainetai*, "to wane." Moreover, when we go to Averroes' commentary of this passage in Book I, Comment 66, we do not find *sunt diversa* but *diversantur*, which presents its own problems. Perhaps *diversantur* was originally *divertantur*, "might be different." Whatever the case, the shift in meaning might be due to Averroes' reliance on the version of Aristotle's text that Themistius quotes in full in his paraphrase. A translation of the Arabic Themistius reads: "in the case of affliction, conceptualization by the intellect and speculation then are both apt to (*khalīqāni*) corrupt in accordance with something else within." The Arabic *khalīqāni*, "apt," might be mistaken for some form of the Arabic *ikhtalafa, yakhtafilu*, "to be different." This suggestion is at best a conjecture.

e   Reading *multa* with MS C for the text's *multam*, "much" at 412.5.

f   From *Commentarium magnum in Aristotelis* De anima *libros*, ed. F. S. Crawford, Book III, Comments 18–20, pp. 437–54.

g   The text's *et cum fuerit separatum, est quod est tantum, non mortale* at 444.10–11, differs from Text 20, where the passage is initially cited. This difference may be because Ibn Rushd was citing from a different Arabic translation of *De anima*, since we know that he had multiple versions available to him. For a discussion of various translations of *De anima* in the medieval Arabic speaking world, see Richard Frank, "Some Fragments of Isḥāq's Translation of the *De anima*," 215–229.

h   There is some textual difficulty here. In the Arabic version of Themistius' *De anima* paraphrase, ʿilal ("ailment" or "affection") is translating Themistius' *pathēma* ("anything that befalls one" or a "passive condition"), which he used instead of Aristotle's *pathē* ("a passive state"). It is not clear how the Latin *diversa* at 446.10, was derived from ʿilal. Although ʿilal in the sense of "affection" may have been confused with the same Arabic word used for "cause," the Latin would then be *causa*.

i   The citation is not the one that appears in Text 20, where the passage is initially cited, nor does the particle "also" (*etiam*) appear in Text 20. Thus, it would seem that here Ibn Rushd is citing from a different Arabic translation of the *De anima* than that of the Text.

j   Following the extant Arabic of this citation; see *Kitāb Arisṭāṭālīs wa-naṣṣ kalāmihi fī n-nafs*, ʿAbd ar-Raḥman Badawī, ed., 75. In both instances of "imagination," the underlying Arabic is *tawahhum*, whereas in the Latin the first instance is *existimatio*, "estimation" at 452.8, and the second is *ymaginatione*, "imagination" at 452.10.

V.   Commentary on *Metaphysics*, Delta 7

a   From *Tafsīr mā baʿd aṭ-ṭabiʿīyāt*, Maure Bouyges, ed., 552–63.

b   The Arabic text leaves off here, noting that the Greek was corrupt.

c   This entire paragraph is lacking in the Latin translation of Ibn Rushd's *Metaphysics* commentary.

AS-SUHRAWARDĪ

Selections from *The Philosophy of Illumination*

a   The translation is based on the edition found in *Ḥikmat al-Ishrāq*, John Walbridge and Hossein Ziai, eds. and trans., 8–11, 42–52, and 58–59.

b   Reading *waḥda* for the text's *waḥdahū*.

c   Although a perhaps more natural reading of this line is "something's possibility is prior to its existence in the intellect," the remainder of the text makes it clear that this is not the intended sense.

d   Since the apodosis is part of a *lau* conditional, the text should be corrected and a *la* added.

Bibliography

Adamson, Peter. *The Arabic Plotinus: A Philosophical Study of the* "Theology of Aristotle." London: Duckworth, 2002.

————. *"Porphyrius Arabus* on Nature and Art: 463F Smith in Context." In *Studies in Porphyry.* Edited by George Karamanolis and Anne Sheppard. London: Institute of Classical Studies, forthcoming.

Alexander of Aphrodisias. *On the Intellect.* In *Alexandri Aphrodisiensis, Praeter commentaria scripta minor, commentaria in Aristotelem Graeca.* I. Bruno, ed. Berlin: Typis et Impensis Georgii Reimer, 1887.

Alon, Ilai. *Socrates in Mediaeval Arabic Literature.* Leiden: Brill, 1995.

Altmann, Alexander, and Stern, Samuel M. *Isaac Israeli.* Westport, CT: Greenwood Press, 1958.

Aristotle. *De anima (Kitāb an-Nafs),* in *Kitāb Arisṭāṭālis wa-naṣṣ kalāmihī fī n-nafs.* Edited by ʿAbd ar-Raḥman Badawī. Cairo: Maktabat al-Nahḍa l-Miṣrīya, 1954.

————. *Posterior Analytics (Kitāb al-Burhān),* in *Manṭiq Arisṭū.* Edited by ʿAbd ar-Raḥmān Badawī. Vol. 2. Beirut: Dār al-Qalam, 1980.

————. *Posterior Analytics.* English translated by Jonathan Barnes. Oxford: Clarendon Press, 1994.

Bertolacci, Amos. "On the Arabic Translations of Aristotle's *Metaphysics.*" *Arabic Sciences and Philosophy* 15 (2005): 241–75.

————. "The Doctrine of Material and Formal Causality in the *Ilāhiyyāt* of Avicenna's *Kitāb al-Shifāʾ.*" *Quaestio* 2 (2002): 125–54.

Black, Deborah L. "Knowledge (*ʿilm*) and certitude (*yaqīn*) in al-Fārābī's Epistemology." *Arabic Sciences and Philosophy* 16 (2006), 11–45.

D'Ancona, Cristina. "Greek into Arabic: Neoplatonism in Translation," in *Cambridge Companion to Arabic Philosophy.* Edited by Peter Adamson and Richard C. Taylor. Cambridge, UK: Cambridge University Press, 2005, 10–31.

Daiber, Hans, ed. *Bibliography of Islamic Philosophy.* 2 vols. Leiden: E. J. Brill, 1999.

Davidson, Herbert. *Alfarabi, Avicenna, and Averroes on Intellect.* New York: Oxford University Press, 1992.

Dhanani, Alnoor. *The Physical Theory of Kalām: Atoms, Space, and Void in Basrian Muʿtazilī Cosmology.* Leiden: E. J. Brill, 1994.

Druart, Thérèse-Anne. "Brief Bibliographical Guide in Medieval Islamic Philosophy and Theology." http://philosophy.cua.edu/faculty/tad/biblio.cfm.

————. "The Human Soul's Individuation and Its Survival after the Body's Death: Avicenna on the Causal Relation between Body and Soul." *Arabic Sciences and Philosophy* 10 (2000): 259–73.

Al-Fārābī. *Alfārābī's philosophische Abhandlungen.* Edited by Friedrich Dieterici. Leiden: E. J. Brill, 1890.

————. *Alfarabi's Philosophy of Plato and Aristotle.* Translated by Muhsin Mahdi. Rev. ed. Ithaca, NY: Cornell University Press, 2002. [Includes English translation of al-Fārābī's *Taḥṣīl as-Saʿāda,* "The Attainment of Happiness."]

————. *Alfarabi, the Political Writings: Selected Aphorisms and Other Texts.* Translated by Charles Butterworth. Ithaca, NY: Cornell University Press, 2001.

————. *Al-alfāẓ al-mustaʿmala fī l-manṭiq.* Edited by Muhsin Mahdi. Beirut: Dār al Mashriq, 1968.

————. "Al-Fārābī's *Eisagoge.*" *Islamic Quarterly* 3 (1956): 117–38. Edited and translated by Douglas M. Dunlop.

————. *Al-Fārābī on the Perfect State: Abū Naṣr al-Fārābī's Mabādiʾ Arāʾ Ahl al-Madīnah al-Faḍilah.* Edited and translated by Richard Walzer. Rev. ed. New York, NY: Oxford University Press, 1985.

————. "Kitāb al-Burhān." In *Al-Manṭiq ʿinda al-Fārābī.* Edited by Majid Fakhry. Beirut: Dar al-Mashriq, 1987.

————. *Kitāb al-wāḥid wa-l-waḥda.* Edited by Muhsin Mahdi. Casablanca: Les Éditions Toubkal, 1989.

————. *Opinions* in *Rasāʾil al Fārābī.* Hyderabad: Majlis Daira l-Maʿārif al-ʿUthmānīya, 1926.

————. *Philosophy of Aristotle.* Edited by Muhsin Mahdi. Beirut: Dar Majallat al-Shiʿr, 1961.

————. *Risāla fī l-ʿaql.* Edited by Maurice Bouyges. Beirut: Imprimerie Catholique, 1938.

————. *As-Siyāsa l-madanīya l-mulaqqab bi-mabādiʾ al-mawjūdāt.* Edited by Fauzi Najjār. Beirut: Imprimerie Catholique, 1964.

————. *At-Tanbīh ʿalá sabīl as-saʿāda.* Edited by Jaʿfar Āl Yāsīn. Beirut: Dār al-Manāhil, 1985.

————. "Le traité d'al-Fārābī sur les buts de la metaphysique d'Aristote." *Bulletin de philosophie médiévale* 24 (1982): 38–43. French translation by Thérèse-Anne Druart.

Frank, Richard. "Some Fragments of Isḥāq's Translation of the *De anima.*" *Cahiers de Byrsa* 8 (1958–9): 215–29.

Galen. *De usu partium.* Arabic translations and epitomes in [*Risāla*] *fī manāfiʿ al-aʿḍā.* Edited by Fuat Sezgin. *Geschichte des arabischen Schriftums.* Vol. 3, no. 40. Leiden: E. J. Brill, 1967.

————. *De usu partium.* Edited by Georg Helmreich. Leipzig: Teubner, 1907–1909 (repr. 1968).

————. "Kitāb al-Burhān; Dubitationes in Galenum" in *Dictionnaire des philosophes antiques.* Edited by Richard Goulet. Paris: Éditions du centre national de la recherche scientifique, 1989, 458.

————. *On My Own Opinions*. Edited and translated by Vivian Nutton. *Corpus Medicorum Graecorum*. Vol. 3, bk. 2. Berlin: Akademie Verlag, 1999.

————. *Technē iatrikē*. Edited by Karl Kühn. Vol. I. Leipzig: Prostat in officina libraria Car. Cnoblochii, 1821–1833.

————. *Technē iatrikē (Kitāb al-Ṣināʿa al-Ṭibbīya = Kitāb al-Ṣināʿa al-ṣaghīr)*. Arabic edited by Muḥammad Sālim. Cairo: Al-Hayʾa l-Miṣriya l-Amma li-l-Kitāb, 1988.

Al-Ghazālī. *Freedom and Fulfillment: An Annotated Translation of Al-Ghazālī's al-Munqidh min al-ḍalāl and Other Relevant Works of al-Ghazālī*. Translated by Richard J. McCarthy. Library of Classical Arabic Literature. Vol. 4. Boston: Twayne Publishers, 1980.

————. "Ghazali's Chapter on Divine Power in the *Iqtiṣād*." *Arabic Science and Philosophy* 4 (1994), 279–315. Translated by Michael E. Murmura.

————. *The Incoherence of the Philosophers*. Translated by Michael E. Marmura. Islamic Translation Series. Provo, UT: Brigham Young University Press, 1997.

————. *Iqtiṣād fī l-iʿtiqād*. Edited by ʿAbdallah Muḥammad al-Khalīlī. Beirut: Dār al-Kutub al-ʿIlmīya, 2004.

————. *Miʿyār al-ʿilm*. Edited by Ahmad Shams ad-Dīn. Beirut: Dār al-Kutub al-ʿIlmīya, 1990.

————. *Niche of Lights*. Edited and translated by David Buchman. Islamic Translation Series. Provo, UT: Brigham Young University Press, 1998.

Gutas, Dimitri. *Avicenna and the Aristotelian Tradition*. Leiden: E. J. Brill, 1988.

————. *Greek Thought, Arabic Culture: The Graeco-Arabic Translation Movement in Baghdad and Early ʿAbbāsid Society (2nd–4th/8th–10th Centuries)*. London and New York: Routledge, 1998.

————. "Intuition and Thinking," in *Aspects of Avicenna*. Edited by Robert Wisnovsky Princeton, NJ: Marcus Wiener Publishers, 2001, 1–38.

Hasse, Dag N. "Avicenna on Abstraction," in *Aspects of Avicenna*. Edited by Robert Wisnovsky. Princeton, NJ: Marcus Wiener Publishers, 2001.

————. *Avicenna's* De Anima *in the Latin West*. London: Warburg Institute, 2000.

Hyman, Arthur, and Walsh, James, eds. *Philosophy in the Middle Ages*. Indianapolis, IN: Hackett Publishing Company, 1983.

Ibn Bājja. "Commentary on [Aristotle's] *De anima*," in *ʿIlm al-Nafs*. Translated by Muḥammad Maʿṣūmī. Pakistan Historical Society Publication, 26. Karachi: Pakistan Historical Society, 1961.

————. "Commentary on [Aristotle's] *Meteorology*," in *Aristotle's "Meteorology" and Its Reception in the Arab World*. Translated by Paul Lettinck. Aristoteles Semitico-Latinus, 10. Leiden: E. J. Brill, 1999.

————. "Commentary on [Aristotle's] *Physics*," in *Sharḥ as-samāʿ aṭ-ṭabīʿī li-Arisṭūṭālīs*. Edited by Majid Fakhry. Beirut: Dār an-Nahār li-n-Nashr, 1973.

————. "Commentary on [Aristotle's] *Physics*," in *Shurūḥāt as-samāʿ aṭ-ṭabīʿī*. Edited by Maʿan Ziyāda. Beirut: Dār al-Kindī, 1978.

————. "Conjunction of the Intellect with Man," in *Rasāʾil Ibn Bājja l-Ilāhīya*. Edited by Majid Fakhry. Beirut: Dār an-Nahār li-n-Nashr, 1968.

————. "The Governance of the Solitary." *Journal of the Royal Asiatic Society* (1945): 61–81. Partially translated by Douglas M. Dunlop

————. "The Governance of the Solitary." Partial translation by Lawrence Berman, in *Medieval Political Philosophy: A Source Book*. Edited by Ralph Lerner and Muhsin Mahdi. Ithaca, NY: Cornell University Press, 1972.

————. "The Governance of the Solitary," in *Rasāʾil Ibn Bājja l-Ilāhīya*. Edited by Majid Fakhry. Beirut: Dār an-Nahār li-n-Nashr, 1968.

————. "Tratado de Avempace sobre la Unión de Intelecto con el Hombre." *Al-Andalus* 7 (1942): 1–47. Edited and Spanish translation by Miguel Asín Palacios.

Ibn an-Nadīm. *The Fihrist: A 10th Century AD Survey of Islamic Culture*. Translated by Bayard Dodge. Great Books of the Islamic World. Chicago: KAZI Publications, 1998.

Ibn Rushd. *Aristotelis opera cum Averrois commentariis*. Vol. 8. *De Physico Auditu*. Venice: apud Junctas, 1562. (repr.: Frankfurt a. M.: Minerva, 1962).

————. *Averroes' Commentary on Plato's* Republic. Edited and translated by Erwin I. J. Rosenthal. University of Cambridge Oriental Publications, vol. I. Cambridge, UK: Cambridge University Press, 1956.

————. *Averroes' Long Commentary on* the De Anima. Translated by Richard C. Taylor. New Haven, CT: Yale University Press, forthcoming.

————. *Averroes' Middle Commentaries on Aristotle's* Categories *and* De interpretatione. Translated by Charles Butterworth. Princeton, NJ: Princeton University Press, 1983.

————. *Averroes on Plato's* Republic. Translated by Ralph Lerner. Ithaca, NY: Cornell University Press, 1974.

————. *Commentarium Magnum in Aristotelis De anima Libros*. Edited by Stuart F. Crawford. *Corpus Commentariorum Averrois in Aristotelem*. Vol. 6. Cambridge, MA: The Medieval Academy of America, 1953.

————. *Decisive Treatise*. In *Averroes on the Harmony of Religion and Philosophy*. Translated by George F. Hourani. London: Luzac, 1961. Reprinted with the permission of the E. J. W. Gibb Memorial Trust.

————. *Decisive Treatise and Epistle Dedicatory*. Translated by Charles E. Butterworth. Islamic Translation Series. Provo, UT: Brigham Young University Press, 2001.

————. *De substantia orbis*. Edited and translated by Arthur Hyman. Medieval Academy Books, 96. Cambridge, MA: Medieval Academy of America, 1986.

————. *The Epistle on the Possibility of Conjunction with the Active Intellect*. Edited and translated by Kalman P. Bland. Moreshet Series, 7. New York: Ktav Publishing House, 1982.

————. *Ibn Rushd's Metaphysics: A Translation with Introduction of Ibn Rushd's Commentary on Aristotle's* Metaphysics, Book Lām. Translated by Charles Genequand. Islamic Philosophy and Theology; Texts and Studies, I. Leiden: E. J. Brill, 1986.

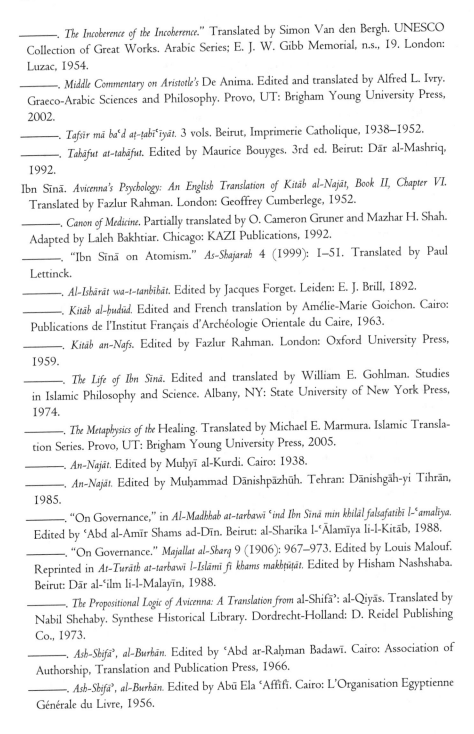

————. *The Incoherence of the Incoherence."* Translated by Simon Van den Bergh. UNESCO Collection of Great Works. Arabic Series; E. J. W. Gibb Memorial, n.s., 19. London: Luzac, 1954.

————. *Middle Commentary on Aristotle's De Anima.* Edited and translated by Alfred L. Ivry. Graeco-Arabic Sciences and Philosophy. Provo, UT: Brigham Young University Press, 2002.

————. *Tafsīr mā baʿd aṭ-ṭabīʿīyāt.* 3 vols. Beirut, Imprimerie Catholique, 1938–1952.

————. *Tahāfut at-tahāfut.* Edited by Maurice Bouyges. 3rd ed. Beirut: Dār al-Mashriq, 1992.

Ibn Sīnā. *Avicenna's Psychology: An English Translation of Kitāb al-Najāt, Book II, Chapter VI.* Translated by Fazlur Rahman. London: Geoffrey Cumberlege, 1952.

————. *Canon of Medicine.* Partially translated by O. Cameron Gruner and Mazhar H. Shah. Adapted by Laleh Bakhtiar. Chicago: KAZI Publications, 1992.

————. "Ibn Sīnā on Atomism." *As-Shajarah* 4 (1999): 1–51. Translated by Paul Lettinck.

————. *Al-Ishārāt wa-t-tanbīhāt.* Edited by Jacques Forget. Leiden: E. J. Brill, 1892.

————. *Kitāb al-ḥudūd.* Edited and French translation by Amélie-Marie Goichon. Cairo: Publications de l'Institut Français d'Archéologie Orientale du Caire, 1963.

————. *Kitāb an-Nafs.* Edited by Fazlur Rahman. London: Oxford University Press, 1959.

————. *The Life of Ibn Sīnā.* Edited and translated by William E. Gohlman. Studies in Islamic Philosophy and Science. Albany, NY: State University of New York Press, 1974.

————. *The Metaphysics of the Healing.* Translated by Michael E. Marmura. Islamic Translation Series. Provo, UT: Brigham Young University Press, 2005.

————. *An-Najāt.* Edited by Muḥyī al-Kurdi. Cairo: 1938.

————. *An-Najāt.* Edited by Muḥammad Dānishpāzhūh. Tehran: Dānishgāh-yi Tihrān, 1985.

————. "On Governance," in *Al-Madhhab at-tarbawī ʿind Ibn Sīnā min khilāl falsafatihī l-ʿamalīya.* Edited by ʿAbd al-Amīr Shams ad-Dīn. Beirut: al-Sharika l-ʿĀlamīya li-l-Kitāb, 1988.

————. "On Governance." *Majallat al-Sharq* 9 (1906): 967–973. Edited by Louis Malouf. Reprinted in *At-Turāth at-tarbawī l-Islāmī fī khams makhṭūṭāt.* Edited by Hisham Nashshaba. Beirut: Dār al-ʿilm li-l-Malayīn, 1988.

————. *The Propositional Logic of Avicenna: A Translation from al-Shifāʾ: al-Qiyās.* Translated by Nabil Shehaby. Synthese Historical Library. Dordrecht-Holland: D. Reidel Publishing Co., 1973.

————. *Ash-Shifāʾ, al-Burhān.* Edited by ʿAbd ar-Raḥman Badawī. Cairo: Association of Authorship, Translation and Publication Press, 1966.

————. *Ash-Shifāʾ, al-Burhān.* Edited by Abū Ela ʿAffīfī. Cairo: L'Organisation Egyptienne Générale du Livre, 1956.

———. *Ash-Shifāʾ, al-Ilāhīyāt*. Edited by George Anawatī, Muḥammad Mūsá, Sulaymān Dunyā and Saʿīd Zāyed. 2 Vols. Cairo: Organisation Générale des Imprimeries Gouvernamentales, 1960.

———. *Ash-Shifāʾ, al-Madkhal*. Edited by Maḥmud al-Hudayrī, Fuʾad al-Ahwānī and George Anawatī. Cairo: Organisation Générale des Imprimeries Gouvernamentales, 1952.

———. *Ash-Shifāʾ, aṭ-Ṭabīʿīyāt*. Edited by Jaʿfar Āl Yāsīn. Beirut, Dār al-Manāhil, 1996.

———. *Ash-Shifāʾ, aṭ-Ṭabīʿīyāt*. Edited by Saʿīd Zāyed. Cairo: The General Egyptian Book Organization, 1983.

Ibn Ṭufayl. *Hayy Ben Yaqdhân, Roman Philosophique d'Ibn Thofail*. Edited by Léon Gauthier. Beirut: Imprimerie Catholique, 1936.

———. *Ḥayy ibn Yaqẓān*. Edited by Ahmad Ameen. Damascus: Dār al-Madá li-th-Thaqāfa wa-n-Nashr, 2001.

———. *Ibn Ṭufayl's Ḥayy ibn Yaqẓān, a Philosophical Tale*. Translated by Lenn E. Goodman. Library of Classical Arabic Literature, I. New York: Twayne Publishers, 1972.

Janssens, Jules L. *An Annotated Bibliography on Ibn Sīnā (1970–1989)*. Louvain-la-Neuve: Leuven University Press, 1991.

———. *An Annotated Bibliography on Ibn Sīnā: First Supplement (1990–1994)*. Louvain-la-Neuve: Leuven University Press, 1999.

———. "Experience (*tajriba*) in Classical Arabic Philosophy (al-Fārābī–Avicenna)." *Quaestio* 4 (2004): 45–62.

Khalidi, Muhammad Ali. *Medieval Islamic Philosophical Writings*. Cambridge Texts in the History of Philosophy. Cambridge: Cambridge University Press, 2005.

Al-Kindī, "The Explanation of the Proximate Efficient Cause for Generation and Corruption," in *Rasāʾil al-Kindī l-falsafiya*. Vol. I. Edited by Muhammad Abū Rīda. Cairo: Dār al-Fikr al-ʿArabī 1950–1953.

———. *Al-Kindī's Metaphysics: A Translation of Yaʿqub Ibn Ishaq al-Kindī's Treatise "On First Philosophy."* Translated by Alfred L. Ivry. Albany, NY: State University of New York Press, 1974.

———. "On Divine Unity and the Finitude of the World's Body," in "Al-Kindi's Risala fi Wahdaniya Allah wa Tanahi Jirm al-ʿAlam." *Islamic Studies* 17 (1978): 185–201. Translated by F. A. Shamsi.

———. "On Divine Unity and the Finitude of the World's Body," in *Oeuvres philosophiques et scientifiques d'al-Kindī*. Edited and French translation by Roshdi Rashed and Jean Jolivet. Leiden: E. J. Brill, 1997.

———. "On the Intellect," in *Rasāʾil āl-Kindī al-falsafiya*. Vol. I. Edited by Muhammad Abū Rīda. Cairo: Dār al-Fikr al-ʿArabī 1950–1953.

———. "On the Means of Dispelling Sorrows," in "The Epistle of Yaʿqūb ibn Isḥāq al-Kindī on the Device for Dispelling Sorrows." Translated by Ghada Jayyusi-Lehn. *British Journal of Middle Eastern Studies* 29 (2002): 121–35.

————. "On the Means of Dispelling Sorrows," in "Uno scritto morale inedito di al-Kindī." Edited, and Italian translation by Helmut Ritter and Richard Walzer. *Memorie Della Reale, Accademia Nazionale Dei Lincei, Classe Di Scienze Morali, Storiche e Filologiche.* 6th ser., vol. 8 (1938): 5–63; Arabic text, 31–47.

————. *The Philosophical Works of al-Kindī.* Translated by Peter Adamson and Peter E. Pormann. Karachi: Oxford University Press, forthcoming.

Kraemer, Joel. *Philosophy in the Renaissance of Islam: Abū Sulaymān and His Circle.* Leiden: E. J. Brill, 1986. (Includes translations of several treatises by as-Sijistānī.)

Kuhn, Thomas. "Ptolemaic Astronomy," in *The Copernican Revolution: Planetary Astronomy in the Development of Western Thought.* Cambridge, MA: Harvard University Press, 1957.

Kukkonen, Taneli. "No Man Is an Island: Nature and Neo-Platonic Ethics in *Ḥayy ibn Yaqẓān.*" *Journal of the History of Philosophy* (forthcoming, 2007).

Lane, Edward W., *An Arabic-English Lexicon.* Beirut: Libraire du Liban, 1968.

Lerner, R. and Mahdi, M., eds. *Medieval Political Philosophy.* Ithaca, NY: Cornell University Press, 1972.

Lettinck, Paul. *Aristotle's* Physics *and Its Reception in the Arabic World.* Aristoteles Semitico-Latinus. vol. 7. Leiden and New York: E. J. Brill, 1994.

Marmura, Micheal E. "Avicenna's 'Flying Man' in Context," in *Probing in Islamic Philosophy.* Binghamton, NY: Global Academic Publishing, 2005.

————. "Ghazālī's Chapter on Divine Power in the *Iqtiṣād.*" *Arabic Science and Philosophy* 4 (1994): 279–315.

Mattá, Abū Bishr "Commentary on [Aristotle's] *Physics,*" in *aṭ-Ṭabīʿa.* 2 vols. Edited by ʿAbd ar-Raḥman Badawī. Cairo: al-Hayʾa l-Miṣrīya l-ʿāmma li-l-Kitāb, 1964–65.

———— "The Discussion between Abu Bishr Mattá and Abū Saʿīd as-Sīrāfī on the Merits of Logic and Grammar." *Journal for the Royal Asiatic Society* (1905): 79–129. Translated by David S. Margoliouth.

McCarthy, Richard J. "Al-Kindī's Treatise on the Intellect." *Islamic Studies* 3.2 (1964): 119–49.

McGinnis, Jon. "Scientific Methodologies in Medieval Islam." *Journal of the History of Philosophy* 41 (2003): 307–27.

Nasr, Seyyed H., and Aminrazavi, Mehdi, eds. *An Anthology of Philosophy in Persia.* 2 vols. Oxford: Oxford University Press, 1999.

Owen, G. E. L. "Zeno and the Mathematicians," in *Logic, Science, and Dialectic: Collected Papers in Greek Philosophy.* Ithaca, NY: Cornell University Press, 1986.

Peters, F. E. *Aristotle and the Arabs.* New York: New York University Press, 1968.

Pines, Shlomo. "Aristotle's *Politics* in Arabic Philosophy." *Israel Oriental Studies* 5 (1975): 150–60. Reprinted in *The Collected Works of Shlomo Pines.* Vol. 2. *Studies in Arabic Versions of Greek Texts and in Mediaeval Sciences.* Edited by Sarah Stroumsa. Jerusalem: The Magnes Press, 1986, 257–58.

———. "Rāzī critique de Galien," in *The Collected Works of Shlomo Pines*. Vol. 2. *Studies in Arabic Versions of Greek Texts and in Mediaeval Sciences*. Edited by Sarah Stroumsa. Jerusalem: The Magnes Press 1986.

Porphyry. *Porphyry the Phoenician, Isagoge*. Translated by Edward Warren. Toronto: Pontifical Institute of Medieval Studies, 1975.

———. *Eisagoge*. Arabic edited by Aḥmad al-Ahwānī. Cairo: Dār Iḥyaʾ al-Kutub al-ʿArabīya, 1952.

Ar-Rāzī. "Apologia pro Vita Sua." Translated by A. J. Arberry. *Aspects of Islamic Civilization*. Ann Arbor: University of Michigan Press, 1967.

———. *Kitāb ash-shukūk ʿalá Jālīnūs*. Edited by Mahdī Muḥaqqiq. Tehran: al-Maʿhad al-ʿalī al-ʿalamī li-l-fikr wa-l-ḥaḍāra l-Islāmīya, 1993.

———. *Opera philosophica fragmentaque quae supersunt*. Edited by Paul Kraus. Cairo: Fuʾad I University, 1939.

———. "The Philosopher's Way of Life," in "Raziana I, la conduite du Philosophe, traité ethique de Muhammad b. Zakariyya al-Razi." Edited by Paul Kraus. *Orientalia* n.s. 4 (1935): 300–334.

———. *The Spiritual Physick of Rhazes*. Translated by A. J. Arberry. Wisdom of the East Series. London: Murray, 1950.

as-Sijistānī, Abū Sulymān. "On the Proper Perfection of the Human Species," in *Muntakhab Ṣiwān al-ḥikma*. Edited by ʿAbd ar-Raḥman Badawī. Tehran: Bunyād-i Farhang-i Īran, 1974.

Stern, S. M. "The First in Thought Is the Last in Action: The History of a Saying Attributed to Aristotle." *Journal of Semitic Studies* 7 (1962): 234–52.

As-Suhrawardī. *The Book of Radiance*. Edited and translated by Hossein Ziai. Bibliotheca Iranica, Intellectual Traditions Series, vol. 1. Costa Mesa, CA: Mazda Publishers, 1998.

———. *Ḥikmat al-ishrāq*. Edited and translated by John Walbridge and Hossein Ziai. Islamic Translation Series. Provo, UT: Brigham Young University Press, 1999.

———. *The Philosophical Allegories and Mystical Treatises*. Translated by Wheeler M. Thackston Jr. Bibliotheca Iranica. Intellectual Traditions Series, 2. Costa Mesa, CA: Mazda Publishers, 1999.

Taylor, Richard C. "Remarks on *Cogitatio* in Averroes' *Commentarium Magnum in Aristotelis De anima Libros*," in *Averroes and the Aristotelian Tradition*. Edited by Gerhart Endress and Jan A. Aertsen. Leiden: E. J. Brill, 1999.

———. "Separate Material Intellect in Averroes' Mature Philosophy," in *Words, Texts, and Concepts, Cruising the Mediterranean Sea*. Edited by Rüdiger Arnzen and Jörn Thielmann. Leuven: Peeters, 2004.

Wisnovsky, Robert. *Avicenna's Metaphysics in Context*. Ithaca, NY: Cornell University Press, 2003.

———. "Final and Efficient Causality in Avicenna's Cosmology and Theology." *Quaestio* 2 (2002): 97–123.

————. "Notes on Avicenna's Concept of Thingness (*Shay'iyya*)." *Arabic Sciences and Philosophy* 10 (2000): 181–221.

Wolfson, Harry A. *The Philosophy of Kalam*. Cambridge, MA: Harvard University Press, 1976.

Wright, William. *A Grammar of the Arabic Language*, 3rd ed. 2 vols. Cambridge, UK: Cambridge University Press, 1896, 1898.

Yaḥyá Ibn 'Adī. "Establishing the Nature of the Possible," in "Yaḥyá Ibn 'Adī: über den Nachweis der Nature des Möglichen, Edition und Einleitung." *Zeitschrift für Geschichte der arabischen-islamischen Wissenschaften* 5 (1989): 281–96; 63–97 [Arabic].

————. "On the Attribution of Knowledge (*Fī iḍāfa l-'ilm*)," in *Maqālāt Yaḥyá bin 'Adī al-falsafiya*. Edited by Saḥbān Kalīfāt. Amman: Publications of the University of Jordan, 1988, 185–87.

————. *The Reformation of Morals: A Parallel English-Arabic Text*. Translated by Sidney. H. Griffith. Provo, UT: Brigham Young University Press, 2002.

Ziai, Hossein. "Shihāb al-Dīn Suhrawardī: Founder of the Illuminationist School," in *History of Islamic Philosophy*. Edited by S. H. Nasr and O. Leaman. Routledge History of World Philosophies. Vol. I. London and New York: Routledge, 1996.

Glossary/Index: English/Arabic

TRANSLATORS' NOTE: Although the following glossary is a relatively complete list of all the technical terms that occur in this anthology, it does not attempt to index all of the occurrences of every term. Frequently, only a single reference is given for a term in order that the reader can see the word in context. Still, in the case of certain historically important concepts, such as form, matter, and intellect, we have tried to track the development of that idea both within a single philosopher as well as from one philosopher to another. We have also have tried to mark those places where either an author devotes an extended discussion to a topic, or a certain argument turns on a particular concept.

403

Glossary/Index: Arabic-English

416